HANDBOOK OF PUBLIC TRANSPORT RESEARCH

RESEARCH HANDBOOKS IN TRANSPORT STUDIES

This important and timely series brings together critical and thought-provoking contributions on the most pressing topics and issues in transport studies. Comprising specially commissioned chapters from leading academics these comprehensive *Research Handbooks* feature cutting-edge research, help to define the field and are written with a global readership in mind. Equally useful as reference tools or high-level introductions to specific topics, issues, methods, innovations and debates, these *Handbooks* will be an essential resource for academic researchers and postgraduate students in transport studies and related disciplines.

Titles in this series include:

Handbook of Sustainable Transport
Edited by Carey Curtis

Handbook of Public Transport Research
Edited by Graham Currie

Handbook of Public Transport Research

Edited by

Graham Currie

Professor of Public Transport, Public Transport Research Group, Institute of Transport Studies, Department of Civil Engineering, Monash University, Australia

RESEARCH HANDBOOKS IN TRANSPORT STUDIES

Edward Elgar
PUBLISHING

Cheltenham, UK • Northampton, MA, USA

Cover image: The Oculus, World Trade Center Station, New York City by Patrick Robert Doyle on Unsplash.

Published by
Edward Elgar Publishing Limited
The Lypiatts
15 Lansdown Road
Cheltenham
Glos GL50 2JA
UK

Edward Elgar Publishing, Inc.
William Pratt House
9 Dewey Court
Northampton
Massachusetts 01060
USA

Paperback edition 2023

A catalogue record for this book
is available from the British Library

Library of Congress Control Number: 2021932270

This book is available electronically in the **Elgar**online
Geography, Planning and Tourism subject collection
http://dx.doi.org/10.4337/9781788978668

ISBN 978 1 78897 865 1 (cased)
ISBN 978 1 78897 866 8 (eBook)
ISBN 978 1 0353 1552 9 (paperback)

Typeset by Servis Filmsetting Ltd, Stockport, Cheshire
Printed and bound by CPI Group (UK) Ltd, Croydon, CR0 4YY

Contents

v

Contributors

Aaron Antrim, Trillium Solutions Inc., USA

Laura Aston, Monash University, Australia

Sean Barbeau, University of South Florida, USA

Maria Börjesson, Swedish National Road and Transport Research Institute, Stockholm and Linköping University, Sweden

Candace Brakewood, University of Tennessee, USA

Jeffrey Brown, Florida State University, USA

Oded Cats, TU Delft, Netherlands

Avishai (Avi) Ceder, Technion-Israel Institute of Technology, Israel

Mike Corby, IBI Group, Canada

Selby Coxon, Monash University, Australia

Miles Crumley, TriMet, USA

Boer Cui, McGill University, Canada

Graham Currie, Monash University, Australia

Alexa Delbosc, Monash University, Australia

Felipe Delgado, Pontificia Universidad Catolica de Chile, Chile

James DeWeese, McGill University, Canada

Ehab Diab, University of Saskatchewan, Canada

Ahmed El-Geneidy, McGill University, Canada

Masoud Fadaei, AFRY, Stockholm, Sweden

Nicholas Fournier, Monash University, Australia and University of California, Berkeley, USA

Ilya Fridman, Monash University, Australia

Margareta Friman, Karlstad University, Sweden

Ricardo Giesen, Pontificia Universidad Catolica de Chile, Chile

Anne Halvorsen, Metropolitan Transportation Authority, New York Transit, New York, USA

Madalena Harreman-Fernandes, McGill University, Canada

Wen Xun Hu, University of Toronto, Canada

Omar Ibarra-Rojas, Universidad Autonoma de Nuevo Leon, Mexico

Md Kamruzzaman, Monash University, Australia

Haris N. Koutsopoulos, Northeastern University, Boston, USA

Lisa Li, University of Toronto, Canada

Tao Liu, Southwest Jiaotong University, China

Emma Lucken, University of California, Berkeley, USA

Zhenliang Ma, Monash University, Melbourne, Australia

Joel Mendez, University of Kansas, USA

Vincent Moug, Queensland College of Art, Griffith University, Australia

Carlyn Muir, Monash University, Australia

Juan Carlos Munoz, Pontificia Universidad Catolica de Chile, Chile

Robbie Napper, Monash University, Australia

Dristi Neog, Westfield State University, USA

John Preston, University of Southampton, UK

Mustafizur Rahaman, Monash University, Australia and Phillip Boyle and Associates

James Reynolds, Monash University, Australia

Susan Shaheen, University of California, Berkeley, USA

Amer Shalaby, University of Toronto, Canada

Niels van Oort, TU Delft, Netherlands

Wijnand Veeneman, TU Delft, Netherlands

Kari Watkins, Georgia Tech, USA

Andrew Wong, IBI Group, Canada

James Wood, University of Texas at Arlington, USA

Menno Yap, TU Delft, Netherlands

Jinhua Zhao, Massachusetts Institute of Technology, USA

Daniel Zhou, IBI Group, Canada

1. Introduction to the *Handbook of Public Transport Research*

Graham Currie

1.1 PUBLIC TRANSPORT – INTERESTING, INTELLECTUALLY CHALLENGING AND IMPORTANT

This *Handbook of Public Transport Research* aims to provide a comprehensive overview of the latest research in a growing field: the field of research on urban public transport. The quantity of public transport related research papers has doubled in the last nine years. Why? For two reasons.

First, researchers have been increasingly inspired by the topic. It is an applied and practical topic affecting the quality of life of billions of people. It is also a field with significant challenges, seeking new and original solutions. These challenges range from the difficult interface of engineering, operations and human perceptions in user satisfaction and performance management, to the tricky balance between prudent financial management, operations planning and the social access goals making subsidies essential. These challenges require a multi-disciplinary perspective to wicked problems in Engineering, Planning, Psychology and Design, which is why the field is intellectually as well as tactically challenging. The foundation of many of these challenges is the conflicting congestion and environmental relief, and the social equity objectives that justify public transport in cities.

Secondly, public transport in cities is growing globally and indeed is expected to grow significantly into the future as mega cities multiply and increasingly become the focus of human development. In 2007, for the first time in history, more than half of the world's population lived in cities (United Nations Population Fund 2007). Humanity's urban population is expected to double between 2000 and 2030. The twenty-first century is considered the 'Urban Millennium' where cities and how they function have a principal influence on the human race and its future (United Nations Population Fund 2007). Travel in most world cities has been dominated by the private car (Cosgrove et al. 2009), which is both a problem and an opportunity for public transport expansion:

- Traffic congestion is widely recognised as a major and growing global problem (Cervero 1991; Downs 1992; Arnott and Small 1994). In Australia congestion costs $Aust 9.4 billion p.a. (2005) and is expected to rise to $Aust 20.4 billion by 2020 (Bureau of Transport and Regional Economics 2007).
- If humanity is to live in cities, urban liveability and the quality of urban living is of critical importance. Yet there are important social impacts of car traffic on urban liveability (Vuchic 1999) including the separation of urban communities by busy roads and impacts on social disadvantage (Rosenbloom 2007).
- The climate crisis is often manifest in cities and in private car travel which was the only sector of the UK economy for which environmental emissions in 2007 were

higher than in 1990 (Woodcock et al. 2007). They are also increasing globally and remain a major focus of concern for greenhouse gas and climate change (Bureau of Infrastructure Transport and Regional Economics 2009).

- Obesity and an aging population are major concerns for the future of humanity. Strong links have been established between physical activity and health (British Medical Association 1997) (Dora and Phillips 2000). Public transport use involves more physical activity compared to car travel, suggesting growing health concerns as car use increases (Woodcock et al. 2007).
- Motorised transport is over 95 per cent dependent on oil and accounts for almost half of world use of oil (Woodcock et al. 2007). There is a growing consensus that oil reserves are falling and that the costs of transport will increase as a result (Dodson and Sipe 2008). These issues suggest significant risks associated with car-dependent transport futures.

1.2   PUBLIC TRANSPORT RESEARCH

All aspects of public transport warrant a research focus including ridership, user behaviour, planning, policy and operations. An implied and often hidden objective of this research is to improve how public transport systems are developed and operated using insights from research.

It is important that practitioners as well as academics understand what research is. Research concerns the development of *entirely new knowledge* to find new insights into problems in public transport. It does not concern the use of existing knowledge, which is what the consulting and planning industry adopts to solve the problems. By its very nature, research in public transport is thus new, innovative and original. It is also a very powerful tool because of this.

The field of public transport research is also necessarily broad and multi-disciplinary. Topics range from psychology to engineering, from governance to operations and from theory to practice. A flavour of contemporary research in public transport has been research that combines disciplines to provide new insights. This is never quite as easy as it sounds since each discipline has a language that is often indecipherable to others and practices that limit flexibility. Addressing these barriers is both necessary and a personal motivation. A significant power to solve problems in public transport comes from cross-disciplinary research. The public transport field is also useful for researchers because it is notably prolific in generating numerous complex, confounding and 'wicked' problems that need a cross-disciplinary solution.

The field of public transport research is also by nature practical or practice focused and thus less theoretical than most academic research. I have always seen this as a significant advantage since I consider it the purpose of academia: to help solve problems in the real world. However, not everyone in academia agrees and indeed there are significant barriers between practitioners and academia. There is much truth in the view that the 'ivory towers' of academia are remote from the reality of everyday concerns. For example, research papers in leading journals are difficult to read and access for most practitioners. Public transport research has a significant challenge in making it easier for practitioners to access and understand research. This is another motivation and rationale for this *Handbook*.

1.3 BOOK AIMS AND APPROACH

This book aims to provide a comprehensive overview of the latest research in the field. So my first major challenge in assembling the book was to find the latest, most interesting research from the best researchers. I had a significant advantage in being able to do this; in 2010 my research team (The Public Transport Research Group at Monash University) developed a free research tool to help the world public transport industry get better access to research and researchers in the field. It is called the World Transit Research Clearinghouse[1] and is a free database on the web which has gathered all published research papers in the world in the field. So I reviewed the database, found the best researchers and invited them to contribute. The good news is that they said yes.

A side benefit of this approach is that the book is necessarily international in flavour. Although research applications may cover public transport systems in their native countries, the research and its findings focus on the international implications for all public transport. The book has a total of 49 authors from nine countries, from 22 universities and five private sector agencies.

I had another important advantage which I also used for this book: I am fortunate to know and work with some of the most promising young researchers who are doing tremendous and important work. There is an obvious element of 'blowing our own trumpet' in some of this; authors from the Public Transport Research Group provide six of the 20 main content chapters of the book. However, this is justified by more than just my familiarity with their research; independent evidence supports the status of our outputs in the field.[2] I hope you, dear reader, will be as inspired as I am by their work.

One last point of focus for the book is that it is very public transport mode neutral; I don't care if the wheels have rubber or steel or indeed if there are any wheels at all. What matters is quality, and we can learn a lot about that from all public transport modes, but most of all from our users and their experiences.

1.4 BOOK STRUCTURE AND CHAPTERS

The book includes 21 chapters, 20 chapters of content papers plus this Introduction. It is structured around five parts:

- *I. Research Foundations, Trends and Futures* – which includes 'research on research'; findings from two separate meta-studies of research in the field of public transport to provide insight on what the field is, how it has been changing and where it might be going in future.
- *II. User Perspectives* – comprising four chapters on user focused research and the insights it provides on how public transport can better consider user needs in service design and management.
- *III. Policy Perspectives* – including four chapters covering the strategic issues of governance, road space management and funding.
- *IV. Planning and Operational Perspectives* – including seven chapters on issues as diverse as operational control, reliability and network resilience.

- ● *V. Service Development and Future Perspectives* – with three chapters exploring mobility futures, advances in customer information and ways to improve bus systems.

Chapters in the book are now outlined:

I.   Research Foundations, Trends and Futures

Chapter 2: 'World transit research: state of the art' explores the field of public transport research using the World Transit Research Clearinghouse database as a source. Research trends and patterns are explored including geographical spread of publications, citation rates and leading authorship patterns.

Chapter 3: 'Methodologies for empirical research on the link between the built environment and transit use' presents a meta-study on the complex but important field of research linking the built environment in cities to public transport ridership. This chapter provides an overview of the theoretical frameworks, sampling and estimation methods and indicators relevant to designing empirical built environment and transit use research. Case studies are used to demonstrate the trade-offs that need to be considered when choosing between alternative approaches.

II.   User Perspectives

Chapter 4: 'Transit customer satisfaction research: is the customer always right?' presents research results on new approaches to customer satisfaction measurement. It uses customer complaint data integrated with real-time service operations data as a new tool to understand customer perspectives.

Chapter 5: 'Personal safety on public transport: research frontiers and new tools for an old problem' presents new tools to address a major problem for public transport: crime and perceptions of crime. It describes results of the first research project ever to quantify factors affecting perceptions of safety (POS) at stations and the relative influences of station design quality, anti-social behaviour (ASB), crime rates and individual psychological and social-demographic factors.

Chapter 6: 'The power of design to enrich the public transport experience' comes from the emerging field of design research and illustrates how designers explore problems in the field of public transport and how this can enhance understanding of the customer experience. It includes a range of examples from the authors' work in public transport.

Chapter 7: 'The paradigm shift in revenue protection research and practice' presents the findings of an innovative research project exploring the motivations of passengers who fare evade and how to mitigate the problem. This research provided new tools to help understand fare evaders and to improve management of the issue. The research had considerable impact, reducing evasion by over half and saving billions of dollars in cities that adopted the approaches identified.

III.   Policy Perspectives

Chapter 8: 'The governance of public transport: towards integrated design' explores theories and research in the field of public transport governance from a wider set of perspectives. It explores interactions from the various agencies and their functional regulatory perspectives including a review of levels of governance and the mechanisms of governance models. It includes recommendations on designing governance and its mechanisms into the future.

Chapter 9: 'The total social cost (TSC) of public transport modes' explores the concept of the Total Social Cost (a summation of operator, user and external costs) as a means of understanding public transport modes and their impact. Several international applications are used to explore this concept. Prospects for the use of this concept into the future are also discussed.

Chapter 10: 'New approaches and insights to managing on-road public transport priority' presents a new perspective on an old problem: successful implementation of on-road traffic priority for buses and trams. This approach moves on from 'techno rationalist' engineering perspectives of the problem to recognise and deal with the perceived intractable problem of politics and power which often constrains the development of priority in cities where car-based priorities dominate politics. The field of policy studies is described and pragmatic approaches to managing the problem of power and politics are presented.

Chapter 11: 'Paying for public transport' presents the results of research exploring the efficacy of alternative funding options for public transport with a focus on options explored in the United States. The chapter discusses use of these options in real-world circumstances, and assesses their strengths and limitations. The chapter concludes with reflections on the funding mechanisms and calls for additional research on their use.

IV. Planning and Operational Perspectives

Chapter 12: 'Public transport network resilience' presents the concepts of network resilience in public transport including the properties of service disruptions, methods of measuring resilience and disruption impacts. Approaches to mitigation of disruption impacts and methods of improving network resilience are reviewed.

Chapter 13: 'Service reliability: a planning and operations perspective' is a review of service reliability research in public transport. Definitions, impacts, indicators and improvement measures are presented and discussed. Indicators to understand the level of service reliability are presented and the chapter concludes by addressing how to improve service reliability through an appropriate design of public transport networks and schedules, in addition to control measures.

Chapter 14: 'Rail transit disruption management: a comprehensive review of strategies and approaches' provides a critical review of the state of knowledge in rail disruption management strategies, modelling, and analysis, with special emphasis placed on unplanned disruptions. The chapter summarises lessons learned from research and identifies gaps and future directions for research in the field.

Chapter 15: 'Demand management in urban railway systems: strategy, design, evaluation, monitoring and technology' synthesises demand management strategies and technologies in traffic and public transport, and develops a general public transport demand management (PTDM) framework including novel methodologies using fare card data for problem identification, design, evaluation and monitoring. Case studies illustrate successful applications of these approaches in practice.

Chapter 16: 'Transit signal priority: research and practice review and future needs' provides a detailed review of transit signal priority systems, research literature and industry practices to derive insights on successes and challenges in real-world implementations. It also identifies possible future research directions including the significant potential of more advanced control systems.

Chapter 17: 'ACES technologies and public transport operations and control' presents an analysis of the impacts and opportunities for public transport systems of four technological trends related to operations and control: Autonomous, Connected, Electric and Shared (ACES) vehicles. Policy-setting for better implementation of operations control is discussed as are challenges in implementing transitions in the technologies of control.

Chapter 18: 'Research in public transport vehicle scheduling' reviews the latest research, approaches and computerised software packages to address transit vehicle scheduling problems (VSPs). The focus is on practical methods and tools for scheduling vehicles in transit agencies from around the world. Case study examples and applications are described and future directions for research in the field are discussed.

V.   Service Development and Future Perspectives

Chapter 19: 'Incorporating Mobility-on-Demand (MOD) and Mobility-as-a-Service (MaaS) automotive services into public transportation' focuses primarily on Mobility-on-Demand services, particularly microtransit and transportation network companies (TNCs, also known as ridesourcing and ridesharing), and their integration with public transportation service in the USA. An analysis of partnership models is provided and a state of the art review of modelling of their impacts is presented. New research frontiers in the field are outlined.

Chapter 20: 'Large increases in bus use in Sweden: lessons learned' explores two case studies in Sweden where bus systems have been improved and examines the implications for practice in the field. Improvement measures, their design and implementation are described, including the impacts these had on ridership and customer satisfaction. Implications for research and practice are outlined.

Chapter 21: 'Advances in transit customer information' describes the history and benefits of transit information as practice has evolved from printed schedules to ubiquitous real-time information. It explores contemporary standardised data formats that have enabled a transit data revolution, especially the General Transit Feed Specification, as well as related web and mobile applications. Futures for transit information including Mobility-as-a-Service (MaaS) applications are also discussed.

1.5   WHEN A BOOK IS MORE THAN A BOOK

As is fitting with a book exploring research advances in planning practice including new approaches and technologies, this book also offers readers an alternative approach to better understand the research and researchers presented in this book. To supplement chapters in this book the Public Transport Research Group at Monash University has interviewed selected authors and will present these as selected episodes of our *Researching Transit* podcast series. Researching Transit can be found on all major podcast platforms or accessed via our website.[3] Search for podcast interviews with authors of chapters in this *Handbook*.

NOTES

1. See www.worldtransitresearch.info.
2. In 2015, an independent world review of academic research in the field of public transport (Heilig and Voß 2015) found that public transport research at Monash University was the leading research group in Australia and among the top three in the world.
3. See www.ptrg.info and click on the podcast option on the homepage.

REFERENCES

Arnott, R. and K. Small (1994). 'The economics of traffic congestion'. *American Scientist*, **82**(5): 446–55.

British Medical Association (1997). *Road Transport and Health*. London: Chameleon Press.

Bureau of Infrastructure Transport and Regional Economics (2009). 'Greenhouse gas emissions from Australian transport: Projections to 2020'. Working Paper No. 73. Canberra: Department of Infrastructure, Transport, Regional Development and Local Government.

Bureau of Transport and Regional Economics (2007). 'Estimating urban traffic and congestion cost trends for Australian cities'. Working Paper No. 71. Canberra: Department of Transport and Regional Services.

Cervero, R. (1991). 'Congestion, growth and public choices'. Reprint No. 51. Berkeley, CA: University of California Transportation Center.

Cosgrove, D., D. Gargett and D. Mitchell (2009). 'Urban passenger transport: How people move about in Australian cities'. Information Sheet No. 31. Canberra: Bureau of Infrastructure, Transport and Regional Economics.

Dodson, J. and N. Sipe (2008). 'Shocking the suburbs: Urban location, homeownership and oil vulnerability in the Australian city'. *Housing Studies*, **23**(3): 377–401.

Dora, C. and M. Phillips (eds) (2000). *Transport, Environment and Health*. WHO Regional Publications. Copenhagen: World Health Organization.

Downs, A. (1992). *Stuck in Traffic: Coping with Peak-hour Traffic Congestion*. Washington, DC: Brookings Institution.

Heilig, L. and S. Voß (2015). 'A scientometric analysis of public transport research'. *Journal of Public Transportation*, **18**(2): 111–41.

Rosenbloom, S. (2007). 'Lessons for Australia from the US: An Amercian looks at transportation and social exclusion'. In Graham Currie, Janet Stanley and John Stanley (eds), *No Way to Go: Transport and Social Disadvantage in Australian Communities*. Melbourne: Monash University Publishing.

United Nations Population Fund (2007). *State of World Population 2007: Unleashing the Potential of Urban Growth*. New York: United Nations Population Fund.

Vuchic, V. (1999). *Transportation for Livable Cities*. New Brunswick, NJ: Center for Urban Policy Research.

Woodcock, J., D. Banister, P. Edwards, A. Prentice and I. Roberts (2007). 'Energy and transport'. *Lancet*, **370**(9592): 1078–88.

PART I

RESEARCH FOUNDATIONS, TRENDS AND FUTURES

2. World transit research: state of the art
Nicholas Fournier and Graham Currie

2.1 INTRODUCTION

This chapter is a high-level exploration of research in public transport using a research database, the World Transit Research Clearinghouse,[1] as a resource to understand trends and patterns of research publications in the field.

Providing public transport can be challenging due to a multitude of factors that span many professional and academic disciplines, from operations and economics to land use policy and planning, as well as softer sciences on the social and behavioural factors regarding public transport. This complexity is a major challenge to the public transport profession; some authors have characterised the industry by the types of disciplines adopted to solve problems in public transport (Veeneman 2002). The disciplines provide a coherent framework to understand a specific area of knowledge. However, problems lie when practitioners and planners must work between disciplines as the understanding of issues and even use of technical terms can act as barriers to understanding.

A large and rapidly growing body of academic research literature is seeking to investigate, understand, and provide solutions to the challenges facing public transport in contemporary society. Outcomes of this research are as useful to transport practitioners and policy makers as medical research is to doctors. However, access to research is not easy for practitioners who must deal with the day-to-day pressures of delivering public transport to cities. There is a vast array of journals and research papers on numerous topics and covering many disciplines. While this is an important resource to practitioners, it is far from being readily accessible or even understandable to industry. There is a growing need to bridge the gap between the potential for academic research to aid a diverse and changing public transport industry and the barriers to access and understandability which that industry has to understand academic research.

In July 2010, the Public Transport Research Group at Monash University developed the World Transit Research (WTR) Clearinghouse to bridge this gap. The purpose of WTR is to help transit practitioners and researchers access quality research on transit using a structured database of research papers from the leading academic research journals and selected research from industry. At the end of 2019, this database includes over 7500 records linked to publish research in the industry. The system is now used by over a quarter of a million users from over 170 countries and over 8000 cities and towns.

This chapter adopts the WTR database as a tool to explore what the current state of the art is with public transport research. In particular it investigates the types/themes of research covered, trends in publication, trends in authorship and citation and the geographical patterns of research. The objective is to provide a broader insight on the trends, patterns and relationships of academic research in public transport. The research in this chapter researches research itself so is an exploration of what research is doing and who does it. This is not new; environmental communication in research was explored to better understand public communication in science (Pleasant et al. 2002). Within public transport itself a 'scientometric' analysis of digital publications was also undertaken focusing on the 5-year period 2009 to 2013 (Heilig and Voß 2015). This review covers the full history of all published digital research (spanning 39 years) and includes new insights on the historical development of research over this time.

The chapter is organised as follows: first the WTR database, its rationale, design and usage are outlined. Then methods adopted to analyse the database are described. Results and discussion then follow. The chapter concludes with a summary of key findings and implications for future knowledge development in this area.

2.2   THE WORLD TRANSIT RESEARCH CLEARINGHOUSE

WTR commenced operations in July 2010 after a period of about six months in terms of design and construction of the clearinghouse structure and the compilation of the database of records. Some 3500 records were loaded prior to start-up, representing digital publications written in English in the field prior to this date. The database has now more than doubled to over 7500 in a period of nine years.

All records are digital, hence the system leveraged the increasing digitisation and online availability of research materials from printed materials. This transition was largely complete by 2010 when WTR commenced. WTR research content does not represent all knowledge; rather it covers digital and on-line accessible knowledge which from around 2010, when the database started, represents almost all publications in the field.

The database was developed at Monash University but with cooperation with a wide range of research publishers who permit free access to research abstracts and links to web pages where user-paid access to source research is often needed via a paywall to access copyright material. The database also holds some free-access downloadable research material where copyright rules and the authors permit.

A major value of the database is the ability to search using a keyword structure developed to represent a structure of knowledge in the public transport industry. Table 2.1 illustrates the database structure built around nine knowledge themes: planning, operations, land use, policy, ridership, technology, organisation, infrastructure and economics. All research records entered into the database are tagged within this knowledge structure, which allows website users to search readily for material on the database. In addition a newsletter is published every two months, detailing the new publications in the field (Public Transport Research Group 2019); this is circulated to a user opt-in email list. Access to each newsletter is also advertised in broadcast industry websites such as the US Transportation Research Board E-Newsletter (Transportation Research Board 2020).

The WTR database is updated daily as research is published; much of this is now through automated digital research publication bulletins using set keywords from publishing agents. All entries are vetted by the database director to ensure relevance to the world public transport industry. The research tends to focus on research in developed world and urban settings.

A review of WTR and its users was undertaken in 2012 including a survey of users (Currie et al. 2012). Only about a third of website users were from academia, consultants and Government policy makers represented over half of users, and transport providers

Table 2.1   WTR database structure: topic and subject area classifier

Infrastructure	Policy	Technology	Planning
Bus/tram lane	Congestion	Alternative fuels	Education
Bus/tram priority	Disability	Automatic vehicle	Environmental
Busway	Environment	monitoring	impact
Fleet management	Equity	Emissions	History
Interchange/	Fares	Geographic information	Integration
transfer	Parking	systems	Marketing/promotion
Maintenance	Social exclusion	Intelligent transport	Methods
Right of way	Sustainable	systems	Network design
Rolling stock		Management information	Personal safety/crime
Station		systems	Promotion
Stop		Passenger information	Public consultation
Track		Ticketing systems	Route design
Traffic signals			Safety/accidents
Vehicle			Service improvement

Operations	Organisation	Land use	Service level
			Service quality
Capacity	Performance	Impacts	Service rationalisation
Coordination	Competition	Planning	Signage/information
Crowding	Contracting	Smart growth	Standards
Frequency	Governance	Transit oriented	Surveys
Performance	Management	development	Terrorism
Reliability	Nationalisation	Urban density	Travel demand
Scheduling	Privatisation	Urban design	management
Service span	Regulation	Urban sprawl	
Traffic	Structures		
	Workforce planning		

Mode	Place	Ridership	Economics
Bike	Africa	Attitudes	Appraisal/evaluation
Bus	Airport	Behaviour	Benefits
Bus rapid transit	Asia	Commuting	Capital costs
Car	Australasia	Demand	Economies of scale
Carpool	Central Business	Disadvantage	Fare revenue
Community	District (CBD)	Drivers	Finance
transport	Europe	Elasticity	Operating costs
Demand responsive	Low density	Forecasting	Pricing
transit	North America	Growth	Profitability
Ferry	Oceania	Mode choice	Revenue
Mass transit	Rural	Modelling	Subsidy
Other	South America	Old people	Value capture
Paratransit	Universities	Perceptions	Value of time
Park and ride	Urban	Young people	Willingness to pay
Pedestrian			
Rail			
School bus			
Subway/metro			
Taxi			
Tram/light rail			

some 9 per cent. The main active use of the research on the database was to be kept informed; however, about a quarter said they cited WTR research in their own reports and 13 per cent said they used the research to develop policy, and 7 per cent an actual service.

2.3   ANALYSIS APPROACH

The analysis aims to explore four perspectives: overall trends, geography, themes and authors. Within each is an overall analysis of research paper volume, trends over time, and citations. Several different analysis and visualisation techniques were utilised, such as classical research impact measures as well as slightly more sophisticated *n*-gram analysis of subject/topic areas to reveal the interaction of topics. To achieve this, several different data sources were combined to form an analysis database for this chapter.

The WTR database provides the central basis for the records analysed but this was supplemented by an analysis using Elsevier's Scopus database for a sample of WTR records.

2.3.1   Word Transit Research Database Records

The WTR database contains meta-data for a curated repository of over 7500 publications relating to public transport. The database contains several basic features:

- Paper title;
- Authors;
- Journal publication;
- Abstract (if available);
- Authors;
- Document type (article, conference, report, thesis, etc.);
- Keywords;
- Publication date;
- Subject area.

In addition to the basic meta-data, there is the 'subject area' field, which contains a code (string) classifying all subject areas relevant in the paper and their topic grouping. As opposed to user defined keywords, this provides a more structured taxonomy of research subjects which are catalogued and classified when a paper is entered into the database. The breakdown of the subject area is composed of two parts, the overall 'theme' and the 'topic', as defined in Table 2.1.

2.3.2   Elsevier Scopus Database

To supplement the basic meta-data provided in the WTR database, Elsevier's Scopus database was used. Adopting Scopus' application programming protocol (API), the database was searched using WTR publication title and digital object identifier (DOI), if available. If the publication record was found in the database, additional features for analysis, such as number of citations, city, and country were extracted and added to the local WTR database. Although WTR has some 7500 total documents, only 5408 were cross-referenced in the Scopus database. This is because WTR includes conference papers, reports, newsletters, and so on, and other documents published through universities or other institutions which are considered useful for the public transport industry but are not included in Scopus.

2.4 RESULTS

The analysis results are structured as follows: overall database, geography, modes, themes and authors. Within each section, the analysis focuses on the total volume of publications, the trends over time, and the citations for each.

2.4.1 Overall Database

At the time of writing (April 2020), the WTR database is comprised of 7670 documents in total. The vast majority of documents are journal articles at 84.6 per cent, followed by reports and conference papers at 9.6 per cent and 4.7 per cent, respectively. All remaining document types make up less than 1 per cent of the database (Table 2.2).

Volume and trends
Although the WTR database was established in 2010, it was initially populated using all relevant articles available electronically before this time. Thus, the database provides a reasonable sample of all digital records of transit research and its growth since 2010, as shown in Figure 2.1. The earliest record in the database is 1980; however, there is no doubt that earlier research documents exist but are merely not captured in the database due to many publications not being digitised and catalogued in any contemporary searchable academic database. As such, the pre-2010 data represents a record of the growth of digital online availability of research, but since 2010 it is a good representation of all research in the field.

Table 2.2   WTR database document type composition

Document Type	Number in database	Per cent of database (%)
Article	6271	84.6
Report	713	9.6
Conference	351	4.7
Newsletter	56	0.8
Book	6	0.08
Policy document	5	0.07
Discussion	4	0.05
Research paper	3	0.04
Working paper	2	0.03
Survey	1	0.01
Thesis	1	0.01
Electronic	1	0.01
Editorial	1	0.01
Total	7415	100

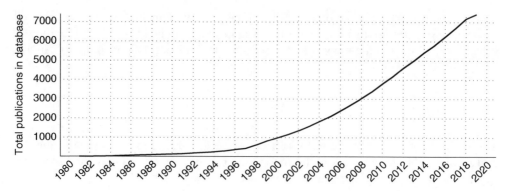

Figure 2.1   Publications by year in WTR database

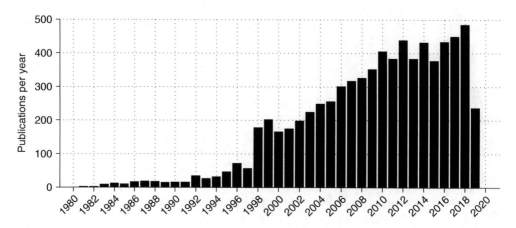

Figure 2.2   Number of papers published per year in the WTR database

Between 2010 and 2019, the number of records in the database more than doubled; this represents a compound annual growth rate of about 7.75 per cent, or a doubling of research in the field every 9.3 years.

The rate of growth is presented annually in Figure 2.2.[2] In 2010 just over 400 papers were published in the public transport field, representing just over 7.8 a week. In 2018, the latest full year of records, this had increased to almost 500 a year: a 20 per cent increase or broadly 9.3 new papers a week.

Leading journals in database
The WTR database contains approximately 256^3 different journals. By research publication volume, the database is dominated by *Transportation Research Record*, the journal of the Transportation Research Board's annual meeting in Washington, DC, USA, representing 35 per cent of the whole database. The next largest journal publication is substantially less, at just 8 per cent, which is *Transportation Research Part A: Policy and Practice*.

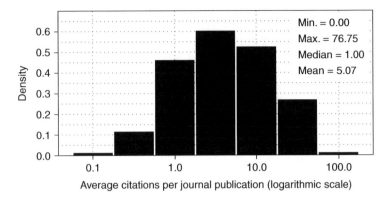

Figure 2.3 *Distribution of average citations per publication of journals*

Citation of research papers is a common metric which speaks to academic value, since citation implies it is valued as a source by other researchers. The average number of citations per publication is shown in Figure 2.3. On average, papers in the field are cited just slightly over five times. The distribution of average citation per journal publication is extremely skewed, but when plotted on a logarithmic scale (i.e., log-normal distribution), it takes a more 'normal' Gaussian distribution. The minimum citation rate is 0, with a maximum of 76.75, a mean of 5.07, and a median of 1.00. The majority of journals have a very low citation rate of between 1 to 10 citations per publication, and there are a few outliers with extremely high citation rates.

A more detailed perspective of the leading journals in the database is shown in Table 2.3, which is created by combining the journals that are in either or both the top ten by publication volume or top ten by citation rate.

This illustrates a very skewed citation rate between journals. The *Institute of Electrical and Electronic Engineers (IEEE) Transactions on Intelligent Transportation Systems* appears to be the top cited journal with an average of 76.75 citations per article. Behind this is *Transportmetrica* and *Transportation Research Part B: Methodological*, with averages of 52.5 and 40.8 citations per publication, respectively. There is some suggestion in these patterns that journals associated with technology have higher citation rates. It should be noted, however, that having fewer publications per journal can also tend to inflate the citation rate. Regardless, *IEEE* as a leading journal may be indicative of the amount of interest generated in recent years regarding technologically driven disruption and hype in the transportation industry (e.g., demand responsive and autonomous vehicles).

2.4.2 Geography

The location of a publication was determined by the location of author affiliation. When a paper possesses multiple authors from different locations, a fractional allocation was given by dividing by the number of different author locations. For example, a paper with two authors in New York City and one in Melbourne would be given a weight of 2/3 to New York and 1/3 to Melbourne. The total number of papers per location is then the sum of all these values.

Table 2.3   Top most cited or productive academic journals in WTR database

Journal	N	Citations per publication	Proportion of database (%)
Transportation Research Record	1848	8.78	32.08
Other (Not top ten cited or published)	1339	3.21	23.24
Transportation Research Part A: Policy and Practice	466	28.98	8.09
Transport Policy	336	27.79	5.83
Transportation Research Part B: Methodological	306	40.83	5.31
Transportation Research Part C: Emerging Technologies	263	32.90	4.57
Journal of Transport Geography	227	19.19	3.94
Research in Transportation Economics	194	6.04	3.37
Journal of Public Transportation	173	7.56	3.00
ITE Journal	164	2.20	2.85
Transportation	154	23.65	2.67
Transportation Research Part D: Transport and Environment	151	34.79	2.62
Transportation Research Part E: Logistics and Transportation Review	81	33.44	1.41
IEEE Transactions on Intelligent Transportation Systems	32	76.75	0.56
Environment and Planning A	14	34.07	0.24
Journal of Transport Economics and Policy	5	33.00	0.09
Environment and Planning B: Planning and Design	4	36.50	0.07
Transportmetrica	2	52.50	0.03
Journal of Advanced Transportation	2	33.00	0.03

Volume

The average number of publications per country in the database is 65.8 with a max of 1845.5.[4] Table 2.4 shows the overall number and proportion of papers in the database by country, as well as the average number and rate of publication per year. The United States represents the majority of the database and produces over six times more publications than the next most productive country. This demonstrates a limited geographic diversity of spread of countries who publish research in the field. However, there are several countries which show very strong growth rates in publications over the analysis period, including China, which is currently the second largest country by volume.

The pattern of geographic publication in Table 2.4 is also influenced by the use of publications written in English in the database. Despite this, non-English-speaking countries such as China and European countries represent a large share of the field.

Figure 2.4 shows the overall distribution of publications by city location around the world. Again, the majority of publications come from North America (i.e., the United States) and Europe, with a substantial number also coming from Asia. However, there does appear to be a considerable number of publications coming from sparse yet concentrated locations, such as Australia and Chile. These two standout locations are revealed in Table 2.5 as Santiago, Chile, with 97.5 publications and in Australia are Melbourne, Sydney and Brisbane, with 136, 101.3 and 85.5 publications, respectively. With the average number publications per city at just 6.8 and 65.8 per country, these leading cities have remarkably high productivity in the WTR database.

Table 2.4   Leading publishing countries/states in WTR database

Country/State	Total publications	Proportion of database (%)	Average number of publications per annum (2010–19)	Compound annual growth rate (2010–19) (%)
United States	1845.50	40.00	82.24	5.62
China	441.33	9.57	40.55	18.61
Australia	409.50	8.88	31.45	12.18
United Kingdom	340.83	7.39	18.13	7.07
Canada	261.00	5.66	18.91	11.30
Netherlands	203.00	4.40	13.34	9.86
Spain	135.50	2.94	10.19	11.85
Sweden	114.50	2.48	9.20	13.87
Germany	112.33	2.43	8.82	12.54
Chile	100.50	2.18	9.54	17.53
France	96.83	2.10	5.99	8.84
Italy	92.50	2.00	6.68	11.34
Hong Kong	87.33	1.89	5.60	9.96
Taiwan	70.17	1.52	4.28	8.68
South Korea	68.50	1.48	4.42	9.17
New Zealand	67.50	1.46	5.90	15.78
Switzerland	57.83	1.25	4.94	16.01
India	55.50	1.20	4.60	13.75
Singapore	53.50	1.16	4.20	13.35

Trends

Figure 2.5 expands upon Figure 2.1 to include WTR database composition by country and publication year. The United States has always represented the largest contributor since 2010, but research in the rest of the world has increasingly grown to represent a higher share of all publications. The UK, China and Australia are the next highest in share of publication countries in recent years after the USA.

2.4.3   Modes

Although transport 'mode' is technically only one of the classification themes, it is unique in that it is relevant to almost all publications. For this reason, a more detailed analysis is given to mode because of its relative importance in transit research.

Paper volume by mode

The most prominent modes in the database are bus, rail and the US-based umbrella term of 'mass transit', representing 25.7 per cent, 19.8 per cent and 11 per cent, respectively. All other modes make up a small percentage of the database. However, other modes appear to garner a relatively high number of average citations per publication. This means that despite their small share, they attract considerable attention (Table 2.6).

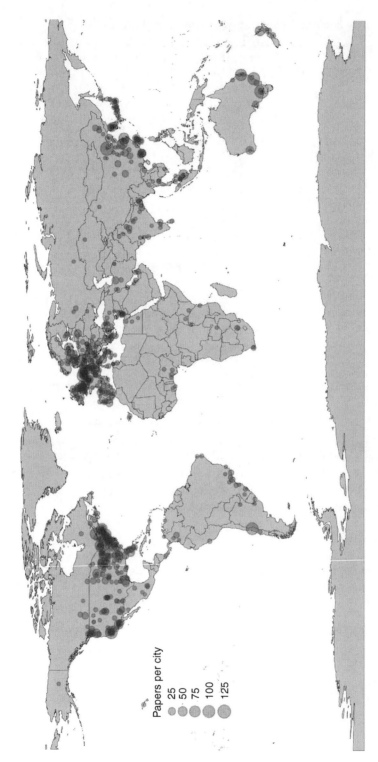

Figure 2.4   City and quantity of publications in WTR database

Table 2.5   Leading cities by publication volume in WTR database

City	Country	Number of publications
Melbourne	Australia	136.0
Beijing	China	133.3
Delft	Netherlands	105.0
Berkeley	United States	102.5
Sydney	Australia	101.3
Santiago	Chile	97.5
New York	United States	95.7
Montreal	Canada	89.0
London	United Kingdom	86.3
Brisbane	Australia	84.5
Cambridge	United States	72.5
Shanghai	China	69.8
Chicago	United States	65.8

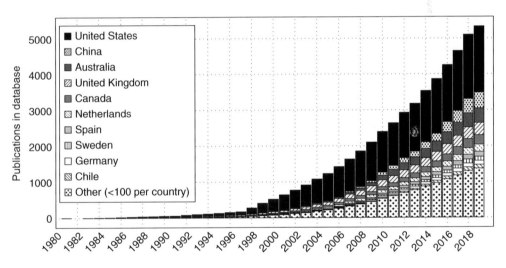

Figure 2.5   Total publications in database by country and year

Mode trends

Figure 2.6 presents the proportion of papers in the database by mode and year of publication. Papers on bus are the most common (28 per cent) but in global public transport terms, bus is likely to represent more than half of all services. This suggests some under-representation of bus in global transit research. Papers on bus and rail represent the highest share of papers throughout the years, while 'mass transit' has largely faded away in recent years. However, it appears that mass transit has been replaced by more mode-specific terminology, such as 'subway/metro', 'bus', 'tram/light rail' and 'bus rapid transit'. Trend data also illustrates the growth in bus rapid transit literature from about the year 2000 onwards and more recently an increasing interest in bike and park and ride.

Table 2.6   WTR database composition by mode

Mode	N	Citations per publication	Proportion in database (%)
Bus	1821	14.80	28.31
Rail	1402	15.50	21.80
Mass transit	780	24.23	12.13
Subway/metro	563	15.31	8.75
Tram/light rail	370	8.73	5.75
Car	323	16.79	5.02
Bus rapid transit	283	8.21	4.40
Pedestrian	277	27.27	4.31
Bike	225	23.81	3.50
Park and ride	73	11.51	1.13
Paratransit	72	15.29	1.12
Demand responsive transit	59	13.85	0.92
Carpool	43	12.63	0.67
Other	39	6.87	0.61
Taxi	38	17.68	0.59
Ferry	38	3.45	0.59
School bus	20	18.15	0.31
Community transport	6	11.5	0.09

Citation rates per paper by transit mode

Similar to evaluating journal impact, papers focusing on mode type can be evaluated by average citation per publication as a means to gauge academic research interest (Figure 2.7). Although bus and rail dominate the database by volume of publications, other modes yield a high number of average citations per paper, such as pedestrians and bikes. This means that despite their relatively small research volume, they attract a robust number of research citations. However, the average citation per publication rate for very rare research areas may be inflated simply because there are so few publications in that research area. For example, school bus has only 20 publications, yet the citation rate is 18.15 citations per publication. This might also be seen as a research opportunity, since publishing research in this area seems to have a better impact in terms of citation.

2.4.4   Research Themes

Using the WTR database structure subject area classification in Table 2.1, the topics in the database were analysed by volume and trend.

Volume

Table 2.7 summarises overall volume of publication themes to provide a general sense of database composition by theme. In general, ridership, planning and operations are the leading three themes, comprising 53.3 per cent of the entire database. However, the other themes are not to be discounted as they still represent a sizeable proportion of the

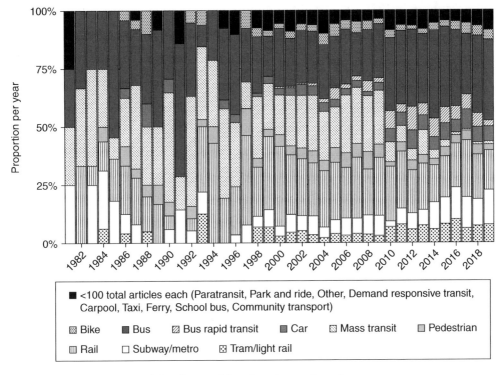

Figure 2.6   Proportion of database publications by mode and year

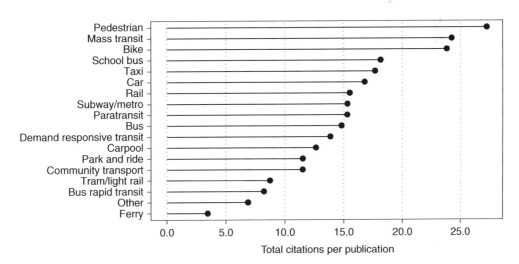

Figure 2.7   Citations per publication by mode: WTR research database content

Table 2.7   Volume of database themes

Theme	N	Citations per publication	Proportion in database (%)
Planning	3628	14.29	19.72
Ridership	3595	18.62	19.54
Operations	2587	18.44	14.06
Infrastructure	2012	17.64	10.94
Land use	1571	17.17	8.54
Economics	1469	12.98	7.98
Policy	1271	16.52	6.91
Technology	1155	15.46	6.28
Organisation	1028	11.04	5.59
Literature review	81	17.43	0.44

Table 2.8   Top topics and themes by volume in database

Topic	Theme	N	Citations per publication
Planning	Land use	715	19.03
Surveys	Planning	654	14.29
Traffic	Operations	610	22.71
Behaviour	Ridership	608	12.34
Commuting	Ridership	579	24.63
Performance	Organisation	545	12.71
Performance	Operations	545	12.71
Mode Choice	Ridership	533	23.68
Demand	Ridership	526	22.62
Vehicle	Infrastructure	520	23.83
Impacts	Land use	421	12.74
Scheduling	Operations	392	25.83
Other (<1% of database)		12638	14.98

database, particularly infrastructure, land use and economics, which still account for 27.5 per cent of the database.

The individual publication topics were far less concentrated (Table 2.8), with all topics representing less than 4 per cent of the database and 65.5 per cent being composed of topics that represent 2 per cent or less. In general, this means that the topics are very dispersed and no single topic stands out. By citation performance, scheduling, commuting, vehicles and mode choice have the highest citation rates.

Topic trends

Topic areas tend to evolve over time. Figure 2.8 shows the proportion of topic themes in the database by publication year. This illustrates a gradual decline in the volume of publications regarding infrastructure, organisation and economics, while planning, ridership and

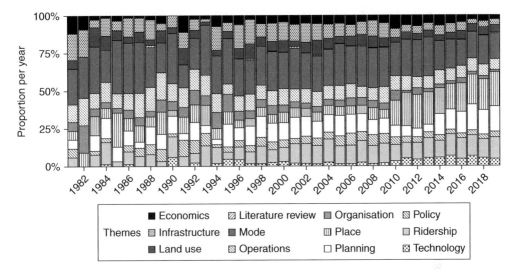

Figure 2.8   Proportion of database by topic theme and year

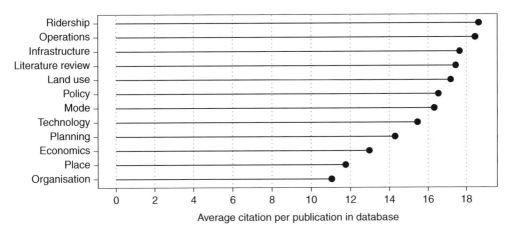

Figure 2.9   Average citation per publication by topic theme in database

technology have grown. The planning topic in particular has seen substantial growth in recent years. This could be interpreted as indicative of developed nations shifting focus away from major infrastructure projects and towards a more refined planning-based approach.

Topic citations

As with mode, publications classified by topic can be gauged by average citation per publication. Results of this are shown in Figure 2.9. Although planning publications are growing and now represent the largest proportion of the database, they have a relatively low rank in terms of average citations per publication. The top topic themes by average citation per publication are ridership, operations and infrastructure. Literature review is

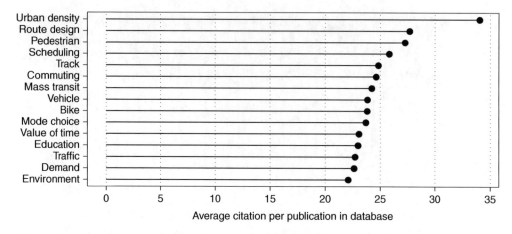

Figure 2.10   Average citation per publication by topic in database

fourth ranked in terms of citation, despite it having the least number of publications of this theme, just 81 in total (see Table 2.7). This clearly suggests literature reviews have much academic value in terms of citation performance; authors aiming for academic impact should take note of this finding.

The top 15 most cited individual topic areas are displayed in Figure 2.10. Most topics are relatively evenly cited with one major exception: urban density is a clear outlier, with an average of 34 citations per publication. The next nearest are route design and pedestrian at 27.7 and 27.3, respectively. It is interesting that urban density is so prominent, yet is ranked 111th by volume. This might be illustrative of the wider cross-disciplinary interest in the topic for both the land use, governance as well as the transport planning community. It is clear that urban density is an important yet potentially underrepresented topic for research in public transport.

2.4.5   Authors

Authors are also compared using total associated publications and academic citations for WTR content. Author publications and citations in WTR were counted based on publications cross-referenced in the Scopus database. It should be noted that authors may have a greater number of public transport publications/citations if those articles are not found in Scopus.

Author volume

The top 20 most productive authors in terms of research volume in the WTR database are shown in Figure 2.11. Graham Currie is top by volume, with over 104 published articles in public transport, with next authors in order of volume including Avishai Ceder, Ahmed El-Geneidy, David Hensher and Corinne Mulley, with 61, 56, 56 and 52 publications respectively. One additional factor included is whether the publication is as first author or not (shown as dark black line and dot). The proportion of lead-authored papers varies among authors, and can largely depend upon the field, resources, nature of research

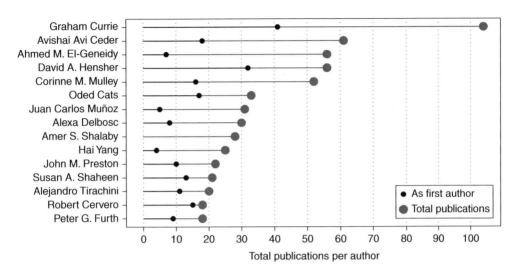

Figure 2.11   Top published authors in WTR database

supervision and academic culture of authorship. For example, some fields are prone to having a greater number of single authored papers, such as urban planning, compared to engineering fields, which are frequently co-authored in teams of researchers.

In general, the top five authors by volume are also the top five authors by first author authorship; however David Hensher, ranked fourth in this analysis, is ranked second by first author publication volume.

Author citations
Total citations per author (not per publication) are shown in Figure 2.12. An interesting result here is that many of the most cited authors do not appear in the list of most published authors, for example Robert Cervero and Kara Kockelman. These authors possess relatively few public transport publications in the WTR database, but those publications are heavily cited. Within the field, Robert Cervero, David Hensher and Graham Currie are the most cited, with Kara Kockelman a close fourth.

Author impact
Average citation rate per publication is compared for authors in this analysis. The distribution of overall paper citation rates for authors is shown in Figure 2.13, revealing a highly skewed distribution with a long tail of few authors having a very high citation rate. For clarity, it is logarithmically scaled, revealing a generally log-normal distribution. The mean citation rate (average citation per publication) is 15.88, has a median of 5.0, and a minimum and maximum of 0 and 1478, respectively.

Another perspective is illustrated in Figure 2.14 where total publications versus average citations per author are plotted. This effectively shows the author impact of articles in the database from both the perspective of publication volume and overall citations. Authors in the top left have fewer but higher impact articles, and those in the lower right have a high publication rate but fewer citations per publication.

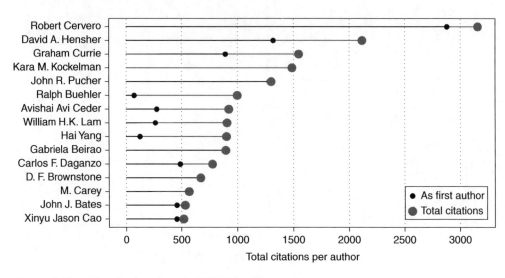

Figure 2.12   Top cited authors in WTR database content

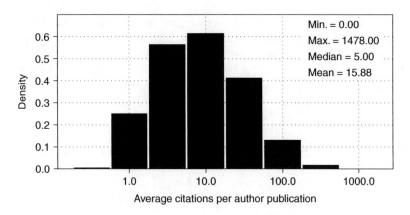

Figure 2.13   Distribution of average citations per author publication

For clarity, Figure 2.14 is plotted on a logarithmic scale along the vertical axis. In general, there are two extremes, authors with very few but very high impact publications (e.g., Kara Kockelman) and authors with a high volume of publications but lower impact per publication (e.g., Graham Currie).

2.5   CONCLUSIONS

This chapter explores the current state of public transport research using an analysis of the World Transit Research database, a clearinghouse of research publications aimed at improving industry access to research. It covers the entire history of digital research publications in the field up to the end of the year 2019.

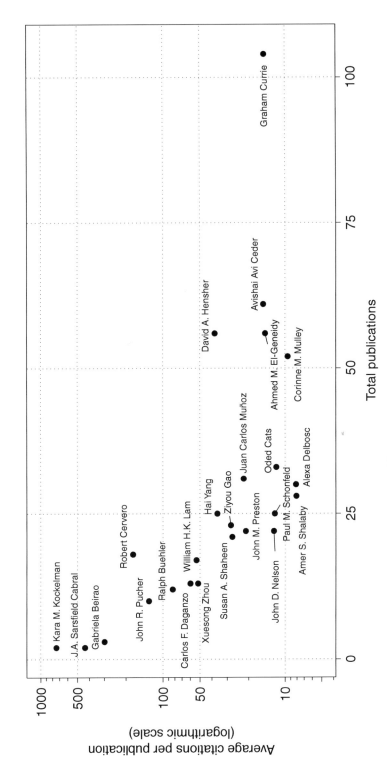

Figure 2.14 Leading authors: top 15 most published and/or most cited

Public transport research is mainly comprised of academic papers, at 84.6 per cent, following by reports and conference papers, at 9.6 per cent and 4.7 per cent, respectively. The remaining items represent less than 1 per cent of the database. The database is currently growing rapidly from an average of 7.7 papers a week in 2010 to 9.6 a week in 2018. The average compound growth rate of public transport research papers is 7.75 per cent a year, which implies research in the field doubles every 9 years.

By volume, the journal *Transportation Research Record* has the largest share of research papers in public transport, representing 32.1 per cent of the database. However, this has a citation rate of only 8.78 citations per publication. That is quite low compared to the highest citation rate of 76.75 for the *IEEE Transactions on Intelligent Transportation Systems*, but is still above the mean journal value of 5.07. The United States represents the largest proportion of the research in the field, at 34.6 per cent, followed by China, Australia and the United Kingdom, at 8.3 per cent, 7.7 per cent and 6.4 per cent, respectively. The countries with the fastest growing publication rates are China, Chile, Switzerland and New Zealand.

Generally, the most common mode in publications is 'bus', followed by 'rail', but 'pedestrians', 'mass transit' and 'bikes' are the most cited modes in papers. An interesting trend is a decline of the term 'mass transit' and its replacement with more specific public transport terminology, such as 'bus rapid transit', 'tram/light rail', and 'subway/metro'. Major themes in the database are 'planning', 'ridership', 'operations' and 'infrastructure', with 'planning' and 'ridership' representing 40 per cent of publications in the database alone. Planning is also the fastest growing theme for papers in the field, and has overtaken operations and infrastructure by total volume of publications in the last decade.

The leading authors in the database by volume and citation rate, respectively, are Graham Currie, with over 100 verifiable publications in the database, and Kara Kockelman, with an average citation rate of over 750 citations per publication. The average number of publications in the database per author is 1.1, with an average citation rate of 15.88 citations per publication.

Overall, results show that the volume of transit research is rapidly expanding and diversifying. Planning and ridership are key themes in public transport research and are outpacing the more supply-side themes of operations and infrastructure. There is also some evidence that public transport research is diversifying from techno-rationalist operations and engineering fields into social and psychological sciences. With a substantial growth rate in both the volume (doubling every nine years) and diversity of research (expanding into non-technical fields) practitioners will have a better range of research to support their efforts but the scale of the research search and assimilation tasks will also increase substantially into the future. Researchers in the public transport field should be proud of their success but should also be aware of the challenges that practitioners have in comprehending a vastly expanding field. The World Transit Research clearinghouse is increasingly becoming an essential resource to an expanding global industry seeking to leverage the benefits of an expanding and increasingly sophisticated knowledge base in public transport research.

NOTES

1. See www.worldtransitresearch.info.
2. The figure for 2019 appears to be lower because not all 2019 publications had been added to the WTR database at the time of writing.
3. This number does not count the 994 documents where the publisher was missing from the catalogue record. This was due to privately or institutionally published articles.
4. The average number of publications per country was calculated excluding countries with zero publications.

REFERENCES

Currie, G., A. Delbosc and P. Forbes (2012). 'World transit research: Trends in need, supply and use'. *Transportation Research Record: Journal of the Transportation Research Board*, **2276**(1): 1–8.
Heilig, L. and S. Voß (2015). 'A scientometric analysis of public transport research'. *Journal of Public Transportation*, **18**(2): 111–41.
Pleasant, A., J. Good, J. Shanahan and B. Cohen (2002). 'The literature of environmental communication'. *Public Understanding of Science*, **11**: 197–205.
Public Transport Research Group (2019). 'World Transit Research October 2019 Newsletter'. *World Transit Research Newsletter*.
Transportation Research Board (2020). 'TRB transportation research e-newsletter'. Accessed 4 December 2019 at http://www.trb.org/Main/Newsletter-130326.aspx.
Veeneman, W. (2002). *Mind the Gap: Bridging Theories and Practice for the Organisation of Metropolitan Public Transport*. Delft: TRAIL Research School.

3. Methodologies for empirical research on the link between the built environment and transit use

Laura Aston, Graham Currie, Md Kamruzzaman and Alexa Delbosc

3.1 CONTEXT FOR BUILT ENVIRONMENT AND TRANSIT USE RESEARCH

Growth in urban populations, and the associated demand for access to goods, amenities and employment, is placing increasing pressure on urban transportation networks. Demand for urban transportation derives from the need for people and goods to move between different locations (Mitchell and Rapkin 1954). The location and intensity of land uses, as well as the configuration of transportation networks, therefore underpins demand for travel. Interest in the relationship between these built environment characteristics and travel demand has grown over the last century, in response to a range of technological developments, environmental concerns and urban challenges (Banister et al. 2007; Miller 2019). Urban public transport offers an efficient mobility solution for cities faced with growing demand for travel (Banister 2005). Research focused on understanding associations between the built environment and transit use (BE-TU) is therefore particularly relevant to the continued prosperity and liveability of cities.

Knowledge of the factors driving demand for travel by transit is important for two key reasons. First, investment decisions about the supply and operation of transport rely on accurate predictions of demand. Effective investment in transit is underpinned by reliable predictions. Second, knowledge of the drivers of transit ridership also helps policy makers design strategies to influence demand.

Chapter Overview

This chapter introduces approaches to examining associations between the built environment and transit use. A definition of the built environment in the context of transit use is provided following this chapter outline. Section 3.2 provides an overview of the components of causal research design. Theoretical frameworks used to explain the mechanisms driving empirical results in land use and travel behaviour research are introduced. Section 3.3 explores study design considerations for analysing the BE-TU relationship. Three key areas are discussed: sampling, data and estimation methods. Section 3.4 provides guidance on indicators that are commonly used to quantify properties of the built environment. This includes a useful summary of relevant variables for those looking to measure the built environment as an explanatory factor for other research, as well as for research focused on understanding the impacts of transit on the built environment. Section 3.5 introduces future directions for empirical BE-TU research. The chapter concludes by summarising issues related to the generalisability of research, including recommendations and state of the art approaches for addressing them.

The focus of this chapter is on empirical methods. For more information regarding models that simulate land use or transport, readers are referred to recently published reviews of the frameworks and approaches that underpin transport and land use, or integrated urban modelling, including Miller (2019); Wegener and Spiekerman (2018) and Moeckel et al. (2019).

Defining the Built Environment in the Context of Transit Use

The built environment is a relevant factor to consider in the context of most travel behaviour studies, not only those that aim to better understand the specific urban design and land use interventions that impact transit use. Furthermore, the impact of transit on the built environment is also an important topic of research.

Definitions of the built environment in this context have evolved in response to knowledge development and advancements in data collection methods. Early travel behaviour research defined land use with respect to buildings and infrastructure and their purpose, and the intensity of occupants or users of the land (Mitchell and Rapkin 1954). A series of empirical studies and meta-analyses gave rise to the convention of using several 'D-variables' to represent the built environment in research. The original built form factors of Density, Diversity and Design (Cervero and Kockelman 1997) have been expanded to include Destination accessibility and Distance to transit (Ewing and Cervero 2010).

The availability of big data sets and techniques for aggregating and analysing them has given rise to a new era of BE-TU research. Metrics for measuring walkability, in terms of access to local amenities and services, have proliferated (Boulange et al. 2017; Park et al. 2017; Woldeamanuel and Kent 2016). Network-level accessibility, and the factors that impact the relative ease and competitiveness of transit travel to places across a network, have also gained increased attention (Levinson et al. 2017; Renne et al. 2016). This chapter offers guidance for researchers seeking to measure the evolving dimensions of the built environment that impact transit use.

3.2   FRAMEWORKS THAT FIT: APPLYING BUILT ENVIRONMENT AND TRANSIT USE RESEARCH

The methods for quantifying the built environment outlined in this chapter should be considered as part of an overall research strategy that is fit-for-purpose. Many possible combinations of sampling strategies, estimation methods and data sources are available for empirical BE-TU investigation. To promote generalisability between findings, researchers must strive to design their study in keeping with the assumptions of the theoretical framework within which travel behaviour is conceptualised (Boarnet and Crane 2001a). This chapter first introduces some of the economic, psychological and systems-based frameworks that may be used. It then distinguishes causal and correlational research, before outlining some of the considerations for study design that might impact particular applications of research.

Theoretical Frameworks for Understanding Built Environment Impacts on Transit

Research exploring travel behaviour is underpinned by the recognition that the need to travel derives from a desire to access activities in different locations. Early theoretical frameworks considered the size, function, relationship to neighbouring land uses and connection to transportation networks as four key influences of the built environment on travel behaviour (Mitchell and Rapkin 1954, p. 16). Theories, and some useful sources that address them, include:

- Urban design theories of travel demand (Boarnet and Crane 2001b; Litman and Steele 2017);
- Generalised cost and utility (Ben-Akiva 1985; Domencich and McFadden 1975; Hensher 2015b);
- Activity-space theory (Fan 2007).

Such theories suggest that the built environment can provide a competitive advantage for particular modes. This has fuelled interest in the strategic context for integrated BE-TU research.

Psychological frameworks are increasingly used to conceptualise built environment impacts on travel behaviour from a behavioural perspective. Frameworks include:

- Learning theory and cognitive dissonance theory (De Vos et al. 2018; van de Coevering et al. 2018);
- Attitudes and perceptions (Dill et al. 2014; Spears et al. 2013; van Wee et al. 2019);
- Mobility biographies (Jain et al. 2020; Scheiner 2018).

Finally, City Science offers a system-based conceptual framework that recognises the transportation–land use relationship as part of a complex urban system (Batty 2013; West 2017). It seeks to identify general rules which may predict growth and behaviour of transportation networks.

Designing research that is consistent with a framework is important for two reasons. The framework can help interpret results and identify those that are unexpected. Second, frameworks are essential for adapting results from research to policy. Research that lacks a theoretical framework therefore has limited generalisability to real-world applications.

Distinguishing Causal and Correlational Research

Travel behaviour research warrants bespoke study design that fits the data and can appropriately test new hypotheses. Causal study design is the gold standard for evaluating the impacts of an intervention, such as land use change, on behaviour (Khander et al. 2010). Causal research provides findings that can be generalised, based on the proof of a cause-and-effect relationship. This is important for policy-making. In order to make causal inferences about research findings, four criteria must be met. These include (Singleton 2005):

1. Associations: a statistically significant relationship between the cause and effect;

2. Non-spuriousness: a relationship that cannot be attributed to third factors, such as another variable or interaction (collinearity) between variables;
3. Time precedence/order: the cause precedes the effect;
4. Theoretical causal mechanisms: a plausible explanation for why the alleged cause should produce the observed effect.

Establishing these conditions is a difficult task in transport and land use research. First, experimental research requires the analysis of treatment groups compared to a control group, before and after an intervention (Creswell 2009). In the case of the built environment and travel behaviour research, this requires observing the mode choice of individuals following changes to the built environment. Identifying and collecting travel behaviour data for large samples of individuals, over sufficient time to allow changes in travel behaviour to manifest themselves, poses ethical and logistical challenges. As a result, most empirical research is non-experimental, or observational, in nature. A comprehensive review of the literature reveals that only 10 per cent of BE-TU studies use multi-year data (Aston et al. 2020b).

Observational studies typically adopt cross-sectional sampling techniques, using data measured for a single point in time for a particular study area (usually a city or network). Such studies do not control for the temporal sequence of the built environment change preceding the travel behaviour change, which is a requirement for establishing causal relationships between variables (Creswell 2009).

Despite the challenges posed by causal research design in BE-TU empirical analysis, appreciation for the long-range nature of travel decision making, and advances in data collection, have seen an increased emphasis on multi-period research design and behavioural analyses. Longitudinal studies, with data collected two or more years apart, is increasingly being used to enable inferences to be drawn about the direction of causality between changes in the built environment and changes in travel behaviour (van de Coevering et al. 2018). As an alternative, some researchers leverage quasi-longitudinal study design, in which individuals who have recently experienced a built environment change are asked about their travel mode choice before and after the change (Cao et al. 2007; Handy et al. 2005; Yang et al. 2017). This approach has even been extended to consider attitudes toward travel before and after residential relocation, by asking respondents to report on their relative perceptions of particular modes before and after relocation (De Vos et al. 2018).

Applications in Demand Forecasting

Neighbourhood built environment factors are an important input to reliable ridership and mode split models (Cervero 2002). Similarly, trip generation rates should differentiate between automobile and transit modes, so as not to overestimate the vehicle trip inducements of new developments (De Gruyter 2019). Evidence obtained through causal and non-causal study design alike can provide useful inputs for these forecasting applications. For example, sketch plans and direct ridership models are used to predict transit use based on the observed properties of the built environment (Lane et al. 2006).

In such applications, cross-sectional models of the BE-TU association can improve the accuracy of travel models. However, correlational findings are more susceptible to unreliability, because their magnitude is dependent on the variables and study design used to estimate them (van de Coevering et al. 2015). This means they are context-dependent, with limited transferability outside the research setting. Furthermore, the BE-TU relationship is weak, which means predictions are likely to be imprecise (Aston et al. 2020b). As a result, transit and land use models must typically be re-specified and calibrated for each new forecasting application.

Carefully designed studies can minimise errors and increase the reliability of predictions associated with empirical evidence. This requires matching the estimation strategy to the data chosen and including relevant external variables (see section 3.3). Best practice approaches to research design may not always be clear or available. In such cases, sensitivity testing the association of BE-TU under different research specifications can provide prediction intervals which can highlight the precision (or lack) associated with specific correlations (Aston et al. 2020b).

Applications in Travel Behaviour and Mode Choice Policy

Many planning strategies have been developed to promote sustainable travel behaviours by integrating transit services with the built environment (Banister et al. 2007; Stevens 2017). These include Smart Growth, Transit-Oriented Development, Compact Development and New Urbanism. Causal research methods are most useful for policy because they facilitate the formulation of behavioural frameworks that explain built environment impacts on transit use. Such frameworks are not circumstantial: they provide a logic that is more flexible in the face of diverse contexts, policies and geographic factors (Handy 1996). Behavioural understanding of the relationship is therefore fundamental for successful policy formulation. Observational research does not explain the behavioural mechanisms underpinning transit use behaviours, which makes it difficult to design travel behaviour policies from them (Boarnet 2011; Handy 1996). However, many of the conditions for causal research can be satisfied within the observational study design paradigm, to maximise the policy-applicability of primary research. These are outlined in section 3.3.

Although psychological theory has gained currency for its ability to provide transferrable behavioural explanations of travel behaviour, its application to transit use is still underdeveloped. Readers are referred to the psychology literature, and to recent reviews of the application of psychological frameworks in built environment and travel behaviour, for more detailed guidance on the development of causal experiments (Dill et al. 2014; Scheiner 2018; van Wee et al. 2019).

3.3   METHODOLOGICAL CONCEPTS IN EMPIRICAL BUILT ENVIRONMENT AND PUBLIC TRANSPORT RESEARCH

Regardless of whether a researcher aims to design a causal experiment, carefully designed studies are important for maximising the reliability of results (Aston et al. 2020b; Elvik 2005a). Key considerations for BE-TU research design, discussed in this section, are:

1. Sampling strategy;
2. Data;

3.   Unit of analysis;
4.   Analysis method;
5.   Alternative explanations.

This section first presents options for collecting observations. It then presents an overview of the type of data used to represent the dependent variable. A framework for conceptualising the relevant unit of analysis for built environment variables is introduced. Considerations for choosing statistical methods to estimate relationships between variables are presented. Common third factors that may provide alternative explanations for travel behaviour relationships with transit use are outlined, as well as methods for accounting for them with study design.

Scope and Sampling

Researchers must first determine the temporal and geographic scope of their study. Contextual differences from network to network constrain most studies to a single city or urban area. For studies geared to developing forecasting models, it is common to take a census of all transit sites. For policy-oriented research, which is geared more towards individual mode choices, or proof-of-concept for factors affecting transit ridership, it is pragmatic to construct a cross-sectional sample of randomly selected sites or individuals (Hensher and Button 2008). Cross-sectional data provides a snapshot of quantitative evidence for a single time period. Mainly due to their limited temporal scope, they do not establish whether the association is the result of a causal interaction between the variables (van de Coevering et al. 2015).

Longitudinal methods leverage repeat observations of the same sample over multiple time points. Panel surveys, a type of longitudinal data, use repeat observations of the same individuals over time. Provided the corresponding built environment data can be obtained, these methods can be used to draw causal inference (van de Coevering et al. 2015). Cross-sequential studies, involving multiple cross-sections of different individuals at different time points, are another alternative that can facilitate quasi-experimental research. Chapter 14 in the *Handbook of Transport Modelling* provides more information about sampling techniques (Stopher 2008).

Cross-sectional samples continue to dominate BE-TU research. Despite causal limitations, there are many ways researchers can make valid contributions using cross-sectional methods. Researchers should acknowledge the limitations of single-period and cross-sectional studies with respect to causal inference, while adopting appropriate methods to suit the data and the problem, as described in the following sections.

Data Types

There are two types of variable for which data is needed in BE-TU research: data for transit travel and data for independent factors that can impact it.

Travel behaviour can be quantified in terms of actual use (revealed preferences) or intended use (stated preference). Revealed preference data is often easier to obtain: many authorities routinely collect evidence on travel behaviours as part of national travel surveys or census, while most transit authorities collect ridership data. Rose and Bliemer

(2008) offer guidance on the design of robust and reliable stated preference surveys for travel behaviour research. Survey data about attitudes and preferences can also provide insight about BE-TU linkages. Such surveys typically leverage Likert scales, which ask respondents to rank their agreement with statements about transit modes (De Vos 2018; Ton et al. 2019). Attitudinal data provides valuable insights about the behavioural mechanisms by which the built environment impacts transit use.

The built environment is typically quantified with objective indicators of population, land use type or intensity, street configurations or amenity counts. These 'measured' data sources are the subject of section 3.4 of this chapter. Despite the prevalence of objectively measured built environment measures in the field, subjective or perceptual indicators are also increasingly important for unlocking behavioural insights (Appleyard 2010). Perceptual indicators must be carefully developed to ensure that the perceptual variables accurately reflect individuals' perception of a built environment quality (Ewing and Handy 2009). Handy et al. (2005) document the design of a survey to measure respondents' perception of the neighbourhood built environment. The survey asks respondents to indicate their level of agreement with statements about modal preferences and use according to a five-point scale ranging from 1 ('strongly disagree') to 5 ('strongly agree').

Other factors, such as transit-user attitudes and transit service frequency, also impact travel behaviour. These can be accounted for through careful study design (see the subsection below: 'Accounting for Alternative Explanations') as well as direct measurement, using the types of data described above.

Unit of Analysis

The unit of analysis chosen to measure the built environment is also an important consideration. Transit-oriented development principles recognise the existence of zones of use around a transit facility (Monzón et al. 2016). Four zones are relevant for the measurement of built environment variables and other explanatory factors relevant to transit use. These are the transit facility, transfer zone, access–egress catchment and network/region. Spatial definitions of these zones are summarised in Table 3.1. These zones can be applied to the transit zone (as depicted in Figure 3.1), to individuals or households, or to trip ends.

Geographic information systems and other software are available to facilitate the aggregation of built environment and socio-demographic data to different spatial units. Chapter 15 in the *Handbook of Transport Modelling* provides an introduction to the use of Geographic Information Systems in Transportation (Dueker and Peng 2008).

Table 3.1   Definition of built environment spatial catchments relevant to transit use

Unit	Spatial definition
Facility (F)	Property of the transit facility
Transfer zone (T)	160m Euclidian buffer
Access–egress (neighbourhood) catchment (N)	Bus modes: 300–800 metres
	Rail modes: 400–1600 metres
Network/Region (R)	Defined by extent of urban transit network

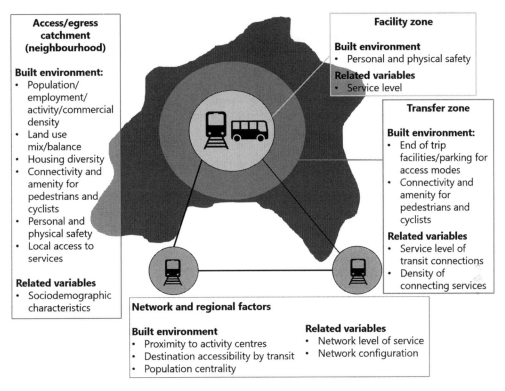

Source: Adapted from Torabi Kachousangi et al. (2019).

Figure 3.1 Level of influence of built environment and related variables impacting transit use

Land use within the access and egress catchments represents the generators and attractors of travel demand. Active transport is the method most commonly used to access transit. This puts transit users in contact with the built environment when accessing transit. Catchment boundaries can be defined in a number of ways. Radial methods involve generating a buffer corresponding to a radial distance from the transit facility (aggregate analysis) or household (disaggregate). Advances in spatial methods and the availability of street network datasets have seen 'walk' catchments supplant Euclidian methods of radial catchment generation. Walk catchments, which typically follow the street network, or pavement where available, provide a more accurate reflection of the land use that can be accessed by a pedestrian (Boulange et al. 2017). In locations where cycling is a popular first and last mile transit mode, catchments may be more accurately defined based on cycling distance (Kager and Harms 2017).

A final consideration for the measurement of built environment variables is whether to examine trip origins, destinations, tour stops or a combination of all. Most studies examine trip origins, which are typically associated with residential locations (Aston et al. 2020b). This is especially true in disaggregate studies that examine household (residential) variables. However, impacts at the destination, which are typically associated with trip attractors such as employment locations and retail centres, are also important (Cervero 2002; Chakour and Eluru 2016; Frank et al. 2008).

Aggregate and Disaggregate Estimation Strategies

Estimation strategies in transport modelling require an understanding of econometric methods and assumptions. Many sources exist to guide researchers on the selection of appropriate econometric models, depending on the nature of the data and relationships of interest (Hair et al. 2014; Wooldridge 2016).

A crucial distinction in BE-TU research is whether the travel behaviour data is collected for individuals and households (disaggregate) or in aggregate. The selection of aggregate or disaggregate data constrains subsequent choices about data and inferences that can be drawn from the results. Certain estimation methods may be favoured for use with aggregate or disaggregate data. The estimation methods and data sources typically associated with each are summarised in Table 3.2.

Access to appropriate data may predetermine the choice of whether to use aggregate or disaggregate data. Disaggregate data usually comes from household surveys, face-to-face surveys or census data. Built environment variables are measured around the home, workplace, or access/egress route of individual subjects. Individual data from disaggregate sources can also be aggregated before modelling. For example, ridership data often harvested from smartcard or ticketing data from transit authorities may also be aggregated to the level of a transit station catchment.

Researchers who have the choice to use aggregate or disaggregate data should consider the application of their research, and the importance of explaining individual differences, when choosing between approaches. Aggregating data before modelling captures more latent factors, but cannot link them to individual traits and is therefore associated with greater risk of spurious correlations (Ben-Akiva 1985). Aggregate data is important for policy, since efficient policies target populations rather than individuals.

Methods to estimate mode choice probabilities fall under the family of estimation methods known as discrete choice methods. Discrete choice methods are commonly used when examining travel behaviour from the perspective of economic utility. For example, logistic models transform discrete responses using a logistic function to model

Table 3.2   Estimation methods and data sources for analysis

	Data source	Estimation methods
Aggregate methods	• Revealed preferences, including: patronage, census or travel surveys • Stated preference	• OLS regression • Multiplicative regression • Bootstrapped regression • Two-stage least squares regression (2SLS)
Disaggregate methods	• Census • Travel survey • Stated preference	• Logistic regression • Negative binomial regression • Probit regression

the probability that an individual will choose transit relative to one (binomial) or many (multinomial) other mode choices. This probability is often transformed into an odds ratio, which expresses the odds of an individual choosing transit in response to a change in the independent (built environment) variable. Count data of individual-level ridership or trips adhere to a distribution known as the Poisson distribution. Negative binomial regression is commonly used to model the association of such data with independent variables in travel behaviour. The coefficient produced in Poisson regression is also a probability, which can be transformed to yield a rate ratio, with a similar interpretation to the odds ratio. Readers are referred to Ben-Akiva (1985) and Hensher (2015a) for more on the specification and interpretation of discrete choice models.

Aggregate modelling techniques typically adopt ordinary least squares (OLS) regression. OLS models a direct linear relationship between variables, although the variables themselves may be transformed to suit the data. (Ortúzar and Willumsen 2011). The unstandardised coefficients from linear regression models, 'B', represent the strength of association between the independent and dependent variables. They may be standardised to facilitate comparison of the relative strength of association across the predictors in a model. The standardised coefficient is referred to as the 'Beta' or 'β' coefficient. Variants on the traditional OLS aggregate modelling approach include multiplicative models, used in direct demand forecasting; two-stage least squares regression, used to capture the effects of instrumental variables; and bootstrapped regression, which usually involves iterating simple linear models to determine which variables to include in a multivariate model.

Several permutations can be applied to either family of model. Decay factors or geographic weighting can be used to assign greater importance to the built environment in closer proximity to transit stations (Cardozo et al. 2012). Multi-level modelling can be used to embed hierarchies or nested decisions when modelling relationships (Boulange et al. 2017; Koppelman and Bhat 2006; Renne et al. 2016).

Measuring the Unobserved with Structural Equations

Two trends have occurred which have led to the rise of a third type of estimation method: Structural Equation Modelling (SEM). The causal-limitations of combining cross-sectional data with OLS estimation methods, and the increased emphasis on attitudinal and perceptual data, have increased the prevalence of structural equations in travel behaviour research. Structural equations combine multiple regression techniques with factor analysis, allowing researchers to model a set of relationships between latent variables (Golob 2003). Structural equations are flexible in that they allow for multiple dependence relationships and can accommodate bidirectional impacts. Prior to estimating relationships using structural equations, a measurement model must first be developed to represent latent variables. Measurable variables are chosen to represent latent constructs, such as neighbourhood character or attitudes toward transit, using exploratory factor analysis. Structural models are suited to testing and validating directional models which represent the interaction between the built environment, attitudes and mode choice (Aditjandra et al. 2016; Cao et al. 2007). Causal inference from SEM is still bounded by many conditions, including the use of multi-year data (Bollen 1989).

CASE STUDY: COMPARING THE USE OF TRAVEL BEHAVIOUR METRICS FOR BUS AND RAIL STUDIES

This chapter presents insights about the study design leveraged in 187 empirical built environment and transit use studies, conducted since 2000. Characteristics of these studies have been coded into an open-source empirical meta-database available on *Bridges* at: https://doi.org/10.26180/5d921ac827289.

The BE-TU meta-database provides a comprehensive repository of empirical research in the field, to facilitate easier and more robust knowledge development in the field. The database contains information about sampling, data, estimation methods and variables, as described in the sections that follow. By assembling all of the information in BE-TU together, it is possible to gain insights about over- and underrepresented fields of research, as well as to quickly and comprehensively scan existing evidence to find the relevant literature. Figure 3.2 provides a visualisation created using the BE-TU meta-database.

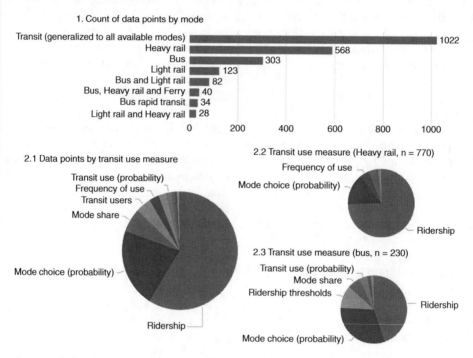

Source: Authors' summary of data in the BE-TU meta-database (Aston et al. 2019).

Figure 3.2   Visualisation of modes and metrics used in prior research

The first chart reveals a tendency of studies to report estimates for transit in general, rather than specific modes. The most common transit use metric reported is ridership, followed by mode choice. The most common individual modes studied are rail and bus. While heavy rail studies predominantly analyse ridership, bus studies are more balanced in assessing ridership, mode choice and ridership thresholds. This pattern may reflect the ease of acquisition of ridership data for rail.

Accounting for Alternative Explanations

Robust research ensures that alternative explanations for an observed relationship are accounted for. Failure to account for factors other than the built environment that may explain transit use, 'third factors', limits the reliability and validity of observations about the variables of interest. Third factors make it more likely to detect significant effects when there are none (Type II error), and for significant relationships to be masked or suppressed (Alonso 1968; MacKinnon et al. 2000).

Mitchell and Rapkin (1954) provided one of the first extensive catalogues of variables relevant to the characterisation of transport and land use interaction. These included attributes of the trip-maker, the vehicle and the trip itself. Boarnet (2011) argues that upstream policy factors and urban genesis are also crucial to policy-relevant research. Empirical evidence supports this claim, with an examination of transit-oriented development success factors finding recurring themes among institutional and commercial arrangements (Thomas and Bertolini 2017). These include political stability, the level of government responsible for transport policy, relationships between actors, public participation, and development certainty for interdisciplinary implementation teams, and certainty for developers.

Table 3.3 summarises non-built environment variables using five categories that are relevant considerations when examining BE-TU: attributes of the trip-maker, attributes of the trip, contextual factors, policy, network context and geographic context.

These factors can be mapped to the '7D' framework for built environment and travel behaviour, which has been developed and strengthened through repeat syntheses of empirical research (Ewing and Cervero 2001, 2010).[1] The '7D' framework recognises Demographics (trip-maker), Demand management (policy) and Destination accessibility or Distance to transit as important considerations for understanding the BE-TU relationship.

Other factors that impact the reproducibility of findings from one context to the next include geographic factors such as weather (Abenoza et al. 2019), regional cultural norms (Haustein and Nielsen 2016; Heinen et al. 2011) and social influences (Maness et al. 2015). Study design aspects, including the scope of the sample, transport modes, data type and unit of analysis can also impact results (Aston et al. 2020b).

Accounting for Alternative Explanations: Self-selection

Attitude-induced transit propensity is one of many logistical challenges in studies that seek to establish causality between the BE and TU. The choice to live in a transit-friendly neighbourhood may coincide with an individual's preference to use transit (association), or it may induce a change in the individual's travel behaviour in favour of higher transit use (causality) (Cao et al. 2009). Similarly, socio-economic factors may influence a household's choice of travel mode. Socio-demographic and attitudinal predisposition to use transit may confound or mask transit ridership patterns if not controlled. The following factors are recognised as variables related to self-selection.

Socio-demographic (Greenwald and Boarnet 2001):

- Educational attainment;
- Per-capita income;
- Migration mix.

Table 3.3   Factors that explain travel behaviour

Type of variable	Examples of explanatory factors
Trip-maker	• Individual demographic characteristics including age, sex, education, employment industry and income • Household characteristics including access to vehicles, composition and size • Individual travel attitudes and preferences
Trip and vehicle	• Trip purpose • Linked or unlinked nature of trip • Transfer penalties • Comfort • Reliability • Trip length and duration • Level of service
Upstream (policy) factors	• Land development policy • Institutional arrangements including actors, level of authority for transport planning, integration with other planning functions • Political stability • Development controls and certainty • Normative travel behaviours • Transit system franchising/operation • Fare structure
Network context	• Network configuration • Network-level supply of transit service • Ratio of transit to other modal infrastructure and services
Geographic context	• Topography • Weather and climate

Source: Mitchell and Rapkin (1954), Thomas and Bertolini (2017), Abenoza et al. (2019).

It is worth noting that automobile ownership is considered an invalid socio-demographic control in travel behaviour research, due to evidence that it is influenced by attitudes and the built environment (Næss 2009). It should not be used to account for self-selection.
    Attitudinal (Cao et al. 2009):

• Stated preference for residential location and lifestyle;
• Revealed preference for lifestyle;
• Personality.

Studies that account for self-selection control these variables either explicitly with direct questioning or statistical control, non-explicitly by using instrumental variables or two-stage least squares regression, or by segmenting or matching the sample (Mokhtarian and Cao 2008). Another approach is to use longitudinal study design, so that individual attitudes and preferences are controlled over multiple study years. The approach recommended for its ability to account for self-selection is longitudinal structural equations modelling, with statistical control of explicit measures of self-selection (Mokhtarian and Cao 2008).

Readers are referred to the review papers for a complete overview of nine distinct approaches to control self-selection, as well as their strengths, weaknesses and applications (Cao et al. 2009; Mokhtarian and Cao 2008). For more information on propensity matching techniques, readers are referred to examples of its applications in travel behaviour research (Cao and Fan 2012; Nasri et al. 2018) and to Heinrich et al. (2010) for theoretical guidance.

3.4   QUANTIFYING BUILT ENVIRONMENT VARIABLES

There are many possible measures that can be used to quantify the built environment. These are often determined by the availability of data (Rajabifard et al. 2017). In the time that has elapsed since Ewing and Cervero estimated elasticities for transit use and the D-variables (2010), data sources and techniques for acquisition have rapidly evolved (Welch and Widita 2019). New data sources have in turn unlocked the potential for new research insights. For example, a recent empirical study of Shanghai's metro ridership used open source land use point data to classify land use types (An et al. 2019). The ability to collect information on accessibility efficiently has facilitated network-level comparison of regional access quality, which is gaining growing recognition as an important contributor to travel behaviour (Mahmoudi and Zhang 2018; Renne et al. 2016). The remainder of this section provides methods and assumptions for choosing built environment variables and aggregating data for indicators to facilitate robust analysis of impacts on transit use.

Density

Four types of Density are commonly measured, including population, jobs, commercial, and combination densities, often expressed as 'activity' density (Table 3.4). Densities may be measured per total area, or net area, where net is defined as land dedicated to a particular use, although these nuances were not differentiated in the present analysis. Density is typically measured at the neighbourhood scale, that is, within a catchment area encompassing the person, household, or transit facility of interest.

Diversity

Three distinct measures of Diversity, or 'mix' of activity types, are commonly measured. The most common variable measures the extent to which land use is balanced across multiple land use types. Different techniques are available for calculating this measure, often referred to as 'entropy', that is, a measure of the disorder of land uses. Equation 3.1 is an adaptation of the Shannon entropy formula[2] for application in quantifying the mixture of land use.

$$-\frac{\sum_k [(p_{ik})\,(\ln_{p_{ik}})]}{\ln_k} \qquad (3.1)(\text{Cervero 2002})$$

Where
k = number of land uses;
p = the proportion of the catchment occupied by land use type i.

Table 3.4   Standardised indicators for Density

Indicator	Definition	F	T	N	R
Employment density	Gross or net jobs or employment per area (total or by type of employment)			✓	
Population density	Gross or net households, dwellings or persons per total area			✓	
Activity density	Active floor space ratio, sum of jobs and population and/or commercial/retail opportunities per area			✓	
Commercial density	Commercial or retail density, number of establishments, commercial or retail land use proportion			✓	

Notes: Unit of analysis: F: facility; T: transfer zone; N: access/egress (neighbourhood); R: region/network.

Table 3.5   Standardised indicators for Diversity

Indicator	Definition	F	T	N	R
Land use mix	Mix of land use (floor area), vertical mix of land use, Bhat/Shannon/Simpson/Heip/McIntosh/Smith-Wilson measures of entropy or diversity			✓	
Housing mix	Mix of housing type, mix of housing affordability, mix of tenure type			✓	
Attraction/generation balance	Jobs–housing balance, ratio of trip origins to trip destinations (normalised)			✓	

Notes: Unit of analysis: F: facility; T: transfer zone; N: access/egress (neighbourhood); R: region/network.

The inclusion of the denominator normalises the index to 1 by setting the total number of land uses equal to k. Greater disorder in the arrangement of land uses is considered to represent more activity participation opportunities. Entropy scales are usually expressed as a score out of 1, where the closer to 1 the score, the greater the disorder among land uses. Entropy scales might calculate a score for a predefined number of land uses (Diversity), or they may omit the normalisation step and instead measure the 'evenness' of land uses based on the number of land uses present. The second type of Diversity focuses on housing. Similar scales may be applied as for land use Diversity; however, the focus is on measuring the Diversity in housing type, tenure type, or average rent or real estate values. The third Diversity measure is land use balance. This measures the evenness of two types of land use, typically one land use associated with trip attractions, and one associated with trip generation. Retail or employment area are common trip-end land uses, while residential Density is commonly used to represent trip origins (see Table 3.5). Equation 3.2 sets out a balance formula to represent the evenness of housing (pop) and retail employment (Emp_{retail}).

$$1 - \frac{[ABS(Pop. - Emp_{retail})]}{Pop. + Emp_{retail}} \qquad (3.2) \; (\text{Cervero 2002})$$

When an area contains only two land uses to begin with, the diversity score being measured approximates to a measure of evenness akin to 'balance'. Diversity is also typically measured at the neighbourhood scale.

Design

Design refers to how pedestrian 'friendly' or 'unfriendly' the urban form is. To date, research has assumed that since the most common access modes for transit are active modes (bicycle or walking), design treatments that make for more pleasant cycle or pedestrian journeys are also transit-oriented design.

At the neighbourhood and transfer-zone levels, urban design measures include building setback, proportion of activated street frontage, landscaping, street furniture and bicycle parking. Categorical indicators of pedestrian or cycle amenity at the micro or neighbourhood level are also commonly collected using 'dummy' variables. These denote the presence of features such as pavements, classical housing or gridded street networks. Perception of personal safety and security, or features that improve physical safety, are another type of Design variable. These can be quantified for the immediate vicinity of facility or transfer zone, or for a neighbourhood. The most common transit-friendly Design measures are those which quantify the connectivity of active mode transport facilities, at the neighbourhood level. These can include the number of intersections (crossing opportunities), or the length of bike or pedestrian paths.

Conversely, increasing 'auto-friendly' design is typically associated with lower transit use. Measures of auto-friendly design measure the length or density of roads, dis-amenity or inaccessibility (Table 3.6).

Accessibility

As with Design, Accessibility can be divided into access that favours transit use ('transit-friendly'), and Access that favours auto use ('auto-friendly') (see Table 3.7). When measured at the neighbourhood level, Accessibility refers to the number of local activity-participation opportunities. 'Local access' quantifies activity participation. Unlike Diversity measures, local access is usually targeted at pedestrian-oriented land uses, and relies on point sources about activity types. A common local access measure is the Walk Score™, which has led this indicator to often receiving the label of 'walkability'. To capture the accessibility benefits of 'agglomeration' in high-density developments, a dummy variable is often used to categorise sites as being in an 'accessible location', such as a Central Business District (CBD) or a transit-oriented development (TOD). Regional accessibility is captured by measuring the proximity of a site to job centres in networks with strong urban cores, or as a continuous measure of the number of jobs accessible on the transit network. Centrality is another macro-level variable that approximates the evenness of density in an urban area, or the connectivity of a transit node to other parts of the network. The latter has a close overlap with measures of regional accessibility. Decentralisation or sprawl is also measured to capture auto-orientation on the network level.

Table 3.6   Standardised indicators for Design

Indicator		Definition	F	T	N	R
Transit-friendly	Pedestrian and cycle amenities	Pedestrian or cycle amenities: canopy, pleasantness, street furniture, facilities, building setback, % pedestrian-oriented buildings	✓	✓		
	Pedestrian and cycle amenities (categorical)	As above, using 'dummy' variables, neighbourhood type, building age, presence of pavement, grid street network	✓	✓		
	Personal and physical safety	Lighting, perception of security, kerbs, shoulder width, perception of safety from vehicle traffic	✓	✓	✓	
	Pedestrian and cycle connectivity	Total path length, number of pedestrian crossings, average footpath width, footpath density, crossing density, link to node ratio, intersection density, syntactical accessibility	✓	✓		
Auto-friendly	Automobile connectivity	Road network density, block size, path impedances, road length per capita, cul-de-sac or dead-end density, street segment length				✓
	Dis-amenity, inaccessible (categorical)	Appearance, upkeep, homogeneity, lack of safety/security, isolation or lack of local access, curvilinear street type, new development, located in low transit/low access/low density area				✓

Notes: Unit of analysis: F: facility; T: transfer zone; N: access/egress (neighbourhood); R: region/network.

Which Indicators are the Important Ones?

The proliferation of data sources presents researchers with a new challenge: where once the availability (or lack of) data was a constraint on research, the myriad possible sources of data now demand greater discernment. Which variables are most relevant for examining transit use? Which data sources are most representative of the chosen variables?

When selecting variables to include in analysis, it is important to consider which variables are theoretically relevant to the relationship. Different indicators relate differently to transit use, and this may depend on the research context. Indicators and findings from studies contained within the BE-TU meta-database[3] illustrate the impact that variable selection might have. For example, Figure 3.3 provides a visualisation of the rate at which 16 indicators were identified as significant in the expected direction ('Theoretically Consistent'), insignificant, or significant in the opposite direction to hypotheses ('Theoretically Inconsistent').

Almost half of empirical findings across all indicators do not show a significant relationship with transit use, illustrated by the light grey region in Figure 3.3. Indicators of high transit Accessibility, including local access and network or city centrality – are most often associated with significant increases in transit use, followed by Density.

Table 3.7   Standardised indicators for Accessibility

Indicator		Definition	F	T	N	R
Transit-friendly	Local access/walkability	Walk Score™, local living score, count of services/mixed use opportunities, perception of convenience of access to amenities and activities		✓		
	Accessible destination (categorical)	Located in CBD, TOD or close to transit, high density, above average density		✓	✓	
	Regional accessibility	Density of stops, employment/activities accessible by transit, distance to transit, network coverage				✓
	Centrality	Proportion of population within CBD, compactness index, betweenness centrality, degree centrality				✓
Auto-friendly	Decentrality	Sprawl index, distribution of population or employment, city shape, distance to CBD				✓

Notes: Unit of analysis: F: facility; T: transfer zone; N: access/egress (neighbourhood); R: region/network.

Meta-averages provide another means of evaluating the relative importance of indicators. Meta-analysis considers many studies together to produce summary effects that are more generalisable than the findings from any one study (Borenstein et al. 2009). Meta-analysis was conducted on the data from the BE-TU database in a recent empirical study (Aston et al. 2020a). The study converted effect sizes into elasticities, where sufficient information was available to do so. The elasticities for built environment indicators listed in Table 3.8 represent the percentage change in transit use that would be expected in the built environment indicator increased by 1 per cent.

Eight of the 12 indicators examined have significant, positive associations with ridership.[4] All of the elasticities are less than 1, with the largest being for land use mix, with meta-elasticity equal to 0.26. This implies that transit use is weakly related to the built environment, or that the relationship is 'inelastic'.

Three Density indicators show significant meta-elasticities with transit use. The largest is for Commercial density ($\varepsilon = 0.15$), followed by Population density ($\varepsilon = 0.10$) and Employment density ($\varepsilon = 0.08$). Despite having high theoretical consistency, Activity density does not have a significant association with transit use. This demonstrates the need for caution when interpreting results, as they may vary depending on which subset of studies is being examined.

Fifty-six per cent of findings for Diversity are not significant (Figure 3.3). However, a relatively small proportion of findings are contrary to hypothesised values (9 per cent). Furthermore, land use mix has the largest average elasticity with transit use ($\varepsilon = 0.26$) and jobs–housing diversity has the third strongest ($\varepsilon = 0.16$). The relatively large elasticities for Diversity but low rate of significant findings can be explained by the fact that indicators of diversity tend to be measured on a ratio scale capped at 1. Observations vary within a narrow range. For a given sample, if a small number of observations are negative, it may

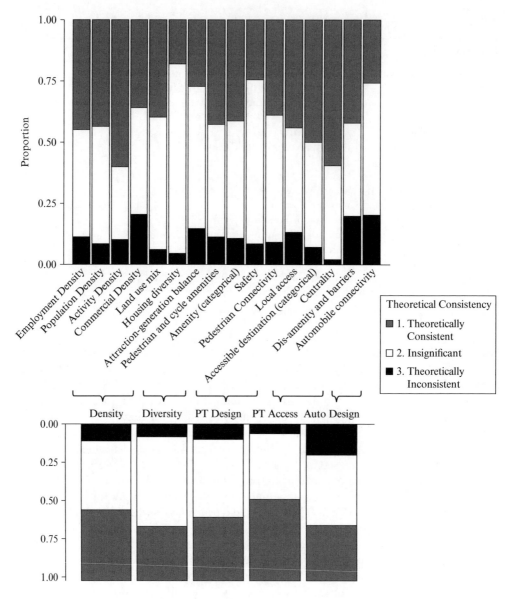

Source: Authors' summary of data in the BE-TU meta-database (Aston et al. 2019).

Figure 3.3   *Plot of results for built environment indicators (segmented by Theoretical Consistency)*[5]

result in the overall finding being insignificant. The use of a ratio scale with maximum equal to 1 makes diversity a more precise predictor of transit use than other variables.

Transit-friendly Design indicators are associated with increased transit use in 40 per cent of findings. The second largest meta-elasticity is Pedestrian and cycle connectivity

Table 3.8   Meta-elasticities for the relationship between BE and TU

BE indicator	n	Meta-elasticity ε
Land use mix	42	0.26*
Connectivity	52	0.17**
Jobs–housing balance	25	0.16*
Commercial density	27	0.15*
Population density	99	0.10*
Employment density	74	0.08**
Safety	4	0.07**
Local access	23	0.06***
Amenity	14	0.00***
Activity density	25	0.24
Population centrality	24	0.65
Housing mix	9	0.00

Note: Significance level: * $p < 0.05$; ** $p < 0.01$; ***$p < 0.001$.

($\varepsilon = 0.17$). Figure 3.3 suggests that auto-oriented design is less consistent at predicting decreased transit use than transit-friendly design is at predicting increased transit use.

The research literature finds that transit-friendly Accessibility is associated with increased transit use in the majority of cases. Of the two Accessibility indicators included in meta-analysis, only local access relates significantly to transit use, with meta-elasticity equal to 0.06.

Variables with high theoretical consistency do not necessarily show high average meta-elasticities. Indicators associated with significant meta-elasticities are not necessarily those that show high theoretical consistency, and vice versa. Differences in the sample, as well as precision-weighting of elasticities[6] account for some of the difference. However, the two measures also convey different aspects of indicator reliability. While meta-elasticities are more useful for understanding the relative importance of indicators, theoretical consistency serves as a reminder that findings vary significantly from study to study. This underscores the importance of clearly presenting assumptions and procedures when selecting and aggregating variables for analysis.

3.5   FUTURE DIRECTIONS

Several key trends are occurring in BE-TU research. These can be divided into three themes. First, changes are occurring in the subject matter of research, with new modes disrupting the public transport sector, and a diversification of the geographic coverage of research (Aston et al. 2020c). Second, shifts in the theoretical frameworks for BE-TU are occurring. Greater emphasis is being placed on developing behavioural explanations for travel behaviour (Dill et al. 2014). Third, measurement techniques are rapidly evolving, in response to data and technological advancements (Moeckel et al. 2019). The implications of these trends for BE-TU methodologies are summarised in Table 3.9, along with resources for further reading on each topic.

Table 3.9   Trends impacting empirical BE-TU research design

Implications		Further reading
1. Subject matter and context		
Diversification of geographic locations with diverse urban and transportation contexts		(Hu and Iseki 2018)
Expanding repertoire of transit modes, as well as technologies that offer first and last mile solutions to transit		(Torabi Kachousangi et al. 2019)
2. Shifts in conceptual understanding		
Application of psychological theories to explain impacts of the built environment on attitudes towards modes	Theoretical underpinnings	(Ajzen and Fishbein 1980; Dill et al. 2014; van Wee et al. 2019)
	Measuring attitudes and perceptions	(De Vos et al. 2018; Handy et al. 2005)
Context sensitive and human centred design		(Monzón et al. 2016; Tomitsch 2018)
3. Data and methods		
New data sources, machine learning algorithms and replicable programming are improving the efficiency and precision of measuring BE-TU	Challenges in big data	(Welch and Widita 2019)
	Novel data sources	(An et al. 2019; Pourebrahim et al. 2019) (Tu et al. 2018)
	Online data repositories	(Geertman et al. 2015; Ramsey and Bell 2014)
	Multi-country studies	(Woods and Masthoff 2017) (Mahmoudi and Zhang 2018)

Table 3.10   Best practice recommendations for designing empirical BE-TU research

Study design	Best practice
Explanatory variables (includes BE)	Control all theoretical relevant variables while maintaining statistical power for a given sample size (Alonso 1968; Elvik 2005b).
	Account for self-selection and the relative regional accessibility of a sample site or individual's locations in the network (Cao et al. 2009; Renne et al. 2016).
Collinearity	Remove collinearity of explanatory variables (e.g. by forming factors).
Data	Use disaggregate (individual-level) data that measures perceptions or stated preferences (Dill et al. 2014; Handy et al. 2005).
Market segmentation	Segmentation of samples by population, trips purpose, and mode of transit will produce more precise estimates where a particular segment is of interest. Evidence suggests results can vary significantly when transit modes are examined individually (Aston et al. 2020b).
Time periods	Multi-period (Creswell 2009; van de Coevering et al. 2015).
Estimation method	Structural equations (Mokhtarian and Cao 2008).
Unit of analysis	Buffer size: $400 < x \leq 800$ m aligns to most planning conventions. Guerra et al. (2011) suggest choosing based on data availability and quality. Buffer type: Walk or access/egress route catchment. Journey leg: Measure built environment at origins, destinations and stops along the way where applicable.

3.6 SUMMARY

The approaches outlined in this chapter respond to the specific challenges of built environment research. A summary of best practice approaches to sampling and indicator selection is provided in Table 3.10.

Advances in the conceptual and methodological understanding of public transport interactions with the built environment offer means of generating increasingly robust and transferable insights. Irrespective of the overall strategy chosen by researchers, adherence to best practice and acknowledgement of a study's limitations will ensure that researchers can make valid and valuable contributions to BE-TU knowledge development.

NOTES

1. The first three Ds refer specifically to the built environment, and include Density, Diversity and Design (introduced in detail in section 3.4) (Cervero and Kockelman 1997).
2. Shannon's entropy was first developed as a measure of the complexity of communication (Shannon 1948).
3. Accessible on *Bridges* at: https://doi.org/10.26180/5d921ac827289.
4. The association of amenity with ridership was neutral for practical purposes.
5. Increasing values for variables such as Density and Diversity, as well as pedestrian-scale Design are typically associated with higher transit use, while increases in automobile connectivity are associated with decreasing transit use (Boulange et al. 2017; Ewing and Cervero 2010). Significant findings that accord with these directions of association between built environment indicators and transit use are 'Theoretically Consistent'.
6. Meta-elasticities are weighted for precision: studies that are more reliable (denoted by lower standard errors) are given greater importance when estimating the elasticity.

REFERENCES

Abenoza, R.F., Liu, C., Cats, O. and Susilo, Y.O. 2019, 'What is the role of weather, built-environment and accessibility geographical characteristics in influencing travelers' experience?', *Transportation Research Part A*, vol. 122, pp. 34–50.

Aditjandra, P.T., Cao, X. and Mulley, C. 2016, 'Exploring changes in public transport use and walking following residential relocation: A British case study', *Journal of Transport and Land Use*, vol. 9, no. 3, pp. 77–95.

Ajzen, I. and Fishbein, M. 1980, *Understanding attitudes and predicting social behavior*, Englewood Cliffs, NJ: Prentice-Hall.

Alonso, W. 1968, 'Predicting best with imperfect data', *Journal of the American Institute of Planners*, vol. 34, no. 4, pp. 248–55.

An, D., Tong, X., Liu, K. and Chan, E.H.W. 2019, 'Understanding the impact of built environment on metro ridership using open source in Shanghai', *Cities*, vol. 93, pp. 177–87.

Appleyard, B.S. 2010, 'New methods to measure urban environments for consumer behavior research: Individual access corridor analysis of environmentally sustainable travel to rapid transit', ProQuest LLC, via Compendex.

Aston, L., Currie, G., Delbosc, A., Kamruzzaman, M. and Teller, D. 2020a, 'Exploring built environment impacts on transit use: An updated meta-analysis', Paper under review.

Aston, L., Currie, G., Delbosc, A., Kamruzzaman, M. and Teller, D. 2020b, 'Study design impacts on built environment and transit use research', *Journal of Transport Geography*, vol. 82.

Aston, L., Currie, G., Kamruzzaman, M., Delbosc, A. and Teller, D. 2019, *BE-TU: Built environment and transit use meta-database*, 10 January 2020 edn, Bridges.

Aston, L., Currie, G., Kamruzzaman, M., Delbosc, A. and Teller, D. 2020c, 'The BE-TU (Built Environment – Transit Use) Open-Access Meta-Database: Rationale, Development and Applications', *Journal of Transport and Land Use*.

Banister, D. 2005, *Unsustainable transport: City transport in the new century*, Abingdon: Taylor & Francis.

Banister, D., Marshall, S. and Blackledge, D. 2007, 'Land use and transport: The context', in S. Marshall and D. Banister (eds), *Land Use and Transport*, Oxford: Elsevier, pp. 6–17.

Batty, M. 2013, *The new science of cities*, Cambridge, MA: MIT Press.

Ben-Akiva, M.E. 1985, *Discrete choice analysis: Theory and application to travel demand*, Cambridge, MA: MIT Press.

Boarnet, M. 2011, 'A broader context for land use and travel behavior, and a research agenda', *Journal of the American Planning Association*, vol. 77, no. 3, pp. 197–213.

Boarnet, M. and Crane, R. 2001a, 'The influence of land use on travel behavior: Specification and estimation strategies', *Transportation Research Part A: Policy and Practice*, vol. 35, no. 9, pp. 823–45.

Boarnet, M. and Crane, R. 2001b, *Travel by design: The influence of urban form on travel*, Oxford: Oxford University Press.

Bollen, K.A. 1989, *Structural equations with latent variables*, New York: John Wiley & Sons.

Borenstein, M., Hedges, L.V., Higgins, J. and Rothstein, H. 2009, *Introduction to meta-analysis*, Chichester: John Wiley & Sons.

Boulange, C., Gunn, L., Giles-Corti, B., Mavoa, S., Pettit, C. and Badland, H. 2017, 'Examining associations between urban design attributes and transport mode choice for walking, cycling, public transport and private motor vehicle trips', *Journal of Transport & Health*, vol. 6, pp. 155–66.

Cao, X. and Fan, Y. 2012, 'Exploring the influences of density on travel behavior using propensity score matching', *Environment and Planning B: Planning and Design*, vol. 39, no. 3, pp. 459–70.

Cao, X., Mokhtarian, P.L. and Handy, S. 2007, 'Do changes in neighborhood characteristics lead to changes in travel behavior? A structural equations modeling approach', *Transportation*, vol. 34, no. 5, pp. 535–56.

Cao, X., Mokhtarian, P.L. and Handy, S.L. 2009, 'Examining the impacts of residential self-selection on travel behaviour: A focus on empirical findings', *Transport Reviews*, vol. 29, no. 3, pp. 359–95.

Cardozo, O.D., Garcia-Palomares, J.C. and Gutierrez, J. 2012, 'Application of geographically weighted regression to the direct forecasting of transit ridership at station-level', *Applied Geography*, vol. 34, pp. 548–58.

Cervero, R. 2002, 'Built environment and mode choice: Toward a normative framework', *Transportation Research Part D*, vol. 7, no. 2002, pp. 265–84.

Cervero, R. and Kockelman, K. 1997, 'Travel demand and the 3Ds: Density, diversity, and design', *Transportation Research Part D: Transport and Environment*, vol. 2, no. 3, pp. 199–219.

Chakour, V. and Eluru, N. 2016, 'Examining the influence of stop level infrastructure and built environment on bus ridership in Montreal', *Journal of Transport Geography*, vol. 51, pp. 205–17.

Creswell, J.W. 2009, *Research design: Qualitative, quantitative, and mixed methods approaches*, 3rd edn, Thousand Oaks, CA: Sage Publications.

De Gruyter, C. 2019, 'Multimodal trip generation from land use developments: International synthesis and future directions', *Transportation Research Record*, vol. 2673, no. 3, pp. 136–52.

De Vos, J. 2018, 'Do people travel with their preferred travel mode? Analysing the extent of travel mode dissonance and its effect on travel satisfaction', *Transportation Research Part A: Policy and Practice*, vol. 117, pp. 261–74.

De Vos, J., Ettema, D. and Witlox, F. 2018, 'Changing travel behaviour and attitudes following a residential relocation', *Journal of Transport Geography*, vol. 73, pp. 131–47.

Dill, J., Mohr, C. and Ma, L. 2014, 'How can psychological theory help cities increase walking and bicycling?', *Journal of the American Planning Association*, vol. 80, no. 1, pp. 36–51.

Domencich, T.A. and McFadden, D. 1975, *Urban travel demand: A behavioral analysis*, Amsterdam: North-Holland Publishing and New York: Elsevier.

Dueker, K.J. and Peng, Z.R. 2008, 'Geographic Information Systems for Transport (GIS-T)', in D.A. Hensher and K.J. Button (eds), *Handbook of Transport Modelling*, 2nd edn, Emerald Group Publishing, online version, pp. 303–28, accessed 19 November 2017.

Elvik, R. 2005a, 'Can we trust the results of meta-analyses?: A systematic approach to sensitivity analysis in meta-analyses', *Transportation Research Record: Journal of the Transportation Research Board*, vol. 1908, pp. 221–9.

Elvik, R. 2005b, 'Introductory guide to systematic reviews and meta-analysis', *Transportation Research Record: Journal of the Transportation Research Board*, vol. 1908, pp. 230–35.

Ewing, R. and Cervero, R. 2001, 'Travel and the built environment: A synthesis', *Transportation Research Record: Journal of the Transportation Research Board*, vol. 1780, pp. 87–114.

Ewing, R. and Cervero, R. 2010, 'Travel and the built environment: A meta-analysis', *Journal of the American Planning Association*, vol. 76, no. 3, pp. 265–94.

Ewing, R. and Handy, S. 2009, 'Measuring the unmeasurable: Urban design qualities related to walkability', *Journal of Urban Design*, vol. 14, no. 1, pp. 65–84.

Fan, Y. 2007, *The built environment, activity space, and time allocation: An activity-based framework for modeling the land use and travel connection*, ProQuest Dissertations Publishing.

Frank, L., Bradley, M., Kavage, S., Chapman, J. and Lawton, T.K. 2008, 'Urban form, travel time, and cost relationships with tour complexity and mode choice', *Transportation*, vol. 35, no. 1, pp. 37–54.

Geertman, S., Ferreira, J., Goodspeed, R. and Stillwell, J.C.H. (eds) 2015, *Planning support systems and smart cities*, Cham: Springer.

Golob, T.F. 2003, 'Structural equation modeling for travel behavior research', *Transportation Research Part B: Methodological*, vol. 37, no. 1, pp. 1–25.

Greenwald, M.J. and Boarnet, M.G. 2001, *Built environment as determinant of walking behavior: Analyzing nonwork pedestrian travel in Portland, Oregon*, Transportation Research Record, vol. 1780, no. 1.

Guerra, E., Cervero, R. and Tischler, D. 2011, *The half-mile circle: Does it best represent transit station catchments?*, Berkeley, CA: University of California Transportation Center.

Hair, J.F., Black, W.C., Babin, B.J. and Anderson, R.E. 2014, *Multivariate data analysis*, 7th edn, Harlow: Pearson Education.

Handy, S. 1996, 'Methodologies for exploring the link between urban form and travel behavior', *Transportation Research Part D: Transport and Environment*, vol. 1, no. 2, pp. 151–65.

Handy, S., Cao, X. and Mokhtarian, P. 2005, 'Correlation or causality between the built environment and travel behavior? Evidence from Northern California', *Transportation Research Part D: Transport and Environment*, vol. 10, no. 6, pp. 427–44.

Haustein, S. and Nielsen, T.A.S. 2016, 'European mobility cultures: A survey-based cluster analysis across 28 European countries', *Journal of Transport Geography*, vol. 54, pp. 173–80.

Heinen, E., Maat, K. and van Wee, B. 2011, 'The role of attitudes toward characteristics of bicycle commuting on the choice to cycle to work over various distances', *Transportation Research Part D*, vol. 16, no. 2, pp. 102–109.

Heinrich, C., Maffioli, A. and Vazquez, G. 2010, *A primer for applying propensity-score matching*, No. IDB-TN-161, Washington, DC: Inter-American Development Bank.

Hensher, D. 2015a, *Applied choice analysis*, 2nd edn, Cambridge: Cambridge University Press.

Hensher, D. 2015b, 'Choice and utility', in *Applied choice analysis*, 2nd edn, Cambridge: Cambridge University Press.

Hensher, D. and Button, K. 2008, *Handbook of transport modelling*, 2nd edn, Bingley: Emerald Group Publishing.

Hu, L. and Iseki, H. 2018, 'Land use and transportation planning in a diverse world', *Transport Policy*, accessed at https://doi.org/10.1016/j.tranpol.2018.11.016.

Jain, T., Johnson, M. and Rose, G. 2020, 'Exploring the process of travel behaviour change and mobility trajectories associated with car share adoption', *Travel Behaviour and Society*, vol. 18, pp. 117–31.

Kager, R. and Harms, L. 2017, *Synergies from improved bicycle-transit integration: Towards an integrated urban mobility system*, Paris: Organisation for Economic Cooperation and Development (OECD).

Khander, S.R., Koolwal, G.B. and Samad, H.A. 2010, *Handbook on impact evaluation: Quantitative Methods And Practices*, Washington, DC: The World Bank.

Koppelman, F.S. and Bhat, C. 2006, *A self instructing course in mode choice modeling: Multinomial and nested logit models*. Federal Transit Administration, Washington, DC. See also http://www.ce.utexas.edu/prof/bhat/COURSES/LM_Draft_060131Final-060630.pdf.

Lane, C., DiCarlantonio, M. and Usvyat, L. 2006, 'Sketch models to forecast commuter and light rail ridership: Update to TCRP Report 16', *Transportation Research Record: Journal of the Transportation Research Board*, vol. 1986, no. 1, pp. 198–210.

Levinson, D., Marshall, W. and Axhausen, K. 2017, *Elements of access*, Sydney, Australia: Network Design Lab.

Litman, T. and Steele, R. 2017, *Land use impacts on transport: How land use factors affect travel behavior*, Victoria Transport Policy Institute, accessed 24 June 2017.

MacKinnon, D., Krull, J. and Lockwood, C. 2000, 'Equivalence of the mediation, confounding and suppression effect', *Prevention Science*, vol. 1, no. 4, pp. 173–81.

Mahmoudi, J. and Zhang, L. 2018, 'Impact of county-level built environment and regional accessibility on walking: A Washington, DC–Baltimore case study', *Journal of Urban Planning and Development*, vol. 144, no. 3.

Maness, M., Cirillo, C. and Dugundji, E.R. 2015, 'Generalized behavioral framework for choice models of social influence: Behavioral and data concerns in travel behavior', *Journal of Transport Geography*, vol. 46, no. Supplement C, pp. 137–50.

Miller, E.J. 2019, 'Integrated modeling: Past, present, and future', *Journal of Transport and Land Use*, vol. 11, no. 1, pp. 387–99.

Mitchell, R.B. and Rapkin, C. 1954, *Urban traffic: A function of land use*, New York: Columbia University Press.

Moeckel, R., Garcia, C.L., Chou, A.T.M. and Okrah, M.B. 2019, 'Trends in integrated land use/transport modeling: An evaluation of the state of the art', *Journal of Transport and Land Use*, vol. 12, no. 1.

Mokhtarian, P.L. and Cao, X. 2008, 'Examining the impacts of residential self-selection on travel behavior: A focus on methodologies', *Transportation Research*, vol. 42, no. 3, pp. 204–28.

Monzón, A., Hernández, S. and Di Ciommo, F. 2016, 'Efficient urban interchanges: The City-HUB model', *Transportation Research Procedia*, vol. 14, no. C, pp. 1124–33.

Næss, P. 2009, 'Residential self-selection and appropriate control variables in land use: Travel studies', *Transport Reviews*, vol. 29, no. 3, pp. 293–324.

Nasri, A., Carrion, C., Zhang, L. and Baghaei, B. 2018, 'Using propensity score matching technique to address self-selection in transit-oriented development (TOD) areas', *Transportation*, pp. 1–13.

Ortúzar, J.D. and Willumsen, L.G. 2011, *Modelling transport*, 4th edn, Chichester: John Wiley & Sons.

Park, S., Choi, K. and Lee, J.S. 2017, 'Operationalization of path walkability for sustainable transportation', *International Journal of Sustainable Transportation*, vol. 11, no. 7, pp. 471–85.

Pourebrahim, N., Sultana, S., Niakanlahiji, A. and Thill, J.C. 2019, 'Trip distribution modeling with Twitter data', *Computers, Environment and Urban Systems*, vol. 77.

Rajabifard, A., Bishop, I., Eagleson, S., Pettit, C., Badland, H., Day, J., Furler, J., Kalantari, M., Sturup, S. and White, M. 2017, 'Using an online data portal and prototype analysis tools in an investigation of spatial livability planning', *International Journal of E-Planning Research (IJEPR)*, vol. 6, no. 2, pp. 1–21.

Ramsey, K. and Bell, A. 2014, *Smart location database user guide version 2.0*, U.S. Environmental Protection Agency Office of Sustainable Communities.

Renne, J., Hamidi, S. and Ewing, R. 2016, 'Transit commuting, the network accessibility effect, and the built environment in station areas across the United States', *Research in Transportation Economics*, vol. 60, pp. 35–43.

Rose, J.M. and Bliemer, M.C.J. 2008, 'Stated preference experimental design strategies', in D.A. Hensher and K.J. Button (eds), *Handbook of Transport Modelling*, 2nd edn, Emerald Group Publishing, online version, pp. 151–80, accessed 19 November 2017, via Knovel.

Scheiner, J. 2018, 'Why is there change in travel behaviour? In search of a theoretical framework for mobility biographies', *Erdkunde Archive for Scientific Geography*, vol. 72, no. 1, pp. 41–62.

Shannon, C.E. 1948, 'A mathematical theory of communication', *Bell System Technical Journal*, vol. 27, pp. 379–423, 623–56.

Singleton, R. 2005, *Approaches to social research*, 4th edn, New York: Oxford University Press.

Spears, S., Houston, D. and Boarnet, M.G. 2013, 'Illuminating the unseen in transit use: A framework for examining the effect of attitudes and perceptions on travel behavior', *Transportation Research Part A: Policy and Practice*, vol. 58, pp. 40–53.

Stevens, M.R. 2017, 'Does compact development make people drive less?', *Journal of the American Planning Association*, vol. 83, no. 1, pp. 7–18.

Stopher, P.S. 2008, 'Survey and sampling strategies', in D.A. Hensher and K.J. Button (eds), *Handbook of Transport Modelling*, 2nd edn, Emerald Group Publishing, online version, pp. 279–302, accessed 19 November 2017, via Knovel.

Thomas, R. and Bertolini, L. 2017, 'Defining critical success factors in TOD implementation using rough set analysis', *Journal of Transport and Land Use*, vol. 10, no. 1, pp. 139–54.

Tomitsch, M. 2018, *Making cities smarter: Designing interactive urban applications*, Berlin: Jovis Publishers.

Ton, D., Zomer, L-B., Schneider, F., Hoogendoorn-Lanser, S., Duives, D., Cats, O. and Hoogendoorn, S. 2019, 'Latent classes of daily mobility patterns: The relationship with attitudes towards modes', *Transportation*.

Torabi Kachousangi, F., Van Oort, N. and Hoogendoorn, S. 2019, 'The future of intermodal hubs', in M. Triggianese, R. Cavallo, N. Baron and J. Kuijper (eds), *Stations as Nodes: Exploring the role of stations in future metropolitan areas from a French and Dutch perspective*, Delft: TU Delft Open, pp. 57–62.

Tu, W., Cao, R., Yue, Y., Zhou, B., Li, Q. and Li, Q. 2018, 'Spatial variations in urban public ridership derived from GPS trajectories and smart card data', *Journal of Transport Geography*, vol. 69, pp. 45–57.

van de Coevering, P., Maat, K. and Van Wee, B. 2015, 'Multi-period research designs for identifying causal effects of built environment characteristics on travel behaviour', *Transport Reviews*, vol. 35, no. 4, pp. 1–21.

van de Coevering, P., Maat, K. and Van Wee, B. 2018, 'Residential self-selection, reverse causality and residential dissonance: A latent class transition model of interactions between the built environment, travel attitudes and travel behavior', *Transportation Research Part A*, vol. 118, pp. 466–79.

van Wee, B., De Vos, J. and Maat, K. 2019, 'Impacts of the built environment and travel behaviour on attitudes: Theories underpinning the reverse causality hypothesis', *Journal of Transport Geography*, vol. 80, p. 102540.

Wegener, M. and Spiekerman, K. 2018, 'Multi-level urban models: Integration across space, time and policies', *Journal of Transport and Land Use*, vol. 11, no. 1.

Welch, T.F. and Widita, A. 2019, 'Big data in public transportation: A review of sources and methods', *Transport Reviews*, pp. 1–24.

West, G.B. 2017, *Scale: The universal laws of growth, innovation, sustainability, and the pace of life in organisms, cities, economies, and companies*, New York: Penguin Press.

Woldeamanuel, M. and Kent, A. 2016, 'Measuring walk access to transit in terms of sidewalk availability, quality, and connectivity', *Journal of Urban Planning and Development*, vol. 142, no. 2.

Woods, R. and Masthoff, J. 2017, 'A comparison of car driving, public transport and cycling experiences in three European cities', *Transportation Research Part A*, vol. 103, pp. 211–22.

Wooldridge, J.M. 2016, *Introductory econometrics: A modern approach*, 6th edn, Boston, MA: Cengage Learning.

Yang, M., Wu, J., Rasouli, S., Cirillo, C. and Li, D. 2017, 'Exploring the impact of residential relocation on modal shift in commute trips: Evidence from a quasi-longitudinal analysis', *Transport Policy*, vol. 59, pp. 142–52.

PART II

USER PERSPECTIVES

4. Transit customer satisfaction research: is the customer always right?

Madalena Harreman-Fernandes, Ehab Diab, Boer Cui, James DeWeese, Miles Crumley and Ahmed El-Geneidy

4.1 INTRODUCTION

In recent years, public transport agencies have come to value the benefits of incorporating customer satisfaction in their decision-making process (Eboli et al., 2018). Among other things, customer satisfaction is an important indicator of customer loyalty (van Lierop and El-Geneidy, 2016). Understanding the determinants of customer satisfaction can therefore help agencies determine how best to retain the existing riders and attract new ones to increase growth and profitability of the system (Diab et al., 2017).

Many public transport agencies regularly collect surveys to gauge customer satisfaction. But the process of designing a survey is time-consuming and expensive due, in part, to the caution that must be exercised to minimize response biases. In particular, changes in question order or wording can systematically affect the way respondents answer questions related to satisfaction in travel surveys (Grise et al., 2019). Moreover, poorly designed or closed-ended surveys may cause policymakers to overlook important aspects of real or perceived service quality by failing to elicit information about unforeseen topics (Whitfield and Baker, 1992). In response to this, researchers have recommended user-oriented, qualitative methods to assess perceived quality of service. These methods include the use of open-ended questions that allow respondents to express their satisfaction or – more often – dissatisfaction freely (Bankauskaite and Saarelma, 2003; Pichert et al., 1998).

Several public transport agencies use the number of complaints received in a certain period of time by their customer service centers as an indicator of customer satisfaction levels. Yet a disconnect might exist between the service quality captured in satisfaction surveys or complaint data and objectively measured state of service (van Lierop and El-Geneidy, 2017). Occasionally this disconnect is to the transport agencies' benefit. For example, riders tend to overestimate their actual time savings from new services (El-Geneidy and Surprenant-Legault, 2010). At other times, this disconnect is to the agencies' detriment: perceived waiting time is often longer than reality (Watkins et al., 2011). Therefore, it is prudent to validate the satisfaction surveys or complaints received with actual service data. Doing so will provide a more complete picture of the performance of the public transport system, enabling it to target service problems more effectively.

This chapter reviews current practices in transit customer satisfaction research and their strengths and weaknesses, including, to our knowledge, the first study to analyze and assess the usefulness of customer complaints to evaluate transit service. In this study, customer comment and suggestion data provided by the Tri-County Metropolitan Transportation District of Oregon (TriMet) agency of the Portland, Oregon, metropolitan region was analyzed and linked to real-world operations data. Data was provided for the

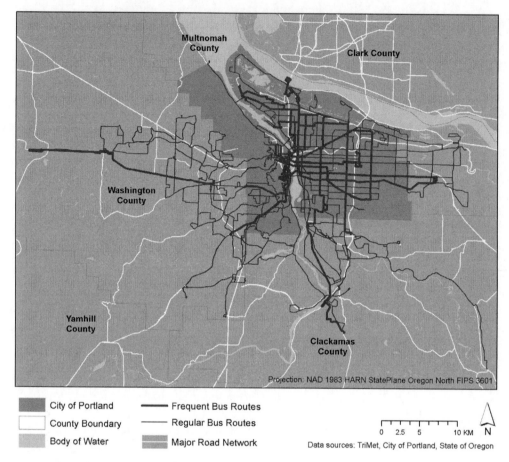

Figure 4.1   Bus routes operated by TriMet

period between August 2018 and January 2019 for the 84 regular and two night bus routes shown in Figure 4.1 (TriMet, 2019b). This approach enabled us to evaluate the validity of feedback received. In presenting this research, we hope to provide an overview of best practices and current limitations of transit customer satisfaction research and establish the use of complaint data as an important first step to evaluate route level performance and inform policy decisions.

4.2   MEASURING CUSTOMER SATISFACTION WITH PUBLIC TRANSIT

Customer Satisfaction

Public transport professionals tend to focus on the technical aspects of service provision where the common belief is that improvements made to measurable characteristics, such as travel time, cost and frequency, would directly lead to an increase in ridership. However, it has been shown that it is the perceived quality of service, conveyed through riders' level of satisfaction (Chen et al., 2007), which actually dictates their behavioral intentions (Abou-Zeid et al., 2012). Furthermore, satisfaction has been found to positively influence customer loyalty and willingness to recommend the service to others (van Lierop and El-Geneidy, 2016; van Lierop et al., 2018). While satisfaction with public transport is dependent on the attitude and personal characteristics of the rider, the quality of both quantitative and qualitative, off-board and on-board service attributes still has an impact (Eboli and Mazzulla, 2009; Tyrinopoulos and Antoniou, 2008; Mouwen, 2015; Hensher et al., 2003). For example, van Lierop and El-Geneidy (2017) found that the overall satisfaction of passengers on an express bus route in Vancouver, Canada, was largely dependent on their satisfaction with crowding, service frequency, onboard safety and cleanliness.

Satisfaction and Objective Service Quality

While understanding riders' satisfaction levels regarding various service attributes is a critical first step when deciding where to make investments to improve the quality of the public transport system, researchers argue that without linking satisfaction with objective service performance measures, the process is incomplete (Carrel et al., 2016; Friman and Fellesson, 2009; Allen et al., 2019). First, knowing that riders are dissatisfied with a particular service does not tell us how they will react to changes in service. Secondly, it has been shown that there is a marked difference between perceived and actual quality of service (van Lierop and El-Geneidy, 2017; Diab et al., 2015), with waiting time being an example. It is important to understand the reasons behind this difference when identifying the appropriate policy intervention. Watkins et al. (2011) found that the provision of real-time information mediated the difference between perceived and actual waiting times, emphasizing the importance of real-time information when assessing user satisfaction. More recently, Carrel et al. (2016) used surveys, automatic vehicle location (AVL), and smartphone tracking data to connect survey responses with respondents' on-route experience to understand how they experienced unreliability throughout the duration of their trips. A clear link between reported satisfaction with delays and measured delays was established where satisfaction decreased as travel time increased.

Critical Incidents (CIs)

Other researchers have approached customer satisfaction differently, using the critical incident technique which states that *critical incidents* (CIs) (Bitner et al., 1990) are the main factors determining customer satisfaction and thus perceived service quality. Specifically, Friman et al. (2001) argued that in the delivery of public transport service, dissatisfying or negative critical incidents (NCIs), such as perceived dangerous driving, are more impactful than positive ones. NCIs directly affect satisfaction with specific service attributes (e.g. delays are attributed to unreliability of service). Therefore, they concluded that the frequency of NCIs has an indirect impact on overall satisfaction. This hypothesis was recently confirmed by researchers through the use of structural equation modeling (Allen et al., 2018).

Measuring Perceived Service Quality

In most studies examining customer satisfaction, including those that were mentioned earlier in this chapter, satisfaction was measured quantitatively: respondents were asked to rate their satisfaction based on the Likert or similar numerical scales. However, researchers argue that these strictly formulated (i.e. closed-ended) survey questions can be problematic for multiple reasons: first, they can result in misleading responses due to poor survey or question design and, second, they can limit the opportunity for customers to express concerns about aspects of the service not addressed in the questions (Whitfield and Baker, 1992; Bankauskaite and Saarelma, 2003). Additionally, responses can be influenced by a recall bias from a previous NCI unrelated to the questions being asked.

In the transport planning field, researchers have observed (Grise et al., 2019; dell'Olio et al., 2010) that question order and/or wording impact survey responses. Specifically, Grise et al. (2019) found that when surveying respondent satisfaction regarding their typical and last commute trips, there were significant systematic differences in the way respondents answered questions depending on question wording and the order in which they appeared. Question order effects were similarly observed by dell'Olio et al. (2010).

As there is no best practice in place for the design of customer satisfaction surveys to avoid these issues, researchers studying patient satisfaction in the healthcare field (O'Cathain and Thomas, 2004; Whitfield and Baker, 1992) have suggested that more attention should be placed on qualitative methods. These methods may include using responses from open-ended questions where customers can provide their input directly, especially concerning events that resulted in dissatisfaction (Williams et al., 1998) such as NCIs. Some researchers of the impact of NCIs on perceived quality of public transport service used customer complaints, both archived and from face-to-face interviews, which were categorized and then analyzed. They found that, in addition to service unreliability, users also frequently complained about employee behavior (Friman et al., 1998).

On the other hand, researchers studying customer complaint behavior have recognized that there is a variety of personal factors that determine whether a customer would report a complaint (Kim et al., 2003; Stephens and Gwinner, 1998; Thøgersen et al., 2009; Raval, 2020). In addition, it has been reported that up to two-thirds of dissatisfied customers do not complain, but instead cope with their dissatisfaction by quietly exiting the system or communicating negative word-of-mouth assessments (Richins, 1983).

To address these shortcomings of customer complaint data, some have advocated that quantitative methods (i.e. customer ratings obtained from all survey respondents) and qualitative methods (i.e. customer complaints from willing respondents) should be used together to measure perceived quality (Cunningham et al., 1997). However, no study has examined public transport customer complaints alongside objective measures of system performance, using a similar method performed by Carrel et al. (2016) where they used ratings instead of complaints, to assess the validity of complaints when measuring perceived quality.

4.3   USING COMPLAINTS AND OPERATIONS DATA

Complaints Data

To better understand the types of bus-related public transit CIs that users feel most strongly about, recent research conducted at McGill University analyzed user complaint data obtained from the TriMet transport agency in Portland, Oregon. In total, 4021 complaints were received from August 2018 to January 2019. Complaints were collected through multiple sources (e.g. phone, text, online, Twitter) (TriMet, 2019a) and then entered into a database. As such, no standard procedure was followed regarding their initial entry and categorization. To perform the analysis, the data required additional collation and cleaning by the researchers.

Categorization of Complaints

To analyze the user complaints and link them directly to system performance, they were first reclassified into 18 standard categories and unnecessary duplicates were removed. We relied on the non-standardized categories entered by TriMet customer service representatives to guide our development of standard categories. Each complaint record was then reclassified into the appropriate category, or categories if they addressed multiple issues. Example categories included Personnel Commendation, Pass-up, Policies and Procedures, Signage, Stop Request/Complaint, and so on. Duplicate records of the same category were removed; however those that spanned multiple categories, for example a complaint concerning a rude operator (Personnel Complaint) who was also speeding (Vehicle Operation), were kept as multiple records for analysis. A total of 3838 complaint records were left for analysis. Subcategory descriptions were also created to further isolate different types of complaints to facilitate analysis if needed. For example, 'Failure to deploy ramp/kneel' under 'ADA Complaint'.

Complaints Analysis

Time of complaint

Of the 3838 records, 3643 complaints were associated with a particular event date and time. The other records were the result of either the event being non time-specific (e.g. bus shelter cleanliness), recurring, or details being omitted when they were submitted or entered into the database. The distribution of the number of complaints by time and period of day can be seen in Figure 4.2. Complaints were most frequently reported during peak periods (between 6 am and 9 am and 3 pm and 6 pm), when commute ridership is highest. This is presumably due to users being under greater time pressure on their journey to and from work and, therefore, more likely to be negatively impacted by poor service performance.

Complaint topics

To generate standardized classifications, we were guided both by the existing unstandardized descriptors in the data and the broad categories adopted in other studies of public transport satisfaction and operations. See for example Gao et al. (2016), Kamaruddin

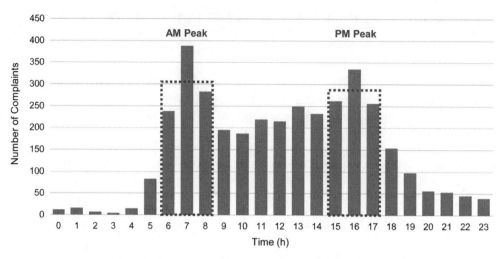

Figure 4.2   Distribution of the number of complaints by event time

et al. (2017) and Van Lierop and El-Geneidy (2016). The top-level classifications related to different aspects of customer satisfaction included information, safety, service, and travel environment. Within these higher-level classifications, we nested more specific categories of complaints derived from the data itself. The complaints fall under the following topics: ADA (Americans with Disabilities Act) Compliance, Comfort, Customer Service, Fare, Information, Physical Facilities, Policy, Reliability, Safety and Security, and Service. Similar to previous studies that looked at satisfaction with public transport (van Lierop and El-Geneidy, 2017; Friman et al., 1998), the most common topics (making up 80 percent of total complaints) concerned Reliability, Customer Service, and Safety and Security (see Figure 4.3).

Nearly half (47 percent) of complaints concerned the reliability of TriMet's bus service. Complaints that fall under Reliability include: Deviation from Schedule, Overload, Pass-up, Vehicle Operations, and Reroute Issues/Concerns. A majority of these complaints (54 percent) were about vehicle pass-ups, where the operator failed to pick up a waiting passenger or stop at the proper location when requested. This was followed by 39 percent of complaints concerning deviations from schedule (e.g. late/early arrivals, no show buses). As expected, this suggests that being able to plan and rely on the service to get to one's destination on time is a priority for passengers (Diab et al., 2015). If users are unable to do so, they may look to other options, as demonstrated by one of the complaints:

> This morning 10/12/18 at bus stop xxxx the '7:00 am' bus drove right by us at a high rate of speed. They stopped at the next stop down the street and picked up the people there but did not pick us up. There were 3 of us waiting. The next bus (according to your app) never showed up and the 3rd bus was late, so I ended up taking an Uber to work. I was late.

Complaints about customer service made up 20 percent of total complaints and consisted of two categories: Personnel Complaints (66 percent) and Personnel Commendations (34 percent). While the majority of customer service comments received were negative,

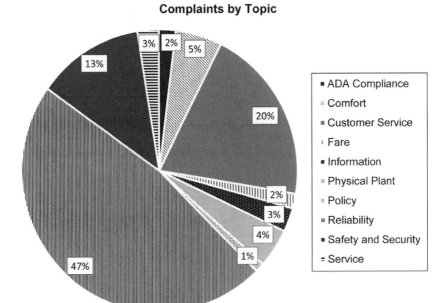

Figure 4.3 Percentage of complaints by topic

having over a third being unprompted positive feedback about personnel is significant. In fact, nearly all positive comments received were regarding personnel specifically. This indicates that interactions between operators and the public, both positive and negative, are an important component of user opinion of the service.

Safety and Security is another topic that users felt strongly about, with 13 percent of complaints on the topic. This includes Accident Reports, Vehicle Operation, Safety Issues/Suggestions, Stop Requests/Complaints, and Vehicle Requests/Complaints. An overwhelming majority (80 percent) of these complaints reported reckless driving by the operator, including distracted driving, erratic or aggressive driving, failing to yield, running red lights, conflicts with other road users, rough rides, speeding, unsafe lane changes, and other poor driving behavior. Collecting the appropriate information regarding the time of day when the incident occurred as well as the location is critical for the public transport agency to verify the situation and conduct any actions related to training and monitoring of a driver.

Link Between Complaints and System Performance

Data and methodology
The study also sought to understand the association between passenger complaints and real-world system performance measures. To do so, four of the routes with the highest total number of complaints were identified for analysis (see Figure 4.4). Many complaints, such as those regarding cleanliness, vandalism, emergencies, and violence, were not logically related to service operations and were excluded from our analysis. This left a total of

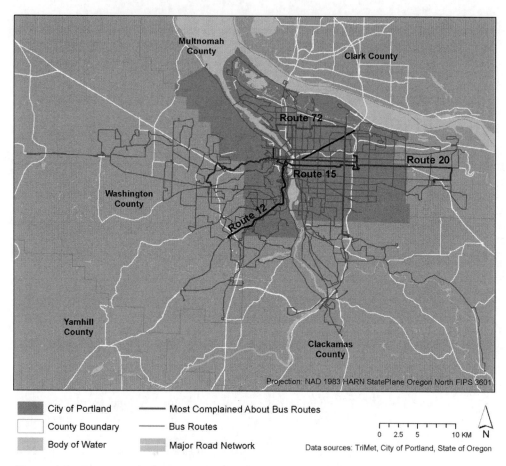

Figure 4.4   Routes with the most complaints

382 complaints spanning the high-level classifications of Vehicle Operations, Deviations from Schedule, and Pass-ups. Within the remaining complaints, we identified the four subcategories that (1) displayed the highest individual frequencies and (2) could be associated with particular times, locations and event data. These subcategories encompassed 315 individual complaints with the following distribution: Pass-ups (200 complaints), Late Arrival/Departure (56 complaints), Early Arrival/Departure (30 complaints), and Rough Ride/Driving Behavior (29 complaints).

Bus service operational data from TriMet's bus dispatch system which includes detailed AVL and automatic passenger counting (APC) systems was acquired for these four routes for the period between 1 August 2018 and 31 January 2019. All TriMet buses are equipped with such systems, which allowed for a detailed picture of operations for each route and its constituent trips during the study period.

Using the AVL/APC data, several performance measures were estimated for each trip: travel time, average and maximum passenger load and average and maximum stop delay. TriMet's AVL/APC data also provided the maximum speed reached between every two

Table 4.1   Routes linked to operations data

Route	Length (km)	Number of Stops	Peak Headway (min)	Daily Ridership (2018)	Filtered Operational Complaints
Route 12: Barbur/Sandy Blvd	25.29	82	<10	8200	69
Route 15: Belmont/NW 23rd	19.76	72	<10	8160	73
Route 20: Burnside/Stark	43.05	135	<1	11020	104
Route 72: Killingsworth/82nd	27.13	106	<10	14750	69

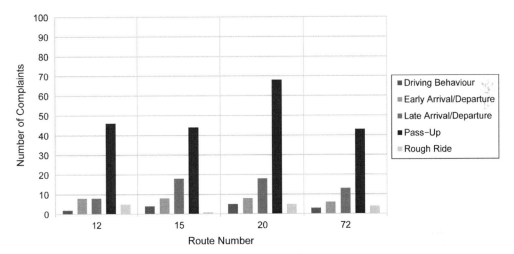

Figure 4.5   Number of complaints by operations subcategories

consecutive stops (i.e., stop-to-stop segment). The average maximum speed for each trip was calculated using this information. Trips with incomplete records, a malfunctioning APC system or missing stop information were removed from the analysis.

A total of 205 complaints were successfully linked. For each of these trips (those with a complaint), we also retained the trip immediately before and after for analysis to better understand the causes and later impacts of the CI that led to the complaint. Additionally, a random sample of trips (around 10 percent of trips) from the four routes was kept for comparison purposes.

Complaints association with performance measures
Table 4.1 summarizes the physical characteristics, ridership, and number of complaints for the four routes linked to operations data. According to recent TriMet ridership estimates (TriMet, 2019a), these routes have the highest daily ridership in the region. The number of complaints received for these routes ranged between 69 and 104 per route, with a majority of complaints concerning pass-ups (see Figure 4.5).

As seen in Table 4.2, the maximum and average trip loads of trips with pass-up complaints were slightly higher compared to random trips and trips right before and

Table 4.2   Trip performance measures broken down by complaint types

	# of Trips	Max. Trip Load	Avg. Trip Load	% of Stops Made	Max. Segment Speed	Avg. Stop Delay
Random trips	925.00	23.84	10.73	0.49	24.64	122.62
Pass-up						
Trip with complaint	141.00	24.11	11.24	0.49	**25.48**	**154.29**
One trip after complaint	133.00	22.27	10.34	0.48	**25.24**	128.82
One trip before complaint	138.00	22.64	10.19	0.48	**25.33**	116.75
Late Arrival/Departure						
Trip with complaint	28.00	**28.25**	**12.80**	0.48	25.17	**497.06**
One trip after complaint	28.00	**19.96**	9.48	**0.43**	25.87	117.04
One trip before complaint	25.00	25.24	11.68	0.47	25.12	107.45
Early Arrival/Departure						
Trip with complaint	14.00	26.57	11.43	0.50	24.42	102.51
One trip after complaint	14.00	16.79	8.27	0.49	23.34	156.22
One trip before complaint	14.00	24.00	10.22	0.51	23.55	119.55
Rough Ride/Driving Behavior						
Trip with complaint	22.00	**27.27**	**12.11**	0.50	**26.14**	138.18
One trip after complaint	21.00	20.14	9.09	0.46	25.08	103.64
One trip before complaint	22.00	24.73	10.12	0.47	25.17	92.08

Note: Bold indicates significance at 95%.

after, although not to a significant degree. However, these trips also had statistically significant higher maximum speeds between stops, as well as higher average stop delays in comparison to random trips. This suggests that pass-up associated trips were usually late and overcrowded compared to other trips. This may have led operators to speed and skip passengers at stops, resulting in the pass-up complaints. Trips before and after pass-up complaints did not have significantly different average stop delays compared to random trips. Interestingly, they did have higher average maximum speeds.

Trips associated with Late Arrival/Departure complaints had significantly higher loads and greater delays at stops compared to random trips. This affirms that these trips were running late and capturing more passengers than they should have. In contrast, subsequent trips stopped less frequently to serve passengers, with statistically significant higher average speeds and smaller passenger loads. This is indicative of a typical bus-bunching situation (Verbich et al., 2016), where late buses that capture more riders lead to further delays and result in the following buses travelling faster and with fewer passengers.

Trips with complaints about Early Arrival/Departure did not show any significant difference compared to random trips, which may be attributed to the small sample size of these trips. Finally, trips with Rough Ride/Driving Behaviour complaints had significantly higher average passenger loads and speeds. Numerous explanations are possible. For example, drivers with heavily loaded buses could perhaps feel greater pressure, causing them to increase their driving speed. It is also conceivable that higher passenger loads, corresponding to a greater number of people standing, could render passengers more susceptible to a rough ride. Future research with a larger database of complaints could allow for greater disaggregation in the analysis, which might better explain the results for this category.

4.4   CONCLUSIONS AND FUTURE RESEARCH

Data Limitations

Customer complaints provide a useful indication of perceived service quality, particularly when verified using system performance data. There are limitations to the use of customer complaints compared to other sources of satisfaction data. The primary limitation is the lack of standardization in terms of how the complaints are collected, recorded and stored within and across agencies. This makes it difficult for researchers to be able to compare the results between transit systems and for agencies to be able to analyze and use the feedback received given the amount of data cleaning that is involved. Additionally, complaint data represents a very small sample of users, so it is difficult to make generalizations based on comments and suggestions that may not be representative of the entire ridership base. However, complaints provide useful insight regarding potential deficiencies in service that can be further investigated through comparison with actual system performance.

Recommendations for Public Transit Agencies

To facilitate data tabulation and improve the usefulness of comments and suggestions collected, we recommend that public transit agencies adopt the following standards when recording customer complaints:

1. Adopt standard categories for complaints while including 'Other' as an option; this both streamlines the entry process and reduces the need for data cleaning later and, to the extent possible, align time, date and location stamps with formatting in AVL/APC data.
2. Create separate fields describing whether comments/suggestions submitted were for a particular event or a recurring issue.
3. Similarly, implement fields for whether complaints were submitted by the user or by a third party; for example, some complaints were also entered under the category of 'Witness' or 'Third Party' to describe a complaint made on the behalf of another user (e.g. someone witnessing a pass-up); these duplicate records were excluded from our analysis as they are not a descriptor of the type of complaint and would best be included as a separate field for data filtering purposes.
4. List how the complaint was reported; since the level of complaint detail seems to vary depending on the method with which it was filed, this would inform agencies which platforms are best for collecting more detailed and useful feedback.

4.5   CONCLUSION

Accurately measuring perceived and actual transit customer satisfaction is challenging. There are many things to consider when determining how best to collect and analyze customer satisfaction data: response bias, customer characteristics and attitudes, representation of ridership base, validity of complaints, how negative and positive transit experiences impact travel behavior, and so on. Previous methods relied on customer satisfaction surveys, interviews, and/or the number of complaints received to evaluate perceived customer satisfaction with the transit service provided. A recent study at McGill University used self-reported customer complaints and objective bus service operations data in an attempt to better understand the actual factors that led to the complaints. The results of the study indicate that using complaints can provide useful insight regarding potential deficiencies in service that can be further confirmed through comparison with actual system performance. This can inform researchers, practitioners and transport agencies which deficiencies have the greatest impact on customer satisfaction (enough to file a complaint) and where to make improvements based on the causal factors of the complaint. However, since complaints typically arise from a vocal few riders, it is important to complement complaint and/or operations data with other methods to assess general customer satisfaction and what is working well with the service. Further research following the loyalty of a user following a complaint or negative/positive experience is also needed to determine the relationship between actual and perceived satisfaction with the transit service provided.

REFERENCES

Abou-Zeid, M., Witter, R., Bierlaire, M., Kaufmann, V. and Ben-Akiva, M. 2012. Happiness and travel mode switching: Findings from a Swiss public transportation experiment. *Transport Policy*, 19, 93–104.

Allen, J., Eboli, L., Mazzulla, G. and Ortuzar, J. 2018. Effect of critical incidents on public transport satisfaction and loyalty: An Ordinal Probit SEM-MIMIC approach. *Transportation*, 1–57.

Allen, J., Munoz, J. and Ortuzar, J. 2019. On the effect of operational service attributes on transit satisfaction. *Transportation*, 47, 2307–36.

Bankauskaite, V. and Saarelma, O. 2003. Why are people dissatisfied with medical care services in Lithuania? A qualitative study using responses to open-ended questions. *Journal of Quality in Health Care*, 15, 23–9.

Bitner, M., Booms, B. and Tetreault, M. 1990. The service encounter: Diagnosing favorable and unfavorable incidents. *Journal of Marketing*, 54, 71–84.

Carrel, A., Mishalani, R., Sengupta, R. and Walker, J. 2016. In pursuit of the happy transit rider: Dissecting satisfaction using daily surveys and tracking data. *Journal of Intelligent Transportation Systems*, 20, 345–62.

Chen, C., Gong, H. and Paaswell, R. 2007. Role of the built environment on mode choice decisions: Additional evidence on the impact of density. *Transportation*, 35, 285–99.

Cunningham, L., Young, C. and Lee, M. 1997. Developing customer-based measures of overall transportation service quality in Colorado: Quantative and qualitative approaches. *Journal of Public Transportation*, 1, 1–21.

dell'Olio, L., Ibeas, A. and Cecín, P. 2010. Modelling user perception of bus transit quality. *Transport Policy*, 17, 388–97.

Diab, E., Badami, M. and El-Geneidy, A. 2015. Bus transit service reliability and improvement strategies: Integrating the perspectives of passengers and transit agencies in North America. *Transport Reviews*, 23, 292–328.

Diab, E., Van Lierop, D. and El-Geneidy, A. 2017. Recommending transit: Disentangling users' willingness to recommend transit and their intended continued use. *Travel Behaviour and Society*, 6, 1–9.

Eboli, L. and Mazzulla, G. 2009. A new customer satisfaction index for evaluating transit service quality. *Journal of Public Transportation*, 12, 21–37.

Eboli, L., Forciniti, C. and Mazzulla, G. 2018. Spatial variation of the perceived transit service quality at rail stations. *Transportation Research Part A: Policy and Practice*, 114, 67–83.

El-Geneidy, A. and Surprenant-Legault, J. 2010. Limited bus stop service: An evaluation of an implementation strategy. *Public Transport: Planning and Operations*, 2, 291–306.

Friman, M. and Fellesson, M. 2009. Service supply and customer satisfaction in public transportation: The quality paradox. *Journal of Public Transportation*, 12, 57–69.

Friman, M., Edvardsson, B. and Garling, T. 1998. Perceived service quality attributes in public transport: Inferences from complaints and negative critical incidents. *Journal of Public Transportation*, 2, 67–89.

Friman, M., Edvardsson, B. and Garling, T. 2001. Frequency of negative critical incidents and satisfaction with public transport services. *Journal of Retailing and Consumer Services*, 8, 95–104.

Gao, L., Yu, Y. and Liang, W. 2016. Public transit customer satisfaction dimensions discovery from online reviews. *Urban Rail Transit*, 2, 146–52.

Grise, E., Cui, B., Turim, A., Manaugh, K. and El-Geneidy, A. 2019. The impacts of varying survey design on reported trip satisfaction. *Transportation Research Part F: Traffic Psychology and Behaviour*, 60, 761–9.

Hensher, D., Stopher, P. and Bullock, P. 2003. Service quality: Developing a service quality index in the provision of commercial bus contracts. *Transportation Research Part A: Policy and Practice*, 37, 499–517.

Kamaruddin, R., Osman, I. and Pei, C.A.C. 2017. Customer expectations and its relationship towards public transport in Klang Valley. *Journal of ASIAN Behavioural Studies*, 2, 29–39.

Kim, C., Kim, S., Im, S. and Shin, C. 2003. The effect of attitude and perception on consumer complaint intentions. *Journal of Consumer Marketing*, 20, 352–71.

Mouwen, A. 2015. Drivers of customer satisfaction with public transport services. *Transportation Research Part A: Policy and Practice*, 78, 1–20.

O'Cathain, A. and Thomas, K. 2004. 'Any other comments?' Open questions on questionnaires – a bane or a bonus to research? *BMC Medical Research Methodology*, 4, 25.

Pichert, J., Miller, C., Hollo, A., Gauld-Jaeger, J., Federspiel, C. and Hickson, G. 1998. What health professionals can do to identify and resolve patient dissatisfaction. *Joint Commission Journal on Quality Improvement*, 24, 303–12.

Raval, D. 2020. Whose voice do we hear in the marketplace? Evidence from consumer complaining behavior. *Marketing Science*, 39, 168–87.

Richins, M. 1983. Negative word-of-mouth by dissatisfied consumers: A pilot study. *Journal of Marketing*, 47, 68–78.

Stephens, N. and Gwinner, K. 1998. Why don't some people complain? A cognitive–emotive process model of consumer complaint behavior. *Journal of Marketing Science*, 26, 172–89.

Thøgersen, J., Juhl, H. and Poulsen, C. 2009. Complaining: A function of attitude, personality, and situation. *Psychology & Marketing*, 26, 760–77.

TriMet 2019a. Help Center [Online]. Accessed 27 July 2019 at https://support.trimet.org/hc/en-us.

TriMet 2019b. TriMet [Online]. Accessed 22 July 2019 at https://trimet.org/.

Tyrinopoulos, Y. and Antoniou, C. 2008. Public transit user satisfaction: Variability and policy implications. *Transport Policy*, 15, 260–72.

Van Lierop, D. and El-Geneidy, A. 2016. Enjoying loyality: The relationship between service quality, customer satisfaction and behavioral intentions in public transit. *Research in Transportation Economics*, 59, 50–59.

Van Lierop, D. and El-Geneidy, A. 2017. Perceived reality: Understanding the relationship between customer perceptions and operational characteristics. *Transportation Research Record: Journal of the Transport Research Board*, 2652, 87–97.

Van Lierop, D., Badami, M. and El-Geneidy, A. 2018. What influences satisfaction and loyalty in public transport? A review of the literature. *Transport Reviews*, 38, 52–72.

Verbich, D., Diab, E. and El-Geneidy, A. 2016. Have they bunched yet? An exploratory study of the impacts of bus bunching on dwell and running time. *Public Transport*, 8, 225–42.

Watkins, K., Ferris, B., Borning, A., Rutherford, G. and Layton, G. 2011. Where is my bus? Impact of mobile real-time information on the perceived and actual wait time of transit riders. *Transportation Research Part A: Policy and Practice*, 45, 839–48.

Whitfield, M. and Baker, R. 1992. Measuring patient satisfaction for audit in general practice. *Quality and Safety in Healthcare*, 1, 151–2.

Williams, B., Coyle, J. and Healy, D. 1998. The meaning of patient satisfaction: An explanation of high reported levels. *Social Science & Medicine*, 47, 1351–9.

5. Personal safety on public transport: research frontiers and new tools for an old problem

Graham Currie, Mustafizur Rahaman, Carlyn Muir and Alexa Delbosc

5.1 INTRODUCTION

A range of research suggests that personal safety and fear of crime on public transport acts to reduce its attractiveness:

- studies in the UK suggest 10 per cent of the population would reconsider using public transport if their fears were addressed (Crime Concern 2004);
- an analysis of influences on satisfaction with bus journeys in Edinburgh found that safety was the most commonly cited concern (Stradling et al. 2007);
- a majority of car drivers in inner Los Angeles claimed they would use transit if public buses were perceived as safe and clean (Loukaitou-Sideris 1999b).

Concerns about personal safety on public transport are common, popular, and often alarmist topics for media coverage (e.g. Millar 2009; Sexton 2009; van den Berg 2009). Despite this, there is much debate about the actual effects of crime on public transport and how this relates to the beliefs held by passengers and potential passengers. Some Government statistics suggest that crime rates on public transport are falling, whereas media and political commentary suggests the opposite (Gardiner 2009). A study in Australia found that concern for personal safety was one of the least cited barriers to taking public transport to work (lack of service and inconvenience were far more important factors; Australian Bureau of Statistics 2009). A survey of customer satisfaction in Sydney suggests that 90 per cent of bus and train passengers are satisfied with their level of safety (Transport Data Centre 2009).

A similar debate is being held within academic circles concerning the impact of actual crime on perceptions of safety on public transport. It has been suggested that media coverage itself is acting to influence perceptions (Crime Concern 2002). Some researchers emphasise that perceptions are not related to actual experiences of crime (Box et al. 1988) and others maintain that psychological factors play a role in negative perceptions of safety (Thomas 2009). Regardless, crime rates on public transport are likely to impact both actual and perceived personal safety: higher patronage results in less opportunity for crime to occur, and larger groups make people *feel* safer (Cozens et al. 2003a).

Despite much interest in the topic, there is a lack of systematic research on factors affecting the perceptions of personal safety on public transport. In addition, methodologies employed in the limited research available are not very sophisticated; conclusions are often drawn almost exclusively from anecdotes or from qualitative focus groups or comparative analyses (Reed et al. 2000; Cozens et al. 2003b; Crime Concern 2004). A few exceptions exist, such as simple regression analyses used in Wallace et al. (1999), Morse and Benjamin (1997) and Delbosc and Currie (2012).

This chapter reports on a largely unpublished PhD research programme which was able to quantitatively establish factors affecting the perceptions of personal safety of rail travellers using stations and the relative size of these impacts.[1] The research background, methods adopted and findings are presented in the following sections. The chapter concludes with a discussion on implications of the research for practice and an outline of opportunities for future research in the field.

5.2   RESEARCH CONTEXT

5.2.1   Crime and the Perception of Personal Safety

Crime and perceptions of personal safety are clearly interrelated. Criminology studies have found that being a victim, a witness, or possessing knowledge of crime, and also crime rate in the local neighbourhood are associated with lower perceptions of personal safety and higher fear of crime (Balkin 1978; Skogan and Maxfield 1981; Heath 1984; O'Keefe 1984; Hough et al. 1985; Liu et al. 1998; Lane and Meeker 2003; Banks 2005; Hedayati Marzbali et al. 2012a; Nellis and Savage 2012; Abdullah et al. 2013).

Public transportation is certainly vulnerable to crime (Levine and Wachs 1986; Carr and Spring 1993; Clarke 1997; Smith and Clarke 2000; Newton 2004). Offenders can target the system itself, employees, or passengers at the stations and on board vehicles, and commit a range of offences (e.g., vandalism or fare evasion, assaults on ticket collectors, pickpocketing, etc.) (Benjamin et al. 1994; Smith and Clarke 2000). A number of research publications have considered various factors related to crime in the public transport context. However, little research has explored the empirical relationship between the experience and witnessing of crime and threatening behaviour, crime at stations and in surrounding areas, and passengers' perceptions of personal safety. In addition, the combined influence of these factors is yet to be considered in a model of personal safety perceptions. *Thus, it's worth investigating the relationships between crime rates, passengers' exposure to crime and threatening behaviour at stations and in surrounding neighbourhoods, and their perceptions of safety.*

5.2.2   Anti-social Behaviour and the Perception of Personal Safety

Anti-Social Behaviour (ASB) is described as behaviours that are undesirable or unacceptable but not criminal in nature (Millie 2008b). Some research has concluded that ASB can adversely impact individual mental health, community cohesion and quality of life through long-term effects of harassment, intimidation and fear of crime (Maxfield 1984; Green et al. 2002; Flint et al. 2007; Millie 2008a).

However, little research has focused on anti-social behaviour (ASB) in the context of public transport. Most of the related studies have explored the behavioural aspects of ASB and some suggested measures/policies to prevent ASB (Abbott 2004; Granville and Campbell-Jack 2005; Moore 2010; Moore 2012; Coxon et al. 2013). *However, the link between passengers' perceptions of personal safety and concern with, or the experience of, ASB has not been considered previously in published research.*

5.2.3   Design Quality and the Perception of Personal Safety

Previous studies have identified that the physical environment is related to fear of crime – for example, dilapidated physical surroundings and neighbourhoods, abandoned or burned-out buildings, unmanaged property, litter, graffiti, unkempt blocks and/or houses, and abandoned cars, are associated with higher fear of crime (Hunter 1978; Maxfield 1984; Box et al. 1988; LaGrange et al. 1992). Crime Prevention Through Environmental Design (CPTED) is a multi-disciplinary concept which focuses on designing the built environment in a way that reduces crime. CPTED consists of several general elements: Surveillance (formal and natural), Access control (e.g., fencing), Motivation reinforcement (e.g., alarms, gates), Maintenance/image control (e.g., cleanliness), Territoriality and Activity support. CPTED principles have primarily been studied in the context of residential developments and found to be effective in reducing crime and fear of crime (Painter and Tilley 1999; Hedayati 2009; Hedayati Marzbali et al. 2012a), which has led to interest in applying the principles in other domains.

The effect of various formal surveillance measures, access control features and regular maintenance of transport facilities has been studied separately (Loukaitou-Sideris 1994; La Vigne 1997; Loukaitou-Sideris 1999a; Wachs et al. 2015). Generally, CPTED studies in the context of public transport are qualitative in nature (La Vigne 1996a; 1996b; Cozens et al. 2003b; Cozens and van der Linde 2015). However, no existing research has evaluated the relationship between CPTED and passengers' perceptions of personal safety. In addition, to date, no study has attempted to benchmark the existing CPTED design quality of stations. *As a result, it is worth quantifying the quality of station design in a CPTED framework and linking this with passengers' perceptions of personal safety at stations.*

5.2.4   Individual Differences in Perception of Safety

A substantial body of research has explored how personal, social and psychological characteristics of people act to influence fear of crime and perceptions of personal safety. Lower perceptions of personal security and safety, and higher fear of crime (regardless of context), have been described for several groups: for instance, the elderly (Antunes et al. 1977; Cook et al. 1978; Patterson and Ralston 1983), women (Gordon et al. 1980; Warr 1985; Lynch and Atkins 1988; Stanko 1995; Smith 2008), economically disadvantaged groups and ethnic minorities (Taylor and Hale 1986).

In the context of public transport, a substantial number of studies have investigated the influence of gender and age on safety perceptions (Lynch and Atkins 1988; Loukaitou-Sideris and Fink 2008; Smith 2008; Currie et al. 2010; Currie et al. 2013). They have found that women and young people have lower perceptions of personal safety than males and other age groups. In addition, some studies have explored the link between perceptions of personal safety and several psychological traits (Delbosc and Currie 2012; Currie et al. 2013). *As a result, it is worth investigating how demographics and psycho-social characteristics of the individual interact with perceptions of crime, ASB, and features of station design in influencing overall perceptions of personal safety.*

5.3   RESEARCH APPROACH

Given the limited evidence quantifying the relationships between the various factors involved in perceptions of safety and environmental design, the current research aimed to explore rail passenger perceptions of safety at stations, and associations with station design quality, crime and anti-social behaviour. This included developing a new method to better understand design quality of stations using Crime Prevention Through Environmental Design (CPTED) principles. The other main research task was to model a comprehensive range of factors which might affect the perceptions of safety (POS) at stations, including:

- the crime rate at stations and in local neighbourhoods;
- the experience of, or witnessing of criminal and threatening behaviour at stations and in local neighbourhoods;
- station design quality;
- passenger satisfaction with CPTED features at stations;
- passenger experience of and concerns with anti-social behaviour (ASB);
- individual demographics.

5.3.1   CPTED Station Audit Tool

CPTED quality in terms of built form applications has most commonly been applied in the field of housing and then described according to its impact on fear of crime and victimisation (Minnery and Lim 2005; Abdullah et al. 2012; Hedayati Marzbali et al. 2012a; 2012b; Sakip et al. 2012). These studies have measured CPTED at the level of individual dwellings, streets and neighbourhoods. For each construct, several indicators were considered and scores were provided for each of the indicators based on the characteristics observed.

However, there is limited research measuring CPTED principles on public transport. Cozens et al. (2003a) measured the situational safety measures at 15 stations along the Valley Line in the UK, using a dichotomous scale (yes = 1/no = 0). For those stations under consideration, the presence of a staffed ticket office, CCTV, help point, public access, real-time/electronic information, high throughput level, lack of visual obstruction and so on were scored either 0 or 1, depending on their presence or absence. An accumulated score was termed the situational index (SI). Liggett et al. (2001) measured the surrounding physical environment for the highest crime bus stops in Chicago, USA. They counted the presence of negative environmental features like the presence of bars and liquor shops, and bus stop characteristics such as the existence of bus shelters, visibility, and lighting; and street characteristics and so on.

The current research sought to develop an objective measure of a station's qualities in relation to CPTED design principles. A framework and audit tool was developed using the Principle Dimension and Component Dimensions indicated in Figure 5.1.

The full details of the methodology are detailed in Rahaman et al. (2016).[2] The concepts adopted are outlined below.

The station CPTED index has five Principle Components: Surveillance; Access Control; Motivation Reinforcement; Maintenance; and Territoriality/Activity Support.

It comprises a weighted, multi-criteria scorecard approach with each Principle Dimension divided into several component indicators (shown in Figure 5.1). These have

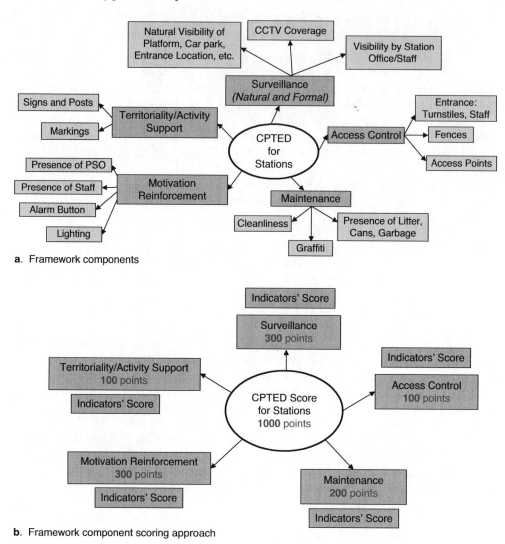

a. Framework components

b. Framework component scoring approach

Figure 5.1   Framework for CPTED station design audit and indicator

a score set and relative significance weighting. Individual scores are from 0 to 10. The weighting of the dimensions are based on existing published research and likely impact on station design. Depending on the ranking of the safety measures of the public transport facilities in the existing research, the main dimensions, namely surveillance, access control, motivation reinforcement, maintenance and territoriality/activity support, have been prioritised (Morgan 1996; Hamilton 2003; Stafford and Pettersson 2004; Hamilton 2007).

Component indicators of each of the key dimensions are measured by on-site observation of stations (a period of between two to three hours is required to complete the audit at each station, depending on their size).

Table 5.1 shows an example of the audit specification for the scales used to measure

Table 5.1 Scales to measure Access Control and Motivation Reinforcement dimensions

Access Control

No.	Criteria	Scale	Weight	Max Score
Location: Platforms				
1	Turnstiles	0=Not at entry 10=Present at entry	2.5	25
2	Staff	0=Not at entry 5=Present at office 10=Present at entry	4	40
3	Entrance/Exit	0=More than 3 Locations; 5=2 Locations; 10=One Location	1	10
		Maximum weighted score for Platforms		75
Location: Station area				
4	Entrance/Exit at each side	0=More than 3 Locations; 5=2 Locations; 10=One Location	0.5	5
5	Fencing	0=Not present 10=Present	2	20
		Maximum weighted score for Station area		25
		Maximum total weighted score for Access Control		100

Motivation Reinforcement

No.	Location	Scale	Weight	Max Score
Criteria: CCTV				
1	Notification	0=Not present	10=Present	1	5
2	Platforms	0=Not present	10=Present	1.5	15
3	Waiting area	0=Not present	10=Present	1.5	15
4	Circulation area	0=Not present	10=Present	0.5	10
5	Entry/Exits	0=Not present	10=Present	0.5	5
		Maximum weighted score for CCTV		50
Criteria: PSO (Protective Service Officer; or On Site Transit Police)				
6	At station	0=Not appointed 10=Appointed 7 days 5=Appointed on Weekdays/Weekends	5	50
Criteria: Police booth/Station				
7	At station	0=Not within .5 km radius 7.5=Visible platforms 5=Within .5 km radius 10=Located just outside	1.5	15

Table 5.1 (continued)

Motivation Reinforcement

No.	Location	Scale	Weight	Max Score
Criteria: Railway Staff				
8	At station	0= Not appointed	10= Appointed 7 days	4	40
		5= Appointed on weekdays			
		5= During office hours	10= Until last train	4	40
			Maximum weighted score for Railway Staff		80
Criteria: Alarm button				
9	At platform	0= Not present	10= Present	1.5	15
		5= Not near entrance	10= Located near entrance	0.25	2.5
10	At waiting area	0= Not present	10= Present	0.75	5
			Maximum weighted score for Alarm button		25
Criteria: Lighting				
12	At Platforms	0= Dark places (>9 spots);		2	20
		2.5= Dark places (7–9 spots);			
		5= Dark places (3–6 spots);			
		10= Dark Places (0–2 spots)			
14	At Car park				20
16	At Circulation area				20
18	Access/egress routes				80
			Maximum weighted score for Lighting		80
			Maximum total weighted score for Motivation Reinforcement		300

Source: Rahaman et al. (2016).

the Access Control and Motivational Reinforcement dimensions of the audit (the other dimensions are detailed in Rahaman et al. 2016). Access control considers features controlling illegitimate access to the platforms and station areas. Staff presence and turnstiles are effective in averting illegal access. In addition, fewer entrances are thought to be efficacious in managing platform access. Considering this, the highest weight is provided to staff presence at the entrance, followed by turnstiles and number of entrance points to the platforms.

Motivation reinforcement influences willingness to commit an offence. The 'presence of railway staff' and 'proper illuminations' have been cited most by the users (Hamilton 2003; Stafford and Pettersson 2004; Currie et al. 2010; Delbosc and Currie 2012). For that reason, the presence of staff and proper lighting has been given the highest weight to measure motivation reinforcement. This is followed by provision of PSO (Protective Service Officer; transit police) and CCTV, alarm button and presence of police booth at or outside the station premises.

An aggregated score to measure the quality of the train stations in terms of crime prevention and reduction measures is developed using component scores and relative weighting. Each station can get a maximum possible weighted score of 1000 points. The surveillance and motivation reinforcement dimensions have the highest weighted score of 300 points, followed by maintenance (score of 200 points), access control (score of 100 points) and territoriality/activity support (score of 100 points).

5.3.2 Perception of Safety (POS) Modelling Approach

The primary modelling tool was a Structural Equation Model (SEM) of factors affecting passenger Perceptions of Safety (POS). SEM is a quantitative analytical technique which adopts a hypothesis-testing (i.e., confirmatory approach) method to specify, estimate and test theoretical relationships among variables (Bentler 1990; Blunch 2008; Abdullah et al. 2012; Awang 2012; Byrne 2013). It is a multivariate data analysis procedure which includes a combination of various procedures: analysis of covariance, regression and factor analysis. SEM represents causal relationships between multiple variables which might be observable or unobservable (latent) in nature (Bentler 1988). There are two types of variables in these models: observed measurement and latent variables.

There are seven observed variables in the proposed SEM (shown in Table 5.2). Among those, crime data was collected from the Crime Statistics Agency (police-reported data), and CPTED scores of the case study stations were compiled through audits using the method described above.

Five latent variables (Table 5.3) were proposed: perception of safety; satisfaction with CPTED features; level of concern about ASB; experience of ASB; and feelings of safety in the neighbourhood. Each is comprised of several items addressing their underlying constructs, the items being collected in stations in a user survey.

The behavioural variables collected above were assembled from a station intercept survey where all passengers were intercepted and asked if they wanted to participate. A self-complete questionnaire was distributed with free mail return. The survey took 15–17 minutes to complete. A target of at least 50 full valid responses per station was sought and largely achieved at each station surveyed.

Six case study stations were selected for analysis including two stations with low crime rates (L), two stations with medium crime rates (M), and two with high crime rates (H).

Table 5.2   Observed variables and coded labels – SEM of perception of safety

Variables	Coded label of the variable in SEM	Variable measurement type
Crime rate at the stations	Crimerate_station	Continuous
Crime rate in the neighbourhood	Crimerate_neighbr	Continuous
CPTED design quality of the stations	CPTEDscore	Continuous
Trust in others	Trust_people	Continuous
Experience of threatening behaviour on trains and at stations	Exp_threat_tr	Categorical
Experience of threatening behaviour in neighbourhood	Exp_threat_neibr	Categorical
Demography of the user	Female	Categorical

The intercept survey was implemented in each of these stations and a CPTED audit also completed for each.[3]

5.4   RESULTS

5.4.1   Station CPTED Scores

Figure 5.2 shows the CPTED design results from the audits of the selected stations.

The overall mean CPTED scores of the case study stations were 845 out of 1000, which reveals that security features are generally well addressed at the sample stations. Between stations, overall scores varied between 824 (low) for Medium Crime Rate, to 876 (high) for High Crime Rate. The result did not find much variation in the total CPTED scores of the stations although the crime rates varied across them. The primary reason for the difference in scores across the stations was the surveillance, access control and maintenance dimensions. However, there are similar scores for the motivation reinforcement and territoriality/activity support dimensions across the case study stations. Indeed overall there is not too much variation in total aggregate scores between the case study stations, yet there is much variation in crime rate.

A stand-out finding from the analysis is that High Crime Rate stations in general also have good (high) CPTED scores. The implication is that CPTED quality has little direct association with actual crime. One explanation is that, in general, high crime rate stations have had targeted investment, suggesting better quality CPTED design at those stations.

5.4.2   Station Perception of Safety Modelling

Structural Equation Models adopt a hypothesis-testing method to explore and test theoretical relationships among variables. Figure 5.3 shows the hypothesised model developed in the research.

This posits that Perceptions of Safety (POS) will be related to overall feelings of safety in the neighbourhood local to the station and satisfaction with CPTED design features. Further, the level of concern for anti-social behaviour (ASB) and the individual's

Table 5.3   Latent variables and their coded labels – SEM of perceptions of safety

No.	Variables	Coded label of the variables in SEM	Items in the variable	Coded label of the items in SEM
1.	Perception of safety of the passengers (POS) (6 items)	POS	While riding trains during the day	riding
			While waiting at train stations during the day	waiting
			While walking along the approach to the rail stations during the day	walking
			While riding trains after dark	riding_dark
			While waiting at rail stations after dark	waiting_dark
			While walking along the approach to the rail stations after dark	walking_dark
2.	Experience of ASB (9 items)	EXP_ASB	Someone playing loud music	music
			Someone smoking	Smoking
			Someone being noisy	Noisy
			Someone deliberately damaging the train station	Damage
			Someone being drunk on the trains	drunk_tr
			Someone being drunk at the station premises	drunk_st
			Someone putting their feet on the seats	feet
			Someone not vacating priority seats	No vacate
			Begging at and around the train stations	begging
3.	Concerns about ASB (2 items)	Con_ASB	ASB on trains	Train
			ASB at stations	Station
4.	Feeling safe in the neighbourhood (4 items)	feelsafe_ neighbr	At home during the day	Home_d
			At home after dark	Home_dark
			While walking in the neighbourhood streets during day	Street_d
			While walking in the neighbourhood streets after dark	Street_dark
5.	Satisfaction with the CPTED elements (11 items)	SAT_CPTED	CCTV coverage of the station	CCTV
			Visibility by other people (from other platforms and outside street/area)	Visibility
			Presence of railway staff at the stations	Staff
			Presence of emergency button (red panic button)	BTN
			Presence of Protective Service Officer (PSO)	PSO
			Turnstiles/ gates at the platform entrance	Turnstiles
			Fencing off station area	Fencing
			Lighting of the station area	Lighting

Table 5.3   (continued)

No.	Variables	Coded label of the variables in SEM	Items in the variable	Coded label of the items in SEM
			Cleanliness of the station area (Platforms, car park etc.)	Clean
			Absence of graffiti at the station area (platforms, waiting area, walls)	Graffiti
			Proper signs and markings at the stations	Signs

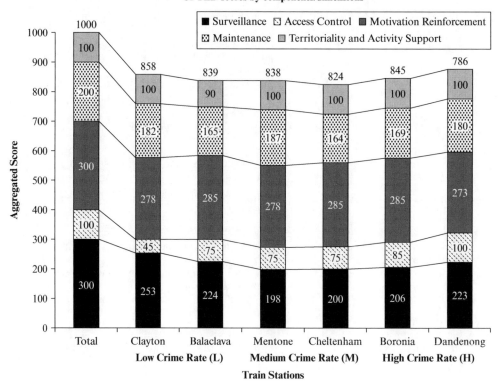

Figure 5.2   CPTED station scores

experience of ASB will add to direct influences such as station crime rate, neighbourhood crime rate, CPTED design score and a range of personal variables including trust in others, experience of being threatened in the neighbourhood, and on the train. Gender and travel at night variables were also thought to be important.

Figure 5.4 shows the final results of SEM outcome resulting from the statistical modelling. The results show an overall good model fit. The Global Fit Index is 0.90, TLI

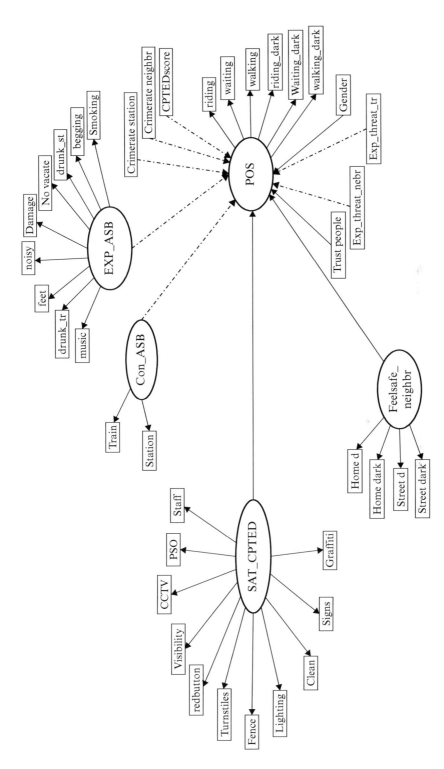

Figure 5.3   Hypothesised SEM – factors affecting stations' POS

81

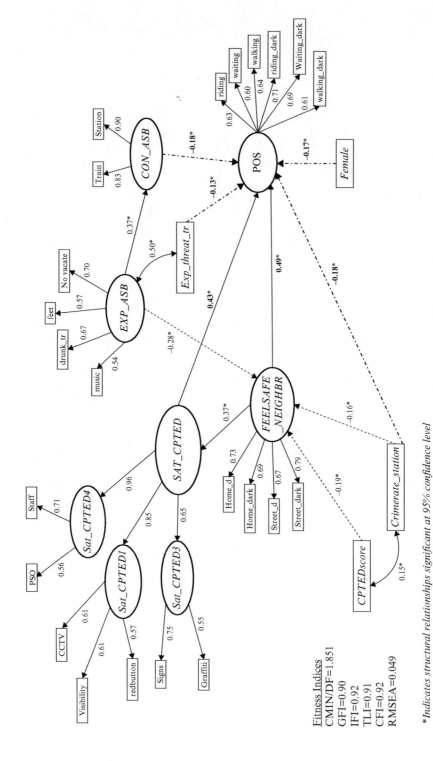

*Indicates structural relationships significant at 95% confidence level

Figure 5.4   SEM outcome – factors affecting stations' POS

Fitness Indices
CMIN/DF=1.851
GFI=0.90
IFI=0.92
TLI=0.91
CFI=0.92
RMSEA=0.049

Table 5.4   Direct, indirect and total effects of variables on perceptions of safety

Variables	Direct effect on POS	Indirect path	Indirect effect on POS	Total effect
Feelings of safety in the neighbourhood	0.49	via 'satisfaction with CPTED features'	0.37*0.43 = 0.16	0.65
Satisfaction with CPTED features	0.43	none		0.43
Crime rate at stations	−0.18	via 'feelings of safety in neighbourhood'	0.16*−0.49 = −0.08	−0.26
Experience of ASB	none	via 'concern about ASB' and 'feelings of safety in neighbourhood'	(−0.28*0.49) + (0.37* −0.18) = −0.20	−0.20
Level of concerns about ASB	−0.18	none		−0.18
Being a woman	−0.17	none		−0.17
Experience of threatening behaviour at stations/trains	−0.13	none		−0.13
CPTED score	none	via 'feelings of safety in neighbourhood'	−0.19*0.49 = −0.1	−0.1

is 0.91, CFI is 0.92 and RMSEA is 0.05. All model fit indices satisfy the conditional values for a good overall fit. The total effects of variables on POS, including both direct and indirect effects, are presented in Table 5.4. Indirect effects are calculated by multiplying the coefficients along the causal paths. These are summed with direct effects to calculate the total effects. These effect pathways are presented and discussed relative a series of hypothesised relationships as follows.

Several hypothesised links impacting POS were tested in the analysis:

Hypothesis H1:   There is a positive association between 'Satisfaction with CPTED features' at stations and passenger POS.

The path analysis in both the proposed and modified SEM confirms a positive relationship between these variables. According to the modified SEM, this relationship is statistically significant and thus supports hypothesis H1. The direct standardised path coefficient is 0.43. *This is the second largest effect in the model.*

Hypothesis H2:   Higher 'Experience of anti-social behaviour (ASB)' while using trains and stations, is associated with lower POS.

The direct regression path in the hypothesised SEM does not indicate a significant relationship between the 'experience of ASB' and 'POS'. The hypothesised model shows a standardised regression weight (β) = 0.03, which is not significant at the .05 confidence level. However, the modification index suggests indirect effects on 'POS' through two variables, namely 'concern about ASB' and 'feelings of safety in the neighbourhood'. The total indirect effect is −.19, which is relatively small.

Hypothesis H3:   Higher 'Level of concerns about ASB' occurring on trains and at stations is associated with lower POS.

The outcome of the modified SEM model supports this hypothesis. The estimated standard path coefficient $\beta = -0.18$ at $p < .05$. The result indicates that a higher 'concern about ASB' is associated with a lower 'POS', although the effect is relatively small.

Hypothesis H4:   'Feelings of safety in the neighbourhood' has a positive influence on the POS.

'Feelings of safety in the neighbourhood' was found to be a strong predictor of POS at stations from both the proposed hypothesised and modified SEM model. According to the modified SEM model (Figure 5.3), the standardised estimated coefficient $\beta = 0.50$, together with the indirect effect (through satisfaction with CPTED features at station), the total effect is 0.65. *This is the largest effect in the model. It also had an unexpected impact on the model: three variables indirectly influenced POS through their impact on this variable.*

Hypothesis H5:   The higher the 'Rate of crime' at the stations and in the surrounding area, the lower will be the POS.

The crime rate at stations is a significant predictor of POS and the SEM outcome supports hypothesis H5. The modified SEM showed a path coefficient $\beta = -0.18$ ($p < .05$), which implies that higher crime rate at the train station causes lower POS. It also had an indirect effect through feeling safe in the neighbourhood, with a total effect of $-.26$, which was *the third-largest effect in the model.*

Hypothesis H6:   The lower the 'CPTED design quality' of the stations, the lower will be the POS.

The standardised path coefficient both in the hypothesised and modified SEM model does not support the proposed hypothesis H6. There is no significant direct relationship between 'CPTED design quality' of train stations and POS. However, the indirect effect through feeling safe in the neighbourhood was significant but in the opposite direction to the prediction $(-.07)$.

Hypothesis H7:   Higher 'Trust in others' is associated with higher POS.

The result of the hypothesised SEM model *does not* support this hypothesis: the estimated standardised coefficient $\beta = 0.03$ at $p > .05$. That is why the modified SEM model (Figure 5.3) excludes this variable.

Hypothesis H8:   Higher 'Experience of crime and threatening behaviour' at the stations and in the surrounding area is associated with lower POS.

The path coefficient of the hypothesised and the modified SEM model shows that experiencing high threatening behaviour while at stations and using trains is associated with lower POS, as per H8. However, the effect is small, $\beta = -0.13$. If passengers have personal experience of being verbally abused or threatened and/or have witnessed these kinds of behaviours at stations, then they have lower POS. However, the model outcome *does not* find any association between experience of actual crime and passengers' POS. This is likely to be due to significantly lower reporting of actual experience of crime (such as physical assault, fighting or robbery) at stations and on trains by the passengers that participated in the survey.

Hypothesis H9: Women will have lower POS than men.

The female gender variable has also been found to be a predictor of the POS, with a $\beta = -0.17$ ($p < .05$). The model shows that female passengers have lower perceptions of safety than males.

Interestingly, some unanticipated correlations were also found in the analysis:

- A positive correlation was found between 'CPTED design score' and 'crime rate at stations' with a coefficient of .15 which was statistically significant. In addition, CPTED design score and crime at stations showed negative influence on 'satisfaction with CPTED'. However, the degree of influence was very weak and statistically insignificant at 95 per cent confidence level.
- The 'Experience of ASB' and 'Experience of threatening behaviour' in the rail environment were strongly correlated ($r = .50$). This unsurprising result showed that those with higher experience of threatening behaviour also have a higher experience of ASB while using trains.
- Analysis also revealed several new path links. For example, passengers' satisfaction with CPTED features was influenced by their feelings of safety in their neighbourhood. In addition, experience of ASB, crime rate at the stations and CPTED score of the stations negatively influence feelings of safety in the neighbourhood. It was also found that experience of ASB increases concern about ASB.

5.5   CONCLUSIONS

5.5.1   Key Findings and Observations

The outcomes of the SEM show that 'feelings of safety in the local neighbourhood' has the strongest association with the POS. This outcome is unexpected because the majority of previous studies on the topic concluded that crime prevention measures are the most effective way to deal with passengers' POS (Del Castillo 1992; Webb and Laycock 1992; Weidner 1996; Batley et al. 2012). This may be because previous studies focused on crime and crime-related factors, and did not have a comprehensive model including social and design factors such as feelings of safety in the surrounding neighbourhood, trust in others, ASB and CPTED factors. However, this outcome is similar to the findings of Delbosc and Currie (2012) and Vilalta (2011), who also found that feelings of safety in the neighbourhood is one of the key factors that affects transit users' POS. It suggests that it is necessary to focus on safety perceptions in the wider community when addressing perceptions of safety at stations.

Although published research suggests that various security and crime preventative measures (e.g., CCTV, staff and alarm button) are effective in reducing fear of crime, the concept of CPTED, which combines a range of security measures as well as security by design, has not yet been considered in this perspective (Angel 1968; Balkin 1978; Box et al. 1988; Austin et al. 2002). This research has focused on two factors related to CPTED design quality of stations, namely: 'satisfaction with CPTED features' at the station and 'CPTED scores of stations' in the SEM model. The outcomes in relation to the CPTED factors have shown some interesting and important results. They suggest that '*satisfaction* with CPTED features' is the second highest influential factor for POS after 'feelings of safety in the neighbourhood'. Although previous studies measured passengers' perception of and satisfaction with various crime prevention measures (Reed et al. 2000; Tyrinopoulos and Antoniou 2008; Budiono 2009), how these factors affect their POS has not yet been addressed. The outcomes of the SEM model also show that actual CPTED design quality of stations *does not* have any direct influence on POS, and its degree of indirect effect on POS is the lowest among the other factors in the study. This implies that *passengers' awareness of and satisfaction with the security measures at stations is more important than the actual CPTED features at stations* while taking passengers' POS into consideration.

This study reveals that ASB is an important factor influencing passenger POS. Although ASB in the context of public transportation has been addressed in previous studies, they are limited to the behavioural aspects of ASB on transit and at the stops/ stations, and their prevention strategies (Abbott 2004; Scott 2008; Moon et al. 2009; Moore 2010; 2011; 2012). However, none of the previous studies measured the empirical relationship of ASB with passengers' POS.

In this study, passengers' level of 'concern with ASB' while using trains and at stations directly influences their POS. However, the SEM outcome shows that 'experience of ASB' while using trains does not affect POS directly. The effect of this variable on POS is mediated by the 'level of concern with ASB' and 'feelings of safety in the neighbourhood'. In addition, this result also suggests that the day-to-day experience of ASB escalates passengers' level of concern with ASB, which in turn reduces their perceptions of safety at stations. Thus, this study finds that tackling and reducing ASBs in the rail environment is necessary to deal with passengers' POS. Yet *overall these results imply that it is the fear of crime or ASB that drives perceptions, not actual experience.*

Similar to the outcomes of the existing studies, the SEM outcomes confirm that crime at the stations influences passenger POS (Antunes et al. 1977; Balkin 1978; Garofalo 1981; Box et al. 1988; Cozens et al. 2003b; Abdullah et al. 2013; Breetzke and Pearson 2014). In addition, the outcomes show that passengers who have experienced and/or witnessed threatening behaviour at stations have lower POS. However, the model outcome does not find any association between experience of actual crime and passengers' POS. This is due to significantly lower reporting of actual experience of crime (such as physical assault, fighting or robbery) at stations and on trains by the passengers who participated in the survey.

5.5.2 Implications for Practice

An obvious implication for practice is the CPTED scale method which can be readily applied to measure the security designs of stations, to assist rail operators in checking existing situational crime prevention measures in situ at stations. Moreover, a comparative assessment of the station security design in light of station CPTED scores would assist policy makers in identifying potential stations for design enhancement and to prioritise budget allocation accordingly.

In terms of addressing POS in the community, results suggest that it is necessary to concentrate on improving safety perceptions among the wider community in the first place in order to enhance the perceptions of safety at stations. This suggests a need to consider working beyond the station boundary and extending a focus to secure the surrounding areas of the stations. Improvement of the landscape for secure movement, the provision of adequate lighting and introducing various security features in local areas are appropriate measures. In addition, rail operators and planners could work with policy makers to reduce criminal activities in the local station area to address both safety perceptions in the community and at stations. For example, protective service officers (POS) could work with the local police to enhance the vigilance of the surrounding areas near the stations in order to ensure safety and the security of passengers and local people.

The strong association between passenger satisfaction with CPTED features and their POS suggests that in addition to designing and equipping with security features there are a number of ancillary actions which are also important in dealing with POS. While policy makers and operators need to make arrangements for proper natural and formal surveillance features, routine maintenance, providing territorial boundaries and advising supported activities, and applying various crime prevention measures (i.e., appointing staff, PSO, alarm buttons and adequate lighting, etc.), they also need to put great emphasis on publicising the security features to the passengers. This can be achieved in various ways. For example, the station operators could highlight and emphasise the CCTV cameras at the station premises using flashing lights and/or white borders around them. In addition, the presence of staff, PSO and other security information could be emphasised to passengers using a digital display board at the entrance to the station areas.

Results also emphasise the need for managing ASB at stations and on trains due to its negative effect on POS. One approach might be using a campaign to increase tolerance of ASB and advise acceptable behaviour at stations, as suggested in other studies (Moore 2010; 2012), In addition, measures such as warnings and/or fines could be enforced to better manage ASB on trains and at stations.

5.5.3 Research Futures

The research has a number of limitations which should be addressed in future studies. The CPTED scale is a preliminary design and could be improved through a more comprehensive testing of passenger perceptions of actual safety measures and their performance. The scale could also be improved by testing of auditor bias in its application; this should also act to improve the advice to auditors in the scale's design.

The POS modelling adopted a cross-sectional (point in time) comparison of stations. A longitudinal study would have many merits to expand understanding of changes and factors influencing perceptions over time. It would also be of much interest to understand the before versus after impacts of the introduction of personal safety mitigation measures at stations to better understand their value.

There is clearly much potential to adopt the methods described in this chapter to better understand and mitigate fear of crime and its influence in public transport. The advances described in this chapter suggest powerful new tools are available to address an old problem in a growing global industry.

NOTES

1. This is the work of PhD researcher Dr Mustafizur Rahaman whose research topic was 'Exploring Passenger Personal Safety Perceptions at Stations and Associations with Crime, Anti-Social Behaviour and Design Quality', Monash University 2017. Dr Rahaman's supervisors were Professor Graham Currie, Dr Carlyn Muir and Dr Alexa Delbosc.
2. This paper won the 'William W. Millar Award' for the best paper in the field of Public Transport at the Annual Meeting of the Transportation Research Board, Washington, DC, USA 2017.
3. None of the survey stations are named in the research; this is to avoid possible stigmatisation of stations given association of crime data to particular locations.

REFERENCES

Abbott, J. (2004). 'Preventing anti-social behaviour on public transport'. *Eurotransport*, **2**(4).
Abdullah, A., N.A. Razak, M.N.M. Salleh and S.R.M. Sakip (2012). 'Validating crime prevention through environmental design using structural equation model'. *Procedia – Social and Behavioral Sciences*, **36**(0): 591–601.
Abdullah, A., M.H. Marzbali, H. Woolley, A. Bahauddin and N.Z. Maliki (2013). 'Testing for individual factors for the fear of crime using a multiple indicator-multiple cause model'. *European Journal on Criminal Policy and Research*, **20**: 1–22.
Angel, S. (1968). 'Discouraging crime through city planning', Center for Planning and Development Research, Institute of Urban and Regional Development, University of California.
Antunes, G.E., F.L. Cook, T.D. Cook and W.G. Skogan (1977). 'Patterns of personal crime against the elderly: Findings from a national survey'. *The Gerontologist*, **17**(4): 321–7.
Austin, D.M., L.A. Furr and M. Spine (2002). 'The effects of neighborhood conditions on perceptions of safety'. *Journal of Criminal Justice*, **30**(5): 417–27.
Australian Bureau of Statistics (2009). Environmental issues: Waste management and transport use. Canberra: ABS.
Awang, Z. (2012). *Structural Equation Modeling Using AMOS Graphic*. Malaysia: Penerbit Universiti Teknologi MARA.
Balkin, S. (1978). 'Victimization rates, safety and fear of crime'. *Social Problems*, **26**(3): 343–58.
Banks, M. (2005). 'Spaces of (in) security: Media and fear of crime in a local context'. *Crime, Media, Culture*, **1**(2): 169–87.
Batley, R., M. Rogerson, J. Nellthorp, M. Wardman, A. Hirschfield, A.D. Newton, J. Shires et al. (2012). 'Evaluating measures to improve personal security and the value of their benefits'. Project Report. Rail Safety and Standards Board. Accessed December 2020 at http://eprints.hud.ac.uk/id/eprint/14650/.
Benjamin, J.M., D.T. Hartgen, T.W. Owens and M.L. Hardiman (1994). 'Perception and incidence of crime on public transit in small systems in the southeast'. *Transportation Research Record*, **1433**: 195–200.
Bentler, P.M. (1988). 'Causal modeling via structural equation systems'. In J.R. Nesselroade and R.B. Cattell (eds), *Handbook of Multivariate Experimental Psychology*. New York: Springer, pp. 317–35.
Bentler, P.M. (1990). 'Comparative fit indexes in structural models'. *Psychological Bulletin*, **107**(2): 238.
Blunch, N. (2008). *Introduction to Structural Equation Modelling Using SPSS and AMOS*. Thousand Oaks, CA: Sage.
Box, S., C. Hale and G. Andrews (1988). 'Explaining fear of crime'. *British Journal of Criminology*, **28**(3): 340–56.
Breetzke, G.D. and A.L. Pearson (2014). 'The fear factor: Examining the spatial variability of recorded crime on the fear of crime'. *Applied Geography*, **46**(0): 45–52.

Budiono, O.A. (2009). 'Customer satisfaction in public bus transport: A study of travelers' perception in Indonesia'. Msc thesis, Karlstad University. Accessed December 2020 at http://www.diva-portal.org/smash/get/diva2:232419/FULLTEXT01.pdf.

Byrne, B.M. (2013). *Structural Equation Modeling with AMOS: Basic Concepts, Applications, and Programming.* New York: Routledge.

Carr, K. and G. Spring (1993). 'Public transport safety: A community right and a communal responsibility'. *Crime Prevention Studies*, **1**: 147–55.

Clarke, R.V.G. (1997). *Situational Crime Prevention.* Monsey, NY: Criminal Justice Press.

Cook, F.L., W.G. Skogan, T.D. Cook and G.E. Antunes (1978). 'Criminal victimization of the elderly: The physical and economic consequences'. *The Gerontologist*, **18**(4): 338–49.

Coxon, S., R. Napper and A. De Bono (2013). 'Design strategies for mitigating the impact of anti-social behavior upon suburban rail timetables'. *Crime Prevention & Community Safety*, **15**(3): 192–206.

Cozens, P. and T. van der Linde (2015). 'Perceptions of Crime Prevention Through Environmental Design (CPTED) at Australian railway stations'. *Journal of Public Transportation*, **18**(4): 5.

Cozens, P., R. Neale, J. Whitaker and D. Hillier (2003a). 'Investigating personal safety at railway stations using "virtual reality" technology'. *Facilities*, **21**(7/8): 188–94.

Cozens, P., R. Neale, J. Whitaker and D. Hillier (2003b). 'Managing crime and fear of crime at railway stations: A case study in South Wales (UK)'. *International Journal of Transport Management*, **1**: 121–32.

Crime Concern (2002). 'People's perceptions of personal security and their concerns about crime on public transport: Literature review'. London: Department for Transport.

Crime Concern (2004). 'People's perceptions of personal security and their concerns about crime on public transport: Research findings'. London: Department for Transport.

Currie, G., A. Delbosc and S. Mahmoud (2010). Perceptions and realities of personal safety on public transport for young people in Melbourne. Paper presented at the *Australian Transportation Research Forum*. Canberra: ACT.

Currie, G., A. Delbosc and S. Mahmoud (2013). 'Factors influencing young peoples' perceptions of personal safety on public transport'. *Journal of Public Transportation*, **16**(1).

Del Castillo, V.R. (1992). 'Fear of crime in the New York City subway'. ETD Collection for Fordham University. Accessed December 2020 at https://research.library.fordham.edu/dissertations/AAI9223811.

Delbosc, A. and G. Currie (2012). 'Modelling the causes and impacts of personal safety perceptions on public transport ridership'. *Transport Policy*, **24**: 302–309.

Flint, J., S. Green, C. Hunter, J. Nixon, S. Parr, J. Manning, I. Wilson, H. Pawson, E. Davidson and D. Sanderson (2007). 'The impact of local antisocial behaviour strategies at the neighbourhood level'. Scottish Government Social Research.

Gardiner, A. (2009). 'Public transport attacks soar in Victoria'. *Herald Sun*, 9 September.

Garofalo, J. (1981). 'The fear of crime: Causes and consequences'. *Journal of Criminal Law and Criminology*, **82**: 839–57.

Gordon, M.T., S. Riger, R.K. Le Bailly and L. Heath (1980). 'Crime, women, and the quality of urban life'. *Signs*, **5**(53).

Granville, S. and D. Campbell-Jack (2005). 'Anti-social behaviour on buses'. Scottish Executive Social Research.

Green, G., J.M. Gilbertson and M.F. Grimsley (2002). 'Fear of crime and health in residential tower blocks: A case study in Liverpool, UK'. *The European Journal of Public Health*, **12**(1): 10–15.

Hamilton, B.A. (2003). 'Investigation into public transport passenger safety and security on the arterial road network'. Melbourne: VicRoads R&D Project.

Hamilton, B.A. (2007). 'Personal security in public transport travel: Problems, issues and solution'. Land Transport New Zealand Research Report.

Heath, L. (1984). 'Impact of newspaper crime reports on fear of crime: Multimethodological investigation'. *Journal of Personality and Social Psychology*, **47**: 263–76.

Hedayati, M. (2009). 'Perception of crime and an assessment of crime prevention through environmental design (CPTED) elements in a housing area: A case study of Minden Heights in Penang'. Pulau Pinang: University Science Malaysia.

Hedayati Marzbali, M., A. Abdullah, N.A. Razak and M.J. Maghsoodi Tilaki (2012a). 'The influence of crime prevention through environmental design on victimisation and fear of crime'. *Journal of Environmental Psychology*, **32**(2): 79–88.

Hedayati Marzbali, M., A. Abdullah, N.A. Razak and M.J. Maghsoodi Tilaki (2012b). 'Validating crime prevention through environmental design construct through checklist using structural equation modelling'. *International Journal of Law, Crime and Justice*, **40**(2): 82–99.

Hough, J.M., P. Mayhew and G. Britain (1985). *Taking Account of Crime: Key Findings from the Second British Crime Survey.* London: HM Stationery Office.

Hunter, A. (1978). 'Symbols of incivility: social disorder and fear of crime in urban neighborhoods'. Paper presented at the Annual Meeting of the American Society of Criminology, Dallas, TX.

La Vigne, N.G. (1996a). 'Crime prevention through the design and management of the built environment: The case of the DC Metro'. Doctoral dissertation. Rutgers University.

La Vigne, N.G. (1996b). 'Safe transport: Security by design on the Washington metro'. In R.V. Clarke, *Preventing Mass Transit Crime*. Monsey, NY: Criminal Justice Press, accessed at www. popcenter. org/Library/ CrimePrevention 2006: 05.

La Vigne, N.G. (1997). *Visibility and Vigilance: Metro's Situational Approach to Preventing Subway Crime*. US Department of Justice, Office of Justice Programs, National Institute of Justice.

LaGrange, R.L., K.F. Ferraro and M. Supancic (1992). 'Perceived risk and fear of crime: Role of social and physical incivilities'. *Journal of Research in Crime and Delinquency*, **29**(3): 311–34.

Lane, J. and J.W. Meeker (2003). 'Women's and men's fear of gang crimes: Sexual and nonsexual assault as perceptually contemporaneous offenses'. *Justice Quarterly*, **20**(2): 337–71.

Levine, N. and Wachs, M. (1986). 'Bus crime in Los Angeles: Victims and public impact'. *Transportation Research Journal*, **20**(4): 285–93.

Liggett, R., A. Loukaitou-Sideris and H. Iseki (2001). 'Bus stop–environment connection: Do characteristics of the built environment correlate with bus stop crime?' *Transportation Research Record: Journal of the Transportation Research Board*, **1760**(1): 20–27.

Liu, S., J.-C. Huang and G.L. Brown (1998). 'Information and risk perception: A dynamic adjustment process'. *Risk Analysis*, **18**(6): 689–99.

Loukaitou-Sideris, A. (1994). 'Reviving transit corridors and transit riding'. *Access*, **4**: 27–32.

Loukaitou-Sideris, A. (1999a). 'Hot spots of bus stop crime: The importance of environmental attributes'. *Journal of the American Planning Association*, **65**(4): 395–411.

Loukaitou-Sideris, A. (1999b). 'Inner city commercial strips: Evolution, decay: retrofit?' *Town Planning Review*, **68**(1): 1–29.

Loukaitou-Sideris, A. and C. Fink (2008). 'Addressing women's fear of victimization in transportation settings: A survey of US transit agencies'. *Urban Affairs Review*, **48**(4).

Lynch, G. and S. Atkins (1988). 'The influence of personal security fears on women's travel patterns'. *Transportation*, **15**(3): 257–77.

Maxfield, M.G. (1984). 'The limits of vulnerability in explaining fear of crime: A comparative neighborhood analysis'. *Journal of Research in Crime and Delinquency*, **21**(3): 233–50.

Millar, P. (2009). 'Train gang bashes Indian student'. *The Age*. Melbourne.

Millie, A. (2008a). *Anti-Social Behaviour*. Maidenhead: McGraw-Hill International.

Millie, A. (2008b). 'Anti-social behaviour, behavioural expectations and an urban aesthetic'. *British Journal of Criminology*, **48**(3): 379–94.

Minnery, J.R. and B. Lim (2005). 'Measuring crime prevention through environmental design'. *Journal of Architectural and Planning Research*, **22**(4): 330–41.

Moon, D., A. Walker, R. Murphy, J. Flatley, J. Parfrement-Hopkins and P. Hall (2009). 'Perceptions of crime and anti-social behaviour: Findings from the 2008/09 British Crime Survey'. London: Home Office.

Moore, S. (2010). 'Preventing anti-social behaviour on public transport: An alternative route & quest'. *Crime Prevention & Community Safety*, **12**(3): 176–93.

Moore, S. (2011). 'Understanding and managing anti-social behaviour on public transport through value change: The considerate travel campaign'. *Transport Policy*, **18**(1): 53–9.

Moore, S. (2012). 'Buses from Beirut: Young people, bus travel and anti-social behaviour'. *Youth & Policy*, (108): 20.

Morgan, S.T. (1996). 'Fear of crime project'. Final report for CityRail, Sydney, Australia.

Morse, L.B. and J.M. Benjamin (1997). 'Analysis of feeling of security on public transit among residents of small urban area'. *Transportation Research Record*, **1557**: 28–31.

Nellis, A.M. and J. Savage (2012). 'Does watching the news affect fear of terrorism? The importance of media exposure on terrorism fear'. *Crime & Delinquency*, **58**(5): 748–68.

Newton, A.D. (2004). 'Crime on public transport: "Static" and "non-static" (moving) crime events'. *Western Criminology Review*, **5**(3): 25–42.

O'Keefe, G.J. (1984). 'Public views on crime: Television exposure and media credibility'. In R.N. Bostrom (ed.), *Communication Yearbook 8*. Beverly Hills, CA: Sage, pp. 514–35.

Painter, K. and N. Tilley (1999). *Surveillance of Public Space: CCTV, Street Lighting and Crime Prevention*, Monsey, NY: Criminal Justice Press.

Patterson, A.H. and P.A. Ralston (1983). 'Fear of crime and fear of public transportation among the elderly'. Pennsylvania State University. College of Human Development. Urban Mass Transportation Administration. University Research and Training Program, UMTA.

Rahaman, M., G. Currie and C. Muir (2016). 'Development and application of a scale to measure station design quality for personal safety'. *Transportation Research Record: Journal of the Transportation Research Board*, **2540**: 1–12.

Reed, T.B., R.R. Wallace and D.A. Rodriguez (2000). 'Transit passenger perceptions of transit-related crime reduction measures'. *Transportation Research Record*, **1731**: 130–41.

Sakip, S.R.M., N. Johari and M.N.M. Salleh (2012). 'The relationship between crime prevention through environmental design and fear of crime'. *Procedia – Social and Behavioral Sciences*, **68**(0): 628–36.

Scott, K. (2008). 'A study of anti-social behaviour on Dublin bus routes'. Master's Dissertation. Dublin Institute of Technology, September.

Sexton, R. (2009). 'Scary night trains rated network's biggest problem'. *The Age*. Melbourne.

Skogan, W.G. and M.G. Maxfield (1981). *Coping with Crime: Individual and Neighborhood Reactions*, Beverly Hills, CA: Sage Publications.

Smith, M.J. (2008). 'Addressing the security needs of women passengers on public transport'. *Security Journal*, **21**(1): 117–33.

Smith, M.J. and R.V. Clarke (2000). 'Crime and public transport'. *Crime and Justice*, **27**: 169–233.

Stafford, J. and G. Pettersson (2004). 'People's perceptions of personal security and their concerns about crime on public transport'. Report prepared for Crime Concern and Department for Transport.

Stanko, E.A. (1995). 'Women, crime, and fear'. *The ANNALS of the American Academy of Political and Social Science*, **539**: 46–58.

Stradling, S., M. Carreno, T. Rye and A. Noble (2007). 'Passenger perceptions and the ideal urban bus journey experience'. *Transport Policy*, **14**: 283–92.

Taylor, R.B. and M. Hale (1986). 'Testing alternative models of fear of crime'. *The Journal of Criminal Law and Criminology*, **77**(1): 151–89.

Thomas, J. (2009). *The Social Environment of Public Transport*. Doctoral thesis. University of Wellington, New Zealand.

Transport Data Centre (2009). '2007 household travel survey summary report'. NSW Ministry of Transport.

Tyrinopoulos, Y. and C. Antoniou (2008). 'Public transit user satisfaction: Variability and policy implications'. *Transport Policy*, **15**(4): 260–72.

van den Berg, L. (2009). 'Young fear attack on late-night trains'. *Herald Sun*. Melbourne, Australia.

Vilalta, C.J. (2011). 'Fear of crime in public transport: Research in Mexico City'. *Crime Prevention & Community Safety*, **13**(3): 171–86.

Wachs, M., C.N. Fink, A. Loukaitou-Sideris and B.D. Taylor (2015). *Securing Transportation Systems*, Hoboken, NJ: John Wiley & Sons.

Wallace, R.R., D.A. Rodriguez, C. White and J. Levine (1999). 'Who noticed, who cares? Passenger reactions to transit safety measures'. *Transportation Research Record*, **1666**: 133–8.

Warr, M. (1985). 'Fear of rape among urban women'. *Social Problems*, **32**(3): 238–50.

Webb, B. and G. Laycock (1992). 'Reducing crime on the London underground: An evaluation of three pilot projects'. Crime Prevention Unit Series, paper no. 30.

Weidner, R.R. (1996). 'Target-hardening at a New York city subway station: Decreased fare evasion – at what price'. *Crime Prevention Studies*, **6**: 117–32.

6. The power of design to enrich the public transport experience

Selby Coxon, Robbie Napper, Ilya Fridman and Vincent Moug

1. AN INTRODUCTION TO A DESIGN APPROACH

Every object created by human beings has been 'designed', whether the design be inept or highly professional. The organised, planned and thoughtful assemblage of cultural and material resources lies at the heart of the designer's being. As a profession, it is a broad church embracing the highly technical at one end and high art at the other. Its central purpose is to balance technology and visual elegance to engender positive human experiences. Design captures an 'intent' by organising a sum of parts so as to convey meaning. Taking design seriously makes demands upon us. It requires us to open ourselves up to the idea that we are affected by our surroundings, that we are emotionally vulnerable to the colour of interior walls and that our sense of purpose could be derailed by an uncomfortable bus seat. Design at its most accomplished will constitute some small resistance to visual and tactile anarchy and chaos. Satisfaction can be derived from the careful composition of two surfaces brought together in a neat join or the wash of light over a shiny train window (De Botton 2006). If we accept this notion, what might good design look like?

Roland Barthes, the French social theorist, observed the 'intense amorous studiousness' with which people at the Paris Auto show of 1950 looked upon a new model of automobile. 'The bodywork, the lines of union, the upholstery palpated, the seats tried, the doors caressed, the cushions fondled, the vehicle is conceived with passion from unknown artists and consumed in image if not usage by a population that perceives a whole magical object'. The management of stylistic aesthetic detail helps determine the specific ways a product will be understood and used (Norman 2004). Traditional ergonomic theories argue that objects should be shaped by affordances; that is, their shape should communicate their use or action. At the very least, the shape of an object should limit the likelihood of misuse. Designers labour over an aesthetic that creates the sweeping curve or up lift button and brings into existence the very affordances that make a product usable and desirable.

An interest in the appearance of our methods of conveyance evolved, as so many technologies before, when the original inconvenience had been overcome. A simple lashed together horse and cart gave way to the exuberance of a gilded stage-coach. Mere function no longer satisfactory and adornment to reflect wealth, status or purpose became required. The foundation of what we might call the coordinated design of infrastructure and associated graphical collateral, is most often associated with London Transport in the decade before the Second World War and in particular its visionary chief executive Frank Pick. Although a transport administrator and manager by profession rather than a designer, he maintained a strong interest and enthusiasm for design, especially its manifestation in public life. He steered the development of London Transport's identity, which included the roundel logo and associated Johnson typeface. An enduring brand even today, nearly one hundred years later. The pioneering approach of Pick's career was that he moved deftly between highly operational work and an appetite for carefully orchestrated visual communication. This included consistent station signage, Charles Holden's station architecture, and Harry Beck's daring non-topographical and diagrammatic Underground rail map, a map that was once 'too strange' and now the standard approach for networks around the world. Pick was a Modernist seeking 'a bold simplicity that is unmistakably twentieth century' and the designs he commissioned from seating textiles to bus shelters during the 1920s and 1930s established a new standard for public transport station infrastructure. A top to bottom approach unseen at the time and seldom emulated since.

The rapid expansion of a privately owned vehicle fleet over the second half of the twentieth century has put Public Transport, as an aspirational mode of choice, firmly on the back foot. The position is solidified by an approach to automotive design that creates a milieu of functional, aesthetic and haptic experiences that contribute to the pleasure of driving or travelling by car. For a passenger on public transport, many of these pleasures of interaction are lost. Automotive design attempts to induce in the consumers' consciousness the status of owning and driving that possession of a car will bring. Cars facilitate personal goals. For public transport the goal in the mind of the passenger is much simpler: to get from A to B. There is no status associated with riding public transport.

However, there are signs that our transport landscape is changing and the pendulum is swinging back to the public domain. A declining rate at which young people are taking up driving (Delbosc and Currie 2013). Higher city densities and associated congestion misery along with a much greater awareness of the ecological and economic impacts of private motor vehicles are driving enthusiasm towards a re-imagined public and shared transport landscape. The rapid expansion of digitally mediated mobility choices through ubiquitous smartphone use is providing an opportunity for public transport offerings to return to ascendency. Understanding and mediating these socio-technical changes will be a role that design, and its methodological approach, is well placed to deliver and enrich.

The chapter is structured to follow the British Design Council's *Double Diamond* model, where each section describes how designers navigate through the ambiguity of complex challenges to create innovative transport solutions through four stages: *Discover, Define, Develop, Deliver* (Figure 6.1).

2.   DISCOVER

Designers hold an ability to navigate the changing transport landscape through a variety of methods that enable them to *discover* problems, conflicts and opportunities during early project development stages. Methods during these discovery stages are deliberately divergent in order to gather a broad range of data that may then serve as inspiration for later stages of design work. Reference books provide a general overview of design's discovery methods (see for example Kumar 2012; Martin and Hanington 2012), though these examples are not exclusive to the field of transport and must be configured to ensure their suitability.

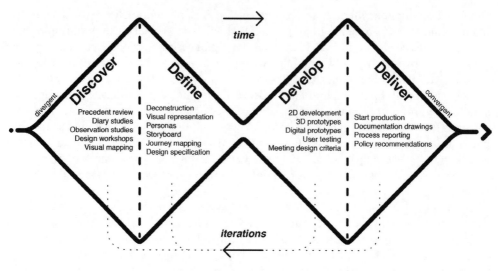

Figure 6.1   Double Diamond design process, based on British Design Council

This section focuses specifically on methods that allow transport designers to review precedents, understand experiences, design with people and map conflicting factors. Examples are drawn upon from a range of projects conducted by the Mobility Design Lab at Monash University to contextualise how methods may be applied within transport-specific contexts.

2.1   Precedent Review

Transport designers can make discoveries by reviewing existing precedents (typically products and services) and making connections between what has been done, what is missing and what is possible. This is as important for designers as reviewing literature during initial stages of a research and development project. By reviewing what already exists, designers can understand how people engage with and perceive it, which in turn leads to opportunities for potential improvements.

Reviewing precedents should be a systematic process of comparing and contrasting existing products and services so that trends and knowledge gaps may be discovered amongst them. Fridman (2016) provides an example of this in a review of battery-electric buses. Comparing a range of vehicles from various manufacturers led to the discovery that large traction batteries were having a negative impact on vehicle size, total weight and ability to accommodate passengers. This inspired the exploration of vehicle designs with alternative battery locations, as well as smaller battery sizes that were a contrast to industry trends (Figure 6.2).

It is also important to review precedents from outside the direct transport mode under consideration. By reviewing precedents from various forms of transport, and even other fields, designers can draw analogous insights that create grounds for innovative exploration within a given context. Napper (2011) provides an example where insights from the airline industry helped to inform a new approach for bus manufacturing in Australia.

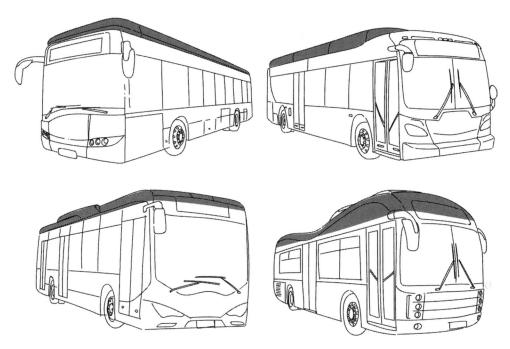

Figure 6.2   Visual analysis of buses from work described in Fridman (2016)

Applying principles of mass-customisation through a standardisation of products and reduction in assembly time resulted in reduced production costs. This allowed for the continued manufacture of high-quality vehicles that could be sold at a competitive price.

2.2   Diary Studies

Diary studies can help designers discover how people interact with and perceive transport services during their day-to-day lives. They are a qualitative, ethnographic research method, a type of cultural probe presented in the form of a daily journal consisting of prompts that can be completed either physically or digitally. Respondents record their thoughts, feelings and experiences over a series of days through creative activities such as writing, drawing and photography during their travels. Once these have been completed, they are returned back to the design team who can analyse the data. Due to their detailed nature, diary studies are typically conducted on small sample sizes where discoveries are mainly intended as inspiration rather than generalisable findings. They help designers to understand the experience of transport users on a more personal and emotional level. Common themes may still emerge when diaries are cross-compared between multiple respondents.

The work of design researcher Sarah Roberts provides an example of how diary studies may be applied in public transport (as described in Roberts et al. 2018). Participants in this study were asked to complete a week-long 'travel diary' that had different daily activities including journey mapping, card sorting and writing a love/break-up letter (written by the participant towards a form of public transport). Many of these are existing research

Source: Image courtesy of Sarah Roberts.

Figure 6.3   Travel diary

methods in their own right that can be used to assist interviews, focus groups or design workshops. Having participants complete them in their daily lives, however, allowed the information to be captured in the moment so that feelings and frustrations could be more accurate. Doing multiple activities throughout the course of the week also helped to contextualise experiences within a greater picture of an individual's travel patterns. This type of emotionally rich, qualitative data is particularly important to designers who are interested in discovering potential ways to improve passenger experience on transport services. In the context of Roberts' research project, diary studies were able to enrich an existing quantitative dataset that was acquired through customer feedback responses submitted to a transport operator. Diaries were constructed to provide a greater context to passenger experiences, beyond isolated comments, which allowed the designer to discover their underlying causes and motivations (Figure 6.3).

2.3   Observation Studies

Semi-structured observations are an essential discovery method utilised by designers to build a baseline understanding of how people interact with existing products and services in their everyday lives. Designers immerse themselves within a given situation when observing people's interaction. This provides a personal understanding of the data they may be working with, which is particularly important when they are new to the field of study or when data within a specific field is lacking. During observations, designers need

Source: Image courtesy of Sarah Roberts.

Figure 6.4 Observation photos

to approach situations with an open mind in order to make new discoveries. They must separate what is actually observed and what they infer from those observations by making creative connections in their own mind. For this reason, observations should be carefully documented using notes, drawings, photographs or video recordings to ensure that they may be analysed later to provide both inspiration and data to inform design decisions.

The work of design researcher Sarah Roberts again provides an example of how observation studies may be conducted in public transport to enrich a designer's understanding of the space they are working in (as described in Roberts et al. 2018). By using public transport bus services for her daily commutes and making observations during these moments, the design researcher immersed herself within the experience and was able to position behaviours that were witnessed against what was experienced by the design researcher herself. Discoveries provided a greater contextual understanding to data collected through other methods as they were made on a more personal and experiential level that allowed the design researcher to empathise with the transport users she was designing for (Figure 6.4).

2.4 Design Workshops

Design workshops are organised events where multiple participants – often including designers, industry stakeholders and transport users – come together to work

Figure 6.5   Design workshop described in Fridman et al. (2018)

collaboratively on a creative task. These sessions often lead to unique discoveries through outcomes that emerge as a result of different participants interacting creatively in the same physical space and time. Like focus groups, design workshops allow participants to exchange views, share perspectives and discuss issues; however, they go beyond this with the end goal of co-created outcomes. The collaborative and creative nature of design workshops enables participants to contribute in a richer way toward discoveries in transport development projects as they can also provide creative input alongside their personal lived experiences and existing perceptions.

Design workshops conducted by Fridman et al. (2018) provide an example of this method's application in public transport (Figure 6.5). Over a series of sessions, groups of participants co-created their ideal bus journey with the help of a toolkit that was developed by the design team. Workshop participants were able to suggest ideas for how bus services could be enhanced in the future by sharing their personal stories, lived experiences and creative inputs during the sessions. The toolkit used in these workshops was developed on the basis of a quantitative dataset found in existing transport literature. Engaging with the activities, participants were also able to enrich the existing data set by providing a layer of qualitative depth to it. This was particularly useful for the design team as it allowed them to discover what the existing data actually meant to people and how it could lead to desirable improvements in future bus services.

2.5   Visual Mapping

Visual mapping is often implemented by designers to discover conflicts, patterns and opportunities within a transport system. This can be done early in a design development project by creating system maps with the assistance of computer software or by simply

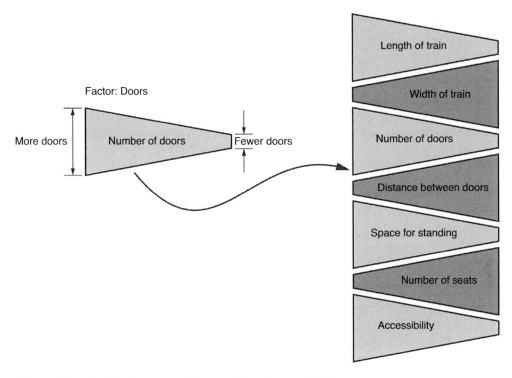

Figure 6.6   Conflicting factors diagram from Coxon (2015)

sketching a diagram using readily available tools such as pen and paper. Visualising complex relationships between system elements allows them to become tangible so that designers can 'make sense' of subjective aspects such as 'service quality' that they have been tasked with improving.

The work of both Coxon (2015) and Fridman (2016) provide examples of how visual mapping can lead to discoveries in public transport. In both projects, conflicting system factors were visually represented to discover how they may be mediated in order to propose design improvements. In the work of Coxon, the visual diagram acted as a source of inspiration for subsequent stages of design activity (Figure 6.6). For Fridman, these diagrams were instead used towards the end of the design process to discover patterns between the literature, existing precedents and new design concepts that were developed.

2.6   From Discovering to Defining

The creative methods outlined in this section provide unique ways to discover new information. Designers may use them to establish grounds for further creative thinking towards more human-centred innovations. Focusing on people's perceptions of and interactions with products, services and systems means that these methods are of a qualitative nature requiring further analysis and processing to *define* specific challenges and opportunities within a given project. This forms the second stage of design activity with a transport development project.

3.   DEFINE

The methods and approach outlined in the *Discover* stage look widely at the problem space demonstrating a variety of ways to mine data and collect information. Much of what emerges about user experience will be messy and it will not be easy to decipher or use to prescribe a direction immediately. Interpretation and synthesising this material to inform and 'bridge' to the creative activity is the role of the *Define* stage in the process. This stage is convergent, framing, clarifying and aiming to be more precise.

Designing is often referred to as 'problem-solving'. Before any problem can be solved it needs to be understood. The methods of the defining stage engage with whatever passenger or operational dissatisfactions have been discovered. They will be relative to the perspective of the person or persons who have raised the issue. The problem may in fact be different from what is initially perceived. For example, a potential purchaser of a new bicycle might well be looking for a response to their mobility problem rather than because they need to own a new bicycle. In the defining stage of the design process it is not enough to describe the literal current state. In analysing discovery data, there will naturally be a tension between what people know of themselves now and the breadth of potential desired situations believed by experts and designers. This issue can be addressed by deconstructing the current state of the problem.

3.1   Deconstruction

Deconstruction methods in design can take a number of forms. This essentially involves breaking the problem into a hierarchy of sub-issues examining their causes and effects. In this way, a 'problem tree' can be created. In Figure 6.7 the problem of elderly passengers falling in trams is analysed and deconstructed to establish the key issues that the designer needs to address.

Fieldwork from the discovery process needs to be carefully documented, catalogued and

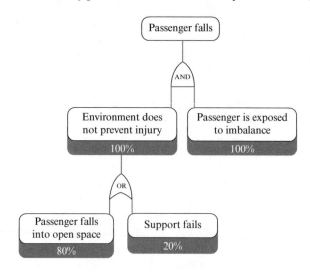

Figure 6.7   An extract from a 'problem tree' analysis by Luke Valenza

captured to assist work during the defining stage. This is achieved by analysing interview transcripts, questionnaires, diaries, photos, videos, observational notes, cognitive maps and diagrams. The manner in which the material is documented and catalogued should be consistent, since different researchers might use different terms or catalogue in different ways. Anything idiosyncratic will make the analysis more difficult.

3.2 Visual Representation

Design methods for problem-solving are made tangible through visualisation. Displaying data in the form of sticky notes and pictures is a popular way to review material and garner insights, placing the array of data into a single field of view. This single field of view enables connections between various points to be drawn physically, not unlike being part of a police investigation with images and connections spread across a wall. These ways of picturing the research material are accessible and engaging. 'Collages' and 'theme boards' are common applications of collected visual imagery. The curating and selecting of images helps determine the criteria a design solution should meet, for example, context, environment, function target users, appearance such as the characteristics of materials, colours, brands and form language, amongst others. The theme board is both analytical and creative (Figure 6.8).

3.3 Personas

Discovery methods often try to garner information around archetypal representations of intended users, capturing their needs, behaviours and values, while not as specific or as accurate as engaging with real people. The coalescence of, say, passenger trip data, demographics, education, employment, ethnicity and family status can help communicate in the create stages ahead of a summary of insights in a people-centred way. The preparation of the personas is usually in a printed form with made-up names and biography reflecting the research that informed such a profile (Figure 6.9).

3.4 Storyboard/Journey Mapping

Particularly important in the Transport sector is the close scrutiny of the detailed nuances of passenger journeys from door to door and with every interaction therein. Each 'touchpoint' is marked out between the service and the passenger's experience. The preparation of such defining devices often begins sketchily, with broad overviews, and then as the designers reflect upon and synthesise their research material they can build a rich picture of the nuances of the passenger's journey. Mapping this narrative against time is invaluable in capturing passengers' intent, exposing the friction points and defining the design problem (Figure 6.10).

3.5 A Design Specification

The creation of a specification is most often drafted as a compilation of all the information gathered, often containing both quantitative as well as qualitative data. Such a specification serves as the benchmark against which the efficacy of the creative design can be evaluated and judged to be successful or not. In this form, it is a 'checklist' and

Source: Courtesy of Samantha Blake.

Figure 6.8   Theme board development

agreement between designer and transport operating company. In most applied research a design specification should follow the following framework:

1. Identify a hierarchy of needs, distinguishing between higher and lower requirements.
2. Practical in either in terms of observable or quantifiable.
3. Have a distinction between *demands* that must be met and *wishes* that might differentiate between ideas.
4. Capture the sources of the specification in a reference list that can be referred back to.

However, there are drawbacks to design specifications if too tightly drawn. Such a technique needs to be carefully crafted so as not to unduly hinder the openness of the creative process to follow. Design is iterative where application to the design problem switches between ideation and defining criteria. Defining too many requirements will limit the possibilities that can emerge in the creative stages.

Designers have a natural tendency to want to conceptualise quickly, which is why it might sometimes be more effective to separate the designer's and the researcher's roles so

PERSONA Chris

Chris is an 18 year old apprentice electrician.
She lives in an outer suburb. This combined with her need to get to different work destinations across the city and her TAFE course during the week means her family bought her a car to enable the travel. She recently passed her driving test, but is still anxious about driving through congested inner city areas. Public transport is not really an option due to work commitments and the weight and quantity of tools she carries.
Today she is travelling...

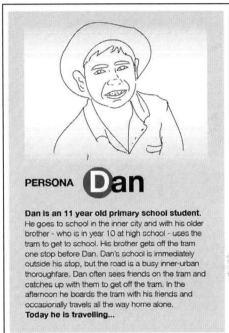

PERSONA Dan

Dan is an 11 year old primary school student.
He goes to school in the inner city and with his older brother - who is in year 10 at high school - uses the tram to get to school. His brother gets off the tram one stop before Dan. Dan's school is immediately outside his stop, but the road is a busy inner-urban thoroughfare. Dan often sees friends on the tram and catches up with them to get off the tram. In the afternoon he boards the tram with his friends and occasionally travels all the way home alone.
Today he is travelling...

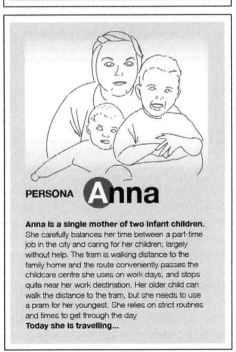

PERSONA Anna

Anna is a single mother of two infant children.
She carefully balances her time between a part-time job in the city and caring for her children; largely without help. The tram is walking distance to the family home and the route conveniently passes the childcare centre she uses on work days, and stops quite near her work destination. Her older child can walk the distance to the tram, but she needs to use a pram for her youngest. She relies on strict routines and times to get through the day
Today she is travelling...

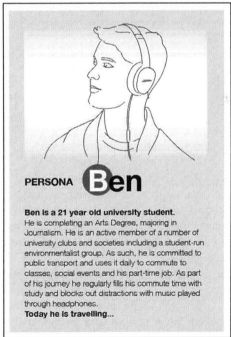

PERSONA Ben

Ben is a 21 year old university student.
He is completing an Arts Degree, majoring in Journalism. He is an active member of a number of university clubs and societies including a student-run environmentalist group. As such, he is committed to public transport and uses it daily to commute to classes, social events and his part-time job. As part of his journey he regularly fills his commute time with study and blocks out distractions with music played through headphones.
Today he is travelling...

Source: Courtesy of Gene Bawden.

Figure 6.9   Personas: insights made real through visualising and description

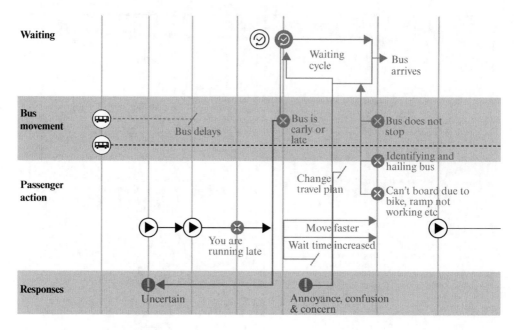

Source: Image courtesy of Lisa Fu.

Figure 6.10   Journey mapping

that a thorough trawl through the material can be achieved (Sanders and Stappers 2016). This is not to undermine the value of those first intuitive steps, but they can be made more robust by verification. Dwelling on new ideas too soon can develop bias or self-fulfilling outcomes and premature conclusions. They should be collected and then parked until the creative stage is in full swing.

3.6   The Generative Creative Stage

The quality of information coming out of any research analysis will, of course, depend upon the quality of the information gathered in. The aspiration is that such information will be rigorous and, once processed, very efficient in problem definition. The methods employed in the definition stage use information to unlock potential opportunities within a given context by making otherwise unrelated connections, creative actions, reflections and visualisations. Defining the problems and opportunities by understanding the information retrieved signifies that the design development process has already begun by building a structural framework for innovation.

The point at which the problem-definition stage and the design-development stage begin is blurred. We pass from what is known about a current issue to what we are going to do about it. We can make this jump at various levels with some low-level insights on raw data that have direct correlation with the research, such as a participant's liking for red buses. We can also apply insights at the higher level of a new hypothesis in which grander plans form to be tested through design, such as how to encourage people to use public transport rather than the private car in the first place. In both cases, the analysis and problem definition have put things together in new ways, revealing opportunities through previously unseen patterns and structures, and thus provoking new ways of thinking about the situation.

4.   DEVELOP

4.1   Translation from Define to Develop

As designers engage further with the design process, the emphasis on framing the 'problem-scoping' activity moves to a 'problem-solving' activity. Here a period of perceptible reasoning follows the preceding informing stages of *Discover* and *Define*. This *Develop* stage marks a shift towards the creation of design propositions where the use of prototyping and visualisation tools comes to the fore. It is in this stage that a broadening evolution of design-led ideas, requirements and attributes is investigated, iterated, tested and evaluated. Conducted in predominantly tangible modes of design activity, the aim is to arrive at a singular preferred or specific range of potential solutions to address the 'design-problem'.

For design practitioners within public transport the scope is considerable given the complexity and large scale of the product-service system. Elements such as way-finding, passenger information displays (PIDs), and ticketing interfaces through to vehicle design and infrastructure configurations present wide-ranging opportunities for designing improved user experiences.

4.2   Development Process

Having identified and synthesised the focus criteria, the process enters this development stage where both cognitive and tangible rationalisation of ideas are investigated. Designers engage with prototyping to 'draw out', in both a literal and metaphorical sense, a response to the design brief. This approach parallels discussions within the preceding 'definition' stage whereby various approaches of physical making and visualisation, methods of design research and practice, are now considered (Wensveen and Matthews 2015). The 'type' of method is chosen in order to provide greatest insights from the information gathering exercise. An example is the use of low-fidelity soft models to get a sense of physical scale or engaging in iterative development to account for or resolve design details elicited from user feedback.

The development phase is not an isolated, or necessarily linear activity with designers operating in a continual loop of making, of testing and iteration – see back to Figure 6.1, returning to the product design specification and discovery documentation to evaluate progression. To do this though, the design first needs to be manifested in some form or composition and this is where designers bring initial concepts to realisation, moving from paper to prototype (Lim et al. 2008).

4.3   Two-dimensional and Three-dimensional Development

Designers often begin with two-dimensional drawing as a basis for exploration and ideation, building a repository of visual propositions, to communicate key concepts and document the thought process (Figure 6.11). Drawing is a valuable skill demanded of designers; an exterior vehicle designer will produce numerous sketches to express elements of forms, texture and colour, aligning to a visual style of the client or consumer market. Drawing gives life to ideas, allowing them to be externalised so that they may be understood, critiqued and improved by others or by the designer themselves. Though the medium of pen and paper-based drawing has experienced a shift to digital aided sketching, the intent remains to capture and document both the designers' intuitive and structured response in a readily accessible and visual form language.

Designers then extend beyond the two-dimensional sketch to engage in three-dimensional physical methods of making and idea testing (Figure 6.12). They translate sketches of vehicle concepts into a series of physical form studies or produce a number of functional prototypes to evaluate dynamic interfaces, for example carriage flip seats on a train. This development period may involve numerous collaborators engaged within the design process, combining expertise of engineers, fabricators, material scientists and users to provide feedback for the designer to synthesise into the project.

The scale of a prototype is often an important factor to consider in Public Transport development as it can be a significant challenge when negotiating projects of large scale. To overcome these constraints, designers engage the use of scaled models, sketch mock-ups and digitally crafted representations, including immersive digital models. Designers then use scales consistent with the subject matter and intent: architectural scales such as 1:50 to 1:100 for small infrastructure models, i.e. tram stops, or 1:4 for automotive form and visual models. Development of full-scale mock-ups of variable resolution is used to test the efficacy of particular design requirements. Low-fidelity timber and foam models can be used to evaluate the spatial requirements of passenger circulation or internal arrangements for disability compliance. Quarter-scale vehicle models make way for full-scale clay models, a combination of CNC milling and hand finishing is used to produce life-size form studies of vehicle concepts, the level of visual fidelity provided by the material itself and post-processes such as graphic vinyl wraps.

4.4   Digital Prototypes for Cognitive Development

Increasingly the use of digitally immersive techniques obtainable via virtual reality (VR) allows designers to test less haptic requirements of large-scale design systems. The design inquiry outcome may be to evaluate cognitive mapping of the user's engagement with the physical design through to gauging user perception around visual elements of the design concepts (Martin and Hanington 2012). This is evidenced in the work of Roberts (2020) where VR was used to test the provision of information for suburban bus services through virtual vehicle models exhibiting new proposals for signage, wayfinding and digital phone applications – see the example in Figure 6.12.

4.5   User Testing

As prototypes serve to provide key insights to designers, they become further integral to the development process as props to engage and evaluate interactions with various stakeholders. User testing is an important method in design development particularly for new product, service or technology systems. Understanding complexities within

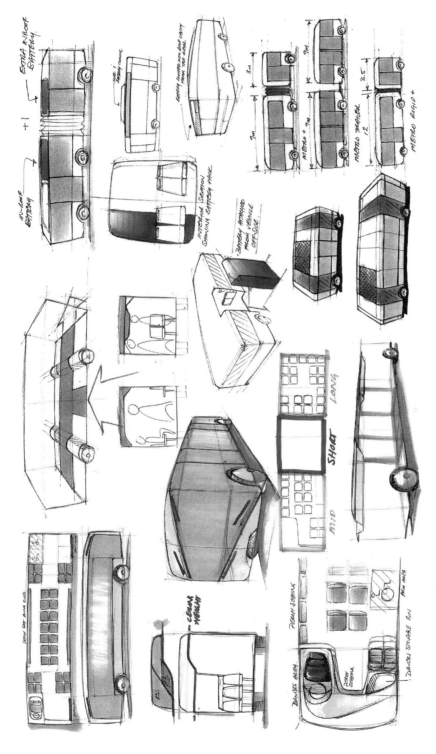

Figure 6.11   Design sketches from Fridman (2016)

Source: Images from Moug (2017) and Roberts (2020).

Figure 6.12   Examples of the wide variety of ways design researchers explore three-dimensional design problems

Public Transport design, of numerous stakeholders, experienced and inexperienced users, and large ecosystems benefits from systematic user testing. Engaging users early and throughout the development process allows their insights to inform and evaluate the design concepts under consideration. Stakeholder walkthroughs, ergonomic analysis, and experiential feedback become primary research as facilitated and informed by close proximity to a prototype 'product', whether a train interior mock-up or digital sketch prototype of a wayfinding system schematic or interface.

Iteration and feedback loops are important stages to incorporate into the prototyping process. By leveraging design methods of user testing and prototyping an emerging and iterative approach within the design process is engaged. The production of a high-fidelity functional or visual prototype may be used to assess a range of evaluation criteria (Houde and Hill 1997). Users provide feedback, functional prototypes are trialled, form studies are assessed, and the development process enters an iterative design feedback loop. In a period of iteration, a preferred design will undergo a number of changes to accommodate qualitative and quantitative feedback. Qualitative changes include aspects such as the look and feel of the product or a refinement of the interface to establish a hierarchy of visual cues or colour palette, while quantitative changes may include aspects such as the size of grab handles or material composition as driven by ergonomic, finite element analysis (FEA) or production methods to resolve the design. Each change may re-enter the feedback loop, re-engaging with user testing and engineering analysis before satisfying the design requirements.

4.6   Meeting the Design Criteria

There is an emphasis on design-led enquiry throughout the *Develop* stage. This involves drawing out and making sense of the problem through divergent exploration in two-dimensional and three-dimensional design activities. At its core, this stage seeks to enact a synthesis in arriving at the design outcome by addressing the previously established design criteria, engaging methods of physical and digital prototyping to identify any constraints or reveal opportunities within any proposed concept. By undertaking empirical and observable studies with users, at scale and within the desired context, the designer can form increasingly reliable conclusions on the concept's suitability – its 'fit for purpose'. The connection between the design, its intended application and ability to be readily understood by the intended audience then position it favourably for delivery to a broader audience.

5.   DELIVER

As illustrated through the first three stages, the design process is supported by a range of versatile methods which we can see being brought to bear on a variety of issues. Classically, design is concerned with the production of some physical thing, and as our societies have moved on from the industrial revolution towards a balance of these things with a growing range of services, we've come to the new terminology that design might be characterised as producing 'interventions'.

5.1   Design as Intervention

This slightly more ambiguous description of design outcomes is useful in the present age, since many physical designs now also have a strong intangible service component. There are now also interventions which are entirely service-based, accompanying the existing array of physical interventions. This last section, *Deliver*, deals with the necessary methods and practices of delivering an intervention to its intended audience and implementing it within a given context. It brings into focus the questions that designers might be asked to which to deliver a response; the formats that these could or should take; and the practical reasons why they might make these choices.

First, some working definitions. The notion of delivering a design intervention can take on several forms. A useful starting point is to consider that it is the culmination of the previous three stages and therefore represents, in our double-diamond methodology, the narrowing down of developments to the most suitable option – see back to Figure 6.1. This might be characterised as taking the most promising idea and performing a 'reduction to practice' task of getting it ready for the physical world. The previous stages will have considered a range of practical issues and ought to have produced, through critical review and iteration, a concept which can meet the rigours of reality. This is not to say that all the work has been done: as a concept is narrowed down towards the delivery stage, we can often witness the most effort-intensive stage of the design process. It is where the details are added – in the case of physical things for production this means the three-dimensional equivalent of dotting i's and crossing the t's – generally referred to as detailed design.

5.2   Deliver What?

Design thrives in well specified conditions as well as those of ambiguity. The extent to which these conditions prevail in any given task can set the tone for what kinds of activities are undertaken in the four stages of the design process. Taking the former, at times a design team is tasked with the design and development of a specific thing, for example a bicycle parking device or a railway interior. For such projects, it is simple enough to envision at least part of the intervention. Taking the latter, design methods are often brought to bear in situations where an ambiguous, perhaps wicked problem needs to be dealt with, and thus we apply research methods in early stages to help figure out what may be done by way of intervention. Most projects will sit somewhere on a continuum between these two extremes of specific and vague, and have sub-parts which display characteristics of both. In developing a bicycle parking device, it was found that an ambiguous and somewhat wicked problem was encountered regarding a user's propensity to squeeze bicycles into small spaces and how this behaviour interacts with the prevailing design standards.

So, the first question to ask was 'deliver what?'. This can range from the highly tangible, through to tangible but non-physical services, all the way to ideas, insights, or information. Some working examples of this spectrum are:

- Designed and manufactured objects/spaces;
- Refined prototypes;
- Two-dimensional work, e.g. communication and motion graphics;
- Services, e.g. wayfinding apps;
- Systems;
- Means of service delivery, e.g. staff training;
- Validated but non-manufactured objects/spaces;
- Insights, e.g. user behaviours connected to the designed environment;
- Information.

What designers have been asked to deliver will therefore greatly shape the manner in which this last stage of work is undertaken, and how the delivery takes place. A physical or digital intervention is often carried out in the established domain of the designer. This will necessitate long hours at the drawing board, iterations of small details negotiated with suppliers, financiers, manufacturers and distributors, and the trading-off of various competing targets such as durability and cost.

Many of these production-level concerns will cascade down the above list, for example the production of printed material or screen-based media carries its own highly technical constraints, especially around legibility. The delivery of services is no less complex when we consider that services are delivered by trained humans as well as digital interfaces and need to be interpreted and meaningful to a vast array of users. At the intangible end, the delivery of information through the design process may not carry manufacturing constraints in the same way a physical product does, but the complexity of the information – remember that design is rarely brought to bear on narrowly scoped quantitative problems – suggests that the effective communication of this information will be more than a written report. An additional consideration is that a design is often accompanied by documentation of the process, a theme we will pick up below.

Having discussed the range of interventions that design may be asked to *deliver*, we now turn to the necessary discussion of what format this delivery might be in. Two primary considerations are the traditional forms these *should* take – and the open-ended consideration of what forms they *could* take.

5.3 Start Production

There are established protocols for many aspects of design delivery, intentionally aligning with the needs of clients and users. A turn-key provision of design will often involve the delivery of one, or many, physical interventions, sometimes reflecting full-scale mass-production and at other times a 'first off' to verify that all is well. Estimated costs for mass, or batch, production are versions of this, as a client will often be conducting strategic work for which the manufactured objects will be needed at a later date. Drawings, as mentioned below, can provide a very high level of certainty about the design and are also broadly interpretable by informed viewers.

The *deliver* phase can also be brought to bear at stages in longer projects. Given that many transport design problems are part of large-scale, multi-year programs such as infrastructure upgrades, technical drawings and their close ally, design visualisation, can carry considerable weight in discussions with local communities. Often the problem with a visual representation of a forthcoming design is that they are of such high quality that the viewer interprets them as a foregone conclusion. Because of this, designers often show emergent ideas in suitable mediums, such as hand drawn sketches to invite more constructive feedback and incite relatively fewer confrontations if they are part of a genuine consultation process.

5.4 Documentation Drawings

When an intervention needs to be communicated, drawing and other means of technical documentation enter the frame. The purpose of the drawing is to enable anyone familiar with the drawing protocols to understand the designer's intent and put the intervention into production. Different fields in transport will have their own protocols: consider for example the difference between the nuances of Civil Engineering and Typography – both essential elements of a well-constructed transport corridor. Also consider the difference in drawings if the design team has been asked to deliver something intangible, for example a process or service rather than a thing.

5.5 Process Reporting

A further consideration is the format of delivery. The design process, as outlined in this chapter, is often cause for some level of concern in more quantitative disciplines, as the core creative process can present an element of mystery to the outsider. A reasonable solution to this problem is that part of the delivery is a documentation of the design process. Thus, we can expect the delivery of any intervention to be accompanied by a report documenting the process by which it was reached, with a simple method being to follow the four stages outlined in this chapter in a report. Documenting the design process in this way underwrites the accountability of the process in the same way that lab notes provide validity to the scientific process.

5.6   Policy Recommendations

The second consideration of delivery format is what form it *could* take. In this we need to consider for what purpose the intervention is being proposed. For example, while it may be field-ready, an additional format of delivery may also make it cabinet or boardroom-ready, or policy-ready. The client and designer should discuss what additional processes will be necessary to strengthen or permit the intervention to take place. An intervention that hasn't cleared red-tape may never actually have an effect in the world, and thus we should consider formats of visualisation, an accompanying statement on policy settings, virtual-reality walk-through, scale models, and site visits as part of the delivery phase of design. These less tangible design elements can be the difference between any of the intervention getting through to production or not.

The delivery phase can be a challenging time for the design process. It requires all previous considerations to be brought together and, as the double-diamond suggests, narrowing down to an eventual intervention. This brings the design process back to the client, and potentially the public, in ways that need to be carefully handled. It deals as much with the established domains of design such as productionisation and technical documentation as it does the delivery of services, policy, and stakeholder consultations. Ultimately the delivery phase is a strong bridge between ideas and the valuable interventions that design can create.

5.7   Illustrative Case: The Wheelie Bike Parking Device

While no one example can illustrate the broad scope of what can be achieved in the double-diamond design process, a worked example is described to provide a concrete illustration of how the process can be applied.

In 2017, a Victorian Department of Transport (DoT) project identified a gap in infrastructure for bicycle parking at railway stations. While low-cost, low-capacity hoops and high-cost, high-capacity parking stations for bicycles are a mainstay of the state's transport network, a middle ground was lacking in which unknown demand for bicycle parking was destined to remain as such. The DoT commissioned a design process to develop a new bicycle parking device, as follows.

The *Discover* process sought to understand the problem space. Using field observations during the morning peak at affected stations where current bicycle parking was at capacity, a rich understanding of bicycle user parking behaviour was reached. The key insight was the trade-off between security and convenience for end users. Some end users met this by utilising cheap 'clunker' bikes for railway access, and others by using sturdy locks in secure areas, such as passenger waiting spaces, which inconvenienced other station users. Bicycle geometry was studied in the field to gather an understanding of technical considerations when storing these somewhat unwieldy vehicles with a database being created to reflect the 'population' of bicycles in this context. This was followed by a desktop study of the relevant standards and an inclusive survey of design precedents.

The *Define* stage was largely carried out through a stakeholder workshop process, gathering views of the relevant authorities, NGOs and user representative bodies to construct a reasonable set of design specifications. These target specifications provided a bridge to the creative process by quantifying, and qualifying, a set of target attributes for the design. An important part of this process was openly debating the trade-offs between some target specifications.

To *Develop* the new bicycle parking device took several methods. First, the same stakeholder group were engaged in the creative process via proxy means of LEGO™ and then full-scale prototype modelling. This important activity served several purposes: as a means of actively engaging stakeholders, documenting their opinions and ideas, putting vague notions to the test in a simulated environment, and demystifying the design process by sharing it. Following this process, the design team developed an array of concepts using paper sketching, CAD modelling, and full-scale physical prototypes in a repeated process of iteration to invent and then test possible solutions against the design specifications, standards, and practicalities in order to reach a design to satisfy and balance these constraints.

The *Deliver* stage consisted of a first-off prototype made in production-accurate materials, technical documentation for manufacture and deployment, a report of the design processes used and documentation of their outputs such as photographs, data and descriptive prose (Figure 6.13). Taking 'The Wheelie' towards delivery consisted of

Figure 6.13   Production model of The Wheelie

a large number of hours in technical documentation, visits to manufacturers to discuss and adjust the design in order to meet cost targets, review of materials and processes for manufacturing, as well as involving the client wherever direction was required on trade-offs. The act of delivery in this project consisted of a review with the original stakeholder group prior to field testing of the prototype.

In the example above, as well as our exploration of the design process more broadly, a closing remark should be made. While the double-diamond approach outlined in this chapter suggests a linear process with a clear ending, the reality is that the design endeavour never really ends. Design projects, like fiction novels, have their own lives that exist within longer spans of time. As one design process comes to a conclusion, forces act on the situation of the present that often precipitate subsequent processes for design intervention. As the needs of society change, and the context of what is technologically possible expands, it is quite normal for a design process to be re-engaged as societies seek to improve their transport services and local environments.

REFERENCES

Coxon, S. (2015) A design study of metropolitan rail carriage interior configuration to improve boarding, alighting, passenger dispersal and dwell time stability (Doctoral dissertation). Monash University, Australia.

De Botton, A. (2006) *The Architecture of Happiness.* New York, NY: Vintage Books.

Delbosc, A. and Currie, G. (2013) Causes of youth licensing decline: A synthesis of evidence. *Transport Review*, 33(3), 271–90.

Fridman, I. (2016) Battery-electric route bus: A platform for vehicle design (Doctoral dissertation). Monash University, Australia.

Fridman, I., Napper, R. and Roberts, S. (2018) Data co-synthesis in developing public product service systems, *CoDesign*, 16(2), 171–87.

Houde, S. and Hill, C. (1997) What do prototypes prototype? In M. Helander, T.K. Landauer and P. Prabhu (eds) *Handbook of Human–Computer Interaction.* Amsterdam: Elsevier, pp. 367–81.

Kumar, V. (2012) *101 Design Methods: A Structured Approach for Driving Innovation in Your Organization.* New York, NY: John Wiley & Sons.

Lim, Y.-K., Stolterman, E. and Tenenberg, J.D. (2008) The anatomy of prototypes: Prototypes as filters, prototypes as manifestations of design ideas. *ACM Transactions on Computer-Human Interaction (TOCHI)*, 15(2), 1–27.

Martin, B. and Hanington, B.M. (2012) *Universal Methods of Design: 100 Ways to Research Complex Problems, Develop Innovative Ideas, and Design Effective Solutions.* Beverly, MA: Rockport Publishers.

Moug, V. (2017) Mind the gap: A design strategy for accessibility compliance and user autonomy at the platform-to-train interface (Doctoral dissertation). Monash University, Australia.

Napper, R. (2011) Designing route buses: From bespoke to mass customisation (Doctoral dissertation). Monash University, Australia.

Norman, D. (2004) *Emotional Design: Why we Love (or Hate) Everyday Things.* New York, NY: Basic Books.

Roberts, S. (2020) Feeling in control: Designing the Melbourne bus user experience (Doctoral dissertation). Monash University, Australia.

Roberts, S., Napper, R. and Coxon, S. (2018) A new way to design buses: A methodological framework for the front end of design, paper presented to the Australasian Transport Research Forum, 30 October–1 November, Darwin, Australia.

Sanders, E. and Stappers, P. (2016) *Convivial Toolbox: Generative Research for the Front End of Design.* Amsterdam: BIS Publishers.

Wensveen, S. and Matthews, B. (2015). Prototypes and prototyping in design research. In P.A. Rodgers and J. Yee (eds) *Routledge Companion to Design Research.* London: Routledge, pp. 262–76.

7. The paradigm shift in revenue protection research and practice

Graham Currie and Alexa Delbosc

7.1 INTRODUCTION

Public transport authorities face a complex set of technical, behavioural, ethical and political challenges in protecting farebox revenue from fraud. All authorities aim to improve user experience and attract riders with open, inclusive and safe public transport. But at the same time they need to reduce revenue loss from fare evasion, often by imposing ticket barriers and hiring expensive inspection staff to stop customers to police their ticketing behaviour. Governments regulating public transport have often been criticised for excessive policing and for even imposing 'martial law' on communities (Bartlett 2019). Politically it's a sensitive issue and in extreme contexts has even been seen as a catalyst for social unrest such as recent riots in Chile. Since these issues are highly problematic and easy solutions are not readily available, it is not uncommon for revenue protection to become a conveniently forgotten issue in public transport.

Globally farebox revenue covers about 76 per cent of all public transport costs in a sample of 98 cities (UITP 2015), although this varies widely globally. Farebox revenue is a key issue in financially difficult times and as needs for investment increase. Hence paying attention to revenue protection is important. Revenue loss is also large; recently London reported losses amounting to over £100 million ($US 130 million) every year (Dilley and Bardo 2019). Santiago in Chile has reported some of the highest rates of fare evaders; some 20 per cent of riders have not paid for a valid ticket (Correa et al. 2017). However, most systems seem to have rates of between 1 and 2 per cent (Multisystems Inc et al. 2002), though barrier free, self-validation (often termed proof-of-payment) ticket systems report rates of around 5 per cent (Dauby and Kovacs 2006). In truth, measuring fare evasion is difficult, and accurate measurement can be expensive so there is much uncertainty about what fare evasion rates are (Multisystems Inc et al. 2002). This is an obvious opportunity for researchers looking to make impact.

This chapter focuses on recent research discoveries which have been applied in practice and found to reduce revenue loss in public transport significantly. It starts with an overview of research in fare evasion. A major study undertaken by the authors in Melbourne is then outlined including key findings. A new market analysis method is then described which quantifies both ridership and population evasion rates. The research impacts of the Melbourne study are then described, followed by an outline of findings of an international follow-on project the authors undertook in 10 cities. The chapter concludes with a summary and discussion of future research directions.

7.2   RESEARCH CONTEXT

Given the scale of the problem of fare evasion, research literature on the topic is quite limited; indeed most of the available research has been published in the last 10 years to 2018 (Barabino et al. 2020). Most research is published in North America and is focused on fare evaders, criminology, economic, technological and operational perspectives.

Three types of research on fare evasion have been identified (Delbosc and Currie 2019) including:

- *The conventional fare evasion perspective:* This is the bulk of published research in the field and has also dominated practice. It focuses on ticketing and access infrastructure design, including barriers, access control, inspection rates and fines (e.g. Clarke 1993; Kooreman 1993; Dauby and Kovacs 2006; Reddy et al. 2011; Barabino et al. 2014).
- *Customer profiling studies:* Including a small set of studies using largely disaggregate data (Beke 2004; Bucciol et al. 2013; Barabino et al. 2015).
- *Customer motivation studies:* A new and growing field which is adopting insights from criminology into fare evasion to better understand why behaviours are occurring. The authors' research described in this chapter forms the basis of this perspective (Delbosc and Currie 2016a; 2016b; Currie and Delbosc 2017).

The strengths, weaknesses, opportunities and threats of fare evasion research in these perspectives are reviewed in Table 7.1.

While conventional research has been successful at establishing how to control a major part of the revenue protection problem, it is expensive and can victimise accidental evaders and act to negatively impact on the customer experience. There are clear opportunities to improve conventional approaches to the problem of fare evasion using big data from smart card ticketing systems. However, a major truth is that prevailing fare evasion rates in today's public transport systems are largely the result of thinking in conventional ways about the problem.

The profiling of fare evaders is an obvious means of targeting the problem; however, there are significant ethical barriers, making profiling a difficult political issue. Profiling is also a limited means of tackling the problem: we might know who the problem is but not why or how to deal with it.

The customer motivations perspective seeks to understand causal factors and motivations recognising that social and human factors including customer psychology can influence behaviours. It is a more nuanced and complex exploration of the problem and, as such, lends itself to an integrated understanding of the solutions and how they may address the problem.

7.3   THE PSYCHOLOGY OF FARE EVASION IN MELBOURNE

The Melbourne case study research programme discussed in this chapter leveraged the above research literature to address the study objective of better understanding the psychology of fare evasion as a means to find approaches to reduce fare evasion.

Table 7.1   SWOT analysis of different fare evasion perspectives

Perspective	Strengths	Weaknesses	Opportunities	Threats
Conventional transit system perspective	Easier to measure and quantify. Easier to control.	Cannot control all aspects of ticket environment, especially in 'open' systems. Ticket inspections can be expensive.	'Big data' could be used to spatially target inspections.	Tends to victimise a high share of accidental evaders; not good for customer satisfaction or authority credibility.
Customer profiling perspective	Somewhat easy to measure and quantify.	Limited use beyond profiling.	Can build a profile for targeting ticket inspections or education/ marketing campaigns.	Ethically questionable to visually 'profile' customers.
Customer motivations perspective	Better understand causal factors which can then be targeted.	Time consuming and complex to measure. Difficult to quantify. Open to self-reporting bias.	Can help target interventions and marketing campaign messages.	Difficult to identify motivations in the field. Marketing alone is unlikely to change behaviour.

Source: Delbosc and Currie (2019).

7.3.1   Scope and Approach

Melbourne, Australia had a population of 4 million in 2011 when revenue loss from fare evasion was estimated to cost a total of \$Aust 79 million p.a. (\$US 54 million) and represented 12 per cent of trips. Fare evasion rates were highest on Melbourne trams at ~20 per cent of trips, which have open access (proof of payment) ticketing. At this point the authors were commissioned by Public Transport Victoria (PTV) to run a research programme to 'understand the psychology behind fare evasion and provide actionable recommendations for use in improving compliance'.

The research design included a conventional literature and practice review of fare evasion/revenue protection research but also explored criminology research to establish if links to motivational factors could provide insights into fare evasion. The major element of the research was primary research of public transport users, notably those involved in fare evasion behaviour. This is problematic since fare evasion is illegal and asking those engaged in crime to self-report behaviours and motivations is unlikely to be successful. The research team developed several strategies to tackle this problem based mainly on the team's experience in behavioural research and by thinking through new ways to address the problem. First the term 'fare evasion' was never used with respondents. It was replaced with carefully tested phrases like 'finding yourself without a valid ticket on public transport'. Next, the research was promoted as an independent university study (and not run by the Authority or Police). This included assurances of anonymity and commitments to this in the ethics research disclosure statements. Lastly, innovative data collection methods were adopted through a third-party market research company who independently managed names and contact details of participants. This included use of anonymous online discussion forums where researchers could chat to respondents without face-to-face contact. These measures undoubtedly helped to get as open and frank a set of views from 'offenders' as is possible; however, an entirely honest and objective set of self-reported results should not be fully expected.

The major research design was 'qual–quant'; qualitative explorations of passenger experience, attitudes, behaviours and motivations to build up a more nuanced and complex pattern of thinking, terms used, ideas and motivations. This was then used to design a quantitative online survey instrument which could be used to measure the scale of behaviours for the market as a whole. Major motivational factor results from the research are now outlined, including: a conceptual model; qualitative perspectives on fare evasion types; cluster analysis; and an empirical model. A separate set of unpublished market analysis outcomes from the research are also presented in the next section.

7.3.2   The Conceptual Model

Figure 7.1 illustrates a conceptual model of the motivations behind fare evasion behaviours developed from the literature review.

This model synthesises constructs from the Theory of Planned Behaviour, including the role of Attitudinal Factors, Social Norms and Perceived Controls on the Intention to Fare Evade. Perceived Control is conceptualised in terms of the risks of being caught and the level of fines if a fare evader is caught. Concepts from the criminology literature on what is termed 'consumer misbehaviour' (a term referring to shoplifting) are adopted to suggest Intention to Evade might be influenced by personality factors. The same research is used to suggest Servicescape perceptions might be influential with regard to Fare Evasion intentions (Tonglet 2006). Servicescape is a term from the research literature on shoplifting/criminology and refers to all aspects customers experience when interfacing with the services offered by businesses.

The concepts in Figure 7.1 are entirely theoretical but provoked the thinking which framed questions explored in the primary research.

7.3.3   Qualitative Perspectives

Qualitative research was used to explore the fare experiences of those involved. This included a range of focus groups and anonymous online discussion forums. They explored the concepts in Figure 7.1 with respondents but also their wider motivations and feelings about fare evasion. This resulted in a new way to understand those involved in fare evasion; Figure 7.2 illustrates the four major types of fare evasion groups which emerged, including how their behaviour, intentions and feelings varied.

A high share of qualitative research respondents had condemning views of fare evasion but accepted they had rarely accidentally been involved due to a range of causes like faulty ticket machines or forgetting a smartcard. These people were embarrassed about being caught and had no intent. 'It's not my fault' evaders were also quite common but

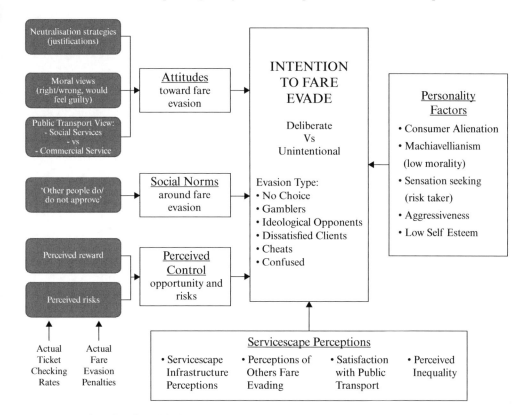

Source: Currie and Delbosc (2017).

Figure 7.1 Theoretical conceptualisation of the psychological influences on fare evasion using an adaption of the theory of planned behaviour

blamed the system if they found themselves without a ticket; they gave some strong views on the injustice of them being caught when 'criminal fare evaders' were out there. Groups 3 and 4 were not common but have very divergent views to groups 1 and 2. 'Calculated Risk Takers' expressed a clear intent to evade but only when conditions were favourable and low risk. Frequency of evasion was often but not always. There were very few people classified as 'Career Evaders' in the qualitative research, but they expressed an absolute intent, always evaded and pride was their main emotion in discussing the topic.

7.3.4 Cluster Analysis

The quantitative research involved an online survey recruited from a market research panel of 31 000 Melbourne residents. Sampling was based on public transport users targeting a high share who 'self-reported' fare evasion: the sample was 700 respondents, 75 per cent of whom had reported fare evasion at least once in the last year and 25 per cent who did not report this. A two-step cluster analysis approach was adopted

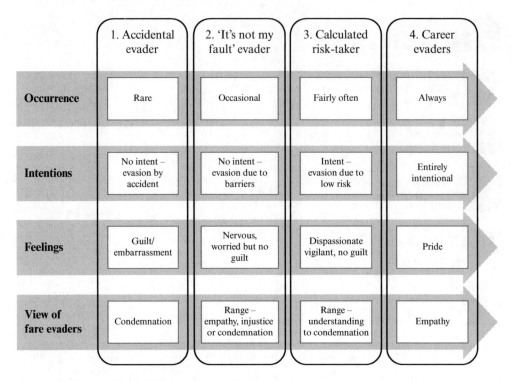

	1. Accidental evader	2. 'It's not my fault' evader	3. Calculated risk-taker	4. Career evaders
Occurrence	Rare	Occasional	Fairly often	Always
Intentions	No intent – evasion by accident	No intent – evasion due to barriers	Intent – evasion due to low risk	Entirely intentional
Feelings	Guilt/ embarrassment	Nervous, worried but no guilt	Dispassionate vigilant, no guilt	Pride
View of fare evaders	Condemnation	Range – empathy, injustice or condemnation	Range – understanding to condemnation	Empathy

Source: Delbosc and Currie (2016b).

Figure 7.2   Fare evasion 'rationale' segments – attitudes and perspectives

(Delbosc and Currie 2016a) to identify if respondents could be categorised into fare evasion behaviour groups using statistical methods (rather than the observational approach used to create the segments in Figure 7.2). Results are shown in Table 7.2, including key characteristics of each of the three groups that emerged. An important part of these results is that an estimate of the size of fare evasion in the market is made, *but* critical here is that the market is measured as people, *not* trips, since the survey is of individuals rather than their travel. We will touch on this again in the next section but it is important to be clear how the market is defined – here it is as people, that is, the public, residents or perhaps they may even be seen as the voting public, as opposed to trips.

Table 7.2 shows that about half of the people using transit at least once a year are 'never evaders' who avoid fare evading at all costs, have strong beliefs in honesty and see the transit system as a social service to benefit everyone. They are more likely to be older, retired and infrequent transit users. Some 35 per cent are 'unintentionally' fare evading. They want to do the right thing but feel that sometimes circumstances get in the way, making it difficult or impossible to pay their fare. They don't typify any particular demographic and see both the commercial and social aspects of the transit system, although they are less satisfied with the service than never evaders. A small but important group are deliberate evaders. They travel frequently, may be

Table 7.2   Fare evasion market cluster summary

	Deliberate evaders	Unintentional evaders	Never evaders
Proportion of transit market*	17.6%	34.8%	47.6%
Frequency of accidental fare evasion	Often	Sometimes	Rarely
Frequency of unintentional fare evasion	Often	Sometimes	Never
Frequency of deliberate fare evasion	Sometimes	Rarely	Never
Frequency of transit use	Frequent riders	Varies	Infrequent riders
Demographics	Young, full-time worker, undergraduate degree	Varies	Older, retired
Personality	Lower self-esteem and honesty, higher sensation-seeking and aggression	Varies	Higher self-esteem and honesty, lower sensation-seeking and aggression
Transit attitudes	Less satisfied	Less satisfied	More satisfied
Commercial vs social service	Commercial service	Both aspects	Social service

Note: * Melbourne residential population who use transit at least once a year. Note this is *not* the number of trips made; it is the number of people who make trips.

Source: Delbosc and Currie (2016a).

well-educated and are likely to be employed. They don't always deliberately fare evade, but they are predisposed to do so. They have lower self-esteem and sense of honesty and a higher predisposition to sensation seeking or risk taking. They are generally unsatisfied with the transit service and see it as a commercial service run only to make money.

7.3.5   The Empirical Model

The research on fare evasion motivation concluded with an empirical analysis to determine which variables have the greatest impact on unintentional and deliberate fare evasion. This built on the conceptual model and findings from the qualitative research reported above. A Structural Equation Modelling (SEM) approach was adopted; this is a pictorial and interactive process where expected links (such as those theorised in Figure 7.1) can be tested from the findings of the quantitative survey. Figure 7.3 illustrates the final form of the models; each are statistically significant.

The latent (or constructed) factors (shown as ovals in the figure) are found to predict unintentional fare evasion. They include honesty, a permissive attitude toward unintentional fare evasion, and competence using the ticketing system. Two observed variables (in boxes) were strongest direct predictors of likelihood to commit fare evasion; they are travelling without validating because of crowding, and travelling without a ticket because they didn't realise they hadn't topped up a smart card's value. Honesty had a medium

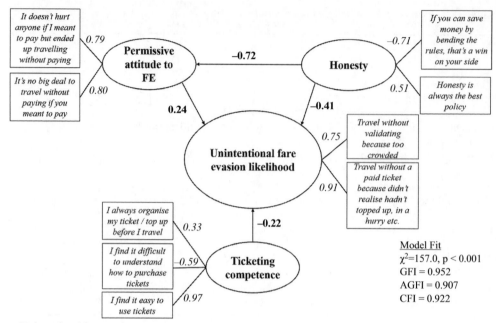

a. Unintentional fare evasion

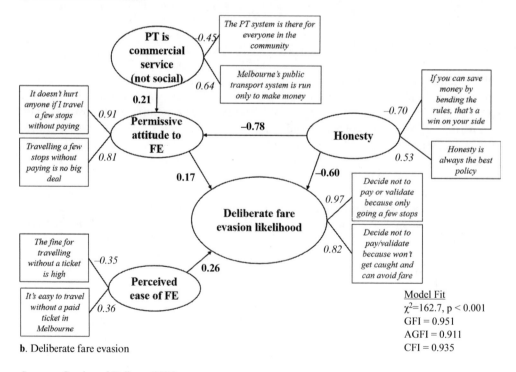

b. Deliberate fare evasion

Source: Currie and Delbosc (2017).

Figure 7.3   SEM predicting unintentional and deliberate fare evasion

effect on unintentional fare evasion (−.41) whereby people who were more honest were less likely to say they would commit unintentional fare evasion in the future. Permissive attitudes toward fare evasion had a small positive effect on fare evasion (.24), and ticketing competence had a small negative effect on fare evasion (−.22). In addition, honesty had a strong indirect effect on permissive attitudes (−.72); people who were more honest were much less likely to have permissive attitudes.

For deliberate fare evasion, three latent variables were found to directly predict deliberate fare evasion: honesty, perceived ease of fare evasion and a permissive attitude toward deliberate fare evasion. An indirect link was also found where people who believed that public transport is operated for commercial and not social functions were more likely to have permissive attitudes to deliberate fare evasion.[1] Two observed variables were the strongest predictors of likelihood to commit deliberate fare evasion: deciding not to pay because they were only going a few stops and deciding not to pay because they don't think they'll get caught. Honesty had a large effect on deliberate fare evasion (−.60) whereby people who were more honest were less likely to say they would commit deliberate fare evasion in the future. Permissive attitudes toward fare evasion had a small effect on fare evasion (.17) and perceived ease of fare evading had a small/moderate effect on fare evasion (.26). In addition, the view that public transport is run for commercial gain had a small effect on permissive attitudes (.21). Finally, honesty had a strong impact on permissive attitudes (−.78): people who were more honest were much less likely to have permissive attitudes.

7.4 FARE EVASION MARKET ANALYSIS

7.4.1 Scope and Approach

This section outlines some (to date unpublished) aspects of the Melbourne research which concerns market size analysis. The rationale for this analysis is that there are two very important ways to understand fare evasion: as a share of:

a. *Trips made:* this more directly relates to revenue lost since fares are commonly charged on a per trip basis.
b. *Population using transit:* this relates to the residential and voting population of a city.

The above are two very different perspectives since often only a few people in the population travel frequently but they represent a high share of total travel, most notably commuters (Larwin 1999).

Frequency of trip was defined and adopted the six groups in Table 7.3 which took part in the online questionnaire.

Respondents were also asked to identify their frequency of fare evasion using the following question:

> Overall, how often in the last year have you found yourself on public transport without a paid or valid ticket or pass? Is it . . .
> (Please answer this question truthfully; all responses are anonymous and results are in confidence)

Table 7.3   Annual trip rates for trip frequency groups selected for analysis

Trip Frequency Category	Trip rate p.a. TRFE*	Equivalent Weekly Trips	Basis for Selection
i. 6–7 days a week	572	11	Assumes an average of 12 trips per week (including some single and some return trips each day) but factors in a 4-week annual leave into a typical commuter working year
ii. 5 days a week	381	7	Assumes an average of 8 trips per week (including some single and some return trips each day) but factors in a 4-week annual leave into a typical commuter working year
iii. 3–4 days a week	214	4	Assumes 6 trips per week including an allowance for some single and return trips during an average week
iv. 1–2 days a week	130	3	Assumes 3 trips per week including an allowance for some single and return trips during an average week
v. At least once a month	24	0.46	Based on 2 trips a month
vi. Less often than once a month	12	0.23	Based on 1 trip per month

Note: *Number of trips each year by a person in that frequency of travel group.

    a.   Always (all the time)
    b.   Almost always (almost all the time)
    c.   Mostly (more than half of the time)
    d.   Regularly (more than a quarter of the time)
    e.   Occasionally (less than a quarter of the time)
    f.   Rarely (it has only happened once or twice)
    g.   Never in the last 12 months.

The first six of these responses represent at least some degree of fare evasion in the last year denoted as SFE_j. Trips involving fare evasion are calculated as follows:

$$TtFE = \sum_{j=1 \text{ to } n2} FE_j * tFE_j * t \qquad (7.1)$$

Where:
$TtFE$ = total trips p.a. involving fare evasion;
FE_j = share of total trips made by respondents in fare evasion frequency group j (equation (7.2));
tFE_j = share of trips that involve fare evasion made by respondents in fare evasion frequency group j (equation (7.3));
t = total annual trips (boardings or unlinked journeys) made by public transport;
$n2$ = number of fare evasion frequency groups (in this case 6).

The share of trips made by respondents in each trip frequency group (*FE_j*) is calculated as follows:

$$FE_j = \sum_{\substack{i=1 \text{ to } n1 \\ j=1 \text{ to } n2}} \frac{SFE_{ij} * TRFE_i}{t} \tag{7.2}$$

Where:
FE_j = share of total trips made by respondents in fare evasion frequency group *j*;
SFE_{ij} = share of survey respondents from the survey in fare evasion frequency group *j* and trip frequency group *i*;
$TRFE_i$ = annual trip rate of people in trip frequency group *i* (see Table 7.1);
t = total annual trips made by public transport;
$n1$ = number of trip frequency groups (in this case 6);
$n2$ = number of fare evasion frequency groups (in this case 6).

The share of trips that involve fare evasion made by respondents in fare evasion frequency groups (*tFE_j*) is thus calculated as follows:

$$tFE_j = \underset{j=1 \text{ to } n2}{SFE_j * STFE_j} \tag{7.3}$$

Where:
tFE_j = share of trips that involve fare evasion made by respondents in fare evasion frequency group *j*;
SFE_j = share of survey respondents from the survey in fare evasion frequency group *j*;
$STFE_j$ = share of trips which involve fare evasion in fare evasion frequency group *j* (see Table 7.2);
$n2$ = number of fare evasion frequency groups (in this case 6).

Table 7.4 shows values for the share of travel involving fare evasion for the six fare evasion frequency groups (*STFE_j*).

The share of the population represented by fare evasion behaviour groups can thus be calculated as follows:

$$TPFE_j = \sum_{\substack{i=1 \text{ to } n1 \\ j=1 \text{ to } n2}} \frac{SFE_{ij} * TRFE_i}{TRFE_i} \tag{7.4}$$

Table 7.4 Share of travel involving fare evasion by fare evasion frequency group

Fare Evasion Frequency Category	Estimated Share of Trips (*STFE_j*)
a. Always (all the time)	100.0%
b. Almost always (almost all the time)	95.0%
c. Mostly (more than half the time)	75.0%
d. Regularly (more than a quarter of the time)	37.5%
e. Occasionally (less than a quarter of the time)	12.5%
f. Rarely (once or twice)	1.0%

Where:

$TPFE_j$ = total population involved in fare evasion in group fare evasion frequency group j;

SFE_{ij} = share of respondents in fare evasion frequency group j and trip rate frequency group i;

$TRFE_i$ = annual trip rate of people in trip frequency group i (see Table 7.1);

$n1$ = number of trip frequency groups (in this case 6);

$n2$ = number of fare evasion frequency groups (in this case 6).

The above approach can establish the total number of individual people involved in fare evasion and also behaviour by individual fare evasion frequency group.

An important aspect of this approach is to identify what we term 'Recidivist' fare evaders and 'Rare' evaders:

- Recidivists Fare Evaders = Riders who fare evade (a) Always (all the time) or (b) Almost always (almost all of the time);
- Rare Fare Evaders = Riders who (f) Rarely fare evade (it has only happened once or twice in the last year).

7.4.2   Results

Table 7.5 shows results developed using the above approach. These have been enhanced by estimating the share of riders, the share of revenue lost and how much revenue loss is involved per fare evasion trip and per person.

These findings suggest a very important discovery about fare evasion: *most revenue loss comes from a very small share of evaders who fare evade all the time*. Termed 'recidivists', this group represents 68 per cent of all revenue lost or \$Aust 802 per person p.a. In Melbourne, a city of 4 million (2012), some 67 200 people are estimated to cause 68 per cent of all revenue loss. The obvious policy implication is that revenue protection should target this group.

Another observation is that prevailing conventional revenue protection methods target *all* users and hence tend to catch those in the 'rare' evader group. This group is a massive 0.6 million people (or 15 per cent of the whole population) yet only represent

Table 7.5   Key fare evader types, scale and estimated revenue loss

Measure	Fare Evader Type	
	Recidivists	Rare
Share of people fare evading at least once p.a.	8%	71%
Share of revenue lost/fare evasion trips	68%	5%
Estimated value of revenue lost p.a.	\$53.9M	\$4.0M
Number of people*	67 200	597 000
Share of Melbourne population	1.7%	14.9%
Lost revenue per person p.a.	\$802.44	\$6.64

Note: * Residents who have fare evaded at least once in the last year.

5 per cent of all revenue lost. It is easy to relate this group to the 'accidental' and 'it's not my fault' evaders noted in the qualitative research. Most conventional revenue protection resources act to catch the rare evaders, yet the qualitative research suggests this group associates them being caught with a strong sense of injustice and a view that authorities are incompetent because they have spent public money catching the wrong people. This observation has important implications for political justification of public transport: it suggests conventional revenue protection approaches spend a lot of time catching the wrong people who will not affect revenue loss to any great extent but as a result will negatively impact their appreciation of public transport and the authorities who run it.

These findings present much opportunity to improve revenue protection practice and performance.

7.5   RESEARCH IMPACT

7.5.1   Key Recommendations for Practice

The major recommendations of the Melbourne research were:

- To target recidivist fare evaders: profiling evidence was available from the surveys suggesting these could often be employed and relatively affluent passengers.
- To be more lenient with first-time evaders: these will mainly comprise those in the rare and accidental fare evader groups. It was recommended that personal details of any first-time evader be recorded and used to target them for training leaflets on how to use the ticketing system (this linked to findings that ticketing competency correlated with accidental evasion). In addition, offender records could be checked in future to see if they are repeat (and potentially recidivist) offenders.

It was also suggested that public attitudes to fare evaders be changed if possible. Recidivist offenders clearly cost the community a lot of money and are actually often quite affluent yet the general public doesn't generally understand this. General societal attitudes to fare evasion were significant factors influencing all types of fare evasion in the analysis.

A final major recommendation was a general increase in both the perception of and actual occurrence of ticket checking. The empirical model demonstrated that perceived ease of fare evasion was important in influencing deliberate evaders. Additional checks or measures that make it seem that ticket checking are increasing would act to influence behaviour.

Additional ticket checking was also suggested by wider findings of the research programme; Figure 7.4 shows an analysis of ticket checking rates (as a share of travel) and measured fare evasion rates (as a share of travel) found for Melbourne tram services. A strong collection was found ($R^2 = 0.63$), implying a doubling of ticket checking rates would reduce tram fare evasion by about a third (a simple elasticity of -0.32).

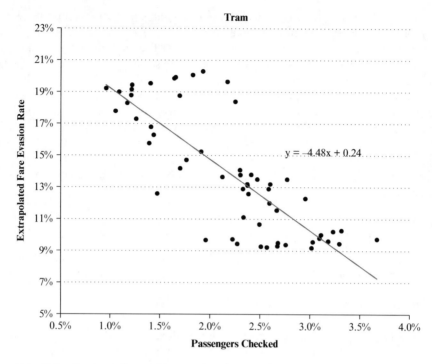

Figure 7.4   Distribution of tram fare evasion rates with share of tickets checked

7.5.2   The 'Freeloader' Campaign

As a result of the research findings, Public Transport Victoria developed a major TV, online and print media campaign around a concept called the 'Freeloader'; this is a derogatory term commonly used in Australia for people who benefit from activities which other people pay for. Promoting the association of this term with recidivist evaders was the major rationale and focus of the campaign.

Figure 7.5 shows an example poster from the campaign which illustrates an innovation developed by PTV to match the research recommendation that 'perceptions' of ticket checking are increasing. They promoted the concept of 'plain clothed' ticket checking staff, the rationale being that riders may well perceive that any passenger could be a ticket checker.[2]

In addition, PTV and their partners both increased the number of actual ticket checking staff and were able to improve the efficiency of existing staff by increasing their hours of actual checking of tickets. A major focus for additional ticket checking was open access (or proof of payment) tram services which had the highest fare evasion rates. Targeting of 'recidivist' offenders and use of a more cautionary approach to first offenders was also adopted.

7.5.3   Revenue Protection Outcomes

Figure 7.6 illustrates the progress of fare compliance rates by mode in Melbourne both before and after the research programme and the Freeloader campaign. Prior to the

Figure 7.5   Poster from the Melbourne 'Freeloader' revenue protection media campaign

research, network-wide fare evasion rates (as a share of travel) were broadly 12 per cent of all trips but as high as 20 per cent for trams. The research and its associated media campaign significantly reduced fare evasion. In 2015 urban fare evasion rates had more than halved: they fell from 12 per cent of trips to 5 per cent of trips, saving some $Aust 45 million p.a. ($US 31 million).

Revenue protection performance improvements were particularly significant for trams; they went from a fare evasion rate of ~20 per cent, where they were the worst performing mode, to 6 per cent, where their revenue protection performance was better than buses. However, the performance of all modes improved.

The outcomes of the research were outstanding, indeed the research remains one of the most successful research projects in terms of financial return[3] and has also had

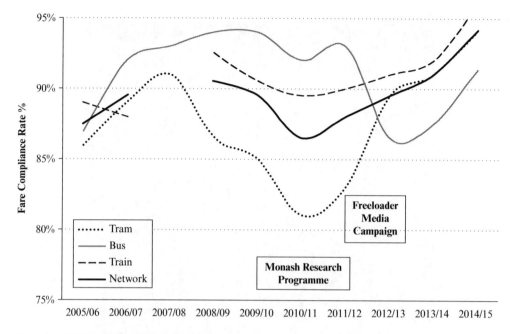

Source: Public Transport Victoria (2016).

Figure 7.6   Melbourne fare compliance before and after the research programme and the 'Freeloader' media campaign

considerable state, national and international recognition academically.[4] The authors have since actively communicated the most successful recommendations with public transport operators in other cities, who have reported considerable success in implementing these ideas.[5] As a result a follow-on project sought to explore if study findings concerning recidivist evaders could be found in other cities.

7.6   INTERNATIONAL RESEARCH

Research was then untaken in 10 international cities to explore the proportion of recidivist and rare evasion as a share of trips and also as a share of the residential population. A major advantage of the methodology developed for the research is the online questionnaire which can be deployed to any city at a relatively modest cost. An international market research agency was commissioned to provide a panel of respondents for 10 English-speaking cities using the fare evasion market analysis method described above. Individual city results are reported in Appendix Table 7A.1 and illustrated in Figure 7.7.

Figure 7.7 shows that in all cities, the vast majority of fare evasion travel is made by recidivists. The recidivist problem is not only a Melbourne issue, it's a problem in all cities studied. As a share of travel, recidivists dominate fare evasion, with most cities having between 60 and 80 per cent of all travel as recidivists. Since travel volume most closely relates to fare revenue, these findings suggest that recidivists are responsible for over half

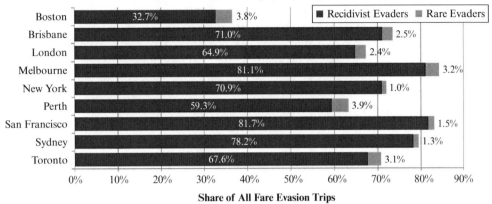

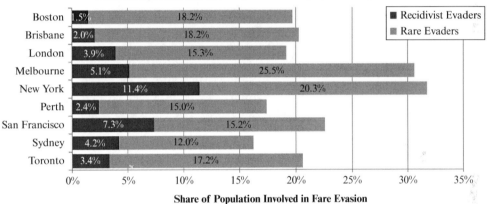

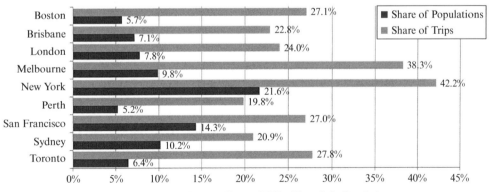

Figure 7.7   Selected estimates of fare evasion metrics by international city

and close to two-thirds of all revenue lost due to fare evasion in all the English-speaking cities in this sample. The population-based analysis of recidivists suggests they represent a comparatively small share of the population (between 1 per cent and 11 per cent, with most values in the 2–5 per cent range). In contrast, 'rare' fare evaders represent hardly any share of all fare evasion trips (between 1 and 4 per cent) but dominate the residential population engaged in fare evasion (between 15 and 25 per cent of the population).

These findings have some important implications for fare evasion mitigation policies in all cities. They suggest that most revenue lost from fare evasion is associated with a small group of people who always/almost always evade fares. Conversely, rare (or accidental) evaders represent a very high share of the population but a very small share of revenue lost (and trips). The strong and clear implication is that mitigation should focus on recidivists as a global industry priority.

7.7   CONCLUSIONS

This chapter describes recent discoveries in fare evasion research and how they have acted to impact practice to more than halve fare evasion in cities. Most research in fare evasion focuses on ticketing and infrastructure design, fines, inspection rates and profiling. A new and emerging area focuses on customer motivations. The authors' research programme on the psychology of fare evasion in Melbourne is described. New models describing factors that may influence evasion have been developed based around the theory of planned behaviour. Qualitative studies identified four types of fare evasion from a motivational perspective: 'accidental', 'it's not my fault' evaders, 'calculated risk takers', and 'career evaders'; the latter are rare but take pride in fare evasion and always evade. Cluster analysis was used to quantitatively identify clusters of behaviour; three resulted: deliberate evaders, unintentional, and never evaders. An empirical model demonstrated that unintentional evaders are affected by honesty, permissive attitudes to evasion and ticketing competence. Deliberate evasion is also driven by honesty but also by perceived control (perceptions of ticket checking rates and fines). A methodology for market analysis estimates is described; results show that in Melbourne, recidivist evaders represent only 67 200 people but account for 68 per cent of revenue loss of $Aust 53 million p.a. ($802 per evader p.a.). Recommendations of the research were applied by PTV with considerable success; fare evasion rates more than halved, from 12 per cent of trips to 5 per cent of trips, saving some $Aust 45 million p.a. ($US 31 million). A follow-on international study of 10 cities demonstrated that the problem of recidivist evaders was apparent in all cities.

So what is the future for research on fare evasion? As suggested in Table 7.1, there is considerable scope for conventional research in the field to benefit from advances in big data associated with smart card systems. However, this chapter has described the relatively new and to an extent immature field of fare evader motivation research. This is very much at its beginning, yet it is clearly having considerable impact. Application of the Melbourne research to other cities is clearly needed. While the international study reported in this chapter suggests consistency in findings, to date the international research has been at a broad and system-wide scale; there is a need to explore the qualitative as well as the quantitative findings in depth in a wider range of cities. An interesting research gap concerns the theoretical model proposed in Figure 7.1; this suggests that 'servicescape perceptions' will influence evasion rates and is based on findings in shoplifting research. No links between servicescape and fare evasion were established in the Melbourne project but it is entirely possible that this finding might be different in other cities.

Overall the research described in this chapter has had considerable impact in academia and in practice. Researchers in public transport need to learn from this success and develop strategies which practitioners can readily apply to improve practice into the future.

NOTES

1. Melbourne transit is operated with private sector (or commercial) franchises under contract to the Government.
2. To our knowledge this is an original innovation: both plain clothes ticket checking and also the idea of promoting it to enhance a perception of increased checking both match discoveries made in the research that perception of ticket checking was as important as actual ticket checking as a key control factor influencing behaviour.
3. Financial savings (excluding costs of the Freeloader campaign) in the year after the research suggested it returned over 450 times total research cost. Total savings at time of writing would be of the order of $225 million since 2015.
4. The authors' research won the Monash University Vice Chancellors award for Economic and Social Research Impact in 2017, the Australasian Road Research Board National Award for Research Impact in 2017. The research paper Currie and Delbosc (2017), 'An empirical model for the psychology of deliberate and unintentional fare evasion', was presented at the 14th World Conference on Transport Research in 2016 and won the Best Paper Prize in Transport Policy at the conference.
5. Transport for NSW reported savings in revenue loss of the order of $Aust 50 million p.a., resulting from recommendations applied to their network. Transport for London reported notable cases of wealthy repeat offenders who they have prosecuted, which correlates directly with the research findings on recidivist evaders.

REFERENCES

Barabino, B., C. Lai and A. Olivo (2020). 'Fare evasion in public transport systems: A review of the literature'. *Public Transport International* **12**: 27–8.
Barabino, B., S. Salis and B. Useli (2014). 'Fare evasion in proof-of-payment transit systems: Deriving the optimum inspection level'. *Transportation Research Part B: Methodological* **70**: 1–17.
Barabino, B., S. Salis and B. Useli (2015). 'What are the determinants in making people free riders in proof-of-payment transit systems? Evidence from Italy'. *Transportation Research Part A: Policy and Practice* **80**: 184–96.
Bartlett, J. (2019). 'Chile students' mass fare-dodging expands into city-wide protest'. *The Guardian*, 18 October.
Beke (2004). *Database Problematische Zwartrijders: Daderprofielen en Criteria voor een Aanpak*. Arnhem: Beke Advies.
Bucciol, A., F. Landini and M. Piovesan (2013). 'Unethical behavior in the field: Demographic characteristics and beliefs of the cheater'. *Journal of Economic Behavior & Organization* **93**: 248–57.
Clarke, R.V. (1993). 'Fare evasion and automatic ticket collection on the London underground'. *Crime Prevention Studies* **1**: 135–46.
Correa, J., T. Harks, V.J.C. Kreuzen and J. Matuschke (2017). 'Fare evasion in transit networks'. *Operations Research* **65**(1): 165–83.
Currie, G. and A. Delbosc (2017). 'An empirical model for the psychology of deliberate and unintentional fare evasion'. *Transport Policy* **54**: 21–9.
Dauby, L. and Z. Kovacs (2006). Fare evasion in light rail systems. *Joint International Light Rail Conference*. St Louis, Missouri, pp. 230–46.
Delbosc, A. and G. Currie (2019). 'Why do people fare evade? A global shift in fare evasion research'. *Transport Reviews* **39**(3): 376–91.
Delbosc, A. and G. Currie (2016a). 'Cluster analysis of fare evasion behaviours in Melbourne, Australia'. *Transport Policy* **50**: 29–36.

Delbosc, A. and G. Currie (2016b). 'Four types of fare evasion: A qualitative study from Melbourne, Australia'. *Transportation Research Part F: Traffic Psychology and Behaviour* **43**: 254–64.

Dilley, S. and M. Bardo (2019). Fare dodging costs London £100m a year. *BBC News*, 1 March.

Kooreman, P. (1993). 'Fare evasion as a result of expected utility maximisation: Some empirical support'. *Journal of Transport Economics and Policy* **27**(1): 69–74.

Larwin, T.F. (1999). 'Urban transit'. In *Transport Planning Handbook*. 2nd edn. Institute of Transportation Engineers, Washington, DC: Prentice Hall. pp. 427–98.

Multisystems Inc, Mundle & Assoc. Inc. and Parsons Transportation Group Inc. (2002). 'A toolkit for self-service, barrier-free fare collection'. *Transit Cooperative Research Program (TCRP) Report 80*. T.R. Board.

Public Transport Victoria (2016). Victorian Official Fare Compliance Series. Accessed December 2020 at https://www.ptv.vic.gov.au/footer/data-and-reporting/revenue-protection-and-fare-compliance/.

Reddy, A.V., J. Kuhls and A. Lu (2011). 'Measuring and controlling subway fare evasion: Improving safety and security at New York City Transit Authority'. *Transportation Research Record* **2216**: 85–99.

Tonglet, M. (2006). 'Consumer misbehaviour: An exploratory study of shoplifting'. *Journal of Consumer Behaviour* **1**(4): 336–54.

UITP (2015). 'Mobility in cities database 2015'. Brussels: International Association of Public Transport.

APPENDIX

Table 7A.1 *Fare evasion market penetration analysis: key summary results –*
International City Survey

City		Fare Evasion Trips (M p.a.)			Residential Population Involved in Fare Evasion		
		Recidivists	Rare	Total	Recidivists	Rare	Total
Boston	Total	7.2	0.8	21.9	29 185	360 128	534 821
	% Fare Evasion	*32.7%*	*3.8%*	*100.0%*	*5.5%*	*67.3%*	*100.0%*
	% Total	*1.9%*	*0.2%*	*5.7%*	*1.5%*	*18.2%*	*27.1%*
Brisbane	Total	9.0	0.3	12.7	27 854	248 278	310 740
	% Fare Evasion	*71.0%*	*2.5%*	*100.0%*	*9.0%*	*79.9%*	*100.0%*
	% Total	*5.1%*	*0.2%*	*7.1%*	*2.0%*	*18.2%*	*22.8%*
London	Total	179.1	6.7	276.0	449 071	1 756 866	2 756 297
	% Fare Evasion	*64.9%*	*2.4%*	*100.0%*	*16.3%*	*63.7%*	*100.0%*
	% Total	*5.0%*	*0.2%*	*7.8%*	*3.9%*	*15.3%*	*24.0%*
Melbourne	Total	41.3	1.6	50.9	182 664	910 727	1 366 866
	% Fare Evasion	*81.1%*	*3.2%*	*100.0%*	*13.4%*	*66.6%*	*100.0%*
	% Total	*8.0%*	*0.3%*	*9.8%*	*5.1%*	*25.5%*	*38.3%*
New York	Total	567.5	7.8	800.1	1 401 689	2 487 060	5 167 608
	% Fare Evasion	*70.9%*	*1.0%*	*100.0%*	*27.1%*	*48.1%*	*100.0%*
	% Total	*15.3%*	*0.2%*	*21.6%*	*11.4%*	*20.3%*	*42.2%*
Perth	Total	4.5	0.3	7.6	26 433	163 821	216 826
	% Fare Evasion	*59.3%*	*3.9%*	*100.0%*	*12.2%*	*75.6%*	*100.0%*
	% Total	*3.1%*	*0.2%*	*5.2%*	*2.4%*	*15.0%*	*19.8%*
San Francisco	Total	49.2	0.9	60.2	152 960	316 423	561 587
	% Fare Evasion	*81.7%*	*1.5%*	*100.0%*	*27.2%*	*56.3%*	*100.0%*
	% Total	*11.7%*	*0.2%*	*14.3%*	*7.3%*	*15.2%*	*27.0%*
Sydney	Total	43.1	0.7	55.0	109 865	315 411	548 617
	% Fare Evasion	*78.2%*	*1.3%*	*100.0%*	*20.0%*	*57.5%*	*100.0%*
	% Total	*8.0%*	*0.1%*	*10.2%*	*4.2%*	*12.0%*	*20.9%*
Toronto	Total	21.8	1.0	32.2	57 657	296 385	477 207
	% Fare Evasion	*67.6%*	*3.1%*	*100.0%*	*12.1%*	*62.1%*	*100.0%*
	% Total	*4.4%*	*0.2%*	*6.4%*	*3.4%*	*17.2%*	*27.8%*

Source: Monash PTRG research on fare evasion rates in international cities.

PART III

POLICY PERSPECTIVES

8. The governance of public transport: towards integrated design
Wijnand Veeneman

8.1 INTRODUCTION

In recent years, governance has been getting a great deal of attention. This is also true in the field of public transport. Governance is often seen as the role that government plays in a sector. From that perspective, governance is framed largely as the interaction between private and public parties, which in public transport is important. The attention given to governance has developed from a first perspective of a changing balance between those two, with a primary focus on the introduction of more competition. Still, governments play an important role in public transport.

Here, this chapter will discuss governance in a slightly wider perspective. The chapter focuses on those interactions between public and private parties, or more specifically authorities and operators, but will look at them from a wider governance perspective. Governance here is defined as the rule sets that condition the interactions between actors with diverging interests, focusing on public transport for this chapter.

The chapter therefore starts with the role of government in public transport. Subsequently, this chapter will introduce two seminal publications on governance, looking at levels of governance (Williamson, 1998) and mechanisms of governance (Powell, 1990). That literature is the basis for the structure of the following discussion of research on governance of public transport and will help understand the key design challenges of governance in the field of public transport.

8.2 A BRIEF HISTORY OF PUBLIC TRANSPORT AND ITS GOVERNANCE

Public transport is a key instrument of policy makers around the world in the field of mobility. As early as the nineteenth century (Chadwick, 1859), the positive potential of public transport was recognised. Over time, the value that policy makers linked to public transport changed, from connecting the country to build a nation in the early years of trains (Martí-Henneberg, 2013) and canals (Shaw, 2014) to efficient use of urban space in our swiftly urbanising world (Litman, 2007). From allowing cities to grow (Jackson, 2018) to providing access to labour possibilities (Sanchez et al., 2004). From helping women participate in the labour market (Matas et al., 2010) to reducing congestion (Aftabuzzaman et al., 2010). From improving health (Rojas-Rueda et al., 2012) to providing mobility for the disabled (Odufuwa, 2007). Many different values were and are attached to the provision of public transport services over time.

Provision of public transport services requires high investments, mainly to provide the necessary infrastructure. In the early years of development, those investments had a high-risk character, and their value was highly dependent on the network effect: the more locations are connected with a system, the higher the value of every connection (Laird et al., 2005). Both elements meant that governments often stepped in in developing the system, because of the possibility to reduce the risk by long-term focus and coordinating between otherwise fragmented services in their jurisdiction (Button, 2010).

With the development of infrastructure for the car and the rise of income levels in many countries, automobility grew. Consequently, the individual modes of transport eroded the potential for the collective and pressure was put on the financial feasibility of public transport. This led to many governments stepping in beyond investing in infrastructure and bearing growing parts of the operational cost, given the expected value of public transport for society.

From the 1980s, the role of government in public transport was reviewed in many Western countries, as performance of many public transport systems was seen as poor and expectations about stronger involvement of the private sector were high. Interestingly, in South America and Asia, the governmental role in providing public transport was strengthened. In the Western countries where these concerns led to the most extreme institutional changes, as in the United Kingdom, it became clear soon enough that public transport does rely on coordination from the public sector.

In recent years, with global urbanisation growing, the role of high capacity public transport as a prerequisite for the metropolis to function and the governmental role in developing a coordinated collective transport system for the metropolis have come into focus. As always, the private sector plays a major role in developing vehicles and infrastructure and also private investors and operators are active around the world to support governments in providing the services to the travellers.

Over history, government has established a strong role in the provision of public transport infrastructure and services, while the exact form in which that role was set up is changing over time. In this chapter, that governmental role will provide our focus when discussing governance of public transport. This is not because of a normative perspective that government will have to play a major role, but because of the empirical observation that government almost always plays a major role in public transport. Which makes sense when looking at our definition of governance below.

8.3   GOVERNANCE IN PUBLIC TRANSPORT

Governance is a term that has been given a wide variety of meanings.[1] In discussing the role of governance in public transport, we will have to take a position in that debate. Governance is seen here as *the rule sets supporting decision-making in a context of actors with diverging interests*. The core actors in public transport obviously are travellers, operators and government, but also these three can be seen as sets with many subsets. Government can be seen as the bureaucratic agencies managing the contracts with operators and as the representative political bodies to which travellers might appeal for better rail services. Operators range from the driver of the bus to the shareholder of the company. Travellers range from regular peak-hour commuters to foreign city trip tourists. These actors all have different interests, or different demands from the public transport system, and many rule sets are in place to organise decision-making in such a multi-actor context.

Most of the key literature on governance does not talk about public transport, with one major exception in the book in which Chisholm (1992) underlines the potential of network coordination (on which more later). However, most literature starts at the general role of government in society, where governance is the process of governing (Bevir, 2012). As the literature develops in the field of public administration, governance gets the connotation of less hierarchical and more network-oriented steering (Stoker, 1998). The rise of this network-of-actors-perspective aligns with the changing role of government, changing in the second half of the twentieth century from focus on being a controlling hierarchy to being one of the actors in a network of societal actors, including civil society and private enterprise. With that shift, the meaning of the word 'governance' changed from one of governmental action based on hierarchy, to a more general term of ways in which decision-making between actors was designed and functioning. As we will see, that included hierarchy as a mechanism, but widened beyond it.

Governance Mechanisms: Hierarchy, Markets and Networks

In our perspective of governance, as introduced in the first paragraph, governance can be based on different mechanisms to project a rule set on actors (see Powell, 1990). *Hierarchy* deals with conflicting interests of actors through unilaterally set rules. We best understand this governance mechanism when looking at governments. Governments create the most visible rule sets in the form of a legal framework, and they have the power to enforce those rules. Hierarchy is also an apparent governance mechanism within organisations, public and private alike, where also power is institutionalised in a hierarchy to coordinate and to deal with possible conflicts, for example between the ministries of finance and transport or between the infrastructure branch and the operations branch of a railway company.

Markets are governance mechanisms that deal with conflicts between actors through competition: the conflict between suppliers is settled by the aggregate of individuals' (or organisations') choices in transactions. Those chosen less often lose by losing market share; those chosen more often win. As public transport competes with other modes and some public transport services compete between each other, the travellers choosing between the offerings in the market eventually settle the conflict between those private and public transport systems.

With *networks* as governance mechanisms (referring to actor networks, not service or infrastructure networks), actors find their way out of conflict through negotiations. In public transport we could illustrate this by the interaction between authorities and operators on a concession. Some buslines might be underused and operator and authority could negotiate a change to the network to make more effective use of the buses and drivers available. The interest of the operator might be to focus on profitable lines or low-cost service provision, while the interest of the authority might be on covering the whole jurisdiction and good peak services. If all interests are on the table and shared solutions are sought, 'network' is the term for this mechanism. The word 'network' underlines the fact that the actors are mutually dependent and more or less on the same plane in terms of power.

In real life, these different mechanisms interact. Hierarchically, governments can set rules providing subsidies for public transport, making it more attractive for travellers. In terms of markets, operators of public transport services then compete with other modes to attract travellers to their services, where the choice of the traveller settles the conflict between modes. In terms of networks, governments might negotiate with neighbourhood inhabitants to set restrictive parking policies, to make public transport more attractive, but also giving the inhabitants a possibly nicer and safer place to live. All governance mechanisms can be used but in essence work differently. In the section on design, this chapter will get back to that interaction.

Levels of Rule Sets

With the above mechanisms, rule sets are projected on the involved actors. These rule sets are laid down in a wide variety of levels. Williamson (1998) provides a framework to structure these rule sets and how they are interlinked (see also Van de Velde, 2019), with a strong economics focus. Here we will look at that framework, again from a perspective of governance in public transport. Williamson had a clear economic take on the levels, starting with economic transaction at the bottom layer. As we use his framework in a public administration context, we do take some liberties, with a stronger focus on the interaction of actors in decision-making and less on transactions (see also Koppenjan and Groenewegen, 2005).

On a first level, part of those rule sets is laid down in *culture*, in what Williamson calls embeddedness. Some cultures have a stronger collective focus, others a stronger individual focus (Hofstede, 2001). When we consider the interaction between two key actors, government and operator, in delivering services, culture can drive difference in dealing with conflicting interests. In a collectively oriented culture, the decision-making at operator level will more often choose for the collective good than in an individual culture. For example, a Japanese operator will have a different position on maximising profit by strategically reducing maintenance of assets he is entrusted with by the government than an Australian operator (Veeneman and Smith, 2016). The balance between collective responsibility and individual profit maximisation is different in both countries and leads to different behaviours. In this way, the culture sets rules for the decision-making of actors to deal with the different interests of the actors.

On a second level, the rule sets are laid down in *laws*. For public transport, the key discourse in the field has been on regulatory regimes. And also, in other parts of the world this is laid down in legal frameworks for the interaction between governments and operators. The European Commission has been pushing for a stronger market orientation in the rule set for the interaction between government and operators. That regulation has been included in national laws that define the roles of governments and private enterprise. Obviously, many more rule sets for public transport are laid down in laws, from safety regulation to rights of passengers, from technical standards to accounting rules. These rule sets apply to all actors in the sector.

On a third level, rule sets are set up by and between actors in public transport themselves on a long-term relation and not aimed at a specific decision. In these *arrangements* two (or possibly more) actors agree on the rules they will abide by. Mostly, one of the actors is in the lead with developing the rule set. When a passenger buys a ticket, the passenger charter is the arrangement providing the rule set with the expectations to both passenger and operator on the service. When an operator wins a concession or a contractor the contract to build a railway, the arrangement is the rule set for both government and operator or contractor.

On a fourth level, actors interact directly with each other, or in the words of Williamson *transactions* take place. When looking at the governance, it is helpful to look at this level with two perspectives. First, the rule sets can be agreed upon by actors active in a specific decision-making *process* dealing with diverging interests. One could think about the decision to build a railway line, cancel a busline or to procure new rolling stock. In such a process, contractual arrangements and legal requirements might require those making the decision to include specific actors, for example inhabitants of the area affected by the busline cancellation. Or the process could have its own rules, for example, when operators procure new rolling stock their internal procurement process might require consulting with internal health and safety experts, driver representatives, financial and maintenance departments, and many more. A second perspective on this fourth level further descends to the many small decisions made by travellers and train drivers, managers and ministers, conductors and civil servants, and many more. All those smaller and bigger decisions eventually tally to the overall performance of the system: its modal split, its efficiency, its sustainability; the value public transport provides to society. All those decisions eventually are conditioned by the rule sets above.

As Williamson states, these levels influence each other and condition each other, down and up. The rule sets on the above levels condition the decision-making, but also the challenges on each level are conditioned by other levels. A culture conditions what you might want to arrange in a contract, a law could condition how you will include passengers in your decision-making on a busline. In addition, Williamson shows how changing the rule sets on these levels has different time scales. Culture is changing more slowly than laws. Laws are changed less often than arrangements such as contracts. And arrangements are changed much less frequently then the choice to organise a specific decision-making process.

As stated, governance can be seen as those rule sets. That means governance is a broad term, and not a great deal of research is aimed at governance as a whole. Mostly, the focus is on a particular level, and for public transport mostly on the two mid-levels: how should the market be regulated in law? What is the best contract form in terms of arrangements? It is relevant though to understand this wider context. Any analysis of governance on those levels is culture dependent: what works in Chile does not necessarily work in China; what works in Australia does not necessarily work in Austria. In addition, it is the direct interaction between actors on the fourth level in which we can study the effects of the rule sets. This is where travellers choose to use the train, where traffic controllers decide to let the intercity train go first, a bus driver does his best for his company to stay on schedule, and so on. And at the same time this last level is the level where the rule sets are tested and challenged. Where growing poverty might trigger behaviours from travellers that erode a culture averse to fare dodging. Where permanence in good performance of bus operators could reduce the need that authorities feel for detailed contracts with harsh penalties. Where laws requiring transport operators to publish their schedules on paper might be overtaken by people planning their trips on smartphones. We'll discuss the literature on public transport below.

8.4   KEY LITERATURE ON GOVERNANCE IN PUBLIC TRANSPORT

When reviewed through the above framework, we see three aspects that come forward most. First, most governance-oriented literature in the field of public transport focuses on possible conflicts of interest between authorities and operators. The STO framework (Van de Velde, 1992) frames the debate on which tasks should be carried out by operators or authorities. Literature is looking for ideal models, often claiming a stronger role in decision-making for operators or authorities.

In addition, a great deal of the literature on these conflicts of interest between operators and authorities focuses on two of the three governance mechanisms: markets and hierarchies. In public transport, these mechanisms have received a great deal of the attention, with discussions about a stronger role for hierarchy by government in South Africa and Chile and discussions about a stronger role for operators through more open markets in Europe and Australia.

Moreover, most of the literature on public transport governance focuses on the lower three levels. They focus on possible changes to the legal system to improve public transport's regulatory systems, or they review contracting strategies aligned with the discussions above. That does make sense when you expect the research to contribute directly to policy decisions that have to be made on the governance of public transport. *Culture* and the way in which it conditions the performance of public transport is relevant when policy makers want to change the performance of a public transport system. However, it changes slowly and is not very malleable for those policy makers. As much of the research into public transport is driven by a policy-related need for change, the way in which culture conditions the performance of public transport is not a common topic in research.

Below, we will look at the key literature on those three levels to provide a *tour d'horizon* of governance literature related to public transport. The examples will focus on the relation between the operator and the authority as the key governance question, even though many other governance questions exist. Some will be mentioned to illustrate the wider field.

8.5   THE LEGAL FRAMEWORK: RULE SET FOR THE WHOLE SECTOR

The legal framework is a blanket type rule set: it applies to the complete sector, often even the complete society. For public transport, a great deal of work is done on how the legal system should deal with the interaction between government and operator, in general. We have already established that government generally plays an important role in public transport. A great deal of work on this topic was developed in the wake of the new public management perspective that challenges the extent to which that governmental role had become dominant. In terms of our framework it is really about the tension between hierarchy and market, and that market perspectives drive a strong involvement of economists (see also Veeneman, 2002).

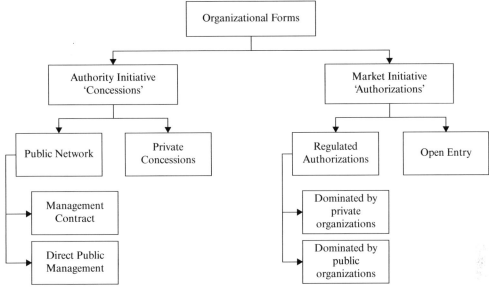

Source: Van de Velde (1999).

Figure 8.1   *Organisational forms in public transport governance*

The Regulatory Regime

Van de Velde (1999) describes four regulatory regimes that can be laid down in a legal framework to condition the relation between operator and authority. The first question is on who has the initiative, the eventual control over what and how services are defined. Is that a decision by the governmental authority (with hierarchy as the key governance mechanism) or by operators (with markets as the key governance mechanism)? In the situation where government authority has the initiative, Van de Velde distinguishes between governmental operators (possibly with a private company managing the provision of services) and private operators executing concessions as defined by the government authority. On the side of market initiative, he distinguishes between open access, where the role of government is highly limited, and authorisations, where government is authorising operators, public and/or private, to run their services (Figure 8.1). As he states: 'the level of authority intervention in the appearance of public transport services increases from right to left, while from top to bottom the level of authority intervention increases in terms of design and production' (Van de Velde, 1999).

A key debate in this field is around the introduction of the open entry model for bus services under Margaret Thatcher in the United Kingdom in the 1980s. The debate is between Gwilliam, Nash and Mackie (1985a, 1985b) on the one hand and Beesley and Glaister (1985) on the other. The discussion clearly shows what the key challenge of a governance system is. Gwilliam et al. underline that government intervention can secure a great deal of different values, such as safety accessibility, and sustainability. This would be hampered by the introduction of the free market. Beesley and Glaister underline that the improved efficiency is a key element of a free market and that governments have a wide variety of policy instruments to secure those values without interfering in this free market.

In his study on regulatory regime changes in Scandinavia and the United Kingdom, Alexandersson (2010) shows how strong the economic focus has been in the debates, with a central role for efficiency. He expects that the changes that will follow throughout Europe will focus more on the wider consequences of a more market oriented regulatory regime. Laurino et al. (2015) show that governments still play a major role in many countries throughout the world.

Ongkittikul and Geerlings (2006) show how these regulatory regimes drive innovation in public transport in different ways. They conclude that in the English regulatory regime innovation was stronger, for better and for worse, than in a Dutch context, with the English adopting a more market and the Dutch a more hierarchical governance mechanism. Veeneman (2016) adds that in a regulatory regime with long-term concessions, innovations occur mostly around the concession changes. In open access oriented regulatory regimes, innovation is more of a constant process.

The debate has long been focusing on a principal issue: should the right to operate be in its core a public or a private matter, with a great deal of debate on property rights in the Americas (Klein et al., 1997; Echeverry et al., 2005). Currently, more focus is given on the interplay between the public and private actors (Hansson, 2013), shifting the discussion from principal economics to practical governance.

On which model of a regulatory regime works best, Van de Velde (2019) has a clear answer: most models can work, depending on the value that policy makers are seeking from the model and a consistency of choices in the regulatory regime. Veeneman (2002) shows how regimes are generally changed to serve a specific value, like efficiency or innovation, but that will trigger reactions to secure other values with other instruments, for example a free market regime can trigger quality contracts to coordinate better between government and operators in Great Britain.

Multilevel Governance

The regulatory regime is a key aspect captured in the legal framework of (most) countries. There is a second aspect that has recently got more attention and is of key importance for the functioning of public transport: the way that jurisdictions are defined and the way in which the legal framework distributes agency on public transport over those entities. Public transport (or the transport system in general) is a layered set of services. The local bus, the high-speed train, and everything in between together provide a complete (though often poorly integrated) set of transport services. Just a local bus or just a high-speed train provides travellers with a rather limited proposition. Integration of those services is an important topic in the research and policy, especially with recent discussions on the potential of mobility-as-a-service as the integrating platform (Audouin and Finger, 2018 and Hirschhorn et al., 2019).

Governments are also layered, from municipalities to supra-national entities, like the European Union. And these different entities have different interests in these different modes (see Figure 8.2). Those interests at a certain level can be defined along two lines: connectivity with other similar jurisdictions and coverage within the own jurisdiction.

Local municipalities generally focus on good bus services linking the key destinations in

Governmental level Type 1 institutions	Expected focus on trip of distances	Expected transport policy focus	Focus
Supra-national, federal and large national	>500 km	High speed rail, air transport, cross boundary transport	Flow
Smaller national and state	50–500 km	Highway system and national railway system	
Regional and metropolitan	5–50 km	Arteries and high capacity public transport	
Local	<5 km	Safety, cycling, walking, parking	Place

Source: Veeneman and Mulley (2018).

Figure 8.2   Governmental levels and public transport policy focus

their city and covering the various origins in the city. Their focus is on local slow modes and their link to the different places. On the other end of the spectrum, large jurisdictions, like major countries and supra-national entities, are focusing on linking their different parts with high-speed railways and air transport. Multi-level governance literature (for example, Marsden and Rye, 2010) investigates this layered character of actors and how governance is successful (or not) in integrating these different perspectives. Veeneman et al. (2015) show how tax revenues on different levels had effects on the funding of public transport during austerity and explain the focus on different modes in public transport. As such, the funding aspect of governance provides agency to different levels and that for a large part drives the decision-making towards a different mix of transport solutions. Veeneman and Mulley (2018) show how spending on different levels can help explain public transport decision outcomes.

Concluding, a relatively new part of the literature is about the rule sets between governmental layers. A more developed part of the literature on the regulatory regime is about the rule sets that condition *how* the relation between government and operator is coming about. This ranges from the free market, in which the relation is limited and initiated by operators with the market as the key mechanism, to government service provision, in which the relation is far more hierarchical, and initiated by the authority. Within the context of the regime, authorities generally develop a specific rule set they want for their interaction with the operator, the contract or arrangement, which is discussed below.

8.6   THE ARRANGEMENTS: CONTRACTS AND CONCESSIONS

While a regulatory regime touches on all actors in a jurisdiction of a government (mostly a country) in the same way, arrangements are those rule sets that are particular and mostly bilateral, devised for and agreed upon by the specific actors they pertain to (Gwilliam and

Scurfield, 1996; Van der Velde et al., 2008). Consequently, the arrangements concern and condition a more specific relation between mostly two actors. As above, a great deal of literature is available on contracting and the incentives in the contract. Here again, the literature is selected that focuses on the relation between authority and operator, mostly contracts. They generally have the form of licences (allowing operators in the market), franchises (giving a non-exclusive right to operate the market) or concessions (giving an exclusive right to the market), but also can be more direct for in-house operators, through direct hierarchical planning and control or service level agreements. That right to operate could be related to pick-up points (stops), lines, networks of a particular mode, or multiple modes in a region. Much of that literature singles out contract elements, such as scope definition (multi-modal or single modal, lines or networks), conditions on the production (like the type of vehicle to be used) and the remuneration (net cost, gross cost, incentive) (Hirschhorn et al., 2018). However, here we will start with the way the arrangement is established.

Relation in the Arrangement

A large part of the literature on governance of public transport looks at how the relation between authority and operator is established. As discussed above, that is often a topic of a regulatory framework, but many jurisdictions provide a broad framework, with many choices to be made by the authorities within that jurisdiction. (See for example for France, Roy and Yvrande-Bilon, 2007; for Sweden, Alexandersson, 2010; for the Netherlands, Veeneman, 2018; for New Zealand, Wallis et al., 2010; and for Australia, Hensher, 2017.)

In this literature, the three governance mechanisms mentioned before play an important role: hierarchy, market, and network. All research mentioned in the paragraph above compares the way the relation between the authority and the operators is established and the related contract along the lines of these mechanisms. For example, Hensher and Stanley (2008) focus on the role of complexity of the scope under contract in the choice between negotiations as network governance and tendering as market governance. Higher complexity (with many more factors and values at play) in the services provided demands more network governance, as in both a hierarchy and a market governance is rather poor at securing the inclusion of all those different perspectives, with market mechanisms having a propensity to single out a customer perspective (not necessarily the traveller, but also governmental clients paying the subsidies) and hierarchy mechanisms to single out the principal perspective.

A key debate in the last decades for many Western countries (for an overview see Van de Velde, 2019) was the move from hierarchical governance mechanisms (organising control over government operators) to market mechanisms (organising competition between mostly private operators). A great deal of the literature looked at the effects of the new governance that emerged or tried to predict the effect of the implementation of specific governance elements. A lot of the literature looks at efficiency (for example Holmgren, 2013; Veeneman et al., 2014). However, Currie et al. (2018) look at the relation between ownership and performance on sustainability.

The contextuality of governance is well illustrated by the fact that other parts of the literature show a move from private small operations to more public control, in both

African (Walters, 2008; Schalekamp and Behrens, 2010) and South American countries (Muñoz and Gschwender, 2008), a transformation from market governance to hierarchy, or more precisely a combination of market and hierarchy.

In many countries this leads to competitive tendering being the governance model of choice, using market mechanisms but giving authorities the possibility to establish agency using competitive control mechanisms: more market governance may give more control to government (Veeneman, 2018), as the agency shifted to the authorities that were using market mechanisms to control operators.

There has long been a debate on the role of authorities and operators in this relation. That debate has settled to a large extent. It is clear that public transport requires a great deal of coordination between all kinds of policy fields (sustainability, social inclusion, spatial development, infrastructure development and much more) and public transport operations. Public transport can deliver public value in many of these areas. This also means there is value in a strong role for governmental authorities. However, public provision of services can lead to loss of efficiency and this is where competition (or benchmarking) can help. This points to tendering as the global preferred model in which governments can set the framework in securing public values and operators deliver the services efficiently (see also Veeneman, 2002).

Scope of the Arrangement

The rule set in the arrangement generally pertains to a specific scope: deliver bus services, build a railway line, or maybe do everything for all modes. Hoekstra et al. (2019) show how multi-modal concessions could simplify coordination in design and operation of bus and train services by putting them all under one contract with one operator and giving a more limited role to the authority. This illustrates how governance literature looks at the coordination question between actors and the scope they are responsible for within the public transport system.

Also, the coordination between different tasks on the rail services is a topic of interest. The arrangements might fragment the tasks in the sector, asking for coordination and specific attention on that coordination in the contracts. In operation and planning we see several examples. Nash (2008) talks about the problem of vertical separation and how the way of contracting can help to overcome that. Mizutani et al. (2015) talk about the coordination needed on rail that allows for multiple operators on the same network (horizontal separation).

Other literature looks at design and construction of rail systems, infrastructure and services. Literature on the alliance and the consortium (for example Priemus, 2009) looks at how actors can be brought together in an arrangement to allow for easier coordination between their possibly conflicting interests. A similar focus arises in the literature on public–private partnerships (Carpintiro and Petersen, 2015) and more complex contracting forms like design-build-operate-and-maintain (Wiss et al., 2000). The literature seeks to set up the arrangements with rule sets that overcome stifling conflicts of interest in those projects (for example Flyvbjerg et al., 2003).

That is not to say that there is no research that looks at rule sets on a different relation than that of operator and authority. For example, all literature on pricing strategies for public transport services and their effect on patronage can be seen as research on a specific contract element in the relation between operator and traveller and how those rules condition the behaviour of the traveller (for example Tirachini et al., 2014).

Remuneration in the Arrangement

Remuneration is also an important topic in the literature on arrangements and contract (Walters and Jansson, 2008). Regularly, public transport provision does not cover its costs completely. Consequently, there is generally funding from the government, often related to specific public values and related goals. This stream provides the authority with agency on public transport. The literature shows three types of basic remuneration in contracts: gross-cost, net-cost and super-incentive, all with a different role in the farebox revenues in the way that the operator is remunerated by the authority (see van de Velde, 2019). With *gross-cost remuneration*, a lump sum is provided to the operator, related to the costs of the provision of the service. That relation could give an incentive to raise costs, as the lump sum simply moves with growing costs. This incentive can be curbed by the way in which the contract is awarded, like through competitive tendering on price, which will be discussed below. London, Copenhagen, Stockholm and Helsinki provide examples of this model of remuneration. With *net-cost remuneration*, the operator receives a lump sum (subsidy) and what travellers pay for the services (farebox revenue). In that case the incentives to the operator is expected to shift their attention towards the traveller, but then also shifts away from other public values that public transport could deliver, such as accessibility, sustainability and safety. These remunerations are widely used in the Netherlands and France, but are less common in those situations where governments take a stronger role. *Super-incentive remuneration* takes a further step, with the subsidy dependent on the revenue stream from the traveller. This provides additional incentives to give attention to the traveller revenue and an additional need to secure the public value of affordability, as operators might focus on maximising the revenue stream and limit the mobility of financially vulnerable groups. This is a less used model, but examples can be seen in Telemarken, Norway and Amstelland/Meerlanden, the Netherlands.

The base model of remuneration is often supplemented with additional incentives in the form of bonuses or penalties (Wallis, 2005). Some of these have a rather narrow focus, driving specific actions on the part of the operator to improve specific service-related performance indicators (see also Hensher and Stanley, 2003), like punctuality (Jansson and Pyddoke, 2010). Other performance indicators and related incentives have a broader focus, like patronage (Pyddoke and Swärdh, 2017), allowing the operator to weigh its different options in terms of service improvements to attract customers.

The total of incentives in the base remuneration and the additional incentives needs to be a highly balanced system of incentives, related to the cost for the operator of providing the service in the way that the authority would like and related to the gains for society that the authority is expecting. Related to the former, providing the operator with an incentive much smaller than the cost to the operator is ineffective: the operator will ignore the incentive. Providing an incentive much larger than the costs to the operator is inefficient, as the operator will profit excessively. An incentive that is much lower than the expected societal gains is a missed opportunity. An incentive much higher than the expected societal gains is a waste of public money.

8.7   THE PROCESSES: DECISION-MAKING AND INTERACTION

As stated above, governance can be set up to be generic for all actors of a specific type, as in a legal framework, or specific for a specific long-term relation between specific actors, in arrangements. But rule sets can also be tied to specific actors in a specific short-term decision-making process. The literature on these *processes* of decision-making is less well developed in the field of the relation between the authority and the operator, although some of it can be found in Veeneman (2016, 2018, 2020). These processes are highly conditioned by the other levels mentioned before, and as such more contingent and less easily generalised in research. The literature on processes focuses on the inclusion of different actors and their perspectives, progress of the decision-making between the actors, providing agency to those that are less well represented, and often seeking ways to create shared solutions for actors that might have very different ideas of what the essence of the problem is.

The literature on value variety because of a multi-actor perspective in decision-making processes exhibits a clear chasm. One part focuses on the inclusion of real actors in the decision-making process, seeking integrated solutions by inclusion and representation of multiple actors (De Bruijn and Ten Heuvelhof, 2018). Another part of the literature focuses on support systems for a single actor to include the different perspectives (Ferretti and Montibeller, 2016). A great example of the latter in public transport can be found at Wang et al. (2019), in their support system for train drivers and Faber and Jorna (2013) for railway planning. For this chapter and its definition of governance, we will focus on the first type, not the support system but the rule set.

Schipper and Gerrits (2018) give a great overview of the roles involved in rail traffic control and how decision-making between them is organised in various European countries. They show how the shared sense-making of the different actors has a different rule set in the countries they researched. A key difference is for example what freedom the traffic controller gets to diverge from predefined plans that were set up with the other actors. Lo et al. (2019) add the way in which the different perspectives are brought to a decision-making process. Steenhuisen and Van Eeten (2008) show how decision-making operational staff are subject to governance that is pushing different actors' values.

In transportation decision-making, the role of public participation is under renewed interest. Vigar (2017) is making a strong case for transport planning and decision-making with a more participative character. He argues that expert knowledge is often limited to a specific perspective and that more participatory approaches allow for more integrated solutions, serving a wider set of values. Also, Mercier et al. (2019) make this point for urban transport decision-making, with De Bruijn and Ten Heuvelhof (2018) who clarify the use of hierarchy and network mechanisms in decision-making processes. Koppenjan et al. (2011) show how, in decision-making in transport projects, hierarchy and network mechanisms are combined to create greater effectiveness.

Concluding, rule sets are also set up for processes making specific decisions. Two important examples from the literature on public transport are how to deal with disruptions in rail traffic and ensure project execution. In addition, participative decision-making and a wider perspective on the value set transport has to deliver on are currently getting more attention in the field of sustainable transport, mostly at a local level. This makes sense as at the local level you can actually get the actors round the table and include them directly in the process, which can only be done at larger scales through representation.

8.8   DESIGNING GOVERNANCE

As governance is defined here as the rule set for decision-making in a world with actors with diverging interest, the rule sets have two key design challenges: which actors and what perspectives to include in the decision-making in an effective way. Excluding actors or limiting access to the decision-making is about focusing power, providing agency to specific actors, and supporting swift and effective decision-making, but effective on a limited set of values. On the other hand, including or admitting actors to the decision-making is about distributing power to multiple actors and can support more integrated solutions and value variety (see Veeneman et al., 2006).

Public transport is generally aimed to support a wider range of public values, from sustainability and safety to spatial accessibility and social inclusion. Many of these values are linked to actors in different ways. Travellers might want relatively empty vehicles; operators relatively full. Cyclists might want zero-emission vehicles, not worrying too much about the cost; travellers might want higher frequencies, not worrying too much about the emissions. The financial department of the operator might see the risks of new infrastructure; the market department see the potential. And so on. And those values have different implications for decisions on public transport.

Those implications can be understood through research, but that research hardly ever covers the full picture, all the value variety of related actors. In that context, governance has to be designed to overcome that narrowness and make decision-making possible with that wider set of actors.

Design on Different Governance Layers

As stated before, the design of governance can work on three layers, legal, arrangements and processes, with the 'design' of culture being mostly out of reach because of the slow pace of change. The legal framework is long-term and for all actors the same; arrangements are medium-term and designed for the specific actors that undersign them; and processes are short-term and set up for specific (generally substantial) decisions.

There are clear relations between these levels. First, higher levels condition lower levels. When culturally something is unacceptable, generally the lower layers are not that concerned with it. For example, Tokyo concession contracts have few demands on vehicle maintenance, as culturally neglecting it would be unacceptable (see Veeneman and Smith, 2016). Also, when something is legally prohibited, contracts can mostly ignore it. Dutch operators legally have to participate in an electronic ticketing system; concessions do not have to reiterate that. Second, lower levels can tweak the higher levels. When something is legally focused on a certain set of values, contracts can be used to secure another set of values. For example, when in the UK the legal system was focused on opening market mechanisms, authorities sought ways to secure specific quality aspects through hierarchy and negotiations, eventually leading to quality contracts (Veeneman, 2002). Third, change of higher levels can be initiated from the observation of failure in lower levels. When it is clear that decisions are made that are not driving efficiency, it might lead the authority to choose new contracts or contracting forms. When those contracts don't help, it might trigger the demand for a different regulatory regime in law. This, in turn, will likely change the culture in the sector. This basically is the path that new public management triggered, after authorities were unhappy about the performance of operators in the 1980s throughout Europe. These interactions between the levels can be taken into account when designing governance, choosing the level to intervene in the governance, aiming for more short-term changes or long-term effects and allowing room in lower levels to mitigate the weaknesses in higher levels.

Design Using Different Governance Mechanisms

Besides these interactions between levels, when designing governance it should also be recognised that governance mechanisms do not operate in isolation. For example, in competitive tendering the phases use different governance mechanisms. The competitive tendering itself clearly uses *market* mechanisms: governments are using their ability to choose an operator to put force behind the rule set. Once the concession period has started, there is a contractual *hierarchy*, with the authority being the principal with the most agency. Moreover, *network* mechanism negotiations are the key mechanism on those aspects where the *operator* has the agency, because they simply have a better understanding of the key decision points than the authority, and that knowledge gives them agency in the decision-making. For example, when designing an efficiently operating network, generally operators know best and authorities better understand that they should build on that knowledge, putting the operators and authorities in a negotiating position, rather than a hierarchical one. The key mechanisms interact through time in this example.

This understanding of the interaction can lead to specific governance designs for specific tasks. For example, concession *management* should be very hierarchical, with the authority focusing on control over the operator in providing the agreed performance. When the agreed performance indicators are not met, a penalty can be applied to underline the hierarchical relation. Concession *development* should be far more oriented towards negotiations, using the knowledge of the operator to design next year's services in line with the policy priorities of the authority. In governance design this generally leads to two different processes of decision-making, with different styles and also different people involved.

This interaction between mechanisms works not only between phases or tasks, but also between concessions. The *possibility* of competitive tendering gives authorities that do not tender (yet) more agency to establish a hierarchy, even when they rely mostly on network mechanisms. In negotiations with an in-house or direct award operator, an authority that can realistically foreshadow future competitive tendering can create far more pressure than an authority that has no (legal) possibility to use competitive tendering. This means the dynamics of the network mechanism change dramatically when the market mechanism can be invoked.

Even levels and mechanisms can be mixed. Veeneman (2016) shows how a Dutch authority in the contract takes a very hierarchical approach, but in the processes for the development of the concession clearly uses network mechanisms. The authority chooses to use hierarchy from the contract to serve as background to which they develop a very reciprocal relation with the operator, very much building on network mechanisms. Those mixed approaches have a clear upside and downside (see also Veeneman, 2002). The upside is that the strengths of the different levels and mechanisms can be used to counter the weaknesses of other levels. The downside is that the role of the different actors can become unclear and the effectiveness of the rules eroded because of that.

8.9   CONCLUSION

We define governance as the rule set under which actors are making decisions that drive the performance of public transport services. What is valued by those actors is highly diverse. In other words, there is a great deal of value variety. The key challenge of the governance is to deal with that value variety.

There is a somewhat problematic tension between the vast majority of the scientific literature on governance and the practice of designing governance (see Hirschhorn, 2020), as sampled above. Researchers generally focus on a specific relation between a governance element (a regulatory framework, a contracting form, a contract type, an actor involvement and role) and a specific performance metric of the system (costs, production, use, and effect as intended by policies, such as congestion reduction). That focus supports sound analysis of the relation between the governance element and the performance of the system. As an example, in the original discussion between Beesley et al. and Nash et al., referred to at the start of this chapter, the focus was very much on efficiency and competition.

However, governments are often looking at a far wider range of values (Beck Jørgenson and Bozeman, 2007; see also Veeneman et al., 2009), following societal demands. Having many public values being secured with many different governance elements can create ineffective and conflicting governance (see also de Bruijn and Dicke, 2006). Various governance elements can secure those different values, but all intervene in the same public transport reality, the same set of actors. And often in that reality they create conflicts.

This chapter can serve as a framework for a more integrated perspective on governance. That framework allows researchers and policy makers to deal with this conflicting character, widening the analysis, away from the earlier narrow focus on competition and efficiency, towards a wider set of governance elements and a more integrated governance design. However, the challenge of designing governance is not one of aiming at one comprehensive design, but far more one of incremental improvements, for which the framework can help to see the strengths and weaknesses of different approaches. That could eventually provide a basis for public transport services that provide a whole lot of value to a whole lot of people.

NOTE

1.   Public administration literature has a wide variety of governance definitions with overlapping and conflicting meanings. A widely accepted distinction is that between institutions and governance, in that institutions concern the rule sets, but also the organisations representing the development, deployment, and enforcement

of those rule sets, like parliaments, regulators, and inspectorates. Governance in that context is often limited to the actions of those organisations. Here we choose a wider, but less often used definition of governance, which embraces institutions and also better fits the public–private context of public transport.

REFERENCES

Aftabuzzaman, M., Currie, G. and Sarvi, M. (2010). Evaluating the congestion relief impacts of public transport in monetary terms. *Journal of Public Transportation*, *13*(1), 1.

Alexandersson, G. (2010). The accidental deregulation. EFI: The Economic Research Institute, Stockholm School of Economics.

Audouin, M. and Finger, M. (2018). The development of Mobility-as-a-Service in the Helsinki metropolitan area: A multi-level governance analysis. *Research in Transportation Business & Management*, *27*, 24–35.

Beck Jørgenson, T. and Bozeman, B. (2007). Public values: An inventory. *Administration and Society*, *39*, 354–81.

Beesley, M.E. and Glaister, S. (1985). Deregulating the bus industry in Britain – (C) a response. *Transport Reviews*, *5*(2), 133–42.

Bevir, M. (2012). *Governance: A Very Short Introduction*. Oxford: Oxford University Press.

Button, K. (2010). *Transport Economics*. Cheltenham, UK and Northampton, MA, USA: Edward Elgar Publishing.

Carpintero, S. and Petersen, O.H. (2015). Bundling and unbundling in public–private partnerships: Implications for risk sharing in urban transport projects. *Project Management Journal*, *46*(4), 35–46.

Chadwick, E. (1859). Results of different principles of legislation and administration in Europe: Of competition for the field, as compared with competition within the field, of service. *Journal of the Statistical Society of London*, *22*(3), 381–420.

Chisholm, D. (1992). *Coordination without Hierarchy: Informal Structures in Multiorganizational Systems*. Berkeley, CA: University of California Press.

Currie, G., Truong, L. and De Gruyter, C. (2018). Regulatory structures and their impact on the sustainability performance of public transport in world cities. *Research in Transportation Economics*, *69*, 494–500.

de Bruijn, H. and Dicke, W. (2006). Strategies for safeguarding public values in liberalized utility sectors. *Public Administration*, *84*(3), 717–35.

de Bruijn, H. and Ten Heuvelhof, E. (2018). *Management in Networks*. Abingdon: Routledge.

Echeverry, J.C., Ibanez, A.M., Moya, A., Hillon, L.C., Cárdenas, M. and Gómez-Lobo, A. (2005). The economics of TransMilenio, a mass transit system for Bogotá. *Economía*, *5*(2), 151–96.

Faber, N.R. and Jorna, R.J. (2013). Dispatching, planning, passenger support, multi-actor systems and organizational structures in the Netherlands railways. In N. Dadashi, A. Scott, J.R. Wilson and A. Mills (eds), *Rail Human Factors: Supporting Reliability, Safety and Cost Reduction*. Boca Raton, FL: CRC Press, pp. 377–88.

Ferretti, V. and Montibeller, G. (2016). Key challenges and meta-choices in designing and applying multi-criteria spatial decision support systems. *Decision Support Systems*, *84*, 41–52.

Flyvbjerg, B., Bruzelius, N. and Rothengatter, W. (2003). *Megaprojects and Risk: An Anatomy of Ambition*. Cambridge: Cambridge University Press.

Gwilliam, K. and Scurfield, R. (1996). Constructing a competitive environment in public road passenger transport (No. TWU–24). Washington, DC: World Bank.

Gwilliam, K.M., Nash, C.A. and Mackie, P.J. (1985a). Deregulating the bus industry in Britain: A rejoinder. *Transport Reviews*, *5*(3), 215–22.

Gwilliam, K.M., Nash, C.A. and Mackie, P.J. (1985b). Deregulating the bus industry in Britain: (B) the case against. *Transport Reviews*, *5*(2), 105–32.

Hansson, L. (2013). Hybrid steering cultures in the governance of public transport: A successful way to meet demands? *Research in Transportation Economics*, *39*(1), 175–84.

Hensher, D.A. (2017). Future bus transport contracts under a mobility as a service (MaaS) regime in the digital age: Are they likely to change? *Transportation Research Part A: Policy and Practice*, *98*, 86–96.

Hensher, D.A. and Stanley, J. (2003). Performance-based quality contracts in bus service provision. *Transportation Research Part A: Policy and Practice*, *37*(6), 519–38.

Hensher, D.A. and Stanley, J. (2008). Transacting under a performance-based contract: The role of negotiation and competitive tendering. *Transportation Research Part A: Policy and Practice*, *42*(9), 1143–51.

Hirschhorn, F. (2020). *En Route to Better Performance: Tackling the Complexities of Public Transport Governance*. Delft: Delft University of Technology.

Hirschhorn, F., Veeneman, W. and van de Velde, D. (2018). Inventory and rating of performance indicators and organisational features in metropolitan public transport: A worldwide Delphi survey. *Research in Transportation Economics*, *69*, 144–56.

Hirschhorn, F., Paulsson, A., Sørensen, C.H. and Veeneman, W. (2019). Public transport regimes and mobility as a service: Governance approaches in Amsterdam, Birmingham, and Helsinki. *Transportation Research Part A: Policy and Practice, 130*, 178–91.

Hoekstra, G., Veeneman, W., van Oort, N. and Goverde, R. (2019).The advantages of multi-modal concessions, two analyses in the Netherlands. *International Conference Series on Competition and Ownership in Land Passenger Transport* (Thredbo), Singapore.

Hofstede, G. (2001). *Culture's Consequences: Comparing Values, Behaviors, Institutions and Organizations Across Nations*. Thousand Oaks, CA: Sage Publications.

Holmgren, J. (2013). The efficiency of public transport operations: An evaluation using stochastic frontier analysis. *Research in Transportation Economics, 39*(1), 50–57.

Jackson, A.A. (2018). *Semi-detached London: Suburban Development, Life and Transport, 1900–39*. Abingdon: Routledge.

Jansson, K. and Pyddoke, R. (2010). Quality incentives and quality outcomes in procured public transport: Case study Stockholm. *Research in Transportation Economics, 29*(1), 11–18.

Klein, D.B., Moore, A.T. and Reja, B. (1997). Curb rights: Eliciting competition and entrepreneurship in urban transit. *The Independent Review, 2*(1), 29–54.

Koppenjan, J. and Groenewegen, J. (2005). Institutional design for complex technological systems. *International Journal of Technology, Policy and Management, 5*(3), 240–57.

Koppenjan, J., Veeneman, W., Van der Voort, H., Ten Heuvelhof, E. and Leijten, M. (2011). Competing management approaches in large engineering projects: The Dutch RandstadRail project. *International Journal of Project Management, 29*(6), 740–50.

Laird, J.J., Nellthorp, J. and Mackie, P.J. (2005). Network effects and total economic impact in transport appraisal. *Transport Policy, 12*(6), 537–44.

Laurino, A., Ramella, F. and Beria, P. (2015). The economic regulation of railway networks: A worldwide survey. *Transportation Research Part A: Policy and Practice, 77*, 202–12.

Litman, T. (2007). Evaluating rail transit benefits: A comment. *Transport Policy, 14*(1), 94–7.

Lo, J.C., Sehic, E. and Meijer, S.A. (2019). Balancing organizational and academic research: Investigating train traffic controller's geographical workspace design and team situation awareness using gaming simulations. *Journal of Rail Transport Planning & Management, 10*, 34–45.

Marsden, G. and Rye, T. (2010). The governance of transport and climate change. *Journal of Transport Geography, 18*(6), 669–78.

Martí-Henneberg, J. (2013). European integration and national models for railway networks (1840–2010). *Journal of Transport Geography, 26*, 126–38.

Matas, A., Raymond, J.L. and Roig, J.L. (2010). Job accessibility and female employment probability: The cases of Barcelona and Madrid. *Urban Studies, 47*(4), 769–87.

Mercier, J., Tremblay-Racicot, F., Carrier, M. and Duarte, F. (2019). The context of sustainable urban transport. In *Governance and Sustainable Urban Transport in the Americas*. Cham: Palgrave Pivot, pp. 31–54.

Mizutani, F., Smith, A., Nash, C. and Uranishi, S. (2015). Comparing the costs of vertical separation, integration, and intermediate organisational structures in European and East Asian Railways. *Journal of Transport Economics and Policy (JTEP), 49*, 496–515.

Muñoz, J.C. and Gschwender, A. (2008). Transantiago: A tale of two cities. *Research in Transportation Economics, 22*(1), 45–53.

Nash, C. (2008). Passenger railway reform in the last 20 years: European experience reconsidered. *Research in Transportation Economics, 22*(1), 61–70.

Odufuwa, B.O. (2007). Towards sustainable public transport for disabled people in Nigerian cities. *Studies on Home and Community Science, 1*(2), 93–101.

Ongkittikul, S. and Geerlings, H. (2006). Opportunities for innovation in public transport: Effects of regulatory reforms on innovative capabilities. *Transport Policy, 13*(4), 283–93.

Powell, W.W. (1990). Neither hierarchy nor market: Network forms of organization. *Research in Organizational Behavior, 12*, 295–336.

Priemus, H. (2009). Do design & construct contracts for infrastructure projects stimulate innovation? The case of the Dutch high speed railway. *Transportation Planning and Technology, 32*(4), 335–53.

Pyddoke, R. and Swärdh, J.E. (2017). The influence of demand incentives in public transport contracts on patronage and costs in medium sized Swedish cities. K2 Working Paper.

Rojas-Rueda, D., De Nazelle, A., Teixidó, O. and Nieuwenhuijsen, M.J. (2012). Replacing car trips by increasing bike and public transport in the greater Barcelona metropolitan area: A health impact assessment study. *Environment International, 49*, 100–109.

Roy, W. and Yvrande-Billon, A. (2007). Ownership, contractual practices and technical efficiency: The case of urban public transport in France. *Journal of Transport Economics and Policy (JTEP), 41*(2), 257–82.

Sanchez, T.W., Shen, Q. and Peng, Z.R. (2004). Transit mobility, jobs access and low-income labour participation in US metropolitan areas. *Urban Studies, 41*(7), 1313–31.

Schalekamp, H. and Behrens, R. (2010). Engaging paratransit on public transport reform initiatives in South Africa: A critique of policy and an investigation of appropriate engagement approaches. *Research in Transportation Economics*, 29(1), 371–8.

Schipper, D. and Gerrits, L. (2018). Differences and similarities in European railway disruption management practices. *Journal of Rail Transport Planning & Management*, 8(1), 42–55.

Shaw, R.E. (2014). *Canals for a Nation: The Canal Era in the United States, 1790–1860*. Lexington, KY: University Press of Kentucky.

Stanley, J. and van de Velde, D. (2008). Risk and reward in public transport contracting. *Research in Transportation Economics*, 22(1), 20–25.

Steenhuisen, B. and van Eeten, M. (2008). Invisible trade-offs of public values: Inside Dutch railways. *Public Money and Management*, 28(3), 147–52.

Stoker, G. (1998). Governance as theory: Five propositions. *International Social Science Journal*, 50(155), 17–28.

Tirachini, A., Hensher, D.A. and Rose, J.M. (2014). Multimodal pricing and optimal design of urban public transport: The interplay between traffic congestion and bus crowding. *Transportation Research Part B: Methodological*, 61, 33–54.

Van de Velde, D.M. (1992). Classifying regulatory structures of public transport. Paper presented at the 6th World Conference on Transport Research, July.

Van de Velde, D.M. (1999). Organisational forms and entrepreneurship in public transport: Classifying organisational forms. *Transport Policy*, 6(3), 147–57.

Van de Velde, D. (2019). *Competition in Public Transport: An Exploratory Research in Institutional Frameworks in the Public Transport Sector*. Doctoral dissertation, Delft University of Technology.

Van de Velde, D., Beck, A., Van Elburg, J. and Terschüren, K.H. (2008). *Contracting in Urban Public Transport*. Amsterdam: European Commission.

Veeneman, W. (2002). *Mind the Gap: Bridging Theories and Practice for the Organisation of Metropolitan Public Transport*. Delft: Delft University of Technology.

Veeneman, W. (2016). Public transport governance in the Netherlands: More recent developments. *Research in Transportation Economics*, 59, 116–22.

Veeneman, W. (2018). Developments in public transport governance in the Netherlands: The maturing of tendering. *Research in Transportation Economics*, 69, 227–34.

Veeneman, W. (2020). Developments in public transport governance in the Netherlands: Authorities on the rise. *Research in Transportation Economics*, forthcoming.

Veeneman, W. and Mulley, C. (2018). Multi-level governance in public transport: Governmental layering and its influence on public transport service solutions. *Research in Transportation Economics*, 69, 430–37.

Veeneman, W. and Smith, A. (2016). Workshop 2 report: Effective institutional design, regulatory frameworks and contract strategies. *Research in Transportation Economics*, 59, 60–64.

Veeneman, W., Dicke, W. and De Bruijne, M. (2009). From clouds to hailstorms: A policy and administrative science perspective on safeguarding public values in networked infrastructures. *International Journal of Public Policy*, 4(5), 414–34.

Veeneman, W., Van de Velde, D. and Lutje Schipholt, L. (2006). The value of bus and train: Public values in public transport. *Proceedings of the European Transport Conference*, Noordwijk.

Veeneman, W., Wilschut, J., Urlings, T., Blank, J. and van de Velde, D. (2014). Efficient frontier analysis of Dutch public transport tendering: A first analysis. *Research in Transportation Economics*, 48, 101–108.

Veeneman, W., Augustin, K., Enoch, M., d'Arcier, B.F., Malpezzi, S. and Wijmenga, N. (2015). Austerity in public transport in Europe: The influence of governance. *Research in Transportation Economics*, 51, 31–9.

Vigar, G. (2017). The four knowledges of transport planning: Enacting a more communicative, trans-disciplinary policy and decision-making. *Transport Policy*, 58, 39–45.

Wallis, I.P. (2005). Patronage incentives in urban public transport contracts: Appraisal of practice and experience to date. In *Competition and Ownership in Land Passenger Transport*. 8th International Conference (Thredbo 8) Transport Engineering Programme, Federal University of Rio de Janeiro, Brazil.

Wallis, I., Bray, D. and Webster, H. (2010). To competitively tender or to negotiate: Weighing up the choices in a mature market. *Research in Transportation Economics*, 29(1), 89–98.

Walters, J. (2008). Overview of public transport policy developments in South Africa. *Research in Transportation Economics*, 22(1), 98–108.

Walters, J. and Jansson, J.O. (2008). Risk and reward in public transportation contracting. *Research in Transportation Economics*, 22(1), 26–30.

Wang, P., Goverde, R.M. and Van Luipen, J. (2019). A connected driver advisory system framework for merging freight trains. *Transportation Research Part C: Emerging Technologies*, 105, 203–21.

Williamson, O.E. (1998). The institutions of governance. *The American Economic Review*, 88(2), 75–9.

Wiss, R.A., Roberts, R.T. and David Phraner, S. (2000). Beyond design-build-operate-maintain: New partnership approach toward fixed guideway transit projects. *Transportation Research Record*, 1704(1), 13–18.

9. The total social cost (TSC) of public transport modes*

John Preston

9.1 INTRODUCTION

This chapter has two motivations. The first is that in public transport research the supply characteristics of public transport are relatively neglected. There are plenty of compendia on the demand for public transport (see Preston, 2015 for a summary, including examples from Australia, Canada, the EU, the UK and the US). However, there is relatively little on supply and hence costs, although for costs it is more difficult to generalise because they are so contingent on local conditions. The second, and inter-related, motivation is the need to determine when public transport is the most suitable form of transport supply and what type of public transport is suitable in what circumstances. One approach to answering this question is to undertake a series of bespoke cost–benefit analyses and then draw general inferences from these specific circumstances. An alternative approach that is the basis of this chapter is to develop a generic tool that can provide strategic answers. We call this tool a social cost model and our work in this area originates with the Tools for Evaluating Strategically Integrated Public Transport (TEST) project funded by the UK's Engineering and Physical Sciences Research Council (EPSRC) between May 2001 and April 2003, although as we shall see this modelling work has a much longer pedigree.

This chapter will be structured as follows. In the next section, we will very briefly outline the total social modelling approach. In subsequent sections, we will provide initial case study research into this topic in the UK and then consider international applications in China, Vietnam and Saudi Arabia. We will then draw some conclusions, particularly with respect to future work.

9.2 TOTAL SOCIAL COST MODELS

The starting point for this research is the pioneering study of Meyer et al. (1965) on the operator costs for different transport modes (auto, bus and rail) in different population density areas which indicated the levels of population (and hence traffic) density that can support conventional public transport. This work was advanced by the likes of Jansson (1984) who developed the concept of social costs as the sum of total producer costs and total user costs, whilst this was further elaborated by Brand and Preston (2003) by the addition of external costs, in particular related to the environment. This work is also influenced by public transport technology assessment by the likes of Vuchic (2007).

Total social costs (TSC) is simply the sum of total operator costs (TOC), total user costs (TUC) and total external costs (TEC):

$$TSC = TOC + TUC + TEC \tag{9.1}$$

where TOC cover all capital investment by infrastructure authorities and operators of the public transport service in addition to recurrent operating and maintenance costs. Capital costs are annualised using a Capital Recovery Factor that requires knowledge of design lives and interest rates (see, for example, Rogers and Duffy, 2012). TUC include passenger walking time and waiting time (collectively referred to as out-of-vehicle time) and in-vehicle time converted into money units using values of time, latterly using meta-studies such as Wardman et al. (2016). TEC accounts for external impacts such as climate change, air pollution, noise and accidents. In the results given in this chapter, congestion is internalised through the user cost calculations but it can be considered an externality in multimodal applications where both public and private transport are considered. It should be noted that within the TSC approach fare is considered a transfer between the operator and user and therefore is not considered. This is an important difference compared to the traditional social welfare approach to public transport in which forms of cost–benefit analysis are used (for example Jansson, 2005 and Preston et al., 2005). This has advantages in generalising the analysis in that pricing is context-specific, but has practical limitations when proffering design guidance for local public transport systems.

Average social cost (ASC) is then given by:

$$ASC = TSC/Q \tag{9.2}$$

where Q is a measure of output (typically passenger km or passenger trips).

Assuming TSC is a function solely of Q, marginal social cost is then given by:[1]

$$MSC = dTSC/dQ \tag{9.3}$$

In practice, it is difficult to observe the change in TSC as a result of a change of just one passenger km. Instead, incremental costs are calculated on the basis of non-marginal changes in passenger km, reflecting indivisibilities in both the demand and supply of public transport. Examples of the TSC approach applied by others include Jakob et al. (2006) and Tirachini et al. (2010), whilst CfIT (2005) demonstrate a practical example that determines when Metro systems might be feasible.

9.3   INITIAL TSC MODELS AND APPLICATIONS IN THE UK

The initial TEST model calculated the TSC (and variants) for up to 15 conventional and advanced public transport technologies for a typical 12 km long urban public transport route in a stand-alone spreadsheet model (Brand and Preston, 2003; 2006). This was based on data collated from 10 case studies, with an emphasis on intermediate public transport modes (such as Light Rapid Transit and variants of Bus Rapid Transit) and one personal rapid transit mode, based on the ULTra system currently operating at the business car park of Heathrow Terminal 5. These case studies are shown in Table 9.1.

The initial results of ASC and MSC are shown by Figures 9.1 and 9.2. In terms of average costs, a series of U-shaped curves are apparent. The downward-sloping portion

Table 9.1   Case studies for the initial TEST model

Rail-based alternatives	Bus-based alternatives
Light rail	*Guided bus*
1. Manchester Metrolink (Phases 1–3)	6. Leeds (Scott Hall Road, East Leeds)
2. Croydon Tramlink	7. Ipswich (*Superoute 66*)
Heavy and dual mode rail	*Conventional bus lane*
3. Robin Hood Line (Nottingham–Worksop)	8. Oxford (London Rd, Banbury Rd)
4. Karlsruhe dual mode rail (track sharing)	9. Heathrow M4 spur motorway bus lane
Personal public transport	*Other forms of Bus Priority*
5. ULTra system (Cardiff pilot scheme)	10. Edinburgh *Greenways*

Source: Brand and Preston (2006).

of these curves reflects fixed costs being spread across more and more traffic units. Such fixed costs are particularly important for systems with dedicated rights of way and signalling. The fixed costs for bus systems using mixed rights of way were determined using the fully allocated costs for Public Service Vehicles (PSVs) determined by Sansom et al. (2001), which was also an important source for input data on external costs. The upward-sloping portion of the U-shaped curve largely reflects congestion on the right of way, on vehicles and at stops. Such congestion costs are particularly marked for fixed track systems and systems with small vehicles, such as personal rapid transit (PRT). The marginal cost curves (or more correctly incremental cost curves as demand is increased in increments of 1000 passengers per direction per day) are upward sloping, their more jagged, saw's teeth, appearance representing the costs of additional vehicles (which is particularly a feature for systems with high capacity fixed vehicle sets).

Figure 9.1 indicates that in terms of social costs, buses are the best alternative up to passenger flows of around 30 000 pdd (passengers per direction per day). Between 30 000 and 60 000 pdd, light rail vehicle (LRV) track sharing (or tram-train as in Karlsruhe) appears to minimise social costs (but opportunities for such systems are limited by railway geography) although at the lower end of this demand range a lot of systems (including modern light rail) are close to the minimum cost frontier. Above 60 000 pdd, heavy rail systems appear to minimise social costs. The opportunities for guided bus systems appear limited but it should be noted we are assuming here that the technology is applied throughout the length of the corridor. In practice, guidance may be only required along a small section of the corridor to achieve most of the benefits, whilst congestion at stops can be reduced by coming off guidance. Modelling such flexible, hybrid systems requires bespoke approaches that are context specific.

However, these initial models have an important weakness in that they assume demand is exogenously fixed. In reality, demand will be endogenous. At a given externally fixed demand level, some public transport technologies will offer a better level of service in terms of in-vehicle and out-of-vehicle times, and hence lower average user costs, than other technologies and hence they would be expected, *inter alia*, to have higher levels of demand than technologies with inferior levels of service.

To overcome this, the initial version of TEST involved integrating a stand-alone

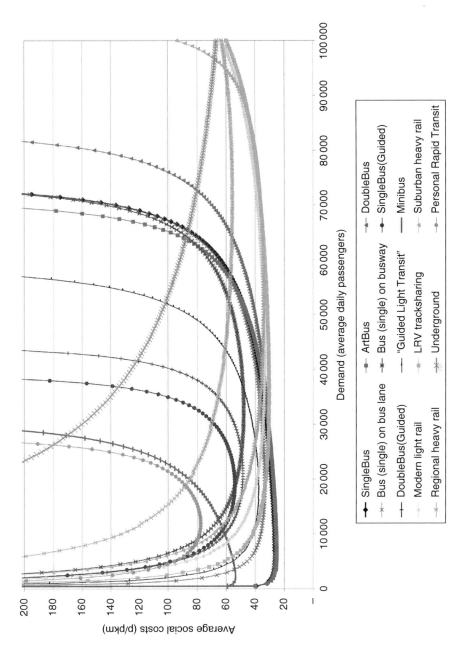

Source: Brand and Preston (2006).

Figure 9.1   Example of average social costs as a function of demand for a 12 km urban PT route (in pence per passenger-km, 2000 prices)

159

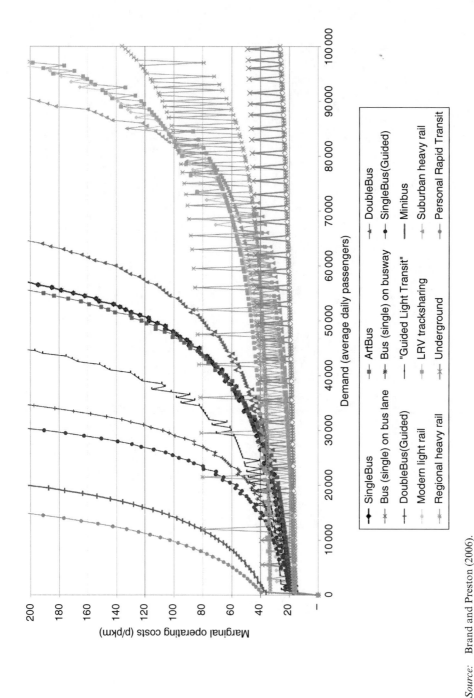

Source: Brand and Preston (2006).

Figure 9.2   Example of marginal social costs as a function of demand for a 12 km urban PT route (in pence per passenger-km, 2000 prices)

spreadsheet model with macroscopic public transport and private transport network assignment models[2] which were used to estimate the demand impacts of a proposed (and to-date unrealised) bus rapid transit system (called Guided Transit Express) between Kidlington, Oxford and Abingdon (Brand and Preston, 2006). This approach was cumbersome, so in follow-up work the impact on demand was assessed using public transport demand elasticities, using compendia such as Balcombe et al. (2004) and an iterative process illustrated by Figure 9.3 (Li and Preston, 2015a). The Social Cost Model (SCM) was used in conjunction with a Demand–Supply Model (DSM) in order to achieve this reconciliation.

The results of this iterative process are shown by Figure 9.4. The x-axis shows the demand level when it is externally fixed and the y-axis shows the demand level when the influences of supply on demand are introduced in the model. The endogenous demand levels are shown as a percentage of the current exogenous demand level to demonstrate the relationship between them.

From Figure 9.4, exogenous demand might be thought of as demand that is fixed at specified headways and journey times. At low demand levels, PRT stands out because of its higher frequency (due to small vehicles) and faster speeds (due to segregated right of way, high acceleration/deceleration rates and low dwell times), and in this case, endogenous demand is greater than exogenous. At high exogenous demand levels, endogenous demand is less than exogenous levels because this high passenger demand level would cause traffic congestion, which lowers vehicle operating speeds. In addition, the vehicles have to spend more time at stations/stops for boarding/alighting passengers.

Figure 9.4 demonstrates the potential attractiveness of 16 public transport technologies at different demand levels. For example, double deck bus technology has a higher ratio of endogenous to exogenous demand than other public transport modes for demand levels between 35000 and 75000 pdd. PRT and Minibus have very high endogenous demand levels compared to other public transport modes, especially before the exogenous demand reaches 21000 pdd. This is because the service intervals are much lower than for other technologies and thus much more attractive, particularly for passengers who value their waiting time highly. The endogenous:exogenous demand ratio for underground is relatively stable and indicates advantages compared to other modes at high exogenous demand levels. The reason is that the service interval of the underground service is very high with a low passenger demand level, but it can provide reasonable wait time and journey time with a high level of demand (from around 80000 pdd onwards), due to its high capacity and operational speed.

For all public transport technologies, the curves in Figure 9.4 exhibit some parabolic features as a result of the changing waiting time and journey time at different demand levels. The waiting time is decreasing at low demand levels due to the increasing service frequency for the increasing passenger numbers. However, the increasing passenger demand would also cause more boarding/alighting time and thus more delays. Journey time for all passengers increases with demand levels for modes with non-dedicated rights of way because speeds reduce when more vehicles are operating on the road. As a result of these phenomena, the curves in Figure 9.4 gradually grow until average user costs reach a minimum and then they start to decline as the modal capacity is reached.

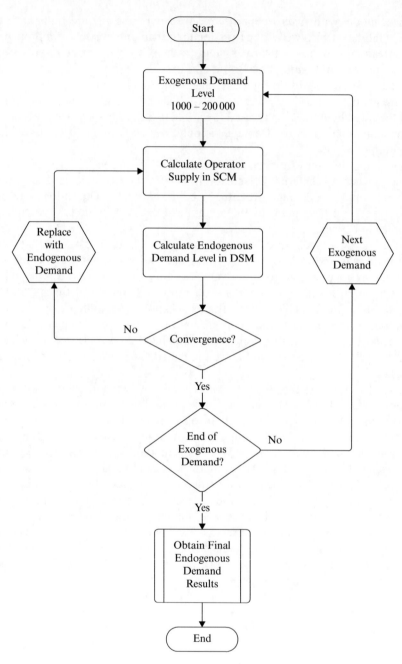

Figure 9.3   Operation procedure of the spreadsheet model

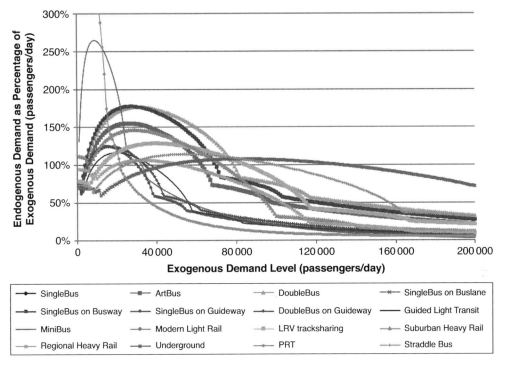

Source: Li and Preston (2015a).

Figure 9.4   Relationship between endogenous demand and exogenous demand

9.4   SUBSEQUENT TSC MODELS: INTERNATIONAL APPLICATIONS

Urban Transport in China

The first international application of our TSC modelling approach was to China. An additional public transport technology, straddle bus (also known as straddling bus or transit elevated bus), was included as it was being considered by a number of Chinese cities at the time (McDermon, 2010). Straddle bus is a new rapid transit concept that was developed by Shenzhen Huashi Future Parking Equipment Company and was launched at the 13th Beijing International High-tech Expo in 2010. The vehicle is designed to straddle two lanes and operate above the general traffic in order to utilise the unused space above private vehicles. The design dimensions of the straddle bus are described in more detail in an elaborate video by China TBS (2012).

Figure 9.5 illustrates the average social cost minimising technology when endogenous demand is taken into account. Minibus shows the lowest average social cost when the daily demand is less than 2000 pdd due to its low vehicle and infrastructure costs but a vehicle capacity of only 16 passengers. When the demand is higher than 2000 pdd, the lower investment but higher capacity advantages of conventional buses stand out by showing

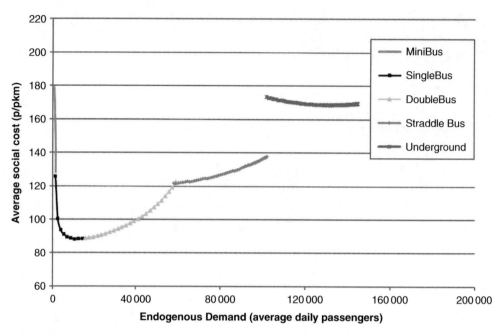

Source: Li and Preston (2015a).

Figure 9.5   Minimum average social cost after applying endogenous demand (pence per passenger km, 2011 prices)

the lowest social costs in the graph. Straddle bus also shows it has potential when the demand level is higher than 57 000 pdd. The higher capacity than normal buses and lower capital investments for vehicles and infrastructures than heavy rail and underground, as well as an electric motive design that lowers the external costs, make it achieve the lowest average social costs within the demand level range of 57 000 to 101 000 pdd. Underground technology has the highest capacity among all the public transport forms modelled for the default values. For demand levels above 101 000 pdd, the underground technology has the lowest average social costs while the costs of almost all other public transport forms are extremely high as the number of vehicles required is more than the infrastructure capacity, and congestion makes the user cost much higher. A noticeable feature is that the cost-minimising frontier is discontinuous between straddle bus and underground. After reaching the demand level of 101 000 pdd, straddle bus becomes less attractive for passengers and the actual demand level falls. This thus represents the capacity limit of this technology. Assumptions concerning vehicle capacity become important. For example, if the assumed fixed formation for suburban heavy rail is increased from three- to four-car units, the gap between straddle bus and underground will be reduced and filled by the curve of suburban heavy rail. Determination of optimal vehicle size and fleet size would require bespoke modelling.

Further improvements to the model are detailed in Li and Preston (2015b). First, the speed-flow equation in the original spreadsheet model assumed that speed decreases according to the ratio of the current frequency and the lane capacity. However, this may vary in different operating environments. Therefore, the speed-flow equation was improved by moving from a linear equation to a piecewise equation that considers the features of different operating environments (after Small, 1992, pp. 71–2). Capacity was determined for four different operating environments (mixed traffic, semi-exclusive, exclusive and grade separated) based on the Transportation Research Board's Transit Capacity and Quality of Service Manual (Ryus et al., 2013, pp. 3–34).

Secondly, the original model assumed that supply was sufficient to meet demand. However, when the level of demand is high for the lower capacity public transport technologies, passengers may find the incoming vehicle full and therefore they have to wait more than one service interval. Queuing theory was therefore applied to investigate the probability of having to wait longer than the expected service headways, which will affect the average passenger waiting time. The extra waiting time for each passenger is calculated and applied in the spreadsheet cost model.

The importance of these assumptions is shown by Figure 9.6. In the original model, the average social cost of a bus operating on a busway was always higher than that of operating in mixed traffic because the fixed costs of providing the exclusive right of way were not offset by the improved operating environment. In the revised model, when the demand level reaches around 51 400 pdd for the 12 km corridor, the advantages of having an exclusive right of way make the single-decker bus in a busway have the lowest average social costs. This is due to more realistic representation of congestion effects, both on the road and on the bus itself.

Straddle bus technology has a further complicating feature that needs to be considered. Turning vehicles are blocked by it when it passes through junctions (and the vehicles

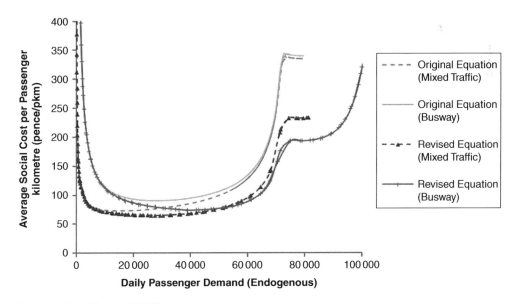

Source: Li and Preston (2015b).

Figure 9.6   *Average social cost of a single-decker bus in mixed traffic and on busway (pence per passenger km, 2011 prices)*

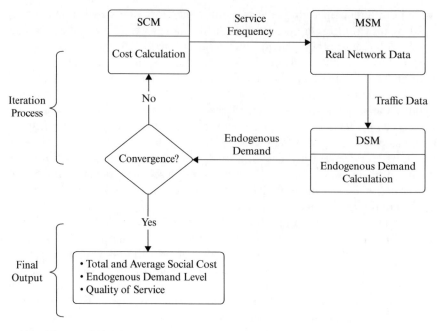

Source: Li and Preston (2015b).

Figure 9.7   Combination of social cost (SCM), demand–supply (DSM) and micro-simulation (MSM) models

would have a length of 38 metres), which would reduce the speed of general traffic. In addition, given the straddle bus is in effect a 'moving tunnel', the behaviour of car drivers underneath could be affected. As a result, a micro-simulation model (MSM) was developed using the VISSIM modelling suite and its Vehicle Actuated Programming (VAP) tool (PTV AG, 2012). As Figure 9.7 shows, this model was then linked with the Social Cost Model (SCM) and a Demand–Supply Model (DSM) (as per Figure 9.3) that endogenises the impact of supply on demand (Li et al., 2016).

The modelling framework was applied to Minzu Avenue in the southern Chinese city of Nanning, which in 2018 had a population of around 7.2 million. A corridor of around 12 km was modelled, with initial demand of 90 000 bus passengers over a modelled period of 11 hours. Initially, just car and bus were modelled, to which straddle bus and Underground rail were added as options. The SCM model was adapted to Chinese circumstances using benefit transfer techniques and a shadow exchange rate based on purchasing power parity (OECD, 2011), whilst the MSM was validated with locally collected traffic data (Li, 2015). Some results are shown by Table 9.2. This suggests that the straddle bus has substantially lower average social costs, although external costs are higher, than those of the proposed Underground system, although external costs are only around 1 per cent of total social costs. The main difference relates to the capital costs borne by the operator, which are much greater for Underground. Underground does produce lower in-vehicle times but this is more than offset by increased out-of-vehicle times. Both systems grow the public transport market compared to the existing bus system. The results suggest that Nanning

Table 9.2   Average cost and endogenous demand results (2011 prices)

	AOC (yuan / pkm)	AUC (yuan / pkm)	AEC (yuan / pkm)	ASC (yuan / pkm)	Endogenous Demand (pax / day)
Straddle Bus	1.24	1.00	0.033	2.27	115058
Underground	3.91	1.31	0.029	5.25	125762

Source: Li et al. (2016).

was not at the time of study ready for an Underground system but an intermediate system such as straddle bus could be appropriate.

In the event, Nanning considered the technology of straddle bus to be immature and instead developed a Metro system. Line 1 (32 km long) was opened in 2016 and covers Minzu Avenue. A total network of 252 km will be completed by 2021, consisting of eight lines.

Urban Transport in Vietnam

Other public transport applications of this approach are being developed. For example, Vu and Preston (2020) consider options for Hanoi, Vietnam. Here motorcycles are the dominant technology and hence this mode was incorporated into the modelling approach, along with taxis and ride sourcing modes such as Uber. In addition, public transport technologies under consideration include elevated Metro (as in Bangkok's Skytrain) and monorail (as in Kuala Lumpur). One urban corridor with a length of 7 km was modelled and characterised using eight transport modes including 125cc Motorcycle, Car, Uber, Taxi, Bus, BRT, Monorail and Elevated Metro. The model required further customisation, particularly with respect to speed-flow characteristics for motorcycles (Nguyen et al., 2007; Nguyen and Sano, 2012), operating costs for cars and taxis, and an appropriate value of time (based on Small and Verhoef, 2007). Some initial results are given by Figure 9.8.

Figure 9.8 shows that when the demand levels range from 1000 to 85000 pdd, the ASC of the motorcycle option is the lowest. When the demand is from 85000 to 125000 pdd, conventional bus shows the lowest ASC. Compared to motorcycles, the much higher capacity of bus is an advantage. Moreover, compared to rail-based technologies, the infrastructure costs and operator costs of bus-based technologies are significantly lower. This seems to be a benefit for conventional bus at low and medium demand levels. BRT is the best mode for a demand range of between 125000 and 220000 pdd although the ASCs of BRT and bus can be similar due to insignificant differences in vehicle capital costs and person capacity of vehicles. When the demand level is between 220000 and 310000 pdd, the ASC of Monorail is lowest, while the Metro has advantages with demand higher than 310000 pdd. Car, Uber and taxi are not cost-minimising modes at any demand level. Note that in this instance demand refers to the entire (motorised) transport market and not solely the (motorised) public transport market. Further work has been undertaken to examine multiple lanes, with the options of mixed traffic operations, and to enhance the model capability in terms of endogenising demand and dealing with multimodality.

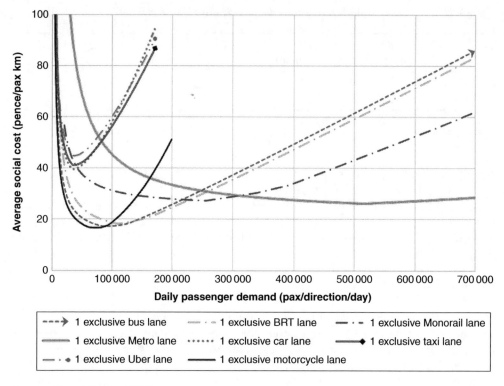

Figure 9.8   *Average social cost as a function of demand for one-lane (per direction) divided corridor (2015 prices)*

Inter-urban Transport in Saudi Arabia

The total social cost modelling approach can be applied to inter-urban public transport as well as intra-urban public transport. A typical distance considered is 500 km – as has been used to develop stylised models of high-speed rail (HSR) services (de Rus and Nombela, 2007). An application for Saudi Arabia has been developed by Almujibah and Preston (2018; 2019). The Riyadh–Dammam corridor is used as a case study (approximately 450 km). As of 2018, this corridor had a classic rail service, with 7 trains per day, a fastest journey time of around three and a half hours and annual patronage of 1.7 million. HSR could bring the journey time down to around one and a half hours (with Maglev offering even further reductions), whilst frequency would be increased. Given rapid economic and population growth, the forecasts are that on this corridor for 2030 HSR would attract 13.21 million passengers and Maglev 16.45 million. It should be noted that these demand levels seem excessive given that total travel (including air, car, coach and rail) between Riyadh and Dammam was only 4.5 million in 2018, with rail having an estimated 38 per cent share, although the 2030 forecasts include intermediate traffic at two additional stops. Some illustrative results in terms of total social costs are given by Table 9.3.

Table 9.3   Total social costs of HSR and Maglev systems (€ million 2009 prices)

	HSR	Maglev
Total Operator Costs	859.79	921.24
Total User Costs	216.77	245.50
Total External Costs	13.54	17.00
Total Social Costs	1090.10	1183.74
Annual Patronage (2030)	13.21	16.45
Average Social Cost	82.52	71.95

Source: Based on Almujibah and Preston (2019).

Table 9.3 shows that although HSR has lower overall total social costs, the Maglev system has almost 25 per cent higher demand due to higher speeds. As a result, average user costs for Maglev are around €14.92, compared to €16.41 for HSR – some 9 per cent lower. Similarly, average social costs for Maglev are 13 per cent lower than for HSR. However, as with straddle bus, Maglev is the less mature technology and it is likely that HSR will be provided on this corridor following the Haramain high speed rail route between Medina, Jeddah and Mecca (453 km, opened October 2018). These findings are also consistent with those for a much shorter inter-city corridor (Edinburgh–Glasgow, around 70 km) where cost–benefit analysis indicated Maglev could be preferable to HSR over a 60-year lifespan (Preston et al., 2009).

Given the uncertainties over the demand forecasts, work is on-going to get better estimates of future demand levels. This has included Stated Preference studies of the choice between air, car, classic rail, coach, HSR and Hyperloop (in essence a Maglev in a vacuum tube), despite some concerns with the feasibility of Hyperloop (see, for example, Hansen, 2019).

9.5   CONCLUSIONS

We have shown that the total social cost modelling approach to public transport has some advantages. It can easily characterise the economics of public transport supply in terms of U-shaped average costs and upward-sloping marginal cost curves (or approximations thereof). It can be used to strategically assess what form of public (or indeed private) transport is appropriate under different circumstances. It can be particularly useful in optioneering when a large number of possible public transport technologies are under consideration.

However, the assumptions concerning the performance of these technologies (vehicle size, acceptable load factor, vehicle performance, infrastructure capacity, etc.) and up-to-date and locally specific data on this performance are crucial. This in turn will require a good set of relevant case studies. As a result, the model is set up so that sensitivity analysis can be performed around the key parameters (including design lives and interest rates) and a move towards a more stochastic approach would be a useful line of further investigation. Furthermore, it is important to endogenise demand and correctly characterise the operating environment, especially in terms of congestion in the vehicle and on the right of way and in multimodal contexts.

Although social cost models can answer the broad question of what type of public transport technology should be operated, specific questions about vehicle size and frequency and the extent to which dedicated rights of way should be provided will require more bespoke approaches, often based on macro- or micro- simulation (or both). Additional analysis will also be required to determine fares and ticketing arrangements as they will critically affect demand levels.

Our work here is based on single corridors, but an obvious extension would be to extend the approach to networks, and some work has been done in this direction (Tirachini et al., 2010). In such cases, modelling interchange becomes crucial, whilst the possibility of mixed mode trips adds extra complexity. Adding new modes to the mix is also important. For short distance trips, walking and particularly cycling should be considered (see, for example, Wang, 2011), possibly along with shared e-bikes and e-scooters. Connected Autonomous Vehicles will also change the supply characteristics for both public and private transport, but this would require dynamic simulations of a type that are beyond the scope of this chapter (see, for example, Cats et al., 2016).

Overall, social costs models might be best suited for strategic level decisions on the appropriateness of a broad type of public transport technology for a particular corridor. This decision then can be validated by more detailed modelling that also considers fares and ticketing. This would involve a move towards project-level cost–benefit analysis, although of course this is not without its own problems (see, for example, Hickman and Dean, 2017).

NOTES

*   This work was initiated at the University of Oxford in collaboration with Christian Brand (still at the University of Oxford) and with the support of EPSRC, the Go-Ahead Group and Mott Macdonald. It has continued at the University of Southampton through doctoral research by Xucheng Li (now at the Shenzhen Urban Transport Planning Center), Hamad Almujibah (also of Taif University) and Minh Tam Vu (also of the National University of Civil Engineering, Hanoi). I am hugely indebted to their contributions. The usual caveat applies.
1. In reality, other factors will also be relevant (not least input prices) and a partial differentiation will be required. However, this is beyond the scope of this chapter. Again, this helps generalise the analysis, but also leads to practical limitations.
2. VIPS (now part of VISUM) was used for public transport and SATURN/CONTRAM for private transport.

REFERENCES

Almujibah, H. and Preston, J. (2018) The Total Social Costs of Constructing and Operating a Maglev Line Using a Case Study of the Riyadh–Dammam Corridor, Saudi Arabia. *Transportation Systems and Technology*, 4, 3, 298–327.
Almujibah, H. and Preston, J. (2019) The Total Social Costs of Constructing and Operating an High-Speed Rail Line Using a Case Study of the Riyadh–Dammam Corridor, Saudi Arabia. *Frontiers in the Built Environment*, 5, 79, 1–18.
Balcombe, R., Mackett, R., Paulley, N., Preston, J., Shires, J., Titheridge, H., Wardman, M. et al. (2004) *The Demand for Public Transport: A Practical Guide*. Crowthorne: Transport Research Laboratory.
Brand, C. and Preston, J. (2003) Which Technology for Urban Public Transport? *Proceedings of the Institution of Civil Engineers: Transport*, 156, 201–10.
Brand, C. and Preston, J. (2006) TEST – A Tool for Evaluating Strategically Integrated Public Transport. Paper presented at the *European Transport Conference*, Strasbourg.

Cats, O., West, J. and Eliasson, J. (2016) A Dynamic Stochastic Model for Evaluating Congestion and Crowding Effects in Transit Systems. *Transportation Research Part B*, 89, 43–57.

CfIT (Commission for Integrated Transport) (2005) *Affordable Mass Transit Guidance. Helping you Choose the Best System for Your Area.* London: CfIT.

China TBS (2012) Incredible way of future transportation – Straddling Bus (3D bus). [Online video] 17 February. Accessed 23 January 2020 at: https://www.youtube.com/watch?v=t1gTzc7-IbQ.

de Rus, G. and Nombela, G. (2007) Is investment in HSR socially profitable? *Journal of Transport Economics and Policy*, 41, 1, 3–23.

Hansen, I.A. (2019) Hyperloop – A System Engineering Analysis. Paper presented at the *World Conference on Transport Research*. Mumbai, 26–31 May.

Hickman, R. and Dean, M. (2017) Incomplete cost – incomplete benefit analysis in transport appraisal. *Transport Reviews*, 38, 6, 689–709.

Jakob, A., Craig, J.L. and Fisher, G. (2006) Transport cost analysis: A case study of the total costs of private and public transport in Auckland. *Environmental Science & Policy*, 9, 1, 55–66.

Jansson, J.O. (1984) *Transport System Optimisation and Pricing.* Chichester: John Wiley & Sons.

Jansson, J.O. (2005) *Key Factors for Boosting the Bus Transport Market in Medium Sized Towns.* In D. Hensher (ed.), *Competition and Ownership in Land Passenger Transport.* Oxford: Elsevier.

Li, X. (2015) *A Comparative Assessment for Innovative Public Transport Technologies.* PhD Thesis, Faculty of Engineering and the Environment, University of Southampton.

Li, X. and Preston, J. (2015a) Assessing the Financial and Social Costs of Public Transport in Differing Operating Environments and with Endogenous Demand. *Transportation Planning and Technology*, 38, 1, 28–43.

Li, X. and Preston, J. (2015b) Reassessing the Financial and Social Costs of Public Transport. *Proceedings of the Institution of Civil Engineers: Transport*, 168, 4, 356–69.

Li, X., Preston, J. and Shrestha, B. (2016) A Model for Evaluating and Comparing Social Cost of Different Public Transport Technologies with Endogenous Demand. Paper presented at the *World Conference on Transport Research*, Shanghai, 10–15 July.

McDermon, D. (2010) Riding High: A Chinese Concept for Bus Transit, *New York Times*, 8 August.

Meyer, J.R., Kain, J.F. and Wohl, M. (1965) *The Urban Transportation Problem.* Cambridge, MA: Harvard University Press.

Nguyen, C.Y. and Sano, K. (2012) Estimating Capacity and Motorcycle Equivalent Units on Urban Roads in Hanoi, Vietnam. *Journal of Transportation Engineering*, 138, 6, 776–85.

Nguyen, C.Y., Sano, K. and Chu, C.M. (2007) Dynamic motorcycle unit and mean stream speed under mixed traffic conditions on urban roads. *Journal of the Eastern Asia Society for Transportation Studies*, 7, 2439–53.

OECD (Organisation for Economic Co-operation and Development) (2011) *Purchasing Power Parities (PPPs) Data.* Paris: OECD.

Preston, J. (2015) Public Transport Demand. In C. Nash (ed.), *Handbook of Research Methods and Applications in Transport Economics and Policy.* Cheltenham, UK and Northampton, MA, USA: Edward Elgar Publishing, pp. 192–211.

Preston, J., Armstrong, J. and Docherty, I. (2009) The Economic Case for High Speed Rail: The Case of Glasgow–Edinburgh. Paper presented at the RGS/IBG Conference, University of Manchester.

Preston, J., Huang, B. and Whelan, G. (2005) *Determining Optimal Bus Service Provision: The Role of Quality in the Service Mix.* In D. Hensher (ed.), *Competition and Ownership in Land Passenger Transport.* Oxford: Elsevier.

PTV AG (2012). *VAP 2.16 User Manual.* Karlsruhe: PTV AG.

Rogers, M. and Duffy, A. (2012) *Engineering Project Appraisal.* Chichester: John Wiley & Sons.

Ryus, P., Danaher, A., Walker, M., Nichols, F., Carter, B., Ellis, E., Cherrington, L. et al. (2013). *Transit Capacity and Quality of Service Manual*, 3rd edn. Washington, DC: Transportation Research Board.

Sansom, T., Nash, C., Mackie, P., Shires, J. and Watkiss, P. (2001) *Surface Transport Costs and Charges: Great Britain 1998.* Report commissioned by the Department of Environment, Transport and the Regions. Institute for Transport Studies, University of Leeds and AEA Technology Environment, Culham.

Small, K.A. (1992) *Urban Transportation Economics.* Chur: Harwood Academic Publishers.

Small, K.A. and Verhoef, E.T. (2007) *The Economics of Urban Transportation.* New York: Routledge.

Tirachini, A., Hensher, D.A. and Jara-Díaz, S.R. (2010) Comparing Operator and Users Costs of Light Rail, Heavy Rail and Bus Rapid Transit over a Radial Public Transport Network. *Research in Transportation Economics*, 29, 1, 231–42.

Vu, T. and Preston, J. (2020) Assessing the Social Costs of Urban Transport Infrastructure Options in Low and Middle Income Countries. *Transportation Planning and Technology*, forthcoming.

Vuchic, V.R. (2007) *Urban Transit Systems and Technology.* Hoboken, NJ: John Wiley & Sons.

Wang, R. (2011) Autos, Transit and Bicycles: Comparing the Costs in Large Chinese Cities. *Transport Policy*, 18, 1, 139–46.

Wardman, M., Chintakayala, P.K. and de Jong, G. (2016) Values of Travel Time in Europe: Review and Meta-Analysis. *Transportation Research Part A: Policy and Practice*, 94, 93–111.

10. New approaches and insights to managing on-road public transport priority

James Reynolds and Graham Currie

10.1 INTRODUCTION

The technical justification for transit priority in congested urban conditions is simple. Buses and streetcars can move people more efficiently than private cars and therefore can make better use of the limited road space and intersection time that is available in urban areas.[1] Clear examples of the potential of prioritising transit are provided by the successful implementation of priority measures in Zurich (Nash 2001; 2003; Mees 2010; Nash et al. 2018) and Curitiba's bus system, which rivals the capacity of heavy rail and has made the city famous as the 'cradle of Bus Rapid Transit' (BRT) (Lindau et al. 2010b). However, implementing transit priority measures is not necessarily easy in practice, particularly in more car-centric cities where opposition may be more likely.

Toronto and Melbourne provide examples of more car-centric cities where some transit priority implementations have been delayed, partially removed or cancelled entirely.[2] The research literature has identified broader issues including that transit signal priority schemes have been quietly removed by some road authorities (Currie 2016). Unfortunately, transport research is yet to come to grips fully with how non-technical factors such as politics, institutions and governance structures can help or hinder transit priority implementation (Ardila-Gomez 2004; Pulichino and Coughlin 2005; Nash et al. 2018), in part because authorities may be 'keener to publish success stories than to share learnings resulting from system failures' (Currie 2016, p. 490). More generally, research in transportation policy journals tends to focus on techno-rational[3] approaches based around normative models,[4] technology development and statistical and quantitative analysis (Mees 2010) despite 'a need to engage with substantive questions of governance which pay greater attention to context, politics, power, resources and legitimacy' (Marsden and Reardon 2017).

This chapter responds to this gap as it relates to on-road transit priority implementation. It outlines a new conceptual framework and pragmatic strategies for transit priority implementation in car-centric cities, which have emerged from a PhD research programme.[5] This research has used case research methodology to examine the empirical context of priority implementation in Melbourne, Toronto, Zurich and Curitiba through the lens of public policy analysis and legitimacy theory. The research findings suggest three approaches for improving the implementation of transit priority in car-centric cities: building legitimacy *before* implementation; *avoiding impacts* on other road users; and building legitimacy *through* implementation.

This chapter is structured as follows: first, the background research context is discussed through an outline of techno-rationalist perspectives, a discussion of the need for new perspectives, and a brief description of public policy analysis and legitimacy theory.

Section 10.3 outlines the case research methodology used in this study and provides a brief summary of the cases that have been examined. A new framework through which to conceptualise the legitimacy of transit priority is presented in section 10.4, followed by a discussion in section 10.5 of three approaches and nine pragmatic strategies for transit priority implementation in car-centric cities. Finally, section 10.6 summarises the key findings, identifies implications for practice, and suggests future research directions.

10.2   RESEARCH CONTEXT

The purpose of transit priority is typically to improve the speed and reliability of on-street transit services. However, priority measures may also impact transit operations, ridership, traffic operations, driver behaviour, mode use, road use efficiency, social equity, cost, safety, risk, land use and issues related to strategic objectives (Waterson et al. 2003; Currie 2016; Litman 2016). These various impacts may be assigned greater or lesser importance during evaluation and policy-making, depending on the perspectives that are adopted by decision-makers. For example, road authorities may tend to oppose transit priority measures that negatively impact traffic flow or decrease road capacity (Vuchic 2007, p. 243).

10.2.1   Techno-rationalist Perspectives

Traffic engineering has historically tended towards evaluation perspectives that emphasise vehicle movement and delay minimisation. This is now giving way to perspectives that emphasise moving people and goods, the accessibility of activities and services, economic efficiency, transit operations, horizontal and vertical social equity, environmental impacts, safety or strategic planning (Litman 2003; 2016; Ryus et al. 2016). However, all of these evaluation perspectives are grounded in techno-rationalist ways of thinking, which are reminiscent of the large-scale transport planning approaches such as the classic four-stage model, the Chicago Area Transportation Study (CATS) planning scheme, the Urban Transportation Planning System, and the Systems Approach (Thomas 1966; Dimitriou 1992, pp. 35–44; Mees 2003b, pp. 1–2; Garrison and Levinson 2006, pp. 283–95; Stopher and Stanley 2014, p. 19; McPherson 2017, pp. 796–7). These are similar to the early periods of public policy analysis from the 1940s to the 1970s when the field was focused on methods of rationally selecting the 'best option' when making decisions (Parsons 1995; Turnpenny et al. 2013).

What might be missed when using this mindset is that it is often political concerns, rather than engineering details, that drive real-world decision-making about transit priority. The optimal technical solution may not matter much when setting policy and allocating limited road space and intersection time. In democracies these choices are instead tested at city council meetings, on the floors of parliamentary bodies and ultimately, albeit indirectly, during elections at the ballot box.

Further complicating transit priority policy is that Currie (2016) suggests that the 'best option' (the 'state of the art') is not just a simple and almost unconditional duty to always favour transit. Rather, the appropriate level of transit priority instead depends on the role of transit in a city, mode share and patterns of use, as shown in the conceptual model in Figure 10.1.

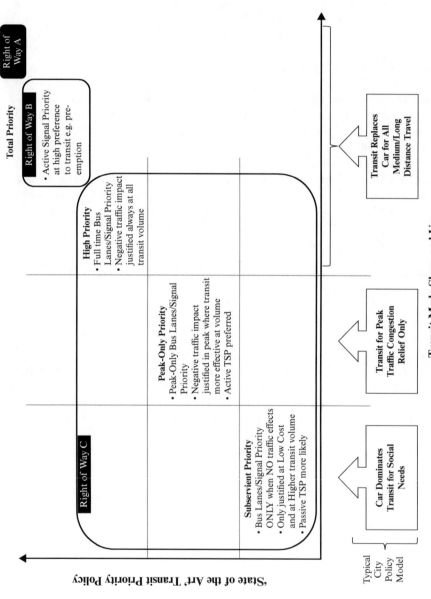

Source: Currie (2016).[6]

Figure 10.1   Conceptual model for the 'state of the art' in on-road public transport priority design

This is a normative model that suggests that:

- if a city is car-centric, but provides transit to allow those who cannot otherwise drive to have at least some motorised mobility, then transit priority should be subservient to, and not impact on, traffic operations;
- if a city is car-centric, but provides transit primarily to improve mobility when traffic demand is at its worst, then transit priority that negatively impacts other road users should only be provided in peak periods when the effectiveness of the road network is already limited by congestion;
- in transit-centric cities, where public transport provides a realistic alternative to the car for trips beyond walking or cycling distance, transit should receive high levels of priority when operating in mixed traffic, or should receive total priority through longitudinal- or grade-separation from other traffic.

Of course, transport policy in the real world is not so clear cut and '[i]n practice all cities probably exhibit aspects of policy of each of the types . . . in separate parts of the city' (Currie 2016, p. 492). However, while a practitioner might be tempted to start drawing boundaries on city maps that match with these three types of policy, this would again be a techno-rational approach, albeit adopting a strategic objectives perspective.

Unfortunately, these types of strategic-level policy planning approaches appear to have sometimes contributed to previous unsuccessful efforts to implement transit priority in car-centric cities. In 'Who Killed Melbourne 2030' Mees (2011) argues that a lack of public consultation and a top-down, secretive and technocratic planning process led to the failure of the city-wide strategic plans (VicDOI 2002; VicDOT 2008; VicPCD 2008). *Melbourne 2030* had provided the motivation for the *Think Tram* programme (Yarra Trams et al. 2004), which initially sought to decrease tram journey times by 25 per cent. However, after public opposition resulted in a compromise partial removal of the pilot project the programme switched to a more consultative approach, and ultimately had only a limited impact on tram speeds and reliability (Currie and Shalaby 2007; Currie et al. 2013). In Toronto, the answer to 'who votes for a mayor like Rob Ford?' (Taylor 2013) perhaps more clearly shows how top-down policies can fail to change political realities. Ford ended the 'war on the car' (Kalinowski and Rider 2010) on his first day in office by cancelling the *Transit City* plan for seven new Light Rail Transit (LRT) lines along arterial roads in the City of Toronto. He had been carried to an election victory by a wave of support from suburban voters, who likely saw at-grade LRT that would reduce road capacity as an attack on their existing, car-orientated mobility.

Transit mode shares have helped to support transit priority implementation programs in Zurich and Curitiba, but may have lessened the cases for prioritising transit in Melbourne and Toronto.[7, 8] However, acceptance that low transit mode shares automatically lead to subservient transit priority, which causes low transit speeds, reliability and attractiveness, and then inevitably circles back around to low transit mode shares again suggests submission to the path dependence of car-dominance and simply giving up in some cities. In Chapter 3, Aston et al. discussed the influence of the built environment on transit use. The results of some modelling-based research suggest that policy should be directed towards building rail transit and increasing nearby urban densities to reduce car-dependence (McIntosh et al. 2014). However, if at-grade LRT is politically infeasible and the expense of subways is difficult to justify in low-density suburbs it might appear impossible to move forward in car-centric cities without burning everything down and starting again (c.f. Gambetta and Hertog (2017)).

10.2.2   The Need for New Perspectives

Activist-academics in urban planning have long since found ways to engage in public debate that does not involve grand plans or normative dreams of how the world 'should' be. For example, Jane Jacobs was involved in protests that ultimately halted the proposed Spadina Expressway, preventing it from running directly through existing suburbs in inner Toronto (Osbaldeston 2008; Laurence 2016), as well as writing a highly influential book on life in urban environments (Jacobs 1961). In Melbourne, Paul Mees was chair of the Public Transport Users Association before moving into academia, but remained very active in public debates on transport and in opposition to some of the more technocrat-led, top-down approaches to policy change (Mees 2000; 2003a; 2003b; 2010; 2011; Burke 2013; Gleeson and Beza 2014).

In contrast, engineering approaches appear to avoid conflict and protests, and instead emphasise that 'dialogue and consensus building are effective processes to resolve various concerns, to lead to "buy in" by stakeholders . . . and to build partnerships for sharing some of the costs' (King 2003, p. 47) when seeking to change policy relating to transit priority. However, practical experience shows that regardless of the technical merits of a proposal, the 'real challenges for preferential treatment are the management of all the stakeholders . . . as conflicting interests are likely to (result in) opposition' (Pulichino 2003, p. 26). This lack of recognition that transit priority is really a political issue is not just a problem for engineers in more car-dominant cities. Deputy Director of the Zurich Transport Authority Ernst Joos' first message to other cities about the success of transit priority implementation in Zurich following the successful passing of the 1977 Citizen's Transit Priority Initiative was that 'if you ask the inhabitants of a town which transport policy should be followed, the citizens will not choose the car' (Joos 1994). However, this appears to overlook that prior to the 1977 vote 49 per cent of journey-to-work travel by the residents of the city was already on transit (Nash 2001, p. 44), that the Citizen's Transit Priority Initiative was passed by only a narrow margin of 51 per cent to 49 per cent, and that further advocacy was required to overcome initial reluctance and actually get the Initiative enacted (Joos 1989; 1990; 1994; Cervero 1998; Nash 2001; 2003; Mees 2010). For a city that is more car-centric than Zurich, where a much smaller proportion of travellers use transit, such success might appear impossible.

The potential for success through staged implementation has previously been identified in the BRT literature (Levinson et al. 2003a, pp. 185–90), but this lacks connection to public policy analysis perspectives provided by the landmark papers of Lindblom (1959; 1979) that introduced the concept of incrementalism. Similarly, transport literature that suggests identifying a champion for transit prioritisation (e.g. Baker et al. 2004, p. 10) lacks clear connection to established theories of implementation and advocacy coalitions (Sabatier 1987; 1988; Jenkins-Smith 1990; Sabatier and Jenkins-Smith 1993; 1999), and empirical research showing that a policy entrepreneur is *not essential* for successful transit priority implementation (Pulichino and Coughlin 2005, p. 85).

There is a large volume of research literature about how Curitiba's BRT system may provide a model for other cities, who should adopt the same technology. However, many appear to have missed the fact that a military dictatorship governed Brazil well into the 1980s, and it is this that helped 'Curibita's mayor to push for an aggressive implementation' (Pulichino 2003, p. 12) of the BRT technology. Engineering researchers are understandably focused on technical innovation rather than political context, but politics, institutional factors and other non-rational factors may help to explain why BRT might have been more difficult to implement in other places. Some of Curitiba's buses and boarding tubes were sent to New York and run on a demonstration loop around the streets of Manhattan for six weeks (Worcam 1993). The trial was successful but ended without permanent adoption of the technology, illustrating a 'failure of technical replica without prior policy making' (Pulichino and Coughlin 2005, pp. 80–81).

The promises of the BRT technology may have suggested that 'many cities that previously could not dream of a quality public transport system may be able to implement systems within a matter of years' (Wright 2010). However, the realities may be better explained by the theories of cross-national policy diffusion, policy transfer, iso-morphism and decoupling,[9] none of which appear to have been widely considered in transit priority literature. Instead BRT continues to battle it out against LRT in the research literature as to which technology is technically superior,[10] despite neither appearing to be politically popular if implementation worsens conditions for other traffic. Meanwhile, the hype surrounding autonomous vehicles may be starting to peak (Currie 2018), but even more outlandish and possibly impractical concepts such as the straddling bus (Fullerton 2017) and the hyperloop continue to compete for limited research and technological development funding. Unfortunately, society appears to be simply rehashing the previous defeats of personal rapid transit, the monorail, and other high-tech, silver-bullet solutions that have tended to fail to deliver on promised technological utopias because of the physics of friction and rolling resistance, path dependency, and other practical challenges.[11]

What is needed is to move beyond the obsession with developing yet more grand technological solutions, and instead to adopt public policy analysis theories to understand how to prioritise our existing on-road transit services in the real-world of public decision-making, institutions and politics (Reynolds et al. 2017). Transport policy research is currently dominated by techno-rationalism (Marsden and Reardon 2017) despite many issues, including transit prioritisation, being decided in political battles over the allocation of street space (Ardila-Gomez 2004; Nash et al. 2018). New approaches to road network operations planning may suggest some ways forward, but transit priority implementation '**cannot be viewed from a purely technical perspective** . . . [and] it is essential to study policy-making processes' (Pulichino and Coughlin 2005, p. 80).[12]

10.2.3   Public Policy Analysis Perspectives

Public policy analysis dates from efforts in the early twentieth century to understand and improve decision- and policy-making (Parsons 1995, p. 17; Caramani 2011; Peters 2011; 2015). There are now a 'wild and ever-escalating cacophony of decision-making theories, models, processes, tools, techniques, and approaches' (Fitzgerald 2002, p. 2) across a wide range of research disciplines. *Rationality* has already been touched on in the above discussion of techno-rationalism in transport research. However, public policy analysis theory provides more precise definitions and insights through concepts such as bounded rationality (also known as 'satisficing' and which involves selecting the first acceptable option), quasi-satisficing (selecting an obviously acceptable option without considering other choices) elimination by aspects, and the policy cycle model (Janis and Mann 1977; Huber 1981; Hickson 1987; Lyles and Thomas 1988; Eisenhardt and Zbaracki 1992; Fischer and Forester 1993; Parsons 1995; Turpin and Marais 2004; Weible et al. 2009; Caramani 2011; Knill and Tosun 2011; Peters 2011). *Institutionalism* focuses on how organisational structures can impact on decision-making (Huber 1981, p.4; Shrivastava and Grant 1985; Parsons 1995; Turpin and Marais 2004, p.145; Caramani 2011; Peters 2011). However, public policy analysis moved beyond these perspectives in the mid-twentieth century during the 'behavioural revolution', which shifted the field towards a greater emphasis on individual decision-makers and politics (Caramani 2011; Peters 2011).

Incrementalism was introduced and refined by Lindblom (1959; 1979). It describes policy as typically changing through only small steps as decision-makers 'muddle through' complex environments. This might involve: *simple incrementalism*, in which decisions are independent; *disjointed incrementalism*; in which policy changes in accordance with general visions or goals; *strategic analysis*, in which policy changes until a specific objective is reached; or *'no longer fiddling'*, in which policy change is no longer incremental.

Political approaches to public policy analysis consider how bargaining between stakeholders, decision-makers and other actors influences policy development (Huber 1981; Shrivastava and Grant 1985; Lyles and Thomas 1988; Eisenhardt and Zbaracki 1992; Das and Bing-Sheng 1999; Turpin and Marais 2004; Caramani 2011; Stopher and Stanley 2014). The early Easton (1965) model conceptualises the political system as a black box, which takes demands and support as inputs and outputs decisions. *Implementation theory* developed out of this and other political models as researchers explored: centralised and *top-down* policy-making; *bottom-up* actions by 'street-level implementers' who are closer to the real problems and so may oppose, reinforce or co-opt central policies; and *hybrid models* that consider how advocacy coalitions, policy brokers and other factors might impact decision-making (Pressman and Wildavsky 1984; Sabatier 1986; Parsons 1995, p.469; Pülzl and Treib 2007; Weible and Sabatier 2007; Weible et al. 2009; Althaus et al. 2013; Weible and Nohrstedt 2013; Stopher and Stanley 2014, pp.322–9; Marsden and Reardon 2017; Reynolds et al. 2017).

Unfortunately, 'some of the most damaging urban transport decisions . . . have been top-down measures imposed by higher-level governments' (Mees 2010, p.159), often based on large-scale strategic approaches to transportation and land-use planning. However, some bottom-up approaches that seek to include citizens in decision-making are already evident in transportation, such as in Local Area Traffic Management, tactical urbanism, and the Movement & Place and Complete Streets frameworks. These can even push into unsanctioned and potentially illegal direct actions undertaken independently by citizens such as: guerrilla gardening and street-art; the invention of the first *woornef*, which was quietly ignored by local officials until formal approval was obtained (Lydon and Garcia 2015, p.28); and a recent protest in Seattle that involved passengers at bus stops stopping drivers from illegally using the transit lane.[13]

The many public policy analysis models may provide new frameworks through which to examine transit priority implementation. However, these do not necessarily provide clear guidance about how to respond to the consistent theme emerging from Nash (2001; 2003); Pulichino (2003); Ardila-Gomez (2004); Pulichino and Coughlin (2005); Nash et al.

(2018) and Marsden and Reardon (2017), which is that implementing priority measures is about politics. For this there is a need to turn to international relations, comparative politics, organisational behaviour and other related fields and the subject of *legitimacy*.

10.2.4 Legitimacy Theory

Legitimacy is important as it 'affects power, and power matters because it creates the ability – in some views, is just the ability – to get things done' (Meyer and Sanklecha 2009, p. 2). It is widely studied in international relations because there are no democratic elections to legitimise international organisations (Buchanan and Keohane 2009, pp. 29–31), but legitimacy also has importance in political science and philosophy because 'politicians and authorities are constantly trying to legitimise their decisions and actions . . . [and] legitimacy assures that political rule is more than merely the raw power of coercion or the strategic force of inducement' (Netelenbos 2016, p. 1). There are various types of *legitimacy*, which are summarised in Table 10.1.

Table 10.1   Forms of legitimacy

Type of legitimacy	Definition	Example
Normative	Relating to the rule of law and the 'right to rule' (Buchanan and Keohane 2009, p. 29).	The law requires a bus lane.
Sociological	Where an entity 'is widely *believed* to have the right to rule' (Buchanan and Keohane 2009, p. 29).	Everyone thinks that there should be a bus lane.
Public consent	Where the agreement of the public with the system of governance and decision-making legitimises the decisions that are made (Meyer and Sanklecha 2009, p. 3).	The public voted for a bus lane.
Reasonableness	Involving compliance with established processes, but also the *fairness* of the processes and outcomes (Meyer and Sanklecha 2009, pp. 5–6; Netelenbos 2016, pp. 226–30).	Buses make more efficient use of road space and the warrants are met, so a bus lane is reasonable.
Unconditional duty	Where there is a 'content-independent obligation to obey' (Meyer and Sanklecha 2009, p. 6).	Other vehicles are not allowed in the bus lane, regardless of whether they delay a bus or not.
Trust	Where there is trust in organisations or authorities, which may occur through a 'subjective leap of faith' (Netelenbos 2016, pp. 119–68).	The transport engineers said that a bus lane was needed, so it must be necessary.
Conditional normative support	Where there is agreement in principle with an idea, but support is dependent on circumstances (Netelenbos 2016, pp. 71–113).	There should always be bus lanes, but only if it does not reduce traffic capacity.

Source: Author's synthesis.

On-road transit priority operates within the context of almost *unconditionally legitimate* traffic laws, backed by enforcement through a sovereign nation's *normative* and *sociological legitimacy* and monopoly on the use of force. However, overlapping issues of *reasonableness, conditionality, public consent* and *trust* are evident in decision-making based on bus lane warrants (Vuchic 2007, p. 245; Litman 2016), driver attitudes to tram lanes (Currie 2009, p. 66), and the wider acceptance of traffic enforcement (Jason and Liotta 1982; Basford et al. 2002; Amanda et al. 2005, p. 406; Norton 2007; Johnson et al. 2011; 2013; Longhurst 2015). Similarly, the 'dehumanisation of cyclists' (Delbosc et al. 2019) and the adversarial legal system that underpins enforcement and policy-making (Hayden 2009; Furness 2010; Lunceford 2012, pp. 74–89; Morhayim 2012; Henderson 2013; Reynolds 2019) all suggest that transit priority implementation exists within a non-techno-rational system where the rule of law is just one of the many sources of legitimacy.

10.3   RESEARCH APPROACH

Case studies involve researchers investigating phenomena in their real world context by examining a small number of cases in great depth while seeking at the same time to make generalisable findings that apply to more than just the cases that are studied (Yin 2009; 2014; 2018; Barratt et al. 2011, p. 329; Ketokivi and Choi 2014). Unfortunately, case research is sometimes misunderstood or rejected by people more familiar with quantitative methods, but it is a well-established method that uses observation, deduction and replication to generate, test or elaborate theory.[14] Yin (2009, p. 8; 2014; 2018) provides clear guidance on case study methodology, which supports its use in studying transit priority implementation because: questions about implementation are about 'how' and 'why', rather than 'what' or 'how much'; and events cannot be fully controlled, which limits the use of experimental methods.

Four cases have been examined in this research: Zurich, Curitiba, Melbourne and Toronto. There have been efforts to implement transit priority in each of these cities, but with varying degrees of success. Fortunately, there is already a large volume of literature about these cities, so instead of further primary data collection, this research examines transit priority implementation through this existing material, but from a new angle through the lens of public policy analysis and legitimacy theory. Cases were interrogated using questions about how or why each type of *legitimacy* was relevant to priority implementation. New theory was developed and elaborated on using cross-case comparison, explanation building and through the drift and iteration that is typical in case research (Bonoma 1984, pp. 204–205; Voss et al. 2002, p. 216).

Table 10.2 provides a brief summary of the cases and implementations studied in this research.[15] In general in the more transit-centric cities: the success in Zurich was legitimised by public votes that rejected moving transit underground and then called for transit priority implementation, but it took time to move away from implementation being conditional on limiting traffic impacts; and in Curitiba legitimacy was built on technical enquiry and seminars that led to the adoption of a new city plan, authority and *normative legitimacy* provided by a military dictatorship, and an incremental approach to introducing busways and further improvements gradually across the city. For the more car-centric cities: transit priority measures in Melbourne were removed because of

Table 10.2 Summary of cases

City	Implementation	Summary
Zurich *Transit-centric* Transit mode share: journey-to-work 76%, all trips 41%.	*Citizen's Transit Priority Initiative*	• Moving streetcars underground and building a U-Bahn were rejected in public ballots in 1962 and 1973 respectively. • A *Citizen's Transit Priority Initiative* was submitted in 1973, but opposed by the city who preferred less ambitious approaches with less impact on traffic. However, the Initiative was narrowly passed by 51% to 49% in 1977. • Transit priority levels have since increased and there has been a gradual shift to a *Waiting Time Zero* policy for transit. • Another ballot initiative in 1991 provided further funding and transit prioritisation continues to the present.
Curitiba *Transit-centric* Transit mode share: journey-to-work 70–75%, all trips 45%	*Structural axes* and *busways* *Direct bus services* and *bus boarding tubes*	• A coup d'état in 1964 resulted in a military dictatorship ruling Brazil. The Mayor of Curitiba became an appointed position. • A competition between planning firms and a seminar series led to a new city plan being adopted in 1965. This called for linear growth along a north–south 'structural axis'. A central busway and one-way streets a block away on either side to provide traffic capacity were added to the plan, but it stalled until Jamie Lerner was appointed Mayor in 1971. • The north–south busway opened in 1974. Lerner's term ended, but his group of technocrats continued to hold power. • More structural axes were added to the city plan, two more busways were built and crosstown services were introduced. • Civilian government gradually returned to Brazil in the 1980s and Lerner was elected as mayor in 1989. • The busways were reaching capacity, and there were plans to introduce LRT. Instead Lerner's team implemented an express bus service on the one-way streets a block from one of the busways, which incorporated boarding tubes to provide off-vehicle fare collection and level-boarding. This was successful and so was introduced on the other axes. • The bus boarding tubes and bi-articulated buses were introduced gradually across the network, replacing the LRT plan.

Table 10.2 (continued)

City	Implementation	Summary
Melbourne *Car-centric* Transit mode share: journey-to-work 14%, all trips 11%	*Think Tram* and the *Clarendon Street Tram Priority Pilot*	• The *Melbourne 2030* plan led to the 2004 *Think Tram* programme, which targeted a 25% decrease in tram journey times. • Clarendon Street was selected as a pilot site. Far side stops, hook turns and other measures were implemented in 2005. Twenty parking spaces were removed to accommodate the far side tram stops, but 29 new spaces were added to nearby streets. • Public opposition led to a compromise. The far side stops were removed and parking was reinstated, but other measures were kept. 'The experience of the Clarendon Street trial . . . led to a more consultative approach being taken' (Currie and Shalaby 2007), and while *Think Tram* was extended the overall improvements to speeds and reliability were small.
	Stud Road bus lanes	• The 2008 *Keeping Melbourne Moving* strategy led to the implementation of 14 km of bus lanes along Stud Road in the eastern suburbs. Most works involved road widening, but in some sections the bus lanes replaced traffic lanes. • There were widespread complaints and a pre-election promise to remove the lanes by the opposition. A change of government in 2010 led to the bus lanes being removed where they had replaced traffic lanes, but retained elsewhere.
Toronto *Car-centric* Transit mode share: journey-to-work 29%, all trips 24%	*Transit City* and the *Eglinton Crosstown LRT*	• The 2007 *Transit City* plan called for seven new LRT lines in the suburban areas of the City of Toronto. Most of the lines were to be at-grade and longitudinally separated from other traffic, but part of the *Eglinton Crosstown LRT* would be below grade because of the existing road reserve being too narrow to safely accommodate LRT. • Rob Ford was elected mayor in 2010 and immediately cancelled *Transit City* in favour of a subway plan. However, *Transit City* was already part-funded by the Province. After negotiation and politics the *Eglinton Crosstown LRT* is now being constructed as per the original plan. Some lines have been incorporated into other plans, but *Transit City* was over.

Source: Authors' synthesis of selected research literature.

protests about the *reasonableness* of the removal of on-street parking and traffic lanes; and in Toronto the election of a new mayor showed that there was *public consent* for moving transit underground because proposed at-grade LRT did not meet the *condition* of avoiding impacts on suburban motorists.

10.4   A TRANSIT PRIORITY LEGITIMACY FRAMEWORK

Figure 10.2 shows a conceptual framework relating transit priority implementation to legitimacy, which has emerged from the case study research. It shows transit priority implementation passing through stages of: (1) *techno-rational legitimacy building*; (2) *inaction, opposition and/or delegitimisation*; and then either (3a) *success over time*, (3b) *mixed success and/or compromise*, or (3c) *failure and/or removal*. The framework suggests that transit priority implementation tends to have a greater likelihood of success and results in larger amounts of prioritisation in transit-centric cities. This appears to be in part due to the *sociological legitimacy* and *reasonableness* of prioritising on-road transit that is inherent in a city where a greater proportion of travellers already use transit.

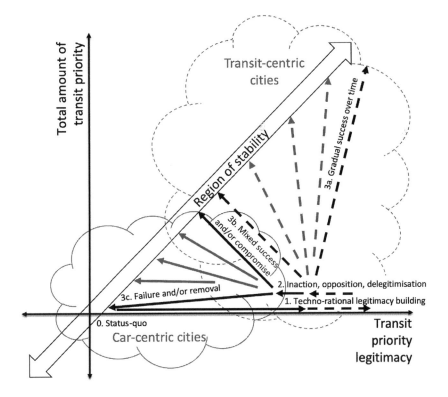

Notes:
1.   Transit-centric cities are indicated by dashed lines, and car-centric cities are indicated by solid lines.
2.   Grey indicates other and similar alternative paths.

Figure 10.2   *Conceptual framework for transit priority implementation and legitimacy*

Transit-centric cities may still experience inaction, opposition, and/or delegitimisation along the way to implementing transit priority measures.[16] However, implementation efforts in these cities appear to be more likely to lead to (3a) *gradual success over time*.

For more car-centric cities, however, the amount of transit priority that is *sociologically legitimate* is likely to be much lower. Regardless of the technical case and *legitimacy by reasonableness* for prioritising on-road transit that might be developed amongst engineers, in a car-centric city it appears unlikely that there will be much support for prioritising transit over other traffic amongst the general public, politicians or policy makers. Hence, (2) *inaction, opposition and/or delegitimisation* appears to be a more likely response to transit priority implementation efforts. This may also be more likely to lead to (3c) *failure and abandonment*, or through (3b) *compromise* to a *mixed success* where only some of the technically appropriate priority is implemented or ultimately retained.

For car-centric cities the (3a) *gradual successes over time* that have occurred in Zurich and Curitiba and the successful implementation of high levels of transit priority might seem almost entirely out of reach. For example:

- the compromise in Melbourne's *Clarendon Street Tram Priority Pilot* related to reinstating just 20 on-street parking spaces, even though 29 new spaces had already been installed on nearby streets (Smith 2005; Currie and Shalaby 2007);
- *Transit City* was branded as a 'war on cars' (Kalinowski and Rider 2010) by its opponents, and Mayor Rob Ford was elected on a wave of support from the suburban, car-dominated areas of the City of Toronto (Taylor 2013).

What are transport practitioners in car-centric cities to do if transit priority that is technically justified is unlikely ever to be *sociologically legitimate* or receive *public consent*? One option might be to *overreach-and-then-compromise*, as an initial push for higher than technically justified levels of transit priority might provide some room to be negotiated down to the technically optimal solution in later bargaining or appeasement. However, such strategies of *direct confrontation*, Machiavellian *political calculation and positioning*, rather than *conflict avoidance*, *trial schemes* and *consensus building* (Isaksson and Richardson 2009) would seem unethical in the short term and likely to reduce *legitimacy through trust* in practitioners over the longer term. Instead, practitioners need pragmatic strategies for implementation in situations where political and public opposition is likely to limit the legitimacy of otherwise technically appropriate levels of transit priority.

10.5　PRAGMATIC STRATEGIES FOR CAR-CENTRIC CITIES

For successful transit priority implementation there is a need to be pragmatic and sensitive to context. In car-centric cities this may mean adapting methods so as to be more conscious of low transit mode shares, the likely lack of *sociological legitimacy* for prioritising transit, and the political realities in places where most voters tend to drive. This research has developed three overall approaches to help practitioners respond to these challenges, which encompass nine pragmatic strategies. The approaches are based on: (a) building legitimacy *before* implementation; (b) *avoiding impacts* on private vehicles; or (c) building legitimacy *through* implementation. These are shown in Table 10.3.

Table 10.3   Pragmatic strategies for transit priority implementation in car-centric cities

Approach	Strategy	Description
(a) Build legitimacy *before* implementation	1. Technical enquiry	Undertake (additional) formal studies and investigations to support the case for transit priority.
	2. Transport planning	Set overall transportation goals and/or visionary plans at the strategic level that support transit prioritisation.
	3. Public processes & hearings	Use formal public policy- and decision-making processes to investigate, debate and demonstrate the appropriateness of transit prioritisation.
(b) *Avoid impacts* on private vehicles	4. Grade separation	Move on-road transit services into their own dedicated right-of-way (elevated or underground) to fully separate transit from other traffic.
	5. Building new capacity	Implement transit priority measures through road widening or other approaches that mean that existing traffic capacity is maintained and the status quo for private motorists is largely unaffected.
	6. Subservient priority	Prioritise transit as much as is possible without impacting (significantly) on other road users.
(c) Build legitimacy *through* implementation	7. Bottom-up and incremental	Increase transit priority gradually through small changes, possibly in conjunction with maintenance (e.g. during track renewal) or other works.
	8. Pop-ups	Prioritise transit using low-cost and temporary intervention, an experimental attitude, and a tactical urbanism style of engagement and small scale change.
	9. Trials	Build support for an experimental implementation to test the viability of permanent transit prioritisation.

Building legitimacy *before* implementation might involve demonstrating *reasonableness* through technical enquiry, generating *normative* and *sociological legitimacy* and an *unconditional duty* to follow visions or goals in a transportation plan, or building *normative* and *sociological* legitimacy through testing *reasonableness* and *public consent* in a public forum. *Avoiding impacts* seeks to limit potential opposition by preventing negative changes for other road users. This might involve: grade-separation to move transit away from other traffic entirely; prioritising transit through the building of new capacity, such as using road widening to create bus lanes; or only implementing subservient priority measures, which improve conditions for transit but do not negatively impact on private motorists. These strategies seek to side-step any legitimacy problems related to the *reasonableness* of transit priority impacts on other road users, lack of *public consent* for degrading traffic capacity, or there being only *conditional normative support* for the idea of improving transit if it does not impact on traffic or on-street parking. In contrast, building legitimacy *through* implementation seeks to use a try-it-and-see approach, which might involve: making only incremental, and hence *reasonable*, changes to the status quo; using a small-scale pop-up implementation that can be removed easily if it is unpopular; or using a formal trial to allow people to experience transit prioritisation without having to commit to permanent implementation.

Figure 10.3 shows how (a) *building legitimacy before implementation* might involve (1) technical enquiry; (2) transport planning; and/or (3) public enquiry.

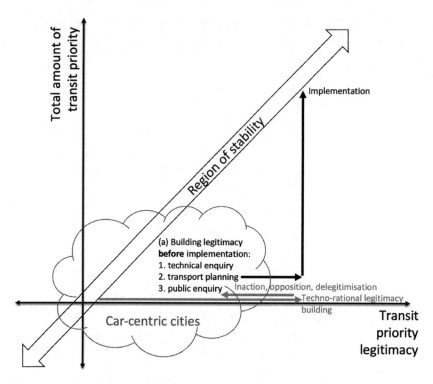

Figure 10.3   Building legitimacy before implementation through (1) technical enquiry; (2) transport planning; and/or (3) public enquiry

Technical enquiry, transport planning and public enquiries are already widely used in engineering and transit planning. However, the emphasis here is to use these to legitimise transit prioritisation *within the broader public policy arena*. For example, in Melbourne the eventual compromise in Clarendon Street was supported by a technical enquiry that studied the impacts of the priority measures on tram speed and reliability, but also community response to the implementation and many other relevant factors. This technical report was written for a non-technical audience of local councillors. It found that 'some elements of the trial have provided benefits' (Smith 2005) and appears to have helped to legitimise removing only the far side stops, rather than the entire scheme, as had been called for by opponents (Quin 2005). In contrast, there does not appear to have been a publicly released technical enquiry into the performance of the Stud Road bus lanes, and so public and political calls for their removal appear to have gone unanswered.

Figure 10.4 shows (b) *avoiding impacts on other road users*, which might involve (4) grade-separation; (5) building new capacity; or (6) subservient priority.

The mixed successes in Toronto provide inspiration for using (4) *grade-separation* as a pragmatic strategy to avoid opposition from private motorists. Mayor Ford cancelled the *Transit City* plan, but he also pushed for more of the Eglinton Crosstown LRT to be moved underground and a switch to subway construction. This appears to have been motivated by a desire to improve transit, but to keep the streets available for the many car drivers who had voted for him. An advantage of grade-separation is that it provides total

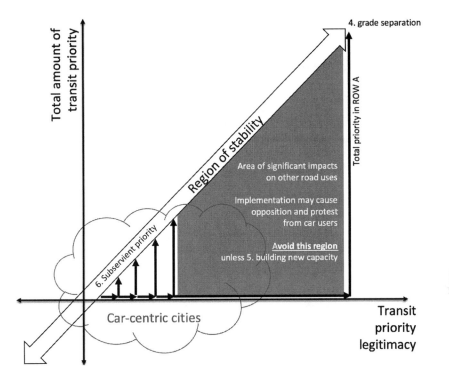

Figure 10.4   Avoiding impacts *on other road users through (4) grade separation; or (5) building new capacity; or (6) subservient priority*

priority for transit and is likely to be supported by motorists because it removes transit from interfering with traffic. However, it may face challenges because of its high costs, potentially causing a lack of *reasonableness*.

Potential opposition from car users is similarly circumvented by (5) *building new capacity* to accommodate transit priority measures. An example of how this may work is provided by the Stud Road bus lanes in Melbourne. Opposition appears to have been primarily about sections where the bus lanes had replaced existing traffic lanes. Sections where the bus lanes had instead been implemented through road widening appear to have been politically acceptable because private motorists had not been made worse off. Ultimately it was only the sections of bus lanes that had replaced existing traffic lanes that were removed (Bernecich 2011a; 2011b; 2011c; The Scarlett Syndrome 2011).

Currie (2016) describes how (6) *subservient priority* involves using measures that have only limited impacts on other road users. This pragmatic strategy is evident in the case examples of: the *bus boarding tubes* in Curitiba, which decreased dwell-time but had no impact on motorists; the initial push by the City of Zurich for a more restrained approach that would have had only limited impacts on other traffic; and the retention of all of the measures that *did not* impact on-street parking in Melbourne's Clarendon Street compromise. The broader political reality in some car-centric cities is that some low-cost and highly effective technical approaches such as painted bus lanes are practically impossible due to opposition and/or protest from motorists, and so might sometimes best be avoided.

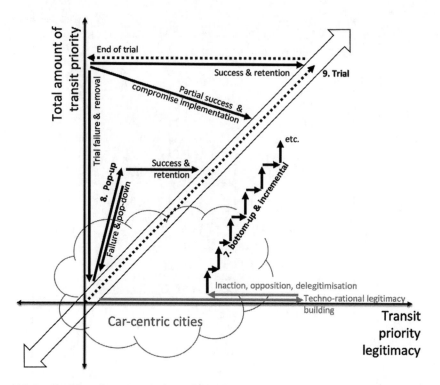

Figure 10.5   Building legitimacy through implementation through (7) bottom-up and incremental implementation; (8) pop-ups; or (9) trials

Figure 10.5 shows (c) *Building legitimacy through implementation* approach, which might include (7) bottom-up and incremental implementation; (8) pop-ups; or (9) trials.

Section 10.2.3 discussed the public policy analysis areas of *implementation theory* and *incrementalism*, which provide the theoretical basis for the pragmatic strategy of (7) *bottom-up and incremental* implementation. Incremental policy change and transit priority implementation is evident in the cases through:

- the gradual shift in Zurich from initial reluctance to a policy of Waiting Time Zero for transit, in part because 'as older employees have retired and younger staff have taken leadership roles, the departments are more fully committed to the transit priority program' (Nash 2001, p. 67);
- the gradual expansion of Curitiba's city plan to add more busways;
- the bus boarding tubes spreading from an initial limited implementation for new express bus services along one structural access, to being adopted across the entire transit network and replacing a proposal to convert to LRT.[17]

Implementation theory suggests that street-level implementors are closer to the real problems and so may have better insights into what may be legitimate in the local context, how small improvements might be made over time, and how transit priority measures might be incorporated into other programmes. Implementers in Melbourne appear to be already using (7) *bottom-up and incremental* implementation through small-scale priority improvements, and by taking opportunities to add separation kerbing during maintenance works and upgrades that are underway to meet federal legislative requirements for level-boarding at tram stops to provide disabled access (Reynolds et al. 2018).

Small-scale (8) *pop-ups* might similarly help to reduce risk in transit priority implementation and, in the words of Mayor Lerner, give people 'a chance to actually see it . . .' (McKibben 2007, p. 65) before committing to anything permanent. Lerner used a pop-up approach to implement the *Rua das Flores* pedestrian mall,[18] the success of which appears to have helped to build legitimacy for the later extensive transit priority implementation across Curitiba. Pop-up bus lanes, 'cone pilots', 'quick build' and 'tactical transit' projects all suggest using a similar approach of implementing transit priority measures temporarily and at a small scale as a low-risk approach (Hovenkotter and Monty 2018; TransitCenter 2018; Garcia and Wall 2019; UCLA Institute of Transportation Studies 2019). The key advantage appears to be that if such implementations do not obtain sufficient *sociological legitimacy* they can simply pop-down again with minimal repercussions.

This contrasts with the more deliberative and likely larger scale approach involved in undertaking a limited-period (9) *trial* implementation of transit priority measures. Such an approach was recently used in King Street in Toronto where city council approval of a one-year transit pilot provided an opportunity to try priority measures and gather extensive data to help demonstrate the *reasonableness* of the scheme, which supported a later decision to make the transit priority measures permanent.[19]

An important point is that the nine pragmatic strategies are not mutually exclusive, but can be combined. Implementers in the cities studied in this research have already been using a mix of these pragmatic strategies[20] and they also appear in various forms in other cities,[21] suggesting that the findings of this research can be generalised to more than just the cases that have been examined. The contribution of this research is not to invent these techniques, but instead to identify and characterise them so that practitioners and researchers will have a syntax with which to discuss, compare and select the combination that best fits their particular circumstances. There is, of course, no guarantee that any one strategy or combination of strategies will be enough to lead to success in every implementation effort. Rather, the pragmatic strategies suggest ways that practitioners can seek to build legitimacy for proposed transit priority measures in the broader community, beyond the rational world of engineering where some form of technical *reasonableness* likely led to transit priority implementation being proposed in the first place.

10.6   CONCLUSIONS

Marsden and Reardon (2017) called for a move beyond techno-rationalism and greater consideration of legitimacy and politics in transportation policy. This chapter has in part responded to this challenge by exploring why the techno-rational arguments supporting the reasonableness of prioritising on-road transit have been successful in some cities, but not in others. The research contribution is a new conceptual framework that relates legitimacy theory to transit priority, and which provides a new way to understand why transit priority measures are accepted or even voted for in transit-centric cities, but might be opposed, protested against and removed in cities that are more orientated towards the car.

The conceptual framework may prove useful as a basis for future research. Further case studies or other research methods might be used to test the new conceptual framework, although the complexity and uniqueness of individual transit priority implementations suggests that using quantitative methods may prove difficult. This does, however, suggest that research involving a large sample of *implementors*, such as through surveys or using a Delphi study, might help gauge the extent to which the new framework matches with the real-world experiences of practitioners in both transit- and car-centric cities. Legitimacy also appears to have wider relevance to other research areas in transport such as cyclist and pedestrian safety and infrastructure, driver behaviour, traffic law enforcement, and the rules and practices underlying road systems. However, it does not appear that transportation researchers have yet explored how legitimacy affects transportation systems and public decision-making about how they should operate, how they actually operate, and the interaction of engineering and politics, and there may be opportunities for further research in these areas.

The outcomes of this research that may be of most relevance to practitioners are the three approaches and nine pragmatic strategies for transit priority implementation. There is already a deep understanding of the technical aspects of transit priority implementation at the tactical and operational levels, and these pragmatic strategies are likely to be familiar to many professionals working in transportation. However, the contribution of this research is to enumerate and categorise these pragmatic strategies, all of which have already been used to some extent in practice, either alone or in combination. Future research might look to expand on this and seek further pragmatic strategies for transit priority implementation, and also to study whether similar frameworks and pragmatic strategies can be applied to other areas of transport, particularly those that are often debated and contested in non-technical policy-making arenas.

Politics may be war (Mao 1967), but engineering instead tends to solve problems through logic, rational thought and technical enquiry. Transit priority implementation appears to span these two extremes and may at times approach a battle for street space (Ardila-Gomez 2004; Nash et al. 2018) or a 'war on cars' (Kalinowski and Rider 2010) in which acceptance of the engineering efficiency and *reasonableness* of prioritising on-road transit is often *conditional* on limiting on-street parking losses, traffic delay or other non-transit impacts. In some cities the supremacy of the car appears to be almost *unconditional*. However, the realisation that society cannot build itself out of traffic congestion has already gained support amongst many practitioners, and is starting to find traction amongst the voting public and politicians. Practitioners seeking to implement on-road transit priority might feel stuck until public policy-making catches up and understands the inevitable need for more sustainable and efficient patterns of road use allocation. Unfortunately, and regardless of the technological brilliance of directly transferring priority technology from transit-centric cities or grand top-down plans, purely techno-rational approaches appear likely to struggle to gain *sociological legitimacy* in car-centric cities for the foreseeable future. In the meantime, now is the time for practitioners to adopt realistic, pragmatic and achievable strategies that have already helped achieve successes in some transit- and car-centric cities, but which may have been under-appreciated in previous techno-rationally focused approaches to understanding or attempting on-road transit priority implementation.

Transit priority implementation needs to be more than just technically appropriate. It also needs to be legitimate through a combination of legality, social acceptance, *public consent* and *reasonableness* within the local context. The pragmatic strategies described in this chapter may help to assist practitioners respond to the opposition, limitations and *conditionalities* commonly placed in car-centric cities on the simple, and from a techno-rational perspective almost *unconditional*, principle that vehicles with many passengers on board should be prioritised in urban conditions.

NOTES

1. City of Munster (1991); Todorovic (2015) and many others have produced photos and illustrations that clearly show the space efficiency of transit, cycling and walking compared to private cars.
2. In Toronto the implementation of a longitudinally separated streetcar alignment along the centre of St Clair Avenue West, with non-mountable kerbs preventing other traffic from crossing onto the tracks, was delayed by opposition and court challenges (Bow 2016). Mayor Rob Ford later declared that the 'war on the car is over' (Kalinowski and Rider 2010) as he cancelled the *Transit City* plan and years of planning for Light Rail Transit (LRT) implementation (Toronto Transit Commission 2007; Metrolinx et al. 2010; Levy 2015; Bow 2017). In Melbourne the *Think Tram* pilot project in Clarendon Street was partially removed in a compromise with local stakeholders (Currie and Shalaby 2007; Currie et al. 2013), while bus lanes on Stud Road in the eastern suburbs were removed following opposition from drivers and a change of the state government (Reid 2010; Tudge 2010; Public Transport Users Association 2011; The Scarlett Syndrome 2011).
3. The concept of techno-rationalism comes from *techno-* ('relating to technology or its use') and *rational* ('based on or in accordance with reason or logic') (Oxford Dictionary 2018b; 2018c), and is reminiscent of top-down technocratic approaches to implementation and policy-making (Torgerson 1985; Sabatier 1986; 1987; 1988; Fischer and Forester 1993; Sabatier 1998). It implies a frame of reference, perhaps common amongst engineers, where society's problems can be overcome through the application of sufficiently advanced technology and the use of rational thinking.
4. A dictionary definition of normative is 'establishing, relating to, or deriving from a standard or norm, especially of behaviour . . .' (Oxford Dictionary 2018a). The term 'normative model' is used in this chapter to describe frameworks, procedures and other prescriptive and authoritative descriptions of how a process *should* be undertaken, in contrast to more descriptive models that authors might use to interrogate or conceptualise how decision-making or policy development is undertaken in practice.
5. This is the work of PhD researcher James Reynolds whose research topic was 'A Framework and Pragmatic Strategies for Transit Priority'. James' supervisors were Professor Graham Currie, Professor Geoff Rose and Alistair Cumming, and the PhD was undertaken at Monash University between 2016 and 2020.
6. In this conceptual model Currie (2016) adopts the Vuchic (1981, pp. 62–3; 2005, pp. 5–6) definitions of transit Right-Of-Way (ROW). These are: ROW A where there is full separation between transit and other traffic, which involves grade separation or a completely independent alignment; ROW B where transit is longitudinally separated from other traffic, but has at-grade intersections; and ROW C where transit operates in mixed traffic, either in its own exclusive (e.g. linemarked) lanes or directly sharing space with other vehicles.
7. Journey-to-work transit mode share was 49 per cent in Zurich in 1970 prior to the ballot on the Citizen's Transit Priority Initiative in 1977 (Nash 2001) and in the order of 70–75 per cent in Curitiba (see note 8) prior to implementation of bus priority measures. In contrast, in Toronto metropolitan area just 23 per cent of journey-to-work trips are by transit, while across Melbourne the figure is only 12 per cent (Statistics Canada 2011; Australian Bureau of Statistics 2017).
8. There are various figures reported for transit mode splits in Curitiba and the exact numbers are unclear due to a lack of household origin and destination surveys or a journey-to-work question on the Brazilian census (Lindau et al. 2010a, p. 17; Mees 2010, p. 118). Regardless of the precise mode split, the transit ridership figures and other statistics reported in the literature suggest that the BRT network provides a realistic and attractive replacement for the car in Curitiba.
9. See the research literature in organisational institutionalism, international relations and comparative politics for a full discussion of these concepts (e.g. Boxenbaum and Jonsson (2017), Andersen (2011), Knill and Tosun (2011) and Peters (2011)). However, in short, the established theoretical knowledge in these areas may help to explain how the success of BRT in Curitiba and other places could apply additional pressures to improve other bus systems to be 'smart', BRT-like, or otherwise better than the status quo as 'organizations conform to "rationalized myths" in society about what constitutes a proper organization . . . [and] as more organizations conform to these myths they become more deeply institutionalized' (Boxenbaum and Jonsson 2017, p. 77). An example that is fictional, but highly illustrative, is provided by a public mob in

Springfield singing in support of building a monorail so as to avoid falling behind 'Brockway, Ogdenville, and North Haverbrook' (O'Brien 1993).

Decoupling describes how organizations might 'seek the legitimacy that adaptation to rationalized myths provides while they engage in technical "business as usual"' (Boxenbaum and Jonsson 2017, p. 78). This may help to explain how new bus livery or minor, yet highly visible, improvements may be an attempt to show progress towards modernisation and that a city is 'keeping up with the Joneses' (or Curitibanos in the case of BRT). As an example from Australia, Hensher et al. (2019) note a tendency for bus services that are branded as being better than a regular bus to actually be *less likely* to have BRT engineering measures that improve service, whereas services that have BRT-style priority measures are not always branded as such.

10. See for example Vuchic et al. (1994); Smith and Hensher (1998); Levinson et al. (2003a; 2003b); Wright (2010); Cervero (2013); Cervero and Dai (2014); Currie and Delbosc (2014); Mulley et al. (2014); Ingvardson and Nielsen (2018).

11. This paragraph is based on a broad review and synthesis of literature including Vuchic et al. (1994); Wright (2001); Levinson et al. (2003b); Pulichino (2003); Vuchic (2005); Currie (2006); Page (2006); Vuchic (2007); Hidalgo and Graftieaux (2008); Osbaldeston (2008); Currie and Delbosc (2010); Lindau et al. (2010a); Wright (2010); Duarte et al. (2011); Cervero (2013); Henke (2013); Cervero and Dai (2014); Currie and Delbosc (2014); Lindau et al. (2014); Mulley et al. (2014); Olesen (2014); Levy (2015); Litman (2015); Marier (2015, pp. 402–403); Ryus et al. (2016); Fullerton (2017); Currie (2018).

12. Bold emphasis is in the original. For details of new approaches such as tactical urbanism, network operations planning, SmartRoads, Movement and Place, and Complete Streets, see Lydon et al. (2012); Pagano (2013); Alisdairi (2014); Finn (2014); Lydon and Garcia (2015); Talen (2015); Voigt (2015); Blumgart (2016); Trailnet (2016); Delbosc et al. (2018); Webb (2018); Smart Growth America (2019).

13. This paragraph is based on review and synthesis of a range of sources including: Engwicht (1999); Mees (2000, p. 7; 2003b, pp. 2–3); Bradbury et al. (2007, pp. 120–21); Jones et al. (2007); Wall (2007); Jones et al. (2008); Jones and Boujenko (2009); Meyrick and Associates (2009); Vanderbilt (2009, p. 191); UKDFT (Department for Transport) (2010); Weeratunga and Luk (2010); Colonna et al. (2012); Morhayim (2012, pp. 52–71); Alisdairi (2014); Jones (2014); Stopher and Stanley (2014, pp. 132–6); Lydon and Garcia (2015, p. 28); Blumgart (2016); Damen and Millican (2017, pp. 688–95); Davis (2017, p. 153); De Gruyter and Wills (2017); Delbosc et al. (2017); Levinson and Krizek (2017, p. 185); Wall (2017b; 2017a); Delbosc et al. (2018); Legacy and Taylor (2018); Ruming (2018); Gorgan (2019); KOMO News (2019); Smart Growth America (2019); Dobson (n.d.). Guerrilla gardening involves citizens taking over space that would be otherwise unused, such as on the nature strip or verge, to grow food, plants and/or flowers. There are many other similar movements such as *chair bombing* (placing new and unofficial seats in public spaces, such as at a bus stop), *guerrilla knitting* or *yarn bombing* (installing knitwear on trees and street furniture) and *street art* or *graffiti* (distinct categories, but which overlap and where the boundaries are very much in the eye of the beholder (Killen et al. 2017, pp. 2–3)).

14. See discussions of the different types of case studies, and common misunderstandings and invalid criticisms about case study research in Bonoma (1984); Benbasat et al. (1987); Eisenhardt (1989); McCutcheon and Meredith (1993); Cavaye (1996); Darke et al. (1998); Meredith (1998); Stuart et al. (2002); Voss et al. (2002); Denscombe (2007); Eisenhardt and Graebner (2007); Siggelkow (2007); Ketokivi and Choi (2014); Roth (2007); Barratt et al. (2011) and Yin (2009; 2014; 2018). For discussion of the scientific rigour involved in case study research see Eisenhardt (1989); Meredith (1998); Stuart et al. (2002); Voss et al. (2002); Denscombe (2007); Siggelkow (2007); Yin (2009); Ketokivi and Choi (2014, p. 239); Yin (2014; 2018). Discussion about case study data analysis methods within and across cases, which have been relevant to this research, are provided in Benbasat et al. (1987, p. 374); Eisenhardt (1989, pp. 539–45); Miles and Huberman (1994); Darke et al. (1998, pp. 284–6); Meredith (1998, pp. 447–9); Stuart et al. (2002, pp. 427–8); Voss et al. (2002, pp. 213–15); Yin (2009); Barratt et al. (2011, p. 331); Yin (2014; 2018).

15. There is insufficient space to list the sources relied upon for all cases and implementations studied in this research that are summarised in Table 10.2. However, details of the transit mode shares shown in Table 10.2 are as follows: the Zurich journey to work value is for 1990 and within the City only (Apel and Pharoah 1995, p. 145; Cervero 1998, p. 303), but the all trips value is from 2015 (Nash et al. 2018, p. 8); for Curitiba these values are consistently shown in the research literature, but their accuracy is unclear; Melbourne figures are for 2006 (journey to work) (Mees 2010, pp. 60–61; Loader 2018) and 2010 (all trips) (Loader 2019); and the Toronto values are from 2011 and for City of Toronto residents only (Transportation Information Steering Committee (TISC) et al. 2018). For this research the precise values are of lesser importance than that Zurich and Curitiba have relatively high transit mode splits, and so represent more transit-centric cities, while Melbourne and Toronto have lower transit mode splits and appear to be generally more car-centric.

16. For example, the City of Zurich initially opposed the Citizen's Transit Priority Initiative as unnecessary. Even after the initiative was passed in a public ballot it took further lobbying and a City Directive to convince planners and politicians to take action (Nash 2001, pp. 66–7). Similarly, in Curitiba there was a

period of inaction after the new city plan was adopted until Jamie Lerner was appointed mayor. The initial implementation of a mall in the central city, which was also part of the City plan adopted in 1965, was met by protests from motorists and objections from shopkeepers who attempted to get the State Governor to remove Lerner as mayor (Dera 1995, pp. 31–2; Meadows 1995; Cervero 1998, p. 271; Hawken et al. 1999, p. 289; Ardila-Gomez 2004; Schwartz 2004, p. 48; McKibben 2007, p. 65).

17. See Rabinovitch and Leitmann (1993, p. 19); Dera (1995, p. 39); Lloyd-Jones (1996); Cervero (1998); Ceneviva (2000, pp. 187–9); Pulichino (2003, p. 60); Ardila-Gomez (2004, pp. 191–203); Schwartz (2004, pp. 93–6); Lindau et al. (2010a).

18. See Hunt (1994, p. 76); Dera (1995, pp. 31–2); Cervero (1998, p. 271); Hawken et al. (1999, p. 289); Kroll (1999); Ardila-Gomez (2004, p. 105); Schwartz (2004, pp. 13, 41–2, 8); McKibben (2007, p. 65); Moore (2007, p. 89).

19. Steps in the King Street Transit Pilot involved (1) a growing recognition over a long time period that something need to be done to improve streetcar performance on King Street (City of Toronto and Toronto Transit Commission 2005; Currie and Shalaby 2007) that eventually led to (2) a visioning study (Keesmaat 2016), and (3) a proposal for a one-year transit priority pilot (City of Toronto et al. 2019), which (4) passed through council (City of Toronto 2017), but was (5) opposed by some businesses (Harris 2018; O'Neil 2018) despite being (6) generally very successful (City of Toronto 2018; City of Toronto et al. 2019) and being ultimately (7) adopted permanently (Bow 2019; City of Toronto 2019).

20. For example, Curitiba's long history of transit priority implementation shows technical enquiry and seminars initially helping to legitimise an overall city plan. This plan was then delivered using a pop-up pedestrian mall, by implementing busways as part of a 'trinary road system' that also provides one-way streets one block away from the busways, and through the expansion of the plan to add further busways and to introduce bus boarding tubes incrementally across the network.

21. For example, the City of Everett's pop-up bus lane (TransitCenter 2018) was implemented through the bottom-up efforts of a local city traffic engineer and mayor, with the bus itself operated by a regional transit authority who appear to have had little to do with the project. The priority implementation appears also to have been subservient to other road users, as the bus lane was only in operation during the morning peak period when the existing on-street parking it replaced was not as needed because shops were not yet open.

REFERENCES

Alisdairi, L. 2014, 'A cry and a demand: Tactical urbanism and the right to the city', Master of Urban Planning thesis, University of Washington.

Althaus, C., Bridgman, P. and Davis, G. 2013, *The Australian Policy Handbook*, 5th edn, Crows Nest, NSW: Allen & Unwin.

Amanda, D., Heather, W., Max, C. and Allan, F.W. 2005, 'Controversies and speed cameras: Lessons learnt internationally', *Journal of Public Health Policy*, vol. 26, no. 4, p. 404.

Andersen, J.G. 2011, 'The impact of public policies', in D Caramani (ed.), *Comparative Politics*, 2nd edn, Oxford: Oxford University Press.

Apel, D. and Pharoah, T.M. 1995, *Transport Concepts in European Cities*, Aldershot, UK and Brookfield, VT, USA: Avebury.

Ardila-Gomez, A. 2004, 'Transit planning in Curitiba and Bogotá: Roles in interaction, risk, and change', PhD thesis, Massachusetts Institute of Technology.

Australian Bureau of Statistics 2017, 'Greater Melbourne: region data summary', Government of Australia, accessed 14 September 2017 at http://stat.abs.gov.au/itt/r.jsp?RegionSummary&region=2GMEL&dataset= ABS_REGIONAL_ASGS&geoconcept=REGION&measure=MEASURE&datasetASGS=ABS_REGION AL_ASGS&datasetLGA=ABS_REGIONAL_LGA&regionLGA=REGION&regionASGS=REGION.

Baker, R.J., Collura, J., Dale, J.J., Head, L., Hemily, B., Ivanovic, M., Jarzab, J.T. et al. 2004, *An Overview of Transit Signal Priority*, 2nd edn, Washington, DC: ITS America.

Barratt, M., Choi, T. and Li, M. 2011, 'Qualitative case studies in operations management: Trends, research outcomes, and future research implications', *Journal of Operations Management*, vol. 29, no. 4, p. 329.

Basford, L., Reid, S., Lester, T., Thomson, J. and Tolmie, A. 2002, *Drivers' Perceptions of Cyclists*, Department for Transport and TRL Limited, UK.

Benbasat, I., Goldstein, D.K. and Mead, M. 1987, 'The case research strategy in studies of information systems', *MIS Quarterly*, vol. 11, no. 3, p. 369.

Bernecich, A. 2011a, 'Bus lanes returned to cars', *Knox Leader*, 5 April.

Bernecich, A. 2011b, 'Horns lock over bus lane', *Knox Leader*, 8 February.

Bernecich, A. 2011c, 'More bus lane pain: Lack of talk set to lead to road chaos', *Knox Leader*, 22 March.

Blumgart, J. 2016, 'Tactical urbanism goes mainstream', *Planning*, vol. 82, p. 8.

Bonoma, T.V. 1984, 'Case research in marketing: Opportunities, problems, and a process', *Journal of Marketing Research*, vol. 21, no. 4, p. 199.

Bow, J. 2016, *The battle of St. Clair*, accessed 5 March 2018 at https://transit.toronto.on.ca/streetcar/4126.shtml.

Bow, J. 2017, *Toronto's Transit City LRT plan*, accessed 23 August 2017 at http://transit.toronto.on.ca/street car/4121.shtml.

Bow, J. 2019, *Route 504 – the King Streetcar*, accessed 24 November 2019 at https://transit.toronto.on.ca/streetcar/4103.shtml.

Boxenbaum, E. and Jonsson, S. 2017, 'Isomorphism, diffusion and decoupling: Concept evolution and theoretical challenges', in R. Greenwood, C. Oliver, T.B. Lawrence and R.E. Meyer (eds), *The SAGE Handbook of Organizational Institutionalism*, 2nd edn, London: SAGE Publications, pp. 77–101.

Bradbury, A., Cameron, A., Castell, B., Jones, P., Pharoah, T., Reid, S. and Young, A. 2007, *Manual for Streets*, Department for Transport, London: Thomas Telford Publishing.

Buchanan, A. and Keohane, R.O. 2009, 'The legitimacy of global governance institutions', in L.H. Meyer (ed.), *Legitimacy, Justice and Public International Law*, New York: Cambridge University Press, pp. 1–28.

Burke, M. 2013, *Vale Paul Mees, Australia's leading transport & land use researcher*, The Conversation Media Group Ltd, accessed 13 November 2019 at https://theconversation.com/vale-paul-mees-australias-leading-tra nsport-and-land-use-researcher-15385.

Caramani, D. 2011, 'Introduction to comparative politics', in D. Caramani (ed.), *Comparative Politics*, 2nd edn, Oxford: Oxford University Press.

Cavaye, A.L.M. 1996, 'Case study research: A multi-faceted research approach for IS', *Information Systems Journal*, vol. 6, no. 3, pp. 227–42.

Ceneviva, C. 2000, 'Operation and use of the integrated public transportation network of Curitiba, Brazil', in M.V.A. Bondada (ed.), *Urban Public Transportation Systems: Implementing Efficient Urban Transit Systems and Enhancing Transit Usage: Proceedings of the First International Conference*, 21–25 March, Miami, FL, American Society of Civil Engineers, Reston, VA, pp. 183–94.

Cervero, R. 1998, *The Transit Metropolis: A Global Inquiry*, Washington, DC: Island Press.

Cervero, R. 2013, *Bus Rapid Transit (BRT): An Efficient and Competitive Mode of Public Transport*, Working Paper 2013-01, Berkeley Institutie of Urban and Regional Development, Unversity of California, Berkeley, CA.

Cervero, R. and Dai, D. 2014, 'BRT TOD: Leveraging transit oriented development with bus rapid transit investments', *Transport Policy*, vol. 36, p. 127.

City of Münster 1991, 'Space required to transport 60 people', accessed 1 April 2020 at https://web.archive. org/web/20190324012201/http://www.bikehub.co.uk/news/sustainability/iconic-waste-of-space-photo-keeps-on-giving/.

City of Toronto 2017, '*Agenda item history – 2017EX26.1: proposed King Street transit pilot – Bathurst Street to Jarvis Street*', accessed 1 February 2019 at http://app.toronto.ca/tmmis/viewAgendaItemHistory.do?item=2017.EX26.1.

City of Toronto 2018, 'King Street transit pilot, data reports and background materials', accessed 5 March 2018 at https://www.toronto.ca/city-government/planning-development/planning-studies-initiatives/king-street-pilot/king-street-transit-pilot-background-materials/.

City of Toronto 2019, 'King Street transit pilot', accessed 1 February 2019 at https://www.toronto.ca/city-gover nment/planning-development/planning-studies-initiatives/king-street-pilot/.

City of Toronto and Toronto Transit Commission 2005, 'Building a transit city', accessed at https://transit. toronto.on.ca/archives/reports/building_a_transit_city.pdf.

City of Toronto et al. 2019, 'The future of King Street: Results of the transit pilot', by City of Toronto, Toronto Transit Commission, Gray, B., Lintern, G., Llewellyn-Thomas, K., Hayward, J., Perttula, J. and Lui, L., Transportation Services, City Planning and Customer Service, Report for Action, EX4.2, accessed at https://www.toronto.ca/legdocs/mmis/2019/ex/bgrd/backgroundfile-131188.pdf.

Colonna, P., Berloco, N. and Circella, G. 2012, 'The interaction between land use and transport planning: A methodological issue', *Procedia – Social and Behavioral Sciences*, vol. 53, no. C, pp. 84–95.

Currie, G. 2006, 'Bus rapid transit in Australasia: Performance, lessons learned and futures', *Journal of Public Transportation*, vol. 9, no. 3, p. 1.

Currie, G. 2009, 'Using a public education campaign to improve driver compliance with streetcar transit lanes', *Transportation Research Record: Journal of the Transportation Research Board*, vol. 2112, pp. 62–9.

Currie, G. 2016, 'Managing on-road public transport', in M.C.J. Bliemer, C. Mulley and C.J. Moutou (eds), *Handbook on Transport and Urban Planning in the Developed World*, Cheltenham, UK and Northampton, MA, USA: Edward Elgar Publishing, pp. 471–97.

Currie, G. 2018, 'Lies, damned lies, AVs, shared mobility, and urban transit futures', *Journal of Public Transportation*, vol. 21, no. 1, pp. 19–30.

Currie, G. and Delbosc, A. 2010, 'Bus Rapid Transit in Australasia: An update on progress', *Built Environment*, vol. 36, no. 3, pp. 328–43.

Currie, G. and Delbosc, A. 2014, 'Assessing Bus Rapid Transit system performance in Australasia', *Research in Transportation Economics*, vol. 48, pp. 142–51.

Currie, G. and Shalaby, A. 2007, 'Success and challenges in modernizing streetcar systems: Experiences in Melbourne, Australia, and Toronto, Canada', *Transportation Research Record: Journal of the Transportation Research Board*, vol. 2006, pp. 31–9.

Currie, G., Goh, K. and Sarvi, M. 2013, 'An analytical approach to measuring the impacts of transit priority', in *Transportation Research Board 92nd Annual Meeting*, Washington, DC.

Damen, P. and Millican, D. 2017, 'Local area traffic management', in A. Delbosc and W. Young (eds), *Traffic Engineering and Management*, 7th edn, Clayton, VIC: Monash University Institute of Transport Studies, pp. 686–709.

Darke, P., Shanks, G. and Broadbent, M. 1998, 'Successfully completing case study research: Combining rigour, relevance and pragmatism', *Information Systems Journal*, vol. 8, no. 4, pp. 273–89.

Das, T.K. and Bing-Sheng, T. 1999, 'Cognitive biases and strategic decision processes: An integrative perspective', *Journal of Management Studies*, vol. 36, no. 6, pp. 757–78.

Davis, G. 2017, 'Applying road hierarchies in practice', in A. Delbosc and W. Young (eds), *Traffic Engineering and Management*, 7th edn, Clayton, VIC: Monash University Institute of Transport Studies, pp. 135–55.

De Gruyter, C. and Wills, P. 2017, 'Transport Impact Assessment', in A. Delbosc and W. Young (eds), *Traffic Engineering and Management*, 7th edn, Clayton, VIC: Monash University Institute of Transport Studies, pp. 156–88.

Delbosc, A., Young, W. and Brindle, R. 2017, 'Road functions, hierarchy and classification', in A. Delbosc and W. Young (eds), *Traffic Engineering and Management*, 7th edn, Clayton, VIC: Monash University Institute of Transport Studies, pp. 115–34.

Delbosc, A., Naznin, F., Haslam, N. and Haworth, N. 2019, 'Dehumanization of cyclists predicts self-reported aggressive behaviour toward them: A pilot study', *Transportation Research Part F: Psychology and Behaviour*, vol. 62, pp. 681–9.

Delbosc, A., Reynolds, J., Marshall, W. and Wall, A. 2018, 'American Complete Streets and Australian SmartRoads: What can we learn from each other?', *Transportation Research Record: Journal of the Transportation Research Board*, vol. 2672(39), pp. 166–76.

Denscombe, M. 2007, *The Good Research Guide*, 2nd edn, Maidenhead: McGraw-Hill International.

Dera, B. 1995, 'Curitiba, Brazil: A planning role model for Halifax', Masters of Urban and Rural Planning thesis, Technical University of Nova Scotia.

Dimitriou, H.T. 1992, *Urban Transport Planning: A Developmental Approach*, London, UK and New York, USA: Routledge.

Dobson, C. n.d., *The Citizen's Handbook*, accessed 16 July 2019 at http://www.citizenshandbook.org/toc.html.

Duarte, F., Firmino, R. and Prestes, O. 2011, 'Learning from failures: Avoiding asymmetrical views of public transportation initiatives in Curitiba', *Journal of Urban Technology*, vol. 18, no. 3, pp. 81–100.

Easton, D. 1965, *A Framework for Political Analysis*, Englewood Cliffs, NJ: Prentice-Hall.

Eisenhardt, K.M. 1989, 'Building theories from case study research', *Academy of Management review*, vol. 14, no. 4.

Eisenhardt, K.M. and Graebner, M.A. 2007, 'Theory building from cases: Opportunities and challenges', *Academy of Management Journal*, vol. 50, no. 1, pp. 25–37.

Eisenhardt, K.M. and Zbaracki, M. 1992, 'Strategic decision making', *Strategic Management Journal*, vol. 13, pp. 17–37.

Engwicht, D. 1999, *Street Reclaiming: Creating Livable Streets and Vibrant Communities*, Sydney, NSW: Pluto Press.

Finn, D. 2014, 'DIY urbanism: Implications for cities', *Journal of Urbanism: International Research on Placemaking and Urban Sustainability*, vol. 7, no. 4, pp. 1–18.

Fischer, F. and Forester, J. 1993, 'Editor's introduction', in F. Fischer and J. Forester (eds), *The Argumentative Turn in Policy Analysis and Planning*, Durham, NC: Duke University Press.

Fitzgerald, S.P. 2002, *Decision Making*, Oxford: Capstone.

Fullerton, J. 2017, 'Failure of China's "straddling bus" shows there's no magic bullet for traffic woes', *The Guardian*, 7 July, accessed at https://www.theguardian.com/sustainable-business/2017/jul/07/failure-china-straddling-bus-no-magic-bullet-traffic-woes.

Furness, Z.M. 2010, *One Less Car: Bicycling and the Politics of Automobility*, Philadelphia, PA: Temple University Press.

Gambetta, D. and Hertog, S. 2017, *Engineers of Jihad: The Curious Connection Between Violent Extremism and Education*, Princeton, NJ: Princeton University Press.

Garcia, A. and Wall, D. 2019, *TCRP Research Report 207: Fast-Tracked: A Tactical Transit Study*, Transit Cooperative Research Program, accessed at https://www.nap.edu/catalog/25571/fast-tracked-a-tactical-transit-study.

Garrison, W.L. and Levinson, D.M. 2006, *The Transportation Experience: Policy, Planning, and Deployment*, New York: Oxford University Press.

Gleeson, B. and Beza, B. 2014, *The Public City: Essays in Honour of Paul Mees*, Carlton, VIC: Melbourne University Press.

Gorgan, E. 2019, 'Viral clip of pedestrian shooing off cars from Seattle bus lane sparks imitators', Autoevolution, accessed 22 September 2019 at https://www.autoevolution.com/news/viral-clip-of-pedestrian-shooing-off-cars-from-seattle-bus-lane-sparks-imitators-136720.html.

Harris, T. 2018, 'Some businesses give an icy middle finger to King St. pilot', *Toronto Star*, 17 January, accessed at https://www.thestar.com/news/gta/2018/01/17/some-businesses-give-an-icy-middle-finger-to-king-st-pilot.html.

Hawken, P., Lovins, L.H. and Lovins, A.B. 1999, *Natural Capitalism: The Next Industrial Revolution*, London: Earthscan.

Hayden, L. 2009, 'Seeing red: Discourse, metaphor, and the implementation of red light cameras in Texas', PhD thesis, University of Texas at Austin.

Henderson, J. 2013, *Street Fight: The Politics of Mobility in San Francisco*, Amherst, MD: Amherst University of Massachusetts Press.

Henke, C. 2013, 'Designing BRT for future rail conversion: Issues, state of practice, and project considerations', paper presented at the Third International Conference on Urban Public Transportation Systems, Paris, accessed at https://doi.org/10.1061/9780784413210.027.

Hensher, D., Wong, Y. and Ho, L. 2019, 'Review of Bus Rapid Transit and branded bus service performance in Australia: From workhorse to thoroughbred', paper presented at Australasian Transport Research Forum, Canberra, ACT, Australia.

Hickson, D. 1987, 'Decision-making at the top of organizations', *Annual Review of Sociology*, vol. 13, pp. 165–92.

Hidalgo, D. and Graftieaux, P. 2008, 'Bus Rapid Transit systems in Latin America and Asia: Results and difficulties in 11 cities', *Transportation Research Record: Journal of the Transportation Research Board*, no. 2072, pp. 77–88.

Hovenkotter, K. and Monty, J. 2018, 'Quick build bus lanes: How US cities are building more lanes faster', paper presented at TransportationCamp DC, Washington, DC.

Huber, G.P. 1981, 'The nature of organizational decision making and the design of decision support systems', *MIS Quarterly*, vol. 5, no. 2, pp. 1–10.

Hunt, J. 1994, 'The urban believer: A report on Jaime Lerner and the rise of Curitiba, Brazil', *Metropolis Magazine*, vol. 13, no. 8, pp. 66–79.

Ingvardson, J.B. and Nielsen, O.A. 2018, 'Effects of new bus and rail rapid transit systems: An international review', *Transport Reviews*, vol. 38, no. 1, pp. 96–116.

Isaksson, K. and Richardson, T. 2009, 'Building legitimacy for risky policies: The cost of avoiding conflict in Stockholm', *Transportation Research Part A*, vol. 43, no. 3, pp. 251–7.

Jacobs, J. 1961, *The Death and Life of Great American Cities*, New York: Random House.

Janis, I.L. and Mann, L. 1977, *Decision Making: A Psychological Analysis of Conflict, Choice, and Commitment*, New York: Free Press.

Jason, L.A. and Liotta, R. 1982, 'Pedestrian jaywalking under facilitating and nonfacilitating conditions', *Journal of Applied Behavior Analysis*, vol. 15, no. 3, pp. 469–73.

Jenkins-Smith, H. 1990, *Democratic Politics and Policy Analysis*, Pacific Grove, CA: Brooks/Cole.

Johnson, M., Charlton, J., Oxley, J. and Newstead, S. 2013, 'Why do cyclists infringe at red lights? An investigation of Australian cyclists' reasons for red light infringement', *Accident Analysis & Prevention*, vol. 50, pp. 840–47.

Johnson, M., Newstead, S., Charlton, J. and Oxley, J. 2011, 'Riding through red lights: The rate, characteristics and risk factors of non-compliant urban commuter cyclists', *Accident Analysis & Prevention*, vol. 43, no. 1, pp. 323–8.

Jones, P. 2014, 'Link and place: Bridging stakeholder divides', in M. Carmona (ed.), *Explorations in Urban Design: An Urban Design Research Primer*, Abingdon: Ashgate Publishing, pp. 90–100.

Jones, P. and Boujenko, N. 2009, '"Link" and "Place": A new approach to street planning and design', paper presented at the Australasian Transport Research Forum, Auckland.

Jones, P., Boujenko, N. and Marshall, S. 2007, *Link & Place: A Guide to Street Planning and Design*, London: Local Transport Today.

Jones, P., Marshall, S. and Boujenko, N. 2008, 'Creating more people-friendly urban streets through "link and place" street planning and design', *IATSS Research*, vol. 32, no. 1, pp. 14–25.

Joos, E. 1989, 'The Zürich model', *Modern Tramway*, vol. 76, March, pp. 75–82.

Joos, E. 1990, 'The Zürich model, light transit to combat congestion', *Public Transport International*, vol. 39, no. 3, pp. 262–85.

Joos, E. 1994, *Economy and Ecology are no Contradictions: Three Messages from Zürich Concerning the New Transport Policy*, Zürich Transport Authority.

Kalinowski, T. and Rider, D. 2010, '"War on the car is over": Ford moves transit underground', *The Star*, 2 December, accessed at https://www.thestar.com/news/city_hall/2010/12/02/war_on_the_car_is_over_ford_moves_transit_underground.html.

Keesmaat, J. 2016, *TOcore Planning Downtown: King Street Visioning Study*, Toronto, ON: Toronto Transit Commission, accessed at https://transit.toronto.on.ca/images/10_King_Street_Visioning_Study_Merged_Updated.pdf.

Ketokivi, M. and Choi, T. 2014, 'Renaissance of case research as a scientific method', *Journal of Operations Management*, vol. 32, no. 5, p. 232.

Killen, A., Coxon, S. and Napper, R. 2017, 'A review of the literature on mitigation strategies for vandalism in rail environments', paper presented at the 39th Australasian Transport Research Forum (ATRF), Auckland.

King, R.D. 2003, *TCRP Synthesis 49: Yield to Bus – State of the Practice*, Washington, DC: Transportation Research Board.

Knill, C. and Tosun, J. 2011, 'Policy-making', in D. Caramani (ed.), *Comparative Politics*, 2nd edn, Oxford: Oxford University Press.

KOMO News 2019, 'Woman forces cars out of bus-only lane, causes social sensation', accessed 22 September 2019 at https://komonews.com/news/local/woman-forces-cars-out-of-bus-only-lane-causes-social-sensation.

Kroll, L. 1999, 'Creative Curitiba (the urban design of Curitiba, Brazil)', *The Architectural Review*, vol. 205, no. 1227, p. 92.

Laurence, P.L. 2016, *Becoming Jane Jacobs*, Philadelphia, PA: University of Pennsylvania Press.

Legacy, C. and Taylor, E. 2018, 'Resisting regeneration: Community opposition and the politicisation of transport-led regeneration in Australian cities', in K. Ruming (ed.), *Urban Regeneration in Australia: Policies, Processes and Projects of Contemporary Urban Change*, Abingdon, UK and New York, USA: Routledge, pp. 333–52.

Levinson, D.M. and Krizek, K.J. 2017, *The End of Traffic and the Future of Access: A Roadmap to the New Transport Landscape*, Sydney, NSW: Network Design Lab.

Levinson, H., Zimmerman, S., Clinger, J., Gast, J., Rutherford, S. and Bruhn, E. 2003a, *TCRP Report 90: Bus Rapid Transit Volume 2: Implementation Guidelines*, Transportation Research Board, Washington, DC, accessed at http://www.tcrponline.org/PDFDocuments/TCRP_RPT_90v2.pdf.

Levinson, H., Zimmerman, S., Clinger, J., Rutherford, S., Smith, R.L., Cracknell, J. and Soberman, R. 2003b, *TCRP Report 90: Bus Rapid Transit Volume 1: Case Studies in Bus Rapid Transit*, Transportation Research Board, Washington, DC.

Levy, E.J. 2015, *Rapid Transit in Toronto: A Century of Plans, Projects, Politics, and Paralysis*, Toronto, ON: BA Consulting Group.

Lindau, L.A., Hidalgo, D. and Facchini, D. 2010a, 'Bus Rapid Transit in Curitiba, Brazil: A look at the outcome after 35 years of bus-oriented development', *Transportation Research Record*, no. 2193, pp. 17–27.

Lindau, L.A., Hidalgo, D. and Facchini, D. 2010b, 'Curitiba, the cradle of Bus Rapid Transit', *Built Environment*, vol. 36, no. 3, pp. 274–82.

Lindau, L.A., Hidalgo, D. and de Almeida Lobo, A. 2014, 'Barriers to planning and implementing Bus Rapid Transit systems', *Research in Transportation Economics*, vol. 48, pp. 9–15.

Lindblom, C.E. 1959, 'The science of "muddling through"', *Public Administration Review*, vol. 19, no. 2, pp. 79–88.

Lindblom, C.E. 1979, 'Still muddling, not yet through', *Public Administration Review*, vol. 39, no. 6, pp. 517–26.

Litman, T. 2003, 'Measuring transportation: Traffic, mobility and accessibility', *ITE Journal*, vol. 73, no. 10, pp. 28–32.

Litman, T. 2015, *Evaluating Public Transit Benefits and Costs*, Victoria, BC: Victoria Transport Policy Institute, accessed at http://www.vtpi.org/tranben.pdf.

Litman, T. 2016, *When are Bus Lanes Warranted? Considering Economic Efficiency, Social Equity and Strategic Planning Goals*, Victoria, BC: Victoria Transport Policy Institute, accessed at http://www.vtpi.org/blw.pdf.

Lloyd-Jones, T. 1996, 'Curitiba: Sustainability by design', *Urban Design Quarterly*, vol. 57, pp. 47–53.

Loader, C. 2018, *Charting Transport: How is the Journey to Work Changing in Melbourne (2006–2016)*, accessed 21 February 2020 at https://chartingtransport.com/category/mode-share/.

Loader, C. 2019, *Charting Transport: Update on Australia Transport Trends (December 2019)*, accessed 21 February 2020 at https://chartingtransport.com/category/mode-share/.

Longhurst, J. 2015, *Bike Battles: A History of Sharing the American Road*, Seattle, WA, USA and London, UK: University of Washington Press.

Lunceford, B. 2012, *Naked Politics: Nudity, Political Action, and the Rhetoric of the Body*, Lanham, MD: Lexington Books.

Lydon, M. and Garcia, A. 2015, *Tactical Urbanism: Short-term Action for Long-term Change*, Washington, DC: Island Press.

Lydon, M., Bartman, D., Garcia, T., Preston, R. and Woudstra, R. 2012, *Tactical Urbanism 2: Short-Term Action, Long-Term Change*, Miami, FL, and New York, NY, USA: The Street Plans Collaborative, accessed at https://issuu.com/streetplanscollaborative/docs/tactical_urbanism_vol_2_final?mode=window&backgroundColor=%23222222.

Lyles, M.A. and Thomas, H. 1988, 'Strategic problem formulation: Biases and assumptions embedded in alternative decision-making models', *Journal of Management Studies*, vol. 25, no. 2, pp. 131–45.

Mao, Z. 1967, *On Protracted War*, 3rd edn, Peking: Foreign Languages Press.

Marier, P. 2015, 'Policy feedback and learning', in E. Araral, S. Fritzen, M. Howlett, M. Ramesh and W. Xun (eds), *Routledge Handbook of Public Policy*, London: Routledge, pp. 401–414.

Marsden, G. and Reardon, L. 2017, 'Questions of governance: Rethinking the study of transportation policy', *Transportation Research Part A: Policy and Practice*, vol. 101, pp. 238–51.

McCutcheon, D. and Meredith, J. 1993, 'Conducting case study research in operations management', *Journal of Operations Management*, vol. 11, no. 3, p. 239.

McIntosh, J., Trubka, R., Kenworthy, J. and Newman, P. 2014, 'The role of urban form and transit in city car dependence: Analysis of 26 global cities from 1960 to 2000', *Transportation Research Part D: Transport and Environment*, vol. 33, pp. 95–110.

McKibben, B. 2007, *Hope, Human and Wild: True Stories of Living Lightly on the Earth*, Minneapolis, MN: Milkweed Editions.

McPherson, C.D. 2017, 'Transport modelling', in A. Delbosc and W. Young (eds), *Traffic Engineering and Management*, 7th edn, Clayton, VIC: Monash University Institute of Transport Studies, pp. 790–837.

Meadows, D. 1995, 'The city of first priorities', *The Whole Earth Review*, no. 85, p. 58.

Mees, P. 2000, *A Very Public Solution: Transport in the Dispersed City*, Carlton South, VIC: Melbourne University Press.

Mees, P. 2003a, 'Paterson's Curse: The attempt to revive metropolitan planning in Melbourne', *Urban Policy and Research*, vol. 21, no. 3, pp. 287–99.

Mees, P. 2003b, 'What happened to the systems approach? Evaluation of alternatives in planning for major transport projects', paper presented at the *26th Australasian Transport Research Forum (ATRF)*, Wellington.

Mees, P. 2010, *Transport for Suburbia: Beyond the Automobile Age*, London, UK and Sterling, VA, USA: Earthscan.

Mees, P. 2011, 'Who killed Melbourne 2030', paper presented at the State of Australian Cities National Conference, Melbourne, VIC.

Meredith, J. 1998, 'Building operations management theory through case and field research', *Journal of Operations Management*, vol. 16, no. 4, p. 441.

Metrolinx, Toronto Transit Commission, City of Toronto and Transit City Group 2010, *Transit City: Eglinton Crosstown Light Rail Transit: Transit Project Assessment Study: Environmental Project Report*, accessed 21 June 2018 at http://thecrosstown.ca/the-project/reports/EglintonCrosstownLRTEnvironmentalProjectReport.

Meyer, L.H. and Sanklecha, P. 2009, 'Introduction: Legitimacy, justice and public international law: Three perspectives on the debate', in L.H. Meyer (ed.), *Legitimacy, Justice and Public International Law*, New York: Cambridge University Press, pp. 1–28.

Meyrick and Associates 2009, *Network Operations Planning Framework*, AP–R338/09, Austroads, Sydney, NSW.

Miles, M.B. and Huberman, A.M. 1994, *Qualitative Data Analysis: An Expanded Sourcebook*, 2nd edn, Thousand Oaks, CA: Sage Publications.

Moore, S.A. 2007, *Alternative Routes to the Sustainable City: Austin, Curitiba, and Frankfurt*, Lanham, MD: Lexington Books.

Morhayim, L. 2012, 'From counterpublics to counterspaces: Livable city advocates' efforts to reshape cities through carfree-streets events', Berkeley, CA: University of California.

Mulley, C., Hensher, D.A. and Rose, J. 2014, 'Do preferences for BRT and LRT vary across geographical jurisdictions? A comparative assessment of six Australian capital cities', *Case Studies on Transport Policy*, vol. 2, no. 1, pp. 1–9.

Nash, A. 2001, *Implementation of Zürich's Transit Priority Program*, San José, CA: Mineta Transportation Institute, San José State University.

Nash, A. 2003, 'Implementing Zurich's transit priority program', *Transportation Research Record: Journal of the Transportation Research Board*, vol. 1835, pp. 59–65.

Nash, A., Corman, F. and Sauter-Servaes, T. 2018, *A Reassessment of Zurich's Public Transport Priority Program*, unpublished.

Netelenbos, B. 2016, *Political Legitimacy Beyond Weber: An Analytical Framework*, London: Palgrave Macmillan.

Norton, P.D. 2007, 'Street rivals: Jaywalking and the invention of the motor age street', *Technology and Culture*, vol. 48, no. 2, pp. 331–59.

O'Brien, C. 1993, *The Simpsons: Marge vs. the Monorail*, 20th Century Fox Television and Gracie Films.

O'Neil, L. 2018, 'Street hockey: The newest form of transit protest on King St', BlogTO, accessed 31 January 2018 at https://www.blogto.com/city/2018/01/street-hockey-newest-form-transit-protest-king-st/.

Olesen, M. 2014, 'Framing light rail projects: Case studies from Bergen, Angers and Bern', *Case Studies on Transport Policy*, vol. 2, no. 1, pp. 10–19.

Osbaldeston, M. 2008, *Unbuilt Toronto: A History of the City That Might Have Been*, Toronto, ON: Dundurn Press.

Oxford Dictionary 2018a, *Normative*, Oxford University Press, accessed 14 December 2018 at https://en.oxfo rddictionaries.com/definition/normative.

Oxford Dictionary 2018b, *Rational*, Oxford University Press, accessed 4 July 2018 at https://en.oxforddictionaries.com/definition/rational.

Oxford Dictionary 2018c, *Techno-*, Oxford University Press, accessed 3 July 2018 at https://en.oxforddictionaries.com/definition/techno-.

Pagano, C. 2013, 'DIY urbanism: Property and process in grassroots city building', *Marquette Law Review*, vol. 97, p. 335.

Page, S. 2006, 'Path dependence', *Quarterly Journal of Political Science*, vol. 1, no. 1, pp. 87–115.

Parsons, W. 1995, *Public Policy: An Introduction to the Theory and Practice of Policy Analysis*, Aldershot, UK and Brookfield, VT, USA: Edward Elgar Publishing.

Peters, B.G. 2011, 'Approaches in comparative politics', in D. Caramani (ed.), *Comparative Politics*, 2nd edn, Oxford: Oxford University Press.

Peters, B.G. 2015, *Advanced Introduction to Public Policy*, Cheltenham, UK and Northampton, MA, USA: Edward Elgar Publishing.

Pressman, J.L. and Wildavsky, A. 1984, *Implementation: How Great Expectations in Washington are Dashed in Oakland: Or, Why it's Amazing that Federal Programs Work at all, this being a Saga of the Economic Development Administration as Told by Two Sympathetic Observers Who Seek to Build Morals on a Foundation of Ruined Hopes*, 3rd edn, Berkeley, CA: University of California Press.

Public Transport Users Association 2011, 'Bus lane removal short-sighted', accessed 21 August 2017 at https://www.ptua.org.au/2011/03/29/stud-rd-bus-lane/.

Pulichino, M. 2003, 'Transit preferential treatment: A public policy-making perspective', Master of Science in Transportation thesis, Massachusetts Institute of Technology.

Pulichino, M. and Coughlin, J.F. 2005, 'Introducing transit preferential treatment: Is a political maverick necessary for public transportation to innovate?', *Journal of Urban Planning and Development*, vol. 131, no. 2, p. 79.

Pülzl, H. and Treib, O. 2007, 'Implementing public policy', in F. Fischer, G.J. Miller and M.S. Sindney (eds), *Handbook of Public Policy Analysis: Theory, Politics, and Methods*, Hoboken, NJ: Taylor & Francis Ltd.

Quin, P. 2005, 'Batchelor's tram experiment fails Clarendon Street', accessed 4 October 2017 at https://web.archive.org/web/20070310184842/http://www.clarendonstcampaign.org:80/.

Rabinovitch, J. and Leitmann, J. 1993, 'Environmental innovation and management in Curitiba, Brazil', in *UMP Working Paper Series*, Banco Mundial, vol. 1.

Reid, M. 2010, 'Fury at Stud Rd bus lane', *Knox Leader*, accessed 10 May 2018 at https://web.archive.org/web/20110513202942/http://knox-leader.whereilive.com.au/news/story/fury-at-stud-rd-bus-lane/.

Reynolds, J. 2019, '"O teach me how I should forget to think"; Safe systems, human factors, institutions and a Montague Street bridge crash', paper presented at the Australasian Transport Research Forum, Canberra, ACT.

Reynolds, J., Currie, G., Rose, G. and Cumming, A. 2017, 'Moving beyond techno-rationalism: New models of transit priority implementation', paper presented at the Australasian Transport Research Forum, Auckland, 27–29 November.

Reynolds, J., Currie, G., Rose, G. and Cumming, A. 2018, 'Top-down versus bottom-up perspectives on streetcar priority', paper presented at Transportation Research Board Annual Meeting, Washington, DC.

Roth, A. 2007, 'Applications of empirical science in manufacturing and service operations', *Manufacturing & Service Operations Management*, vol. 9, no. 4, pp. 353–67.

Ruming, K. 2018, 'Metropolitan strategic plans: Establishing and delivering a vision for urban regeneration and renewal', in K. Ruming (ed.), *Urban Regeneration in Australia: Policies, Processes and Projects of Contemporary Urban Change*, Abingdon, UK and New York, NY, USA: Routledge, pp. 27–50.

Ryus, P., Laustsen, K., Blume, K., Beaird, S. and Langdon, S. 2016, *TCRP Report 183: A Guidebook on Transit-supportive Roadway Strategies*, Washington, DC: Transportation Research Board.

Sabatier, P. 1986, 'Top-down and bottom-up approaches to implementation research: A critical analysis and suggested synthesis', *Journal of Public Policy*, vol. 6, no. 1, pp. 21–48.

Sabatier, P. 1987, 'Knowledge, policy-oriented learning, and policy change: An advocacy coalition framework', *Knowledge*, vol. 8, no. 4, pp. 649–92.

Sabatier, P. 1988, 'An advocacy coalition framework of policy change and the role of policy-oriented learning therein', *Policy Sciences*, vol. 21, no. 2–4, pp. 129–68.

Sabatier, P. 1998, 'The advocacy coalition framework: Revisions and relevance for Europe', *Journal of European Public Policy*, vol. 5, no. 1, pp. 98–130.

Sabatier, P. and Jenkins-Smith, H. 1993, *Policy Change and Learning: An Advocacy Coalition Approach*, Boulder, CO: Westview Press.

Sabatier, P. and Jenkins-Smith, H. 1999, 'The advocacy coaltion framework: An assessment', in P. Sabatier (ed.), *Theories of the Policy Process*, Boulder, CO: Westview Press, pp. 117–68.

Schwartz, H.H. 2004, *Urban Renewal, Municipal Revitalization: The Case of Curitiba, Brazil*, Higher Education Publications.

Shrivastava, P. and Grant, J.H. 1985, 'Empirically derived models of strategic decision-making processes', *Strategic Management Journal*, vol. 6, no. 2, pp. 97–113.

Siggelkow, N. 2007, 'Persuasion with case studies', *Academy of Management Journal*, vol. 50, no. 1, pp. 20–24.

Smart Growth America 2019, *Safety Demonstration Projects: Case Studies from Durham, NC, Huntsville, AL, and Pittsburgh, PA*, accessed at https://smartgrowthamerica.org/resources/safety-demonstration-projects-case-studies-from-durham-nc-huntsville-al-and-pittsburgh-pa/.

Smith, N. and Hensher, D. 1998, 'The future of exclusive busways: The Brazilian experience', *Transport Reviews*, vol. 18, no. 2, pp. 131–52.

Smith, P. 2005, 'Clarendon Street Think Tram trial project', Strategy and Policy Review committee, Policy and Plannning, City of Port Phillip, Melbourne, VIC, accessed 2 October 2017 at http://www.portphillip.vic.gov.au/default/meeting_agenda_archive/o14949.pdf.

Statistics Canada 2011, 'Proportion of workers taking public transit to work, by census metropolitan area and type of public transit, 2011', accessed 30 January 2019 at https://www12.statcan.gc.ca/nhs-enm/2011/as-sa/99-012-x/2011003/c-g/c-g01-eng.cfm.

Stopher, P.R. and Stanley, J. 2014, *Introduction to Transport Policy: A Public Policy View*, Cheltenham, UK and Northampton, MA, USA: Edward Elgar Publishing.

Stuart, I., McCutcheon, D., Handfield, R., McLachlin, R. and Samson, D. 2002, 'Effective case research in operations management: A process perspective. (Statistical data included)', *Journal of Operations Management*, vol. 20, no. 5, p. 419.

Talen, E. 2015, 'Do-it-Yourself urbanism: A history', *Journal of Planning History*, vol. 14, no. 2, pp. 135–48.

Taylor, Z. 2013, 'Who votes for a mayor like Rob Ford?', The Conversation Media Group, accessed 13 November 2019 at https://theconversation.com/who-votes-for-a-mayor-like-rob-ford-20193.

The Scarlett Syndrome 2011, 'Stud Road bus lanes still causing commuters headaches', accessed 10 May 2018 at https://thescarlettsyndrome.wordpress.com/2011/05/14/stud-road-bus-lanes-still-causing-commuters-headaches/.

Thomas, E.N. 1966, 'Introduction to a systems approach to transportation problems', Transportation Center at Northwestern University, Evanston, IL.

Todorovic, F. 2015, Justicia Urbana, UN Habitat, accessed at https://unhabitat.org/the-2015-urban-october-design-competition-winners-announced/.

Torgerson, D. 1985, 'Contextual orientation in policy analysis: The contribution of Harold D. Lasswell', *Policy Sciences*, vol. 18, no. 3, pp. 241–61.

Toronto Transit Commission 2007, 'Meeting minutes, March 21, 2007: Toronto Transit City – Light Rail Plan', Toronto Transit Commission, accessed 19 March 2020 at http://www.ttc.ca/About_the_TTC/Commission_reports_and_information/Commission_meetings/2007/Mar_21_2007/Other/Toronto_Transit_City.pdf.

Trailnet 2016, 'Slow your street: A how-to guide for pop-up traffic calming', accessed at http://www.onestl.org/media/site/documents/reports/bicycle-pedestrian-planning/SlowYourStreets_HowToGuide_Final-v.2_reduced.pdf.

TransitCenter 2018, 'Everett bus lane: The little popup that could', accessed at http://transitcenter.org/2018/01/02/everett-bus-lane-the-little-pop-up-that-could/.

Transportation Information Steering Committee (TISC), R.A. Malatest & Associates Ltd., David Kriger Consultants Inc., HDR Inc. & Data Management Group (DMG) Department of Civil Engineering University of Toronto 2018, *Transportation Tomorrow Survey 2016, TTS 2016: 2016, 2011, 2006, 1996 and 1986 travel summaries for the Greater Toronto & Hamilton Area, March 2018*, accessed at http://dmg.utoronto.ca/pdf/tts/2016/2016TTS_Summaries_GTHA.pdf.

Tudge, A. 2010, 'Stud Road bus lane; sample feedback from residents', accessed 6 April 2018 at http://www.alantudge.com.au/Portals/0/Bus%20lane%20-%20resident%20report.pdf.

Turnpenny, J., Adelle, C. and Jordan, A. 2013, 'Policy appraisal', in E. Araral Jr, S. Fritzen, M. Howlett, M. Ramesh and X. Wu (eds), *Routledge Handbook of Public Policy*, Abingdon: Routledge.

Turpin, S. and Marais, M. 2004, 'Decision-making: Theory and practice', *ORiON*, vol. 20, no. 2, pp. 143–60.

UCLA Institute of Transportation Studies 2019, *Best Practices in Implementing Tactical Transit Lanes*, Berkeley, CA: University of California, accessed at https://www.its.ucla.edu/wp-content/uploads/sites/6/2019/02/Best-Practices-in-Implementing-Tactical-Transit-Lanes-1.pdf.

UKDFT (Department for Transport) 2010, *Manual for Streets 2: Wider Application of the Principles*, London: Chartered Institution of Highways and Transportation, accessed 17 May 2016 at https://www.gov.uk/government/publications/manual-for-streets-2.

Vanderbilt, T. 2009, *Traffic: Why We Drive the Way We Do (and what it says about us)*, New York: Vintage Books.

VicDOI 2002, *Melbourne 2030: Planning for Sustainable Growth*, Melbourne, VIC: Victorian State Government, Department of Infrastructure.

VicDOT 2008, *The Victorian Transport Plan*, Melbourne, VIC: State of Victoria.

VicPCD 2008, *Melbourne 2030: A Planning Update: Melbourne @ 5 million*, Melbourne, VIC: Victorian State Government, Department of Planning and Community.

Voigt, R. 2015, 'The serious game of tactical urbanism', *Municipal World*, vol. 125, no. 5, pp. 15–16, 40.

Voss, C., Tsikriktsis, N. and Frohlich, M. 2002, 'Case research in operations management', *International Journal of Operations & Production Management*, vol. 22, no. 2, pp. 195–219.

Vuchic, V.R. 1981, *Urban Public Transportation: Systems and Technology*, Englewood Cliffs, NJ: Prentice-Hall.

Vuchic, V.R. 2005, *Urban Transit Operations, Planning and Economics*, Hoboken, NJ: John Wiley & Sons.

Vuchic, V.R. 2007, *Urban Transit Systems and Technology*, Hoboken, NJ: John Wiley & Sons.

Vuchic, V.R., Bruun, E.C., Krstanoski, N.B., Shin, Y.E., Kikuchi, S., Chakroborty, P. and Perincherry, V. 1994, *The Bus Transit System: Its Underutilized Potential*, Report for Federal Transit Administration, U.S. Department of Transportation.

Wall, A. 2007, 'Network operation planning: A new approach to managing congestion', paper presented at the *30th Australiasian Transport Research Forum (ATRF)*, Melbourne, VIC.

Wall, A. 2017a, 'A framework for traffic engineering and management', in A. Delbosc and W. Young (eds), *Traffic Engineering and Management*, 7th edn, Clayton, VIC: Monash University Institute of Transport Studies, pp. 1–20.

Wall, A. 2017b, 'Network operation planning', in A. Delbosc and W. Young (eds), *Traffic Engineering and Management*, 7th edn, Clayton, VIC: Monash University Institute of Transport Studies, pp. 619–31.

Waterson, B.J., Rajbhandari, B. and Hounsell, N.B. 2003, 'Simulating the impacts of strong bus priority measures', *Journal of Transportation Engineering*, vol. 129, no. 6, pp. 642–7.

Webb, D. 2018, 'Tactical urbanism: Delineating a critical praxis', *Planning Theory & Practice*, vol. 19, no. 1, pp. 58–73.

Weeratunga, K. and Luk, J. 2010, 'A comparative study of four network operations planning frameworks/guidelines', paper presented at the *24th ARRB Conference*.

Weible, C.M. and Nohrsted, D. 2013, 'The advocacy coalition framework', in E. Araral Jr, S. Fritzen, M. Howlett, M. Ramesh and X. Wu (eds), *Routledge Handbook of Public Policy*, Abingdon: Routledge, pp. 125–37.

Weible, C.M. and Sabatier, P. 2007, 'A guide to the advocacy coalition framework', in F. Fischer, G.J. Miller and M.S. Sindney (eds), *Handbook of Public Policy Analysis: Theory, Politics, and Methods*, Hoboken, NJ: Taylor & Francis.

Weible, C.M., Sabatier, P. and McQueen, K. 2009, 'Themes and variations: Taking stock of the advocacy coalition framework', *Policy Studies Journal*, vol. 37, no. 1, pp. 121–40.

Worcam, N. 1993, 'Boom and bus (Curitiba, Brazil's new high-capacity bus transit system)', *Technology Review*, vol. 96, no. 8, p. 12.

Wright, L. 2001, 'Latin American busways: Moving people rather than cars', *Natural Resources Forum*, vol. 25, no. 2, pp. 121–34.

Wright, L. 2010, 'Bus Rapid Transit: A public transport renaissance', *Built Environment*, vol. 36, no. 3, pp. 269–73.

Yarra Trams, VicDOI and VicRoads 2004, 'Tram Priority Program', VicRoads: Publication Number 01390, Melbourne, accessed at http://www.portphillip.vic.gov.au/default/meeting_agenda_archive/o14950.pdf.

Yin, R.K. 2009, *Case Study Research: Design and Methods*, 4th edn, Thousand Oaks, CA: Sage Publications.

Yin, R.K. 2014, *Case Study Research: Design and Methods*, 5th edn, Thousand Oaks, CA: Sage Publications.

Yin, R.K. 2018, *Case Study Research and Applications: Design and Methods*, 6th edn, Thousand Oaks, CA: Sage Publications.

11. Paying for public transport
Joel Mendez, James Wood, Dristi Neog and Jeffrey Brown

11.1   INTRODUCTION

Public transport services require funding. Funding is needed to purchase, operate and maintain vehicles, pay staff, and make strategic investments to maintain or increase patronage. The purpose of this chapter is to query the research and practitioner literatures to identify the different mechanisms used to pay for public transport, discuss their use in real-world circumstances, and assess their strengths and limitations. The authors draw primarily from United States examples in this review, although some mechanisms are also used elsewhere.

The chapter opens with a discussion of the benefits and costs of public transport and the issue of subsidies in public transport. This opening section is followed by four sections that introduce different types of mechanisms used to pay for public transport. The first set of mechanisms is fare-based mechanisms, including directly paid passenger fares and indirectly paid fares such as employer or university-based pass programs. The second set of mechanisms is locally generated revenue sources including sales taxes, payroll taxes, charges on motorists, and agency-generated advertising revenues. The third set of mechanisms is intergovernmental grants that involve funding transfers to the public transport operator from other government entities. The fourth set of mechanisms is urban development based taxes and fees including joint development strategies, special assessments, and private contributions. The chapter concludes with reflections on the funding mechanisms and calls for additional research on their use.

The Benefits and Costs of Public Transport

Decisions over how to pay for public transport are critically important. They are also integrally bound up with larger public debates over the *purpose* of public transport. Policymakers must grapple with questions such as:

- "What are public transport's benefits and costs?"
- "Why should non-riders pay for public transport?"
- "To whose benefit are public transport planning decisions made?"

Much of this debate, and indeed much of the controversy surrounding public transport, centers on a consideration of its costs and benefits. This is because the *costs* – both financial and non-financial – of public transport are generally more noticeable and "real" to taxpayers than the *benefits* of it. Because of this general sentiment, and the skepticism about public transport that it may generate in societies where financial support depends on voter actions, public transport providers must frequently function as salespeople and persuasive advocates for their systems. They must be prepared to advertise the various

Table 11.1   Typical capital and operating expenses for public transport

	Capital expenses	Operating expenses
Definition	Expenses incurred from construction of transit infrastructure, or from the purchase of depreciating assets (such as vehicles)	Expenses incurred from the operation and maintenance of transit systems
Examples	• Rail construction • Purchase of buses, trams and wheelchair-accessible vehicles • Purchase of existing rail rights-of-way • Construction of transit stops and facilities	• Labor costs for operators and mechanics • Energy costs for powering vehicles • Maintenance of vehicles and facilities • Costs of collecting fares • CCTV/security expenses

benefits of public transport to an audience of riders and non-riders. This is often critical to maintaining a stable financial foundation for the delivery of public transport services.

Public transport has costs and these costs, in turn, necessitate the identification of mechanisms that can be used to pay for public transport services. Public transport costs are generally divided into two categories: capital costs (incurred from building infrastructure and purchasing vehicles) and operating costs (incurred from purchasing fuel, funding operators' wages, etc.) (see Table 11.1). A third category, maintenance costs associated with repairing and preserving vehicles and infrastructure, is sometimes considered separately from operating costs. These costs are often paid by different levels of government, and with different degrees of priority. In US public transport systems, a longstanding pattern of "capital bias" has been observed since the 1970s (Hilton, 1974; Pickrell, 1986). This phenomenon refers to the apparent preference among government agencies for funding very visible capital projects (such as rail transit lines and landmark stations) rather than funding maintenance or operations. Taylor and Samples (2002) assert that this bias has been built in to public transport grants formulas for decades, which ultimately induces service providers to overspend on construction and underspend on maintenance, labor and general operations.

Public transport benefits and their distribution provide the rationale for the selection of many of the mechanisms used to pay for public transport services. Due to the diversity of service types, geographies, and populations served, public transport's benefits may vary considerably (see Table 11.2). A substantial benefit in one location might only yield modest benefit in another location, for example. In order to minimize the effects of this widespread variation, the benefits may be viewed through conceptual frameworks or "lenses" focused on a specific set of benefits or outcomes. This perspective enables policymakers to more effectively observe public transport's diverse benefits as they are applied to specific modes or populations. Litman (2019) divides these outcomes into categories of "Efficiency", which he defines as the relationship between costs and benefits, and "Equity", which he defines as the distribution of costs and benefits and whether they are appropriate. He finds that public transport modes excel at one or the other, and

Table 11.2   Direct and indirect benefits secured by public transport riders and non-riders

	Direct benefits	Indirect benefits
Riders	● Low-cost transportation ● Parking reduction ● Independent mobility ● Access to activity centers	● Crime/safety ● Overall accessibility for all ages and ability levels
Non-riders	● Congestion relief ● Emissions reduction ● Increased safety (fewer traffic accidents) ● "Option value"	● Transit-oriented development ● Transit jobs multiplier ● "Option value"

occasionally both. For example, commuter rail (which tends to serve wealthy commuters who work in professional settings) advances efficiency, but generally not equity. At the same time, paratransit services (which serve people who otherwise might be homebound) are equity-driven and provide little to no measurable efficiency benefit. Buses and light rail offer a mix of efficiency and equity benefits. Given the increasing public pressure to make efficient use of scarce public dollars for the provision of public transport, there is a growing need to understand the best way to pay for it in order to meet consensus-formed goals and satisfy the many constituencies involved in the decision-making process. A review of how we pay for it is a necessary first step in this process.

The Function and Purpose of Subsidies

The need for subsidies for public transport, and the distribution of public transport benefits, combine to explain the development of the non-fare-based funding mechanisms discussed later in this chapter. Virtually all of the world's public transport systems are subsidized with public dollars. This is particularly true in Western Europe, North America and Australasia, where rider fares rarely cover the costs of operating public transport let alone the capital costs of building its infrastructure. In this geopolitical context, public transport is subsidized in part because of its contributions as a public service/good, but also because of its economic benefits to the surrounding community. These economic benefits have become a focal point for researchers and policymakers, centered chiefly on the economic concept of Return on Investment (ROI) as a means of comparing an expenditure's real and potential benefits (Litman, 2007; Chang-fu and Yuan, 2011). ROI comes in many forms and timeframes. For example, adding shelters to bus stops along a popular route might quickly boost ridership or improve customer satisfaction in return for a modest outlay of funds. On the other hand, an urban rail/tram line designed to revitalize a downtrodden area requires a far greater investment and may take several years to generate the desired results. The specific ROI varies by place and transport mode. However, given the political climate in which public transport decisions are made, these outcomes are critical to convincing stakeholders and taxpayers to support an expensive and long-term project.

In addition to questions of immediate versus delayed benefits, considerable attention has been paid to the twin concepts of Transit-Oriented Development (TOD) and Transit-

Adjacent Development (TAD) in cities with rail-based services. Both TOD and TAD are mechanisms for communities to leverage public transport investments into transformative land-use changes. In a number of places, governments have devised funding mechanisms that tax this induced new development for the financial benefit of public transport providers. In addition to these development-focused mechanisms, communities have found other ways to fund public transport, ranging from various forms of fare payment to locally generated sales taxes and motor vehicle tolls and congestion charges.

11.2   FARE-BASED MECHANISMS TO FUND PUBLIC TRANSPORT

Funding for public transport typically comes from four mechanisms: passenger fare revenue, locally raised taxes or fees, intergovernmental grants, and urban development-related taxes or fees. This section discusses fare-based mechanisms, highlighting examples of their everyday use, while later sections address the other mechanisms. Most examples cited throughout this chapter come from North America, but the use of the various funding mechanisms extends beyond the North American context.

Passenger Fares

Passenger fares are an important and common mechanism for paying for public transport. Most service providers require users to pay some form of fare to ride, which is appropriate from an equity perspective as the person who rides is the most direct beneficiary of the service provided. The resulting revenues contribute toward the cost of providing service. However, passenger fares do not provide sufficient revenues to fully cover the costs of providing public transport. In fact, they rarely cover operating costs alone. Table 11.3 reports the ratio of passenger fare revenues to operating costs, which is referred to as farebox recovery ratio, in major cities around the world (World Bank, 2013). The data indicate that in very few cities do fare revenues even meet operating costs, let alone cover the capital costs of the infrastructure and vehicles used to provide service.

Farebox recovery ratios also vary among types of services, largely due to differences in efficiency, or the average number of riders served by a single vehicle. Table 11.4 provides these data for different services in the United States (Office of Budget and Policy, 2018).

Table 11.3   Passenger fare revenues as a proportion of operating costs in major world cities

City	Percent	City	Percent	City	Percent
Hong Kong	118	Mumbai	70	Ahmedabad	51
Curitiba	100	Toronto	67	Paris	51
Singapore	97	London	63	Vancouver	51
Bangalore	95	Seoul	61	Mexico City	42
Santiago	90	Delhi	59	New York	36

Source: Adopted from World Bank (2013, p. 30).

Table 11.4   Passenger fares as a proportion of operating costs for different services in the United States

Rail		Bus		Demand Response		Other	
Heavy rail	63.3	Commuter bus	52.9	Demand response taxi	12.8	Vanpool	78.2
Commuter rail	52.9	Fixed-route bus	23.2	Demand response	7.5	Ferry boat	31.7
Light rail	25.9	Rapid transit bus	32.3				
Streetcar/tram	20.7	Trolley bus	26.6				
Hybrid rail	10.1						

Source: Office of Budget and Policy (2018).

Among all public transport services in the US, the farebox recovery ratio was about 35 percent. However, ratios ranged from 7.5 percent for demand responsive service, door-to-door services typically provided for older adults and/or disabled persons, to 63.3 percent for heavy rail services such as subways.

Because fare revenues are typically not sufficient to support total operating and capital costs, non-fare-based mechanisms such as those discussed in later sections have emerged as sources of financial subsidy. But in this section, the authors discuss the different types of fare mechanisms that are used to fund public transport.

Passenger-paid Fares

Typically, a passenger pays the provider directly for using public transport. However, this direct payment comes in many different forms. Fares may be collected from the rider at the time of use (individual trip payment), or in advance of use (multiple use tickets, tokens, or passes) (McCollom and Pratt, 2004). Fares can be charged as: a single amount which does not vary with use, distance or zone-based fares that increase based on the distance travelled or number of fare zones crossed, or even by the time of day where the fare charged during the time of peak use might exceed that charged when demand for service is lower. In many countries, fares are discounted for particular rider groups such as older adults, youth, or the disabled.

The fares charged by the New York Metropolitan Transportation Authority, North America's largest public transport network, provide an example of how passenger-paid fares are charged in practice. Passengers can pay $3 per individual trip, purchase multiple-use metro cards that offer a discount on the single-use fare ($2.75 per trip), or buy unlimited-ride passes that are valid for 7 days or 30 days. The provider also offers reduced fares (typically priced at half the regular fare) for older adults and disabled persons (Metropolitan Transportation Authority, n.d.).

Passenger-paid fares have strengths and limitations as a funding mechanism. Their greatest strength is their user-based nature, which means they tend to be regarded favorably from both efficiency and equity perspectives. The fare serves as a charge for the amount of service consumed by the rider and their willingness to pay it reflects the value they place on the trip. If riders are not willing to pay a fare then they do not place that level of value on the service. When fares are set appropriately, rider demand can indicate to providers where services might be increased or otherwise improved in a way that would provide additional benefits to their customers. While fare increases are sometimes opposed by users or allied interest groups, charging a fare is relatively non-controversial in most places.

However, passenger-paid fares also have limitations. The act of paying a fare at the time of use might cause some potential riders not to use a service. Providers have responded by using multiple trip ride options that obscure the per-ride charge associated with using public transport in the hope that doing so might encourage some individuals to use it more often. Second, there are collection costs associated with charging fares, including the costs of acquiring and maintaining fare collection equipment and the costs of implementing enforcement strategies to deter fare evasion. In extreme cases, these costs might approach or even exceed the amount of fare revenue collected.

Indirectly Paid Fares

An indirectly paid fare is a charge for using a service that is not paid by the user. Instead, someone else pays the fare on their behalf. For example, employers might purchase the service for their employees or colleges might purchase the service for their students. The fare is thus shifted to some other mechanism of payment. Because the passenger does not have to pay the fare, they might use the service more often, which might, in turn, reduce the need for an employer, college, medical complex, or apartment building to provide parking spaces for automobiles. These other entities pay the provider directly on behalf of the eligible rider population. They might in turn bundle their costs into the rents paid by renters or the fees paid by students at colleges and universities, or choose to provide fare-free access to public transport as an additional benefit to employees or other constituencies. These programs operate under a variety of names, including Eco-Pass, U-Pass, and Fare Share, among numerous others. Service providers offer these programs as a means of raising revenues to fund their operations and a strategy to encourage new riders to use their services (Brown et al., 2001; Meyer and Beimborn, 1998).

The Universal College Student Transit Pass (U-Pass) offered by Los Angeles Metro, serving Los Angeles County (LA), provides students at participating colleges and universities with unlimited rides on all Metro services, including Metro Rail, Metro Rapid and Express buses, and local buses. Metro charges $0.75 per boarding to participating institutions (which include Cal Tech, UCLA, Loyola Marymount University, and a number of other public and private institutions) and also partners with these institutions to offer heavily discounted unlimited ride passes for purchase on their campuses. Institutions often fund these programs through a combination of student fees or subsidies derived from parking revenue (Metro LA a, n.d.).

Smaller service providers also offer these programs. Rogue Valley Transportation District (RVTD) in Medford, Oregon provides a U-Pass program for local schools for just $1.95 per student per month and an employer-based program that allows employers to buy an unlimited ride pass for all employees at $3.85 per employee per month. Additionally, they offer a Fare Share program that lets participating schools and companies share the cost of transit service with their students and employees. They have partnered with the local housing authority to offer the Fare Share program to public housing residents in seven residential complexes in the community. Residence-based programs can also be found in other communities, including in State College, Pennsylvania where the transit agency has partnered with apartment buildings to make available resident passes to their tenants (RVTD, n.d.; West, 2019; Sheader, 2019).

These indirect forms of fare payment have strengths and limitations. A strength is that this arrangement can provide a stable and predictable source of revenue for the provider (based on how pricing is set). The partnerships might also allow the provider to reach a new rider market, which could lead to increased longer-term ridership. These new potential riders might be more likely to use public transport because one of the barriers to use, the act of paying a fare, is removed. And because someone is paying for the service being consumed, there is no pressure on the public to provide additional subsidy support, which increases the program's political appeal. One potential weakness is that because it is not a payment directly from the rider, it could be seen as unfair to burden an organization and/ or individuals in such organizations who do not use the service with higher fees or rents. The level of payment must be negotiated between the public transport provider and the partnering organization and there are risks for both parties. The public transport operator might set the price too low for the amount of service consumed or the partnering entity might accept too high a price in circumstances where usage does not meet expectations. Charges tied to actual use are a good compromise to protect the interests of both parties.

Free Transit

While not a funding mechanism per se, one option for service providers is to not charge a fare for use. This action may encourage higher ridership and thereby justify the channeling of more public funds for the services. The logic here is that public transport provides so many benefits to the community that acquiring these additional benefits is worth the higher costs required to provide free service. Of course, this requires that other funding sources be identified to offset the loss of passenger fare revenues (Volinski, 2012; Hodge et al., 1994).

Tallinn, Estonia stopped charging to ride on public transport in January 2013, becoming the first European Union capital city to offer free service. Officials have since extended free transit to 11 of the 15 counties in the country. In the years since, Tallinn has kept its program free for residents (but not for visitors). Residents register and buy a green card for around $2 per person but they can then ride on public transport for free (O'Sullivan, 2018; Hess, 2017).

The objectives for no-fare programs include service promotion and education, mobility, support of the local economy, and congestion reduction (Hodge et al., 1994). Free service also provides low-income people with easier access to jobs. From a fiscal point of view, such programs also make sense when fare collection costs are higher than the revenues raised. Not collecting a fare can also allow passengers to board and alight from vehicles more quickly, which reduces delays and improves on time performance.

One potential drawback is that ridership gains resulting from providing free public transport might be acquired by shifting people from walking to these services, which indeed occurred in Tallinn (Cats et al., 2017; Hess, 2017; Volinski, 2012). If people are not being shifted from their automobiles, anticipated congestion reduction benefits might not occur. Higher passenger loads might also necessitate acquiring more vehicles and hiring more operators, leading to higher costs and added subsidy requirements. There may also be concerns from riders resulting from homeless people using the service to protect themselves from inclement weather. Finally, eliminating any user payment for the provision of the service may diminish the service's value to the rider. People may start to take it for granted. For a number of these reasons, many cities that have tried free public transport have reintroduced fares for riders (Arizona PIRG Education Fund, 2009).

11.3   LOCALLY GENERATED REVENUES TO FUND PUBLIC TRANSPORT

Public transport depends on subsidies to make up the difference between fare revenues and the cost associated with providing service. Some revenues used to subsidize public transport are generated at the local level, in the communities or regions within which services are provided, through taxes or fees levied on individuals, employers, businesses and motorists, or through a provider's other revenue-generating activities such as the sale of advertising at stops or on vehicles, the use of sponsorships, or the provision of contract services for special events. The most commonly used sources of these local revenues include sales taxes, payroll taxes, charges imposed on motorists, and revenue directly generated by the service provider. The general logic behind their adoption is that public transport provides benefits to the larger community and is therefore a worthy recipient of broader financial support.

Sales Taxes

A common non-user-based, local funding source in the United States is the sales tax, which is a tax that is typically assessed on the sale of goods. The tax is typically set as a percentage of the purchase price of the good being sold and resulting tax revenues are collected from sellers. An increasingly popular revenue source for transportation projects in general, sales taxes are the second largest source of revenue for public transport capital and operating expenses in the United States, behind only passenger fare revenues (Arizona PIRG Education Fund, 2009).

Sales taxes are typically approved through a public vote, and they are often tied to lists of specific projects that are to be funded from tax revenues. Sales tax supporters emphasize the greater local control that this approach to project planning provides, whereas critics focus on the politics behind the selection of projects designed to cater to specific constituencies regardless of their likely impact on transportation users (Litman, 2018; Arizona PIRG Education Fund, 2009; Pula et al., 2015).

Los Angeles County, California has extensive experience with the use of sales taxes to fund regional transportation projects, including public transport. Since the 1980s, voters have passed four major sales tax measures that have generated funding for rail and bus services. Proposition A (1980) raised revenue for rail construction and subsidized local bus fares, Proposition C (1990) raised funds for rail construction, transit security and development of park and ride lots. Measure R (2008) raised funds for highway projects and rail system expansion. Measure M (2016), a landmark measure that was approved by 71 percent of voters, is expected to raise $120 billion over 40 years to expand rail, rapid bus, and bike networks, as well as to make a number of highway and road improvements (Metro LA b, n.d.).

Sales taxes have proven to be relatively popular among voters, are prodigious revenue generators, and, under non-recessionary economic conditions, provide predictable sources of revenue. Their greatest virtue is that they raise significant money by adding small, barely perceptible taxes to a large number of transactions; in Los Angeles, the price of a cup of coffee is increased by about two cents (Goldman et al., 2001). However, sales taxes have also been criticized for leading to ballot box-oriented planning (Lowe et al., 2014) where projects are selected based solely on political criteria as opposed to need, for being regressive with respect to income, particularly when the projects that are funded primarily benefit higher income persons (as with rail projects that attract higher income riders than do local buses), and for being divorced from use of the services being supported (Goldman et al., 2001). Given that sales taxes tend to be limited to goods and not services, there are also concerns about their longer-term revenue generation performance in increasingly service-oriented economies (Arizona PIRG Education Fund, 2009).

Payroll Taxes

Payroll taxes are another locally generated source of funding, although they are less commonly used than sales taxes. These taxes are levied on employers or employees within the taxing jurisdiction, which might be a city, county, state, or other political unit. One rationale for their use is that employers and employees contribute to congested conditions during peak travel times and should therefore help support alternative transport services that might alleviate these conditions. Individuals who commute into a city are therefore subject to this tax, whereas they might be able to avoid other taxes that are levied based on an individual's place of residence.

One of the most discussed payroll taxes is that in Portland, Oregon. In Portland, the Oregon Department of Revenue collects a payroll tax on behalf of Tri-Met, the regional service provider, to support operating expenses. Employers pay the tax directly to the state revenue department, and the state department in turn provides the funds to Tri-Met. In January 2019, the tax rate was 0.7637 percent of the wages paid by an employer and of an individual's net earnings from self-employment for services performed within the Tri-Met district boundary (Tri-Met, n.d.). The Oregon Department of Revenue also administers a tax program for the Lane Transit District, another service provider in the state. In 2017, the state of Oregon implemented an additional state-level tax (one-tenth of 1 percent, or .001) that is collected through withholding from the wages of Oregon residents and non-residents who perform services in Oregon to support public transport across the state (Tri-Met, n.d.; Oregon Department of Revenue, n.d.; Lane Transit District, n.d.).

Payroll tax revenues are correlated with incomes and employment and thus are very sensitive to economic conditions. Very few jurisdictions have implemented such taxes (Goldman et al., 2001), likely due to the relative unpopularity of this and other income-based taxes with many voters. Critics have noted that such taxes increase business costs and might lead to the loss of jobs in the taxing jurisdiction (Litman, 2018). Their administration is relatively straightforward for jurisdictions that impose income taxes, but more challenging for those that lack a tax payment infrastructure. Generally, payroll taxes are seen as progressive with respect to income, as low-income people tend to pay smaller taxes while also potentially benefiting from the services that the revenues fund.

Charges on Motorists

Public transport can also be funded by charging motorists for driving. Indeed, this has become an increasingly popular idea in transport policy circles around the world. Examples of such instruments are road tolls and congestion prices. Road tolls are fees paid for driving on a particular road, bridge, or in a particular area. Congestion pricing refers to tolls that are set higher during peak periods to reduce traffic congestion. A portion of the revenue raised through these mechanisms can then be invested in public transport services in the same locations. The logic behind the adoption of these mechanisms is that motorists impose costs on one another or on society at large for which they should pay, and one logical use of the resulting revenue is to fund services to fund alternative transport services.

London's experience with congestion pricing has served as an example to other large cities, most recently New York. London's congestion charge of £11.50 daily applies to most vehicles driven within the charging zone between 07:00 and 18:00, Monday to Friday. While the original charge was implemented in 2003 and has subsequently increased as the charging zone has been expanded, London also introduced an additional Ultra Low Emission Zone (ULEZ) charge in 2017 to improve air quality. This charge applies at all hours every day in the same area as the congestion charge and applies to cars and vans that do not meet ULEZ emission standards. In addition to aiding the goals of congestion reduction and improving air quality and public health, this charge generates funds that are by law dedicated for transportation projects. From 2003 to 2013, about 46 percent or £1.2 billion (USD $1.8 billion) of net revenue, was invested in public transport services, road and bridge improvements, and walking and cycling programs. Of this amount, £960 million (USD $1.44 billion) was spent on improvements to the bus network alone. The prodigious amounts of money generated through this program, and the notable reductions to automobile congestion, explain the interest in this idea in other large cities (TriState Transportation Campaign, n.d.).

However, congestion pricing, or other charges imposed on motorists, can be politically challenging as motorists and their allies mobilize to block implementation. Critical to implementation is the mobilization of a constituency that can advocate for the projects that might be funded from the revenues generated. In London, proponents had the advantage of an environment where the majority of road congestion is caused by a minority of road users, motorists, in an area where most travelers use public transport (Litman, 2011). Still, under the right conditions, congestion pricing can raise significant revenues. Tolls are not as large a revenue generator as they are typically imposed on very specific facilities. The advancement of technology has made implementation easier than in the past as either mechanism's revenues can be electronically collected (Litman, 2018). Long-term revenue stability of both congestion pricing and tolls may be impacted where people have the ability to adjust their travel decisions to avoid paying a charge or toll by avoiding areas where the charge is applied.

Revenue Generated by the Public Transport Service Provider

Service providers sometimes raise money directly by selling their services or facilities through contracts and/or charter arrangements, or by utilizing their facilities and/

or vehicles for advertising or sponsorships. The most common means of raising these self-generated funds is through advertising. Advertisements may be placed on vehicles, at stops or stations, or on schedules and maps. For example, Chicago Transit Authority (CTA) offers advertising space on their buses as well as rail vehicles. CTA also added 130 digital advertising displays across its rail system between 2017 and 2019. Service providers have also begun using onboard audio advertising (10–15-second-long messages) to generate revenues. For example, Champaign-Urbana Mass Transit District, a much smaller provider in Illinois, has earned about $150 000 over 10 years for audio advertising on its buses (Transitwire.com, 2013; The Daily Illini, 2010). Larger providers could undoubtedly earn much more revenue, although advertising revenues are still likely to account for only a small share of overall public transport funding.

The use of advertising to raise money allows providers to offer more services, maintain existing services, or avoid fare increases. With technological advancements, it is becoming easier to implement this strategy of revenue generation. Technology that allow buses trigger announcements about incoming stops and are federally mandated can now be used to trigger location-specific commercials for audio ads. On the downside, such advertising may be a public nuisance as providers may lose some control over the visual aesthetics or, with the advent of audio advertising, the ambience of their vehicles.

11.4   INTERGOVERNMENTAL GRANTS TO FUND PUBLIC TRANSPORT

In many countries, public transport is financially supported, in part, by higher levels of government, such as national and sub-national governments, through intergovernmental grants. Although in most countries urban transport planning and development is undertaken at the local level, financial and regulatory frameworks are frequently established at the national level, with costs shared by different government levels, although the way this is done varies across countries (Hidalgo et al., 2012). Among the countries that provide national-level funding for public transport are Brazil, India, Mexico, Colombia, Germany, United Kingdom and United States. All of these countries provide national-level funding for public transport infrastructure, although national governments in Germany, United Kingdom and United States also provide support for transit operations (Diaz and Bongardt, 2012).

In the United States, intergovernmental grants provide significant funding for public transport. In 2013, combined state and federal grants accounted for 34 percent of transit operating support alone, slightly more than fares (33 percent) or the combination of local support (22 percent) and directly generated funds (11 percent) (Office of Budget and Policy, 2018). Grant funding is distributed to local service providers to support capital, operations, and/or maintenance programs through a variety of programs. Figure 11.1 illustrates the flow of federal public transport funding from revenue sources into the national highway trust fund and then out to states and other governmental units through the various grants programs that have been created by national transportation legislation (American Association of State Highway and Transportation Officials, 2019; Federal Transit Administration, n.d.). Similar schematics could be produced for many states in the United States and/or for other countries. The intergovernmental grants landscape is quite

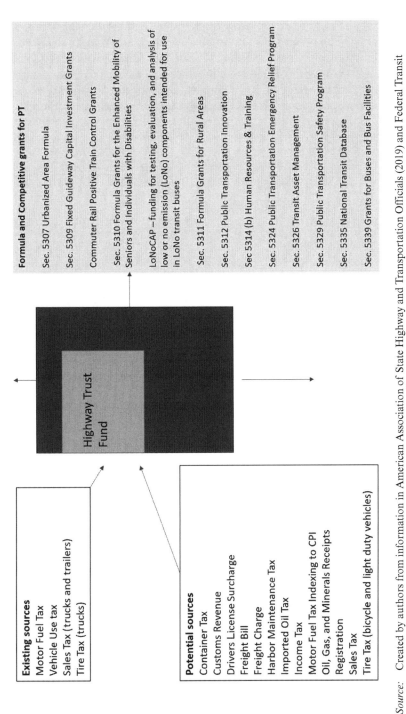

Formula and Competitive grants for PT

Sec. 5307 Urbanized Area Formula

Sec. 5309 Fixed Guideway Capital Investment Grants

Commuter Rail Positive Train Control Grants

Sec. 5310 Formula Grants for the Enhanced Mobility of Seniors and Individuals with Disabilities

LoNoCAP – funding for testing, evaluation, and analysis of low or no emission (LoNo) components intended for use in LoNo transit buses

Sec. 5311 Formula Grants for Rural Areas

Sec. 5312 Public Transportation Innovation

Sec 5314 (b) Human Resources & Training

Sec. 5324 Public Transportation Emergency Relief Program

Sec. 5326 Transit Asset Management

Sec. 5329 Public Transportation Safety Program

Sec. 5335 National Transit Database

Sec. 5339 Grants for Buses and Bus Facilities

Highway Trust Fund

Existing sources
Motor Fuel Tax
Vehicle Use tax
Sales Tax (trucks and trailers)
Tire Tax (trucks)

Potential sources
Container Tax
Customs Revenue
Drivers License Surcharge
Freight Bill
Freight Charge
Harbor Maintenance Tax
Imported Oil Tax
Income Tax
Motor Fuel Tax Indexing to CPI
Oil, Gas, and Minerals Receipts
Registration
Sales Tax
Tire Tax (bicycle and light duty vehicles)

Source: Created by authors from information in American Association of State Highway and Transportation Officials (2019) and Federal Transit Administration (n.d.).

Figure 11.1   Federal public transport funding in the United States

complex with its array of programs, rules and regulations, but provides critical funding for public transport providers.

One rationale for the use of intergovernmental grants to support public transport is to help provide service in communities that might lack the resources to fully fund these services themselves. Another rationale is that such services provide benefits to society at large that extend well beyond the community in which the service is operated, although this rationale might be considered controversial by some. In the United States, among other places, critics have complained about national involvement in local public transport funding because they assert that these services are fundamentally local in their nature and in the extent of their benefits.

11.5 URBAN DEVELOPMENT-RELATED TAXES AND FEES TO FUND PUBLIC TRANSPORT

Policymakers have also sought to capture the value enhancement experienced by properties served by public transport as a means of funding public transport. Property owners may benefit from the provision of new service, or enhancement of existing service in a multitude of ways. Employers may enjoy enhanced labor market access and expand their customer base while residents may gain greater access to essential destinations and reduced travel costs (Salon et al., 2019). These benefits are most concentrated at properties near transit infrastructure and may become capitalized into higher property values (see Table 11.5). Governments may seek to capture this value enhancement through such mechanisms as joint development arrangements, tax increment financing (TIF) districts, special assessment districts (SAD), or by seeking private financial contributions from beneficiaries (Mathur, 2015).

These mechanisms are most likely to be successfully implemented in situations where the presence of public transport has a significant impact on property values. As a result, these mechanisms may be most impactful when implemented in conjunction with rail transit. If implemented in the right way and in the right places, they may generate substantial revenue to help fund much-needed public transport infrastructure or services.

Joint Development

Joint development arrangements provide the public with an opportunity to capture the value enhancement experienced by properties located near public transport improvements. These arrangements commonly require a local government, or public transport provider, to acquire land near a planned project at pre-service market prices. The public entity then partners with the private sector to support the development of a private real estate project on publicly owned land (Salon et al., 2019). These arrangements stipulate either a revenue-sharing or cost-sharing agreement between the public and private entities (Mathur and Smith, 2013). Joint development may allow the public entity to develop additional revenue streams, reduce the cost burden associated with the implementation of public transport improvements, and increase ridership as a result of the densification of public transport service areas (Lari et al., 2009; Mathur and Smith, 2013).

Table 11.5   Property value premiums associated with proximity to public transport

Location	Transit Service	Outcome	Author
Toronto, ON	Spadina Subway Line	$2237 avg. premium for homes in close proximity of transit	Bajic, 1983
New Jersey	PATCO System	Median home price for census tracts immediately served by the rail line were generally 10% higher	Voith, 1991
Philadelphia, PA	SEPTA System	Avg. median home price for census tracts served by SEPTA enjoy a 3.8% premium	Voith, 1991
Atlanta, GA	MARTA East Line	$1000 increase in home price per 30.48 meters closer to transit	Nelson, 1992
Portland, OR	MAX Light Rail	10.6% increase in property values for homes located within 500 meters of transit	Al-Mosaind et al., 1993
Dade County, FL	Miami Metrorail	5% appreciation rate increase in property values	Gatzlaff and Smith, 1993
California	BART system	Homes adjacent to BART would sell for close to 38% more	Cervero, 1996
Chicago, IL	Midway Rail Line	6.89% appreciation in values for properties in proximity to transit	McMillen and McDonald, 2004
San Diego, CA	San Diego Trolley & Coaster Commuter Rail	+10% increase in condominium property value	Duncan, 2008
Houston, TX	MetroRail	Significant increase in property values for residential properties outside 400 meter radius of station	Pan, 2013

Revenue sharing

In a revenue-sharing agreement, a public entity which has acquired land proximate to a pending public transport improvement can sell that land at a premium after project completion (Salon et al., 2019). This arrangement produces a lump-sum payment which can be used for immediate infrastructure development or future capital improvements (Lari et al., 2009). If the public entity desires to retain ownership of that land, they can enter into long-term lease arrangements with developers for ground, air, or subsurface development rights (Salon et al., 2019). This arrangement can produce a consistent stream of revenue over the duration of the agreement which can help offset public transport operating and maintenance costs, and it also provides some flexibility as the public entity can renegotiate lease payments based on future increases in property values (Lari et al., 2009).

The most significant step in operationalizing a joint development agreement is the public acquisition of land near a forthcoming public transport improvement. Suitable land acquisition sites include those which are adjacent to or near improvements and have supportive land use regulations that allow for heightened development activity such as increased densities (Mathur and Smith, 2013). Under such conditions developers are able to increase their potential profit from developing the site. The heightened profitability of a site may increase what developers are willing to pay for it, thus increasing the monetary benefits for the public entity that owns it. Revenue terms then need to be negotiated between the two entities involved. Negotiations may cover the final sale price, monthly lease costs, and revenue sharing. The inclusion of a revenue-sharing component within the joint development agreement requires the private entity to share a portion of the revenue generated from their resulting development project with the public entity. If this is something which is pursued, the revenue structure also needs to be determined. Common structures include the stipulation of minimum guaranteed revenue, Consumer Price Index (CPI) adjusted fixed revenue, or a set percentage of gross revenue which is shared with the public entity (Mathur and Smith, 2013). While fixed lease payments provide a consistent source of revenue, the presence of a revenue-sharing agreement can provide potential for heightened revenue growth.

Washington Metropolitan Area Transit Authority (WMATA) has long been involved in the joint development of real estate. WMATA has dedicated staff who are part of their Office of Real Estate and Station Planning who identify the development potential of properties within their service area and use this information to inform land acquisition decisions. As a result of these efforts, WMATA owns or controls numerous real estate assets throughout the Washington, DC area. Whenever deemed beneficial, WMATA pursues joint development agreements with private developers. One example is the joint development agreement for their Navy Yard east property (WMATA, 2016). In 2007, WMATA entered into a joint development agreement to sell 0.13 acres of property adjacent to their Navy Yard Metro Station to a private developer. This agreement permitted the construction of over 300 residential units and 10000 square feet of retail space. WMATA expected to receive $2.3 million from the agreement and anticipated that the resulting new development would increase ridership.

Cost sharing

In a cost-sharing agreement, a private entity agrees to share costs associated with the construction, operation, and/or maintenance of transit infrastructure. This is something which is often in addition to the agreed-upon final sale or lease price negotiated between these two parties for a property. The inclusion of a cost-sharing element within a joint development agreement is likely to result in the reduction of the ultimate sale or lease value associated with the transaction undertaken between the public and private parties. This type of agreement can also arise when the public entity transfers an incentive to a private entity. Under this scenario, the public awards incentives to a developer, such as density bonuses, in exchange for their commitment to cover costs associated with the implementation of public transport infrastructure. This exchange is mutually beneficial if it increases the earning potential of private developments while decreasing the financial burden for a public entity undertaking public transport improvements.

When entering into cost-sharing agreements, the public entity focuses on costs it incurs as a result of delivering service which could be shifted to the private sector. Such costs can include those associated with the construction of transit stations or corridors, station maintenance, and vehicle acquisition. Agreements may also be made with developers to provide and share amenities, such as auxiliary power generators and ventilation systems, which would serve transit facilities (Transportation for America, 2012). Regardless of the nature of the costs being shifted to the private sector, a timeline needs to be established which details the timeframe within which the private entity is responsible for covering the agreed-upon costs. This can vary from something short, in which there is a one-time payment made to support aspects such as the construction of a public transport facility, or something longer in nature, which may require support for the maintenance of a facility over the life of a lease agreement.

In Philadelphia, the Southeastern Pennsylvania Transportation Authority (SEPTA) has actively pursued cost-sharing joint development agreements. These efforts are undertaken by staff within the Real Estate Department who have expertise regarding the acquisition, development, leasing and sale of SEPTA-owned properties. SEPTA commonly leases commercial space in suburban rail stations at favorable rates and in return the private developer is made responsible for the maintenance and upkeep of public concourses and passageways. This strategy has generated millions of dollars towards station rehabilitation (Lari et al., 2009).

Assessment

The revenue generated via joint development can be fairly limited as it only applies to a small proportion of properties which benefit from public transport access (Lari et al., 2009; United States EPA, 2013). The ability to generate revenue also depends on multiple factors which are outside the service provider's control, most notably the state of the local real estate market. While a strong market can greatly improve the revenue-generating capabilities of this mechanism, a fluctuating market can produce a volatile revenue stream. Local government support is also necessary to facilitate zoning changes whenever deemed necessary (Salon et al., 2019). Due to the complexity of these agreements, it may also be necessary for the public transport provider to have staff with considerable real estate knowledge (United States EPA, 2013; Salon et al., 2019). This can be a substantial barrier for entities which have limited experience and understanding of the development process.

Special Assessment District

Property owners located close to public transport improvements are likely to experience greater benefits than members of the community at large. Special assessment districts are often formed to encompass properties which are considered to experience a heightened benefit as a result of the implementation of a public improvement. Property owners within these districts are assessed regarding a fee which is dedicated to help fund the project which they are benefiting from. This fee can be paid immediately, or a lien can be placed on the property which allows property owners to pay the fee over a set timeframe. Depending on local legislation, revenue generated from assessment districts may be dedicated to help cover capital, operation and maintenance expenditures (United States EPA, 2013). Special assessment districts can also be referred to as benefit assessment districts, business improvement districts, local improvement districts, transportation development districts, or transportation improvement districts, all of which operate under the same defining principles (Lari et al., 2009).

In many areas, special assessment districts may be initiated either by a local government implementing a public improvement or by a majority of property owners who file a petition to collectively fund an improvement project which will benefit them. Once this process is initiated, a feasibility study is conducted in which district boundaries and levy amounts are determined (Zhao and Larson, 2011). There are no consistent guidelines which inform the designation of a district boundary, making it a difficult task to accomplish. Boundary designation is usually left to the discretion of the local government, which employs commonsense judgments to estimate the extent of the heightened benefit emitted from the public improvement. Once the boundary is set, it is necessary to determine the assessment amount which will be levied on properties within the boundary. This amount should be representative of the benefit experienced by each property. This can be difficult to accomplish because assessment values are set before the public improvement is undertaken. As a result, local governments typically employ a "cost method" when setting assessment values in which they attempt to recover a portion of project costs from district properties (Zhao and Larson, 2011). Properties might be assessed to determine fees based on proximity to the improvement, surface area occupied by the property, the property's frontage, or the property's type, for example residential versus commercial. It is also possible to employ a combination of methods in an effort to allocate costs across properties (Zhao and Larson, 2011). There also needs to be a decision on whether the district will exist for a set number of years or until a specified level of revenue is generated. Ultimately, majority support from impacted property owners is often necessary to institute a special assessment district, and a ballot measure may be necessary in order to obtain this support.

The Kansas City Streetcar Authority implemented a special assessment district which supports streetcar service. The district is labeled a transportation development district (TDD) but operates as a special assessment district. Under Missouri statute, a TDD can impose a sales tax and use the revenue generated to support various transportation costs. Two elections were held which allowed registered voters who lived within the TDD to decide whether they agreed to (1) the district's creation and (2) the assessments which would be levied as a result of its establishment. Ultimately, both proposals passed with a ≈63 percent yes vote. The outcome of these elections saw the creation of a TDD which encompasses properties up to half a mile from the streetcar corridor and imposes a 1 percent sales tax and varying property assessments over a 25-year period. The assessment generates roughly $9.5 million in annual revenue, which is utilized to repay bonds and cover system operation and maintenance costs.

The revenue yield from a special assessment district can be substantial as they are typically applied within highly developed areas, or those with considerable planned development (Transportation for America, 2012). Special assessment districts are considered to be equitable as they can assign costs to property owners who are likely to experience heightened benefits resulting from the implementation of a project. While there are many benefits to implementing a SAD, they can be difficult to establish from an administrative standpoint. Perhaps the most difficult aspect of implementing this mechanism is the development of a legally defensible method of calculating assessments (Lari et al., 2009). Once this has been accomplished, SADs are relatively easy to administer as revenue collection is commonly implemented in conjunction with property tax collection (Lari et al., 2009). In most cases, voter approval is necessary to implement a SAD. Efforts to acquire the necessary support can be a barrier for many public transport providers. There may be considerable opposition from local property owners who object to the proposed increases in property taxes. As a result, an extensive outreach and educational campaign is essential in this process. These efforts can be problematic for some service providers due to the time and resources required.

Tax Increment Finance District

The development of a TIF district does not rely on the introduction of a new fee, as do special assessment districts, but instead on the redistribution of future property tax revenue growth. As property values increase, thanks in part to the presence of an improvement, differences between rising property values and a pre-established baseline are diverted to pay for public improvements made within the designated TIF district. These improvements are usually funded through debt, which is later repaid using revenues generated through the TIF district (Lari et al., 2009). The ultimate lifespan of a TIF district is usually stipulated within state statutes. It tends to fluctuate between 20 to 40 years or until a particular project is completed and all debt is paid off (Rolon, 2008; Lari et al., 2009). While this mechanism tries to capture value enhancements experienced by properties within district boundaries resulting from the presence of specific public improvements, it actually captures value enhancements resulting from any reason, including general trends in the real estate market (Salon et al., 2019).

The processes associated with the development of TIF districts are commonly stipulated within statutes. These should be referenced when attempting to operationalize this mechanism as there are likely to be differences across jurisdictions. The governing bodies which have the authority to establish TIF districts should first be identified. The appropriate party may be the municipality itself, redevelopment authorities, or state economic development commissions (Lari et al., 2009). Once the pursuit of the TIF district has been initiated by the appropriate party, it is necessary to establish the district boundary. The designation of this boundary should consider the location of properties which are likely to experience value enhancement benefits as a result of the project being pursued. Once the boundaries have been established it may be necessary to conduct a needs assessment in order to determine if the area under consideration meets the requirements, as stipulated within the state statute, to be designated a TIF district (Lari et al., 2009). If it is ultimately determined that the proposed area meets these requirements, a redevelopment plan needs to be produced. Within this plan, the redevelopment strategy for the area encompassed by the TIF district is established. This strategy is informed by the municipalities' comprehensive land development plan and state legislation which can dictate how revenue generated from TIF districts can be used. The plan may then be required to pass through an approval process before the TIF district designation process can proceed. Once approval has been achieved, the total assessed value for all properties within the proposed district are calculated. Property tax generated at the time the TIF district is established continues to be utilized to support various aspects of the community at large during the life of the TIF district. Property taxes generated due to increases in assessed valuation post-TIF district designation are allocated to a special fund dedicated to support the implementation of public improvement projects within district boundaries.

The Chicago Transit Authority (CTA) has employed TIF districts as a means to generate revenue to fund public transport improvements. Recent efforts to improve rail service will see the modernization of the Red and Purple lines via the reconstruction of several stations and tracks. Perhaps the most significant aspect of this project will see the introduction of a bypass which will facilitate the movement of rolling stock which currently shares a flat rail intersection. In an effort to secure more than $1 billion in federal funding support, the City of Chicago and the CTA were required to provide a local funding match. The Illinois legislature responded by approving the use of a Transit-Tax Increment Financing district which would produce funds to support specified Chicago projects. The use of the TIF district for the projects stipulated above was ultimately approved by the Chicago City Council in 2016 and is actively being utilized to generate $625 million in funds to pay a portion of the local match required for the $1 billion federal funding support.

TIF districts can generate substantial revenue when applied within areas expected to experience considerable value enhancement. TIF districts are less likely to experience public opposition than SADs because they do not impose an additional assessment on property owners. Any opposition which may arise may be due to the equity implications associated with implementing this mechanism. This is largely a result of property taxes allocated to larger community needs being frozen over the life of the TIF district. This may place significant stress on public service providers, which is likely to be compounded by inflationary pressures and population growth, and may lead to a deterioration in service quality (Rolon, 2008; Lari et al., 2009). The presence of a TIF may also lead to displacement of existing residents as property and business owners are not able to afford increasing property taxes arising as property values increase (Lari et al., 2009).

Private Contributions

Private contributions tend to be one-time payments made to help fund a public improvement. These arrangements can be negotiated during the planning stages for an improvement's alignment or stop locations (Transportation for America, 2012). The negotiation may result in changes in alignment or stop location which benefit a developer's property. In exchange, the public entity may request the developer to contribute towards costs associated with the improvement. These contributions are likely to only fund smaller project elements due to their tendency to be smaller-scale, one-time payments (Transportation for America, 2012). Regardless, such arrangements can be beneficial to both parties. The developer benefits from accessibility improvements to their property while the public entity benefits from the reduction of project costs and experiences possible ridership gains as a result of serving an additional activity generator.

One case which highlights the use of private contributions to support public transport projects involves Amazon Inc. and the King County Metro Transit Department. Amazon's private contribution supports the South Lake Union Streetcar Line in Seattle located near Amazon's headquarters. Amazon purchased an additional streetcar vehicle for roughly $3.7 million and agreed to pay its operating costs for ten years. In turn, the service provider reduced headways from 15 minutes to 10 minutes during typical work hours without increasing its own costs. Improved service quality can provide further provider benefits through increased ridership and fare revenue. Amazon benefits by offering a more pleasant commute experience for employees, which in turn may help them improve employee satisfaction, workforce retention, and talent attraction. Additionally, by making their site accessible via public transport, they may be able to reduce costs associated with leasing parking for their employees.

Implementing this strategy successfully depends greatly on many elements of the environment where it is to be employed. Furthering the difficulty of implementing this strategy is the task of convincing private entities to contribute to the costs of a public transport project when there is nothing requiring them to do so. Highlighting the manners in which they are going to directly benefit from the project is essential when attempting to secure private contributions.

11.6 CONCLUSION

This chapter has discussed the logic behind how and why cities pay for public transport, as well as the mechanisms through which communities raise revenues to fund it. The authors used a review of research and practitioner literature to identify funding mechanisms, describe their use in everyday practice, and assess their strengths and limitations. Examples of funding mechanisms and their key strengths and limitations are highlighted in Table 11.6.

Left unsaid in this review, however, is the decision-making around how the revenues produced by these mechanisms are used. This body of knowledge is beyond the scope of this chapter, but it remains critically important to our shared understanding of the many tensions at play in contemporary public transport, such as the following:

Table 11.6 *Summary of funding mechanisms and their principal strengths and limitations*

Mechanism	Key Strength(s)	Key Limitation(s)
Passenger fares	User-based; Willingness to pay reflects demand	Paying fare serves as barrier to use; Collection costs
Indirectly paid fares (passes)	Stable and predictable revenue; Tap into new rider market	Unfair to non-users; Difficulty establishing a price
Free transit	Eliminates money barrier to use	May diminish value to users Necessitates new funding sources
Sales taxes	Predictable revenue in good economic conditions	Divorced from user of service
Payroll taxes	Tax non-resident commuters	Increase business costs
Charges on motorists	Changes relative cost of auto versus transit	Politically difficult
Revenue generated by operator	Not funded by riders or general public	Modest source of funding at best
Joint development	Leverages public transport assets to develop new funding stream	Requires real estate expertise on part of public transport operator; Yield generation is heavily influenced by strength of local real estate market
Special assessment	Captures unearned public transport accessibility benefit from adjacent properties; Yield can be substantial when applied within highly developed areas, or those with considerable planned development	Opposition from property owners
Tax increment finance district	Does not add a new assessment on property	Opportunity cost of forgone general property tax revenue
Private contributions	Voluntary	Limited to specific local circumstances

- Operating vs. Capital vs. Maintenance costs;
- Buses vs. Rail;
- Urban vs. Suburban;
- Benefits for riders vs. Benefits for non-riders.

These decisions have tremendous and lasting impact on the types of public transport services we provide in cities, who uses it and in what numbers, and ultimately helps to fuel and shape the public's image of what public transport is and what it could one day be.

While this chapter has identified some of the funding mechanisms that support the provision of public transport service, a change in mentality may be necessary for some of them to receive broader consideration. Most service providers are primarily focused on providing safe and reliable service and consider the development or implementation of funding mechanisms to be the responsibility of someone else, including a larger governmental entity (Salon et al., 2019). It may be necessary to break from this mentality to explore more innovative ways in which funding can be generated to help providers decrease their reliance on public subsidies and build a level of immunity towards governmental funding shortages.

Research is therefore needed to better understand the decision-making around the selection of funding mechanisms, the strategies used to facilitate their adoption (particularly in the case of more innovative or unusual mechanisms), and the effectiveness of the mechanisms for providing a stable (or increasing) base of support for the operation of public transport services and the attraction of public transport riders. Particularly useful for both researchers and practitioners would be a better understanding of the factors that influence the success or failure of the different mechanisms from both political feasibility and revenue-generating capacity perspectives.

REFERENCES

Al-Mosaind, M.A., K.J. Dueker and J.G. Strathman (1993), 'Light-rail transit stations and property values: A hedonic price approach', *Transportation Research Record*, 1400, 90–94.

American Association of State Highway and Transportation Officials (2019), *Matrix of Illustrative Surface Transportation Revenue Options*, accessed at https://fundingfinance.transportation.org/wp-content/uploads/sites/16/2019/02/Matrix_of_Funding_Options.pdf.

Arizona PIRG Education Fund (2009), *Why and How to Fund Public Transportation*, accessed at https://uspirgedfund.org/sites/pirg/files/reports/Why-and-How-to-Fund-Public-Transportation.pdf.

Bajic, V. (1983), 'The effects of a new subway line on housing prices in Metropolitan Toronto', *Urban Studies*, **20** (2), 147–58.

Brown, J., D.B. Hess and D. Shoup (2001), 'Unlimited access', *Transportation*, **28** (3), 233–67.

Cats, O., Y.O. Susilo and T. Reimal (2017), 'The prospects of fare-free public transport: Evidence from Tallinn', *Transportation*, **44**, 1083–104.

Cervero, R. (1996), 'Transit-based housing in the San Francisco Bay Area: Market profiles and rent premiums', *Transportation Quarterly*, **50** (3), 33–49.

Chang-fu, H. and X. Yuan (2011), 'Research on the role of urban rail transit in promoting economic development', *Procedia Engineering*, **21**, 520–25.

The Daily Illini (2010), 'MTD audio is music to advertisers' ears', accessed 30 November 2019 at https://dailyillini.com/news/2010/09/02/mtd-audio-is-music-to-advertisers-ears/.

Diaz, R. and D. Bongardt (2012), *Financing Sustainable Urban Transport: International Review of Urban Transport Policies and Programmes*, GIZ and EMBARQ, Germany: Federal Ministry for Economic Cooperation and Development (BMZ), accessed at https://www.sustainabletransport.org/archives/1487.

Duncan, M. (2008), 'Comparing rail transit capitalization benefits for single-family and condominium units in

San Diego, California, *Transportation Research Record: Journal of the Transportation Research Board*, **2067**, 120–30.

Federal Transit Administration (n.d.), *Grants Programs*, accessed 1 November 2019 at https://www.transit.dot.gov/funding/grants/grant-programs.

Gatzlaff, D.J. and M.T. Smith (1993), 'The impact of the Miami Metrorail on the value of residences near station locations', *Land Economics*, **69** (1), 54–66.

Goldman, T., S. Colbert and M. Wachs (2001), *Local Option Transportation Taxes in the United States*, UCTC No. 524, Berkeley, CA: The University of California Transportation Centre.

Hess, D.B. (2017), 'Decrypting fare-free public transport in Tallinn, Estonia', *Case Studies on Transport Policy*, **5**, 690–98.

Hidalgo, D., M. Pai, A. Carrigan and A. Bhatt (2012), 'Towards people's cities through land use and transport integration: A review of India's national urban investment program', EMBARQ India.

Hilton, G. (1974), *Federal Transit Subsidies: The Urban Mass Transportation Assistance Program*, Washington, DC: American Enterprise Institute.

Hodge, D.C., J.D. Orrell III and T.R. Strauss (1994), *Fare-Free Policy: Costs, Impacts on Transit Service, and Attainment of Transit System Goals*, Seattle, WA: Washington State Transportation Center, University of Washington.

Lane Transit District (n.d.), Payroll & Self-Employment Tax Information: Lane Transit District, accessed on 30 November 2019 at https://www.ltd.org/payroll-self-employment-tax-information/.

Lari, A.Z., Z. Zhao, D.M. Levinson, M. Iacono, University of Minnesota and Hubert H. Humphrey Institute of Public Affairs (2009), 'Value capture for transportation finance: Technical research report', Minneapolis, MN: Center for Transportation Studies, University of Minnesota.

Litman, T. (2007), 'Evaluating rail transit benefits: A comment', *Transport Policy*, **14** (1), 94–7.

Litman, T. (2011), *London Congestion Pricing: Implications for Other Cities*, Victoria, BC: Victoria Transportation Policy Institute.

Litman, T. (2018), *Local Funding Options for Public Transportation*, Victoria, BC: Victoria Transport Policy Institute.

Litman, T. (2019), *Evaluating Public Transit Benefits and Costs: Best Practices Guidebook*, Victoria, BC: Victoria Transport Policy Institute.

Lowe, K., R. Pendall, J. Gainsborough and M.T. Nguyen (2014), 'Ballot box planning: Rail referenda: Implementation', *Journal of Public Transportation*, **17** (1), 75–98.

Mathur, S. (2015), 'Funding public transportation through special assessment districts: Addressing the equity concerns', *Public Works Management & Policy*, **20** (2), 127–45.

Mathur, S. and A. Smith (2013), 'Land value capture to fund public transportation infrastructure: Examination of joint development projects' revenue yield and stability', *Transport Policy*, **30**, 327–35.

McCollom, B.E. and R.H. Pratt (2004), *Traveler Response to Transportation System Changes Chapter 12: Transit Pricing and Fares*, Washington, DC: Transit Research Cooperative Program, Transportation Research Board.

McMillen, D.P. and J. McDonald (2004), 'Reaction of house prices to a new rapid transit line: Chicago's Midway Line 1983–1999', *Real Estate Economics*, **32** (3), 463–86.

Metro LA a (n.d.), UPass Program: Metro LA Transit website, accessed 30 November 2019 at https://www.metro.net/riding/colleges/u-pass-program.

Metro LA b (n.d.), Proposition A & C and Measure R Sales Taxes: Metro LA Transit website, accessed 30 November 2019 at https://www.metro.net/about/financebudget/taxes/.

Metropolitan Transportation Authority (n.d.), Fares and Metro Cards: Metropolitan Transportation Authority, accessed 30 November at http://web.mta.info/metrocard/mcgtr eng.htm.

Meyer, J. and E.A. Beimborn (1998), 'Usage, impacts, and benefits of innovative transit pass program', *Transportation Research Record: Journal of the Transportation Research Board*, **1618** (1), 131–8.

Nelson, A.C. (1992), 'Effects of elevated heavy-rail transit stations on house prices with respect to neighborhood income', *Transportation Research Record*, 1359, 127–32.

O'Sullivan, F. (2018), *Estonia Will Roll Out Free Public Transit Nationwide*, accessed 30 November 2019 at https://www.citylab.com/transportation/2018/05/estonia-will-roll-out-free-public-transit-nationwide/560648/.

Office of Budget and Policy (2018), *National Transit Summaries and Trends 2017*, Washington, DC: Federal Transit Administration, US Department of Transportation.

Oregon Department of Revenue (n.d.), *Statewide Transit Tax*, accessed 30 November 2018 at https://www.oregon.gov/DOR/programs/businesses/Pages/statewide-transit-tax.aspx.

Pan, Q. (2013), 'The impacts of an urban light rail system on residential property values: A case study of the Houston METRORail Transit Line', *Transportation Planning and Technology*, **36** (2), 145–169.

Pickrell, D.H. (1986), 'Federal operating assistance for urban mass transit: Assessing a decade of experience', *Transportation Research Record*, **1078**, 1–10.

Pula, K., D. Shinkle and J. Rall (2015), *On Track: How States Fund and Support Public Transportation*, Washington, DC: National Conference of State Legislatures.

Rolon, A. (2008), 'Evaluation of value capture mechanisms from linkage capture to special assessment districts', *Transportation Research Record*, **2079** (1), 127–35.

RVTD (n.d.), Group Bus Passes: Rogue Valley Transportation District (RVTD) website, accessed 30 November 2019 at https://www.rvtd.org/Page.asp?NavID=32.

Salon, D., E. Sclar and R. Barone (2019), 'Can location value capture pay for transit? Organizational challenges of transforming theory into practice', *Urban Affairs Review*, **55** (3), 743–71.

Sheader, J. (2019) Public Relations Manager for Centre Area Transportation Authority, State College, PN. Telephone interview, 26 June.

Taylor, B.D. and K. Samples (2002), 'Jobs, jobs, jobs: Political perceptions, economic reality, and capital bias in U.S. transit subsidy policy', *Public Works Management & Policy*, **6** (4), 250–63.

Transitwire.com (2013), 'Transit agencies turn to audio ads', accessed 30 November 2019 at http://www.thetransitwire.com/2013/05/21/transit-agencies-turn-to-audio-ads/.

Transportation for America (2012), 'Thinking outside the farebox: Creative approaches to financing transit projects', Washington, DC: Transportation for America.

Tri-Met (n.d.), Payroll and self-employment tax information: Tri-Met, accessed on 30 November 2019 at https://trimet.org/taxinfo/.

TriState Transportation Campaign (n.d.), 'Road pricing in London, Stockholm and Singapore: A way forward for New York City', accessed 30 November 2019 at http://nyc.streetsblog.org/wp-content/uploads/2018/01/TSTC_A_Way_Forward_CPreport_1.4.18_medium.pdf.

United States Environmental Protection Agency (2013), 'Infrastructure financing options for transit-oriented development', Washington, DC: United States Environmental Protection Agency, Office of Sustainable Communities.

Voith, R. (1991), 'Transportation, sorting and house values', *Real Estate Economics*, **19** (2), 117–37.

Volinski, J. (2012), *Implementation and Outcomes of Free Fare Transit Systems: A Synthesis of Transit Practice*, TCRP Synthesis 101, Washington, DC: Transit Cooperative Research Program.

Washington Metropolitan Area Transit Authority (WMATA) (2016), *Joint Development: WMATA*. Accessed at www.wmata.com/business/real-estate/about-joint-development.cfm.

West, P. (2019), Senior Planner, Rogue Valley Transportation District, Medford, OR. Telephone interview, 11 June.

World Bank (2013), *Planning, Connecting, and Financing Cities – Now: Priorities for City Leaders*, Washington, DC: World Bank.

Zhao, Z. and K. Larson (2011), 'Special assessments as a value capture strategy for public transit finance', *Public Works Management & Policy*, **16** (4), 320–40.

PART IV

PLANNING AND OPERATIONAL PERSPECTIVES

12. Public transport network resilience
Menno Yap and Oded Cats

12.1 INTRODUCTION

For public transport services to be an attractive travel alternative, the network needs to be efficient under normal operations as well as resilient in terms of its capability to withstand and quickly recover from disturbances and disruptions. Disruptions in public transport systems (PTS) are caused for various reasons, including mechanical and technical failures, traffic incidents, strikes, natural hazards, weather conditions, planned construction or maintenance works or targeted attacks. In addition, perturbations from the planned service (e.g. missed departures, large-scale events) may cause knock-on effects that might propagate across the network if not mitigated.

Transport systems are subject to disruptions that may carry substantial implications for network performance and society at large. The importance of disruptions in transport systems stems from their crucial role in the urban metabolism. The 7 July 2005 terror attacks on London's public transport system, the flooding in Amsterdam on 28 July 2014 and the national strike by French train drivers on 5 May 2019 are just a few examples that demonstrate diverse causes of disruptions in public transport systems and are exemplary for the severity of the societal impacts disruptions can have.

Disruptions are however by no means limited to extraordinary events. Service disruptions – ranging from vehicle breakdowns and switch or signal failures to suicide attempts blocking tracks or a suspected item requiring the evacuation of a station – are unfortunately recurrent and costly. For instance, Yap and Cats (2019) report that each day on average about 20 disruption incidents occur that result in a train or line delay of at least two minutes in the Washington, DC metro network. Cats et al. (2016b) analysed data from a dense multi-modal public transport network in the Netherlands and found, for example, that tram vehicle breakdowns alone amount to more than 1800 incidents per year for this network. Consequently, investments in public transport systems are increasingly conscious of or even driven by their implications for the system's capability to withstand disruptions.

The importance of system resilience is acknowledged in a range of social and engineering systems including finance, ecology and critical infrastructure. *Robustness* refers to the overall capability to maintain system integrity and functionality, while *Resilience* refers to system ability to withstand and recover from shocks (Pimm 1984; Rose 2007). *Vulnerability* is commonly used as the reverse term of Robustness (e.g. Snelder 2010). In contrast to power supply, information and water systems, transportation is a socio-technical system. Hence, it is subject to the outcomes of decentralised and interdependent decisions made by numerous autonomous agents. Travellers' response to changing network conditions depends on their preferences and the information available to them. This highlights the potential role of travel information as a mitigation measure. Furthermore, the impact of service disruptions and risk perceptions may extend beyond the direct time losses due to the disproportional effect of extreme negative events on repetitive travellers' decisions, such as mode choice (Cox et al. 2011).

The remainder of this chapter is structured as follows. In section 12.2, we discuss key concepts related to resilience of public transport systems. Section 12.3 discusses the properties of public transport service disruptions. In section 12.4, we introduce different indicators and methods to quantify disruption impacts on resilience. Approaches related to mitigation of disruption impacts and thus improving resilience are discussed in section 12.5. In section 12.6, we show the application of key concepts, disruption properties and resilience impacts to case study networks in the Netherlands and Washington, DC, followed by an outlook towards future research directions in section 12.7.

12.2   KEY CONCEPTS

This section introduces key concepts when studying resilience of public transport networks. We first introduce the *bathtub model*, followed by *multi-layer* and *multi-modal* features of public transport systems, and finally the *resilience cycle*.

The Bathtub Model

The aforementioned notions of *robustness, vulnerability* and *resilience* can be conceptualised using the so-called bathtub model. The bathtub model illustrated in Figure 12.1 sketches how system performance (*y*-axis) changes over time (*x*-axis) in the event of a disruption. The undisrupted level of performance is here indicated as the base level of 100 per cent. A disruption occurring at time t_0 leads to a sudden loss of system performance. The extent of reduction in system performance as a consequence of service disruption is denoted as *vulnerability*. Note that in reality, while the loss of performance is abrupt, some time may elapse before all ramifications are manifested. The remaining functionality of the network in the event of a disruption is referred to as *robustness*. Note that both vulnerability and robustness thus refer to the immediate impact of the disruption once it

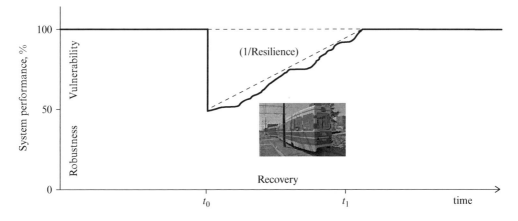

Figure 12.1   The bathtub model, adapted from McDaniels et al. (2008)

occurred. In contrast, *resilience* also considers the time it takes for the system to recover back to full functionality at time t_1. The overall loss in system performance once accounting for the performance during the *recovery time* can be measured by the size of the area under the 100 per cent curve (i.e. assuming a uniform and monotonic rate of recovery in system functionality as time elapses from the disruption start time). Resilience is thus the inverse of the size of this area. In the context of public transport, system performance can be measured in terms of trip production (as opposed to trip cancellations), share of passengers that are not affected, service punctuality or total passenger time losses attributed to the disruption.

The notion of resilience is employed in different disciplines and domains (Reggiani 2013; Modica and Reggiani 2014). In the context of engineering, resilience refers to the impacts of a disruption and the aftermath and the need to design engineering solutions that are safe and reliable. Studies focused on the resilience of critical infrastructure are primarily concerned with the ability to recover system performance and maintain its functionality. In ecological and social sciences, the notion of resilience pertains to the magnitude of stress (e.g. natural or man-made disasters) that a system can absorb before it collapses. In contrast, complex system sciences primarily conceptualise resilience in terms of the presence of notions such as tipping points, transition phases and multiple equilibrium states and related topological properties.

The notions of system *resilience* and *vulnerability* are closely related to system *reliability*. Reliability pertains to stochastic fluctuations in demand and supply resulting in highly recurrent yet small deviations from normal operations, while vulnerability refers to distinguishable incidents or events (Oliveira et al. 2016). Similarly, the aforementioned distinctive incidents are referred to as service *disruptions*, whereas service *disturbances* refer to normal stochasticity in system input, such as variability in passenger volumes or travel times. In the context of public transport, vulnerability (and thus resilience) is thus often understood to encompass discrete events whose cause can be traced, varying from vehicle breakdown and signal failure to crew strikes, terror attacks and flooding. Furthermore, disruptions can be classified as recurrent or non-recurrent based on the disruption frequency and impact (Figure 12.2). The distinction can be based on the probability and

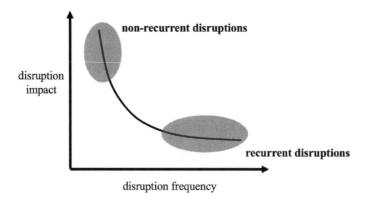

Source: Yap (2020).

Figure 12.2   *Conceptual framework of recurrent and non-recurrent disruptions*

impact of the underlying causes, yet no rigid distinction can be made and the boundaries are fluid since both probabilities and impacts are continuous spectrums. Recurrent PT disruptions, such as a train door malfunctioning or a passenger feeling unwell, occur relatively frequently, whilst the impact is generally small. In contrast, non-recurrent PT disruptions are relatively rare, but typically have larger impacts once they occur. One can think of examples such as a faulty train, signal failure or vehicle derailment. Besides, there are extreme events (such as natural disasters) which form a separate disruption category.

The concept of disruption frequency, or disruption exposure, is typically not considered a component of resilience. To capture both disruption exposure and impact, the concept of risk is often used. *Risk* can be considered the product of disruption probability and disruption impact. Resilience is therefore considered a component of a complete public transport risk analysis (see for example Cats et al. 2016b).

Multi-layer, Multi-modal Networks

While the literature on road transport network resilience offers some relevant concepts and methods, their transferability to the domain of public transport is often limited. PTS are characterised by greater complexity due to the relation between the underlying infrastructure (roads and tracks) layer and the PTS service layer. Moreover, the importance of multi-modality, transfer hubs and intermediate walking links stems from the limited spatial and temporal availability of services and hence lower connectivity when compared with road networks. The *multi-layer* and *multi-modal* characteristics of PTS are discussed in more detail below.

Unlike car traffic networks, public transport systems are also composed of a service layer in addition to the infrastructure layer. The former consists of service stops and lines and their respective properties, such as service frequencies and timetables. It is important to account for the limited spatial and temporal availability of public transport networks since those are likely to have ramifications for system resilience, highlighting the importance of adopting a multi-layer representation (Luo et al. 2019). Note that service disruptions and disturbances can stem from both layers. For example, a switch failure or a signal failure are associated with specific infrastructure elements and may affect all service lines traversing the respective infrastructure, whereas abnormal demand levels or a vehicle breakdown may affect a specific line yet propagate to other lines as a secondary effect. Depending on the disruption, different travel time elements – waiting times, in-vehicle times, walking times or transfer times – of passenger journeys in public transport systems may be affected. This can relate to nominal travel time impacts as well as perceived travel time impacts, such as a more negative in-vehicle time perception resulting from higher crowding levels during a disruption (e.g. Hörcher et al. 2017; Tirachini et al. 2017). Interchanges between services are often particularly susceptible elements in public transport systems.

Another important feature of public transport systems is their multi-modality. This implies that the infrastructure network often consists of several sub-networks such as heavy rail, light rail and roads. On one hand, the presence of separate sub-networks may contribute to system resilience since the impacts of disruptions may be encapsulated, and undisrupted sub-networks may offer redundancy or replacement services. On the other hand, having incompatible sub-networks also means that resources such as rolling stock

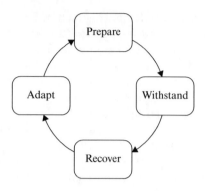

Figure 12.3   The resilience cycle

cannot be reallocated from any service to any service in the event of a disruption, limiting their efficient utilisation. Similarly, while public transport operations are more vulnerable due to their rigidity (e.g. limited detour options, resource-dependent), their centralised control mechanisms allow contingency plans to be devised and disruption management measures to be applied that are based on system optimum conditions.

The Resilience Cycle

Measures to improve system resilience may take place before, during or after a shock to system performance. The concept of *Resilience Cycle* refers to the continuing process of improving a system's ability to cope with shocks. This concept is applicable to many domains, ranging from ecological systems to cybersecurity. As shown in Figure 12.3, it consists of the following steps: (1) Prepare; (2) Withstand; (3) Recover; and (4) Adapt. As implied by the cyclic figure, this is an iterative process that systems and organisations undergo rather than a project with a clear start and end.

In the context of public transport systems the four steps manifest themselves as follows:

- *Prepare:* Service providers can undertake preparatory measures to improve system resilience so that the ramifications of a disruption once occurring are minimised. Such measures include accounting for network robustness when making strategic planning decisions, allocating switches to enable greater flexibility for rerouting trains in the event of a disruption, prioritising maintenance works, or allocating reserve resources to be used in the event of a disruption.
- *Withstand:* The immediate response upon the detection of the disruption. This includes communication with the control centre, the diagnosis, possibly deploying repair staff and informing passengers about the events and their possible consequences. A service provider devises disruption mitigation measures and seeks to ensure that the necessary resources (e.g. tracks, vehicles, crew) can be called upon.
- *Recover:* The deployment of rescheduling measures to the eventual restoration of the planned service. This may involve dispatching, holding and expressing services. It also requires informing passengers on timetable changes. This step corresponds

to the gradual increase in system performance between the two time marks t_0 and t_1 in Figure 12.1.

- *Adapt:* In the aftermath of a disruption, a learning system can be adapted to make itself less prone to disruptions in the future or deploy measures that are likely to be effective for mitigating such disruptions in the future. This includes the re-planning of services in the event of recurrent timetable sliding or missed connections and the re-dimensioning or reallocation of resources to be better positioned to cope with future disruptions.

Of course, in reality, these four conceptual steps do not happen in sequence per se, but rather correspond to different efforts made by the relevant stakeholders – primarily the service operator, the transport authority and the infrastructure manager, if applicable – to improve system resilience.

12.3 PROPERTIES OF SERVICE DISRUPTIONS

This section focuses on the properties of public transport service disruptions. Parts of this section are based on Yap (2020). Disruptions in a PTS can be characterised by the following properties:

- Disruption type;
- Disruption frequency;
- Disruption duration;
- Disruption location.

Recurrent and Non-recurrent Disruptions

Public transport disruptions can be classified based on several dimensions. As discussed in section 12.2, one classification distinguishes between recurrent and non-recurrent disruptions. There is no explicit demarcation between recurrent and non-recurrent disruptions. Instead, they can be considered as two ends of the same scale.

Extreme Events

Extreme events are often considered as a separate disruption category. These events can be natural disasters, such as flooding or hurricanes, or related to human actions such as terror attacks. Attack strategies are usually modelled by removing nodes or links from a PTS (see for example Von Ferber et al. 2009a; Jenelius and Mattson 2015). This type of extreme event can be random or targeted at a specific location or specific public transport service (Candelieri et al. 2019). These events differ substantially from regular recurrent and non-recurrent disruptions in terms of magnitude and behavioural response by passengers, PT service providers and authorities, for which a bespoke research approach is necessary (see for example Markolf et al. 2019).

Planned and Unplanned Disruptions

Another distinction can be made between planned and unplanned disruptions. In scientific literature, the majority of the studies focus on unplanned disruptions (see for example Rodriguez-Nunez and Garcia-Palomares 2014; Zhang et al. 2015). This emphasis can be explained by the disproportionate disutility and dissatisfaction passengers attribute to the impacts of unplanned disruptions. Olsson et al. (2012) illustrate that negative events, such as disruptions, leave a longer lasting mark on customer satisfaction. The impact of planned disruptions – such as planned track maintenance works – is generally smaller than the impact this same disruption would have if unplanned. This is due to awareness and route and mode choice adjustments made by passengers, as well as to planned resource allocation by the service provider in anticipation of a planned disruption. Hence, the unplanned disruption impact can be considered an upper bound for the disruption impact of the same planned disruption. Due to the more predictable nature of planned disruptions, these types of disruptions are less likely to attract the same level of dissatisfaction and attention as a large, unplanned disruption.

The distinction between planned and unplanned disruptions is relevant, as both types result in a different behavioural response from passengers. Most studies concerned with unplanned disruptions focus on en-route choice effects for passengers and assume no demand suppression (e.g. Cats and Jenelius 2014; 2015). Passengers are typically assumed to redistribute over the PT network since no pre-trip awareness is assumed. In contrast, during planned disruptions, the assumption that overall demand for PT remains unchanged does not apply. Due to awareness, passengers might change their mode, destination, departure time or trip frequency choice. The topic of planned disruptions, for example related to maintenance works, is relatively understudied in the field of public transport resilience (Shires et al. 2019). Despite the impact of planned disruptions being – *ceteris paribus* – smaller or equal to the impact of an unplanned disruption, planned disruptions can last much longer. For example, track maintenance works might result in a disruption duration of multiple months (Yap et al. 2018a). Hence, the accumulated impact of a planned disruption over time (e.g. per year) can substantially exceed the impact of unplanned disruptions.

In addition, it should be mentioned that the availability of ride-hailing services, real-time information via smartphones, and increasing acceptance of flexible working arrangements (such as working from home) in many cities might violate the traditional fixed PT demand assumption even for unplanned disruptions. Consequently, mode shifts and trip cancellations can increasingly be observed during unplanned disruptions as well (e.g. Pnevmatikou et al. 2015). This indicates that the behavioural response of passengers during planned and unplanned disruptions tends to converge. This convergence in terms of behavioural response between planned and unplanned disruptions can also be observed for longer-lasting unplanned disruptions, for example a full line suspension starting in the morning peak and lasting for the rest of the day. Information and communication about such disruptions can increase customer awareness, hence allowing for a wider range of responses than public transport route choice only.

Disruption Types, Duration and Location

Disruptions can also be classified according to their cause or the network level on which they occur. Disruptions can, for example, be classified as infrastructure related (e.g. a signalling failure), vehicle related (door malfunctioning), passenger related (a sick or aggressive passenger) or operations related (such as a station overrun or driver error) (Yap and Cats 2019). Disruptions on different public transport network levels, such as the (inter)regional train network, light rail or metro network at the urban agglomeration level, or on the urban tram and bus network can have different characteristics in terms of disruption frequency, duration, impact and spatial distribution over the network (Yap et al. 2018b).

The duration of a disruption consists of two components. The first component is the time between the start of the disruption and the time that the initial incident has been cleared. The second component is the recovery time: the time until the system performance is entirely recovered (i.e. no more passenger impact of the disruption) after clearing the incident. It should be noted that the passenger impact of a disruption can last for a considerable amount of time after the incident itself has been cleared. This is caused by the time required to restore PT fleet and crew in such a way that the original timetable can be executed (e.g. Veelenturf et al. 2012; Yap and Van Oort 2018), and by disruption impact propagation over the total PTS. For example, Malandri et al. (2018) show that knock-on effects on passenger delays can persist for up to six times longer than the duration of the initial disruption itself (the aforementioned first component of disruption duration). Service operators can utilise predictions on disruption duration to determine the recovery period subject to its risk management strategy (Ghaemi et al. 2018b). On one hand, if the recovery period is set too short compared to the realised disruption duration, there is a high likelihood that the time will not be sufficient and there will be a need to reschedule services and re-inform passengers, while on the other hand, if set too long, then the reduced performance due to the disruption is unnecessarily prolonged.

12.4   RESILIENCE IMPACTS OF DISRUPTIONS

Public transport disruptions can have major impacts on passenger and public transport service provider. For example, in Cats et al. (2016b) we calculated that yearly passenger disruption costs resulting from disruptions on one single light rail link in the metropolitan PT network of The Hague and Rotterdam, the Netherlands, can exceed €900 000. Meanwhile, in London all disruptions on Transport for London's underground network during a four-week period from 28 April to 25 May 2019 have resulted in 2.2 million lost customer hours (Transport for London 2019). It is therefore important to be able to quantify the impact PT disruptions have on network resilience. In this section, we address state-of-the-art research related to the resilience impact of public transport disruptions. First, we discuss indicators for resilience in PTS. Second, we discuss methods to quantify resilience impacts of disruptions based on network science indicators, modelling and simulation. Finally, we briefly refer to indicators to identify critical elements in a PTS.

Indicators for Public Transport Resilience

Robustness, redundancy, resourcefulness, rapidity

In transportation studies, a plethora of definitions and indicators for vulnerability, robustness and resilience can be found (see for example Reggiani et al. 2015; Oliveira et al. 2016). One can broadly distinguish between two concepts of resilience, each with its own set of indicators: engineering resilience and ecological resilience (Holling 1973). Indicators for engineering resilience relate to the resistance of a system to disruptions or shocks, and the speed to return to normal conditions (Pimm 1984). Ecological resilience focuses on the magnitude of a shock that can be absorbed before a system changes its structure (Walker et al. 1969).

In line with the most commonly accepted definitions of vulnerability and resilience for transport systems as presented in Figure 12.1, resilience of PTS typically refers to engineering resilience. In line with this definition, resilience indicators can thus pertain to the ability of a PTS to absorb shocks, and/or the ability of a PTS to recover from a shock. Bruneau and Reinhorn (2003) and Leobons et al. (2019) refer to the *4R-framework*, which consists of four properties of resilience to which indicators typically refer: Robustness, Redundancy, Resourcefulness and Rapidity. *Robustness* indicators refer to the ability of a PTS to withstand the initial disruption impact, for example by measuring the direct impact on travel time, travel costs or connectivity directly after the disruption occurs. *Redundancy* indicators – such as the number of alternative routes or modes available in a PTS – refer to the alternative travel options provided by the PTS during a disruption, which therefore influences the system performance under shocks. Indicators for *Resourcefulness* refer to the availability of resources (drivers, vehicles, assets), which influences the time required to start the recovery process. *Rapidity* indicators relate to the speed with which the disrupted PTS returns to normal operations (recovery time).

Resilience indicators for passenger disruption impacts

In this part, we further discuss several resilience indicators for the impact of PTS disruptions. In particular, we focus on resilience indicators aimed to reflect the passenger impacts of disruptions. From a passenger perspective, indicators for resilience of PTS should quantify the accumulated passenger impact of a disruption – typically measured in terms of loss of travel time, travel costs and crowding/comfort – since the initial disruption occurs and during the whole recovery time, in line with Figure 12.1. The aim of these indicators is to measure the extent to which the realised passenger journey deviates from the scheduled or expected passenger journey. Appropriate passenger-oriented indicators should reflect the impact on the total passenger journey, including in-vehicle time, waiting time, walking time, crowding and the number of transfers.

Vehicle-oriented indicators are the most traditional type of indicators used, which are still used by many public transport authorities and service providers worldwide. Punctuality-based indicators measure the percentage of PT trips that depart or arrive with a delay of a certain maximum number of minutes from/at a set of predefined stations. For example, for the Dutch railway network this threshold is set to five minutes (Vromans 2005). Additionally, average punctuality can be calculated for each PT line (e.g. Van Oort 2011). For high-frequency urban PT networks, vehicle regularity is often more important than punctuality. Hence, many studies focusing on urban PT networks use the

Coefficient of Variation (CoV) of actual headways as indicator instead of punctuality (see for example Engelson and Fosgerau 2011). This has also led to the introduction of such regularity-based metrics as part of business operations as discussed by Cats (2014). Based on the CoV, the additional waiting time and variation in waiting time for PT passengers caused by irregularity of PT supply during disruptions can be computed (see for example Turnquist and Bowman 1980; Van Oort 2011).

In recent years, passive data from Automated Vehicle Location (AVL), Automated Fare Collection (AFC) and Automated Passenger Count (APC) systems have become widely available in the PT sector, as well as data from GPS and mobile phone (e.g. Trépanier and Yamamoto 2015). These data sources provide opportunities to quantify abovementioned indicators in a fast and automated manner. The availability of AVL data with scheduled and realised vehicle departure and arrival times enables automated quantification of the punctuality and regularity indicators for all PT trips. A clear disadvantage of the punctuality- or regularity-based metrics above is that all trips are weighted equally, regardless of the number of passengers affected. Passenger-weighted train punctuality aims to correct for this, by weighting arrival punctuality based on the expected passenger volumes per train (Vromans 2005). For capturing the full passenger disruption impacts, this metric is however still problematic due to its focus on separate train trips. None of the abovementioned metrics incorporates how a single PT vehicle delay affects the complete passenger journey, including the possibility of missed connections to other trains, or to trams and buses at the urban PT network level (as for example considered by Lee et al. 2014).

In response to the limitations of vehicle-oriented indicators, researchers and selected PT authorities have gradually adopted more passenger-oriented indicators to measure passenger resilience impacts of disruptions. Excess Journey Time (EJT) – for example implemented by Transport for London for London's underground network – compares the realised passenger journey time with the scheduled journey time (Zhao et al. 2013; Hendren et al. 2015). Based on tap in and tap out data resulting from AFC systems, realised and scheduled times can be compared for the total passenger journey per origin-destination (OD) pair. This also enables quantifying the Reliability Buffer Time (RBT) for individual passenger journeys as indicator (Koutsopoulos et al. 2019). The RBT typically equals the difference between the 95th and 50th percentile of observed journey times. To capture the complete passenger disruption impact, the difference in *perceived* journey times should be captured in addition to the difference in nominal journey times. When expressed in monetary terms, passenger disruption impacts can then be expressed as welfare change between realised and scheduled journey (Cats and Jenelius 2014).

Overall, it is important to note that in scientific research the development and application of passenger-oriented disruption impact indicators is gradually becoming the standard. The dominance of supply-oriented indicators in the public transport industry however indicates there is still a road ahead in translating and implementing passenger-oriented indicators into practice. This poses extra requirements for these indicators, such as being scalable, easy to communicate and fast to compute. Besides, most indicators do consider only the direct passenger impacts of a disruption. Wider economic or societal impacts, such as loss of productivity, increased road network congestion or emission levels when ride-hailing services would be used more often during PT disruptions, are rarely quantified.

Resilience indicators for disruption impacts on PT service provider

Another note we would like to make is the potential discrepancy between passenger-oriented or societal resilience indicators typically proposed in scientific research, and – in some cases – the need for financial, operator-oriented disruption impact indicators in practice. Public transport disruptions can result in substantial financial costs for the PT service provider, for example due to rescheduling costs of fleet and personnel (e.g. resulting in personnel overtime payments). This can be particularly relevant in the event of complex fleet and driver schedules. For example, interlining vehicles between different public transport lines, or drivers who perform their duties on multiple vehicles and lines during one shift, can result in disruption impact propagation over the wider public transport network (see for example Yap and Van Oort 2018). If passenger reimbursement schemes are in place, in which passengers fares are waived if delays exceed a certain threshold (for example applied for the metro networks in Washington, DC and London, and the Dutch national rail network), revenue losses can be another important financial component of disruption impact for the service provider. Another area of interest here is customer satisfaction. If monetary incentives are incorporated in contractual agreements between public transport authority and service providers based on customer satisfaction levels, one can expect disruptions to result in additional financial costs for the service provider via decreased satisfaction levels. For example, in Sweden the impacts of disruptions and in particular the quality of information provided during unplanned disruptions are rated consistently unsatisfactory by customers (Cats et al. 2015). The challenge here is the ability to quantify the relation between a lack of PTS resilience and the impact on customer dissatisfaction.

In summary, we see the development of models and tools which can quantify resilience indicators related to monetised, financial disruption costs for the service provider, next to the societal impacts for passengers, as an important challenge for future PT resilience research. Such indicators would enable quantifying additional disruption costs, as well as monetising additional benefits of potential robustness or resilience measures, resulting in a more complete and informed trade-off between costs and benefits of measures in appraisal studies.

Quantification of Disruption Resilience Impact

This section discusses different methods to quantify resilience of a PTS in the event of a disruption occurring.

Network science models

One approach to quantify disruption resilience impacts in a PTS is the use of network science models, by assessing topological and structural properties of PT networks. A literature review on network science applications in public transport is for example provided by Dimitrov and Ceder (2016). An appropriate network representation is critical in these approaches. Examples are studies using an L-space network representation (nodes reflecting stops, connected with links if a PT service connects two stops consecutively) or a P-space representation (nodes reflecting stops, connected with links if two nodes are connected by a direct PT route) (von Ferber et al. 2009b). As illustration, Derrible and Kennedy (2010) assess the robustness of 33 metro networks worldwide based on network science models. Disruption impacts can be assessed by removing (a sequence of) nodes or links. This enables assessing the impact of a disruption on connectivity, based on the number of origin-destination pairs which cannot be reached (directly) any more, or assessing the impact on travel time by computing the updated shortest path length between all OD pairs (e.g. using the Dijkstra algorithm). Hence, network topology approaches are a simple and fast way primarily to assess network robustness (Zhang et al. 2015). Notwithstanding, these approaches are not able to capture the more complex and dynamic passenger choice behaviour during disruptions, which illustrates that these simplified approaches come at the cost of accuracy. Full resilience impacts including recovery time are often not assessed.

Macroscopic models

The use of frequency-based or schedule-based macroscopic PT assignment models is another approach which is traditionally used to quantify PT disruption impacts (Gentile et al. 2016). In some cases, these assignment models are combined with variable demand models to capture mode choice impacts, in particular in the event of planned disruptions. Macroscopic models are relatively simple models which typically allow for the quantification of impacts of many disruption instances within reasonable computation times. The main limitation of these assignment models is their assumption that passenger route choice is determined before the journey starts, based on knowledge on how PT services are amended in response to a disruption. This means these models might be used to quantify the impact of planned disruptions, where passengers are aware of the disruption and consecutive service adjustments when commencing their journey. However, these models are unable to (fully) incorporate the dynamics of especially unplanned PT disruptions. Typically, passengers become aware of unplanned disruptions during their journey, requiring them to adjust their route during their journey, often based on limited information of the service adjustments or disruption duration. Whilst some models are capable of incorporating some passenger dynamics, detailed underlying behavioural models for this are often lacking. Most models assume a stable PT service network during the disruption, thereby neglecting the transition from undisrupted to disrupted network and the recovery time the PT system needs once the disruption itself is cleared. As such, they are by definition unable to reflect non-equilibrium conditions which are likely to characterise the disrupted situation. This also entails that full resilience impacts – including the impact during recovery time – are typically not captured in these models. In addition, the dynamic interaction between PT demand and supply during disruptions or delays, which can result in vehicle queuing or bunching, cannot be captured in static assignment models.

Mesoscopic and microscopic models

To quantify the impacts of unplanned disruption impacts more accurately there is a need for more advanced, dynamic PT assignment models, which are able to capture the demand and supply dynamics and their interactions during disruptions. In recent years, there have been several developments to use this type of model in transportation, instead of the aforementioned traditional macroscopic assignment models. For example, Cats et al. (2016a) use BusMezzo, a dynamic, mesoscopic PT assignment model, for urban and metropolitan PT networks. As individual PT vehicles and passengers are simulated, it is possible to account for dynamic, en-route passenger route choice and test the impact of real-time information provision or day-to-day learning effects (Cats and Jenelius 2014) for complete and partial service degradations (Cats and Jenelius 2018). The ability of these models to capture a higher level of detail does however come at the cost of (sometimes) longer computation times and the requirement of more detailed model inputs, for example regarding underlying passenger behaviour.

For heavy rail, rescheduling greatly depends on the remaining track capacity given the signalling system in place. As a consequence, microscopic or mesoscopic simulation models such as Open Track (Nash and Huerlimann 2004) are often used to quantify impacts of heavy rail disruptions. These models specifically incorporate railway characteristics such as a signalling system, acceleration and braking characteristics of different rolling stock types and block lengths. These simulation models focus primarily on simulating trains, whilst passengers and their route choices are often incorporated in a simplified way. It should however be noted that not incorporating the full, dynamic interactions between PT demand and supply is typically less problematic for heavy rail networks, compared to high-frequency urban PT systems. Early departures from stations are often prohibited due to the signalling system in place. Effectively, this implies that bunching between subsequent train services is less likely to occur, as trains are subject to holding until their scheduled departure time at the majority of the stations. Additionally, heavy rail networks have a lower network density than urban PT networks, which means that the number of feasible route alternatives available to passengers will be more limited than for dense urban networks. Hence, train simulation models are often used to quantify disruption impacts for heavy rail networks, in contrast to macroscopic or mesoscopic passenger assignment models being used for urban PT systems.

Model combinations and integration
Disruption impacts can propagate between different levels of a public transport network. As an illustration, a train network disruption can result in missed transfers to the urban tram or bus network, thereby affecting the journey time and crowding levels on the urban PT network level. Because of the different types of models typically used to quantify disruption impacts for heavy rail and urban PT networks, quantification of resilience impacts of disruptions for the integrated multi-level PT network including propagation to other network levels can be challenging.

Recent methods to capture interactions between different PT network levels propose the use of a combination of different models. Inputs and outputs are then transferred between the different models. For example, Blume et al. (2019) combine a discrete event simulation to simulate vehicle movements and an agent-based model for passenger route choice decisions for this purpose. Yap et al. (2020) combine an optimisation-based model for train vehicle rescheduling with an agent-based model for simulation of urban vehicles and passenger assignment over the total, multi-level PT network.

Machine learning methods
More recently, one can find studies adopting machine learning approaches aimed at quantifying PT disruption impacts in a data-driven manner. Typically, these approaches require a disruption log file as input, which contains information about the properties of past disruptions (e.g. start time, cause, location and duration). Disruptions and disturbances may also be deduced from realised vehicle movements based on AVL

systems. The passenger disruption impact, on the other hand, can be obtained empirically from data from AFC systems. Hence, machine learning models can be developed which attribute observed passenger disruption impacts to the different individual disruptions. Consequently, a prediction model can be developed to quantify the impacts of future disruptions. For example, Marra and Corman (2019) applied machine learning to connect relatively small PT disturbances to the empirically measured delay impact for the case study network of Zurich. In addition, Yap and Cats (2019) developed machine learning models to quantify impacts of disruptions on the Washington, DC metro network.

Identification of Critical Network Elements

Several methods can be found in scientific literature, aimed to identify the most critical elements (nodes or links) in a PTS. Depending on whether only the direct impact on system performance after a disruption is incorporated, or if also the impact during the recovery is taken into account, criticality can relate to network robustness or resilience.

Two different approaches are broadly distinguished in literature to identify critical network elements: pre-selection methods and full computation methods. In the latter approach, disruption impacts are quantified for all nodes or links in the transport network, which enables listing the contribution of each node/link to network robustness (e.g. Knoop et al. 2008) or resilience (e.g. Yap and Cats 2019). The disadvantage is that these methods can be very time consuming when considering large, real-world transport networks, as a large number of model runs might be required. The first approach uses indicators to pre-select a smaller number of nodes or links which are expected to influence network robustness or resilience the most. In a second step, full disruption impacts are only quantified for these selected nodes or links, thereby reducing the required number of model runs. However, the disadvantage is that there is no guarantee that the most critical nodes or links are selected and hence identified. In addition, the most critical elements can be dependent on the context, as the ranking of critical elements might differ during different days of the week or times of the day.

There are a variety of indicators developed in the scientific literature for pre-selection methods to identify critical nodes or links in a PTS. It should however be mentioned that almost all indicators relate to network robustness rather than resilience, as the system's ability to recover from disruptions is hardly incorporated in these indicators. Pre-selection indicators for road networks are, for example, the volume/capacity ratio of links or the Incident Impact Factor (e.g. Tampère et al. 2007). For PT networks, potential indicators found in literature are node degree, betweenness centrality, or PT link volume (e.g. Bell 2003; Cats and Jenelius 2014). Cats et al. (2016b) propose an indicator which considers both passenger volume (as a proxy for disruption impact) and disruption exposure in the pre-selection process. In different studies, pre-selection methods are applied to metro networks (e.g. Derrible and Kennedy 2010), urban PT networks (e.g. Cats and Jenelius 2014) or to multi-level PT networks (Yap et al. 2018b). While most studies have focused on node or link criticality in the case of full breakdown, many disruptions involve a partial capacity reduction, for which Cats et al. (2017) propose measuring the rapidity of network performance degradation to support the prioritisation of mitigation measures.

12.5   MITIGATING THE IMPACTS OF SERVICE DISRUPTIONS

Following the discussion related to resilience indicators and resilience quantification in section 12.4, this section focuses on mitigation of the impact of service disruptions aimed to improve PTS resilience. Measures to minimise the impacts of service disruptions can take place prior to or once a disruption occurs (Figure 12.3) as planners may already take system resilience into consideration as part of service preparation. As illustrated in the bathtub model in Figure 12.1, resilience of a PTS relates to the total impact of a disruption, once this disruption occurs. In line with this conceptual model, this entails that there are different disruption properties which can mitigate disruption impacts, given the occurrence of a certain disruption type on a certain location in the network. The instantaneous disruption impact when a disruption occurs at t_0 determines how much the system performance is reduced (vulnerability), reflected by the height of the vertical axis of the area reflecting resilience in this figure. Recovery time refers to the time the PTS requires to return to its regular performance, since the start of the disruption at t_0. Therefore, the slope of the resilience area in Figure 12.1 corresponds to the pace of system recovery. In summary, improving the resilience of a PTS can be realised by decisions affecting one (or multiple) of these properties: reducing the initial disruption impact, or reducing recovery time. Each of these actions reduces the surface of the area, thereby increasing resilience.

Effectively all efforts to make the public transport system more resilient give rise to a dilemma between efficiency and redundancy. In a world of infinite resources, a system can always be made more reliable and more resilient by introducing redundancy at all planning levels: from additional infrastructure capacity to additional buffers in the timetable to reserve rolling stock and crew. All of these measures involve the deployment of considerable resources and significant investments and operational costs. By the same token, a system can become close to perfectly punctual or perfectly safe by either reducing speeds or deploying considerable additional resources while compromising system efficiency. This points to the fundamental dilemma between efficiency and resilience. While efficiency considerations call for lean planning and operations, resilience considerations call for introducing more redundancy to reduce system fragility to shocks and improve its ability to withstand those. Ultimately, the risk management strategies undertaken by the planning authorities and operating entities determine the extent to which the system is designed for optimising efficiency under normal circumstances as opposed to ensuring its performance under most and abnormal circumstances. Note however that this strategy is often implicit and seldom articulated.

The impacts of service disruptions can be effectively mitigated when making long-term strategic planning decisions such as network and service design. The robustness and resilience impacts of new infrastructure investments can be analysed as part of their evaluation (Rodriguez-Nunez and Garcia-Palomares 2014; Jenelius and Cats 2015; Cats 2016) as well as the benefits of allocating reserve capacity on service segments that are otherwise overloaded in the event of disruptions (Cats and Jenelius 2015). At the tactical planning level, timetables can be designed so that there is sufficient slack to prevent adverse consequences in the event of the disruption (Besinovic et al. 2016; Sels et al. 2016; Gkiotsalitis and Cats 2018). Robust timetable design then requires a trade-off between performance under normal operations and performance under abnormal conditions.

Once a disruption has been detected, service providers may deploy (reactive) real-time management measures aimed at reducing its ramifications. Such measures may be directed at either supply or demand management. Either way, these measures aim at reallocating (in either time or space) supply to better match the demand patterns given the disruption or steering the demand so that it is better distributed given the supply available. Supply management measures include the rescheduling of services including changes in dispatching (Blume et al. 2019; Gkiotsalitis et al. 2020), stop-skipping (Altazin et al. 2017), short-turning (Ghaemi et al. 2018a) or reassigning heavy rail to tracks (Gao et al. 2016; Ghaemi et al. 2017; Xu et al. 2017; van der Hurk et al. 2018). Demand management pertains to real-time information provision informing passengers on the delay (Cats et al. 2011; Cats and Jenelius 2014; van der Hurk et al. 2018) and thereby allowing them to make adjustments to their travel plans.

12.6   CASE STUDY APPLICATIONS

Case Study Networks

We illustrate disruption properties and the quantification and mitigation of disruption resilience impacts as introduced in this chapter using two case study networks.

The first case study we use is the multi-level PT network of the southern part of the Randstad, the Netherlands. The Randstad is the most important economic area of the Netherlands, located in the western part of the country. The southern part of the Randstad contains about 2.2 million inhabitants and captures the cities of The Hague and Rotterdam. In this case study, we consider the (inter)regional train network level, together with the metro/light rail network connecting the agglomerations of The Hague and Rotterdam, plus the urban tram networks of these two cities. Case study results are based on Cats et al. (2016b) and Yap et al. (2018b).

Second, we use the metro network of Washington, DC, which is administered by the Washington Metropolitan Area Transit Authority (WMATA). This metro network consists of six lines indicated by different colours: the Red line, Green line, Yellow line, Blue line, Orange line and Silver line. The total length of the metro network is about 190 km and contains – at the time we performed our research – 95 metro stations. This network covers the wider metropolitan area of Washington, DC. The case study results are based on Yap and Cats (2019) and Yap and Cats (2020).

Disruption Properties

To obtain insights related to disruption properties, one typically starts with a log file consisting of all logged disturbances and disruptions. Generally, public transport authorities and/or service providers are data owners of such log files.

Randstad multi-level public transport network
For the Randstad case study in the Netherlands, we used disruption log data of the train network for a period of 2.5 years. Besides, we had access to 18 weeks' disruption data from the urban PT service providers in this area. Results in Figure 12.4 show that 46 per cent of all disruptions on the metro/light rail network level are vehicle related. For urban tram

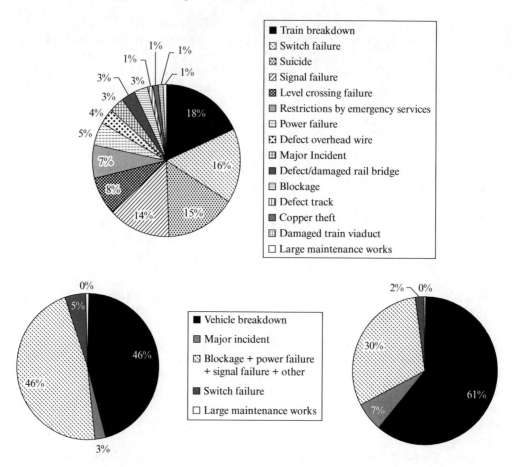

Source: Cats et al. (2016b).

Figure 12.4   Relative disruption frequency for train (top), metro/light rail (left) and tram (right)

networks, the proportion of 61 per cent vehicle-related disruptions is shown to be even higher. For the regional train network level, train-related disruptions account for only 18 per cent of all disruptions. Infrastructure-related disruptions do account for the majority of the disruptions. For example, switch failures, signal failures and level crossing failures are together responsible for 38 per cent of all disruptions. This case study also shows that, on average, train network disruptions last substantially longer than metro/light rail or urban network disruptions. The average duration of a train network disruption for this case study was equal to 128 minutes, compared to 67 minutes (metro/light rail) and 76 minutes (tram), respectively.

Washington, DC, metro network

For the Washington, DC case study, incident log data was received for a period of 13 months, resulting in 21 868 incident records. In the data processing phase, disruptions

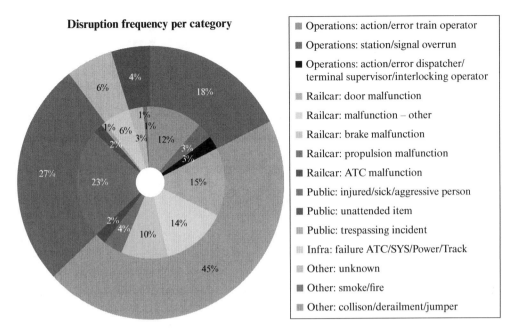

Disruption frequency per category

- ■ Operations: action/error train operator
- ■ Operations: station/signal overrun
- ■ Operations: action/error dispatcher/
  terminal supervisor/interlocking operator
- ▨ Railcar: door malfunction
- ▨ Railcar: malfunction – other
- ▨ Railcar: brake malfunction
- ■ Railcar: propulsion malfunction
- ■ Railcar: ATC malfunction
- ■ Public: injured/sick/aggressive person
- ■ Public: unattended item
- ▨ Public: trespassing incident
- ▨ Infra: failure ATC/SYS/Power/Track
- ▨ Other: unknown
- ■ Other: smoke/fire
- ▨ Other: collison/derailment/jumper

Source: Yap and Cats (2020).

Figure 12.5   Relative disruption frequency per category

were distinguished from disturbances (related to reliability rather than vulnerability or resilience). In addition, disruptions were grouped into a select number of 15 distinguishable disruption types. After processing, 4263 separate and distinguishable disruptions were remaining from the incident list.

Figure 12.5 shows the distribution of disruptions over the 15 disruption categories. For the Washington case study network, it can be seen that injured/sick/aggressive passengers (23 per cent) and vehicle door malfunctioning (15 per cent) are the most frequently observed disruption types. When these 15 disruption types are aggregated into five broader categories – vehicle, infrastructure, passenger, operations, other – we see that 45 per cent of all disruptions are classified as vehicle-related disruptions. Interestingly, this proportion is very similar to the percentage vehicle-related disruptions of 46 per cent found for the Randstad case study network in the Netherlands. Vehicle and passenger-related disruptions together are responsible for more than 70 per cent of all empirically observed disruptions. On the other hand, the contribution of infrastructure-related disruptions (6 per cent) and other disruptions (4 per cent) is relatively small.

In Figure 12.6, we show the spatial distribution of observed disruptions over the Washington metro network. It can be seen that most disruptions occur at stations located in the central area of the network, as train frequencies and passenger volumes as important disruption sources are highest here. Besides, terminal stations are relatively often exposed to disruptions. An explanation for this is that disruptions often arise at the terminal station, for example when testing the train or if a driver or train arrives late from the depot. Stations with the lowest disruption frequency are generally located on branches

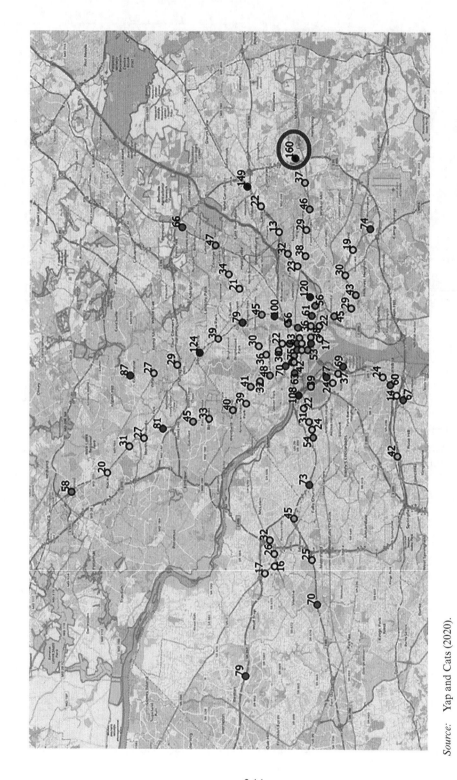

Source: Yap and Cats (2020).

Figure 12.6 Spatial distribution of disruptions

of the different metro lines, being non-terminal and non-transfer stations served by one line only. For the specific case study network, most disruptions occurred at Large Town Center station (circled in Figure 12.6).

Disruption Resilience Impacts and Mitigation

Randstad multi-level public transport network

For the Randstad case study network, the integrated, multi-level PT network consisting of the train, metro, light rail, tram and bus services in the southern part of the Randstad is considered. Disruption impacts were monetised for one light rail link between the two stations Laan van NOI and Forepark, which showed to be particularly critical, by comparing the generalised journey times for all passengers between disrupted and undisrupted circumstances. When summed over a time period of 10 years, the monetised societal disruption impacts caused by disruptions on this specific link – used to quantify (the inverse of) PTS resilience – were predicted to be equal to €4.3 million (Figure 12.7, left).

For this case study, we also tested potential mitigation measures to reduce the disruption impacts for the studied light rail link and hence to improve network resilience. We tested how the availability of the nearby train network could be used to alleviate parts of the disruption impacts for light rail passengers. Therefore, a scenario was tested in which intercity train services on the parallel train route temporarily called at the local train stations near the disruption location at the light rail network, to provide a better, more frequent alternative for affected passengers. Whilst this measure increased in-vehicle

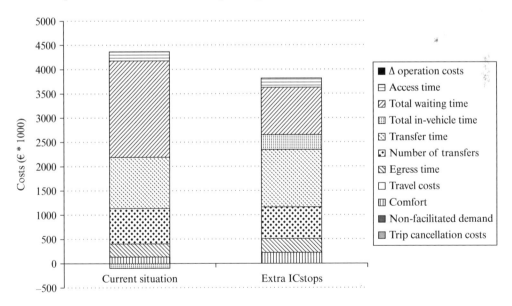

Source: Yap et al. (2018b).

Figure 12.7   *Impact of disruption on the light rail link Laan van NOI–Forepark without mitigation (left), and after testing a potential mitigation measure (right)*

time for the through passengers in the intercity train service, these costs were outweighed by the travel time benefits for the affected light rail passengers, as shown in Figure 12.7 (right). For this same 10-year period, the new total disruption impact was predicted to be equal to €3.9 million, hence realising an 8 per cent resilience improvement pertaining to this link. This case study illustrates how the resilience value of potential measures can be quantified and in a next step be contrasted to their estimated costs in a cost–benefit analysis framework.

Washington, DC, metro network
For the prediction of disruption resilience impacts for the Washington, DC, metro network a different approach was adopted. We used machine learning to predict the passenger delays resulting from different disruptions, which was used to express the reduction in network resilience. The study aim here was to predict the impact of each of the 15 distinguished disruption types for each of the 95 metro stations, during different time periods of the day and days of the week. We developed a supervised learning model which uses network topology indicators, timetable data (from AVL or from General Transit Feed Specification (GTFS) files), passenger data (from AFC systems) and disruption log data as input, and uses the observed passenger delays (obtained from AFC systems) as target.

After testing different machine learning models, a random forest regressor showed to provide the best prediction results. As a result, the total yearly number of passenger delay hours was predicted for each metro station (aggregated over all disruption types), such that stations could be ranked based on their impact on PT network resilience. The yearly passenger delay hours of the least resilient station *Gallery Place* equals almost 77 000, whilst this value equals almost 43 000 for the most resilient station *Stadium-Armory*. Results also showed that transfer stations have a relatively large impact on network resilience, as five of the eight transfer stations of the case study network were among the top-10 least resilient stations. On a network level, 5.9 million passenger delay hours were predicted for the total metro network per year. By applying an unsupervised learning clustering technique, different metro stations could be grouped together based on their disruption characteristics. For this particular case study network, five different station clusters could be distinguished (Figure 12.8). The cluster of most critical stations consists of four transfer stations and the main train station Union Station. Stations located at the end of the branches of the different lines were grouped together as a cluster of least critical stations.

12.7   DISCUSSION AND OUTLOOK

Public transport network resilience is gaining growing attention in recent decades and is expected to become increasingly important in the foreseen future. Major global trends such as the increasing pressures on public transport infrastructure caused by urbanisation and the prevalence of climate-related hazards and security threats contribute to the risk factors. At the same time, the rising expectations from public transport service provision and the increasingly competitive environment direct growing attention to level of service guarantees by stakeholders in the public transport sector.

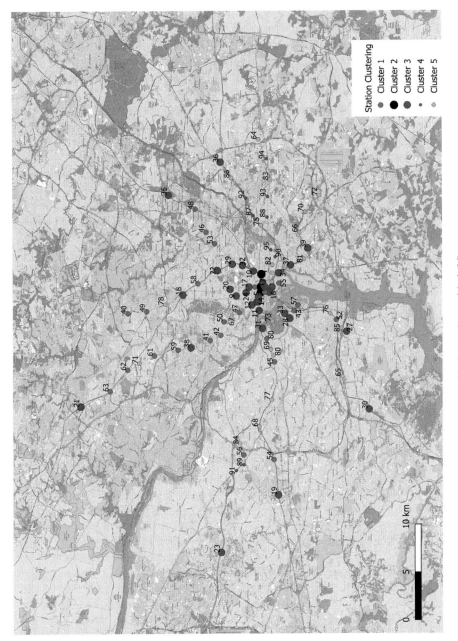

Note: Numbers refer to the ranking of all 95 stations from most critical (1) to least critical (95).

Source: Yap and Cats (2020).

Figure 12.8   Station ranking and clustering

In the public transport planning arena, we believe that the most pressing developments in relation to public transport resilience are:

- Examining the notion of 'optimal resilience' by using the trade-off between efficiency and resilience. This involves developing methods to make this trade-off explicit and quantifiable, and to develop methods to determine the target resilience level of a PT network by incorporating information on uncertainties and a risk management strategy. This can be applied to various planning levels such as the allocation of reserve capacity, switches and buffer times.
- Incorporating resilience into cost–benefit analysis practices to enable the evaluation of resilience-related benefits as part of project appraisal. This applies not only to infrastructure investments (e.g. new lines, switches) but also to planning and policy measures (e.g. timetable design, decentralisation).
- Developing decision support systems that allow analysing and assessing the impacts of alternative measures based on current and predicted system states, such as rolling stock circulation and passenger flows. Such systems may not only support online decisions in response to disruptions, but also the deployment of proactive contingency measures.
- Considering the wider impacts of reducing the occurrence and impacts of public transport disruptions. This includes their inclusion in contractual agreements and related incentive schemes, understanding the impacts of disruption management on user satisfaction as well as the long-term impacts of system resilience on user retention and loyalty, mode choice and the impacts on overall urban and social resilience.

The development of concepts, methods and tools in the domain of public transport resilience requires expertise from a wide range of scientific disciplines. Network science and complex systems engineering provide important insights into the overall public transport network structure properties and their implications for network connectivity in the event of breakdowns (e.g. Ash and Newth 2007; Zhang et al. 2015).

Notwithstanding, such approaches neglect fundamental properties of transport systems and public transport networks in particular, thus hampering their value for the transport planning community, as pointed out by Dupuy (2013). As evident from the previous sections, the transport modelling discipline offers sound theories and methods for evaluating system resilience. Transport models enable devising and testing by means of simulation and optimisation different measures ranging from network design to tactical planning and real-time control. Data science analytics play an important role in not only empirically underpinning the models developed but also offering forecasting techniques (e.g. Zilko et al. 2016; Yap and Cats 2019). To be effective, emerging data science and artificial intelligence techniques should however be embedded in the wider context of policymaking and governance. Moreover, there is a need to design mechanisms to steer stakeholders to embrace the resilience cycle in their business operations. Finally, the electrification and automation of public transport fleets also call for developing new models that account for the so-called multi-layer inter-dependency between different infrastructures (e.g. transport and power grid, transport and communication) and aspects such as cybersecurity.

REFERENCES

Altazin, E., Dauzere-Peres, S., Ramond, F. and Trefond, S. (2017). Rescheduling through stop-skipping in dense railway systems. *Transportation Research Part C*, 79, 73–84.

Ash, J. and Newth, D. (2007). Optimizing complex networks for resilience against cascading failure. *Physica A*, 380, 673–83.

Bell, M.G.H. (2003). The use of game theory to measure the vulnerability of stochastic networks. *IEEE Transactions on Reliability*, 52, 63–8.

Besinovic, N., Goverde, R.M.P., Quaglietta, E. and Roberti, R. (2016). An integrated micro–macro approach to robust railway timetabling. *Transportation Research Part B*, 87, 14–32.

Blume, S.O.P., Cardin, M-A. and Sansavini, G. (2019). Dynamic disruption simulation in large-scale urban rail transit systems. *Complex Systems Design & Management*, 129–40.

Bruneau, M. and Reinhorn, A. (2007). Exploring the concept of seismic resilience for acute care facilities. *Earthquake Spectra*, 23, 41–62.

Candelieri, A., Galuzzi, B.G., Giordani, I. and Archetti, F. (2019). Vulnerability of public transportation networks against directed attacks and cascading failures. *Public Transport*, 11, 27–49.

Cats, O. (2014). Regularity-driven bus operations: Principles, implementation and business models. *Transport Policy*, 36, 223–30.

Cats, O. (2016). The robustness value of public transport development plans. *Journal of Transport Geography*, 51, 236–46.

Cats, O. and Jenelius, E. (2014). Dynamic vulnerability analysis of public transport networks: Mitigation effects of real-time information. *Networks and Spatial Economics*, 14, 435–63.

Cats, O. and Jenelius, E. (2015). Planning for the unexpected: The value of reserve capacity for public transport network robustness. *Transportation Research Part A*, 81, 47–61.

Cats, O. and Jenelius, E. (2018). Beyond a complete failure: The impact of partial capacity degradation on public transport network vulnerability. *Transportmetrica B*, 6, 77–96.

Cats, O., Koppenol, G-J. and Warnier, M. (2017). Robustness assessment of link capacity reduction for complex networks: Application for public transport systems. *Reliability Engineering & System Safety*, 167, 544–53.

Cats, O., West, J. and Eliasson, J. (2016a). A dynamic stochastic model for evaluating congestion and crowding effects in transit systems. *Transportation Research Part B*, 89, 43–57.

Cats, O., Yap, M.D. and Van Oort, N. (2016b). Exposing the role of exposure: Public transport network risk analysis. *Transportation Research Part A*, 88, 1–14.

Cats, O., Abenoza, R.F., Liu, C. and Susilo, Y. (2015). Identifying priority areas based on a thirteen years evolution of satisfaction with public transport and its determinants. *Transportation Research Record*, 2538, 86–95.

Cats, O., Koutsopoulos, H.N., Burghout, W. and Toledo, T. (2011). Effect of real-time transit information on dynamic passenger path choice. *Transportation Research Record*, 2217, 46–54.

Cox, A., Prager, F. and Rose, A. (2011). Transportation security and the role of resilience: A foundation for operational metrics. *Transport Policy*, 18, 307–17.

Derrible, S. and Kennedy, C. (2010). The complexity and robustness of metro networks. *Physica A*, 389, 3678–91.

Dimitrov, S.D. and Ceder, A. (2016). A method of examining the structure and topological properties of public-transport networks. *Physica A*, 451, 373–87.

Dupuy, G. (2013). Network geometry and the urban railway system: The potential benefits to geographers of harnessing inputs from 'naïve' outsiders. *Journal of Transport Geography*, 33, 85–94.

Engelson, L. and Fosgerau, M. (2011). Additive measures of travel time variability. *Transportation Research Part B*, 45, 1560–71.

Gao, Y., Kroon, L., Schmidt, M. and Yang, L. (2016). Rescheduling a metro line in an over-crowded situation after disruptions. *Transportation Research Part B*, 93, 425–49.

Gentile, G., Florian, M., Hamdouch, Y., Cats, O. and Nuzzolo, A. (2016). The theory of transit assignment: Basic modelling frameworks. In G. Gentile and K. Noekel (eds), *Modelling Public Transport Passenger Flows in the Era of Intelligent Transport Systems* (pp. 287–386). Cham: Springer International Publishing.

Ghaemi, N., Cats, O. and Goverde, R.M.P. (2017). A microscopic model for optimal train short-turnings during complete blockages. *Transportation Research Part B*, 105, 423–37.

Ghaemi, N., Cats, O. and Goverde, R.M.P. (2018a). Macroscopic multiple-station short-turning model in case of complete railway blockages. *Transportation Research Part B*, 113, 113–32.

Ghaemi, N., Zilko, A., Yan, F., Cats, O., Kurowicka, D. and Goverde, R.M.P. (2018b). Impact of railway disruption predictions and rescheduling on passenger delays. *Journal of Rail Transport Planning & Management*, 8 (2), 103–22.

Gkiotsalitis, K. and Cats, O. (2018). Reliable frequency determination: Incorporating information on service uncertainty when setting dispatching headways. *Transportation Research Part C*, 88, 187–207.

Gkiotsalitis, K., Eikenbroek, O.A.L and Cats, O. (2020). An exact method for real-time rescheduling after disturbances in metro lines. Paper presented at the *99th Transportation Research Board Annual Meeting*, Washington, DC, January.

Hendren, P., Antos, J., Carney, Y. and Harcum, R. (2015). Transit travel time reliability: Shifting the focus from vehicles to customers. *Transportation Research Record*, 2535, 35–44.

Holling, C.S. (1973). Resilience and stability of ecological systems. *Annual Review of Ecology, Evolution and Systematics*, 4, 1–23.

Hörcher, D., Graham, D.J. and Anderson, R.J. (2017). Crowding cost estimation with large scale smart card and vehicle location data. *Transportation Research Part B*, 95, 105–25.

Jenelius, E. and Cats, O. (2015). The value of new public transport links for network robustness and redundancy. *Transportmetrica A*, 11 (9), 819–35.

Jenelius, E. and Mattson, L.-G. (2015). Road network vulnerability analysis: Conceptualization, implementation and application. *Computers, Environment and Urban Systems*, 49, 136–47.

Knoop, V.L., Hoogendoorn, S.P. and van Zuylen, H.J. (2008). The influence of spillback modelling when assessing consequences of blockings in a road network. *European Journal of Transportation and Infrastructure Research*, 8, 287–300.

Koutsopoulos, H.N., Ma, Z., Noursalehi, P. and Zhu, Y. (2019). Transit data analytics for planning, monitoring, control, and information. In C. Antoniou, L. Dimitriou and F. Pereira (eds), *Mobility Patterns, Big Data and Transport Analytics* (pp. 229–61). Amsterdam: Elsevier.

Lee, A., Van Oort, N. and Van Nes, R. (2014). Service reliability in a network context: Impact of synchronizing schedules in long headway services. *Transportation Research Record*, 2417, 18–26.

Leobons, C.M., Campos, V.B.G. and Bandeira, R.A.M. (2019). Assessing urban transportation systems resilience: A proposal of indicators. *Transportation Research Procedia*, 37, 322–9.

Luo, D., Cats, O., van Lint, H. and Currie, G. (2019). Integrating network science and public transport accessibility analysis for comparative assessment. *Journal of Transport Geography*, 80, 1–10.

Malandri, C., Fonzone, A. and Cats, O. (2018). Recovery time and propagation effects of passenger transport disruptions. *Physica A: Statistical Mechanics and its Applications*, 505, 7–17.

Markolf, S.A., Hoehne, C., Fraser, A., Chester, M.V. and Shane Underwood, B. (2019). Transportation resilience to climate change and extreme weather events: Beyond risk and robustness. *Transport Policy*, 74, 174–86.

Marra, A.D. and Corman, F. (2019). From delay to disruption: The impact of service degradation on public transport networks. *Proceedings of the 8th Symposium of the European Association for Research in Transportation (hEART 2019)*, Budapest.

McDaniels, T., Chang, S., Cole, D., Mikawoz, J. and Longstaff, H. (2008). Fostering resilience to extreme events within infrastructure systems: Characterizing decision contexts for mitigation and adaptation. *Global Environmental Change*, 18, 310–18.

Modica, M. and Reggiani, A. (2014). Spatial economic resilience: Overview and perspectives. *Networks and Spatial Economics*, 15 (2), 211–33.

Nash, A. and Huerlimann, D. (2004). Railroad simulation using Open Track. *Advances in Transport*, 15, 45–54.

Oliveira, E.L., Portugal, L.S. and Junior, W.P. (2016). Indicators of reliability and vulnerability: Similarities and differences in ranking links of a complex road system. *Transportation Research Part A*, 88, 195–208.

Olsson, L.E., Friman, M., Pareigis, J. and Edvardsson, B. (2012). Measuring service experience: Applying the satisfaction with travel scale in public transport. *Journal of Retailing and Consumer Services*, 19, 413–18.

Pimm, S.L. (1984). The complexity and stability of ecosystems. *Nature*, 307, 321–6.

Pnevmatikou, A.M., Karlaftis, M.G. and Kepaptsoglou, K. (2015). Metro service disruptions: How do people choose to travel? *Transportation*, 42, 933–49.

Reggiani, A. (2013). Network resilience for transport security: Some methodological considerations. *Transport Policy*, 28, 63–8.

Reggiani, A., Nijkamp, P. and Lanzi, D. (2015). Transport resilience and vulnerability: The role of connectivity. *Transportation Research Part A*, 81, 4–15.

Rodriguez-Nunez, E. and Garcia-Palomares, J.C. (2014). Measuring the vulnerability of public transport networks. *Journal of Transport Geography*, 35, 50–63.

Rose, A. (2007). Economic resilience to natural and man-made disasters: Multidisciplinary origins and contextual dimensions. *Environmental Hazards*, 7, 383–98.

Sels, P., Dewilde, T., Cattrysse, D. and Vansteenwegen, P. (2016). Reducing the passenger travel time in practice by the automated construction of a robust railway timetable. *Transportation Research Part B*, 84, 124–56.

Shires, J.D., Ojeda-Cabral, M. and Wardman, M. (2019). The impact of planned disruptions on rail passenger demand. *Transportation*. 46 (5), 1807–37.

Snelder, M. (2010). *Designing Robust Road Networks. A General Design Method Applied to the Netherlands* (Ph.D. thesis). Delft: Delft University of Technology.

Tampère, C.M.J., Stada, J., Immers, B., Peetermans, E. and Organe, K. (2007). Methodology for identifying vulnerable sections in a national road network. *Transportation Research Record*, 2012, 1–10.

Tirachini, A., Hurtubia, R., Dekker, T. and Daziano, R.A. (2017). Estimation of crowding discomfort in public transport: Results from Santiago de Chile. *Transportation Research Part A*, 103, 311–26.

Transport for London (2019). Underground service performance. 17 October. Accessed at https://tfl.gov.uk/corporate/publications-and-reports/underground-services-performance.

Trépanier, M. and Yamamoto, T. (2015). Workshop synthesis: System based passive data streams systems: Smart cards, phone data, GPS. *Transportation Research Procedia*, 11, 340–49.

Turnquist, M.A. and Bowman, L.A. (1980). The effects of network structure on reliability of transit service. *Transportation Research Part B*, 14, 79–86.

Van der Hurk, E., Kroon, L. and Maroti, G. (2018). Passenger advice and rolling stock rescheduling under uncertainty for disruption management. *Transportation Science*, 52 (6), 1297–588.

Van Oort, N. (2011). *Service Reliability and Urban Public Transport Design* (Ph.D. Thesis). TRAIL PhD Thesis Series, Delft.

Veelenturf, L.P., Potthoff, D., Huisman, D. and Kroon, L.G. (2012). Railway crew rescheduling with retiming. *Transportation Research Part C*, 20, 95–110.

Von Ferber, C., Holovatch, T. and Holovatch, Y. (2009a). *Attack Vulnerability of Public Transport Networks*. In C. Appert-Rolland, F. Chevoir, P. Gondret, S. Lassarre, J.P. Lebacque and M. Schreckenberg (eds), *Traffic and Granular Flow'07*. Berlin and Heidelberg: Springer.

Von Ferber, C., Holovatch, T., Holovatch, Y. and Palchykov, V. (2009b). Public transport networks: Empirical analysis and modeling. *The European Physical Journal B*, 68, 261–75.

Vromans, M.J.C.M. (2005). *Reliability of Railway Systems* (Ph.D. Thesis). Rotterdam: Erasmus University.

Walker, B.H., Ludwig, D., Holling, C.S. and Peterman, R.M. (1969). Stability of semi-arid savannah grazing systems. *Ecology*, 69, 473–98.

Xu, P., Corman, F., Peng, Q. and Luan, X. (2017). A train rescheduling model integrating speed management during disruptions of high-speed traffic under a quasi-moving block system. *Transportation Research Part B*, 104, 638–66.

Yap, M.D. (2020). *Measuring, Predicting and Controlling Disruptions for Urban Public Transport* (Ph.D. Thesis). Delft: Delft University of Technology.

Yap, M.D. and Cats, O. (2019). Analysis and prediction of disruptions in metro networks. *IEEE Proceedings of the 6th IEEE International Conference on Models and Technologies for Intelligent Transportation Systems (MT-ITS)*, Cracow.

Yap, M.D. and Cats, O. (2020). Predicting disruptions and their passenger delay impacts for public transport stops. *Transportation*. Accessed at https://doi.org/10.1007/s11116-020-10109-9.

Yap, M.D. and van Oort, N. (2018). Driver schedule efficiency vs. public transport robustness: A framework to quantify this trade-off based on passive data. Paper presented at the *Conference on Advanced Systems in Public Transport (CASPT)*, Brisbane.

Yap, M.D., Nijënstein, S. and van Oort, N. (2018a). Improving predictions of public transport usage during disturbances based on smart card data. *Transport Policy*, 61, 84–95.

Yap, M.D., van Oort, N., van Nes, R. and van Arem, B. (2018b). Identification and quantification of link vulnerability in multi-level public transport networks: A passenger perspective. *Transportation*, 45, 1161–80.

Yap, M.D., Cats, O., Törnquist Krasemann, J., Van Oort, N. and Hoogendoorn, S.P. (2020). Quantification and control of disruption propagation in multi-level public transport networks (under review).

Zhang, X., Miller-Hooks, E. and Denny, K. (2015). Assessing the role of network topology in transportation network resilience. *Journal of Transport Geography*, 46, 35–45.

Zhao, J., Frumin, M., Wilson, N.H.M. and Zhao, Z. (2013). Unified estimator for excess journey time under heterogeneous passenger incidence behavior using smartcard data. *Transportation Research Part C*, 34, 70–88.

Zilko, A., Kurowicka, D. and Goverde, R.M.P. (2016). Modeling railway disruption lengths with copula Bayesian networks. *Transportation Research Part C*, 68, 350–68.

13. Service reliability: a planning and operations perspective*

Niels van Oort

1. INTRODUCTION

This chapter addresses service reliability in urban public transport. Definitions, impacts, indicators and improvement measures will be presented and discussed. This chapter is partially based on Van Oort (2011) and related papers (Van Oort and Van Nes, 2009a; Van Oort, 2016).

Service reliability is defined as a certainty of service aspects compared to the schedule (such as travel time (including waiting), arrival time and crowding levels), as perceived by the public transport user. The level of reliability depends on the variability of the system itself and the customer expectation of this variability. Service variability is defined as a distribution of the output values of public transport supply, such as vehicle trip time, vehicle departure time and headways. Unreliability arises when the passenger does not get the service he/she expects given the schedule (Van Oort, 2011).

To prioritize quality factors in public transport, Peek and Van Hagen (2002) introduced the "pyramid of Maslow for public transport". This pyramid consists of different layers representing requirements set by public transport customers. In the lower part of the pyramid are dissatisfiers, which are elements that must be provided in a sufficient manner. If they are not, passengers will be likely to avoid using public transport by not travelling or by changing their travel mode. In the upper part are satisfiers, which are additional quality aspects. The satisfiers are related to passengers' experience, in particular to their perception of the complete journey, including waiting and transferring (Van Hagen and Van Oort, 2019). Reliability along with safety and speed form the base of the pyramid and therefore carry the highest importance.

For decades, reliability-related attributes have been found among the most important service attributes for passengers in a variety of situations (Prashker, 1977; Black and Towriss, 1991). Balcombe et al. (2004) report that service reliability is considered by passengers to be twice as important as frequency. König and Axhausen (2002) conclude that reliability of the transportation system is a decisive factor in user choice behaviour. As studied by Soza-Parra et al. (2019), both passenger density and the number of vehicles a passenger had to wait for to board are significant satisfaction drivers. The European Association of Transport Authorities (EMTA, 2017) defines good public transport as "a reliable service at an affordable price, run by a safe and easy accessible vehicle at a consistent level of quality", also stressing the importance of service reliability.

In order to understand and improve service reliability, it is important to consider how the passenger perceives service variability and reacts to it. In order to gain insights into the interaction process of variability and reliability, a conceptual description of the supply and demand sides of public transport is provided in section 2. The main subject of section 3 is what the impacts of unreliability in public transport are on operations and on passengers. Section 4 addresses indicators and section 5 presents how to improve service reliability through an appropriate design of public transport networks and schedules, in addition to control measures.

2.   ELEMENTS OF SERVICE RELIABILITY IN PUBLIC TRANSPORT

In this section, service reliability in public transport is further conceptualized. Both the supply and demand sides of public transport are addressed including their interaction, which is of main importance in understanding service reliability.

2.1   Public Transport Supply

Looking at the supply side, a single vehicle trip is the basis of operations. Operations are often either schedule-based or headway-based, where the focus regarding the latter is only on the successive headways between the vehicles instead of on the exact departure (and arrival) times at the terminals and stops. In schedule-based operations, vehicle trips are scheduled in time and space resulting in departure and arrival times at all stops along the route from one terminal to another. In addition to these exact departure times at a stop, the number of trips within each period is important. They set the frequency, which determines for passengers the number of possible departures per period and the headways between successive vehicles.

In the schedule, every vehicle trip is planned in a deterministic way and no variation is accounted for. In most cases, schedules are designed for longer periods (e.g. winter or summer months), and trips in homogeneous periods per day are treated similarly. In an ideal situation, vehicles depart on time from the terminal and drive perfectly according to the schedule and with an even headway. During operations, however, actual vehicle trips suffer from disturbances, resulting in variations over the homogeneous periods per day and over longer periods. Deviations and variations of the supply side may be categorized into two source types (Van Oort, 2011):

- *Terminal departure time variability:* this is the distribution of vehicle departure times at the terminal.
- *Vehicle trip time variability:* this is the distribution of vehicle trip times along the route.

There are several internal and external reasons for these deviations affecting service variability. Figure 13.1 shows the main causes of service variability, indicating whether they affect departure time variability or trip time variability (Van Oort, 2011).

2.1.1   Terminal departure variability
Departure variability at the terminal determines the offset of trip deviation according to the schedule (as illustrated by Figure 13.2). Variability occurs if departure times vary in the extent to which they deviate from the schedule (for instance, late and early departures

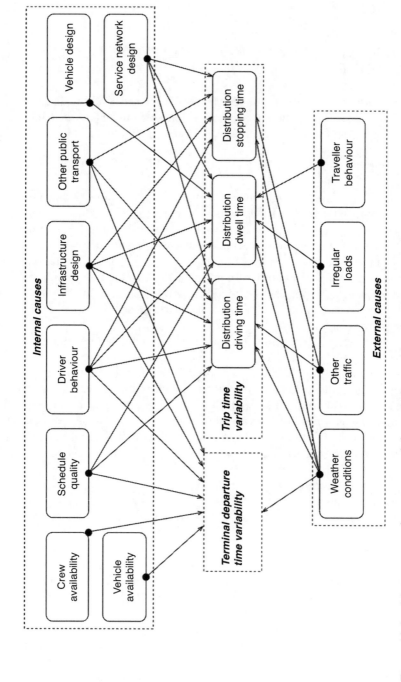

Figure 13.1   Main causes of service variability in urban public transport (Van Oort, 2011)

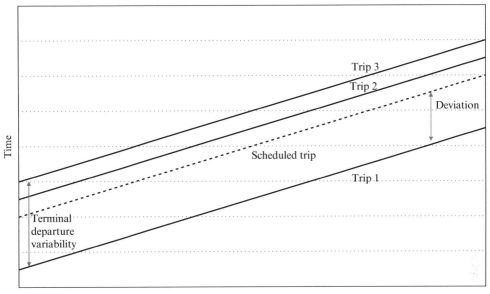

Note: Dotted line is the scheduled service; solid lines are fictitious examples of trips corresponding to the scheduled trip.

Figure 13.2   Variability of service due to terminal departure time variability (Van Oort, 2011)

on the same route at the same terminal). When considering the terminal process, the following causes of variability may be identified:

- *Schedule quality:* If the schedule is loose (longer scheduled trip times than actually needed), drivers tend to depart late (depending on their attitude and driving style). The opposite case is a tight schedule that may lead to early departures. Another issue of schedule quality is the amount of slack in layover time. The amount of slack determines the possibility to recover from an arrival delay of the previous trip.
- *Crew availability:* To depart on time, it is necessary that resources are available and ready on time. Delays in previous vehicle trips or at the beginning of a driver's shift may create departure delays (see e.g. Yap and Van Oort, 2018).
- *Vehicle availability:* In addition to crew availability, the vehicle should be ready and available on time as well.
- *Terminal infrastructure configuration:* Especially in rail-bound traffic, the design of terminals may influence the departure delay. If the provided capacity is not sufficient, delays are to be expected (see e.g. Van Oort and Van Nes, 2010).
- *Driver behaviour:* A crucial aspect is how disciplined drivers are to depart on time and whether they adjust their departure time if delays are expected (as e.g. described by Imram et al., 2019).

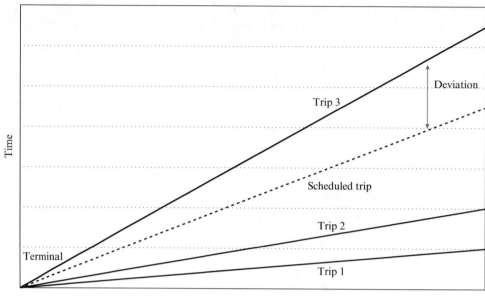

Distance from terminal

Note: Dotted line is the scheduled service; solid lines are fictitious examples of trips corresponding to the scheduled trip.

Figure 13.3   Variability of service due to trip time variability along the route (Van Oort, 2011)

2.1.2   Vehicle trip time variability

Vehicle trip time variability may arise along the route, as indicated by Figure 13.3. In general, this variability increases along the line due to a chain of stochastic events (Veiseth et al., 2007; Van Oort and Van Nes, 2009b).

Concerning the vehicle trip time, three sub-elements may be distinguished, namely: driving, unplanned stopping and dwell time. Driving time is the time the vehicle is actually driving from one stop to another and unplanned stopping time is the time spent on waiting (else other than dwelling). Unplanned stopping happens at locations where no boarding and alighting is allowed, for instance, at traffic lights. Dwell time in turn is the time used for boarding and alighting at a stop. All these time elements may vary over time and across vehicles and together affect the variability of total trip times, expressed in a trip time distribution. Most researchers agree on the basic factors affecting trip times (see e.g. Abkowitz and Tozzi, 1987; Strathman et al., 2000). The causes presented below are responsible for actual driving time and stopping time variability (Van Oort, 2011).

Internal causes:

- *Driver behaviour:* The driving style of every driver differs, resulting in faster or slower trips, creating variability in driving times (see e.g. Imram et al., 2019).
- *Other public transport:* Both on the same route and at junctions, other public transport may affect the driving and stopping time variability. In the case of signallized

sections, this influence is usually even greater, especially when frequencies are close to the theoretical capacity of a track or junction.

- *Infrastructure configuration:* The infrastructure configuration (stops, (dedicated) lanes, junctions (with or without traffic lights)) may affect the capacity and the interaction with other public transport or traffic in such a way that service variability occurs.
- *Service network configuration:* Examples are the number of lines on the same route or stop and the line length. Multiple lines may be presented in the schedule as a frequent and coordinated service, while in practice variability increases with the interaction between different public transport lines (see e.g. Van Oort and Van Nes, 2009c) and coordination may be lost.
- *Schedule quality:* The schedule may affect drivers' behaviour. If the trip time is not planned correctly, some drivers may drive according to the schedule and some may drive as they are used to.

External causes:

- *Other traffic:* The influence of other traffic is mainly visible at junctions and non-exclusive tracks and lanes. The extent to which this cause affects time variability depends, amongst others, on traffic light priority schemes, right of way configurations and traffic volumes.
- *Weather conditions:* Different kinds of weather and how drivers adapt their driving behaviour may result in variability (Hofmann and Mahony, 2005; Mesbah et al., 2015).

In the literature, a lot of attention is paid to the effects of dwell time variability (see e.g. Lin and Wilson, 1992; Li et al., 2006). At an aggregate level, more stops per line lead to a higher level of variability. Apart from this, the following causes of variability in dwell times may be distinguished.

Internal causes:

- *Driver behaviour:* Drivers differ in how fast they open and close doors and the extent to which they wait for late passengers (Phillips et al., 2015).
- *Vehicle design:* Weidmann (1995), Lee et al. (2008) and Fernandez and Tyler (2010) showed the impact of the number and position of vehicle doors enabling an optimized dwell process. A suboptimal design, related to passenger behaviour, may result in dwell time variability.
- *Platform design:* The platform design may lead to an optimal distribution of passengers over the platform, enabling a smooth dwell process. The width, length, location of sheds and other facilities are important elements, and if the design is suboptimal, crowding might occur at specific doors, leading to variability in dwell times.

External causes:

- *Passenger behaviour:* Several types of passengers have different boarding speeds due to age, experience, luggage, etc. The way passengers make use of all vehicle doors is important too.

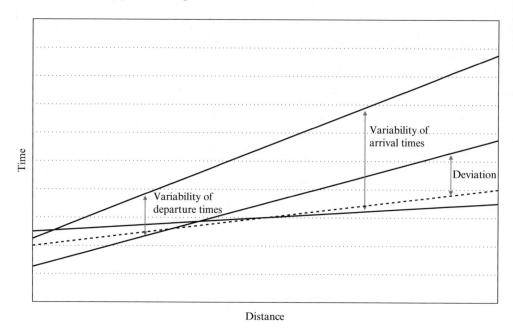

Distance

Note: Dotted line is the scheduled service; solid lines are fictitious examples of trips corresponding to the scheduled trip.

Figure 13.4   Variability of service: example of variability of departure and arrival times
(Van Oort, 2011)

- *Irregular loads:* Due to a different number of people boarding and alighting for every single trip and due to crowding (Currie et al., 2013), variability of dwell times might occur.

2.1.3   Effect of variability in public transport supply

As mentioned above, trip times are stochastic over time, due to a combination of the distribution in terminal departure times and trip time variability. Accordingly, actual departure and arrival times of individual vehicle trips at stops do not match the scheduled times sufficiently, since schedules are deterministic. This phenomenon is illustrated in Figure 13.4. Second, if the focus is set not on the variability of individual trips in time, but on successive trips, headways between successive vehicles at stops are not constant as a result of these distributions. This implies a certain irregularity of vehicle departures at stops, as illustrated by Figure 13.5.

Besides the initial deviations causing variability, as shown above, deviation propagation is quite common in urban public transport. Deviation propagation may be considered in two ways. The first category is the knock-on of delays at the terminal. Arriving late at the terminal limits the possibilities of punctual departure for the next trip (mostly in the opposite direction). The second type of deviation propagation occurs on the line itself. In that case, more than one vehicle is affected. This type of propagation is often referred to as bunching (Fonzone et al., 2015; Verbich et al., 2016; Chapman and Michel, 1978).

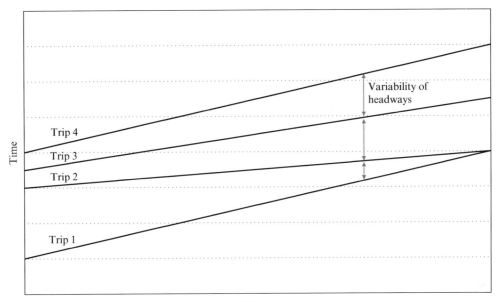

Distance

Note: Presented lines are fictitious examples of successive trips on a route.

Figure 13.5 *Variability of headways between successive trips at stops along the route (Van Oort, 2011)*

If a vehicle suffers from an initial delay (d), the actual headway between this vehicle and its predecessor increases ($H+d$). Due to this longer headway, the number of passengers at the stop waiting for this vehicle increases as well. Because of the larger number of people, dwell time is extended. The extended dwell time creates an additional delay and thus the headway grows even more. This process enforces itself and leads to longer delays. Equation 13.1 (Newel and Potts, 1964) shows how to calculate the (speed of) development of bunching along a line based on an initial delay. It is shown that both the boarding speed and the passenger arrival rate at the platform (factor "k") are key aspects of bunching development speed.

$$\Delta T_{n,m} = \frac{(n-i+m-j)!}{(n-i)! \cdot (m-j)} \cdot \left(\frac{-k}{1-k}\right)^{n-j} \cdot \left(\frac{1}{1-k}\right)^{m-j} \cdot \Delta T_{i,j} \qquad (13.1)$$

where:
$\Delta T_{n,m}$ = Delay of vehicle n at stop m due to initial delay vehicle i at stop j;
k = Ratio passenger arrival at stop [pass/s] and boarding speed [pass/s];
$\Delta T_{i,j}$ = Initial delay.
When one looks at the headway between the vehicle and its successor, this mechanism works the other way around. Due to the initial delay, the headway shrinks ($H-d$) and the number of passengers waiting for the successor decreases. This enables shorter dwell times, which decreases the headway even more. This loop enforces itself as well,

resulting in bunched vehicles. The successor reaches the vehicle and they become bunched.

2.2   Interaction Between Public Transport Supply and Demand

The passenger journey from its origin to its destination consists of multiple steps. The first part of passenger journey time is the access time, which is the time needed between the origin and the departure stop (usually made on foot or by bicycle; see Rijsman et al. (2019) for typical catchment areas and thus access distances). At the departure stop, waiting time occurs between arrival of the passenger and departure of the vehicle. Two arrival patterns may be distinguished. Passengers may arrive at random or they may plan their arrival according to the schedule. In the latter case, some waiting time at the origin may occur as well. This waiting time is referred to as hidden waiting time and arises due to a discrepancy between the preferred departure time and the available departure time. Sometimes the first vehicle is too crowded to enter, so passengers have to wait for the next one. After boarding the vehicle, the next element is moving (or in-vehicle time) until the destination stop is reached. During public transport journeys, one or sometimes more transfers may be necessary. If so, the passenger needs to transfer to the stop of the next vehicle and wait there for the next departure. The final stop is seldom the destination for the passenger, so some egress time from the stop to the destination is unavoidable. Shelat et al. (2018) present typical modal split numbers regarding the egress part. Obviously, walking is the main mode, but due to recent technology and societal developments, it is expected that the use of shared bicycles and e-scooters will grow (Ma et al., 2020).

All these time elements related to the total journey are stochastic in real life due to the variability of different trips in a single period and the variability of a single trip over different days. Figure 13.6 illustrates differences and relations between the demand and supply sides. Passenger waiting time is determined by actual headways and departure times next to passenger arrival time at the stop. This arrival pattern consists of two types, namely: random arrivals and schedule-based arrivals. In addition, passenger in-vehicle time is equal to the vehicle trip time and, together with the departure time, the arrival time at the destination stop is set. From an aggregated passenger perspective, the distribution of total passenger travel time (and as a result the distribution of passenger arrival time) is the most interesting one, since it covers the complete journey.

3.   IMPACTS OF SERVICE RELIABILITY ON PASSENGERS

In the previous section, it was shown that the level of service reliability results from the interaction between the supply and demand sides. In literature, several types of reliability have been distinguished to express the effects of this interaction with a special focus on travel time reliability. The passenger mainly experiences the following effects (Noland and Polak, 2002; Van Oort and Van Nes, 2009c; Muñoz et al., 2020):

- impacts on the duration of travel time components (in-vehicle and waiting time), which lead to arriving early or late;

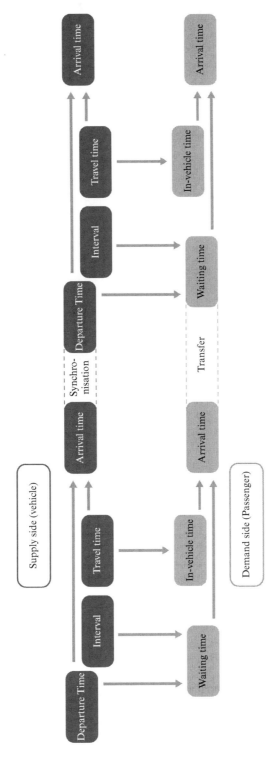

Figure 13.6 Interaction of components on demand and supply sides (Van Oort, 2011)

- impacts on the variability of travel time components (departure, arrival, in-vehicle and waiting time), which lead to uncertainty of the actual travel time;
- impact on the probability of finding a seat and (over)crowding, which affects the comfort level of the journey and might result in denied boarding and extended dwell times.

The aspects are described and analysed in this section.

3.1   Duration of Travel Time Components

Travel time is a key component in all kinds of travellers' decisions. Irregular transport services influence in-vehicle times as well as waiting times, the latter both at the first stop and at transfer nodes. Concerning waiting time, two scenarios are distinguished: waiting when passengers arrive at random (mainly high frequency systems) and when they plan their arrival according to the schedule (mainly low frequency systems). In the case of transfers, waiting time depends on the arrival pattern of feeder vehicles.

3.1.1   In-vehicle time
Variability in vehicle trip times on the supply side results in variability of the passenger in-vehicle time on the demand side. This may result in longer or shorter in-vehicle times for some passengers. If the in-vehicle time is compared to the schedule, the effect depends on the method of planning and publishing trip times in the schedule (e.g. a tight or loose schedule). If a public transport planner uses the average of actual or expected trip times to determine the scheduled trip time, the difference between the scheduled and actual average in-vehicle time per passenger is minimized. In the case of bunching (section 2.1.3), the average in-vehicle time per passenger is extended. More passengers suffer from the delay caused by extended dwell times than the number of passengers benefiting from a faster successive vehicle, because the slowest vehicle collects the majority of travellers.

3.1.2   Waiting time when passengers arrive at the departure stop at random
When passengers arrive at their departure stop uniformly distributed and services are regular, average waiting time per passenger is equal to half the headway between the departing vehicles (Welding, 1957). In theory, half of the passengers would have a shorter waiting time and half of them would encounter more. However, when headways are irregular, the average waiting time per passenger increases. Headways are both longer and shorter than scheduled, but the number of passengers benefiting from shorter headways is smaller than the number suffering from longer headways and waiting times (Welding, 1957; Van Oort and Van Nes, 2009c).

3.1.3   Waiting time when passengers plan their arrival at the departure stop
Literature on the passenger arrival rate and according waiting times when passengers adjust their arrival to the scheduled departure is limited. In Vuchic (2005), a relationship is given showing the average waiting time as a function of the headway, divided into random arrival and planned arrival of passengers and a mixed area in between. The random arrivals lead to waiting times of half the headway as discussed above, while the case of planned arrivals yields an average waiting time of five minutes. In the area in between, the waiting time is the highest.

In the case of passengers planning their arrival at the departure stop, schedule adherence is crucial. For passengers, the difference between early and late departing vehicles is of great importance. Early vehicles might lead to waiting the full headway. Late vehicles only extend waiting time by the amount of delay, which is much less most of the time, especially for large-headway services. The variability of the supply side thus affects the passenger waiting time in an asymmetrical way.

3.2 Variability of Passenger Travel Time Components

In addition to the effect of the supply side variability on the average travel time extension, there is also an effect on the travel time distribution. Due to the combination of the passenger arrival pattern and the variability in departure times and headways, passenger waiting time varies. The variability in vehicle trip time creates a distribution in passenger in-vehicle and arrival time. Equation 13.2 shows the variation of $\tilde{T}^{journey}_{l,j-k}$ in the case of independency of waiting time and in-vehicle time. Due to the expected correlation between these two, this equation may underestimate the variation.

$$Var(\tilde{T}^{journey}_{l,j-k}) = Var(\tilde{T}^{sched,waiting}_{l,j}) + Var(\tilde{T}^{add,\,waiting}_{l,j}) + Var(\tilde{T}^{add,in-vehicle}_{l,j-k}) \quad (13.2)$$

where:

$\tilde{T}^{journey}_{l,j-k}$ = passenger travel time from stop j to stop k on line l (including waiting);

$\tilde{T}^{sched,\,waiting}_{l,j}$ = waiting time according to the schedule per passenger at stop j on line l;

$\tilde{T}^{add,waiting}_{l,j}$ = additional waiting time per passenger due to service variability at stop j on line l;

$\tilde{T}^{add,in-vehicle}_{l,j-k}$ = additional in-vehicle time due to service variability between stop j and k on line l.

The variability in these three elements leads to passenger uncertainty about the service and, consequently, passengers may consider an extra time buffer when comparing travel alternatives. Furth and Muller (2006) state that this time is a function of the perceived service variability. They propose the difference between the 95-percentile value and the average of travel time as the value for this "reliability buffer time". In choices with regard to mode or route, passengers may consider the probability of an uncertain arrival time. Equation 13.3 shows this component (T^{budget}), which is assumed to be a constant per passenger over all their trips, but different per individual passenger. Added to the calculation of travel time per passenger, it results in an expression for the experienced travel time ($\tilde{T}^{journey,exp}_{l,j-k}$).

$$E(\tilde{T}^{journey,exp}_{l,j-k}) = E(\tilde{T}^{journey,sched}_{l,j-k}) + E(\tilde{T}^{add,waiting}_{l,j}) + E(\tilde{T}^{add,in-vehicle}_{l,j-k}) + T^{budget}$$

$$(13.3)$$

where:
$\tilde{T}^{journey,exp}_{l,j-k}$ = passenger travel time from stop j to stop k on line l;
T^{budget} = travel time budget of passengers due to service variability.

3.3   Probability of Finding a Seat and (Over)Crowding

In addition to the influence on travel time, variability also affects the level of comfort by decreasing the probability of securing a seat in a vehicle or creating overcrowding. This effect of service variability is primarily relevant if passengers arrive at the departure stop at random. Due to bunching, vehicles have alternating shorter and longer headways than scheduled. When a vehicle is delayed and the headway is longer, the number of passengers is greater than the expected average per vehicle. This additional number of passengers may lead to capacity problems in the vehicle. More people have to stand or are not even able to enter the vehicle at all. In the case when passengers consult the schedule to arrive at their departure stop, crowding may occur if passengers miss the vehicle (for instance, due to early departure) and board the next one. In this way, the second vehicle suffers from double loads at stops.

Wardman and Whelan (2010) indicate the value of crowding related to travel time. A meta-analysis of 135 valuation studies is reported, finding the travel time valuations to vary with the load factor and journey purpose. The seating multiplier (as a relative weight compared to in-vehicle time) averages 1.15 for load factors between 60 per cent and 100 per cent and almost 1.5 for load factors higher than 100 per cent. These numbers indicate a substantial impact of crowding on passenger perception.

4.   INDICATORS OF SERVICE RELIABILITY

In order to improve service reliability of a public transport system, it is essential to monitor and predict its level with proper indicators. The commonly used indicators do not completely focus on passenger impacts. In fact, they focus more on service variability of the system (Van Oort, 2016). However, section 3 demonstrated the importance of considering the demand side while assessing service reliability. This section presents the traditionally used indicators and introduces new indicators enabling an enhanced quantification of service reliability.

4.1   Traditionally Used Indicators

In practice, commonly used indicators focus either on punctuality, the extent to which the scheduled departure times are met, or on regularity, namely the headway variation. The percentage of trips performed within a predefined bandwidth is a useful reliability indicator. Equation 13.4 expresses this indicator for an average departure deviation on a complete line. Actual data is used to determine the relative frequency of deviations within a bandwidth. As addressed by Van Oort (2014) in detail, the values of δ^{min} and δ^{max} are of main importance and do vary a lot among operators and authorities worldwide and within specific countries.

$$P_l = \frac{\sum_{j=1}^{n_{l,j}} \sum_{i=1}^{n_{l,i}} P_{l,i,j}(\delta^{min} < \tilde{D}_{l,i,j}^{act} - D_{l,i,j}^{sched} < \delta^{max})}{n_{l,i} * n_{l,j}} \qquad (13.4)$$

where:

P_l = relative frequency of vehicles on line *l* having a schedule deviation between δ^{min} and δ^{max};

$P_{l,i,j}$ = relative frequency of vehicle *i* on line *l* having a schedule deviation between δ^{min} and δ^{max} at stop *j*;

$\tilde{D}^{act}_{l,i,j}$ = actual departure time of vehicle *i* on stop *j* on line *l*:

$D^{sched}_{l,i,j}$ = scheduled departure time of vehicle *i* on stop *j* on line *l*;

δ^{min} = lower bound bandwidth schedule deviation;

δ^{max} = upper bound bandwidth schedule deviation;

$n_{l,i}$ = number of trips on line *l*;

$n_{l,j}$ = number of stops on line *l*.

Punctuality may also be defined as an (average) deviation from the timetable at a specific stop, a set of stops, or for all stops on a line. Equation 13.5 shows the latter. This formulation has an important shortcoming. It does not indicate whether vehicles depart too early or too late, which has a large impact on passenger waiting time. If only a set of stops is considered, the location of the stops may be of influence. Important to note is that negative delays are not compensated for by positive delays.

$$p_l = \frac{\sum_{j}^{n_{l,j}} \sum_{i}^{n_{l,i}} \tilde{D}^{act}_{l,i,j} - D^{sched}_{l,i,j} \text{(}}{n_{l,j} * n_{l,i}} \tag{13.5}$$

where:

p_l = average punctuality on line *l*.

Irregularity is used to express headway deviations. Hakkesteegt and Muller (1981) introduced the PRDM (percentage regularity deviation mean), which shows the average deviation from the scheduled headway as a percentage of the scheduled headway. The calculation of the PRDM per stop is shown in equation 13.6; however a calculation for the total line is also possible.

$$PRDM_{l,j} = \frac{\sum_{i} \left| \frac{H^{sched}_{l,i} - \tilde{H}^{act}_{l,i,j}}{H^{sched}_{l,i}} \right|}{n_{l,j}} \tag{13.6}$$

where:

$PRDM_{l,j}$ = relative regularity for line *l* at stop *j*;

$H^{sched}_{l,i}$ = scheduled headway for vehicle *i* on line *l*;

$\tilde{H}^{act}_{l,i,j}$ = actual headway for vehicle *i* on line *l* at stop *j*;

$n_{l,j}$ = number of vehicles on line *l* departing at stop *j*.

All the indicators presented focus purely on characteristics of the supply side. Notwithstanding, the indicators for punctuality and regularity are linked with the assumptions on the arrival pattern of travellers, that is, arrivals based on the timetable and uniformly distributed arrivals, respectively. More important is the fact that these measures make no distinction between stops having a high or low demand. Punctuality and regularity have a strong influence on waiting time and are thus most important for stops having large numbers of passengers. Furthermore, these indicators do not quantify the variability impact on travellers, such as extra travel time, as discussed in section 3. Mazloumi et al. (2008) state that focusing on on-time vehicles only is not sufficient. Therefore, the next section presents new indicators that are better suited to measure service reliability.

4.2   Passenger-oriented Indicators

Adopting a passenger perspective would ideally require indicators for the door-to-door journey instead of punctuality or regularity at stops. Some researchers propose the standard deviation of the actual route travel times as an appropriate criterion for measuring travel time reliability (see e.g. Tseng, 2008). In addition to this, the coefficient of variation of route travel time (CoV) as well as the difference between the 90th and 50th percentile of travel time are proposed for describing travel time reliability. Tseng (2008) shows that these indicators are transformable into each other and the transformation rates depend on the travel time distribution as well. In the literature, travel time reliability has also been defined as the inverse of the standard deviation of journey times (e.g. Sterman and Schofer, 1976). In this section, new indicators are introduced, namely additional travel time and reliability buffer time, enabling the expression of unreliability in a way that better connects to the real impacts on passengers.

4.2.1   Additional travel time

As shown in section 3, service variability may lead to an extension of the passenger average travel time, since the average waiting time may be increased by irregular, early or late vehicles. To express this effect of service variability more effectively than through punctuality and regularity, a new indicator is introduced, called average additional travel time (Van Oort and Van Nes, 2009c; Van Oort, 2014).

In a situation without service variability, the travel time consists of access, waiting, in-vehicle and egress time. Next to regularity and schedule adherence, passenger waiting time depends on the arrival pattern of passengers. In-vehicle time is determined by the scheduled vehicle trip time. Access and egress times are the result of the line and stop spacing.

Due to the variability in actual vehicle trip times and the corresponding deviations of scheduled vehicle departure times and headways, waiting times at stops increase, leading to longer travel times than planned. Access and egress times are not directly affected by variability in operations. In-vehicle time in turn gets affected by variability, but this may result in an extension of travel time for some passengers and a decrease for others. The net effect depends on the scheduled trip time (tight or loose schedule). If the vehicle trip time variability is fixed, no additional in-vehicle time per passenger will arise. After calculating all individual additional travel times, the final indicator, average additional travel time per passenger, may be calculated.

With the average additional travel time per passenger as an unreliability impact indicator, the focus on quantifying service reliability shifts from the supply side (variability) to the impacts on the demand side. Using this indicator, an increase or decrease of the average total travel time due to changes in service variability may be properly expressed. This enables the analysis of an introduction of new instruments and the comparison of several network designs or timetable proposals in, for instance, cost−benefit evaluation (see Van Oort, 2016 for an application of a new, reliable tram line) or advanced transport modelling (see Van Oort et al., 2015 for an approach to incorporate service reliability in conventional transport models). The additional travel time indicator also enables the trade-off between speed and service reliability to be dealt with (Furth and Muller, 2009). Using the supply-oriented indicators only, would lead to a focus on the match between the schedule and operations, which might result in suboptimal timetables. For instance, decreasing speed in the timetable might improve this match. As the schedule (and operations) might become slower, it is obvious that this solution will not necessarily lead to an increase in the overall service quality.

When calculating the additional travel time, two situations have to be distinguished, namely: planned or random arrivals of passengers at the stop. If passengers arrive at random, exact departure times are no longer relevant, meaning that passengers do not use any schedule. Sometimes, operators do not even provide departure times, but just show the headway during different periods. Main assumptions in the calculations are (Van Oort, 2011):

- the examined period is homogeneous concerning scheduled departure times, trip times and scheduled headways (for instance, rush-hour on working days in a month);
- the passenger pattern on the line is fixed;
- all passengers are able to board the first arriving vehicle.

If passengers arrive at the stop at random, the additional travel time is calculated using the coefficient of variation (CoV) of the actual headways ($\tilde{H}_{l,j}^{act}$). The additional waiting time can then be computed using equation 13.7, stemming from Welding (1957). If the service is regular, the covariance equals zero, and the average waiting time equals zero as well. The additional waiting time can be calculated in a similar way using the PRDM (equation 13.6; Hakkesteegt and Muller, 1981). Assuming no change in the actual vehicle trip times, the total average additional travel time per passenger is equal to the average additional waiting time per passenger.

$$E(\tilde{T}_{l,j}^{Add,waiting}) = \frac{E(\tilde{H}_{l,j}^{act})}{2} * (CoV^2(\tilde{H}_{l,j}^{act})) \tag{13.7}$$

where:
$E(\tilde{T}_{l,j}^{Add,waiting})$ = average additional waiting time per passenger due to unreliability of line l at stop j.

Based on the average additional travel time per passenger per stop, one can calculate the average additional travel time per passenger on the complete line. To do this, the proportion or percentage of boarding passengers per stop is used ($\alpha_{l,j}$), as shown by equation 13.8 (Van Oort, 2011). Using the proportion of passengers makes the indicator independent from the actual number of passengers.

$$E(\tilde{T}_{l}^{Add,waiting}) = \sum_{j} (\alpha_{l,j} * E(\tilde{T}_{l,j}^{Add,waiting})) \quad \text{with} \quad \sum_{j} \alpha_{l,j} = 1 \tag{13.8}$$

where:
$\alpha_{l,j}$ = proportion of passengers of line l boarding at stop j.

If passengers plan their arrival at the stop according to the schedule, another method of calculating additional travel time is necessary. Equations 13.9 and 13.10 show this method (Van Oort, 2011). Passengers are assumed to arrive randomly between the scheduled departure time minus τ_{early} and plus τ_{late}. Moreover, it is assumed that they do not experience any additional waiting time if the vehicle departs within this time window. There is a difference between public transport services running ahead of schedule and driving late. Driving ahead (i.e. departing before the scheduled departure time minus τ_{early}) leads to a waiting time equal to the headway (H_l^{sched}; assuming punctual departure of the successive vehicle). Especially in the case of low frequencies, this leads to a substantial increase in passenger waiting time. Driving late creates an additional waiting time equal to the delay ($\tilde{d}_{l,i,j}^{departure}$). Just as before, the additional waiting time is first calculated per stop (equations 13.9 and 13.10) and next computed as a weighted average for all passengers on the line (equation 13.8).

$$
\begin{aligned}
\tilde{T}_{l,i,j}^{Add,waiting} &= H_l^{sched} & if & \quad \tilde{d}_{l,i,j}^{departure} \leq -\tau_{early} \\
\tilde{T}_{l,i,j}^{Add,waiting} &= 0 & if & \quad -\tau_{early} < \tilde{d}_{l,i,j}^{departure} < \tau_{late} \\
\tilde{T}_{l,i,j}^{Add,waiting} &= \tilde{d}_{l,i,j}^{departure} & if & \quad \tilde{d}_{l,i,j}^{departure} \geq \tau_{late}
\end{aligned}
\tag{13.9}
$$

$$
E(\tilde{T}_{l,j}^{Add,waiting}) = \frac{\sum_i E(\tilde{T}_{l,i,j}^{Add,waiting})}{n_{l,i}}
\tag{13.10}
$$

where:

$E(\tilde{T}_{l,i,j}^{Add,waiting})$ = average additional waiting time per passenger due to unreliability of vehicle i on line l at stop j;

H_l^{sched} = scheduled headway on line l;

$\tilde{d}_{l,i,j}^{departure}$ = departure deviation of vehicle i at stop j on line l;

τ_{early} = lower bound of arrival bandwidth of passengers at departure stop;

τ_{late} = upper bound of arrival bandwidth of passengers at departure stop;

$n_{l,i}$ = number of trips on line l.

4.2.2   Reliability buffer time

The average additional travel time per passenger is a proper indicator for the impacts of service variability on passengers. However, it only addresses the average extension of travel time and does not express the variability itself, which contributes to the quality decrease as well. To incorporate this effect, research of Furth and Muller (2006) is useful. They state that besides the average travel time, the 95th percentile value of travel time should be considered, as passengers have to budget extra time for the variability in actual travel time. This additional time is called reliability buffer time (RBT) and may be used to express T^{budget} in equation 13.3.

Ideally, RBT should be calculated for the whole journey. However, based on the data available for operators and authorities, it is possible to determine RBT only for the two main components of a journey, namely waiting and in-vehicle time. The weighted sum of these two RBT indicators might be used as an approximation of the actual RBT used by passengers. To take variability explicitly into account, RBT is considered as a time component in total travel time for passengers. The effect of RBT on passenger departure behaviour at home is not incorporated. More research is required on this topic.

Equation 13.11 enables the calculation of RBT with variability in waiting times and equation 13.12 is used to calculate the average RBT per passenger on the line. Similarly, equations 13.13 and 13.14 show the calculation of RBT with regard to in-vehicle times using the proportion of through passengers ($\beta_{l,j}$).

$$RBT_{l,j}^{waiting} = T_{l,j}^{waiting, 95\%} - E(\widetilde{T}_{l,j}^{waiting}) \tag{13.11}$$

$$RBT_{l}^{waiting} = \sum_{j=1}^{n_{l,j}} (\alpha_{l,j} * RBT_{l,j}^{waiting}) \quad \text{with} \quad \sum_{j} \alpha_{l,j} = 1 \tag{13.12}$$

$$RBT_{l,j}^{in-vehicle} = T_{l,j}^{in-vehicle, 95\%} - E(\widetilde{T}_{l,j}^{in-vehicle}) \tag{13.13}$$

$$RBT_{l}^{in-vehicle} = \sum_{j=1}^{n_{l,j-1}} (\beta_{l,j} * RBT_{l,j}^{in-vehicle}) \quad \text{with} \quad \sum_{j} \beta_{l,j} = 1 \tag{13.14}$$

where:

$RBT_{l,j}^{waiting}$ = Reliability Buffer Time at stop j on line l due to variability in waiting time;

$T_{l,j}^{waiting, 95\%}$ = 95th percentile value of waiting time due to vehicle i at stop j on line l;

$\alpha_{l,j}$ = proportion of passengers of line l boarding at stop j;

$T_{l,j}^{in-vehicle, 95\%}$ = 95th percentile value of in-vehicle time due to vehicle i between stop j and $j+1$ on line l;

$RBT_{l,j}^{in-vehicle}$ = Reliability Buffer Time at stop j on line l due to variability in in-vehicle time;

$\beta_{l,j}$ = proportion of passengers of line l travelling between stop j and $j+1$.

Figure 13.7 illustrates the average additional travel time per passenger (T^{udd}) and the variability of actual travel time. RBT is presented in this figure as well. The scheduled journey time $T^{journey, sched}$ consists of the scheduled waiting and in-vehicle time.

4.2.3 Level of crowding

In addition to the extension of travel time and the reliability buffer time, variability may also result in a loss of comfort due to (over)crowding (see e.g. Wardman and Whelan, 2010; Yap et al., 2018) and denied boarding and extended dwell times (see e.g. Muñoz et al., 2020). This topic is mainly relevant for short-headway services. In such a scenario, ridership is high and even small discrepancies lead to significant deviations in the vehicle occupancy. Overcrowding occurs due to unequal headways as they result in uneven loads of vehicles. In the case of headway deviations, overcrowding always takes place simultaneously with "undercrowding", when vehicles are (much) less occupied than planned. Similar to waiting times, only a few passengers benefit from this, while most passengers experience overcrowding. Given the correlation between headways and overcrowding, the indicators of headway deviations are good for assessing the overcrowding level as well (e.g. PRDM in equation 13.6). For calculating the crowding impacts on (extended) dwell times and on service reliability, Muñoz et al. (2020) provide more insights.

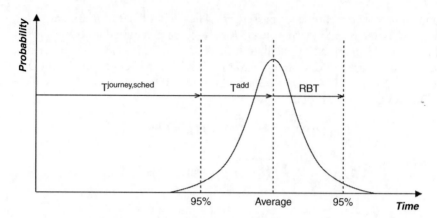

Figure 13.7   Scheduled passenger journey time ($T^{journey, \, sched}$), average additional travel time per passenger (T^{add}) and reliability buffer time (RBT) (Van Oort, 2011)

5.   IMPROVING SERVICE RELIABILITY

To improve the level of service reliability, one could either adjust operations to the planning, or the other way around. Van Oort and Van Nes (2009a), Ibarra-Rojas et al. (2015) and Diab et al. (2015) show that to achieve a high level of service, both strategic, tactical and operational measures are necessary. They provide overviews of measures, as also presented in the following sections.

5.1   Operational Instruments

Operational instruments for improving service reliability are shown in Figure 13.8. These measures have a responsive character and only get used after disturbances have occurred. However, to apply some of these instruments successfully, special conditions at the planning level are required in order to maximize their impact. Section 5.1.1 presents the operational instruments without conditions at a higher level. The instruments that do require such conditions are described in section 5.1.2.

5.1.1   Operational instruments without planning conditions
In literature and practice, many references are available of measures, which are helpful during operations. All instruments are reductive, meaning they do not affect the cause itself, but only reduce (part of) its effects.

Skipping stops   Skipping stops means that some (minor) stops on the route are not served. When a vehicle is late and has to catch up, skipping stops may speed up the vehicle, thereby decreasing the delay. However, passengers travelling to those stops have to alight and transfer to the successive vehicle. Information to passengers, both at the platform and in the vehicle, is thus very important. This strategy is only useful if the number of passengers travelling over the "skip-stop part" is large (and also the number of passengers in the opposite direction, benefiting from increased service reliability) and the number of

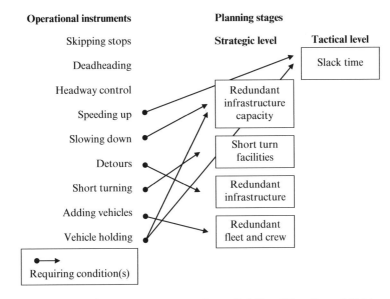

Figure 13.8   Operational instruments improving reliability (Van Oort, 2011)

boardings at this section is low. In Eberlein et al. (1998) and Liu et al. (2013), more details on conditions and trade-offs of this instrument are provided.

Deadheading   A special mode of skipping stops is deadheading, implying that the last part of the route is not served for passengers. The vehicles speed up, because dwelling does not take place any more. Due to this, the next trip (in the opposite direction) may depart from the terminal on time. Again, passenger information is the key success factor of this instrument. Similar to the skip-stop strategy, the trade-off between passengers on the last part of the route and passengers in the opposite direction is essential. Deadheading can be applied for one vehicle trip or all trips on the route. Eberlein et al. (1998) present detailed research on deadheading.

Headway control   Headway control implies regulation of time intervals between successive vehicles. When headways are short and passengers tend to arrive at the departure stop at random, exact departure times are of little interest and headways become more important. If they are constant, the average waiting time and overcrowding are minimized. When a vehicle is delayed in short headway services, headway control may be applied. Figure 13.9 shows the principle of headway control (Van Oort and Van Nes, 2009c). Due to a delay, the headway before the vehicle increases and the headway behind it decreases. By delaying these vehicles, regularity will partly restore. This control can be applied to all vehicles on the line or only a fixed number near the delayed one. Either the control room may be in charge or the driver him/herself. In both cases, actual information on vehicle location and headway adherence should be available. Speeding up the delayed vehicle may be helpful as well, but is often hard due to safety restrictions. In Pangilinan et al. (2008), Delgado et al. (2009), Van der Werff et al. (2019) and Imram et al. (2019), multiple cases of headway control and their impacts are presented.

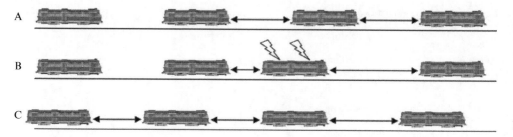

Note: A: Equal headways; B: Imbalanced headways due to a delayed vehicle; C: Partly restored regularity.

Figure 13.9   Principle of headway control (Van Oort, 2009a)

5.1.2   Operational instruments requiring planning conditions
A special category of operational instruments is the one with measures requiring specific choices at the tactical and strategic levels to maximize their impact. Without such conditions, some instruments can still be applied, but service variability might not get reduced or even increase. During the design process (of both networks and schedules), it is important to consider these instruments already, often several years before the actual operations.

Speeding up vehicles   Speeding up vehicles may consist of increasing driving speed as well as decreasing stopping times. If a vehicle is delayed, the theoretically easiest solution is to speed it up. First, traffic safety is crucial when this instrument is applied. Another important issue is the schedule design. The amount and location of slack time in the schedule determines the extent to which speeding up is possible. If an operational speed of 25 km/h is possible and the trip times are based on 20 km/h, speeding up is relatively easy. If trips are designed on an average of 24.5 km/h, speeding up gets harder and the effect is smaller. Chang et al. (2003) present more detailed research on this topic.

Detours   A detour is an alternative route between parts of the original route. Detours are a very effective measure in the case of blocked infrastructure, but also when infrastructure is still available (i.e. recurrent delays are experienced). Detour routes could sometimes enable vehicles to catch up (e.g. by shortcuts) and increase schedule adherence, similar to the skip-stop instrument. An important condition is that the detour infrastructure should be available (in time and space), and especially in rail-bound systems, it should be designed and constructed additionally. This requires attention at the strategic level and increases the infrastructure costs. In Tahmasseby (2009) and Roelofsen et al. (2018), detours related to infrastructure design are analysed and presented.

Short turning   Short turning means that a vehicle turns in the opposite direction somewhere along the route. This instrument can be applied if the infrastructure is blocked and in recurrent delay situations. When a vehicle is short turned, it only provides service on a part of the route. In this way, the vehicle "wins" twice the trip time from the short turn node to the terminal. To apply this instrument, a short turn facility should be available. For road-bound public transport, this is easier than in the case of rail services. Moreover, the capacity of the short turn facility should be sufficient (Van Oort and Van Nes, 2010). Information provision to passengers is of main importance as well. Short turning can be applied for one vehicle trip or all trips in a certain period. More information on short turning is provided by, for instance, Shen and Wilson (2001) and Roelofsen et al. (2018).

Vehicle holding A very common operational instrument is holding (Dessouky et al., 2003; Delgado et al., 2012; Berrebi et al., 2018). Holding implies stopping a vehicle if it runs before schedule at a certain location called the holding point. At the holding point, a decision on holding is taken, based on the actual schedule adherence and the holding strategy (e.g. applying maximum holding time). This requires choices at the tactical level, as the method of schedule design (e.g. tight vs. loose) directly influences the holding process. Besides, the capacity of the holding point should be sufficient, implying some redundant infrastructure capacity. More details on holding will be presented in section 5.2.2.

5.2 Planning Instruments

In section 5.1, the first category of responsive instruments is presented, whereas the second category consists of preventive ones (see Table 13.1). One of the possibilities in preventing service variability is driver education and training. Issues may be, for example, a driving style or the illness ratio with regard to crew availability. Passengers can be coached as well. Showing the effects of boarding through one door instead of spreading over all doors is an example of passenger education. Another instrument is platform design, which encourages passengers to distribute over the platform, enabling smoother boarding. Vehicle design also has an influence, with regard to the interior (possible throughput, method of ticket selling (e.g. vending machines or drivers)) and the exterior

Table 13.1   Preventive instruments for service reliability control (Van Oort, 2011)

Instrument	Level	Causes affected
Training and education of drivers	Operational/Tactical	Drivers' behaviour, crew availability
Passenger education	Operational/Tactical	Passenger behaviour
Spare drivers	Tactical	Crew availability
Vehicle maintenance and spare vehicles	Tactical	Vehicle availability
Trip time determination	Tactical	Schedule quality
Interior and exterior vehicle design	Strategic	Vehicle design
Priority at traffic lights	Strategic	Other traffic
Platform design	Strategic	Passenger behaviour
Terminal and stop (capacity) design	Strategic	Infrastructure configuration, other public transport
Exclusive lanes	Strategic	Infrastructure configuration, other public transport, other traffic
Coordination of lines	Strategic	Service network configuration
Length of lines	Strategic	Service network configuration
Stopping distance	Strategic	Service network configuration
Synchronization of lines	Strategic	Service network configuration

(number and size of doors). In addition, spare drivers and vehicles determine to what extent the variability can be prevented when the actual crew or fleet availability is limited. Other instruments of Table 13.1 are described in the following subsections.

5.2.1   Improving reliability by network design
At the strategic level, two layers are distinguished, namely: the infrastructure layer and the service network layer. Separated per layer, the possibilities for improving service reliability are summarized below.

Infrastructure layer   In the strategic design of public transport, choices are made on infrastructure facilities, including terminals and stops, links and intersections. The following instruments are relevant to service reliability.

- *Terminal design:* Capacity constraints limit the number of possible vehicles turning per hour, depending on the specific configuration of the terminal, such as switch locations before or after the stop (as addressed by Van Oort and Van Nes, 2010). The dynamic character of actual operations has a negative impact on the capacity that can be used.
- *Exclusive lanes:* With the introduction of exclusive lanes for public transport, driving times are less affected and unplanned stopping times decrease, which helps to achieve a higher level of service reliability (Vuchic, 2005; Ceder, 2007).
- *Stop design:* Similar to terminal design, stop design may limit vehicle capacity. Combined with high intensities and variability, this might lead to additional delays.
- *Priority at traffic lights:* Introducing priority at traffic lights may decrease (variability in) stopping times. Several studies have been performed on this topic (Ceder, 2007; Currie and Shalaby, 2008). Besides the absolute priority (public transport never has to stop or even brake), the conditional priority has been introduced (Muller and Furth, 2000). In this case, only late vehicles receive priority, whereas early vehicles have to wait. The influence of the schedule parameters is of extreme importance, as a tight schedule results in all vehicles being late and thus receiving priority.

Service network layer

- *Stopping distance:* Differences in dwell times occur partly because of variation in number of passengers. If there are no passengers at a stop and nobody wants to get out, the vehicle does not need to stop and there is no dwell time. During the network design, attention should be paid to this variation to determine the stop spacing. It is best to always have passengers at a stop, so the vehicle needs to stop every time, which prevents large distributions from occurring. The optimal stop spacing is a trade-off between a few more aspects (Van Nes and Bovy, 2000; Van Nes, 2002), but service reliability should be considered as well.
- *Length of lines:* Long lines offer many direct connections serving many stops. However, the longer the line, the higher the probability of increasing service variability. At the design stage, both effects should be considered as a trade-off. At this moment, service reliability is not explicitly incorporated at the strategic level, which may lead to suboptimal designs. In Van Oort and Van Nes (2009b), it is

demonstrated that shorter lines might yield shorter travel times due to higher service reliability (and compensating for additional transfers).

- *Coordination of lines:* In urban public transport networks, it is very common to provide several lines on the same route. At a specific branch of the network, combined frequencies are high and many direct connections are offered. Although this design choice seems to improve the network quality at the strategic level, it actually depends on the quality of service at the operational level. In the design process, the expected variability should be taken explicitly into account with coordination of the timetable, as addressed by Van Oort and Van Nes (2009c).
- *Synchronization of lines:* In a public transport network, it is hardly possible to connect all origins and destinations, so transfers are unavoidable. To reduce one of the negative impacts of transfers, being passenger waiting time, a synchronization of lines may be applied (Yap et al., 2019). Frequencies and schedules are synchronized, enabling smooth transfers between the lines. In fact, this instrument is thus relevant at both strategic and tactical stage. Lee et al. (2014) demonstrate the impacts of synchronization of service reliability.

5.2.2   Improving reliability by timetable design and vehicle holding

To influence service reliability positively at the tactical level, slack time allocation in trip and dwell times, with or without a holding strategy are addressed here. Planning a tight or loose schedule might have a major impact on passengers. The main issue of driving early or driving late should be considered while designing schedules.

Section 5.1 already presented holding as an operational instrument, yet this also requires much attention at the tactical level. The amount of holding depends on the schedule type. If the schedule is optimized concerning holding strategies, this instrument is preventive as well. A trade-off between service reliability and travel speed would arise.

Holding implies that vehicles arriving early have to wait until they are on schedule again. This way, service reliability is improved downstream from the holding point. However, the passengers who are already in the vehicle during the holding process will suffer from additional travel time leading to a conflict of interests with passengers downstream. The amount of holding depends on the schedule. If trip times are designed tightly, not many vehicles will operate ahead of schedule and holding will not be applied very much. However, if trip times are designed in such a way that the schedule is very loose, many vehicles will be held due to earliness.

The instrument of vehicle holding does not affect the infrastructure design. However, attention must be paid to the capacity of the holding point. The vehicles held may block vehicles of other lines. Costs of operations are unaffected, as cycle time is considered to be fixed. The benefits of vehicle holding are reduced average additional travel time per passenger (for both existing and new passengers), an improved service reliability and the related growth of ridership and revenues. Using empirical research, a line could facilitate on average 5–10 per cent more passenger journeys due to enhanced service reliability that increases the effective frequency (see e.g. Van Oort et al., 2012).

Vehicle holding is divided into a number of categories, which are shown in Table 13.2. First of all, a distinction is made between long and short headways. The type of holding strategy is differentiated as well, where one strategy holds vehicles when they are ahead of

Table 13.2   Categories of vehicle holding

		Long-headway services	Short-headway services
Holding strategy	Schedule-based	X	X
	Headway-based		X
Holding location	All stops	X	
	Few stops	X	X

schedule and the other one when the headway ahead is too short. The last differentiation is where the holding takes place, namely at all stops or at only a few main stops.

In Van Oort et al. (2010) and Van Oort et al. (2012), it was found that vehicle holding at least at two stops per line using percentile values of 35–65 to determine the scheduled trip time, yield the most reliable services and least additional travel times for all passengers.

NOTE

*   This chapter is based on (ongoing) work of the Smart Public Transport Lab of Delft University of Technology. Special thanks to Yaroslav Kholodov, Menno Yap and Laurens Boertje for their support.

REFERENCES

Abkowitz, M. and J. Tozzi (1987), Research contributing to managing transit service reliability, *Journal of Advanced Transportation*, Vol. 21 (Spring), pp. 47–65.

Balcombe, R., R. Mackett, N. Paulley, J. Preston, J. Shires, H. Titheridge, M. Wardman et al. (2004), *The Demand for Public Transport: A Practical Guide*, TRL Report, TRL 593.

Berrebi, S.J., E. Hans, N. Chiabaut, J.A. Laval, L. Leclercq and K.E. Watkins (2018), Comparing bus holding methods with and without real-time predictions, *Transportation Research Part C: Emerging Technologies*, Vol. 87, pp. 197–211.

Black, I. and J.G. Towriss (1991), Quantifying the value of uncertainty in travel time, *Proceedings of 18th PTRC*, Seminar H, London.

Ceder, A. (2007), *Public Transit Planning and Operation, Theory, Modelling and Practice*, London: Elsevier.

Chang, J., J. Collura, F. Dion and H. Rakha (2003), Evaluation of service reliability impacts of traffic signal priority strategies for bus transit. *Transportation Research Record*, No. 1841, pp. 23–31.

Chapman, R.A. and J.F. Michel (1978), Modelling the tendency of buses to form pairs, *Transportation Science*, Vol. 12, No. 2, pp. 165–75.

Currie, G. and A. Shalaby (2008), Active transit signal priority for streetcars: Experience in Melbourne, Australia, and Toronto, Canada, *Transportation Research Record*, No. 2042, pp. 41–9.

Currie, G., A. Delbosc, S. Harrison and M. Sarvi (2013), Impact of crowding on streetcar dwell time, *Transportation Research Record*, No. 2353, pp. 100–106.

Delgado, F., J. Munoz and R. Giesen (2012), How much can holding and/or limiting boarding improve transit performance? *Transportation Research Part B: Methodological*, Vol. 46, No. 9, pp. 1202–17.

Delgado, F., J. Munoz, R. Giesen and A. Cipriano (2009), Real-time control of buses in a transit corridor based on vehicle holding and boarding limits, *Transportation Research Record*, No. 2090, pp. 59–67.

Dessouky, M., R. Hall, L. Zhang and A. Singh (2003), Real time control of buses for schedule coordination at a terminal, *Transportation Research*, No. 37A, pp. 145–63.

Diab, E.I., M.G. Badami and A.M. El-Geneidy (2015), Bus transit service reliability and improvement strategies: Integrating the perspectives of passengers and transit agencies in North America, *Transport Reviews*, Vol. 35, No. 3, pp. 292–328.

Eberlein, X.J., N.H.M. Wilson and C. Barnhart (1998), The real-time deadheading problem in transit operations control, *Transportation Research*, No. 32B, pp. 77–100.

EMTA (2017), Quality of public transport, *Eurotransport*, Vol. 15, No. 4.

Fernandez, R. and N. Tyler (2010), Influence of platform height, door width and fare collection on bus dwell time: Laboratory evidence for Santiago de Chile, in: *Proceedings of 89th Annual Meeting of Transportation Research Board*, Washington, DC.

Fonzone, A., J.D. Schmöcker and R. Liu (2015), A model of bus bunching under reliability-based passenger arrival patterns, *Transportation Research Part C: Emerging Technologies*, Vol. 59, pp. 164–82.

Furth, P.G. and T.H.J. Muller (2006), Service reliability and hidden waiting time: Insights from automated vehicle location data, *Transportation Research Record*, No. 1995, pp. 79–87.

Furth, P.G. and T.H.J. Muller (2009), Optimality conditions for public transport schedules with timepoint holding, *Public Transport*, Vol. 1, pp. 87–102.

Hakkesteegt, P. and T.H.J. Muller (1981), Research increasing regularity, *Verkeerskundige Werkdagen*, pp. 415–36 [in Dutch].

Hofmann, M. and M.O. Mahony (2005), The impact of adverse weather conditions on urban bus performance measures, *Proceedings of the 8th International IEEE Conference on Intelligent Transportation Systems*, Vienna.

Ibarra-Rojas, O.J., F. Delgado, R. Giesen and J.C. Muñoz (2015), Planning, operation, and control of bus transport systems: A literature review, *Transportation Research Part B: Methodological*, Vol. 77, pp. 38–75.

Imran, A., N. Van Oort, O. Cats, S. Hoogendoorn and P. Van der Pot (2019), Combining speed adjustment and holding control for regularity-based transit operations, *Proceedings of IEEE MT-ITS Conference*, Krakow.

König, A. and K.W. Axhausen (2002), The reliability of the transportation system and its influence on the choice behaviour, *Proceedings of the 2nd Swiss Transportation Research Conference*, Monte Verità.

Lee, A., N. Van Oort and R. Van Nes (2014), Service reliability in a network context, *Transportation Research Record*, Vol. 2417, pp. 18–26.

Lee, Y.C., W. Daamen and P. Wiggenraad (2008), Boarding and alighting behavior of public transport passengers, *Proceedings of 87th Annual meeting Transportation Research Board*, Washington, DC.

Li, M., F. Zhao, L. Chow, H. Zhang and S. Li (2006), Simulation model for estimating bus dwell time by simultaneously considering numbers of disembarking and boarding passengers, *Transportation Research Record*, No. 1971, pp. 59–65.

Lin, T. and N. Wilson (1992), Dwell time relationships for light rail systems, *Transportation Research Record*, No. 1361, pp. 287–95.

Liu, H., Y. Yan, X. Qu and Y. Zhang (2013), Bus stop-skipping scheme with random travel time, *Transportation Research Part C: Emerging Technologies*, Vol. 35, pp. 46–56.

Ma, X., Y. Yuan, N. Van Oort and S. Hoogendoorn (2020), Bike-sharing systems' impact on modal shift: A case study in Delft, the Netherlands, *Journal of Cleaner Production*, Vol. 259, 20 June.

Mazloumi, E., G. Curry and S. Majid (2008), Assessing measures of transit travel time variability and reliability using AVL data, *Proceedings of 87th Annual Meeting of Transportation Research Board*, Washington, DC.

Mesbah, M., J. Lin and G. Currie (2015), "Weather" transit is reliable? Using AVL data to explore tram performance in Melbourne, Australia. *Journal of Traffic and Transportation Engineering* [English edn], Vol. 2, No. 3, pp. 125–35.

Muller, T.H.J. and P.G. Furth (2000), Conditional bus priority at signalized intersections: Better service with less traffic disruption, *Transportation Research Record*, No. 1731, pp. 23–30.

Muñoz, J.C., J. Soza-Parra and S. Raveau (2020), A comprehensive perspective of unreliable public transport services' costs, *Transportmetrica A: Transport Science*, Vol. 16, No. 3, pp. 734–48.

Newel, G.F. and R.B. Potts (1964), Maintaining a bus schedule, *Proceedings of the Second Conference of the Australian Road Research Board*.

Noland, R. and J. Polak (2002), Travel time variability: A review of theoretical and empirical issues, *Transport Reviews*, Vol. 22, pp. 39–54.

Pangilinan, C., N.H.M. Wilson and A. Moore (2008), Bus supervision deployment strategies and the use of real-time AVL for improved bus service reliability, *Proceedings of 87th Annual Meeting of Transportation Research Board*, Washington, DC.

Peek, G.J. and M. Van Hagen, (2002), Creating synergy in and around stations: Three strategies, *Journal of Transportation Research Record*, Vol. 1793, pp. 1–6.

Phillips, W., A. del Rio, J.C. Muñoz, F. Delgado and R. Giesen (2015), Quantifying the effects of driver non-compliance and communication system failure in the performance of real-time bus control strategies, *Transportation Research Part A: Policy and Practice*, Vol. 78, pp. 463–72.

Prashker, J. (1977), *Development of a "Reliability of Travel Modes" Variable for Mode-Choice Models*, PhD dissertation, Northwestern University.

Rijsman, L., N. Van Oort, D. Ton, S. Hoogendoorn, E. Molin and T. Teijl (2019), Walking and bicycle catchment areas of tram stops: Factors and insights, *Proceedings of IEEE MT-ITS Conference*, Krakow.

Roelofsen, D., O. Cats, N. Van Oort and S. Hoogendoorn (2018), Assessing disruption management strategies in rail-bound urban public transport from a passenger perspective, paper presented at the *Conference on Advanced Systems in Public Transport and TransitData (CASPT)*, Brisbane, July.

Shelat, S., R. Huisman and N. Van Oort (2018), Analysing the trip and user characteristics of the combined bicycle and transit mode, *Research in Transportation Economics*, Vol. 69, pp. 68–76.

Shen, S. and N.H.M. Wilson (2001), Optimal integrated real-time disruption control model for rail transit systems, in S. Voss and J. Daduna (eds), *Computer-Aided Scheduling of Public Transport: Lecture Notes in Economics and Mathematical Systems 505*, pp. 335–64, Berlin: Springer-Verlag.

Soza-Parra, J., S. Raveau, J.C. Muñoz and O. Cats (2019), The underlying effect of public transport reliability on users' satisfaction, *Transportation Research Part A: Policy and Practice*, Vol. 126, pp. 83–93.

Sterman, B.P. and J.L. Schofer (1976), Factors affecting reliability of urban bus services, *Transport Engineering Journal*, Vol. 102, No. 1, pp. 147–59.

Strathman, J.G., T. Kimple, K. Dueker, R. Gerhart and S. Callas (2000), Service reliability impacts of computer-aided dispatching and automatic location technology: A Tri-Met case study, *Transportation Quarterly*, Vol. 54, No. 3, pp. 85–102.

Tahmassseby, S. (2009), *Reliability in Urban Public Transport Network Assessment and Design*, PhD thesis, Department of Transport and Planning, Faculty of Civil Engineering and Geosciences, Delft University of Technology.

Tseng, Y.Y. (2008), *Valuation of Travel Time Reliability in Passenger Transport*, PhD thesis, Vrije Universiteit, Amsterdam.

Van der Werff, E., N. Van Oort, O. Cats and S. Hoogendoorn (2019), Robust control for regulating frequent bus service: Supporting the implementation of headway-based holding strategies, *Transportation Research Record*, Vol. 2673, No. 9, pp. 654–65.

Van Hagen, M. and N. Van Oort (2019), Improving railway passengers experience: Two perspectives, *Journal of Traffic and Transportation Engineering*, Vol. 7, pp. 97–110.

Van Nes, R. (2002), *Design of Multimodal Transport Networks: A Hierarchical Approach*, TRAIL Thesis Series T2002/5, TRAIL Research School, Delft.

Van Nes, R. and P.H.L. Bovy (2000), The importance of objectives in urban transit network design, *Transportation Research Record*, No. 1735, pp. 25–34.

Van Oort, N. (2011), Service reliability and urban public transport design, T2011/2, TRAIL PhD Thesis Series, Delft University of Technology.

Van Oort, N. (2014), Incorporating service reliability in public transport design and performance requirements, *Research in Transportation Economics*, Vol. 48, December, pp. 92–100.

Van Oort, N. (2016). Incorporating enhanced service reliability of public transport in cost–benefit analyses. *Public Transport*, Vol. 8, No.1, pp. 143–60.

Van Oort, N. and R. Van Nes (2009a), Control of public transport operations to improve reliability: Theory and practice, *Transportation Research Record*, No. 2112, pp. 70–76.

Van Oort, N. and R. Van Nes (2009b), Line length versus operational reliability: Network design dilemma in urban public transportation, *Transportation Research Record*, No. 2112, pp. 104–10.

Van Oort, N. and R. Van Nes (2009c), Regularity analysis for optimizing urban transit network design, *Public Transport*, Vol. 1, No. 2, pp. 155–68.

Van Oort, N. and R. Van Nes (2010), The impact of rail terminal design on transit service reliability, *Transportation Research Record*, No. 2146, pp. 109–18.

Van Oort, N., T. Brands, E. de Romph and J.A. Flores (2015), Unreliability effects in public transport modelling, *International Journal of Transportation*, Vol. 3, No.1, pp. 113–30.

Van Oort, N., J.W. Boterman, and R. Van Nes (2012), The impact of scheduling on service reliability: Trip-time determination and holding points in long-headway services. *Public Transport*, Vol. 4, No. 1, pp. 39–56.

Van Oort, N., N.H.M. Wilson and R. Van Nes (2010), Reliability improvement in short headway transit services: Schedule-based and headway-based holding strategies, *Transportation Research Record*, No. 2143, pp. 67–76.

Veiseth, M., N. Olsson and I.A.F. Saetermo (2007), Infrastructure's influence on rail punctuality, *Proceedings of Urban Transport*, XII, Coimbra.

Verbich, D., E. Diab and A. El-Geneidy (2016), Have they bunched yet? An exploratory study of the impacts of bus bunching on dwell and running times. *Public Transport*, Vol. 8, No. 2, pp. 225–42.

Vuchic, V.R. (2005), *Urban Transit, Operations, Planning and Economics*, Hoboken, NJ: John Wiley and Sons.

Wardman, M. and G. Whelan (2010), 20 years of rail crowding valuation studies: Evidence and lessons from British experience, *Proceedings of 89th Annual Meeting of Transportation Research Board*, Washington, DC.

Weidmann, U. (1995), *Grundlagen zur Berechnung der Fahrgastwechselzeit*, Schriftenreihe des IVT No. 106, Institut für Verkehrsplanung und Transporttechnik, ETH Zürich [in German].

Welding, P.I. (1957), The instability of a close interval service, *Operational Research Quarterly*, Vol. 8, No.3, pp. 133–48.

Yap, M. and N. Van Oort (2018), Driver schedule efficiency vs. public transport robustness: A framework to quantify this trade-off based on passive data, paper presented at the *Conference on Advanced Systems in Public Transport and TransitData (CASPT)*, Brisbane.

Yap, M., O. Cats and B. Van Arem (2018), Crowding valuation in urban tram and bus transportation based on smart card data. *Transportmetrica A: Transport Science*, Vol. 16, No. 1, pp. 23–42.

Yap, M., D. Luo, O. Cats, N. Van Oort and S. Hoogendoorn (2019), Where shall we sync? Clustering passenger flows to identify urban public transport hubs and their key synchronization priorities, *Transportation Research Part C*, No. 98, 433–48.

14. Rail transit disruption management: a comprehensive review of strategies and approaches
Amer Shalaby, Lisa Li and Ehab Diab

14.1 INTRODUCTION

An ever-growing number of cities around the world are investing in urban rail systems to achieve target mobility, environmental and economic goals. The family of urban rail systems includes commuter rail, metro, Light Rail Transit (LRT), and streetcar modes. These systems are capable of transporting large volumes of passengers in a timely and efficient manner, thus providing an important means for personal mobility in congested urban areas. However, these systems suffer frequently from unexpected operational problems and incidents of numerous types, which lead to unplanned service *disruptions*. Transit service disruptions are usually defined as unexpected interruptions that suspend service provision. Disruptions can rapidly cause the quality of service provided to the public to deteriorate, leading to a significant decline in users' satisfaction and weakening the transit system's ability to retain existing users or attract new ones. Additionally, these delays impose significant direct cost on both users and operators and additional indirect cost on society. It is rare to find studies that quantify the full cost of rail service delays. One exception is the recent study by Stringer (2017), which was concerned with quantifying the economic cost of passenger delays due to both recurrent and non-recurrent sources of service delays in the New York metro system. That cost was estimated to be upward of USD 389 million annually.

Rail-based transit service disruptions occur due to a wide array of unexpected events such as equipment failure (e.g., signal and switch problems), passenger-related issues (e.g., medical emergencies, injuries, violence), security problems (e.g., police investigations), crew issues (train operator shortage and errors), and other external factors such as extreme weather conditions (Diab and Shalaby, 2019). In response to unplanned disruptions, public transport authorities utilize several disruption management strategies to mitigate and minimize the negative impacts of these unexpected events on users and the system at large.

In recent years, a considerable body of research on disruption management has been conducted, proposing and evaluating various management strategies. These can be broken down broadly into two major categories: supply management and demand management strategies. The former category includes actions taken by the transit agency to replace and/or restore the service. In contrast, demand management strategies refer to actions taken by transit authorities to manage passenger flows and user experience. One of the most common supply management strategies used in response to rail-system service disruption is *bus bridging*, which is sometimes referred to as "replacement bus service", "substitute bus service" or "temporary bus shuttle service". This strategy involves replacing the suspended passenger train service with a shuttle bus service in order to restore and maintain the connectivity along the affected rail segment.

This chapter aims at synthesizing the state of knowledge in disruption management, modelling and analysis, with special focus placed on unplanned disruptions in urban rail systems. To achieve this objective, a systematic review of the literature is presented. The scope of this chapter excludes route management and service reliability improvement strategies. It also does not concern itself with bus operation issues (e.g., bus bunching and delays) or transit crew and workforce management aspects (i.e., extraboard planning). The chapter begins with a discussion of the used terminology and adopted methodology of the literature review. Next, it presents a synthesis of the recent empirical research on disruption management strategies, with special emphasis placed on understanding the formulated models and approaches. Finally, it provides concluding remarks on the reviewed literature.

14.2 CONCEPTS AND TERMINOLOGIES

As noted earlier, rail service disruptions occur due to many unexpected events that prohibit transit authorities from delivering their normal scheduled services. Disruption can vary in duration, ranging from a few minutes to several hours. In the literature, disruptions of relatively short duration, often referred to as "minor disruptions", are usually dealt with by either doing nothing or rescheduling and rerouting the service. Crew or rolling stock rescheduling is often not considered. In contrast, "major disruptions" generally refer to relatively longer disruptions that require the cancellation of a number of trips in the timetable. According to recent studies, the metro system of Toronto experience more than 12 000 incidents a year, approximately 1000 of which are classified as "major" (Louie et al., 2017; Diab and Shalaby, 2019). These major disruptions usually require a temporary closure of the railway tracks or stations and the allocation of new resources such as shuttle bus services to restore the lost connectivity between stations. They may also require rescheduling and rerouting the service and subsequently rescheduling the rolling stock and crews. When rescheduling occurs, the modified timetable should ideally be communicated to passengers to adjust their arrival times at stops as needed.

14.3 LITERATURE REVIEW METHODOLOGY

A systematic literature review method was used to identify all publications in the academic literature related to rail transit disruption management, and to analyse and understand gaps in knowledge which represent opportunities for future research. The scope of this review is limited to rail disruption management, common strategies, and modelling and analysis approaches. The modes considered in this review include metro, commuter rail and light rail transit.

The adopted literature review method consisted of two sequential phases. The first involved a search on the Web of Knowledge, Scopus and Transport Research International Documentation (TRID) online article databases as of August 2019. TRID is the largest online database of transportation research, containing more than 1.2 million records of transportation research record (TRID, 2013). The search consisted of the following terms within the "title" search field: "(transit OR rail* OR train) AND (disruption OR

Table 14.1   Inclusion and exclusion criteria

Inclusion criteria	Exclusion criteria
• Full articles	• Abstracts and short articles
• Peer reviewed	• Conference proceedings
• English records	• Non peer-reviewed work
• Focused on transit service disruption/ interruption	• All languages other than English
• Focused on bus bridging issues	• Focused on bus/rail route operations, reliability, bunching, and scheduling issues
• Focused on users' behaviour and demand during disruptions	• Focused on crew management and extraboard optimization
• Published as of August 2019	• Focused on trip distribution and transit assignment methods
• Published over the past 10 years	• Focused on modelling transit system resilience and factors affecting the duration or the number of interruptions
	• Focused on flex transit systems, on-demand services, specialized bus services or school service
	• Focused on natural disaster management and disaster evacuation
	• Focused on planned suspension of service (e.g., due to maintenance)

disruption management OR service disruption)", "(transit OR rail* OR train) AND (disruption management OR service disruption) AND (model* OR simulation)", OR "(Bus bridging)". The search was restricted to full-article publications only. Conference proceedings and abstracts were not considered. Additionally, the search was restricted to publications in English related to transportation, urban studies, social sciences and engineering. Finally, the search focused only on publications dated within the past 10 years. Once the database search was complete, the relevant articles were identified based on a predetermined detailed set of inclusion and exclusion criteria which are outlined in Table 14.1. The second phase of the search strategy began by examining the reference lists of all articles resulting from the first phase in order to identify new articles. The same set of inclusion and exclusion criteria were applied to the articles identified in the second phase. Finally, the identified articles from both phases were fully reviewed and synthesized.

The first phase of the search returned 391 papers. Out of these papers, 335 were disqualified due to their irrelevance and application of inclusion and exclusion criteria. Once the database had been reduced to 56 relevant articles, the second phase of the search strategy started. The reference lists of all the articles in the database were examined based on the predetermined set of inclusion and exclusion criteria. This phase yielded 16 additional full articles. Finally, all articles (56 + 16 = 72 articles in total) resulting from the previous process were reviewed in detail. It should be noted that there was a considerable spike in the number of papers published over the last five years. In total, 51 articles (~70 per cent of the sample) since 2015 focused on rail transit service disruption. The reviewed papers were classified into three categories, namely: "bus bridging studies", "other supply management studies" and "demand management studies". The papers reviewed in the three categories are summarized and tabulated in Appendix Tables 14A.1, 14A.2 and 14A.3.

14.4   ACADEMIC LITERATURE OVERVIEW

Planning for transit service disruptions is distinct from traditional system planning under normal operating conditions. Traditional system planning is typically done for a relatively long time horizon (a few weeks or months). In contrast, rail service disruption management has a much shorter time horizon, aiming to mitigate and minimize the impacts of unexpected events on the system and users over periods shorter than several hours. Over the past few years, a growing number of studies have investigated the factors influencing the severity of rail service disruptions. For example, Louie et al. (2017) assessed empirically the impacts of several factors including train type, personal and station (e.g., interchange stations) on metro system disruption duration in Toronto, while Diab and Shalaby (2019) investigated the effects of outdoor tracks and weather conditions. Zilko et al. (2016) developed a model to predict the duration of disruption based on several factors using historical track circuit data acquired from the Dutch Network. Several researchers have also investigated the impacts of the breakdown of one rail service on other modal services in integrated multimodal transit systems. For example, Diab and Shalaby (2018) looked into how metro system interruptions impact bus and streetcar service quality in Toronto.

Other studies conducted industry surveys to understand the most common disruption management practices and strategies. Schmöcker et al. (2005) explored what practices are employed in the industry and how various characteristics in a rail network influence the type of strategies used during a disruption. The researchers used a structured interview approach combined with a quantitative analysis of six transit agencies around the world. They found the most common practice employed by the interviewed agencies involved deploying bus bridging services and short-turning trains. The quantitative analysis also revealed that metro systems with fewer constraints and newer technology (e.g. automatic train operation) can recover faster after a disruption. Pender et al. (2013) used an online survey to understand the disruption response strategies used by 71 international rail transit agencies. They found the most common strategies include deploying bus bridging services, using parallel public transport network, transferring passengers to other rail lines, and track crossovers (or switches) which allow trains to move from one track to another. The researchers indicated that 45 per cent of the surveyed agencies pulled buses from existing scheduled bus services to serve as shuttle buses during rail disruption, while some agencies used spare buses in their bus-bridging strategy. Spare buses are usually drawn from the older (almost retired) portion of the bus fleet for use in various tasks. In contrast, most of the surveyed transit agencies indicated not having a strategic reserve of buses solely for bus-bridging purposes. Other research work focused on recovery models and algorithms for real-time railway rescheduling (Cacchiani et al., 2014). This chapter synthesizes the recent academic literature on rail transit disruption management, grouped broadly into the three categories of bus bridging studies, supply management studies and demand management studies.

14.5 BUS BRIDGING STUDIES

Overview

Several studies focused on the bus bridging as a rail disruption management strategy. In total, 16 papers investigated various aspects of the bus bridging strategy (Appendix Table 14A.1). Most of these studies attempted to develop effective bus bridging plans by optimizing bus routes and vehicle allocation. For example, Kepaptsoglou and Karlaftis (2009) proposed a framework for deploying an optimal bus bridging network with the objective of maximizing passenger welfare in terms of increasing bus bridging capacity while minimizing travel times and operational effects on the rest of the bus network. The framework focused on re-allocating the closest available buses from the bus network to serve in the temporary bus bridging network. The framework consisted of two major sequential steps. The first aimed at designing the bridging routes by determining their layouts and frequencies, while the second allocated buses to the designed routes. The route layouts were determined using a shortest path algorithm with further modification achieved using a heuristic. A Genetic Algorithm (GA) model was implemented to obtain the optimal set of routes and optimal allocation of buses. Candidate buses were considered not only from regular bus routes but also from reserve bus fleets at existing depots.

Other studies considered the process of dispatching buses from a set of pre-designated depots to affected locations (Hu et al., 2016; Wang et al., 2016). For example, Jin et al. (2016) proposed a method for designing optimal bus bridging services and routes during a rail network disruption. Their method identified a set of good candidate bus bridging routes based on commuter demand and using a column generation algorithm. An integrated optimization model was used subsequently to simultaneously execute route selection, frequency determination and bus resource allocation. In determining the bus bridging routes, both intuitive options (routes that align directly with the lost train service operations) and non-intuitive options (express or short routes) were considered. Buses were sourced from specific locations in the network.

Hu et al. (2016) proposed a model for planning bus bridging routes for both upstream and downstream directions along a rail transit line, whereby buses can be dispatched from a set of pre-designated depots. The researchers developed a customized GA-based model to optimally design the bus bridging network. In this network, each bus is dispatched from a depot to a given disrupted station, following which it provides a steady service between the disrupted station and a layover (or a turnover) station to transport passengers. Based on this work, Wang et al. (2016) proposed later an integer programming model that optimizes the path for each bus so as to minimize the total bus travel time. The developed model demonstrated superior computational performance over the GA-based model. Nevertheless, both studies assumed that each bus could only serve one bridging route, which limits the service flexibility. In addition, the two studies did not consider dynamic passenger arrivals during rail service disruptions.

In order to overcome the previous limitations, Gu et al. (2018) proposed a flexible bus bridging plan that assigns buses to different bus bridging routes and develops associated schedules with the goal of minimizing bus bridging time and reducing passenger delays. In that method, once buses are dispatched from depots, they will be operated based on a bridging plan that lists the stations to serve in sequence instead of route frequencies.

The study used a two-stage model to optimize the bridging strategy. The first stage was framed as a mixed integer linear programming (MILP) model with the objective of minimizing bus bridging time, while the second stage was formulated as an integer linear programming (ILP) model with the objective of minimizing total passenger delay. A Weighted Shortest Processing Time (WSPT) heuristic was developed as the solution algorithm of the model. In this line of research, Yang et al. (2017) developed a strategy tailored to achieve specific passenger flow requirements, while optimizing bus bridging services to reduce overcrowding. The researchers used a two-stage mathematical modelling procedure. The first stage determined the stations and time periods for implementing a passenger flow control strategy, while the second identified the optimal bus-bridging services. MILPs were formulated and solved to find the optimal demand-responsive flow control pattern and bus-bridging services. Deng et al. (2018) focused on determining an optimal bus bridging route, while incorporating station capacity as a constraint.

Two studies discussed when bus bridging services should be initiated, while accounting for the uncertainty associated with the expected duration of a disruption (Itani et al., 2019; Zhang and Lo, 2018). By trading off bus bridging initiation cost and passenger delay cost, Zhang and Lo (2018) found the optimal time to initiate shuttle bus services to be between 17 and 49 minutes after the onset of an incident. The wide range reflects the multitude of influencing factors and the associated uncertainties.

Alternative uncertainties that have been considered when devising a bus bridging dispatch scheme include the number of actual passengers affected by the metro disruption and the stochasticity of traffic flow (Lv et al., 2015). Other studies considered the behaviour of passengers and their willingness to use bus bridging services during service interruptions (Wang et al., 2014; Yang et al., 2018). Based on a passenger survey, Yang et al. (2018) observed that people's perception of the metro service generally improves when bus bridging services are provided during unplanned disruptions, but if shuttle buses arrive late, passengers will quickly seek alternative modes (e.g. walking, hailing a taxi). Similarly, Wang et al. (2014) performed large-scale Monte Carlo simulations in a hypothetical case study, demonstrating a range of mathematical conclusions about demand modelling of passengers waiting for bus bridging services during rail disruptions by accounting for balking and reneging. The researchers found that passenger demand is greatly overestimated when models do not consider balking or reneging.

Some studies focused on the physical features of the rail system, such as the locations of the rail crossovers and reserve depot and the associated impacts on bus bridging operations (Pender et al., 2014a; 2012), while other studies investigated bus bridging management practices using real-world data (Diab et al., 2018; Itani et al., 2019). For example, Pender et al. (2012) conducted a cost–benefit analysis to investigate the importance of crossovers to bus bridging strategies during unplanned rail disruptions. The researchers quantified user and operational impacts of alternative crossover plans for a case study of unplanned service disruptions on a suburban rail line in Melbourne. In calculating the user cost, a value of 20 minutes was assumed as an additional delay time, which was required for shuttle buses to reach passengers of the first disrupted rail trip. The results showed that an additional crossover can lower user rail disruption costs by 78–96 per cent, while bus operating costs can be reduced by 63–93 per cent.

Using 36 months of unplanned rail disruption data for Melbourne, Pender et al. (2014a) explored the effect of satellite reserve bus depot locations on the effectiveness and performance of bus bridging plans. The authors used a deterministic approach to determining the best satellite depot locations for reserve buses in order to deploy effective bus bridging services during rail disruption. The study showed that the identified satellite locations significantly improved bus bridging services, specifically the response times. However, the employed approach did not consider variability in key bus briding variables such as travel time fluctuations, variability in demand by time of day, and disruption likelihoods and scenarios where the required number of buses are not available. In essence, the study assumed the existence of a dedicated and reserved bus fleet for such purposes, which are stationed at specific bus depot locations.

Diab et al. (2018) used detailed metro and streetcar shuttle service reports (logs) in 2015 to explore the effects of pulling buses from regular routes to provide shuttle services in response to metro and streetcar service interruptions in Toronto. The paper developed a detailed and replicable framework for bus bridging analysis. The system response time was decomposed into three major components: Initial Response Time, Bus Pull out Time, and Bus Deadhead Time. The bus system recovery time included Bus Service Time on the shuttle service and Bus Returning Time to the original routes. The paper showed that in-field practices in Toronto often resulted in inefficient scenarios such as frequent cases involving buses dispatched yet unutilized. The paper also showed considerable fluctuations in the response and recovery times by mode (i.e., metro and streetcar) and over time (especially during the winter season), highlighting the challenge of managing disruption along the two rail systems.

In another study by the same authors, the performance of bus bridging strategies in Toronto was evaluated with respect to user delays (Itani et al., 2019), utilizing a user delay modelling tool, which was developed based on macroscopic queuing principles. The study also assessed alternative bus bridging policies with respect to the relative effects of four factors: (1) initial dispatch direction of shuttle buses; (2) dispatch time (i.e., the response time for requesting shuttle buses); (3) uncertainty in predicting the incident duration; and (4) reduction of metro passengers demand because of disruption. This work was most recently extended to develop a tool to advise transit operators with bus bridging schemes in real time, while minimizing total user delays (Itani et al., 2020). Given information about the incident and network characteristics, the model generates the optimal number of shuttle buses needed and which bus routes they should be dispatched from, using a constrained GA method. The optimal plans proposed by the model were then compared to real-life case studies to determine the potential impacts on delays. It was observed that the optimal plans could potentially reduce total user delays by more than 50 per cent.

Summary

A sizable portion of the reviewed literature has focused exclusively on how bus bridging services can be used and optimized to reconnect the rail network in the event of unexpected service disruption of the rail system. The main objective of these studies was to minimize bus bridging time and/or reduce passenger delay. Most studies focused on dispatching buses from a set of pre-designated depots/locations, with an underlying assumption that reserve bus fleet dedicated to such events is available. Nevertheless, Diab et al. (2018) and Pender et al. (2013) indicated that some transit agencies rely solely on pulling buses from scheduled services, with no reserved bus fleet or operators available for shuttle services. Additionally, only very few studies looked into when bus bridging services should be initiated for different types of incidents and associated conditions.

The systematic literature review revealed that bus bridging optimization models rarely incorporated demand prediction capabilities. As indicated by several researchers, this limitation may lead to overestimation of passenger demand during and after disruptions. Therefore, there is a need to integrate demand modelling into bus bridging optimization models. Similarly, it was rare to find studies that used detailed disruption data in combination with shuttle service data to understand the different service aspects during rail disruption. Accordingly, there is a limited understanding of the real-world performance of bus bridging strategies and the resulting impacts on users and transit agencies.

14.6   OTHER SUPPLY MANAGEMENT STUDIES

Overview

A large number of studies proposed methods for managing the supply side of operations during service disruption. A total of 45 studies tackled supply management aspects, among which 26 focused solely on reconstructing the timetables of the rail network (Appendix Table 14A.2). The remaining studies focused on either rescheduling the rolling stock and crews during disruptions or addressing other service management issues. Rescheduling rail timetables is usually addressed through two tasks, the first concerned with trip re-timing (when a train should enter a blocked section) and the second with re-routing trains (which route should be selected from a set of feasible possible routing options). For example, Corman et al. (2010) used ROMA (Railway Traffic Optimization by Means of Alternative Graphs) to investigate the rescheduling of rail services in terms of arrival and departure times of trains and local re-routing strategies to respond in real time to unexpected events.

Meng and Zhou (2011) focused on the optimization of dispatching schedules for a relatively long rolling horizon, while considering uncertain disruption durations and variable running times of trains. To achieve that, the authors employed a stochastic integer program with a multi-layer branching solution procedure. Corman and D'Ariano (2012) used an alternative graph (AG) to perform an assessment of dispatching measures for managing railway traffic disruption. Several disruption resolution scenarios involving cancellation of services, rerouting and shuttle trains were considered, and each feasible plan was evaluated with respect to travel times, frequency of services, and delay propagation. Narayanaswami and Rangaraj (2013) formulated an MILP model for rescheduling disrupted train movements on both directions of a single track layout with the objective of minimizing total delay of all trains at their destinations. The model rescheduled the train trips affected by disruption to other times after the expected end of disruption. The conflicts arising between these delayed trains and the trains originally scheduled after the ending time of disruption are resolved by reordering trains at stations.

Cadarso et al. (2013) also formulated an MILP model to optimize timetables and rolling stock schedules while accounting for passengers' behaviour. The study considered complete train cancellation and emergency train insertion to achieve the objective functions of minimizing operational cost, denied passenger boardings and service deviations. Based on the earlier work of Cadarso et al. (2013), Binder et al. (2017) proposed an ILP model to balance the three objectives of passenger satisfaction, operational cost, and deviation from the original timetable to create a new timetable after a disruption occurs. To achieve that, they included three additional dispatching strategies, namely partial cancellation, delaying, and global rerouting, with the main objective of minimizing operational cost, service deviations and passenger inconvenience.

Zhan et al. (2015) developed an MILP model for train rescheduling in cases of complete track blockage at a macroscopic level. The model incorporated cancelling, retiming and reordering trains. Disruption length was assumed fixed and available when the disruption starts. The model's objective was to minimize train delays and cancellations. Using the same objective in a subsequent study, the authors developed another model for partial segment blockage, while taking into account uncertain and variable disruption lengths (Zhan et al., 2016). However, the study did not consider short-turn operations, which was considered by other researchers. For example, Ghaemi et al. (2018) developed an MILP model for complete track blockages at a macroscopic level, with two short-turn station candidates considered for each train. Zhu and Goverde (2019) presented an MILP rescheduling model at a macroscopic level where flexible stopping (i.e., skipping stops and adding stops) and flexible short-turning (i.e., full choice of short-turn stations) were integrated with other common dispatching strategies (i.e., retiming, reordering and cancelling). In contrast to previous studies, Ghaemi et al. (2017a) proposed a similar MILP model to deal with complete track blockage at the microscopic level to guarantee the feasibility and practicability of the solution.

While most of the previous research focused solely on operations by accounting for the operator's perspective, fewer studies incorporated the passenger behaviour and route choices (van der Hurk et al., 2018; Binder et al., 2017; Corman et al., 2017). For example, Corman et al. (2017) integrated the passenger travel choices with the timetable rescheduling problem in a single model, which was formulated as an MILP model at a microscopic level. Kroon et al. (2015) developed a rolling stock rescheduling model that takes into account the dynamic passenger flow extracted from a simulation model. The same simulation model was used later by Veelenturf et al. (2017).

Several papers presented models that focused on how to reschedule the rolling stock during a disruption in a manner compatible with a revised timetable (Haahr et al., 2016; Kroon et al., 2015; Lusby et al., 2017; Tomiyama et al., 2018; Budai et al., 2010). Rescheduling rolling stock units during a disruption is a challenging problem that is regularly encountered by railway operators (Lusby et al., 2017). Only a few studies considered rescheduling both the timetable and rolling stock simultaneously (Veelenturf et al., 2017; Cadarso et al., 2013; 2015).

Other studies focused on examining how crew scheduling can be optimized once new timetables and rolling stock schedules are generated (Potthoff et al., 2010; Veelenturf et al., 2016b; 2012; Verhaegh et al., 2017). A number of studies focused on crew scheduling issues from different perspectives. For example, Verhaegh et al. (2017) proposed an ILP method for rescheduling crews during short disruptions by inserting uncovered tasks in a feasible set of duties. Veelenturf et al. (2012) presented a model to solve railway crew rescheduling with retiming to prevent the cancellation of trains without a driver.

While previous studies have focused mainly on rescheduling of a single mode (i.e., railway) in cases of service disruption, it is rare to find studies that treated the rescheduling or rerouting of multiple modes. One exception is a study that aimed at providing sufficient capacity on all routes of a multimodal network consisting of metro, tram and bus modes to satisfy demand during disruptions (Kiefer et al., 2016). Another study evaluated the strategy of transit agencies contracting with a second party to serve passengers during rail disruptions (Zeng et al., 2012). The study investigated the cost effectiveness for a transit agency to outsource bridging services to a taxi company for providing commuters with a means to reach their destination when tram services are suspended due to short-term disruptions. Their study assessed different pricing schemes and concluded that both parties (i.e., transit agency and taxi company) could benefit economically from such partnership.

Summary

By far, the majority of the reviewed research studies focused on the supply side of disruption management. This body of research developed various methods for rescheduling either the timetable or rolling stock and crew schedules during rail service disruptions (Table 14.2). Most recently (over the past five years), an emerging volume of literature integrated more flexible operational strategies such as flexible stopping and flexible short-turning with traditional dispatching strategies (i.e., retiming, reordering and cancelling). Additionally, a growing number of studies incorporated passengers' behaviour and route choices into the supply management models. This was mainly done by estimating passenger flows from simulation models as inputs into the supply management models. However, it was less common to find studies that considered the rescheduling of trip timetables, rolling stock and crew schedules simultaneously.

Various approaches have been used in supply management studies to tackle rail transit disruptions. These studies commonly formulated the problem in mathematical programming frameworks. The most common modelling approaches were (in order of frequency) MILP, ILP, simulation models, and AG. In fact, most of the recent studies employed MILP and ILP formulations with heuristic-based solutions to achieve adequate computational times for use in real-time applications. Simulation models were also used, albeit less commonly. When they were employed, simulation models usually served to provide passenger flow as input into rolling stock or timetable rescheduling models. Only a few studies incorporated the rescheduling tool ROMA (railway traffic optimization by means of alternative graphs) within the railway traffic simulation environment EGTRAIN, to predict possible conflicts and find the optimal strategies that minimize the maximum consecutive delay on the network.

Several studies used microscopic models to examine disruption management strategies at the detailed operational level, whereas macroscopic models were used in various studies to analyse network level effects of service disruption. The microscopic approach is generally in line with the traditional approach of route management used by many railway systems, where blocking time graphs and actual data are used to compute detailed running times and headways. In contrast, the macroscopic level studies modelled the railway system at a higher level, where detailed information about block sections and signals were not taken into account. Therefore, railway network modelling at the macroscopic level may oversimplify the system by omitting certain details, which means that the real-life feasibility of the solution may not guaranteed.

Table 14.2 Summary of other supply management studies' methodological approaches

Study scope	Number of studies	Methods						Objectives			Dispatching decisions			Levels		
		ILP	MILP	SM	AG	Data analysis	More than one method	Operations oriented	Passenger oriented	Mixed objectives	Traditional dispatching	Flexible dispatching	Both	Macroscopic	Microscopic	Mixed levels
Timetable rescheduling	26	4	13	2	3		4	20	3	3	17	4	2	15	9	2
Rolling stock rescheduling	7	3	2			1	1	3	2							
Crew rescheduling	4		1			3		2								
Management	3		1			2	1	1	1		1	2				
More than one	5	2	2				1	1		2				3		
Grand Total	45	9	19	2	3	6	7	27	6	5	18	6	2	18	9	2

Notes:

Methods: Integer linear programming (ILP), Mixed Integer Linear Program (MILP), Simulation (SM), Alternative Graph (AG).

Dispatching decisions: Traditional dispatching strategies (Cancelling, Rerouting, Delaying, Reordering, Train Insertion) and flexible dispatching strategies (short-turning, flexible short-turning, stop-skipping, adding a stop).

Objectives: Operations oriented (Minimize operational cost, train delays, train deviations, and cancellations) and Passenger oriented (reduce passenger inconveniences, passenger delays or number of denied passengers).

14.7   PASSENGER DEMAND AND FLOW MANAGEMENT STUDIES

Overview

Fewer studies (12 out of 71) addressed demand management during rail service disruptions (Appendix Table 14A.3). Several studies were mainly focused on how to control the flow of passengers or manage crowds during service disruptions to reduce the user and system delay. For example, van der Hurk et al. (2018) investigated the benefits of advising travellers on which alternative routes to take while rescheduling the rolling stock. They used a mathematical optimization model coupled with a passenger flow simulation model to determine the best routing options for affected travellers through the network considering the rescheduled rolling stock. The main objective was to minimize passenger inconvenience in terms of a weighted sum of waiting time, in-vehicle time, and transfers, and to achieve this at a reasonable operating cost. In order to make this approach more realistic, the study assumed that passengers may disregard the route guidance advisory. Their results indicated that providing travel advice helps manage the transit service better compared to solely optimizing the rolling stock schedule.

Yang et al. (2017) developed a mixed integer linear programming model for managing passenger flows and optimizing bus bridging services. To reduce overcrowding, the study aimed at determining the candidate stations for implementing flow management actions and the corresponding time windows. The main strategy considered for managing passenger inflow at certain stations was to provide additional bus bridging services for passengers. However, this study did not present a clear understanding of how passengers would respond to such a strategy.

Other studies investigated the application of social media during rail disruptions. For example, Pender et al. (2014b) looked into the role of social media in managing demand during unplanned passenger rail disruptions through an international survey of 86 agencies on current practices. The results showed that 88 per cent of the surveyed agencies used social media for information provision, with the vast majority using Twitter and Facebook coming in second place. Twitter enabled real-time, two-way communication between transit agencies and users, while Facebook was more suited to marketing. Therefore, Twitter was mainly used to advise passengers about the location and duration of service disruptions and alternative options (i.e., shuttle bus services). The agencies identified the lack of resources (e.g., support staff) and skills as barriers to social media deployment for communication and demand management. The study also indicated that the benefits of social media deployment need to be quantified accurately in order to assess its cost-effectiveness.

Douglass et al. (2018) conducted a passenger survey to investigate the use of social media for trip planning, specifically during disruptions and delays. The results showed that the majority of people of different age groups across travel purposes checked social media sites before starting their journey, indicating that social media could influence personal travel behaviour. Hosseini et al. (2018) analysed Twitter data for three transit agencies in Canada, while integrating the analysis of the participants' social networks and contents of their Twitter discussions. They also developed a lexicon of customer satisfaction to support consistent comparison across transit agencies and to enable comparison to findings of customer surveys. This analysis was performed for normal days and days with service disruptions. Safety and security issues were the most frequently discussed topics on all days with or without disruptions and across most groups. Discussions about safety issues and the need for further information increased significantly during disruptions, particularly during rush hours. Additionally, El-Diraby et al. (2019) developed a methodology for linking social, semantic and sentiment analyses to support analysing transit customers' satisfaction while accounting for the impact of service disruptions.

Several studies used surveys and statistical models to investigate passengers' travel behaviour and mode choices in response to rail service disruptions (Bai and Kattan, 2014; Teng and Liu, 2015; Lin et al., 2018; Murray-Tuite et al., 2014). Bai and Kattan (2014) used a stated preference survey to examine the impact of information provision on passengers' en-route mode choice. Two scenarios were examined: an estimated arrival time of 10 min for the next LRT and an LRT service disruption with no information on expected recovery time. The results showed that various factors had strong influences on travellers' behavioural responses to the provided information including socioeconomic attributes (e.g., age, gender), experience with an advanced passenger information system, and experience with transit and the LRT system. Similarly, Teng and Liu (2015) conducted an SP survey for metro riders and found that most respondents considered using a shuttle bus service if provided.

Lin et al. (2018) developed a joint revealed preference (RP) and stated preference (SP) survey to investigate transit user mode choice in response to metro disruptions. They found about two-thirds of the respondents would wait for the metro to resume services. The imputed value of time was about $84/h per passenger, which was much higher than typical values during normal operating conditions. Murray-Tuite et al. (2014) investigated passengers' behavioural responses to the Washington, DC Metrorail collision in 2009. They found that respondents preferred not to make mode or travel choice changes. In contrast, the most common change was avoiding the first and last train cars.

Other studies used simulation models to investigate the impact of disruptions of various lengths and the possible benefits of disruption information provision. For example, Hua and Ong (2018) explored the effect of disruption information provision using a dynamic schedule-based transit assignment model within a network simulation framework. The results showed the effect of information penetration rate on the network performance, which confirmed theoretically the important role of communicating disruption information to passengers.

Similarly, Leng and Corman (2020) used an agent-based microsimulation approach to model how passengers would behave in a multimodal transit system when they are provided with varying degrees of information about service disruption. Three different scenarios about when information was made available to passengers (in advance, in a timely manner and never) were compared using MATSim. The scenarios were scored in terms of passenger satisfaction, which was estimated based on average delay time and the total number of affected agents. The results showed that the difference in passenger satisfaction between the "Advance Information" scenario and the "Timely Information" scenario was slight, provided that full details about the incident were given.

Srikukenthiran and Shalaby (2017) used a simulation platform to model the crowd dynamics and passenger behaviour in a disruption scenario. The microsimulation platform, called Nexus, allows passenger agents to move between simulation services (station, train, surface vehicle), and have their routes determined by a transit assignment module which incorporates the effects of information provision on route choice behaviour. The framework was used for analysing the impacts of disruptions of various lengths and testing a response strategy related to the provision of information to travellers. The results showed that the timely provision of information on the disruption (type and duration) and alternative options could effectively reduce overcrowding at affected stations.

Summary

Compared to supply management, there have been fewer studies on demand management during rail service disruptions. Several studies focused on mitigating the impacts of service interruptions by managing crowds and controlling the flow of passengers via information provision or providing additional bus shuttle services. These studies used various analytical models including simulation and mathematical programming models.

Other studies investigated the application of social media during rail disruptions through surveys of travellers and transit agencies. Social media, particularly Twitter, was found to be an effective tool for advising users in real time on rail service disruptions issues and alternative routes and options. Twitter was also found to be an effective means of two-way communication between transit agencies and users. Most recently, other studies developed methodologies for analysing Twitter data to understand the frequency of discussions and the content of these discussions during service interruptions to analyse customer experience and satisfaction.

Several studies developed surveys to investigate passengers' travel behaviour and mode choices in response to rail service disruptions, suggesting that various factors had strong influence on travellers' behavioural responses to the provided information. Nevertheless, these studies relied on SP surveys, which only solicit respondents' travel choices under a set of hypothetical service disruption scenarios. In contrast, joint RP and SP surveys were recently employed to measure behavioural responses to service disruption more realistically. Survey results showed that a considerable number of respondents would wait for the rail service to resume. While there are several studies in the literature about crowd flow management under "normal" conditions or during events (King et al., 2014; Zhao et al., 2009; Muñoz et al., 2018), very little work has been done on the study of crowd flow management at times of rail service disruption.

14.8   SUMMARY AND LESSON LEARNED

Over the past 10 years, a large body of research has focused on formulating and testing various strategies and actions to manage rail service disruptions in a timely and efficient manner. This section summarizes and synthesizes the literature which was reviewed in the previous sections and detailed in the Appendix tables, in an attempt to highlight key features and draw useful lessons. For clarity purposes, the issues and lessons learned are summarized in Table 14.3.

Table 14.3   Overview of issues and the lessons learned from the literature

Issues	Methods	Lessons learned/reflections
A. Bus bridging studies		
Recent studies focused on proposing a flexible bus bridging plan that allocates buses to different bus bridging routes with the goal of minimizing bus bridging time and reducing passenger delay	Optimization models	Flexible bus bridging plans can reduce users' delays and improve bus bridging efficiency compared to traditional ad hoc plans
Most of the studies dispatched buses from a set of pre-designated depots and locations within the system or did not consider bus locations while developing optimization models.	Optimization models	This oversimplifies the problem of sourcing buses for shuttle service operations. As indicated by Pender et al. (2013) transit agencies usually do not have a dedicated bus fleet for bus bridging purposes.
Most of the bus bridging optimization models used historical passenger data or simulation models to represent passenger volumes.	Optimization models	Passenger surveys showed that demand during major disruptions is significantly reduced compared to normal operating conditions. Therefore, incorporating demand models is important.
Only one study incorporated station capacity constraints while designing bus bridging routes.	Optimization models	Incorporating station capacity as a constraint increased passengers' total travel time.
A few studies focused on quantifying the impacts of physical features of the rail system, such as rail crossovers and reserve depot locations.	Data analysis	These studies showed that better planning of these features can significantly reduce bus bridging operating costs.
Very few studies explored when bus bridging services should be initiated, or investigated bus bridging operations using real-world data.	Data analysis	The timely dispatch of shuttles can significantly reduce passenger delays at the disrupted stations. Ad hoc practices can result in inefficient operations such as frequent cases involving buses dispatched yet unutilized. More evaluation studies of industry practices using real-world data are needed to assess the effectiveness of various bus bridging practices.
B. Other supply management studies		
Rescheduling the rail service timetable during disruption gained extensive attention from researchers over the past decade (see Table 14A.2).	Optimization models	Rescheduling timetables is well-established in the literature and usually includes the two steps of rerouting trains and retiming trips
Most recently, several studies have rather employed the comprehensive objective of minimizing users' delays and operational cost. Additionally, these studies integrated flexible operational strategies such as flexible stopping and short-turning with traditional dispatching strategies (retiming, reordering, and cancelling).	Optimization models	Optimization models indicated that reducing users' delay does not necessarily lead to decreasing the system operating costs. Flexible stopping and short-turning reduced system operating cost and improved system efficiency.

Table 14.3 (continued)

Issues	Methods	Lessons learned/reflections
A large number of studies established mixed integer linear programming and integer linear program formulations with heuristic-based solutions.	Optimization models	This helped achieve adequate computational times for use in real-time applications.
Recently, a growing number of studies have incorporated route choice behaviour into the supply management models.	Optimization models	This was mainly done by using simulation models to estimate passenger flows or using basic passengers' assignment models.
C. Passenger demand and flow management studies		
Recently, studies used analytical models to understand the possible impacts of information provision.	Simulation models	These studies demonstrated that larger penetration of information can alleviate congestion in the system and reduce the concentration of passenger flow and overcrowding.
Both transit agencies and users recognize the importance of social media and its role in influencing users' travel behaviour and perception during rail service disruption.	Surveys	Social media, particularly Twitter, allows agencies to send messages in real time for updating transit related information. However, the benefits of social media are yet to be quantified and assessed.
Only a limited number of studies analysed Twitter data to understand people's reactions and discussions during transit service disruptions	Semantic and sentiment analyses	These studies found a spike in discussions about safety and need for further information, particularly for rush hour disruptions.
Several studies evaluated the impact of information provision on passengers' mode choices.	Surveys and econometric models	Overall, users indicated their preference for metro service to resume or for shuttle buses. However, various factors had strong influences on travellers' behavioural responses including socioeconomic attributes.

14.9   CONCLUDING REMARKS AND FUTURE DIRECTIONS

This chapter provides an overview of the state of the art in rail service disruption management. A systematic literature review method was employed to identify and assess recent studies related to the topic on hand. The literature review revealed an impressive number of recent studies on managing the supply side of the transport system during rail service disruptions, while fewer studies were found addressing demand management issues.

The body of research pertaining to the bus bridging management strategy has mostly focused on developing methods of dispatching buses from a set of pre-designated depots/locations within the system. While this indeed is relevant and applicable to some transit agencies, many others rely on pulling buses from scheduled bus routes or using spare buses if available, with no strategic reserve of buses and drivers solely dedicated to bus-bridging purposes. Therefore, new analytical tools that help transit agencies determine optimal bus bridging solutions under such constraints are needed. Such optimization models should minimize system-wide user delays and operator cost by determining the optimal number of required shuttle buses and the routes from which such buses should be pulled in addition to shuttle bus route networks. Additionally, given the unpredictability of the duration of disruptions, questions related to bus bridging service deployment timing should receive more attention in future research. The ability to predict in real time the length of a service disruption once it starts is highly desirable. Perhaps data-driven models using Machine Learning methods could be explored to provide such capability.

As seen in the literature review, there have been disproportionately fewer efforts to explore the effectiveness of bus bridging field practices using real-world data, perhaps due to the lack of such data or the difficulty of acquiring it. Further empirical research is required to investigate in more detail the relative effectiveness of bus bridging practices, ideally across different systems. Actual location and ridership data on regular and shuttle bus operations, which can be obtained from automated data collection systems (e.g. AVL, APC, etc.), combined with incident log data can be utilized effectively to undertake such research.

One of the common disruption management strategies indicated by transit agencies is utilizing a parallel bus network to provide customers with mobility means during rail disruption (Pender et al., 2013). Such a strategy though may cause severe delays along those bus routes or trigger additional problems. There is a dearth of studies that consider and optimize different public transport modes in an integrated manner to reduce the negative impacts of rail service disruptions. Such an approach would be helpful for transit agencies that operate rail services in a multimodal urban environment.

The literature review revealed the need for considering unobvious (or non-intuitive) bus bridging route options as opposed to traditional bus bridging routes to reduce system and user delays. A traditional scheme relies on recovering the rail network topology by mimicking the railway service structure. In contrast, a non-intuitive bus bridging network is more sensitive to users' travel requirements that vary according to the day and time period. With the implementation of non-intuitive networks, however, there will be the obvious problem of communicating such new temporary networks to target passengers. This is a critical issue since some of the modelling results in the literature led to very complex and unrestrained bus bridging networks. Therefore, further research that considers the additional challenge of communicating the new networks to passengers is needed. Furthermore, most of the research in this area did not incorporate actual rail station infrastructure and user movement constraints, which can prohibit the implementation of different bus bridging networks due to the limited pick-up bay area capacity and accessibility issues, for example. Therefore, further studies that investigate crowd flow management at times of rail service disruptions are recommended.

Most of the supply management studies focused on rescheduling either the timetable, rolling stock, or crews during rail disruption. However, only a few studies tried optimizing more than one aspect simultaneously. As such, one area of further research is the integration of multiple rescheduling aspects to provide integrated solutions. Passenger demand characteristics during railway or metro disruption could differ considerably from those on a typical day of normal service operations. Passengers may change their travel patterns and use other transportation modes during disruptions to avoid and/or minimize delays. Evidence showed that passenger demand is greatly overestimated during disruptions (Wang et al., 2014). While most supply management optimization models rely on historical data of passenger demand under "normal" operational conditions, there is a tangible need to incorporate passenger demand models that represent behavioural responses and predict demand changes during disruption events, which is hardly considered in the current literature.

Compared to papers on supply management and bus bridging, there have been fewer studies on how demand can be managed during rail service disruptions. These studies mainly focused on mitigating the impacts of service interruptions by managing crowds and controlling the flow of passengers via information provision. However, it is rare to find studies that provided real case studies of the effectiveness of social media or other demand management strategies during rail disruptions.

REFERENCES

Abbink, E., Mobach, D., Fioole, P., Kroon, L., Van der Heijden, E. and Wijngaards, N. 2010. Real-time train driver rescheduling by actor-agent techniques. *Public Transport*, 2, 249–68.

Acuna-Agost, R., Michelon, P., Feillet, D. and Gueye, S. 2011. SAPI: Statistical analysis of propagation of incidents: A new approach for rescheduling trains after disruptions. *European Journal of Operational Research*, 215, 227–43.

Bai, Y. and Kattan, L. 2014. Modeling riders' behavioral responses to real-time information at light rail transit stations. *Transportation Research Record*, 2412, 82–92.

Binder, S., Maknoon, Y. and Bierlaire, M. 2017. The multi-objective railway timetable rescheduling problem. *Transportation Research Part C: Emerging Technologies*, 78, 78–94.

Budai, G., Maróti, G., Dekker, R., Huisman, D. and Kroon, L. 2010. Rescheduling in passenger railways: The rolling stock rebalancing problem. *Journal of Scheduling*, 13, 281–97.

Cacchiani, V., Huisman, D., Kidd, M., Kroon, L., Toth, P., Veelenturf, L. and Wagenaar, J. 2014. An overview of recovery models and algorithms for real-time railway rescheduling. *Transportation Research Part B: Methodological*, 63, 15–37.

Cadarso, L., Marín, A. and Maróti, G. 2013. Recovery of disruptions in rapid transit networks. *Transportation Research Part E: Logistics and Transportation Review*, 53, 15–33.

Cadarso, L., Maroti, G. and Marin, A. 2015. Smooth and controlled recovery planning of disruptions in rapid transit networks. *IEEE Transactions on Intelligent Transportation Systems*, 16, 2192–202.

Corman, F. and D'Ariano, A. 2012. Assessment of advanced dispatching measures for recovering disrupted railway traffic situations. *Transportation Research Record*, 2289, 1–9.

Corman, F. and Quaglietta, E. 2015. Closing the loop in real-time railway control: Framework design and impacts on operations. *Transportation Research Part C: Emerging Technologies*, 54, 15–39.

Corman, F., D'Ariano, A., Pacciarelli, D. and Pranzo, M. 2010. A tabu search algorithm for rerouting trains during rail operations. *Transportation Research Part B: Methodological*, 44, 175–92.

Corman, F., D'Ariano, A., Marra, A., Pacciarelli, D. and Samà, M. 2017. Integrating train scheduling and delay management in real-time railway traffic control. *Transportation Research Part E: Logistics and Transportation Review*, 105, 213–39.

Deng, Y., Ru, X., Dou, Z. and Liang, G. 2018. Design of bus bridging routes in response to disruption of urban rail transit. *Sustainability (Switzerland)*, 10, 4427.

Diab, E. and Shalaby, A. 2018. Subway service down again? Assessing the effects of subway service interruptions on local surface transit performance. *Transportation Research Record*, 2672, 443–54.

Diab, E. and Shalaby, A. 2019. Metro transit system resilience: Understanding the impacts of outdoor tracks and weather conditions on metro system interruptions. *International Journal of Sustainable Transportation*, 1–14.

Diab, E., Feng, G. and Shalaby, A. 2018. Breaking into emergency shuttle service: Aspects and impacts of retracting buses from existing scheduled bus services. *Canadian Journal of Civil Engineering*, 45, 647–58.

Douglass, J., Dissanayake, D., Coifman, B., Chen, W. and Ali, F. 2018. Measuring the effectiveness of a transit agency's social media engagement with travelers. *Transportation Research Record*, 2672, 46–55.

Durand, A., Van Oort, N. and Hoogendoorn, S. 2018. Assessing and improving operational strategies for the benefit of passengers in rail-bound urban transport systems. *Transportation Research Record*, 2672, 421–30.

El-Diraby, T., Shalaby, A. and Hosseini, M. 2019. Linking social, semantic and sentiment analyses to support modeling transit customers' satisfaction: Towards formal study of opinion dynamics. *Sustainable Cities and Society*, 49, 101578.

El Amraoui, A. and Mesghouni, K. 2014. Optimization of a train traffic management problem under uncertainties and disruptions. *Studies in Informatics and Control*, 23, 313–23.

Espinosa-Aranda, J. and García-Ródenas, R. 2013. A demand-based weighted train delay approach for rescheduling railway networks in real time. *Journal of Rail Transport Planning and Management*, 3, 1–13.

Gao, Y., Kroon, L., Schmidt, M. and Yang, L. 2016. Rescheduling a metro line in an over-crowded situation after disruptions. *Transportation Research Part B: Methodological*, 93, 425–49.

Ghaemi, N., Cats, O. and Goverde, R. 2017a. A microscopic model for optimal train short-turnings during complete blockages. *Transportation Research Part B: Methodological*, 105, 423–37.

Ghaemi, N., Cats, O. and Goverde, R. 2017b. Railway disruption management challenges and possible solution directions. *Public Transport*, 9, 343–64.

Ghaemi, N., Cats, O. and Goverde, R. 2018. Macroscopic multiple-station short-turning model in case of complete railway blockages. *Transportation Research Part C: Emerging Technologies*, 89, 113–32.

Gu, W., Yu, J., Ji, Y., Zheng, Y. and Zhang, M. 2018. Plan-based flexible bus bridging operation strategy. *Transportation Research Part C: Emerging Technologies*, 91, 209–29.

Haahr, J., Wagenaar, J., Veelenturf, L. and Kroon, L. 2016. A comparison of two exact methods for passenger railway rolling stock (re)scheduling. *Transportation Research Part E: Logistics and Transportation Review*, 91, 15–32.

Hosseini, M., El-Diraby, T. and Shalaby, A. 2018. Supporting sustainable system adoption: Socio-semantic analysis of transit rider debates on social media. *Sustainable Cities and Society*, 38, 123–36.

Hu, H., Gao, Y., Yu, J., Liu, Z. and Li, X. 2016. Planning bus bridging evacuation during rail transit operation disruption. *Journal of Urban Planning and Development*, 142.

Hua, W. and Ong, P. 2018. Effect of information contagion during train service disruption for an integrated rail-bus transit system. *Public Transport*, 10, 571–94.

Itani, A., Srikukenthiran, S. and Shalaby, A. 2020. Capacity-constrained bus bridging optimization framework. *Transportation Research Record*, 2674, 600–612.

Itani, A., Aboudina, A., Diab, E., Srikukenthiran, S. and Shalaby, A. 2019. Managing unplanned rail disruptions: Policy implications and guidelines towards an effective bus bridging strategy. *Transportation Research Record*, 2673, 473–89.

Jin, J., Teo, K. and Odoni, A. 2016. Optimizing bus bridging services in response to disruptions of urban transit rail networks. *Transportation Science*, 50, 790–804.

Kepaptsoglou, K. and Karlaftis, M. 2009. The bus bridging problem in metro operations: Models and algorithms. *Public Transport*, 1, 275–97.

Kiefer, A., Kritzinger, S. and Doerner, K. 2016. Disruption management for the Viennese public transport provider. *Public Transport*, 8, 161–83.

King, D., Srikukenthiran, S. and Shalaby, A. 2014. Using simulation to analyze crowd congestion and mitigation at Canadian subway interchanges: Case of Bloor-Yonge Station, Toronto, Ontario. *Transportation Research Record*, 2417, 27–36.

Kroon, L., Maróti, G. and Nielsen, L. 2015. Rescheduling of railway rolling stock with dynamic passenger flows. *Transportation Science*, 49, 165–84.

Leng, N. and Corman, F. 2020. The role of information availability to passengers in public transport disruptions: An agent-based simulation approach. *Transportation Research Part A: Policy and Practice*, 133, 214–36.

Lin, T., Srikukenthiran, S., Miller, E. and Shalaby, A. 2018. Subway user behaviour when affected by incidents in Toronto (SUBWAIT) survey: A joint revealed preference and stated preference survey with a trip planner tool. *Canadian Journal of Civil Engineering*, 45, 623–33.

Louie, J., Shalaby, A. and Habib, K. 2017. Modelling the impact of causal and non-causal factors on disruption duration for Toronto's subway system: An exploratory investigation using hazard modelling. *Accident Analysis & Prevention*, 98, 232–40.

Louwerse, I. and Huisman, D. 2014. Adjusting a railway timetable in case of partial or complete blockades. *European Journal of Operational Research*, 235, 583–93.

Lusby, R.M., Haahr, J.T., Larsen, J. and Pisinger, D. 2017. A Branch-and-Price algorithm for railway rolling stock rescheduling. *Transportation Research Part B: Methodological*, 99, 228–50.

Lv, Y., Yan, X.D., Sun, W. and Gao, Z.Y. 2015. A risk-based method for planning of bus–subway corridor evacuation under hybrid uncertainties. *Reliability Engineering & System Safety*, 139, 188–99.

Meng, L. and Zhou, X. 2011. Robust single-track train dispatching model under a dynamic and stochastic environment: A scenario-based rolling horizon solution approach. *Transportation Research Part B: Methodological*, 45, 1080–102.

Mesa, J., Ortega, F. and Pozo, M. 2013. A geometric model for an effective rescheduling after reducing service in public transportation systems. *Computers and Operations Research*, 40, 737–46.

Muñoz, J., Soza-Parra, J., Didier, A. and Silva, C. 2018. Alleviating a subway bottleneck through a platform gate. *Transportation Research Part A: Policy and Practice*, 116, 446–55.

Murray-Tuite, P., Wernstedt, K. and Yin, W. 2014. Behavioral shifts after a fatal rapid transit accident: A multinomial logit model. *Transportation Research Part F: Traffic Psychology and Behaviour*, 24, 218–30.

Narayanaswami, S. and Rangaraj, N. 2013. Modelling disruptions and resolving conflicts optimally in a railway schedule. *Computers and Industrial Engineering*, 64, 469–81.

Nielsen, L., Kroon, L. and Maróti, G. 2012. A rolling horizon approach for disruption management of railway rolling stock. *European Journal of Operational Research*, 220, 496–509.

Ortega, F., Pozo, M. and Puerto, J. 2018. On-line timetable rescheduling in a transit line. *Transportation Science*, 52, 1106–21.

Pender, B., Currie, G., Delbosc, A. and Shiwakoti, N. 2013. Disruption recovery in passenger railways: International survey. *Transportation Research Record*, 2353, 22–32.

Pender, B., Currie, G., Delbosc, A. and Shiwakoti, N. 2014a. Improving bus bridging responses via satellite bus reserve locations. *Journal of Transport Geography*, 34, 202–10.

Pender, B., Currie, G., Delbosc, A. and Shiwakoti, N. 2014b. International study of current and potential social media applications in unplanned passenger rail disruptions. *Transportation Research Record*, 2419, 118–27.

Pender, B., Currie, G., Delbosc, A. and Wang, Y. 2012. Proactive recovery from rail disruptions through provision of track crossovers and bus bridging. *Transportation Research Record*, 2275, 68–76.

Potthoff, D., Huisman, D. and Desaulniers, G. 2010. Column generation with dynamic duty selection for railway crew rescheduling. *Transportation Science*, 44, 493–505.

Samà, M., D'Ariano, A., Corman, F. and Pacciarelli, D. 2017. A variable neighbourhood search for fast train scheduling and routing during disturbed railway traffic situations. *Computers and Operations Research*, 78, 480–99.

Schmöcker, J., Cooper, S. and Adeney, W. 2005. Metro service delay recovery: Comparison of strategies and constraints across systems. *Transportation Research Record*, 1930, 30–37.

Shakibayifar, M., Sheikholeslami, A. and Corman, F. 2018. A simulation-based optimization approach to rescheduling train traffic in uncertain conditions during disruptions. *Scientia Iranica*, 25, 646–62.

Shakibayifar, M., Hassannayebi, E., Mirzahossein, H., Taghikhah, F. and Jafarpur, A. 2019. An intelligent simulation platform for train traffic control under disturbance. *International Journal of Modelling and Simulation*, 39, 135–56.

Srikukenthiran, S. and Shalaby, A. 2017. Enabling large-scale transit microsimulation for disruption response support using the Nexus platform: Proof-of-concept case study of the Greater Toronto Area transit network. *Public Transport*, 9, 411–35.

Stringer, S. 2017. The human cost of subway delays: A survey of New York City riders. New York. Accessed at: https://comptroller.nyc.gov/wp-content/uploads/documents/The-Human-Cost-of-Subway-Delays.pdf.

Teng, J. and Liu, W. 2015. Development of a behavior-based passenger flow assignment model for urban rail transit in section interruption circumstance. *Urban Rail Transit*, 1, 35–46.

Tomiyama, T., Sato, T., Murata, T., Iwamura, S. and Sakamoto, O. 2018. Development of reactive scheduling for rolling stock operation using a constraint model. *Electrical Engineering in Japan* (English translation of Denki Gakkai Ronbunshi), 203, 31–44.

TRID. 2013. *Home page* [Online]. Accessed 15 November 2013 at http://trid.trb.org/.

Van der Hurk, E., Kroon, L. and Maróti, G. 2018. Passenger advice and rolling stock rescheduling under uncertainty for disruption management. *Transportation Science*, 52, 1391–411.

Veelenturf, L., Kroon, L. and Maróti, G. 2017. Passenger oriented railway disruption management by adapting timetables and rolling stock schedules. *Transportation Research Part C: Emerging Technologies*, 80, 133–47.

Veelenturf, L., Potthoff, D., Huisman, D. and Kroon, L. 2012. Railway crew rescheduling with retiming. *Transportation Research Part C: Emerging Technologies*, 20, 95–110.

Veelenturf, L., Kidd, M., Cacchiani, V., Kroon, L. and Toth, P. 2016a. A railway timetable rescheduling approach for handling large-scale disruptions. *Transportation Science*, 50, 841–62.

Veelenturf, L., Potthoff, D., Huisman, D., Kroon, L., Maróti, G. and Wagelmans, A. 2016b. A quasi-robust optimization approach for crew rescheduling. *Transportation Science*, 50, 204–15.

Verhaegh, T., Huisman, D., Fioole, P.J. and Vera, J.C. 2017. A heuristic for real-time crew rescheduling during small disruptions. *Public Transport*, 9, 325–42.

Wagenaar, J., Kroon, L. and Fragkos, I. 2017. Rolling stock rescheduling in passenger railway transportation using dead-heading trips and adjusted passenger demand. *Transportation Research Part B: Methodological*, 101, 140–61.

Wang, Y., Yan, X., Zhou, Y. and Zhang, W. 2016. A feeder-bus dispatch planning model for emergency evacuation in urban rail transit corridors. *PLOS ONE*, 11, e0161644.

Wang, Y., Guo, J., Currie, G., Ceder, A., Dong, W. and Pender, B. 2014. Bus bridging disruption in rail services with frustrated and impatient passengers. *IEEE Transactions on Intelligent Transportation Systems*, 15, 2014–23.

Xu, P., Corman, F., Peng, Q. and Luan, X. 2017a. A timetable rescheduling approach and transition phases for high-speed railway traffic during disruptions. *Transportation Research Record*, 2607, 82–92.

Xu, P., Corman, F., Peng, Q. and Luan, X. 2017b. A train rescheduling model integrating speed management during disruptions of high-speed traffic under a quasi-moving block system. *Transportation Research Part B: Methodological*, 104, 638–66.

Yang, J., Jin, J., Wu, J. and Jiang, X. 2017. Optimizing passenger flow control and bus-bridging service for commuting metro lines. *Computer-Aided Civil and Infrastructure Engineering*, 32, 458–73.

Yang, Y., Ding, H., Chen, F. and Yang, H. 2018. An approach for evaluating connectivity of interrupted rail networks with bus bridging services. *Advances in Mechanical Engineering*, 10.

Yin, H., Wu, J., Sun, H., Qu, Y., Yang, X. and Wang, B. 2018. Optimal bus-bridging service under a metro station disruption. *Journal of Advanced Transportation*, 2018, 1–16.

Yin, J., Wang, Y., Tang, T., Xun, J. and Su, S. 2017. Metro train rescheduling by adding backup trains under disrupted scenarios. *Frontiers of Engineering Management*, 4, 418–27.

Zeng, A., Durach, C. and Fang, Y. 2012. Collaboration decisions on disruption recovery service in urban public tram systems. *Transportation Research Part E: Logistics and Transportation Review*, 48, 578–90.

Zhan, S., Kroon, L., Veelenturf, L. and Wagenaar, J. 2015. Real-time high-speed train rescheduling in case of a complete blockage. *Transportation Research Part B: Methodological*, 78, 182–201.

Zhan, S., Kroon, L., Zhao, J. and Peng, Q. 2016. A rolling horizon approach to the high speed train rescheduling problem in case of a partial segment blockage. *Transportation Research Part E: Logistics and Transportation Review*, 95, 32–61.

Zhang, S. and Lo, H. 2018. Metro disruption management: Optimal initiation time of substitute bus services under uncertain system recovery time. *Transportation Research Part C: Emerging Technologies*, 97, 409–27.

Zhao, G., Zhang, G., Chen, Y. and Wu, P. 2009. Pedestrian simulation research of subway station in special events. Paper presented at the *Ninth International Conference of Chinese Transportation Professionals (ICCTP)*, Harbin, August.

Zhu, Y. and Goverde, R. 2019. Railway timetable rescheduling with flexible stopping and flexible short-turning during disruptions. *Transportation Research Part B: Methodological*, 123, 149–81.

Zilko, A., Kurowicka, D. and Goverde, R. 2016. Modeling railway disruption lengths with Copula Bayesian Networks. *Transportation Research Part C: Emerging Technologies*, 68, 350–68.

APPENDIX

Table 14A.1   Bus bridging studies

Paper	Context	Issues addressed/investigated	Methods/Approaches	Key Findings
1 (Deng et al., 2018)	Tianjin, China	Designed an optimal bus bridging route while incorporating station capacity as a constraint	• Penalty method	• Bus bridging routes generated from the model reduces travel delays. • Direct bridging routes are preferred for short distances while indirect bridging routes are more suitable for longer distances. • Total passenger travel time is improved compared to the scenario with no bus bridging service.
2 (Diab et al., 2018)	Toronto, Canada	Explored the different aspects and impacts of pulling buses from scheduled services in response to metro and streetcar disruptions	• Statistical analysis	• Protocols need to be more flexible and consider additional characteristics, such as seasonal conditions. • Need to inform passengers of scheduled services that are cancelled for emergency shuttle service. • Need for decision support systems to help optimize bus bridging services.
3 (Gu et al., 2018)	Shanghai, China	Developed a flexible bus bridging plan which allocates and schedules buses to different routes with the goal of minimizing bus bridging time and reducing passenger delay	• ILP model • Heuristic algorithm based on Weighted Shortest Processing Time first rule	• Bus bridging time is reduced by 19.4% and 21.1% compared to an alternative strategy and a state-of-the practice strategy, respectively. • Average passenger delay is reduced by 17.1% and 23.7% compared to an alternative strategy and a state-of-the practice strategy, respectively.
4 (Hu et al., 2016)	Shanghai, China	Investigated the best plan to dispatch buses from depots to the disrupted stations	• Customized GA	• The customized GA converges faster and produces a better bus bridging plan compared to a traditional GA.
5 (Itani et al., 2019)	Toronto, Canada	Evaluated the user delays associated with a sample of bus bridging strategies deployed in 2015	• Macroscopic queuing model for user delay estimation	• Having shuttle service initially dispatched at intermediate congested stations can improve performance. • Dispatching shuttle buses 1 minute earlier can save 0.4 minutes per passenger at a disrupted station. • Accurate estimation of the duration of the disruption can prevent excessive passenger delays and under-utilized shuttle buses. • Advising passengers to take other transit lines can greatly reduce delays.

Table 14A.1 (continued)

Paper	Context	Issues addressed/investigated	Methods/Approaches	Key Findings
6 (Jin et al., 2016)	Hypothetical	Designed optimal bus bridging services and routes during a rail network disruption	• Column generation procedure to generate candidate routes & path-based multi-commodity network flow model to determine the best combination of routes	• High potential for using the proposed method in real-world application due to its fast computational time. • Considering non-intuitive bus routes in bus bridging can reduce average delay time.
7 (Kepaptsoglou and Karlaftis, 2009)	Athens, Greece	Proposed a modelling framework for optimizing bus bridging routes and allocating buses to routes	• Genetic Algorithm	• Only a portion of the demand (35%) can be served by the bus bridging service. • The algorithm was tested using a real-world scenario showing adequate performance and potential for use in a decision support system.
8 (Pender et al., 2014a)	Australia	Determined optimal locations for bus reserve satellite depots to provide effective bus bridging services during a rail disruption	• Deterministic model	• Optimal locations of bus depots significantly improves bus bridging services, specifically the response times.
9 (Pender et al., 2012)	Melbourne, Australia	Investigated the importance of crossovers in relation to bus bridging during unplanned rail disruptions	• Cost–benefit analysis accounting for user and operator costs	• Adding a crossover can reduce user rail disruption costs by 78% to 96%. • Only a few rail disruptions annually would make the crossover economically beneficial.
10 (Wang et al., 2014)	Hypothetical	Developed a demand model of passengers waiting for bus bridging services during rail disruptions by accounting for balking and reneging	• Monte Carlo simulations following a Poisson process	• Without taking account of balking and reneging, passenger demand can be six time greater in quantity.
11 (Yang et al., 2017)	Shanghai, China	Developed a strategy for controlling passenger flow and optimizing bus bridging services to reduce overcrowding and improve passengers' satisfaction	• MILP model	• Using flow control strategies with bus bridging services is effective at relieving crowding and improves passengers' satisfaction. • The proposed flow control strategy is more effective than the current practices being used.

# (Reference)	Location	Description	Method	Findings
12 (Yang et al., 2018)	Beijing, China	Investigated the advantages of bus bridging	• Network model based on graph theory • Questionnaire and sensitivity analysis of people's willingness to use bus bridging services	• 35.5% of passengers do not want to use the bus bridging service if it arrives 11 minutes after the disruption. • Bus bridging decreases average travel time and significantly increases network connectivity. • Providing bus bridging services improves people's perception of the metro.
13 (Yin et al., 2018)	Beijing, China	Proposed a method to optimize bus bridging services by minimizing passenger travel times and operating costs	• Discrete choice behaviour model to analyse passenger flow • Genetic algorithm	• Bus bridging services can significantly reduce the negative effects of a station disruption. • If the bus bridging occurs over a long distance (>6 km), passengers prefer to take a taxi.
14 (Zhang and Lo, 2018)	Hong Kong, China	Developed a model to determine the optimal time to deploy bus bridging services during an unplanned rail disruption	• Cost minimizing mathematical model • Sensitivity analysis	• For service disruptions that last for a long duration, even a lower bus bridging service rate is worthwhile. • The range for optimal initiation of bus bridging service is between 17 to 49 minutes, depending on various factors (e.g. cost of initial costs of deploying buses, passenger arrival profile, etc.).
15 (Wang et al., 2016)	Nanjing, China	Presented a model which optimizes shuttle bus dispatching and minimizes travel time of the buses	• ILP model (LINGO)	• The solution proposed in the study produced better solution qualities and shorter computational times than a Genetic Algorithm. • As more time passes after the disruption, fewer buses are needed. • Non-uniform demand at the stations significantly increases cost.
16 (Lv et al., 2015)	Hypothetical	Developed a model which takes account of uncertainties during metro disruptions to create a response plan using shuttle buses and alternative transit routes	• Interval chance-constrained integer programming	• Attempting to evacuate stranded passengers during a metro incident within a shorter time period increases risk. • The waiting time for shuttle buses during a metro disruption greatly influences total evacuation time.

Table 14A.2   Other supply management studies

Paper	Context	Issues addressed/investigated	Methods/Approaches	Key Findings
1 (Binder et al., 2017)	Netherlands	Incorporated three objectives of passenger satisfaction, operational cost, and deviation from the original timetable	• ILP model (CPLEX) • Macroscopic	• Passenger satisfaction improved significantly when operational costs are increased slightly. • Timetables that differ from the original timetable performed better in terms of passenger satisfaction and operational cost.
2 (Cadarso et al., 2013)	Madrid, Spain	Developed an integrated model to optimize timetable and rolling stock rescheduling, while considering passengers' behaviour	• MILP model • Macroscopic level	• Only minimizing operator's cost resulted in very poor service quality for passengers. • Significantly better passenger service can be achieved by slightly increasing operational costs. • More schedule changes led to better service quality.
3 (Cadarso et al., 2015)	Madrid, Spain	Proposed a method to allow controlling recovery lengths and number of schedule changes made during creating a new timetable and rolling stock schedule	• Mathematical model (GAMS/CPLEX)	• Smoothness and controllability can be achieved at a low cost from the perspective of operators and passengers.
4 (Corman and D'Ariano, 2012)	Netherlands	Developed a decision support tool to aid operators in train dispatching in the event of various disruption scenarios	• Alternative graphs	• Most of the proposed timetables have a difficult time in limiting delay propagations.
5 (Corman and Quaglietta, 2015)	Netherlands	Investigated the impact of different control schemes on real-time rail disruption management and presents a traffic control framework	• ROMA (Railway traffic Optimization by Means of Alternative graphs) • Microscopic • Simulation model	• Closed loop approach outperformed an open loop and multiple loop control schemes.
6 (Durand et al., 2018)	Rotterdam, Netherlands	Improved transit disruption management from the perspective of passengers	• Discrete event simulation model	• Societal passenger cost was reduced by up to £7 when the best performing strategy was used.
7 (El Amraoui and Mesghouni, 2014)	Hypothetical	Proposed a method to optimize timetable rescheduling when the duration of a disruption is uncertain	• Extended MILP model using branch-and-bound approach	• Controlling the train speed and waiting time allowed the model to find an effective timetable quickly.

# (Reference)	Location	Description	Model	Findings
8 (Gao et al., 2016)	Beijing, China	Developed a real-time model for rescheduling by optimizing a skip-stop pattern to reduce passengers' total waiting times	• MILP model using iterative heuristic algorithm	• The model's proposed stop-skip pattern performed better than the standard stop pattern that would have been used.
9 (Ghaemi et al., 2017b)	Netherlands	Demonstrated the need for real-time solutions as opposed to predefined plans and for different models for the different transition phases	• MILP model (Gurobi) • Microscopic	• Static contingency plans did not always have feasible solutions depending on the scenario. • The microscopic model determined the optimal platform tracks for short-turning.
10 (Ghaemi et al., 2018)	Netherlands	Developed a model that incorporates short-turning to generate a new timetable and transition plan given a disruption of a known duration	• MILP model (Gurobi) • Macroscopic	• The optimal short-turning solution depended on the start time and the duration of the disruption. More train cancellations were needed when the disruption is longer. • Fast computational time makes the model suitable for real-time applications.
11 (Ghaemi et al., 2017a)	Netherlands	Presented a model to compute a new timetable during a complete blockage while incorporating short-turning	• MILP model • Microscopic level	• The optimal short-turning stations depended on the priority (e.g. minimizing the number of service cancellations, minimizing arrival delays, etc.) of the transit operator. • Under the situation where the cancellation penalty is small, the proposed solution was to short-turn at secondary short-turning station.
12 (Haahr et al., 2016)	Denmark and the Netherlands	Developed a new path-based model that accounts for unit specific constraints to solve the rolling stock rescheduling problem	• MILP model using column and row generation	• The path-based model had longer computational times but demonstrated it can be used in real-time applications.
13 (Meng and Zhou, 2011)	Fujian province, China	Optimized schedules for a relatively long rolling horizon, while selecting and disseminating a robust plan for every period	• A multi-layer branching solution procedure • ILP model • Macroscopic level	• Total train delay time were decreased by a range of 10–30%.
14 (Kiefer et al., 2016)	Vienna, Austria	Developed a model to offer real-time support for transit operators by providing a replacement line plan	• MILP model (CPLEX)	• Allowing more options of the existing plan (e.g. adding new lines are removing existing lines) resulted in better performance.

Table 14A.2 (continued)

Paper	Context	Issues addressed/investigated	Methods/Approaches	Key Findings
15 (Kroon et al., 2015)	Netherlands	Developed a real-time rolling stock rescheduling model that took account of dynamic passenger flow	• ILP model • Passenger flow using a simulation model • Incorporate passenger flow into a model which optimizes the rolling stock schedule	• Average delay of passengers was reduced when dynamic passenger flow was incorporated in the model. • Iterative heuristic approach found a solution fast enough to use in real-world applications.
16 (Lusby et al., 2017)	Copenhagen, Denmark	Rescheduled rolling stock units with a new model that used column generation with disaggregated unit flows	• Branch-and-Price algorithm	• The BAP algorithm found good solutions but to get the optimal solution, the computational time became longer.
17 (Ortega et al., 2018)	Madrid, Spain	Provided real-time rolling stock rescheduling in the scenario where the number of vehicles available was reduced	• MILP model • Macroscopic	• This approach effectively performed rescheduling and outperformed other methods common in the literature.
18 (Potthoff et al., 2010)	Netherlands	Developed a model to provide fast, dynamic crew rescheduling after a new timetable and rolling stock schedule is provided	• Column generation • Lagrangian heuristics	• Experienced dispatchers deemed that the solutions provided by the algorithm outperform solutions that were obtained manually.
19 (Shakibayifar et al., 2019)	Iran	Integrated a discrete event simulation model with a multi-objective optimization algorithm to create real-time train rescheduling after a disruption	• Discrete event simulation model • Multi-objective variable neighbourhood search	• This new approach was capable of finding efficient solutions within a reasonable time and allowed dispatchers to choose their most favourable solutions.
20 (Shakibayifar et al., 2018)	Iran	Designed a simulation-based optimization model to advise dispatchers on how to reschedule trains during a disruption with several uncertainties	• Discrete event simulation model • Multi-objective variable neighbourhood search • Statistical analysis	• The real-world test case showed evidence of the method performing better than other simulation-optimization models in terms of computational times and solution quality.

#	Reference	Country	Description	Method	Findings
21	(Tomiyama et al., 2018)	Hypothetical	Developed a reactive algorithm that rescheduled the rolling stock units using constraints that can be relaxed if necessary	• Constrained mathematical programming	• A solution was be found 44.4% of the time. • For the solved cases, the solutions balanced the objective of improving service quality and minimizing vehicle operation impacts.
22	(Veelenturf et al., 2016a)	Netherlands	Rescheduled a timetable in real-time to minimize the number of cancelled and delayed trains while adhering to multiple constraints	• ILP model (CPLEX) • Macroscopic level	• Fewer trains needed to be cancelled if longer delays are allowed or if rerouting was a feasible solution. • The computational time was reasonable for real-world applications.
23	(Veelenturf et al., 2017)	Netherlands	Developed a real-time model to integrate timetable and rolling stock rescheduling while accounting for passenger flow during transit disruptions	• ILP model • Iterative heuristic approach • Passenger flow using a simulation model • Macroscopic level	• The integrated model reduced total passenger delay by more than 20% without increasing costs from rescheduling the rolling stock.
24	(Veelenturf et al., 2016b)	Netherlands	Developed a real-time approach for crew rescheduling during disruptions with an unknown duration	• MILP model • Two-stage quasi-robust optimization problem • Column generation	• The model provided good quality solutions in contrast to conventional models, which were inappropriate when the duration of the disruption was unknown.
25	(Veelenturf et al., 2012)	Netherlands	Developed a model to solve the real-time crew rescheduling problem with retiming by integrating crew rescheduling with minor timetable adjustments	• ILP model • Column generation • Lagrangian heuristics	• Better solutions were obtained when retiming was incorporated into the model.
26	(Verhaegh et al., 2017)	Netherlands	Provided an algorithm to optimize crew rescheduling during smaller disruptions	• Iterative-deepening depth-first search	• This method provided fast and reliable solutions which performed better than other commonly used methods in the literature.
27	(Wagenaar et al., 2017)	Netherlands	Developed a solution for the rolling stock rescheduling problem that incorporated dead-heading trips and dynamic passenger flow	• MILP model (CPLEX)	• Dead-heading trips reduced the number of cancelled trips and seat shortages.
28	(Xu et al., 2017b)	China	Presented a model for effective disruption management while considering signalling and safety systems	• Alternative graph transformed into a MILP model (CPLEX) • Microscopic	• The proposed approach reduced train delays by 70%. • The optimal solution was obtained 90% of the time under a realistic case study.

Table 14A.2 (continued)

Paper	Context	Issues addressed/investigated	Methods/Approaches	Key Findings
29 (Xu et al., 2017a)	China	Developing a model to consider dynamic interaction between train speed and headway to reduce delays	• Two step MILP model based on alternative graphs (CPLEX)	• Entrance delays played a large role in preventing the system from recovering after a disruption. • The proposed model reduced delay times compared to the solution, while using the same train order as the original timetable.
30 (Zhan et al., 2016)	Beijing–Shanghai	Provided a model for real-world rescheduling of the train services during a partial segment block	• MILP model (CPLEX) • Rolling horizon approach • Macroscopic level	• This method was proven to be effective in a real-world case that had a dense and complex network.
31 (Zhu and Goverde, 2019)	Netherlands	Developed an automatic timetable rescheduling model that considered flexible stopping and flexible short-turning and recommended whether trains should be retimed, reordered or cancelled	• MILP model (Gurobi) • Macroscopic	• Applying a mix of flexible stopping and flexible short-turning reduced passenger delay. • Shortening the recovery duration minimized delays from propagating but will require more trains to be cancelled.
32 (Abbink et al., 2010)	Netherlands	Proposed a crew rescheduling method using multi-agent techniques	• Multi-agent approach	• This method outperformed human dispatchers. • Changing the cost function changed the solution generated.
33 (Acuna-Agost et al., 2011)	France and Chile	Presented a new method which efficiently solves a mixed integer programming model with multiple variables and constraints to reschedule train timetables	• MILP model (CPLEX) • Statistical Analysis of Propagation of Incidents (SAPI)	• SAPI was a feasible and effective method for finding optimal solutions with reasonable computing times.
34 (Corman et al., 2017)	Netherlands	Developed a model to incorporate passengers' perceived quality of service	• MILP model (GLPK) • Microscopic	• Using two case studies from the Dutch railway network, the model showed good quality solutions within a limited computation time.
35 (Budai et al., 2010)	Netherlands	Proposed methods to minimize the off-balances during a rolling stock rescheduling	• ILP model • Iterative heuristic • Two-phase heuristic	• Both methods obtained a solution quickly and can be implemented in real-time disruption management.

Reference	Country	Description	Method	Findings
36 (Corman et al., 2010)	Netherlands	Proposed an improved algorithm for real-time disruption management	• ROMA (Railway traffic Optimization by Means of Alternative graphs) • Tabu search algorithm	• The new method generated solutions that were up to 15% better than previous methods.
37 (Espinosa-Aranda and García-Ródenas, 2013)	Spain	Improved the existing alternative graph models by estimating demand to minimize delays	• Heuristic approach using Avoid Most Delayed Alternative Arc (AMDAA) • ILP (CPLEX) • Macroscopic level	• Algorithms balanced between multiple objectives. • Exact solutions required too much computational time for real-world applications.
38 (Louwerse and Huisman, 2014)	Netherlands	Developed a model to adjust the timetable during a disruption while taking aspects of rolling stock rescheduling into account to allow for earlier communication with passengers		• The results showed that delaying select trains for a few minutes significantly reduced the number of trains needing to be cancelled. • The proposed timetable from the model outperformed current practices.
39 (Mesa et al., 2013)	Madrid, Spain	Presented a new approach for rescheduling the rolling stock using a geometric model to represent the solution	• Geometric optimization	• This method provided a better solution, by 20.9%, than a myopic strategy. • The computational time for this method was shorter than what is required by CPLEX.
40 (Narayana-swami and Rangaraj, 2013)	Hypothetical	Developed a model for rescheduling a disrupted timetable by incorporating conflict-resolving constraints to allow trains that are not impacted to keep their original schedules	• MILP model (GLPK) • Macroscopic level	• Model demonstrated that a non-standard approach need to be used to achieve a global optimum solution. • Model was capable of solving all conflicts that are a result of the disruption.
41 (Nielsen et al., 2012)	Netherlands	Developed a real-time rolling stock rescheduling solution while incorporating local operational detail in a rolling horizon approach	• MILP model with a rolling horizon approach	• A longer horizon provided better solutions but required more computational time. • There was no significant improvement for horizons longer than 3.5 hours.
42 (Samà et al., 2017)	• Italy • Netherlands • Britain	Proposed a new algorithm to reschedule train schedules and compared the performance of this algorithm to other methods in the literature	• Alternative Graph • Variable neighbourhood search • Microscopic	• The proposed method provided better solutions than a state-of-the-art tabu search and a commercial solver.

Table 14A.2 (continued)

Paper	Context	Issues addressed/investigated	Methods/Approaches	Key Findings
43 (Yin et al., 2017)	Hypothetical	Developed a new approach to determine the optimal train rescheduling plan which considered adding back-up trains during a disruption by linearizing the model	• MILP model (CPLEX)	• Adding backup trains was an effective and practical strategy to deploy during a disruption. • The new approach demonstrated that a non-linear model can be linearized and effectively solved by exact algorithms.
44 (Zeng et al., 2012)	Hypothetical	Investigated the cost–benefits of managing public transit disruptions by collaborating with a second party (i.e. taxi company)	• Mathematical modelling • Sensitivity analysis	• Fixed pricing method was more favourable than a linear pricing scheme. • Both parties benefited and reached an equilibrium.
45 (Zhan et al., 2015)	Beijing–Shanghai	Proposed a two-stage approach to minimize the total weighted train delay and the number of cancelled trains, while adhering to headway and station capacity constraints.	• MILP model (CPLEX) • Macroscopic level	• The model provided promising results for reducing the effect of a disruption on passenger service in comparison with a heuristic method used in practice.

Table 14A.3   Demand management studies

Paper	Context	Issues addressed/investigated	Methods/Approaches	Key Findings
1 (Hua and Ong, 2018)	Singapore	Investigated the effects of information provision during transit service disruptions	• Simulation model using information-based dynamic user equilibrium	• Larger penetration of information can alleviate congestion. • Passengers will commonly switch modes if they are informed about a service disruption. • Faster information spread speed can reduce the concentration of passenger flow.
2 (Pender et al., 2014b)	Melbourne, Australia	Investigated the role social media plays in the management of rail disruptions	• Survey of transit agencies (n = 86)	• Twitter was the most commonly used platform. • Agencies indicated a challenge that social media is needed to be constantly managed to prevent the spread of out-of-date information. • Social media can reduce the flow of passengers by notifying travellers about the disruption.
3 (Srikukenthiran and Shalaby, 2017)	Toronto, Canada	Developed a model to capture the effects of crowds during a disruption	• Simulation model	• For minor disruptions (10 minutes), the transit system recovered without any intervention, but longer disruptions produced overcrowded stations that took a long time to dissipate. • Overall, station crowding was reduced when information about the disruption was provided to passengers.
4 (van der Hurk et al., 2018)	Netherlands	Developed an algorithm to advise passengers about which route to take during a disruption while optimizing the rolling stock schedule	• Mathematical optimization algorithm which incorporates passenger flow simulation	• Providing passengers with travel advice improved service quality, even if not all passengers follow the advice given.
5 (Yang et al., 2017)*	Shanghai, China	Established a strategy to control passenger flow and optimize bus bridging services to reduce overcrowding and improve passengers' satisfaction	• MILP model	• Using flow control strategies with bus bridging services was effective at relieving crowding and improved passengers' satisfaction. • The proposed flow control strategy was more effective than the current practices.

Table 14A.3 (continued)

Paper	Context	Issues addressed/investigated	Methods/Approaches	Key Findings
6 (Douglass et al., 2018)	England	Investigated the use of social media for travel planning, specifically during disruptions and delays	• Online survey (n = 240). • Principal Component Analysis. • Cross-tabulation analysis.	• Majority of people checked social media sites before starting their journey. • Less than 30% of people voiced wanting more information related to disruptions and delays.
7 (El-Diraby et al., 2019)	Toronto and Vancouver, Canada	Developed a methodology for using social media data to investigate social networks and semantic networks and to conduct sentiment analysis	• Twitter data. • Social and semantic networks analysis. • Sentiment analysis.	• Analysis of sentiment levels in days with disruption related to public safety incidents showed lower levels of negative attitude compared to regular levels, showing trust in the transit agencies' efforts in protecting them.
8 (Hosseini et al., 2018)	Toronto and Vancouver, Canada	Linked the analysis of user social networks with the contents and analysed the difference in semantics between normal days and days with service interruptions	• Twitter data. • Social and semantic networks analysis. • Sentiment analysis.	• Safety and security were the most frequently discussed topics in all days with or without interruptions and across most groups. • Disruptions were also topics of interest on days with major service disruption.
9 (Lin et al., 2018)	Toronto, Canada	Developed a joint RP and SP survey to investigate transit user mode choice in response to metro disruptions	• Online survey (n = 556). • Multinomial logit (MNL) models.	• Nearly two-thirds of the respondents waited for the metro to resume service. • Value of time was $84/h for metro users facing a severe metro disruption, which was much higher than a typical value during normal operating conditions.

10 (Teng and Liu, 2015)	China	Investigated travel behaviour during disruptions	• Online survey (n = 500). • Multinomial logit (MNL) models.	• First choice of passengers was to stay in the rail system. • More than half of the sample were interested in the shuttle bus service.
11 (Bai and Kattan, 2014)	Calgary, Alberta, Canada	Two scenarios were examined: an estimated arrival time of 10 min for the next LRT and an LRT service disruption with no information on expected recovery time	• Online/field survey (n = 505). • Multinomial logit (MNL) models.	• Various factors had strong influences on travellers' behavioural responses including socioeconomic attributes, experience with the advanced passenger information system, and experience with transit and the LRT system.
12 (Murray-Tuite et al., 2014)	Washington, DC	Investigated behavioural responses to the Washington, DC Metrorail collision in 2009	• Online/field survey (n = 300). • Multinomial logit (MNL) models.	• The most common change was avoidance of the first and last train cars. • Respondents also preferred not to make mode or travel choice changes.

Note: * This study also appeared in Appendix Table 14A.1.

15. Demand management in urban railway systems: strategy, design, evaluation, monitoring and technology

Zhenliang Ma, Haris N. Koutsopoulos, Anne Halvorsen and Jinhua Zhao

15.1 INTRODUCTION

Urbanization is increasing globally, with 68 per cent of the world population projected to live in cities by 2050 (United Nations, 2019). The densification of urban areas has led to a rise in urban congestion on roads and public transport systems. Adding capacity in urban rails, such as extending networks, increasing station sizes, or updating signalling systems, to deal with the crowding is often difficult, especially in the short term. Public transport demand management (PTDM), aiming for better utilization of available capacity through influencing customers' mobility behaviour, is a promising alternative to deal with the challenging issue of urban crowding.

Despite its potential in helping with crowding by redistributing demand in space and time, PTDM has received less attention compared to travel demand management (TDM) in car traffic. The TDM strategies in car traffic, such as shifting modes and congestion pricing, cannot be directly transferred to PTDM due to the characteristics and constraints of public transport. The advancement in information and communication technologies (ICT) and data collection systems (smartcards and smartphones) offers opportunities for the development and implementation of innovative PTDM strategies, such as personalized information and incentives.

The chapter provides an overview of PTDM solutions enabled by the availability of extensive public transport data. It discusses new methodologies using automated fare collection (AFC) data to drive problem identification, efficient design, effective evaluation, and monitoring in PTDM development. The discussion is on the application related to urban heavy rail systems (subways) and focuses on the following problems:

- Developing a general framework to structure the development and implementation of PTDM strategies;
- Evaluating and monitoring the effectiveness of PTDM strategies at varied levels of aggregations;
- Designing optimal promotion-based PTDM strategies to maximize performance while saving investment.

First, a PTDM design framework is proposed to help policymakers structure their design process, adapting previously used strategies, or developing new ones. The choice of the type of intervention (e.g., pricing, regulatory, market, etc.) and associated design parameters (e.g., users targeted, spatiotemporal coverage, etc.) are essential elements of the design process. The second area introduces novel approaches for evaluation of PTDM strategies at three levels of aggregation (system, group, and individual levels) by taking advantage of detailed disaggregate AFC data, with a special focus on users' longitudinal behaviour, an important but less understood area in PTDM. The last area uses available information on how the system is used by passengers and provides systematic approaches on how to set the various design parameters that optimize system performance and resource utilization.

Insights and lessons are derived from a systematic study of a pre-peak discount programme using an extensive AFC dataset from the Mass Transit Railway (MTR), Hong Kong. It includes: (a) users' behavioural response to promotions in short-term (shift departure time) and long-term (sustain travel behaviour); (b) the underlying factors (travel patterns from AFC); and (c) the effectiveness of various promotion design structures in space (station/Origin-Destination (OD)-based), time (pre-peak/after-peak), and pricing (step/flat).

15.2   TRAVEL DEMAND MANAGEMENT IN CAR TRAFFIC AND BEHAVIOURAL DRIVERS

Travel Demand Management (TDM) emerged in the 1970s and aims to alter demand patterns in time, space and mode by influencing users' travel behaviour mainly through incentives in the form of rewards (e.g., free travel using public transport) or penalties (e.g., fees, tolls, parking costs, etc.). TDM has broader applications to various travel modes, and its goals have expanded from energy savings to improving accessibility, system performance, and so on. TDM solutions are among the most cost-effective measures, with benefits including congestion reduction, infrastructure savings, increased safety, reduced pollution, and better land use (VTPI, 2014).

In many cities, TDM gains traction when other alternatives are not feasible or effective. There may be no space to add roads, especially in the short term, and further improvements to transport supply may not be possible. TDM policies can often be implemented in shorter time frames than infrastructure projects. In addition, many different stakeholders can be involved in the development of TDM, from various government planning agencies and transit agencies to non-profit groups and employers, allowing for a variety of approaches.

TDM has been implemented in cities around the world in reducing vehicle trips, such as in Singapore, London and Stockholm (Tillema et al., 2013; Gärling and Schuitema, 2007). Gärling and Schuitema (2007) broadly characterize TDM strategies for traffic congestion based on the main mechanisms behind the strategy, including:

- Physical change measures: Park and ride schemes, land use planning, walking/ cycling improvements;
- Legal policies: Prohibiting traffic in some areas, parking controls, reducing speed limits;
- Economic policies: Taxing vehicles or fuel, congestion pricing, lowering transit costs;

- Information and education measures: Individual marketing, public information campaign, social mode.

Various studies highlighted the effectiveness of TDM on shaping travel patterns of individual users by targeting relevant stakeholders and providing meaningful incentives, and also their positive impacts on traffic, safety and the environment (Giuliano, 1992; Ferguson, 1990; Smith and Moniruzzaman, 2014; Litman and Fitzroy, 2018).

Behavioural Change Drivers

A TDM strategy is successful if it can change users' travel behaviour towards sustainable choices, such as shifting to public transport, bicycling, walking or ride-sharing. There is a large body of literature that aims to understand how users make decisions about their travel. In the short term, the decisions can include route, mode, and departure time choices, while the long-term decisions include whether to get a driver's licence, buy a car, and where to live.

Most demand is derived demand: people are taking trips, not for the sake of the trip itself, but because they need to get to work, school, or another time-sensitive activity. Activity-based travel behaviour frameworks (Kitamura, 1988; Axhausen and Gärling, 1992) account for it by recognizing the constraints that influence trip-making. Factors like gender (or household roles), employment, age, household structure, and time and cost constraints play a role in how people structure their trips, though when these factors change, travel may not shift expectedly. According to Kitamura (1988), "travel behaviour depends upon the history of contributing factors and perhaps on the past trajectory of behaviour itself"; a new TDM policy must contend with factors as they are in the present as well as other ingrained habits to find success.

Gärling et al. (2002) develop a framework of TDM impacts drawing on several behavioural theories. Following the activity-based model, people choose among trip chains (rather than trips) based on the attributes of those trips (e.g., purpose, time, cost, comfort, etc.), their characteristics (household structure, income, employment), and situational factors (weather, time of day, time pressure). TDM measures both directly and indirectly influence trip chain attributes and also affect users' goals and intentions through public information.

For a long-term behavioural change, the TDM policy must lead to a shift in beliefs, attitudes and values (Gärling and Schuitema, 2007). The attitudes refer to "a psychological tendency that is expressed by evaluating a particular entity . . . with some degree of favour or disfavour", while beliefs "reflect the subjective probability that an object has a certain outcome" (Schuitema et al., 2010). While dis-/incentives may impact travel choices, travellers will likely revert to their original travel behaviours once the dis-/incentives are removed, unless the dis-/incentives can change the above internal factors. Behavioural theories, such as goal-setting, control, choice, attitude, and habit theories, are usually used to understand the mechanism of internal changes (Gärling and Fujii, 2009).

One example of using these behavioural theories in TDM is to conceptualize what types of users would be more or less susceptible to certain TDM policies. For example, activity-led users are motivated by the time to be at their destinations, benefit-led users desire comfortable journeys, and habit-led users (developed a travel routine) may require disruptive measures to alter their habitual travels. Then, the most relevant theories can be applied to design targeted and effective TDM strategies for users who fall into a particular group.

Underlying these theories are assumptions that humans act rationally and are fully informed about their choices. However, as behavioural economics has found, this is often not true (Kahneman, 2003), and people tend to use heuristics ('rule-of-thumb') to simplify decision-making. People are also less likely to maximize their utility truly because of the associated risks. According to the prospect theory, people's attitude toward risk varies depending on whether they are dealing with gains or losses and if the outcome has a high or low probability. The way a choice is framed can have a significant impact on decisions by changing how different salient attributes are to the decision-maker. Social aspects can also be influential, as people often refer to their peers' decisions for their own travel decisions (from owning a car to how to treat pedestrians while driving) (Gaker et al., 2010; Avineri, 2012). One caveat for these findings is that they are based on experiments in Western cultures and may not be applicable in other places (Dolan et al., 2012).

Behavioural economics has been applied to transportation both for improving models and designing strategies for behavioural change. Avineri (2012) considers influencing travel behaviour to reduce the environmental impacts of driving, while Dolan et al. (2012) perform a more general study of how behavioural economics can be used in policy design to influence travel behaviour. Ben-Elia et al. (2008) conducted experiments to understand how people make route choices based on average travel time and its variability and found that users overestimate the possibility that their trip will be shorter than average. Encouraging more active travel for environmental and health reasons is considered by Zhao and Baird (2014). They used mobile apps to "nudge" users towards active travel modes by providing feedback on their travel patterns and behaviours.

The Basis for Impactful TDM Programmes

According to Loukopoulos (2007), a policy's success is measured by effectiveness, public attitudes toward it, and political feasibility. These dimensions are interrelated and directly impacted by the design of policies and the behavioural change of drivers discussed in the above section. Drawing directly from a TDM behaviour framework, Gärling and Schuitema (2007) identified three critical elements of an effective TDM programme:

- *Reduce the attractiveness of habitual travel*: measures should trigger goal-setting through careful designs. Non-coercive measures that nudge people to make better decisions on their own, such as travel plans and information, may not be enough to reduce the attractiveness of habitual behaviour on their own.
- *Activate user goals for sustainable travel*: reducing the attractiveness of driving can activate goals, and user characteristics (household structure and income) should also be considered. Coercive measures, like pricing and regulations, can force goals more strongly, assuming appropriate alternatives are available.
- *Reduce costs and uncertainty of alternative travels*: encouraging travel planning reduces the uncertainty of adopting a new travel habit. Temporary changes that force people to break old habits can speed up the adoption of new ones. Simplifying

the decisions and steps that users must go through to change behaviour can help reduce their associated mental costs.

TDM policies should be specific to local contexts, including matching incentives to travellers in a particular region and the spatial scale of the programme (e.g., city vs. region-wide) (Meyer, 1999; Gärling and Fujii, 2009). Meyer (1999) reviews TDM studies on reducing car travel and concludes that the dis-/incentives often involve pricing. Steg (2003) suggests three dimensions required for effective pricing strategies: the instruments have immediate consequences, the pricing level is correct, and prices are relevant to the targeted behavioural change (e.g., peak congestion). Maruyama and Sumalee (2007) also highlight the trade-off between effectiveness and simplicity, that is, a sophisticated design may be (theoretically) optimal when considering efficiency, but a more understandable design is likely to have higher approval and among the public and government.

TDM policies can have different characteristics and types. They can be categorized as "push" and "pull" or "hard" and "soft" measures. Hard measures change users' travel opportunities through pricing or work flexibility, while soft measures target shifting users' attitudes, beliefs and values via information or education. Many studies have reported that combinations of these measures are more effective than using just one (Eriksson et al., 2010; Gärling and Fujii, 2009; Richter et al., 2011). Gärling and Fujii (2009) explain that the combined measures could stimulate more psychological variables (cognitive skill, moral obligation, etc.) associated with behavioural change.

Public acceptance, indicated by public attitudes and beliefs, is closely related to the effectiveness of TDM policies. More coercive push measures are typically less accepted than pull measures, even though studies found that push measures have a more significant impact (Eriksson et al., 2006). Eriksson et al. (2008) found that people viewed the pull measures as "effective, fair, and acceptable", while finding the opposite for push measures. Schade and Schlag (2003) identified the factors that impact public acceptance, including information and awareness, perceived effectiveness, attribution of responsibility, social norms and values, individual claims, revenue allocation, equity, and socio-economic impacts. They found that social norms were the most critical factor in explaining acceptance.

Political acceptance is vital for acquiring funding and support in implementing TDM programmes. Gärling and Schuitema (2007) report that political acceptance is often dependent on public opinion, so the factors listed in public acceptance are still relevant. The competing priorities of different levels of government can also play a role. Local governments are more accountable to citizens' day-to-day experiences, while federal governments can take a broader and long-term view of what policies will benefit their transportation systems.

Effective communication is also critical. Schlag and Teubel (1997) summarize essential elements of "intelligent marketing", including creating awareness, communicating the programme's positive impacts for individuals as well as its broader effects on society, and stressing that mobility will not be constrained and people still have a choice. In the Stockholm case, Schuitema et al. (2010) highlight the value of positive publicity by mass media and the city's official website in increasing acceptance levels over initial acceptability estimates.

15.3 TRAVEL DEMAND MANAGEMENT IN PUBLIC TRANSPORT

The studies on car traffic TDM provide a good reference for demand management in public transport. However, many of the TDM strategies for car traffic cannot be directly translated to public transport due to its different characteristics and constraints. For example, increasing peak fares in public transport, similar to congestion pricing in car traffic, tends to be politically unappealing and faces strong opposition from the public (Henn et al., 2011). It could even push people to travel by car if fare surcharges in public transport are set inappropriately (Whelan and Johnson, 2004). Compared to drivers, public transport users have less flexibility in travel choices (e.g., routes, departure times, etc.). Also, they experience only reduced crowding when they travel off-peak while drivers will have lower travel times, fuel costs, and stress levels. According to Maunsell (2007), public transport demand management (PTDM) is more a question of optimization – how to best redistribute users in the network – than in car traffic in which alternative modes are often viable, such as ride-sharing, bicycling and walking.

Effective and efficient demand management policies for public transport have not yet been nearly as well studied or widely deployed. Price discrimination is well-established for dealing with peak period congestion (Cervero, 1990; Mark and Phil, 2006; Zhang et al., 2017a; Wang et al., 2015; Zhang et al., 2014) and research has shown that people are willing to pay to avoid crowding (Prud'homme et al., 2012). A review of the value of crowding research by Li and Hensher (2011) found that while most studies considered only in-vehicle crowding, passengers exhibit a willingness to pay for reduced crowding in access-way, entrance, platform/station, and in-vehicle crowding. Several studies estimate the value of crowding in public transport using smartcard or survey data (Yap et al., 2018; Batarce et al., 2016; Tirachini et al., 2017; Hörcher et al., 2017; Kroes et al., 2014).

Given the concerns from passengers on crowding to improve the attractiveness of public transport, it is important to develop a PTDM design framework to help policy-makers structure their design process, adapt previously used strategies, or develop new ones. Various studies in car traffic have proposed TDM design frameworks to streamline the TDM process (Gärling et al., 2002; Rose, 2007), but very few have reported on PTDM design. Recently, Halvorsen et al. (2019) discussed the main steps for developing PTDM programmes, building on a synthesis of TDM literature and real-world PTDM experience, and illustrated the PTDM design with automated data using a pre-peak discount programme in Hong Kong.

The PTDM strategies that have been implemented or trialled in public transport usually take the form of promotion (e.g., incentives/rewards encouraging off-peak-hour travel using less crowded routes). For example, the "Free Train Trip Before 7:00 am" in Melbourne, "Travel Smart Program" in Mass Rapid Transit (MRT), Singapore, "Early-Bird Fare Discount Promotion" in Mass Transit Railway (MTR), Hong Kong, and "PERKS Reward" trial in Bay Area Rail Transit (BART), San Francisco (Ma and Koutsopoulos, 2019). Empirical studies on the effectiveness of promotion-based PTDM strategies reported 2–5 per cent of users shifting out of peak-hour travel (Currie, 2009; Halvorsen et al., 2016; Douglas et al., 2011), while the "BART PERKS" trial showed that 10 per cent of the participants shifted to travel in an off-peak hour (Greene-Roesel et al., 2018). Providing real-time crowding information (of vehicles on platforms) has also been reported as a form of PTDM (encouraging boarding a less crowded train or car of a train) in cities, such as Tokyo, Paris, Stockholm and San Francisco (Greene-Roesel et al., 2018; Zhang et al., 2017b). A pilot study in Stockholm showed that real-time crowding information provision reduced the share of passengers boarding the first, most crowded trains by 4.3 per cent.

A PTDM strategy is only successful if it can change travel behaviour. The potential scope of the behavioural response to promotion in public transport may include: (a) departure time; (b) access/egress mode and station choice; (c) path choice; and (d) new demand (induced or from mode change). Various empirical studies show that passengers may change their departure times in response to a PTDM strategy (e.g., discount, free trip, etc.). The departure time change is governed by many factors, such as work flexibility, trip length, base trip fare, promotion level, the amount of time to shift, sociodemographic attributes, etc. (Halvorsen et al., 2016; 2019; Henn et al., 2011; Anupriya et al., 2018). In particular, Halvorsen et al. (2019) evaluated the response to an off-peak discount promotion in Hong Kong (offering a 25 per cent discount for passengers completing their trips before morning peak) and evaluated its effectiveness. Using AFC data from before and after the implementation of the promotion, they analysed the impacts at the system, group, and individual levels. At the system level, they reported an overall change of about 2.5 per cent at the beginning. Groups were defined using the spatio-temporal characteristics of trips. Results demonstrate that different user groups had different responses to the promotion. Individual-level analysis using a logit model concluded that the significant factors in changing passengers' behaviour include the amount of time passengers had to shift to take advantage of the promotion, fare savings, work flexibility, and price sensitivity. Halvorsen (2015) reported that during a discount promotion trial in Hong Kong, there was no evidence of passengers switching their destination station to take advantage of the promotion (an edge effect).

No empirical study has investigated the change of access/egress mode and path choices and induced new demand, mainly due to the data unavailability. Theoretically, Ma and Koutsopoulos (2019) argued that path choice is unlikely to be impacted by a station-based discount promotion given relatively small performance improvement (2–5 per cent of passengers changing departure times). This argument is supported by studies on the value of crowding in public transport (Hörcher et al., 2017; Kroes et al., 2014), where the disutility caused by one additional passenger per square metre onboard a train, on average, is equivalent to 11.92 per cent of their travel time. Assume that a PTDM promotion leads to a 5 per cent reduction in the load (or crowding level) and that crowded trains may carry 5–6 passengers per square metre. For a 30-minute trip, the total equivalent travel time will go down from 51.5 minutes (30 * (1 + 6 * 0.1192)) to 50.4 minutes (30 * (1 + 0.1192 * 6 * (1 − 5 per cent))), a difference (1.1 minutes travel time) very unlikely to induce significant path choice changes. Most behavioural studies focus on the short-term response behaviour to promotion. Few studies reported on long-term behaviour change, in which the attrition of responsive passengers can be significant (Halvorsen et al., 2019; Ma et al., 2019a).

Promotion-based PTDM can be inefficient without careful design, as many passengers may benefit from a reward without having to change their behaviour. Very little has been reported in the literature related to the optimal design of such strategies (Ma and Koutsopoulos, 2019). The choice of the type of intervention (e.g., pricing, regulations) and the associated design parameters (e.g., targeted users, spatiotemporal coverage) are important elements of the design process. While the corresponding problem in car traffic TDM, dealing with the optimization of toll locations and pricing levels, has received some attention (Kachroo et al., 2017; Simoni et al., 2019; Pandey and Boyles, 2018; Zangui et al., 2013), PTDM strategies are often developed on a trial-and-error basis. No systematic approach was reported on how to set the various design parameters that optimize system performance and resource utilization. Yang and Tang (2018) describe a fare-reward scheme (FRS) that rewards a commuter with one free trip during shoulder periods after a certain number of paid trips during the peak hours using a one route network. However, public transport systems are complex and the design of a PTDM scheme, deciding when, where, and how much discount or surcharge is implemented, is not trivial. To fill these gaps, Ma and Koutsopoulos (2019) proposed a general framework for the optimal design of PTDM strategies, in particular promotion strategies, to better target passengers based on their contribution to congested sections of the network and their behavioural response. Using empirical data in Hong Kong, the effectiveness of varied promotion design structures is systematically evaluated, including space (station/OD), time (pre-peak/after-peak), and price (flat/step).

15.4   TECHNOLOGY ENABLERS AND PERSONALIZED INCENTIVES

Automated data collection systems are transforming the planning, scheduling, monitoring and operations control of public transport systems. They provide operators with extensive disaggregated data about the state of their system and the movement of passengers within the system (Koutsopoulos et al., 2019). The main categories of automated data sources include:

- Automated vehicle location systems (AVL);
- Automated passenger counting systems (APC);
- Automated fare-collection (AFC, smartcards).

In addition to the above main data sources, passengers also carry sensors (smartphones) that can provide detailed information about how they use the system (Zhao et al., 2018). Many systems also facilitate fare collection using smartphones via QR code sensors or near field communication technology (Jevinger and Persson, 2019).

Data from these sources has different characteristics, both with respect to the information they convey and their availability in time. AVL and APC data has been available for a long time and used for operations planning and scheduling (e.g. run time distributions, busloads, etc.). AFC systems are a rather recent development. They are becoming common among public transport agencies because of the convenience offered to the passengers, and the efficiency with respect to other functions (e.g. accounting). AFC systems are, in general, open or closed (the functionality, mainly dictated by the agency's fare policy). Open systems require that passengers only tap in when they enter the system (e.g. MBTA in Boston). Closed systems require both tapping in and tapping out (e.g. MTR in Hong Kong). As such, they provide direct information about the OD flows. Many systems are hybrid, utilizing an open architecture on the bus side and closed on the subway side (e.g. London).

The above technologies are vehicle or station-based (i.e. they are part of the agency's infrastructure). AVL data is typically available in real-time at the transit control centre. However, APC and AFC data is not communicated in real-time yet (although technically feasible). The data is stored locally and, usually, uploaded overnight. For this reason, real-time applications of AFC data are only recently emerging.

Passengers and infrastructure are increasingly interconnected, allowing effective communication. The introduction of the mobile internet and the apps ecosystem has changed the way public transport systems communicate directly with their customers. These technological advances conveniently link passengers and services. Passengers receive real-time information, for example, about bus arrivals (which alters how waiting times are traditionally estimated), updates about incidents, and provide feedback to operators about the quality of their services. Furthermore, apps and mobile sensors can provide additional information that complements the data collected from smartcard systems, enhancing the development of customer-centric performance metrics, measures of equity and inclusion to inform policy, and better planning of operations and services.

The smartcard enables the customer-centric evaluation, design, monitoring of PTDM programmes at a disaggregated level, and update of the programme. AFC data drives a broad spectrum of behaviour studies in public transport (Pelletier et al., 2011). It provides the opportunity for analysis in demand and choice modelling (Koutsopoulos et al., 2019; Nassir et al., 2017; 2018; Rahbar et al., 2019; Ma et al., 2019b). In addition to aggregate trends of when, where and how passengers travel, AFC data provides detailed information on travel of individuals and specific groups (Goulet-Langlois et al., 2016; Briand et al., 2017; Ma et al., 2013; 2017). Travel patterns (from AFC data) are critical for estimating behavioural attributes of trips (e.g., trip purpose) (Kusakabe and Asakura, 2014; Alsger et al., 2018) or passenger groups (e.g., sensitive to price). These facilitate continuous monitoring of behaviour and optimal design of PTDM strategies (Ma and Koutsopoulos, 2019). For example, based on the empirical and modelling findings using AFC data, MTR recently updated the 2014 pre-peak discount PTDM programme in October 2019 by increasing the fare discount to 35 per cent when exiting the newly designated core urban stations from 7:15 to 8:15 am (http://www.mtr.com.hk/en/customer/main/early_bird_t&c. html).

The communication technologies and smartphones have been transforming the PTDM paradigm – from the generic (one-fits-all) and static approach to an individualized and dynamic manner – in which the PTDM schemes (e.g., behaviour to change, incentive policies, levels, and injection times) are customized to the individuals and tailored to their trips. For example, the Bay Area Rapid Transit (BART) in San Francisco piloted the "BART Perks – Phase II" incentive programme in 2019. It offered personalized incentives to a group of 1900 regular BART riders with varied types of offers: morning-shift early/late, afternoon-shift early/late. Participants receive points for travelling using a specific station at a certain time, which are determined monthly based on changes in predicted congestion patterns and user historical travel patterns and choices (BART, 2019). The evaluation found that participants with offers increased the share of their travel during incentivized periods by 6–20 per cent. The incentive cost per shifted trip was approximately $1 overall, a significant improvement over that of $10 per shifted trip in "BART

Perks – Phase I". The efficiency was achieved primarily by rewarding behaviour change rather than pre-existing behaviour, and by expanding the eligible windows for time shift.

Incentive or reward-based strategies are also experimented with in car traffic and discussed in the new and future urban mobility area with multimodal operations and connected autonomous vehicles (Angelopoulos et al., 2018; Zhu et al., 2020; Xiong et al., 2019; Zhao and Leclercq, 2018; Luo et al., 2019). For example, Los Angeles conducted a 10-week pilot field study in 2013, and 35 per cent of travellers changed their departure times and route choices (Hu et al., 2015). New York City introduced the "Bike Angels" incentive programme in 2017 that offers points for Citi Bike riders who improve the availability of bikes and docks for fellow riders. Riders get various rewards with different point levels (https://www.citibikenyc.com/bikeangels/). Transportation network company (TNC) (e.g., Uber, Lyft) offers trip discounts to improve shareability opportunities by encouraging sharing, walking and waiting (Zhou et al., 2020; Ma et al., 2019c). The incentive programmes are also popular practices across industries, including airlines, hotels, insurance, telecommunications, e-commerce, and on-demand services (Wang and Yang, 2019).

In summary, the potential for incentives or promotion as a base for PTDM is attractive and further enabled by the advancement of ICT, automated data collection systems, and data analytics. By taking advantage of the commonly available smartcard data in public transport, the chapter introduces a new PTDM development framework (process, analysis methods and metrics). Then, we discuss the findings on optimal PTDM designs that have limited resources and evaluate and monitor users' behaviour continuously over time. The findings include empirical and theoretical modelling analysis using a pre-peak discount programme in Hong Kong.

15.5   A NEW FRAMEWORK FOR PUBLIC TRANSPORT DEMAND MANAGEMENT

This section discusses the main steps for developing PTDM programmes, building on a synthesis of previous TDM literature and real-world PTDM experience. PTDM development consists of four main phases: (1) Problem identification and programme goals; (2) Design; (3) Evaluation; and (4) Monitoring.

A key enabler for the adoption of the framework presented below is AFC data. AFC systems are particularly advantageous for PTDM applications, by facilitating a detailed understanding of the spatiotemporal characteristics of individual travel patterns, more in-depth analyses of existing conditions, models to forecast the impacts of design and estimate its costs, and evaluations of congestion relief. Furthermore, AFC data can facilitate a panel analysis of users to provide insights into their behaviour before and after the introduction of a PTDM strategy. AFC data, especially combined with sociodemographic attributes, provide insight into users' constraints, attitudes and other factors that may affect their responsiveness to PTDM and hence, the likelihood of its success.

Problem Identification and Programme Goals

The overarching motivation for a PTDM programme is to reduce peak-hour congestion in the network. Robust policy designs must account for the local context and the particular nature of its demand. To set specific goals of the programme, the congestion patterns, the involved stakeholders, and the time horizon are important considerations.

Though stakeholders may have varied priorities, agency goals will be likely to include decreased congestion at certain times or locations (within a budget constraint). Understanding the spatiotemporal characteristics of the congestion problem as well as user attributes guides policymakers' decisions, e.g., shifting users to different times of day, different routes, or alternative (public transport) modes. Goals may also include more qualitative guidelines, such as policies that are well-received by users or simple to understand. The time horizon may impact the rate at which these goals are to be met, when to place various milestones, and what designs and outcomes are even feasible.

AFC data provide useful information related to the spatiotemporal characteristics of the usage of the system relevant to the PTDM programme. The extent of the congestion problem, including its distribution across times, and individual facilities, as well as specific resource constraints that affect the system's ability to meet demand, can be derived from AFC data. They are important aspects as they guide the nature and type of PTDM strategies appropriate for the problem. For example, Figure 15.1 illustrates the demand patterns at stations for entries (left) and exits (right). These patterns suggest that PTDM attempting to incentivize passengers to change their exit times would be a strong candidate for reducing congestion, particularly between 8:15 and 9:15 am. The spatiotemporal concentration of the entries and exits also suggests that, if station crowding is the motivation for PTDM, exit-based PTDM strategies could be more effective in the morning (compared to entry-based) (Halvorsen et al., 2019).

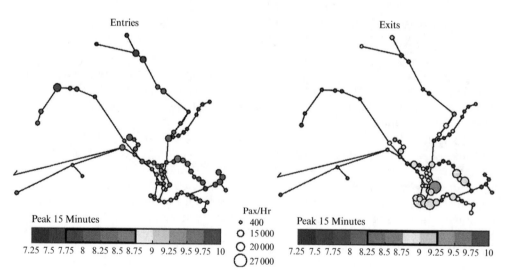

Source: Halvorsen et al. (2019).

Figure 15.1   Demand patterns for station entries and exits

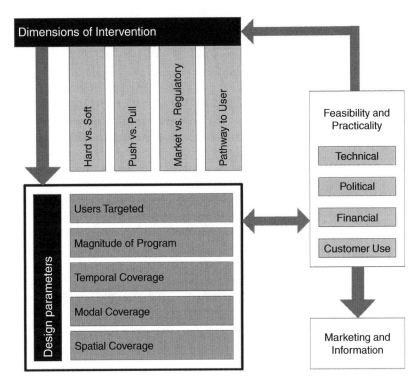

Source: Halvorsen et al. (2019).

Figure 15.2   PTDM design considerations

Design

Figure 15.2 describes a PTDM design process and the key aspects to consider. The first step of PTDM design is determining the dimensions of intervention. Then, various parameters should be set. If any data is already available, it can be used in forecasting to ensure that the effects of the programme approach its aims. After checking the design is feasible, a final step is to determine how to promote the programme through public information and marketing materials. The design process may be an iterative one, as stakeholders' feedback impacts the final design.

The intervention measures may be "hard", changing the attributes of different alternatives (e.g., fares differentials or shaping land use), or "soft", changing users' perceptions of their travel options through, for example, marketing or trip planning tools (Bamberg et al., 2011). Hard measures are further divided into market-based policies, which influence users through prices, and, though less common in public transport, regulatory policies, which set laws to require or promote certain actions. Push measures make one option less appealing to force users away from it (e.g., peak surcharge), while pull measures make another more appealing to attract users (e.g., off-peak discount). Typically, push measures are more effective (Eriksson et al., 2010), though less acceptable to users (Steg and Vlek, 1997). In addition, agencies can manage user demand through several pathways, including customers (entry criteria, pricing, incentives, or information), employers (flexible-hour policies), and broader channels (land use).

The design parameters define how the policy will be implemented. One crucial parameter is the targeted user population: PTDM interventions that target specific users can be more effective or efficient than generic strategies (Bamford et al., 1987), especially incentives. Targeting individuals may be practically infeasible and politically difficult. Instead, the problem can be approached through the use of more homogeneous groups. The magnitude of the programme (e.g., the level of fare differentiation) is a critical parameter, particularly for hard policies (Eriksson et al., 2010). The congestion and crowding analysis carried out in the problem identification stage can be used to establish a policy's temporal, modal and spatial coverage, ensuring that the most overcrowded periods and parts of the system are covered. Another temporal aspect is the programme duration.

The practicality and feasibility of the design, in terms of appropriate technological enablers and implementation costs, is an important consideration. The emergence of mobile sensors and the widespread use of smartcards in recent years have increased the technological options to support innovative strategies. Implementing such options, however, can incur costs, including lost fare revenue, increased staff hours, technology procurement, and marketing. However, some policies may also increase revenue by attracting new customers or reduce cost by allowing the agency to purchase new infrastructure (Currie, 2009).

The policy should have the necessary support of the public and decision-makers. Acceptance levels are shaped by many factors, including problem awareness, perceptions of effectiveness and fairness, perceived responsibility for the problem, and social norms and values (Schlag and Teubel, 1997; Schade and Schlag, 2003). Political acceptance often depends on public opinions (Gärling and Schuitema, 2007), though Schlag and Teubel (1997) point out that politicians may not always perceive public views accurately.

The design must also acknowledge how people will use the system with the policy in place: will users be able to take advantage of loopholes? How will the policy function under service disruptions? Is it so complicated that its effectiveness may be degraded? Maruyama and Sumalee (2007) argue that a complex design may be theoretically optimal, but a more understandable design is likely to have higher participation and approval. Once the design is finalized, a plan for marketing and publicizing the campaign may be instrumental in encouraging fast adoption and broad participation among users.

For example, many PTDM strategies currently being implemented use off-peak discounts to incentivize users to switch from peak periods. Within the context, the various implementations offer station-based promotion schemes, such as the "early bird" promotion in Hong Kong, where passengers exiting the designated stations between 7:15 and 8:15 am receive a 25 per cent discount. The design parameters are the eligible stations, the discount times, and the level of discounts. Figure 15.3 shows an example of the optimal design schemes given constraints on programme goals and budgets, as well as implementation considerations. Figure 15.3a shows an optimal plan for a promotion using a step-discount with station-specific discount times and levels (theoretically the best). Figure 15.3b shows the scheme with a flat discount, discount time and discount levels common to all stations, which trade off the practical issues, such as the ease of communication to users in implementation (Ma and Koutsopoulos, 2019).

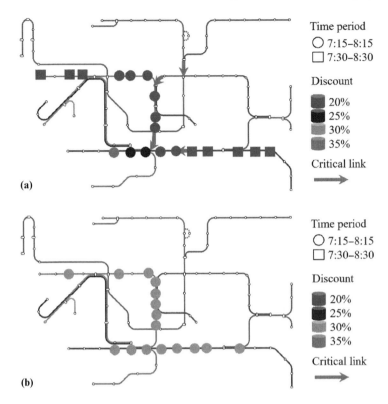

(a)

(b)

Time period
○ 7:15–8:15
☐ 7:30–8:30

Discount
■ 20%
■ 25%
■ 30%
■ 35%

Critical link

Time period
○ 7:15–8:15
☐ 7:30–8:30

Discount
■ 20%
■ 25%
■ 30%
■ 35%

Critical link

Source: Ma and Koutsopoulos (2019).

Figure 15.3 *PTDM design examples: (a) flat discount structure with varied discount time and discount level; (b) flat discount structure, same discount time, and discount levels for all stations*

Evaluation

Figure 15.4 summarizes the evaluation framework of a PTDM programme. It includes: (a) effectiveness of the programme in achieving its desired impact; (b) efficiency in achieving benefits that outweigh costs either from the agency's perspective or from a broader societal view; and (c) acceptability by the public and local decision-makers. While each is important in its own right, these factors are also interrelated. The persistent changes in the effectiveness of PTDM can be evaluated over time (T_1–T_3).

The performance metrics can be categorized as: (a) system impacts, directly related to congestion reduction goals; (b) customer impacts, reflecting other changes users might see in service as a result of system impacts and how they perceive these effects; (c) agency impacts, reflecting resource usage; and (d) social impacts that capture broader effects. Depending on the objectives of the TDM programme, different measurements, supported by AFC data, could be developed and prioritized.

From the behaviour aspect, AFC data facilitates evaluation approaches at three levels of aggregation:

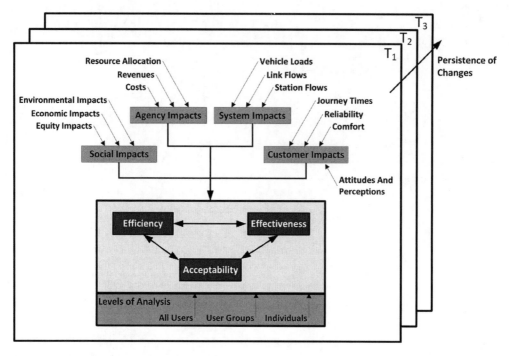

Source: Halvorsen et al. (2019).

Figure 15.4   PTDM evaluation framework

- *System-wide* (all passengers): Fully aggregated passenger data at the system level, that is, link or station flows, is useful from an operational perspective. It gives a basic understanding of how aggregate demand has changed, potentially reflecting service quality and the typical user experience. For agencies with less detailed passenger data, this might be the only type of analysis that is possible (Halvorsen et al., 2016).
- *User groups*: Detailed analysis of user behaviour can provide insight into a policy's particular impacts. Monitoring the behaviour of specific user groups can help understand which characteristics made people more likely to respond to the intervention and how strategies can be adapted to account for differing behaviours. The effectiveness of a group-based analysis depends on the identification of appropriate groups. Using AFC data over a period of time, clustering methods based on a feature vector relevant to the design of the PTDM intervention can be used to identify groups of interest (Ma et al., 2019a).
- *Individual passengers*: Panels of individual users, observed anonymously over time using AFC data, provide a unique tool to monitor passenger behaviour before and after the implementation of a PTDM strategy. This is a powerful means to understand how travel patterns of individuals change in the face of new policies, gain useful insights, and inform the development of improved designs that better account for user heterogeneity and the degree to which individual behaviour changes sustain themselves over time. Changepoint analysis methods can be used to

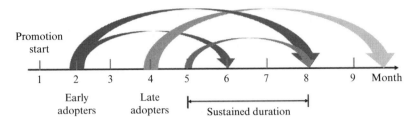

Figure 15.5   Life-span analysis of PTDM adopters

identify systematically users who change their behaviour in response to the PTDM strategy. Based on the inference of users who changed their behaviour, discrete choice models are used to identify the main factors that contribute to passengers' decision to change behaviour, and hence inform more efficient future designs (Halvorsen et al., 2019).

Monitoring

The effectiveness of PTDM programmes may change over time. Monitoring of how impacts change should continue beyond the initial evaluation to capture the medium and long-term changes that the strategy induces (Maunsell, 2007; Currie, 2011). There may be seasonal changes to its impacts, depending on events like holidays and weather. More importantly, long-term user acceptance may change as a result of the "hedonic treadmill", which argues that an intervention alters people's satisfaction with their travel, but over time they adjust and return to their previous satisfaction levels (Brickman and Campbell, 1971). Similarly, public or political acceptance may evolve in such a way that the behavioural levers of PTDM policies become weakened over time.

Figure 15.5 shows a sample life-span analysis of promotion adopters by tracking their behaviour across months after the promotion was implemented. Information such as early and late adopters (depending on when they changed their behaviour) and the corresponding sustained duration can be analysed for different individuals or user groups. That information together with individual travel patterns (extracted from AFC) would provide deep insights on the underlying mechanisms for behaviour change in response to the promotion, and thus will contribute to targeting sustained users in PTDM design or renovating the PTDM strategy periodically to increase its effectiveness.

15.6   EXAMPLES OF PTDM INITIATIVES

The case studies in this section focus on reporting empirical findings on PTDM evaluation and monitoring over time. The impacts of promotion design structures on the effectiveness of the promotion designs are assessed using the optimal promotion design method proposed in Ma and Koutsopoulos (2019). Table 15.1 summarizes the analysis and data used for these analytical components.

Hong Kong's MTR system first introduced a promotion-based PTDM strategy, offering a 25 per cent discount to adult-card users exiting 29 stations during the pre-peak

Table 15.1   Description of data for different analytical components

Analytical Components	Data Description
PTDM evaluation (Halvorsen et al., 2019; Ma et al., 2019a)	PTDM evaluation uses 14751 early shifters identified from "frequent, promotion eligible, and morning travel" panel users in August 2014, and compares their behaviour in October 2014.
PTDM monitoring (Ma et al., 2019a)	PTDM monitoring uses 2187 "consistent shifters" identified from the 14751 early shifters who use the system from October 2014 to October 2016.
PTDM design (Ma and Koutsopoulos, 2019)	PTDM design uses the OD demand matrix derived from AFC transaction records on 26 October 2016, and behavioural response estimated from PTDM evaluation and monitoring analysis.

period, 7:15–8:15 am, in September 2014. It aims to mitigate the congestion on the critical links in the morning peak. MTR system currently includes 11 lines covering 218.2 km (135.6 miles) of rail with 159 stations, including 91 heavy rail stations and 68 light rail stops. The AFC data used are from August 2014 to October 2016. The dataset has over 5 million trips on an average weekday.

PTDM Evaluation and Monitoring

Of all trips between 7:00 and 9:30 am, about 2.5 per cent shifted out of the peak after one month of implementation. With the additional early morning trips that shifted to the pre-peak period, about 3 per cent of all trips between 7:00 and 9:30 am moved into the pre-peak hour. This represents a 10 per cent increase in pre-peak trips. Corresponding changes were not observed among trips made by non-eligible users or to non-eligible stations (Halvorsen et al., 2019). The group-specific analysis highlights the heterogeneous response of different groups. Users with high flexibility, system familiarity, and fare savings, as well as low shifting time are more likely to shift (Ma et al., 2019a).

For passengers who regularly exit between 8:15 and 8:30 am and 8:30 and 8:45 am typically shift to the 8:00–8:15 am period, which is the latest time that they can switch to and still receive the discount. That means that most passengers would only shift their travel time by 15 minutes to take advantage of the discount. Similar behaviour is observed for passengers who shift exit time from the early morning to the promotion period to benefit from the discount. The response in this group is lower, possibly impacted by work flexibility (Ma and Koutsopoulos, 2019).

Initial PTDM monitoring tracked the early shifters from October 2014 (one month after promotion) to October 2016. There is a decreasing trend, with about 65 per cent early shifters (in October 2014) sustaining their travel behaviour after two years. Most early shifters sustain their behaviour for the first two months after promotion (October and November), but there is a sharp decrease in the third month. After that, the decreasing trend becomes more stable. The group-specific analysis indicated that the significant fare savings and relatively high schedule flexibility might lead to more sustained behaviour (Ma et al., 2019a).

An issue with such station-based discount strategies is that the promotion benefits many passengers beyond the ones who actually switch from the peak period, and contribute to critical link reduction, and hence are inefficient. For the pre-peak exit-station based promotion, let period I represent the early morning period, period II, the pre-peak promotion period (with the discount), and period III the peak period. The main groups of passengers are:

- G1: Passengers who usually exit in time period I (off-peak) and shift to time period II (pre-peak) to receive the discount. The change in behaviour of the passengers in this group has no impact on the crowding levels at the critical links during the peak period (although they still receive the discount).
- G2: Passengers who typically exit in time period II. These passengers receive the discount without having to alter their behaviour, and with no benefit to the peak-hour crowding levels.
- G3: Passengers who usually exit in time period III and shift to period II but do not contribute to the congestion during the peak period because they do not use the congested paths or critical links.
- G4: Passengers who usually exit in time period III and shift to time period II. These passengers travel through the critical links, and hence their behavioural change results in a reduction of crowding on the critical links during the peak period III.

Passengers in group G4 are the ones who should be actually targeted by the promotion (referred to as effective passengers), while passengers in groups G1–G3 are not useful since they are not contributing to the load on critical links but still benefit from the promotion (ineffective passengers). Figure 15.6 illustrates the exiting passengers by time period at two such stations, and the corresponding response (based on actual data).

The two stations have very different performance if included in a discount strategy. The relative gain (effective passengers divided by total passengers) shows that the agency needs to provide rewards to 50 users to shift one effective user at station 1 (left), while it needs to reward almost one thousand users at station 2 (right) for every user shifting out

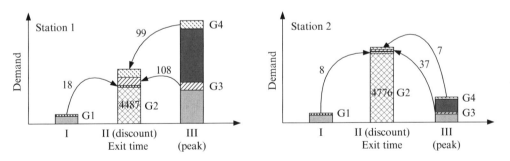

Note: G1–G3 are ineffective passenger groups (dotted shading, large cross-hatched grey, and diagonal shading, respectively). G4 is the effective passenger group (dashed diagonal shading); II indicates the promotion and III the peak period. Numbers indicate passengers in each category.

Source: Ma and Koutsopoulos (2019).

Figure 15.6   Cost efficiency of a station-based promotion

of the peak time period. Besides, the time periods at which users exit the system and pass through the crowded links are different. Hence, it is essential to properly select the stations and times when a promotion is offered.

PTDM Design

The optimal promotion design methodology in Ma and Koutsopoulos (2019) recognizes the role of effective and ineffective passengers explicitly. They formulate the problem to target effective passengers whose behavioural response contributes to the reduction of system congestion. The formulation is general. It can be used to evaluate and optimize a wide range of promotion structures, defined by their spatial (exit/OD based), temporal (pre-peak/after-peak), and discount level characteristics (step/flat).

The main design parameters of interest refer to the promotion in terms of the place (e.g., station, OD pair, routes), whether the discount is based on entry into or exit from the system, time, duration of the discounted time period, and pricing (discount level). These parameters influence where, when and how much discount to be offered to better target effective passengers who contribute to congested links during the peak periods. The implementation of such a strategy is, for example, passengers exiting station X between 7:30 and 8:30 am receive a 30 per cent fare discount. The objective function considered in the application is the minimization of passenger load on critical links during their corresponding congested periods.

Impact of design structures

Figure 15.7 provides a portfolio of schemes that can be adopted by the agency based on given budget constraints and implementation considerations. For example, with a budget of $18 million/year, the reduction of the load at the critical links ranges from 1.50 per cent to 2.10 per cent, compared to the base case of no promotion. By targeting a specific performance level, for example, 1.80 per cent, different strategies can be implemented, however with varying levels of budget. In addition, the fully flexible structure (varied discount times and varied discounts) improves the performance (link load reduction) by 33 per cent compared to the constrained structure (fixed discount times and fixed discounts), indicating that the cost of implementation simplicity (may be favoured by passengers) is relatively significant.

The results show that, regardless of the allocated budget, the performance of a design is bounded and lower than the behavioural response to the promotion. The best strategy is the step-wise discount structure with varied discount time periods by stations, with about 2.1 per cent reduction of the load on critical links. This is achieved at the cost of $20 million per year (in terms of lost revenue due to ineffective passengers receiving the discount without contributing to the reduction of the critical load). An additional budget does not improve performance. Increasing the budget simply adds more stations with only very few effective passengers (and many ineffective passengers).

Other designs, however, have the potential to better target effective users in space and time, including:

- Pre-peak, OD-based promotions. The decision variables include the OD pairs that receive the discount, the amount of discount based on exit time at the destination station, and the (exit) time that the discount is available.

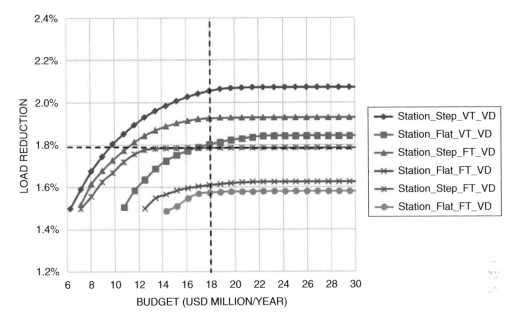

Notes: VT = discount time varies by station; VD = discount level varies by station; FT = discount time is the same for all stations; FD = discount level is the same for all stations.

Source: Ma and Koutsopoulos (2019).

Figure 15.7   Comparison of promotion design effectiveness

- Pre-peak & after-peak, exit station-based promotions. The decision variables include the exit stations that receive the discount, the amount of discount, and the pre-peak and after-peak time periods when the discount is accomplished.

Figure 15.8 shows the comparison results of OD pair-based and pre-peak & after-peak-based design structures. The results show that the OD-based structure is more cost-effective than the exit station-based ones, as it targets the passengers contributing to critical link loads more effectively. It reaches the maximum performance (2.38 per cent) at a budget of around $14 million, using the 2300 candidate OD stations (all OD pairs that contribute to the load on the critical links) and the highest discount level of 35 per cent. Beyond that, regardless of the available budget, no further improvements are possible. OD-based policies, although more effective and easily implementable with AFC systems, may be more challenging to communicate to passengers.

The pre-peak and after-peak structure is also more effective than the corresponding pre-peak only strategy. It gives passengers more flexibility to shift to the most convenient period. For example, it is more likely that a passenger typically exiting in the 9:15 period will shift to the 9:30 discount period than the pre-peak period. The pre-peak & after-peak discount structure requires 17 discounted stations at the cost of $9 million to achieve a 1.8 per cent load reduction, while the pre-peak one requires 29 stations with a cost of $23 million.

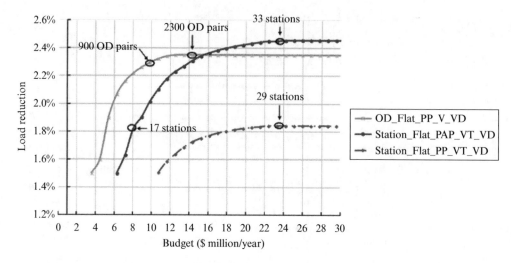

Notes: VT = discount time varies by station; VD = discount level varies by station; PP = discount at the pre-peak time period; PAP = discount at both the pre-peak and after-peak time period.

Source: Ma and Koutsopoulos (2019).

Figure 15.8   Comparison of promotion design effectiveness

15.7   CONCLUSIONS

Many public transport agencies deploy demand management strategies to divert passengers to less crowded routes and time periods. Well-structured PTDM strategies can help agencies better manage the available system capacity when the opportunity and investment to expand are limited. The chapter synthesizes the literature in car traffic TDM and streamlines the important steps of TDM in public transport in light of the role of AFC data in driving design, evaluation and monitoring of PTDM programmes. Case studies are reported for a pre-peak discount programme in Hong Kong (25 per cent fare discount for the designated stations and times). The main findings are:

- Most users shift less than 30 minutes to take advantage of the pre-peak discount, and users with high schedule flexibility, familiarity of the system, and fare savings are more likely to change their behaviour.
- Not all stations contribute effectively to the goals of a promotion. Careful selection of the stations (or ODs) involved in promotion is critical for an effective PTDM design. Hence, the trade-off between design simplicity and efficiency should be considered.
- Defining the discount periods properly is also important given that studies show that the amount of time a passenger has to shift to receive the discount is an important factor in their decision to participate. The common practice of uniform discount during the discount period should be re-evaluated, and the duration and placement of the discount periods relative to the peak period should be considered.

- Optimal promotion design (determine when, where, and how much) has the potential to lead to designs that are equally effective in mitigating crowding, but with more efficient utilization of available resources.
- Under the behaviour assumptions, the performance of the station (or ODs) based promotion strategies are bounded (2.1 per cent load reduction) regardless of the budget invested.

An agency may choose to target a group or not, but could also target different groups with different degrees of intervention. The feasibility of these interventions depends on the users' attitudes towards complexity, partnership opportunities, as well as fiscal implications.

- *Pricing structure*: The discount could be structured more like a rebate, providing a single, large payout over a period of time (e.g., weekly). This may attract those users who overlook small, regular discounts, by accentuating total savings over a period. Another option is to introduce a lottery policy instead of a guaranteed payout. By making users register to have a chance at winning, only those who are more price-sensitive or interested in participating will enter, meaning fewer people who do not change their behaviour are rewarded. Requiring enrolment allows the agency to give users greater rewards or a greater likelihood of winning, particularly if it is willing to pay out the same amount as in a user-wide fare differential scheme.
- *Pricing basis*: Rather than providing a discount based only on the exit station, a promotion could target OD pairs, particular links, or alternative routes. These options better manage uncertainty with travel time, in-vehicle congestion, or the need to change one's departure time, respectively. Discounting travel on less-crowded routes can improve capacity utilization. The integration of smartphone services with public transport payment enables the deployment of such route-based strategies.
- *Targeted customer information*: Providing more individualized information will help users make better travel decisions, conveying the benefits of off-peak travel that best match their needs. Possible strategies include station- or user-specific marketing, or enabling online journey planners, to display time-specific fares and crowding data. Users could also be given specific travel tips through a personalized page on the agency's website (possibly using insights from the group the user belongs to).

As the sophistication of the design of a promotion strategy increases, the complexity of implementation may also increase. While AFC systems facilitate the deployment of many schemes (e.g., based on the exit station), others (such as path-based) may require new sensor technologies to automatically identify the user path or transfer station. More advanced designs also require effective ways to communicate the promotion programme to the public.

Station and discount-based promotions alone are not enough to entirely reduce crowding during the peak period regardless of the budget invested. However, public transport agencies can accomplish the maximum possible load reduction more efficiently if they design their PTDM scheme optimally using methods such as the ones developed in Ma and Koutsopoulos (2019). Gärling and Fujii (2009) argue that combining measures helps activate more of the psychological variables (cognitive skills, moral obligation, etc.) associated with behaviour change.

Examples of reward-based PTDM programmes (offering reward points for certain behaviours) include "Travel Smart" in Singapore and the "BART Perks" pilot programme in San Francisco. Both reported higher response rates than a standard promotion strategy (Greene-Roesel et al., 2018). Hence it is interesting to consider a combination of both discount-based and reward-based strategies to incentivize passengers better. Different reward formats, such as amount, frequency, eligibility criteria for participation (users with "good behaviour") are essential for its design. The optimal design of such hybrid PTDM programmes can be an interesting direction.

ICT technologies and smartphones enable individualized information and incentives. The customized information could also be an effective "non-monetary" incentive, particularly for commuting and time-sensitive travels. Some evidence supports the potential of personalized incentives to manage congestion in systems or applications such as crowding at stations and even to increase ridership at weekends (Luan et al., 2018; Xiong et al., 2019; Zhu et al., 2020). Uncertainty remains as to whether the pilot results would scale up to a larger population and a dedicated source of ongoing funding to scale the programme. Large-scale and evidence-based studies are required in the area.

Demand interventions are quicker and more cost-efficient than adding capacity with new infrastructure. But in the context of public transport, they are often seen as transient solutions. However, when new service is provided, it may be complemented by PTDM policies, giving agencies a broader set of tools to find solutions that best meet their congestion and business needs.

REFERENCES

Alsger, A., Tavassoli, A., Mesbah, M., Ferreira, L. and Hickman, M. 2018. Public transport trip purpose inference using smart card fare data. *Transportation Research Part C: Emerging Technologies*, 87, 123–37.

Angelopoulos, A., Gavalas, D., Konstantopoulos, C., Kypriadis, D. and Pantziou, G. 2018. Incentivized vehicle relocation in vehicle sharing systems. *Transportation Research Part C: Emerging Technologies*, 97, 175–93.

Anupriya, A., Graham, D., Hörcher, D. and Anderson, R.J. 2018. The impact of early bird scheme on commuter trip scheduling in Hong Kong: A causal analysis using travel card data. *Transportation Research Board 97th Annual Meeting*, Washington, DC.

Avineri, E. 2012. On the use and potential of behavioural economics from the perspective of transport and climate change. *Journal of Transport Geography*, 24, 512–21.

Axhausen, K.W. and Gärling, T. 1992. Activity-based approaches to travel analysis: Conceptual frameworks, models, and research problems. *Transport Reviews*, 12, 323–41.

Bamberg, S., Fujii, S., Friman, M. and Gärling, T. 2011. Behaviour theory and soft transport policy measures. *Transport Policy*, 18, 228–35.

Bamford, C.G., Carrick, R.J., Hay, A.M. and Macdonald, R. 1987. The use of association analysis in market segmentation for public transport: A case study of bus passengers in West Yorkshire, UK. *Transportation*, 14, 21–32.

BART 2019. BART Perks Phase II Evaluation Report. San Francisco Bay Area Rapid Transit District.

Batarce, M., Muñoz, J.C. and Ortúzar, J.D.D. 2016. Valuing crowding in public transport: Implications for cost–benefit analysis. *Transportation Research Part A: Policy and Practice*, 91, 358–78.

Ben-Elia, E., Erev, I. and Shiftan, Y. 2008. The combined effect of information and experience on drivers' route-choice behavior. *Transportation*, 35, 165–77.

Briand, A.-S., Côme, E., Trépanier, M. and Oukhellou, L. 2017. Analyzing year-to-year changes in public transport passenger behaviour using smart card data. *Transportation Research Part C: Emerging Technologies*, 79, 274–89.

Brickman, P. and Campbell, D. 1971. *Hedonic Relativism and Planning the Good Society*, New York: Academic Press.

Cervero, R. 1990. Transit pricing research. *Transportation*, 17, 117–39.

Currie, G. 2009. Exploring the impact of the "Free before 7" campaign on reducing overcrowding on Melbourne's trains. 32nd Australasian Transport Research Forum, Auckland.

Currie, G. 2011. Design and impact of a scheme to spread peak rail demand using pre-peak free fares. *European Transport Conference*, Glasgow.

Dolan, P., Hallsworth, M., Halpern, D., King, D., Metcalfe, R. and Vlaev, I. 2012. Influencing behaviour: The mindspace way. *Journal of Economic Psychology*, 33, 264–77.

Douglas, N.J., Henn, L. and Sloan, K. 2011. Modelling the ability of fare to spread AM peak passenger loads using rooftops. *Australasian Transport Research Forum 2011 Proceedings*, Adelaide.

Eriksson, L., Garvill, J. and Nordlund, A.M. 2006. Acceptability of travel demand management measures: The importance of problem awareness, personal norm, freedom, and fairness. *Journal of Environmental Psychology*, 26, 15–26.

Eriksson, L., Garvill, J. and Nordlund, A.M. 2008. Acceptability of single and combined transport policy measures: The importance of environmental and policy specific beliefs. *Transportation Research Part A: Policy and Practice*, 42, 1117–28.

Eriksson, L., Nordlund, A.M. and Garvill, J. 2010. Expected car use reduction in response to structural travel demand management measures. *Transportation Research Part F: Traffic Psychology and Behaviour*, 13, 329–42.

Ferguson, E. 1990. Transportation demand management planning, development, and implementation. *Journal of the American Planning Association*, 56, 442–56.

Gaker, D., Zheng, Y. and Walker, J. 2010. Experimental economics in transportation: Focus on social influences and provision of information. *Transportation Research Record*, 2156, 47–55.

Gärling, T. and Fujii, S. 2009. Travel behavior modification: Theories, methods, and programs. In R. Kitamura, T. Yoshi and T. Yamamoto (eds), *The Expanding Sphere of Travel Behaviour Research*, Bingley: Emerald Group Publishing, pp. 97–128.

Gärling, T. and Schuitema, G. 2007. Travel demand management targeting reduced private car use: Effectiveness, public acceptability and political feasibility. *Journal of Social Issues*, 63, 139–53.

Gärling, T., Eek, D., Loukopoulos, P., Fujii, S., Johansson-Stenman, O., Kitamura, R., Pendyala, R. and Vilhelmson, B. 2002. A conceptual analysis of the impact of travel demand management on private car use. *Transport Policy*, 9, 59–70.

Giuliano, G. 1992. Transportation demand management: Promise or panacea? *Journal of the American Planning Association*, 58, 327–35.

Goulet-Langlois, G., Koutsopoulos, H.N. and Zhao, J. 2016. Inferring patterns in the multi-week activity sequences of public transport users. *Transportation Research Part C: Emerging Technologies*, 64, 1–16.

Greene-Roesel, R., Castiglione, J., Guiriba, C. and Bradley, M. 2018. BART perks: Using incentives to manage transit demand. *97th Transportation Research Board Annual Meeting*. Washington, DC.

Halvorsen, A. 2015. *Improving Transit Demand Management with Smart Card Data: General Framework and Applications*. Master of Science, Masschusetts Institution of Technology.

Halvorsen, A., Koutsopoulos, H.N., Lau, S., Au, T. and Zhao, J. 2016. Reducing subway crowding: Analysis of an off-peak discount experiment in Hong Kong. *Transportation Research Record: Journal of the Transportation Research Board*, 2544, 38–46.

Halvorsen, A., Koutsopoulos, H.N., Ma, Z. and Zhao, J. 2019. Demand management of congested public transport systems: A conceptual framework and application using smart card data. *Transportation*, 47, 2337–65.

Henn, L., Douglas, N. and Sloan, K. 2011. Surveying Sydney rail commuters' willingness to change travel time. *34th Australasian Transport Research Forum*. Adelaide.

Hörcher, D., Graham, D.J. and Anderson, R.J. 2017. Crowding cost estimation with large scale smart card and vehicle location data. *Transportation Research Part B: Methodological*, 95, 105–25.

Hu, X., Chiu, Y.-C. and Zhu, L. 2015. Behavior insights for an incentive-based active demand management platform. *International Journal of Transportation Science and Technology*, 4, 119–33.

Jevinger, Å. and Persson, J.A. 2019. Exploring the potential of using real-time traveler data in public transport disturbance management. *Public Transport*, 11, 413–41.

Kachroo, P., Gupta, S., Agarwal, S. and Ozbay, K. 2017. Optimal control for congestion pricing: Theory, simulation, and evaluation. *IEEE Transactions on Intelligent Transportation Systems*, 18, 1234–40.

Kahneman, D. 2003. Maps of bounded rationality: Psychology for behavioral economics. *American Economic Review*, 93, 1449–75.

Kitamura, R. 1988. An evaluation of activity-based travel analysis. *Transportation*, 15, 9–34.

Koutsopoulos, H.N., Ma, Z., Noursalehi, P. and Zhu, Y. 2019. Transit data analytics for planning, monitoring, control and information. In C. Antoniou, L. Dimitriou and F. Pereira (eds), *Mobility Patterns, Big Data and Transport Analytics*. Amsterdam: Elsevier, pp. 229–61.

Kroes, E., Kouwenhoven, M., Debrincat, L. and Pauget, N. 2014. Value of crowding on public transport in Île-de-France, France. *Transportation Research Record: Journal of the Transportation Research Board*, 2417, 37–45.

Kusakabe, T. and Asakura, Y. 2014. Behavioural data mining of transit smart card data: A data fusion approach. *Transportation Research Part C: Emerging Technologies*, 46, 179–91.

Li, Z. and Hensher, D.A. 2011. Crowding and public transport: A review of willingness to pay evidence and its relevance in project appraisal. *Transport Policy*, 18, 880–87.

Litman, T. and Fitzroy, S. 2018. Safe travels: Evaluating transportation demand management traffic safety impacts. Victoria Transport Policy Institute.

Loukopoulos, P. 2007. A classification of travel demand management measures. In T. Gärling and L. Steg (eds), *Threats from Car Traffic to the Quality of Urban Life: Problems, Causes and Solutions*. Bingley: Emerald Group Publishing.

Luan, W., Liu, G., Jiang, C. and Zhou, M. 2018. MPTR: A maximal-marginal-relevance-based personalized trip recommendation method. *IEEE Transactions on Intelligent Transportation Systems*, 19, 3461–74.

Luo, Q., Saigal, R., Chen, Z. and Yin, Y. 2019. Accelerating the adoption of automated vehicles by subsidies: A dynamic games approach. *Transportation Research Part B: Methodological*, 129, 226–43.

Ma, X., Liu, C., Wen, H., Wang, Y. and Wu, Y.-J. 2017. Understanding commuting patterns using transit smart card data. *Journal of Transport Geography*, 58, 135–45.

Ma, X., Wu, Y.-J., Wang, Y., Chen, F. and Liu, J. 2013. Mining smart card data for transit riders' travel patterns. *Transportation Research Part C: Emerging Technologies*, 36, 1–12.

Ma, Z. and Koutsopoulos, H.N. 2019. Optimal design of promotion based demand management strategies in urban rail systems. *Transportation Research Part C: Emerging Technologies*, 109, 155–73.

Ma, Z., Basu, A.A., Liu, T. and Koutsopoulos, H.N. 2019a. Behavioral response to transit demand management promotions: Sustainability and implications for optimal promotion design. *Transportation Research Board 98th Annual Meeting*, Washington, DC.

Ma, Z., Koutsopoulos, H., Zhu, Y. and Chen, Y. 2019b. Estimating passengers' path choice using automated data in urban rail systems. *TransitData 2019*, Paris.

Ma, Z., Koutsopoulos, H.N. and Zheng, Y. 2019c. Evaluation of on-demand ridesplitting services. *Transportation Research Board 98th Annual Meeting*, Washington, DC.

Mark, S. and Phil, C. 2006. Developments in transit fare policy reform. *29th Australasian Transport Research Forum*. Queensland.

Maruyama, T. and Sumalee, A. 2007. Efficiency and equity comparison of cordon- and area-based road pricing schemes using a trip-chain equilibrium model. *Transportation Research Part A: Policy and Practice*, 41, 655–71.

Maunsell, F. 2007. Demand management techniques: Peak spreading. Department for Transport, Transport for London and Network Rail, London.

Meyer, M.D. 1999. Demand management as an element of transportation policy: Using carrots and sticks to influence travel behavior. *Transportation Research Part A: Policy and Practice*, 33, 575–99.

Nassir, N., Hickman, M. and Ma, Z.-L. 2018. A strategy-based recursive path choice model for public transit smart card data. *Transportation Research Part B: Methodological*.

Nassir, N., Hickman, M. and Ma, Z. 2017. Statistical inference of transit passenger boarding strategies from farecard data. *Transportation Research Record*, 2652, 8–18.

Pandey, V. and Boyles, S.D. 2018. Dynamic pricing for managed lanes with multiple entrances and exits. *Transportation Research Part C: Emerging Technologies*, 96, 304–20.

Pelletier, M.-P., Trépanier, M. and Morency, C. 2011. Smart card data use in public transit: A literature review. *Transportation Research Part C: Emerging Technologies*, 19, 557–68.

Prud'homme, R., Koning, M., Lenormand, L. and Fehr, A. 2012. Public transport congestion costs: The case of the Paris subway. *Transport Policy*, 21, 101–109.

Rahbar, M., Hickman, M., Mesbah, M. and Tavassoli, A. 2019. Calibrating a Bayesian transit assignment model using smart card data. *IEEE Transactions on Intelligent Transportation Systems*, 20, 1574–83.

Richter, J., Friman, M. and Gärling, T. 2011. Soft transport policy measures: Gaps in knowledge. *International Journal of Sustainable Transportation*, 5, 199–215.

Rose, G. 2007. Appraisal and evaluation of travel demand management measures. *30th Australasian Transport Research Forum*, Melbourne.

Schade, J. and Schlag, B. 2003. Acceptability of urban transport pricing strategies. *Transportation Research Part F: Traffic Psychology and Behaviour*, 6, 45–61.

Schlag, B. and Teubel, U. 1997. Public acceptability of transport pricing. *IATSS Research*, 21, 134–42.

Schuitema, G., Steg, L. and Forward, S. 2010. Explaining differences in acceptability before and acceptance after the implementation of a congestion charge in Stockholm. *Transportation Research Part A: Policy and Practice*, 44, 99–109.

Simoni, M.D., Kockelman, K.M., Gurumurthy, K.M. and Bischoff, J. 2019. Congestion pricing in a world of self-driving vehicles: An analysis of different strategies in alternative future scenarios. *Transportation Research Part C: Emerging Technologies*, 98, 167–85.

Smith, B. and Moniruzzaman, M. 2014. Review of TDM appraisal and evaluation tools. Perth, Planning and Transport Research Centre (PATREC).

Steg, L. 2003. Factors influencing the acceptability and effectiveness of transport pricing. In J. Schade and B. Schlag (eds), *Acceptability of Transport Pricing Strategies.* Oxford: Pergamon Press.

Steg, L. and Vlek, C. 1997. The role of problem awareness in willingness-to-change car use and in evaluating relevant policy measures. In T. Rothengatter and E.C. Vaya (eds), *Traffic and Transport Psychology: Theory and Application*, Amsterdam: Elsevier.

Tillema, T., Ben-Elia, E., Ettema, D. and Van Delden, J. 2013. Charging versus rewarding: A comparison of road-pricing and rewarding peak avoidance in the Netherlands. *Transport Policy*, 26, 4–14.

Tirachini, A., Hurtubia, R., Dekker, T. and Daziano, R.A. 2017. Estimation of crowding discomfort in public transport: Results from Santiago de Chile. *Transportation Research Part A: Policy and Practice*, 103, 311–26.

United Nations 2019. *World Urbanization Prospects: The 2018 Revision.* New York: United Nations, Department of Economic and Social Affairs, Population Division.

VTPI. 2014. *Online TDM Encyclopedia* [Online]. Accessed 2019 at http://www.vtpi.org/tdm/.

Wang, H. and Yang, H. 2019. Ridesourcing systems: A framework and review. *Transportation Research Part B: Methodological*, 129, 122–55.

Wang, Z.-J., Li, X.-H. and Chen, F. 2015. Impact evaluation of a mass transit fare change on demand and revenue utilizing smart card data. *Transportation Research Part A: Policy and Practice*, 77, 213–24.

Whelan, G. and Johnson, D. 2004. Modelling the impact of alternative fare structures on train overcrowding. *International Journal of Transport Management*, 2, 51–8.

Xiong, C., Shahabi, M., Zhao, J., Yin, Y., Zhou, X. and Zhang, L. 2019. An integrated and personalized traveler information and incentive scheme for energy efficient mobility systems. *Transportation Research Part C: Emerging Technologies*, 113, 57–3.

Yang, H. and Tang, Y. 2018. Managing rail transit peak-hour congestion with a fare-reward scheme. *Transportation Research Part B: Methodological*, 110, 122–36.

Yap, M., Cats, O. and Van Arem, B. 2018. Crowding valuation in urban tram and bus transportation based on smart card data. *Transportmetrica A: Transport Science*, 1–20.

Zangui, M., Yin, Y., Lawphongpanich, S. and Chen, S. 2013. Differentiated congestion pricing of urban transportation networks with vehicle-tracking technologies. *Transportation Research Part C: Emerging Technologies*, 36, 434–45.

Zhang, J., Yan, X., An, M. and Sun, L. 2017a. The impact of beijing subway's new fare policy on riders' attitude, travel pattern and demand. *Sustainability*, 9, 689.

Zhang, Y., Jenelius, E. and Kottenhoff, K. 2017b. Impact of real-time crowding information: A Stockholm metro pilot study. *Public Transport*, 9, 483–99.

Zhang, Z., Fujii, H. and Managi, S. 2014. How does commuting behavior change due to incentives? An empirical study of the Beijing Subway System. *Transportation Research Part F: Traffic Psychology and Behaviour*, 24, 17–26.

Zhao, C.-L. and Leclercq, L. 2018. Graphical solution for system optimum dynamic traffic assignment with day-based incentive routing strategies. *Transportation Research Part B: Methodological*, 117, 87–100.

Zhao, J. and Baird, T. 2014. "Nudging" active travel: A framework for behavioral interventions using mobile technology. *Transportation Research Board 93rd Annual Meeting.* Washington, DC.

Zhao, Z., Koutsopoulos, H.N. and Zhao, J. 2018. Individual mobility prediction using transit smart card data. *Transportation Research Part C: Emerging Technologies*, 89, 19–34.

Zhou, J., Ma, Z., Hirschmann, S. and Lao, F.Y.K. 2020. Transportation network company service usage in the university community: Service adoption, usage frequency and service type choice. *Transportation Research Board 99th Annual Meeting*, Washington, DC.

Zhu, X., Wang, F., Chen, C. and Reed, D.D. 2020. Personalized incentives for promoting sustainable travel behaviors. *Transportation Research Part C: Emerging Technologies*, 113, 314–31.

16. Transit signal priority: research and practice review and future needs

Amer Shalaby, Wen Xun Hu, Mike Corby, Andrew Wong and Daniel Zhou

INTRODUCTION

Faster operational speed of surface transit vehicles is a highly desirable objective for both passengers and service providers (Vuchic, 2005). However, surface transit services are susceptible to delays due to a wide array of factors. Some are specific to the transit service, while other factors are external to transit operations. The "internal" factors include route configurations, demand characteristics, and fleet conditions. The "external" factors are related to traffic conditions, on-street parking regulations, intersection control treatments, road construction, incidents, and weather conditions. Table 16.1 provides an overview and a short discussion of these sources of delays.

Transit delays can have serious consequences such as longer travel and wait times for passengers, reliability issues (e.g., reduced on-time performance, headway variability and bunching), increased operational cost, and higher emissions. As such, reducing transit delays can benefit passengers and transit operators in a variety of ways. Passengers can benefit from faster service in terms of: (1) travel time savings for existing and potential transit users; (2) wait time savings; (3) improved comfort; and (4) more reliable service. The potential benefits to the transit operators include: (1) increased revenue from new passengers; and (2) reduced investment and operating cost.

Common strategies for reducing transit delay can be categorized into five main groups.

- *Vehicle design and performance* can be improved to increase the operating speed and reduce dwell time. A higher operating speed can be achieved by enhancing acceleration and deceleration performance. Vehicles with low floors, wide doors and efficient interior design can reduce passenger boarding and alighting times effectively.
- *Street and intersection designs* include corridor or site-specific measures, such as dedicated transit lanes, boarding islands/transit bays, curb extensions, queue jump lanes, etc. These measures can reduce transit delays due to the reduced interactions with the general traffic stream.
- *Accelerated operations* can improve speed through various route design strategies, including stop-skipping, expressing and zonal operation. These strategies are often applied to long transit lines with frequent service.
- *Transit stop relocation and consolidation* include widening the spacing between transit stops and alternating nearside and farside stops at corridors with synchronized traffic signals.
- *Transit Signal Priority (TSP)* can reduce signal delays experienced by transit vehicles at signallized intersections.

Table 16.1   *Causes of transit delays*

Category	Sources	Explanation
Internal factors	Route configurations	• Densely spaced stops lead to a higher proportion of time spent on acceleration, deceleration, and dwell time • Circuitous routes and turns are time-consuming
	Fare payment types	• Cash payment increases processing time per passenger compared to tokens, monthly passes, smart cards, off-board fare payments and proof-of-payment
	Demand characteristics	• High passenger load impacts interior circulation, thus increasing passenger service time at transit stops • High demand at stops increases dwell time
	Fleet conditions	• Vehicle type, age and maintenance practices affect vehicle acceleration, speed, and the probability of breakdown
External factors	Traffic conditions	• Slower transit speed and more frequent stops are observed with higher traffic volumes
	On-street parking regulations	• Kerbside parking reduces road capacity and interferes with transit vehicle operation
	Intersection control treatments	• Stop signs and traffic signals increase delays to transit vehicles due to more frequent acceleration, deceleration, and waiting • When traffic signal timing plans are designed exclusively for vehicle traffic flow, transit vehicles incur more delays
	Permissible turning movements	• At signallized intersections where right turning movements are allowed for the general traffic, right-turning vehicle queues often block buses from reaching kerbside stops on the nearside • Permissible left turning movements inflict delays on streetcars/trams travelling in the same lane
	Road construction and incidents	• Road construction and incidents reduce road capacity and adversely affect overall traffic and transit speed
	Weather conditions	• Poor weather conditions, such as snowstorms and heavy rainfall, cause road conditions to deteriorate and can cause transit delays

Other strategies include advanced fare collection systems, such as smart cards and proof-of-payment (off-vehicle payment), direct route layouts, street parking restrictions, yield-to-bus bylaws and driver training programs. Collectively, these measures can mitigate the sources of transit delay substantially.

The chapter is focused exclusively on Transit Signal Priority (TSP). The chapter starts with a detailed overview of TSP types, strategies and system architecture. Next, it presents a review of the TSP research literature and industry practices. Insights on successes and challenges in real-world implementations are also discussed. The chapter then provides a discussion on the lessons learned and possible future research directions, which are followed by concluding remarks.

OVERVIEW OF TSP: TYPES, STRATEGIES, SYSTEM COMPONENTS AND ARCHITECTURE

TSP is one of the key and most widely implemented measures to improve transit speed. Traffic signals have long been recognized as a major source of transit delays, accounting for 10–20 per cent of total travel time (Levinson, 2003) and as high as 25–33 per cent in dense urban centres (Levinson et al., 2003). More severe transit delays are observed in corridors with more densely located signallized intersections (Hu and Shalaby, 2017). TSP has received growing attention since the late 1960s with successful implementations in many cities worldwide. TSP reduces signal delay by modifying the original signal plan (e.g., the start and end time of signal phases,[1] and the sequence of phases) to expedite the passage of transit vehicles through intersections. The most commonly applied signal adjustments include green extension and red truncation. Applications in Toronto and Melbourne on streetcar operations found travel time savings ranging between 6 per cent and 10 per cent due to TSP (Currie and Shalaby, 2008). Experiences in bus operations indicate an average of 15 per cent travel time savings with a maximum reduction of around 25 per cent (e.g., Los Angeles, California), and a maximum signal delay reduction of around 40 per cent (e.g., Tacoma, Washington) (Smith et al., 2005).

This section presents an overview of the various types of TSP control and associated strategies, followed by a discussion of the relevant communication standards, key TSP system components and TSP architecture.

TSP Control Types

There are three main types or forms of TSP, namely: passive, active and adaptive TSP. These are discussed in the following sub-sections.

Passive Transit Signal Priority

Passive TSP is a static type of TSP that does not require a detection system for monitoring the arrivals of transit vehicles at signallized intersections. Passive TSP makes permanent adjustments to the signal timing plan in favour of the transit operation. The performance of passive TSP is greatly affected by variations in the passenger loads, dwell times and general traffic sharing the route. Therefore, passive priority is best implemented along routes with highly predictable transit performance.

Examples of passive TSP include the design of offsets according to transit movements as opposed to general traffic flow, and the provision of additional green time to a phase serving a transit movement that would not be provided otherwise based on traffic demand alone (Stewart and Wong, 2013).

When transit vehicles operate in an exclusive or semi-exclusive right of way, the benefits of coordinating signals for transit vehicles can be more significant, since transit operations are more consistent than in mixed traffic conditions. The main strategies of passive TSP include:

- *Adjustment of cycle length*[2] involves reducing the duration of non-transit serving phases and, as a result, reducing the overall cycle length. The benefit to transit resulting from this strategy is the provision of more opportunities for transit vehicles to clear the intersection. However, this strategy can increase vehicle delay on competing intersection approaches.

- *Splitting phases* involves splitting the phase serving the transit movement into two (or more) phases within a signal cycle. No reduction in cycle length is implemented.
- *Green wave* (area-wide timing plan/signal linking) sets the signal offset values based on the route timetable to enable preferential progression of transit vehicles in a coordinated signal system. This method uses information on transit travel time and dwell time between signalized intersections.

Active Transit Signal Priority

Active TSP makes temporary adjustments to the signal timing plan upon the detection of an approaching transit vehicle. Active TSP can be unconditional or conditional. Unconditional TSP provides priority to all detected buses irrespective of transit operational status. Conditional TSP grants priority only to transit vehicles that meet pre-specified criteria.

Conditional TSP, in a broad sense, uses conditions that are transit- or non-transit-related. Commonly used transit-related criteria include schedule adherence, headway performance and passenger load, while non-transit-related criteria include vehicular and pedestrian safety required intervals, time-of-day restrictions and time since the last priority request. Conditional TSP in this chapter refers strictly to those that use only transit-related criteria.

Unconditional TSP systems can be sub-divided into restrained and unrestrained types. Restrained unconditional TSP provides priority each time it is requested, but after non-transit-related criteria are satisfied (e.g., elapsed time since the last priority request, time of day). An unrestricted unconditional TSP (sometimes referred to as "Absolute TSP") does not have any transit or non-transit-related criteria that limit the activation of transit priority. This latter type is rarely implemented.

Various strategies of active TSP may be applied, including green extension, red truncation, actuated transit phase, phase rotation and phase skipping.

- *Green extension* strategy extends the duration of the green interval to provide extra length for a detected transit vehicle to clear the intersection. Extensions are granted in short intervals as needed, but they get terminated if a maximum extension threshold is reached. As such, the total green extension time per request is variable in nature.
- *Red truncation* (early green) strategy reduces the duration of the red phase to shorten the time left for the return of the next green interval serving the detected transit vehicle. The truncated time of the red phase is often a fixed interval.
- *Actuated transit phase* is often used with other transit-related treatments, such as exclusive left-turn lane for transit vehicles or queue jump lane. Actuated transit phases are only displayed when transit vehicles are detected, for example on an exclusive left-turn lane or queue jump lane. In the latter case, a transit phase is provided immediately before the normal green at intersections with queue jump lanes and nearside stops to avoid merging conflicts of transit vehicles with the general traffic. In these cases, a transit phase is inserted as an additional phase to the normal signal sequence (i.e., *phase insertion*).

- *Phase rotation* modifies the sequence of the normal signal phases. It intends to provide the green interval to a detected transit vehicle earlier in the signal cycle to facilitate faster clearance through the intersection (e.g., reversing a lagging left turn phase into a leading phase following the detection of a left turning bus).
- *Phase skipping* (phase suppression) omits non-priority phases to allow faster clearance of transit vehicles through the intersection. The skipped phase may be served later.

The green extension and red truncation are the most commonly implemented forms of active TSP. All strategies should comply with the minimum phase duration (considering all road users) and maximum green time constraints typically imposed by the traffic control system. It is also fairly common to impose the restriction that only one transit vehicle/request is served with priority per cycle.

In corridors where traffic signal coordination for general traffic already exists, the pre-programmed coordination offsets[3] could be broken due to a TSP event. Offset recovery strategies are often applied to restore the correct offset value after a TSP strategy has been implemented. In order to return to the desired offset, the traffic signal may adjust the phase timings of the next cycle, generally by either extending or reducing the green time of various phases based on the offset correction mode selected. The aggressiveness and length of the recovery period vary by jurisdiction with respect to the restrictions imposed on timing adjustments as well as the signal controller's inherent capabilities. The maximum extension and reduction times are also defined to allow the traffic signal to transition back to the coordinated mode within two to three cycles.

Adaptive Transit Signal Priority

This is a relatively advanced type of TSP that adapts the signal timing of the transit serving phase in accordance with the performance characteristics of the approaching transit vehicle in order to achieve improved transit speed and reliability and/or overall corridor traffic benefits.

Adaptive TSP that aims at optimizing transit performance only can be thought of as an advanced version of conditional TSP. Compared to conditional TSP which is criteria-oriented (based on binary Yes/No rules), adaptive TSP is more objective-oriented. It aims at providing an optimal solution to the predefined objective function that is adaptive to the real-time transit and/or traffic conditions. It determines the magnitude of priority required to achieve the desired objective(s) such as minimizing transit delays and/or maximizing headway regularity.

The second type of adaptive TSP includes TSP methods integrated within adaptive traffic signal control systems, such as SCOOT (Split Cycle Offset Optimization Technique).[4] Under this type, signal timings are adjusted in real time in accordance with the magnitudes and performance characteristics of traffic flows and transit movements at all approaches of the signallized intersection, providing a balanced solution that minimizes the overall transit and traffic delays.

Key Components of Active and Adaptive TSP Systems

The fundamental components of any active or adaptive TSP system include a Priority Request Generator (PRG), a Priority Request Server (PRS), and a Coordinator (CO).

TSP systems typically involve interactions between transit vehicles, the detection system, the traffic signal controller, and potentially the fleet management centre and the traffic management centre (Smith et al., 2005). Each component is described briefly next.

The detection system serves to detect transit vehicles approaching and clearing a signallized intersection. Common detection technologies include loop detection (i.e., in-pavement loop detector and vehicle mounted transponder), infrared detection (i.e., vehicle mounted infrared emitter and infrared detector at intersections), sound-based detection, radio-based detection (i.e., vehicle mounted radio frequency (RF) transponder and RF tag reader at intersections), GPS-based detection and emerging Connected Vehicle (CV) based detection.

The PRG is responsible for generating single or multiple priority requests and can be physically located at different locations (e.g., at the fleet management centre, on the fleet vehicles, at the traffic management centre, within a roadside cabinet, or within the traffic signal controller) (AASHTO, ITE and NEMA, 2014). More discussion on the different options and associated system configurations is presented in the section on TSP Architecture. The PRG sends single or multiple requests of priority to the PRS.

The PRS processes the requests received from the PRG(s) and communicates the request to the CO, which is an integral part of a traffic signal controller, based on predefined TSP control strategies. The PRS can optionally generate logs of all priority requests received and processed.

The CO receives the service requests from the PRS. Depending on the TSP criteria, the CO may or may not adjust the traffic signal settings for transit vehicle prioritization. The CO can also optionally generate logs of all priority requests received and processed.

The Transit Fleet Management Centre's role varies in accordance with the specific architecture that a given TSP system is using. Depending on the source and type of data to receive, there are typically four options (AASHTO, ITE and NEMA, 2014):

- The fleet management centre receives transit vehicle location data from a tracking system, generates priority requests and communicates them to the traffic management centre. This corresponds to the case where the PRG is situated in the fleet management centre.
- The fleet management centre receives transit vehicle location data and sends it to the PRG located in the traffic management centre.
- The fleet management centre receives priority requests from the PRG located in the fleet vehicle and sends it to the traffic management centre.
- The fleet management centre has no functional role.

The Traffic Management Centre, serving primarily as an intermediate agent, receives data or requests from the fleet management centre or the vehicle. Only in the scenario where the PRG is located in the traffic management centre does it fulfill the role of a PRG instead of acting as an intermediary.

Communication System

The PRG, PRS and other components of the TSP system are connected through a communication system, which could be of two types depending on the system's architecture.

The first type provides local communication between transit vehicles and local signal controllers located at intersections via one of the detection technologies outlined in the previous section. The second type provides centralized communication between individual intersections and the fleet/traffic management centres via fibre optic cables or wireless technology. Applications vary among jurisdictions that may require one type or both, depending on the architecture of the TSP system.

TSP Communication Standards

To realize transit preferential treatment under active and adaptive TSP, data and information exchange among multiple components and possibly management centres is required. There are two widely used communication industry standards that are key to TSP field implementation: NTCIP (National Transportation Communications for Intelligent Transportation System (ITS) Protocol) and TCIP (Standard for Transit Communications Interface Profiles). These standards are used as a basis for the method and format of communications between different components of a TSP system.

Given the current interest and push for Connected Vehicles (CV) within the transportation and automotive industry, CV Standards are an emerging topic. Since TSP is one application of CVs through a vehicle to infrastructure (V2I) connection, the TSP industry may be significantly influenced by established CV Standards.

By adhering to a standard-based approach, transit agencies can leverage interoperability (allowing various devices to share a common communications network) and interchangeability (allowing competing vendor products to operate within the same network) within their respective systems. A brief summary of the three standards is provided below:

- The *NTCIP* provides standards to allow for seamless communication among electronic traffic control equipment from different manufacturers to work in the same system (NTCIP, 2014). The NTCIP 1211 (Object Definitions for Signal Control and Prioritization) Version 2 (v02) standard provides the base of and definitions related to the management information of TSP systems through individual parameters that represent the configuration, status, and control information (AASHTO, ITE and NEMA, 2014). NTCIP 2306 (Application Profile for Extensible Markup Language (XML) Message Encoding and Transport in ITS C2C Communications) pertain specifically to the operation and design of TSP systems.
- The *TCIP* is an American Public Transportation Association (APTA) Standard that defines the standardized mechanisms for the exchange of information/data to allow transit agencies and TSP suppliers to create standardized tailored interfaces (USDOT, n.d.). The TCIP WG (Working Group) 10 addresses the transit portions of the NTCIP as it relates to TSP (Y. Li et al., 2008). This standard provides the building blocks for interfaces for various business areas, including TSP.
- The *CV Standards* aim at standardizing software programming codes and formats such that data outputs from individual components of a connected system can be seamlessly interpreted by a shared information system. Fundamentally, it establishes rules on how ITS (Intelligent Transportation Systems) devices, vehicles and management centres are to communicate and how the communication logs

should be stored. The standard applies to both vehicle-to-vehicle (V2V) and vehicle-to-infrastructure (V2I) communications; TSP is considered a form of V2I communication.

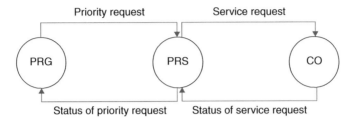

Figure 16.1   General TSP architecture

TSP Architecture

While the industry standards mentioned above ensure seamless communication among components of TSP systems, the TSP architecture defines the framework within which all components (fleet vehicle, PRG, PRS, CO/traffic signal controller, fleet management centre, traffic management centre, and intermediary entities) would operate as a system. There are six alternative physical architectures of TSP systems illustrated in NTCIP 1211 v02. These architectures vary primarily with respect to the physical locations of the PRG and PRS. However, there exist other configurations that only contain PRG or PRS as logical components. In general, to complete a priority service the following steps should be performed (Figure 16.1):

- A (logical or physical) PRG sends a priority request to the PRS.
- The PRS receives the priority request.
- The PRS processes and resolves the priority request(s).
- The PRS sends the status of each priority request back to the PRG.
- The PRS sends the service request(s) to a CO.
- The PRS may log events (of all priority requests received and the service requests exchanged with CO) and send them to the traffic management centre.
- The CO processes the service request(s).
- The CO responds to the PRS with the status of the service request(s).
- The CO implements the priority strategy.
- The CO may log events (of all service requests received and the priority strategies implemented) and send them to the traffic management centre.

The TSP architectures in Figures 16.2, 16.3 and 16.4 share the same configuration for the communication path between PRG, PRS and CO. The differences are with respect to:

- The physical location of the PRG;
- The location of PRS;
- The communication paths linking the PRG and PRS (and whether the management centres are involved).

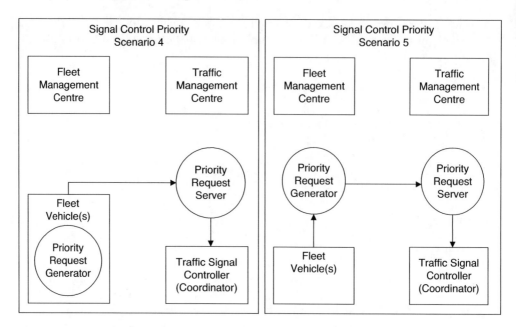

Figure 16.2   V2I system architecture examples (NTCIP, 2017)

Based on the communication paths, TSP system architectures are separated into V2I, C2C and C2I systems.

- *Vehicle-to-Infrastructure (V2I):* V2I systems are a form of distributed system architecture. The PRG is located within the transit vehicle or on the roadside, while the PRS is generally on the roadside. There is direct communication between the vehicle and roadside equipment, while the transit and traffic management centres play no role in TSP systems with such architecture. This setup is commonly used in North America. Moreover, although the TSP communication is a V2I design, the PRS may be embedded in the central traffic signal central system within the traffic management centre, rather than the roadside traffic signal controller. Figure 16.2 illustrates the standard V2I system architectures as per NTCIP scenarios where the PRS is located on the roadside.
- *Centre-to-Centre (C2C):* C2C type systems are a subset of centralized architectures as the PRG and PRS are located within the management centres. Transit vehicles first communicate with the transit fleet management centre, which then relays the priority request to the traffic management centre. The traffic management centre then communicates with the roadside traffic signal controller to initiate TSP. The link between the two management centres is what separates this approach from others. The C2C approach may be cheaper in terms of equipment cost as there is a centralized PRG and PRS unit such that they do not need to be installed on every transit vehicle and TSP enabled intersection. To achieve this, the data exchange messages between management centres have to be well defined and published as a data dictionary. In the current industry, the majority of the ITS elements are

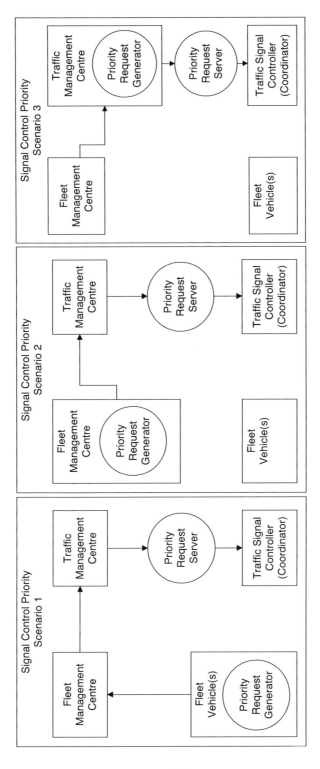

Figure 16.3   C2C system architecture examples (NTCIP, 2017)

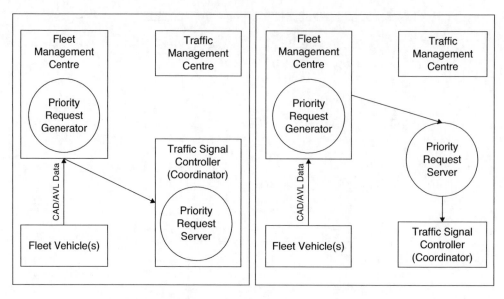

Figure 16.4   C2I system architecture examples

compliant with NTCIP standards. Figure 16.3 illustrates standard C2C system architectures as per NTCIP scenarios; note that it is more common for the PRG to be located in the fleet management centre or on the transit vehicle.

- *Centre-to-Infrastructure (C2I):* A C2I system can be regarded as a mix between C2C and V2I systems. Like a C2C system, transit vehicles communicate with a centralized PRG located in the transit fleet management centre, which communicates directly with roadside PRS units, and the traffic management centre is not involved. This is a modified design as per the scenarios established in the NTCIP 1211. Figure 16.4 illustrates common C2I system architectures in the industry.

REVIEW OF INDUSTRY PRACTICES AND RESEARCH LITERATURE

Early pilot projects and research on TSP date back to the 1960s, following the first field experiment of TSP in Los Angeles County, California. Since then, TSP has been adopted by an increasing number of cities worldwide for signal delay reduction. In the meantime, a plethora of research studies have been conducted to improve TSP control algorithms, propose new ones and evaluate emerging control strategies. The evolution of industry deployments and research developments in TSP over the past few decades have been largely driven by the rapid advancements in CAD/AVL, detection, communication and CV technologies. These trends created a continuous need for novel TSP methodologies to harness the power and capabilities of the new technologies. The next few sections summarize the evolution of industry deployments[5] and research efforts over the past few decades, with more focus placed on literature since 2000. The general trends in the evolution of TSP deployments and academic literature are summarized broadly in Table 16.2.

Table 16.2   *Evolution of TSP deployments and research*

Period	Industry Deployments	Research Literature Emphasis	Common Technology
1970s–1980s	Demonstration projects	Findings from demonstration projects	
1990s	First-generation TSP (unconditional TSP)	Unconditional and conditional TSP	Loop detectors
2000s	Second-generation TSP (conditional TSP)	Conditional and adaptive TSP, with reduced emphasis on unconditional TSP	AVL
	Third-generation TSP (advanced TSP)		AVL and CV

The 1970s and 1980s

The 1970s witnessed a booming interest in a variety of transit/HOV (high-occupancy vehicle) preferential treatments, and TSP was one of them. The field applications in the 1970s were mainly demonstration projects of passive or unconditional TSPs (El-Reedy and Ashworth, 1978; Vincent et al., 1978), while various research studies reported results of these projects and evaluations of the effectiveness of TSP in reducing transit delays. These studies also explored challenges and side-effects of this rising technology.

A large proportion of projects and studies in the 1970s focused on bus pre-emption strategies instead of TSP. The former type suspends the normal traffic signal plan to provide a special control mode for transit vehicles as defined in the NTCIP 1202 version 2 (Smith et al., 2005), which is more interruptive than TSP. However, TSP applications in the early years were referred to frequently as pre-emption treatments (e.g., Benevelli et al., 1983). At that time, the development of TSP control was significantly limited by communication technologies.

The earliest TSP experiment was demonstrated in Los Angeles County in 1967, in which signal priorities were manually activated by staff at two intersections. Green extension and red truncation were applied at the time. This experiment showed a reduction in the average bus trip time of 10–20 per cent (Evans and Skiles, 1970).

Demonstration projects were also established in Sacramento, California; Nice, France; Miami, Florida; and Concord, California. These projects provided field data for evaluations of early TSP systems which were reported in Elias (1976), Cottinet (1977), Wattleworth et al. (1977) and TJKM (1978), respectively. These studies showed the ability of TSP in reducing transit delays, albeit with increased delays incurred by the side street traffic.

However, data collected from field experiments to support further exploration of TSP possibilities were very limited. Researchers started to use other tools, including simulation models (e.g., Ludwick, 1975; 1976; Lieberman et al., 1978; Salter and Shahi, 1979; Benevelli et al., 1983) and analytical models (e.g., Jacobson and Sheffi, 1981; Yedlin and Lieberman, 1981; Radwan and Hurley Jr, 1982). In the 1970s and 1980s, the utilization of simulations for research purposes and at the design stage of TSP was restricted by the inherent level of complexity and the cost associated with simulation (Jacobson and Sheffi, 1981).

The 1990s

The pilot projects and research studies from the 1970s to 1980s justified the benefits and pointed out challenges of TSP, which laid a foundation for large-scale TSP implementations in the industry in the 1990s. The active TSP systems deployed in the 1990s, typically unconditional TSP, are considered the first-generation TSP deployments in the industry.

First-generation TSP
The unconditional TSP deployed in the 1990s had two common characteristics: (1) transit vehicle detection technology relied on transponders with loop detectors (embedded in the roadway pavement) or infrared emitters/receivers as a form of V2I communication; (2) transit vehicles generated priority requests regardless of the vehicle's operational characteristics.

While unconditional TSP is beneficial to transit vehicle travel time, under some conditions, the following issues were observed (Corby and Wong, 2016):

- Due to the inability of the system to distinguish between transit vehicles, vehicles running behind schedule may not receive higher priority over upstream on-time vehicles, which may result in reliability issues.
- For effective transit services along TSP enabled corridors/routes, only transit vehicles with the appropriate equipment (e.g., transponders, infrared emitters) installed could be used and assigned. Hence, transit agencies had reduced flexibility in vehicle scheduling.
- Damage to TSP infrastructure during road construction events, specifically loop detectors/antennae and associated feeder cables would limit and adversely impact the operation of TSP.
- Regular maintenance is required to keep infrared detection lenses aligned and cleaned.
- It is unable to effectively collect transit related data and diagnose issues related to the TSP system.
- It cannot provide TSP based on factors such as schedule adherence and number of onboard passengers, etc.

Operationally, these TSP systems had a fixed Priority Operating Zone (POZ)/detection zone, which is defined spatially between an upstream location where the transit priority request (i.e., check-in point) is issued and the location where the transit vehicle clears the signallized intersection (i.e., check-out point). When a transit vehicle has checked in, a priority request is sent through the transit vehicle detection system to the roadside traffic signal controller. The traffic signal controller then uses a TSP algorithm to advance the transit vehicle through the signallized intersection. This type of TSP system operates unconditionally and does not take into account a transit vehicle's lateness when approving priority requests. Currently, the Toronto Transit Commission (TTC) in Canada still operates an unconditional TSP system, which has a transponder-based transit vehicle detection system (City of Toronto, n.d.) for both buses and streetcars.

Research studies of the 1990s

A sizable body of research work in that era focused on addressing the limitations of unconditional TSP, specifically the associated side-effects on transit performance and delays to the general traffic (Yagar and Han, 1994). Most notably, several studies developed conditional TSP control methods with priority decisions based on various performance indices (e.g. Al-Sahili and Taylo, 1995; Chang et al., 1995).

The noticeable advancement in technologies in the 1990s influenced TSP research efforts to some extent. The literature shows several studies on active TSP algorithms utilizing data transmitted from detection systems, such as induction loops (Bowen et al., 1994; Chang et al., 1996) and AVL syste35ms (Bowen et al., 1994). It is noteworthy that, unlike loop detectors which were prevalent in the 1990s, AVL systems were not widely implemented in the field and utilized in TSP applications until the 2000s.

The 2000s

The rapid advancements in detection, tracking and communication technologies over the past 20 years have fostered new opportunities for advancing TSP concepts and strategies, which have received considerable attention from the industry and research community. The industry deployments from the early 2000s until now have been mainly of the conditional TSP type, which is generally defined as the second-generation TSP. While the third-generation, advanced TSPs (including interoperable and adaptive TSP), have been implemented in some areas recently, they are still not the mainstream.

While TSP implementations in the field have mostly belonged to the second-generation conditional TSP, numerous research efforts have been undertaken to advance the state of the art in TSP systems using various analytical methods. In this section, the second- and third-generation TSPs are described, followed by a synthesis of the research studies over the past 20 years.

Second-generation TSP

Following research efforts and technological developments in the 1990s, conditional TSPs began to dominate the market in the early 2000s. As technology began to improve in the form of increased computing power/memory, GPS technology, and wireless communications, the TSP industry began adopting new technologies to enhance TSP system capabilities. The catalyst to these changes was the integration of CAD/AVL technology into the traditional TSP system.

CAD/AVL technology allowed transit operators to track and collect transit vehicle locations and event activities in real time. The availability of real-time transit data along with the improvements in communication technology allowed for the application of conditional TSP logic. Using data feeds from CAD/AVL equipment as well as onboard equipment (e.g., door movements, stop request push button or pull chords, automated passenger counters, etc.), TSP systems had the capability to determine which specific vehicles should be granted a TSP call (e.g., by vehicle ID, by vehicle type) and when a priority request should be activated, cancelled, or re-activated. For example, the TSP call can be cancelled when the transit door is open and reactivated when the transit door is closed. The advancements in communications technology also provided the option for a centralized PRG and PRS configuration, which reduced the amount of required roadside and vehicular onboard equipment.

Individual traffic/transit agencies have used conditional TSP logic that is unique to their system, but all systems have generally exhibited the following characteristics:

- The transit agency may define various TSP priority strategies based on time-of-day, day-of-week needs, vehicle condition, vehicle type, or a combination of factors.
- CAD/AVL technology is used to collect and communicate transit vehicle operation information (i.e., vehicle location, schedule adherence, estimated arrival time, and vehicle occupancy) to the PRG.
- The CAD/AVL system may either continuously communicate with the PRG to determine the priority or only provide information at pre-defined locations, known as "timing points".
- The communication among PRG, PRS and CO follows one of the TSP architecture scenarios demonstrated in Figures 16.2, 16.3 and 16.4.
- There is a high level of flexibility for the type of system architecture that can be implemented. Conditional TSP systems can function as V2I, C2C, or C2I.
- The system has less impact on general traffic and pedestrian operations, as TSP is only provided when necessary (i.e., when predetermined conditions are met). Conditional TSP allows jurisdictions to better align themselves with their overarching roadway hierarchy (e.g., general traffic vs. transit vehicles vs. pedestrians vs. cyclists).

The conditional TSP implemented in York Region, Canada, demonstrates the basic principles of the conditional TSP system, which is common in North America. Using transit vehicle information provided by the CAD/AVL system, the Region developed two priority levels with respect to its schedule delay that dictated the amount of TSP green extension time a transit vehicle would receive (York Region, 2010). The same CAD/AVL system with conditional TSP of the York Region has also been implemented in some cities in Europe and Asia.

The most used criterion for granting priority under conditional TSP has been schedule adherence (i.e., TSP granted to late buses only). Cities including but not limited to Oakland and Los Angeles, USA; Cardiff, UK; Genoa, Italy; Helsinki, Finland; Toulouse, France; and Sydney, Australia have implemented conditional TSP systems that serve priority for late buses (Lin et al., 2015).

Although this system represented a significant improvement over the first generation, there are still issues from a transit planning and operational perspective. Second-generation systems typically rely on proprietary system components that vary by vendor. Consequently, transit vehicles that cross municipal boundaries may not benefit from TSP services provided by other jurisdictions if they use different vendor equipment. To overcome this challenge, some transit agencies may install two onboard TSP systems with limited onboard storage available, or two roadside units. In addition, extra effort is often required to integrate the CAD/AVL system with the TSP detection system (both physical and software).

Third-generation TSP

The third-generation TSP includes interoperable TSP and adaptive TSP. The first type addresses the above-mentioned problem of the second-generation TSP and avoids the associated extra cost due to the doubling of the equipment to enable cross-boundary TSP service. The second type, Adaptive TSP, extends the capabilities of conditional TSP by providing tailored solutions in response to real-time transit and traffic conditions.

In the last 10 years, many jurisdictions began utilizing a standards-based approach to TSP deployments, using open communication protocols that are interoperable. An interoperable system implies that as long as a transit vehicle has the hardware to access the communication network, it is able to request a priority from the jurisdictions with TSP-enabled intersections given a common message set. An example of a standards-based TSP protocol is the CV standard. Operationally, the third-generation systems function in a similar manner to the second-generation TSP systems.

In Chicago, Illinois, the Regional Transportation Authority (RTA) developed a Regional Transit Signal Priority Implementation Program (RTSPIP) with multiple local transit and traffic agencies. The goal was to develop and implement a regionally interoperable TSP system. Through the programme, the region developed an open communication protocol establishing a V2I relationship between transit vehicles and roadside traffic signal controllers using wireless communication technologies. The programme also established a regional TSP message set that is compliant with NTCIP 1211 standards. This allows different transit operators within the region (both local and regional transit services) to request priority at any TSP-enabled intersection, as the entire region communicates using the same 5.9GHz and message set under the RTSPIP (RTA, n.d.). In addition, RTA also released a virtual PRG-PRS testing tool to help traffic signal control and CAD/AVL vendors to meet the open communication protocol standards prior to field testing and implementation.

The Utah Department of Transportation (UDOT) in the USA has been actively involved in CV testing and implementation. This is an example of early application of leading-edge standards-based TSP using CV technologies. The UDOT uses their new multi-modal signal control system to broadcast Signal Phasing and Timing (SPaT) data to support TSP operations to improve transit reliability (Felice, 2018).

Field applications of adaptive TSP have mostly been of the second type mentioned in the section "Adaptive Transit Priority", namely TSP algorithms integrated with adaptive traffic signal control systems. We are still in the early stage of large-scale applications of adaptive TSP systems. This would be a gradual process evolving from the second-generation TSP. The common practice now is integrating adaptive traffic signal control systems with the second-generation, conditional TSP.

The Public Transport Information & Priority Systems (PTIPS) in Melbourne, Australia was implemented to provide conditional priority to trams over general traffic in an effort to improve transit service reliability. PTIPS is integrated with the Sydney Coordinated Adaptive Traffic System (SCATS), which is an adaptive signal control system that allows for the communication of bus information to traffic signal controllers (Corby and Wong, 2016). Since 2008, all 600 signallized intersection serving trams are equipped with both PTIPS and SCATS.

The integration of conditional TSP with adaptive traffic signal control system can be also found in London, UK. Transport for London (TfL) has procured an AVL system for fleet management, passenger information and TSP, which is known as iBUS (Bowen et al., 2007). The TSP system in London is integrated with the SCOOT-based Urban Traffic Control (UTC) system, which uses differential priority that determines the priority level request on the basis of bus headway regularity (Hounsell and Shrestha, 2005).

Research studies of the 2000s
The rapid advancement in TSP technologies and field implementations over the past 20 years has been paralleled, and in part informed, by a plethora of research studies that aimed at advancing TSP concepts and strategies.

The large body of knowledge produced by research studies over the past 20 years is reviewed in this section. Table 16.3 summarizes the TSP literature since 2000 based on a review of 80 TSP papers/reports, although only 45 are reported in the table. These consist mainly of research papers proposing new TSP algorithms or those evaluating the performance of existing TSP systems. The latter category includes only articles with sufficient details on the TSP algorithms under evaluation.

The TSP types included in this review are active TSP (unconditional and conditional) and adaptive TSP. Passive TSP is excluded as it has received little attention in recent years, with the exception of a few cases where both passive and active TSP were implemented at different intersections along the same corridor (e.g., Kim et al., 2018). The TSP studies are further categorized in terms of: (1) vehicle location technology which is one of the key system components that determines the type of data available and hence influences the choice of TSP algorithm; (2) scale of the TSP system, which reflects its complexity with respect to coordination among opposite directions and among adjacent intersections; (3) strategy used which specifies which signal phases were modified to provide priority and how; (4) methodological approach applied to achieve the desired objectives; and (5) evaluation method for assessing the effectiveness of TSP and its impact on other road users.

Table 16.3 is intended to summarize the recent research trends, extract insights and identify gaps and recommendations for future research. Cells with larger numbers of articles represent areas that have attracted more attention over the past 20 years. For example, reading the table vertically, it can be observed that many research studies focused on conditional TSP, among which loop detectors were the most used technology for transit vehicle detection (more information is provided in the sub-section "Technology" below).

Table 16.3 is also able to imply relationships between the abovementioned categories. For example, reading the table horizontally, it is apparent that traditional strategies (e.g., green extension, red truncation and phase insertion) were less frequently used in adaptive TSP. The length and sequence of phases were more often adjusted to provide more flexible control (more information is provided in the sub-section "Strategy" below). To provide another example, AI methods were mainly applied in adaptive TSP. The sub-sections below provide a summary and analysis of Table 16.3 with a discussion of the most noticeable trends.

TSP control type Unconditional TSP, the first-generation TSP in field deployments (section "First-generation TSP"), has featured less frequently in research efforts since 2000. Some studies of this type of priority introduced new features to the algorithms for more advanced priority control, such as travel time/arrival prediction models and performance indices capturing conflicting requests.

Table 16.3   Summary of TSP literature since 2000

		Active TSP		Adaptive TSP
		Unconditional TSP	Conditional TSP	
Technology	detector	(Dion and Rakha, 2005) (Lee et al., 2005)* (Kim and Rilett, 2005)* (Muthuswamy et al., 2007) (Zlatkovic et al., 2012)* (Ding et al., 2015)*	(Janos and Furth, 2002)* (Wadjas and Furth, 2003)* (Li et al., 2007)* (Ma et al., 2010)* (Ma et al., 2013a)* (Ma et al., 2013b)* (Kim et al., 2018)*	(Liu et al., 2003)* (Ling and Shalaby, 2003)* (Zhou et al., 2007)* (Lee and Shalaby, 2013)* (Han et al., 2014)* (Zeng et al., 2014)* (Ghanim and Abu-Lebdeh, 2015)* (Hu et al., 2020)*
	AVL/GPS	(Ekeila et al., 2009)* (Lin et al., 2013)*	(Balke et al., 2000)* (Delgado et al., 2015)* (Zhou et al., 2017)* (Ye and Xu, 2017)* (Anderson and Daganzo, 2019)	(Liao and Davis, 2007)* (M. Li et al., 2008)* (Li et al., 2011)* (Ghanim and Abu-Lebdeh, 2015)* (Shabestary and Abdulhai, 2019)*
	CV	(He et al., 2011)*	(Hu et al., 2014)* (Hu et al., 2015)* (Hu et al., 2016)*	(He et al., 2014)* (Zeng et al., 2015)*
Scale	multi-directional	(Zlatkovic et al., 2012)* (Lin et al., 2013)* (Xu et al., 2016)*	(Wadjas and Furth, 2003)* (Ma and Bai, 2008)* (Ma et al., 2013a)* (Ye and Xu, 2017)*	(M. Li et al., 2008)* (Christofa and Skabardonis, 2011)* (Zeng et al., 2015)*
	coordinated		(Li et al., 2007)* (Ma et al., 2010)* (Ma et al., 2013b)* (Hu et al., 2015)*	
Strategy	GE		(Delgado et al., 2015)*: GE, holding control	
	GE, RT	(Dion and Rakha, 2005) (Muthuswamy et al., 2007) (Stevanovic et al., 2008)* (Lin et al., 2013)* (Xu et al., 2016)*	(Wadjas and Furth, 2003)* (Ma et al., 2013b)* (Ye and Xu, 2017)* (Kim et al., 2018)*	(Liao and Davis, 2007)* (M. Li et al., 2008)* (He et al., 2014)* (Han et al., 2014)*

Table 16.3   (continued)

Method	Active TSP		Adaptive TSP
	Unconditional TSP	Conditional TSP	
GE, RT, phase insertion	(Kim and Rilett, 2005)*; (Ekeila et al., 2009)*: *GE, RT, cycle extension*; (Zlatkovic et al., 2012)*: *GE, RT, phase rotation*; (Shi et al., 2017)*	(Balke et al., 2000)*; (Ma and Bai, 2008)*; (Zhou et al., 2017)*	
GE, RT, GT	(Lee et al., 2005)*	(Janos and Furth, 2002)*	(Lee and Shalaby, 2013)*: *GE, RT, GT, queue clearance*; (Hu et al., 2020)*: *GE, GT*
other	(He et al., 2011)*; (Ding et al., 2015)*	(Li et al., 2007)*: *offset, lengths of green*; (Ma et al., 2010)*: *GE, RT, phase insertion, GT, RE*; (Ma et al., 2013a)*; (Hu et al., 2014)*: *green reallocation*; (Hu et al., 2015)*: *green reallocation*; (Hu et al., 2016)*: *green reallocation*	(Liu et al., 2003)*: *green reallocation*; (Ling and Shalaby, 2003)*: *length of EW/NS green*; (Zhou et al., 2007)*; (Christofa and Skabardonis, 2011)*: *green reallocation*; (Li et al., 2011)*: *length of green*; (Ghanim and Abu-Lebdeh, 2015)*; (Shabestary and Abdulhai, 2019)*
rule-based TSP control logic	(Dion and Rakha, 2005); (Zlatkovic et al., 2012)*; (Lin et al., 2013)*	(Janos and Furth, 2002)*; (Kim, Cheng and Chang, 2018)*	

rule-based TSP with arrival/ travel time prediction model	(Lee et al., 2005)* (Kim and Rilett, 2005)* (Muthuswamy et al., 2007)	(Balke, Dudek and Urbanik II, 2000)* (Wadjas and Furth, 2003)* (Hu et al., 2014)* (Zhou et al., 2017)*	(Liao and Davis, 2007)* (Lee and Shalaby, 2013)*
mathematical programming	(Ding et al., 2015)*: *fuzzy compromise approach* (Xu et al., 2016)* (Shi et al., 2017)*	(Li et al., 2007)* (Ma et al., 2010)* (Ma et al., 2013b)* (Delgado et al., 2015)* (Hu et al., 2015)* (Hu et al., 2016)* (Ye and Xu, 2017)* (Ma et al., 2013a)*	(M. Li et al., 2008)* (Christofa and Skabardonis, 2011)* (Li et al., 2011)* (He et al., 2014)* (Han et al., 2014)* (Zeng et al., 2014)* (Zeng et al., 2015)* (Liu et al., 2003)* (Mirchandani and Lucas, 2004)* (Ghanim and Abu-Lebdeh, 2015)* (Ling and Shalaby, 2003)*: *RL* (Zhou et al., 2007)*: *parallel GA* (Ghanim and Abu-Lebdeh, 2015)*: *GA* (Shabestary and Abdulhai, 2019)*: *Deep RL* (Hu et al., 2020)*: *Deep RL*
dynamic programming	(Ekeila et al., 2009)*		
AI	(Stevanovic et al., 2008)*: *GA*		
other	(He et al., 2011)*: *heuristic algorithm*	(Ma and Bai, 2008)*: *decision trees*	

Table 16.3   (continued)

		Active TSP		Adaptive TSP
		Unconditional TSP	Conditional TSP	
Evaluation	HIL simulation simulation	(Zlatkovic et al., 2012)*: *software-in-the-loop*	(Balke et al., 2000)*	(Liu et al., 2003)*
		(Lee et al., 2005)*	(Skabardonis, 2000)*	(M. Li et al., 2008)*
		(Kim and Rilett, 2005)*	(Janos and Furth, 2002)*	(Ling and Shalaby, 2003)*
		(Muthuswamy et al., 2007)	(Wadjas and Furth, 2003)*	(Mirchandani and Lucas, 2004)*
		(Stevanovic et al., 2008)*	(Li et al., 2007)*	(Liao and Davis, 2007)*
		(Ekeila et al., 2009)*	(Ma et al., 2013b)*	(Zhou et al., 2007)*
		(He et al., 2011)*	(Ma et al., 2013a)*	(Christofa and Skabardonis, 2011)*
		(Lin et al., 2013)*	(Hu et al., 2014)*	(Lee and Shalaby, 2013)*
		(Ding et al., 2015)*	(Delgado et al., 2015)*	(He et al., 2014)*
		(Xu et al., 2016)*	(Hu et al., 2015)*	(Han et al., 2014)*
			(Hu et al., 2016)*	(Zeng et al., 2014)*
			(Zhou et al., 2017)*	(Ghanim and Abu-Lebdeh, 2015)*
			(Kim et al., 2018)*	(Zeng et al., 2015)*
				(Shabestary and Abdulhai, 2019)*
				(Hu et al., 2020)*
	field test	(Shi et al., 2017)*	(Furth and Muller, n.d.)	(Liu et al., 2003)*
			(Ma et al., 2010)*	(M. Li et al., 2008)*
			(Ye and Xu, 2017)*	

Notes:
* Paper/report proposed new TSP strategies, otherwise implemented TSP strategies in the field were evaluated.
GT: green truncation.
Papers/reports which do not strictly belong to the assigned category are supplemented with additional explanations; in the cells of AI methods, the specific methods used are noted to provide additional information.
Only the papers/reports that included a control logic for conflicting requests are placed in the "multi-directional TSP" category. All papers/reports not categorized as "multi-directional TSP" are considered uni-directional.

Conditional TSP has been more prevalent in the literature, corresponding to the second-generation TSP described earlier (section "Second-generation TSP"). On the research front, there was a noticeable emphasis of developing more detailed criteria for assessing the conditions under which TSP should be granted to maximize the benefits. Similar to the industry practice, the most frequently investigated criterion in conditional TSP research studies has been based on schedule adherence (on-time performance). Other criteria were related to vehicle headway maintenance and occupancy, while roadside criteria included time since the last priority and time of day.

While on-time performance is an appropriate reliability measure for medium to low frequency lines, service reliability of high-frequency lines is better measured by headway regularity. This measure has been considered in very few studies of conditional TSP compared to on-time performance. Similar patterns are observed in the industry. One exception is the London iBUS TSP system, which is among the very few deployments that take into account headway performance as a criterion for conditional TSP.

Another criterion frequently used in conditional TSP since 2000 is based on whether the target transit vehicle is predicted to clear the intersection during the maximum priority window. This criterion addresses a critical concern in the operation of TSP systems, namely "failed priority", which occurs when the granted priority is not utilized by the target transit vehicle to clear the intersection. Failed priority clearly inflicts unnecessary delays on side street traffic without benefiting the transit movement. However, the effectiveness of this type of TSP system requires an accurate prediction model of bus travel time/arrival time at the stop line (more details on this topic are provided in the sub-section "Method").

In addition to conditional TSP, there has been a significant amount of effort made towards the development of adaptive TSP systems. The first type of adaptive TSP reacts adaptively to real-time transit performance by determining the optimal signal timing plan for a predefined objective (e.g., Hu et al., 2020). The second type of adaptive TSP endeavours to balance transit and traffic delays, commonly by applying weight factors to represent the importance of transit relative to traffic. Weights can be dependent on the number of passengers onboard or vehicle lateness. Adaptive TSP also resolves issues related to excessive delays incurred by non-prioritized traffic. Moreover, these TSP systems can potentially overcome the drawbacks of active TSP, which are not capable of reacting to real-time variations in traffic flows (Ekeila et al., 2009).

Technology Detection technologies are essential to active and adaptive TSP systems for feeding transit location information to the control module, based on which priority service is initialized. Induction loop detectors were most commonly considered in the literature, in line with early field implementations. However, detectors are only able to provide discrete detection times. Variabilities along the route are not captured. AVL/GPS and CV technologies have received a growing attention in recent research studies for their capability of providing continuous real-time data to support more robust TSP control logic. This is also the ongoing trend in the industry where many major cities around the world have introduced AVL systems (Hounsell et al., 2012).

Scale Conflicting priority requests from multiple transit lines and/or directions have been considered by a growing number of research studies, which are categorized in the table as "multi-directional TSP". The capability of handling conflicting priority requests is clearly crucial at intersections with multiple transit lines and in multiple directions. The traditional First-Come-First-Served (FCFS) logic may not be the optimal choice if, for example, the priority granted to the first arriving transit vehicle would exacerbate the lateness of the next vehicle arriving in a conflicting direction. Therefore, more advanced logic is necessary to resolve such conflicts (e.g., Xu et al., 2016). Recent studies also investigated balancing priority requests from other road users, like emergency vehicles, commercial trucks and pedestrians (e.g., He et al., 2014).

Single-intersection TSP problems have been more prevalent over the past two decades, particularly in earlier years. All papers/reports included in Table 16.3, but not categorized as "coordinated TSP", are considered uncoordinated TSPs designed at the single intersection level. Coordinated TSP studies on the other hand are rather limited due to the complex nature of the problem, and rarely exist in field deployments. Only those proposed coordination algorithms between adjacent intersections are placed in this category (coordinated TSP). TSP algorithms implemented with coordinated traffic signal control systems are not considered coordinated TSPs if no integration modules were developed explicitly within the TSP algorithms for coordination.

Coordinated TSP can offer benefits to transit performance and signal control systems in a variety of ways, such as ensuring the gain at one intersection is not wasted at the next and creating multiplier effects of benefits along the route. A study which proposed a TSP logic that enables bus/signal cooperation and coordination among consecutive signals under a CV environment has shown in simulation experiments significant reduction in bus delays, between 35 per cent and 68 per cent (Hu et al., 2015).

Strategy More than one TSP strategy has been considered simultaneously in recent research studies. The green extension (GE) and red truncation (RT) have been the most commonly applied strategies in research. They have also sometimes been coupled with other strategies, such as phase insertion to provide additional flexibility. For example, when a bus arrives at the beginning of a red phase, RT would be unable to provide immediate clearance. Phase insertion or phase rotation in this case would be better options. Some TSP algorithms do not strictly fall into any of the defined categories, and therefore they have been placed within the table in the most relevant cells with additional explanation provided (e.g., Zlatkovic et al., 2012).

Under adaptive TSP, the optimal values of key decision variables, such as the length of transit green, are determined and applied. While traditional strategies (e.g., GE and RT) would still be used, more flexible strategies that alter the sequences and lengths of signal phases have been explored as a promising direction due to their adaptability.

Method While the traditional method of executing the TSP control logic has largely been rule based, such an approach has declined in use in recent times due to its limited capability of serving sophisticated goals. Rule-based TSP tended to be combined with prediction models or optimization modules to enhance performance. Using the results from a prediction model, a rule-based TSP can follow a set of rules to make a strategy selection. When combined with optimization modules, the rules are used to decide whether to call the optimization module.

Arrival/travel time prediction models provide critical input to rule-based TSP logic to help minimize "failed priority" cases, particularly at intersections with nearside stops (the reduced effectiveness of TSP at nearside stops is one of the main concerns of TSP, which is further discussed in the section "Lessons Learned"). These models may explicitly include a dwell time prediction component to capture uncertainties of passenger service time. Arrival time models based on historical data could possibly yield inaccurate predictions (Hu et al., 2014). Therefore, real-time traffic and transit data has been used in recent studies to improve the accuracy of the prediction models.

Mathematical programming methods have been frequently applied for the development of optimal TSP logic over the past 20 years. Linear programming, mixed integer programming and dynamic programming have all been used in different TSP studies. The main concern with mathematical programming methods is the requirement of an explicit formulation and representation of system performance, which is usually oversimplified for complex dynamic operations. For example, mathematical programming methods have commonly made the assumption of deterministic traffic flow (e.g., Delgado et al., 2015; Hu et al., 2015).

Machine Learning and Artificial Intelligent (AI) approaches have been increasingly applied in TSP optimization studies as they can provide faster solutions compared to mathematical programming. Most of these applications have been focused on adaptive TSP. For example, Genetic Algorithms (GA) have been used in several TSP studies with reported success (e.g., Zhou et al., 2007; Stevanovic et al., 2008; Ghanim and Abu-Lebdeh, 2015). Several AI methods, like Reinforcement Learning (RL), overcome the limitation of mathematical programming of requiring one or more pre-specified models of the transportation environment as part of its formulation. AI methods can be coupled with simulation models for the training phase of the machine learning agents. Due to the rapid development of machine learning algorithms and their increasing capability of fast processing of big data, they have strong potential for future use in TSP research and development. This tendency has been observed in recent studies on adaptive traffic signal control systems (Genders and Razavi, 2016; Shabestary and Abdulhai, 2018).

Evaluation Assessing the performance of TSP algorithms and their impact on traffic is an important step of algorithm development and validation. Recent research investigated the TSP performance based on a number of measurements of effectiveness (MOEs), including transit travel times, variations in transit travel times, delays to transit and traffic (in both prioritized and non-prioritized directions), total person delays, impact on pedestrians, and transit reliability performance (e.g., headway deviations and variability).

Traffic simulation has been extensively used for evaluating existing and proposed TSP algorithms. It outperforms analytical models for its ability to model complex scenarios with sufficient accuracy and computational speed. Hardware-in-the-loop (HIL) or software-in-the-loop simulation have also been applied to allow for the testing and integration of TSP algorithms in combination with vendor signal control systems (Balke et al., 2000; Zlatkovic et al., 2012).

Summary of TSP research trends It can be inferred from Table 16.3 that conditional TSP has attracted a lot of research attention over the past 20 years, perhaps due to its widespread field implementations. It is also noticeable that research efforts concerned with unconditional TSP have been on the decline, while a growing number of studies have shifted attention to adaptive TSP. With the provision of AVL/GPS and CV technologies, the adaptive TSP is expected to grow in importance at least in the near future. Although a majority of studies focused on TSP at the single-intersection single-direction level, fewer studies developed algorithms capable of providing optimal solutions for conflicting priority requests in a coordinated fashion. Such challenging problems could benefit from the rapid development of advanced optimization methods, including AI. Moreover, simulation will continue to be the main testbed for the development and evaluation of future TSP algorithms.

LESSONS LEARNED AND PROMISING FUTURE TSP DIRECTIONS

Lessons Learned

The TSP systems deployed in the field and proposed in the literature have evolved rapidly since the 1970s, from manually activated TSP to advanced TSP that can act adaptively to optimize real-time transit and traffic flows. While significant achievements have been made, opportunities for further improvements remain. The following comments summarize lessons learned from the review of recent industry practices and research literature.

TSP with nearside stops
The positioning of transit stops in relation to a TSP enabled intersection is an important factor to consider when determining the TSP logic and setting its parameters. In general, farside stops are preferred over nearside stops due to the reduced travel time magnitude and variability in the POZ. The negative effect of nearside stops on the effectiveness of TSP has been recognized and addressed in both real-world applications and research studies.

Various TSP strategies have been considered to mitigate the impact of dwell time variability at intersections with nearside stops. For example, some jurisdictions have adopted an approach where TSP can only be requested at nearside stops once passengers have completed boarding and alighting and the doors have closed. This method removes the need to predict dwell time but could result in greater transit signal delay due to the limited time window of action.

Another strategy to mitigate the impact of stopping at nearside stops on TSP performance is to cancel any TSP call if a stop request is activated through on-board push buttons or pull cords. Transit agencies have also developed strategies to decrease dwell time magnitude and variability by allowing boarding and alighting from all doors, implementing more efficient fare payment systems, and reducing stop density along a transit route.

The use of prediction models for estimating the travel time in the POZ, including dwell time, is a key approach to addressing issues related to nearside stops in the literature (see section reviewing literature in the 2000s). Accurate predictions mitigate the effect of dwell time uncertainties on TSP performance.

TSP and general traffic

When a priority is given to a transit movement, it inevitably induces delay to non-prioritized traffic. This is a well-recognized issue with TSP implementation and the impact on general traffic is always considered as one of the performance indicators of TSP systems. The methods used to reduce the impact on non-prioritized traffic include:

- Provide priority to transit vehicles only in cases where TSP would improve transit performance, so as to reduce the number of priorities granted. The performance of TSP relies heavily on accurate prediction capabilities, which in turn require high-quality, real-time data on transit and traffic vehicles.
- Offer compensation to provide extra green time to the non-prioritized direction in the signal cycle after a TSP action (Skabardonis, 2000). However, compensation could interrupt signal coordination and create unbalanced queues along different approaches.
- Develop signal control algorithms that use multi-objective functions which simultaneously minimize transit and traffic delay (e.g., adaptive traffic signal control). The integration of traffic and transit signal control is receiving more research focus of late.

TSP in saturated traffic

When transit vehicles operate in a mixed-traffic road segment with traffic volumes near capacity levels, TSP becomes ineffective as transit vehicles get trapped in queues. This situation can be addressed either by applying TSP only when the traffic flow is below saturation or deploying traffic control strategies at the corridor or sub-network levels to improve traffic flow conditions. The second type of adaptive TSP (section "Adaptive transit priority"), which also considers optimizing traffic flow, offers a promising option. Providing transit with dedicated lanes is another effective solution to mitigate the impacts of traffic on TSP performance.

TSP with coordinated traffic signal control

As TSP modifies the background traffic signal cycle, it is likely to interfere with any signal coordination scheme in place. Offset recovery/transitioning algorithm (refer to the above section "Active transit signal priority") is sometimes applied after a TSP service to bring the signal back into coordination mode.

In order to return to the desired offset, the traffic signal may adjust phase timings, either by extending or reducing the green time of various phases based on the offset correction mode selected. The aggressiveness and length of the recovery period depend largely on the jurisdiction's restrictions on timing adjustments as well as the signal controller's inherent capabilities.

As noted earlier, offset recovery may take a few cycles to complete, which could be interrupted again by a new priority request before the signal restores coordination, depending on the logic developed in the traffic signal controller. Some conditional TSPs set rules to avoid frequent priority calls within a predefined time interval to ensure full restoration of the signal coordination.

Effect of active TSP on transit reliability

Unconditional TSP that provides priority treatment to all detected transit vehicles may in fact result in the unintended consequence of deteriorating transit reliability. When priority is granted to a bus running ahead of schedule or close to the previous bus, this may exacerbate headway/schedule deviation and can induce bunching.

Some conditional TSPs address this issue partially by providing TSP treatment to late transit vehicles only. While this solution can improve schedule adherence/on-time performance for low-frequency service (e.g., headway > 10 minutes), it is less applicable to high-frequency service, which is more concerned with headway regularity than punctuality. Additionally, conditional TSP is typically insensitive to the degree of schedule deviation (i.e. it treats a bus late by a few minutes similarly to a bus late by a few seconds). As such, it rarely provides different levels of priority as needed.

Very few real-world applications, like the London iBUS, consider headway regularity as a criterion for conditional priority. As mentioned in the sub-section "TSP Control Type", conditional TSP based on headway performance has received little attention in previous research efforts. In order to improve the reliability of transit lines explicitly, TSP methods should be further developed to provide priority levels adaptively in accordance with the degree of deviation in the schedule (for low-frequency lines) and headway (for high-frequency lines). Such methods should also consider coordinated TSP among successive intersections to maximize reliability performance (e.g., separate two paired buses and restore the planned headway over a series of coordinated actions along a number of consecutive intersections).

TSP architecture in the literature

Although NTCIP and TCIP standards are key references for field implementation in recent times, research studies hardly identify the underlying TSP architecture of their investigated systems. Such terms as PRG and PRS are hardly used in research papers. Only a few studies concerned with evaluating existing TSP systems identified these systems in terms of their specific TSP architecture (e.g., Hounsell and Shrestha, 2005). This is an obvious gap between research and industry in recent times. Without considering the architecture explicitly when developing a new TSP algorithm, the applicability of such an algorithm for implementation in the field becomes limited.

Future Directions

Currently, a large portion of the existing TSP systems operate in a similar way to the second-generation conditional systems. While some jurisdictions are beginning to adopt the standards-based approach, it is still viewed as a relatively new trend. Given the current status of field implementation, conditional TSP is also the type of TSP investigated the most in the literature. Moreover, most TSP deployments in the field and proposed in the literature are applicable to single intersections with no coordination among multiple directions and multiple intersections.

There is a need for further research into TSP systems with advanced conditional and adaptive TSP capabilities supported by emerging communication technologies (e.g., CV). Future TSP systems are not expected to operate in stand-alone modes, but instead they are likely to operate more collaboratively with other systems in the transportation network within and across municipalities as we move closer towards smart cities. This calls for more research and development efforts directed towards developing such systems.

Coordinated TSP (on a corridor or network level) which involves communication among signallized intersections would also be a future direction. Coordinated TSP will enhance the benefit of priority treatments implemented at the intersection level. Compared with implementing uncoordinated TSP along a corridor, coordination makes it possible to apply less frequent modifications to the signal plan at individual intersections, producing an overall higher gain at the corridor level. The research study by (Hu et al., 2015) indicates a promising benefit of reducing signal delays by deploying coordinated TSP. Additionally, coordinated TSP may be necessary for advanced TSP methods that explicitly tackle service reliability issues which can be resolved more effectively through coordinated actions at successive intersections.

In the current technological climate, with artificial intelligence and open data being areas of heavy interest, TSP systems are beginning to apply innovative ideas which include the use of adaptive TSP. Similarly, as CV systems gain more traction, the TSP industry can anticipate a heavy emphasis on future consolidated CV standards, as transit vehicles operating in a TSP system can be viewed as connected vehicles with a V2I connection. Research interests in the past two decades have shifted towards this direction of developing adaptive TSP algorithms and deploying CV technologies for this communication system. Given the movement towards Smart City and Big Data, there is a strong trend of collecting detailed data on transit vehicle performance. As an example, many CAD/AVL systems can report second-by-second position information on each transit vehicle, along with the status of the vehicle (e.g., operating on a route, stopped at a transit stop, passenger stop request active/inactive, door open/closed, etc.). Similarly, traffic signal control systems can also report details on signallized intersection operation (e.g., cycle-by-cycle phase duration, TSP active/inactive, detector input, etc.). Combining this information through data analytic techniques allows traffic engineers and transit service planners to collaborate and adjust transit and traffic operations to achieve their desired outcome.

CONCLUSION

TSP is one of the most important and effective strategies for reducing signal delays for transit vehicles, and it has received much attention and experienced tremendous progress in both industry and research alike. TSP advancements have largely been driven by the development of new communication and detection technologies. This chapter provides a comprehensive background on TSP systems, including control types, key system components, industrial communication standards and the TSP architecture. A review of the industry practices and literature is followed with a focused assessment of research developments over the past 20 years. The lessons learned and future directions of TSP are discussed based on the review. Based on recent trends, future developments of TSP systems are likely to continue to be driven by advancements of detection and communication technologies and innovative analytical methods. Tremendous potential exists for developing more advanced TSP control that is: (1) adaptive in providing the right amount of priority for each transit vehicle according to its operational conditions; (2) integrative of priority actions among successive intersections; (3) holistic in its consideration of other road users; (4) effective with minimum priority failures; and (5) less interruptive to the traffic signal plan. Additionally, future TSP systems will be based on emerging standards to enable interoperability of TSP equipped vehicles across various jurisdictions.

NOTES

1.   A signal phase is defined as the right-of-way, yellow change and red clearance intervals in a cycle that are assigned to an independent traffic movement or combination of traffic movements (U.S. Department of Transportation Federal Highway Administration, 2009).
2.   Cycle length is the time required for one complete sequence of signal indications (U.S. Department of Transportation Federal Highway Administration, 2009).
3.   Offset is the time relationship between coordinated phases, and it is defined as the delay of the start time of a phase relative to the start time of the reference phase. In a corridor with synchronized signal timing among its intersections, a unique offset value is assigned to each signallized intersection.
4.   SCOOT is a real-time, on-line, adaptive traffic control system that continuously measures traffic demand on all approaches to intersections in a network and optimizes the signal timing at each intersection to minimize traffic delay and stops (Siemens, no date).
5.   In this section, the review of the industry practice is largely based on Corby and Wong (2016) and (2019).

REFERENCES

AASHTO, ITE and NEMA (2014) "NTCIP 1211: National transportation communications for ITS protocol object definitions for Signal Control and Prioritization (SCP)". Accessed at: https://www.ntcip.org/wp-con tent/uploads/2018/11/NTCIP1211-v0224j.pdf.

Al-Sahili, K. and Taylo, W.C. (1995) "RR-745: Bus Preemption Signal (BPS): An application of an Advanced Public Transportation System (APTS)". No. GLCTTR 61-95/01.

Anderson, P. and Daganzo, C.F. (2019) "Effect of transit signal priority on bus service reliability", *Transportation Research Part B: Methodological*. doi: 10.1016/j.trb.2019.01.016.

Balke, K.N., Dudek, C.L. and Urbanik II, T. (2000) "Development and evaluation of intelligent bus priority concept", *Transportation Research Record*, 1727, pp. 12–19.

Benevelli, D.A., Radwan, A.E. and Hurley, J.J.W. (1983) "Evaluation of a bus preemption strategy by use of computer simulation", *Transportation Research Record*, 906, pp. 60–67.

Bowen, G.T., Bretherton, R.D., Landles, J.R. and Cook, D.J. (1994) "Active bus priority in SCOOT", in *Seventh International Conference on Road Traffic Monitoring and Control*, pp. 73–6. doi: https://doi.org/10.1049/cp:19 940428.

Bowen, T., Head, J.R., Hounsell, N.B., Palmer, S, and Shrestha, B.P. (2007) "Expanding the boundaries of bus priority at traffic signals in London", in *Proceedings of 6th European Congress on Intelligent Transport Systems and Services*, 18–20 June, Aalborg.

Chang, G.L., Vasudevan, M. and Su, C.C. (1995) "Bus-preemption under adaptive signal control environments", *Transportation Research Record*, 1494, pp. 146–54.

Chang, G.L., Vasudevan, M. and Su, C.C. (1996) "Modelling and evaluation of adaptive bus-preemption control with and without automatic vehicle location systems", *Transportation Research Part A: Policy and Practice*, 30(4), pp. 251–68. doi: 10.1016/0965-8564(95)00026-7.

Christofa, E. and Skabardonis, A. (2011) "Traffic signal optimization with application of transit signal priority to an isolated intersection", *Transportation Research Record*, (2259), pp. 192–201. doi: 10.3141/2259-18.

City of Toronto (no date) Traffic signal prioritization. Accessed 27 November 2019 at: https://www.toronto. ca/services-payments/streets-parking-transportation/traffic-management/traffic-signals-street-signs/traffic-si gnal-operations/traffic-signal-prioritization/.

Corby, M. and Wong, A. (2016) Consulting services for development of city of Toronto's Transit Signal Priority strategy. City of Toronto.

Corby, M. and Wong, A. (2019) Consulting services for region of Durham: Traffic engineering and operations TSP signal timing parameters and centre-to-centre architecture assessment. Durham Region.

Cottinet, M. (1977) *Prise en Compte des Autobus sur un Itinéraire Coordonné*. Prepared for the Institut de Recherche des Transports, Arcueil, France.

Currie, G. and Shalaby, A. (2008) "Active transit signal priority for streetcars: Experience in Melbourne,

Australia, and Toronto, Canada", *Transportation Research Record: Journal of the Transportation Research Board*, 2042, pp. 41–9. doi: 10.3141/2042-05.

Delgado, F., Muñoz, J.C., Giesen, R. and Wilson, N.H.M. (2015) "Integrated real-time transit signal priority control for high-frequency segregated transit services", *Transportation Research Record: Journal of the Transportation Research Board*, 2533, pp. 28–38. doi: 10.3141/2533-04.

Ding, J., Yang, M., Wang, W., Xu, C. and Bao, Y. (2015) "Strategy for multiobjective transit signal priority with prediction of bus dwell time at stops", *Transportation Research Record: Journal of the Transportation Research Board*, 2488, pp. 10–19. doi: 10.3141/2488-02.

Dion, F. and Rakha, H. (2005) "Integration of transit signal priority within adaptive traffic control systems", paper presented at the 84th Annual Meeting of the Transportation Research Board, Washington, DC.

Ekeila, W., Sayed, T. and El Esawey, M. (2009) "Development of dynamic transit signal priority strategy", *Transportation Research Record: Journal of the Transportation Research Board*, (2111), pp. 1–9. doi: 10.3141/2111-01.

El-Reedy, T.Y. and Ashworth, R. (1978) "The effect of bus detection on the performance of a traffic signal controlled intersection", *Transportation Research*, 12(5), pp. 337–42. doi: 10.1016/0041-1647(78)90009-6.

Elias, W.J. (1976) "The Greenback experiment: Signal pre-emption for express buses: A demonstration project". Report DMT-014. Sacramento, California.

Evans, H.K. and Skiles, G.W. (1970) "Improving public transit through bus preemption of traffic signals", *Traffic Quarterly*, 24(4), pp. 531–43.

Felice, C. (2018) "Creating road intersection MAP data for MMITSS 'The NMAP File': UDOT's methodology in creating NMAP files". Utah Department of Transportation.

Furth, P.G. and Muller, T.H.J. (2000) "Conditional bus priority at signalized intersections: Better service with less traffic disruption", *Transportation Research Record*, 1731(1), 23–30.

Genders, W. and Razavi, S. (2016) "Using a deep reinforcement learning agent for traffic signal control". Accessed at https://arxiv.org/pdf/1611.01142.pdf.

Ghanim, M.S. and Abu-Lebdeh, G. (2015) "Real-time dynamic transit signal priority optimization for coordinated traffic networks using genetic algorithms and artificial neural networks", *Journal of Intelligent Transportation Systems: Technology, Planning, and Operations*, 19(4), pp. 327–38. doi: 10.1080/15472450.2014. 936292.

Han, X., Li, P., Sikder, R., Qiu, Z. and Kim, A. (2014) "Development and evaluation of adaptive transit signal priority control with updated transit delay model", *Transportation Research Record*, 2438(2438), pp. 45–54. doi: 10.3141/2438-05.

He, Q., Head, K.L. and Ding, J. (2011) "Heuristic algorithm for priority traffic signal control", *Transportation Research Record: Journal of the Transportation Research Board*, 2259 (1), pp. 1–7. doi: 10.3141/2259-01.

He, Q., Head, K.L. and Ding, J. (2014) "Multi-modal traffic signal control with priority, signal actuation and coordination", *Transportation Research Part C: Emerging Technologies*, 46, pp. 65–82. doi: 10.1016/j. trc.2014.05.001.

Hounsell, N.B. and Shrestha, B.P. (2005) "AVL based bus priority at traffic signals: A review and case study of architectures", *European Journal of Transport and Infrastructure Research*, 5(1).

Hounsell, N.B., Shrestha, B.P. and Wong, A. (2012) "Data management and applications in a world-leading bus fleet", *Transportation Research Part C: Emerging Technologies*, 22, pp. 76–87. doi: 10.1016/j. trc.2011.12.005.

Hu, J., Park, B.B. and Lee, Y.J. (2015) "Coordinated transit signal priority supporting transit progression under Connected Vehicle Technology", *Transportation Research Part C: Emerging Technologies*, 55, pp. 393–408. doi: 10.1016/j.trc.2014.12.005.

Hu, J., Park, B.B. and Lee, Y.J. (2016) "Transit signal priority accommodating conflicting requests under Connected Vehicles technology", *Transportation Research Part C: Emerging Technologies*, 69, pp. 173–92. doi: 10.1016/j.trc.2016.06.001.

Hu, J., Park, B. and Parkany, A.E. (2014) "Transit signal priority with connected vehicle technology", *Transportation Research Record: Journal of the Transportation Research*, 2418, pp. 20–29. doi: 10.3141/2418-03.

Hu, W.X. and Shalaby, A. (2017) "Use of automated vehicle location data for route- and segment-level analyses of bus route reliability and speed", *Transportation Research Record: Journal of the Transportation Research Board*, 2649, pp. 9–19. doi: 10.3141/2649-02.

Hu, W.X., Shalaby, A. and Abdulhai, B. (2020) "Transportation research record dual-objective transit signal priority for improving speed and reliability of high- frequency lines: A deep reinforcement learning approach", poster presented at the *Transportation Research Board (TRB) 99th Annual Meeting*, Washington, DC.

Jacobson, J. and Sheffi, Y. (1981) "Analytical model of traffic delays under bus signal preemption: Theory and application", *Transportation Research Part B*, 15(2), pp. 127–38. doi: 10.1016/0191-2615(81)90039-4.

Janos, M. and Furth, P.G. (2002) "Bus priority with highly interruptible traffic signal control: Simulation of San Juan's Avenida Ponce de Leon". *Transportation Research Record*, 1811(1), 157–165.

Kim, H., Cheng, Y. and Chang, G.L. (2018) "An arterial-based transit signal priority control system", *Article*

Transportation Research Record: Journal of the Transportation Research Board, 2672(18), pp. 1–14. doi: 10.1177/0361198118782753.

Kim, W. and Rilett, L.R. (2005) "Improved transit signal priority system for networks with nearside bus stops", *Transportation Research Record: Journal of the Transportation Research*, (1925), pp. 205–14. doi: 10.3141/1925-21.

Lee, J. and Shalaby, A. (2013) "Rule-based transit signal priority control method using a real-time transit travel time prediction model", *Canadian Journal of Civil Engineering*, 40, pp. 68–75. doi: 10.1139/cjce-2011-0344.

Lee, J., Shalaby, A., Greenough, J., Bowie, M. and Hung, S. (2005) "Advanced transit signal priority control with online microsimulation-based transit prediction model", *Transportation Research Record: Journal of the Transportation Research Board*, 1925, pp. 185–94. doi: 10.3141/1925-19.

Levinson, H.S. (2003) "Bus rapid transit on city streets: How does it work", paper presented at the *2nd Urban Street Symposium*, Anaheim.

Levinson, H.S., Zimmerman, S., Clinger, J., Gast, J., Rutherford, S. and Bruhn, E. (2003) *TCRP Report 90: Bus Rapid Transit: Volume 2: Implementation Guide*, Transportation Research Board.

Li, M., Wu, G., Li, Y., Bu, F. and Zhang, W.B. (2007) "Active signal priority for light rail transit at grade crossings", *Transportation Research Record*, (2035), pp. 141–9. doi: 10.3141/2035-16.

Li, M., Zhou, K., Yin, Y., Tan, C.W., Zhang, W.B., Sun, S., Leung, K. et al. (2008) *Toward Deployment of Adaptive Transit Signal Priority (ATSP)*, Report No. CA06-0703, California Department of Transportation.

Li, M., Yin, Y., Zhang, W.B., Zhou, K. and Nakamura, H. (2011) "Modeling and implementation of adaptive transit signal priority on actuated control systems", *Computer-Aided Civil and Infrastructure Engineering*, 26, pp. 270–84. doi: 10.1111/j.1467-8667.2010.00677.x.

Li, Y., Koonce, P., Li, M., Zhou, K., Li, Y., Beaird, S., Zhang, W.B. et al. (2008) *Transit Signal Priority Research Tools*. Washington, DC: US Department of Transportation

Liao, C.F. and Davis, G.A. (2007) "Simulation study of bus signal priority strategy: Taking advantage of global positioning system, automated vehicle location system, and wireless communications", *Transportation Research Record*, (2034), pp. 82–91. doi: 10.3141/2034-10.

Lieberman, E.B., Muzyka, A. and Schmeider, D. (1978) Abridgment: "Bus priority signal control: Simulation analysis of two strategies", *Transportation Research Record*, 663, pp. 26–8.

Lin, Y., Yang, X. and Chang, G.L. (2013) "Transit priority strategies for multiple routes under headway-based operations", *Transportation Research Record: Journal of the Transportation Research*, 2356, pp. 34–43. doi: 10.3141/2356-05.

Lin, Y., Yang, X., Zou, N. and Franz, M. (2015) "Transit signal priority control at signalized intersections: A comprehensive review", *Transportation Letters: The International Journal of Transportation Research*, 7(3), pp. 168–80. doi: 10.1179/1942787514Y.0000000044.

Ling, K. and Shalaby, A. (2003) "Automated transit headway control via adaptive signal priority", *Journal of Advanced Transportation*, 38(1), pp. 45–67. doi: 10.1002/atr.5670380105.

Liu, H., Skabardonis, A. and Zhang, W.B. (2003) "A dynamic model for adaptive bus signal priority", paper presented at the 82nd Annual Meeting of the Transportation Research Board, Washington, DC.

Ludwick, J.S. (1975) "Simulation of an unconditional preemption bus priority system", *Transportation Research Record*, no. 536, pp. 1–10.

Ludwick, J.S. (1976) "Bus Priority System: Simulation and analysis". Final Report prepared by the MITRE Corporation, for the US Department of Transportation, Report UTMA-VA-06-0026-1.

Ma, W. and Bai, Y. (2008) "Serve sequence optimization approach for multiple bus priority requests based on decision tree", in *Plan, Build, and Manage Transportation Infrastructure in China. Proceedings of the Seventh International Conference of Chinese Transportation Professional (ICCTP)*, 21–22 May 2007, pp. 605–15.

Ma, W., Liu, Y. and Yang, X. (2013a) "A dynamic programming approach for optimal signal priority control upon multiple high-frequency bus requests", *Journal of Intelligent Transportation Systems*, 17(4), pp. 282–93. doi: 10.1080/15472450.2012.729380.

Ma, W., Yang, X. and Liu, Y. (2010) "Development and evaluation of a coordinated and conditional bus priority approach", *Transportation Research Record: Journal of the Transportation Research Board*, 2145(1), pp. 49–58. doi: 10.3141/2145-06.

Ma, W., Ni, W., Head, L. and Zhao, J. (2013b) "Effective coordinated optimization model for transit priority control under arterial progression", *Transportation Research Record*, (2356), pp. 71–83. doi: 10.3141/2356-09.

Mirchandani, P.B. and Lucas, D.E. (2004) "Integrated transit priority and rail/emergency preemption in real-time traffic adaptive signal control", *Journal of Intelligent Transportation Systems*, 8(2), pp. 101–15. doi: 10.1080/15472450490437799.

Muthuswamy, S., McShane, W.R. and Daniel, J.R. (2007) "Evaluation of transit signal priority and optimal signal timing plans in transit and traffic operations", *Transportation Research Record: Journal of the Transportation Research*, (2034), pp. 92–102. doi: 10.3141/2034-11.

NTCIP (2017) NTCIP 1211 version v02A-SE.03.

Radwan, A.E. and Hurley Jr, J.W. (1982) "Analytical model of bus preemption signal system: A macroscopic approach", *Transportation Quarterly*, January. Accessed 19 November 2019 at: https://babel.hathitrust.org/cgi/pt?id=mdp.39015021808632&view=1up&seq=135.

RTA (Regional Transportation Authority) (no date) "Regional Transit Signal Priority (TSP) implementation program". Accessed 27 November 2019 at: http://www.rtams.org/rtams/transitSignalPriority.jsp.

Salter, R.J. and Shahi, J. (1979) "Prediction of effects of bus-priority schemes by using computer simulation techniques", *Transportation Research Record*, 718, 1–5.

Shabestary, S.M.A. and Abdulhai, B. (2018) "Deep learning vs. discrete reinforcement learning for adaptive traffic signal control", *IEEE Conference on Intelligent Transportation Systems, Proceedings, ITSC*, pp. 286–93. doi: 10.1109/ITSC.2018.8569549.

Shabestary, S.M.A. and Abdulhai, B. (2019) "Multimodal iNtelligent Deep (MiND) traffic signal controller", paper presented at the *22nd IEEE International Conference on Intelligent Transportation Systems*, pp. 4532–9.

Shi, J., Sun, Y., Schonfeld, P. and Qi, J. (2017) "Joint optimization of tram timetables and signal timing adjustments at intersections", *Transportation Research Part C: Emerging Technologies*, 83, pp. 104–119. doi: 10.1016/j.trc.2017.07.014.

Siemens (no date) *SCOOT Adaptive Traffic Control | Traffic Management | USA*. Accessed 23 March 2020 at: https://new.siemens.com/us/en/products/mobility/road-solutions/traffic-management/scoot-adaptive-traffic-control.html.

Skabardonis, A. (2000) "Control strategies for transit priority", *Transportation Research Record: Journal of the Transportation Research Board*, 1727, pp. 20–26.

Smith, H.R., Hemily, B. and Ivanovic, M. (2005) *Transit Signal Priority (TSP): A Planning and Implementation Handbook*. Washington, DC: ITS America, US Department of Transportation.

Stevanovic, J., Stevanovic, A., Martin, P.T. and Bauer, T. (2008) "Stochastic optimization of traffic control and transit priority settings in VISSIM", *Transportation Research Part C: Emerging Technologies*, 16(3), pp. 332–49. doi: 10.1016/j.trc.2008.01.002.

Stewart, R. and Wong, R. (2013) "Guidelines for planning and implementation of Transit Priority Measures (TPM) in urban areas", paper presented at the Annual Conference of the Transportation Association of Canada, Ottawa: Transportation Association of Canada, pp. 1–16.

TJKM (1978) "Evaluation of bus priority signal system". Report prepared for the City of Concord, California.

US Department of Transportation Federal Highway Administration (2009) *Manual on Uniform Traffic Control Devices for Streets and Highways*, FHWA.

USDOT (no date) *ITS Standards Program | Fact Sheets | ITS Standards Fact Sheets*. Accessed 13 October 2019 at: https://www.standards.its.dot.gov/Factsheets/Factsheet/37.

Vincent, R.A., Cooper, B.R. and Wood, K. (1978) "Bus-actuated signal control at isolated intersections: Simulation studies of bus priority". Transport and Road Research Laboratory (TRRL), TRRL Lab Report 814.

Vuchic, V.R. (2005) *Urban Transit: Operations, Planning, and Economics*. Hoboken, NJ: John Wiley & Sons.

Wadjas, Y. and Furth, P.G. (2003) "Transit signal priority along arterials using advanced detection", *Transportation Research Record*, (1856), pp. 220–30. doi: 10.3141/1856-24.

Wattleworth, J.A., Courage, K.G. and Wallace, C.E. (1977) "Evaluation of bus-priority strategies on Northwest Seventh Avenue in Miami", *Transportation Research Record*, 6, pp. 32–5.

Xu, M., Ye, Z., Sun, H. and Wang, W. (2016) "Optimization model for transit signal priority under conflicting priority requests", *Transportation Research Record: Journal of the Transportation Research*, 2539, pp. 140–48. doi: 10.3141/2539-16.

Yagar, S. and Han, B. (1994) "A procedure for real-time signal control that considers transit interference and priority", *Transportation Research Part B: Methodological*, 28(4), pp. 315–31.

Ye, Z. and Xu, M. (2017) "Decision model for resolving conflicting transit signal priority requests", *IEEE Transactions on Intelligent Transportation Systems*, 18(1), pp. 59–68.

Yedlin, M. and Lieberman, E.B. (1981) "Analytic and simulation studies of factors that influence bus-signal-priority strategies", *Transportation Research Record*, 798, pp. 26–9.

York Region (2010) *Transit Priority Measures to Get You There Faster*. Accessed 27 November 2019 at: http://www.vivanext.com/blog/tag/congestion/page/4/.

Zeng, X., Sun, X., Zhang, Y. and Quadrifoglio, L. (2015) "Person-based adaptive priority signal control with connected-vehicle information", *Transportation Research Record: Journal of the Transportation Research*, 2487, pp. 78–87. doi: 10.3141/2487-07.

Zeng, X., Zhang, Y., Balke, K.N. and Yin, K. (2014) "A real-time transit signal priority control model considering stochastic bus arrival time", *IEEE Transactions on Intelligent Transportation Systems*, 15(4), pp. 1657–66.

Zhou, G., Gan, A. and Shen, L.D. (2007) "Optimization of adaptive transit signal priority using parallel genetic algorithm", *Tsinghua Science and Technology*, 12(2). doi: 10.1016/S1007-0214(07)70020-2.

Zhou, L., Wang, Y. and Liu, Y. (2017) "Active signal priority control method for bus rapid transit based on

Vehicle Infrastructure Integration", *International Journal of Transportation Science and Technology*, 6(2), pp. 99–109. doi: 10.1016/j.ijtst.2017.06.001.

Zlatkovic, M., Stevanovic, A. and Martin, P.T. (2012) "Development and evaluation of algorithm for resolution of conflicting transit signal priority requests", *Transportation Research Record: Journal of the Transportation Research Board*, (2311), pp. 167–75. doi: 10.3141/2311-16.

17. ACES technologies and public transport operations and control*

Juan Carlos Munoz, Ricardo Giesen, Felipe Delgado and Omar Ibarra-Rojas

17.1 INTRODUCTION

The transport industry is going through major technology innovations that promise to change many of its distinctive characteristics significantly. Autonomous, Connected, Electric and Shared vehicles, known as ACES are expected to be very disruptive in an industry that has been reluctant to adopt technology changes of this magnitude in the past decades (Adler et al., 2019). The potential impact of implementing the latter technologies goes well beyond the level of service to be experienced by the passengers, or the typical transport externalities such as congestion, pollution, and reducing the number of accidents. Indeed, ACES would probably also trigger important changes in urban forms and public finances.

In this chapter, we analyze some opportunities and threats that these technologies pose for urban public transport. The arrival of these technologies occurs in a moment when urbanization, motorization, car use, traffic accidents, pollution and congestion are all on the rise. Furthermore, in many cities, public transport is also losing modal share (Sustainable Mobility for All, 2017).

ACES technologies open very attractive opportunities for surface public transport such as buses. Through the concept of Bus Rapid Transit (BRT), the bus service has tried to mimic the level of service provided by the underground Metro (Munoz and Paget-Seekins, 2015). The focus has been placed on a segregated corridor and off-board payment stations. However, through automation buses may increase their safety and reliability performances. Through vehicle connectivity buses may keep headway regularity more effectively and provide more precise information to passengers. Through electrification, buses may become more environmentally friendly, provide a more silent and smoother ride, and reduce their operating costs. These attributes are easier to achieve when buses operate in segregated corridors in which they experience a context more isolated from external perturbations. We argue that BRT corridors are the first place in which these technologies should be tested and implemented. According to BRTdata.org there are already more than 170 cities with BRT-type corridors, serving over 33 million passengers every day (BRT Centre of Excellence et al., 2019). Most of these services face difficulties in keeping their users satisfied and in preventing them from using a car when they can afford it. Thus, these new technologies (ACES) may become a key opportunity for these services to improve the level of service they deliver, and start winning the hearts of their users.

We will analyze the impact of these technologies not just for public transport users, but also for the operator and the city. Their impact is quite different if they are analyzed in combination. We also analyze possible public policies that should be implemented to ensure that the use of ACES technologies improves the quality of life and sustainability of cities where they are implemented.

The use of ACES also presents a very important threat to collective transport since they might encourage the use of single-occupancy vehicles, thus reducing the demand for public transport, affecting the level of service that public transport can offer, or encouraging urban sprawl, which makes public transport less effective in addressing urban mobility needs.

A very important reason behind the current declining trend in transit ridership in many cities is the entrance of app-driven taxi services, also known as Transportation Network Companies (TNC), such as Uber, Lyft, Cabify or Didi. Such a trend might accelerate if airbnb-type services are adopted, in which car owners might rent their cars for given trips. Thus, even if vehicle ownership might decline due to these services, vehicle miles driven would still face a continuous growth. Can big cities prescind from massive public transport to address their mobility needs? Certainly not. Urban mobility increases with income, and cities are growing in surface, inhabitants and are capturing most of the economic growth. So we should expect to see more and longer trips in cities worldwide. In such a context these trips cannot be accommodated through single-occupancy motorized trips. There is simply no capacity for this, even if enhanced technologies allow us to drive our vehicles closer to each other. We should recognize that our streets are not just to move across the city, but also lively places to walk and meet. The public space role of urban life conflicts with a vision of streets becoming just high capacity corridors. Thus, large cities need an efficient network of massive public transport to connect peripheral areas and business districts. Can we rely on underground public transport only? Although the Metro is a key player in any large city, it is also quite rigid in its operation; any disturbance in a train or at a station usually affects all trains in both directions. Also, Metros are not only very expensive to build, but also, to provide a fast trip across the city, stations must be installed far from each other, which forces some passengers to combine their trips with other modes of transport. This is especially true for those who walk slowly, for example the elderly, and those who cannot afford living next to Metro stations. People expect public transport to be accessible, which means that surface public transport (bus, tram or light rail transit (LRT)) should remain an important player. Finally, if we expect car drivers to be attracted by public transport, then this mode should be visible to them, providing a desirable level of service. An underground service that cannot be seen is more difficult to engage the car driver.

In this context, we analyze how ACES technologies should affect and impact public transport. Some of these technologies will require a strong normative framework and public infrastructure to benefit the society, while in other cases, providing a free market competition with standard technologies might suffice. Getting this policy response right or wrong may have important consequences for the efficiency, livability and sustainability of cities involved. Also, in some cases, the transition during which these technologies are implemented may pose some important challenges that will be highlighted.

17.2　AUTONOMOUS

Autonomous or driverless vehicles (AV) can be categorized depending on the level of automation from 0 to 5 (NHTSA, 2020). Most of the attention in the manufacturing industry and in the media related to implementing this technology has been placed on individual cars. People have been captivated by the idea of what is called Level 5 of Full automation, in which the vehicle moves while its occupants do other activities, such as read, work or even sleep, representing a reduction of generalized costs for private car users (see Correia et al., 2019). Most of the impacts of automation to public transport described in this section correspond to Level 4 or lower; thus we assume in the case of buses that a driver is always sitting behind the wheel.

According to Becker and Axhausen (2017), AV seems to be more appealing for young men and those owning a vehicle in urban contexts. However, such a vision faces huge technological challenges due to the very different contexts that cars must navigate and the transition during which AV and older vehicles will share the roads. The dream may turn into an illusion or a nightmare, since in cities, where cars' operational costs are severely underpriced, this technology would encourage their use. This might have severely damaging consequences for cities in terms of congestion, urban sprawl, pollution, vehicle-miles, and obesity, among others.

Particularly during rush hours in which many trips simultaneously head towards a few heavily congested areas, car use should be hindered. Many cities worldwide have started to turn such a vision into action, banning or discouraging car use in certain congested areas. Instead, cities are encouraging the so-called sustainable transport modes: mostly non-motorized, like walking and bikes, and massive public transport. In this context, autonomous vehicle technology may play an important role in urban mobility if it is focused on buses and trolleys instead. Public transport offers many advantages over cars to be the first testbed for autonomous technology, especially if their vehicles for collective use run in corridors that are segregated from general traffic.

Bus, tram or LRT service in segregated corridors operate under conditions that are very predictable regarding the interactions with traffic signals, other vehicles and pedestrians. Thus, public transport operating in segregated corridors has shown to reduce fatalities, especially if safety considerations and operations are both simultaneously designed as part of an integrated approach (Duduta and Lindau, 2015). Still, in this context automation should improve safety performance even further.

Automation should also smooth the ride for its users. By controlling the trajectory of each vehicle, acceleration and deceleration could be constrained to certain acceptable levels. Also, curbside docking at stops would be much more precise, reducing dwell times and speeding up buses, which increases the transport capacity (see Childress et al., 2015). Such precision will be especially relevant for users with limited mobility. Also, through eco-driving, an autonomous vehicle should reduce its operational costs and emissions. These are all important gains. When these automated vehicles are also connected through a communication technology among themselves or with other equipment along the route, new opportunities arise; one of the clearest is to keep regular headways which provides important benefits for the user (detailed in the next section).

For public transport operators, autonomous vehicles might allow them to reduce an important operational cost: the drivers. According to Walker (2011), "Driver labor, and related time-based costs, are the dominant element – often 70% or more – of transit operating budgets in the developed world". In the developing world it is lower, but still significant. However, it is hard to imagine these vehicles completely prescinding from drivers, even if they circulate in segregated corridors. Different types of manoeuvring will probably still be needed, requiring drivers. In the case of buses, they might still need to get out of corridors and visit local neighborhoods in which drivers should be needed. Thus, these interventions should probably aim at a high level of automation, or what is called Level 4. Note that in Metro lines fully automated trains have been operated only recently, and the uninterrupted operational conditions faced by trains will probably never be experienced at the surface.

AV buses can also play an important role in covering the first and last mile of a public transport trip. Many cities have been structured around low-density neighborhoods where providing public transport service is not cost-efficient. By eliminating the cost of the driver, a small Level 5 AV bus covering these neighborhoods at a slow and safe speed might become an attractive solution. As Metz (2018) states, "Autonomous on-demand minibuses could fill the present gap between high capacity, low cost buses and rail services and low capacity, high cost taxis."

Also, by improving their safety performance, crashes should be significantly less frequent (Li and Kockelman, 2016). Since road accidents should be fewer and less severe, the cost for bus operators should decline. Some very infrequent accidents might arise from technology failures. But overall, even though autonomous vehicles are expect to be more expensive than standard vehicles, there are also cost reductions that should justify the investment (see Abe, 2019). Also, as soon as the technology becomes widely used, its cost should drop and eventually become absorbed in the features of a standard vehicle.

Authorities should encourage the testing of these new technologies and eventually require them to be used in the new fleet for their cities. As soon as connectivity across vehicles and between vehicles and infrastructure becomes a standard, the authority should facilitate testbeds for experimenting with these technologies. Once they are successfully proven and they offer a convenient cost–benefit ratio, automation should be adopted by cities in their public transport corridors. An unexpected hurdle may be that many of these corridors are operated by private companies, which could be hard to convince, especially if they are controlled by the drivers. Bus operators worldwide have been a very slow adopter of innovative technologies that do not trigger a direct economic benefit for them. Thus, transit authorities would need to request these innovations to bus operators as part of their regulated contract framework.

The transition during which automated buses and non-automated vehicles coexist on the roads is also a concern. Non-automated vehicles might aggressively benefit from knowing that the automated bus will react, avoiding a crash. There are significant ethical dilemmas that these vehicles should be programmed to address, which might be different depending on the cultural and constitutional local context. Local policies should address them for their local context.

Finally, autonomous vehicles bring new concerns to public policies. First, the legislation should incorporate how to deal with accidents involving driverless vehicles. Second, autonomous vehicles may prove to be subject to cyber-terrorist acts, requiring a proactive policy that develops tools to identify and punish those behind these acts.

Thus, we foresee that AV technology will be embraced by the public transport industry. The beginning of this relationship has been, so far, quite timid. But as Lazarus et al. (2018) indicate, "the convergence of shared mobility, automation, and public transit is in its nascent stages". Some of the opportunities offered by shared mobility and the flexibility it requires from public transport services will be discussed later in this chapter.

17.3   CONNECTED

Communication technologies are allowing vehicles, passengers and infrastructure to be connected as was never before possible, opening the possibility for a more seamless ride for the passengers and a more cost-effective operation for the operators. One of the main opportunities to be addressed through this enhanced connectivity is improving the reliability of the user experience, that is, a level of service that does not significantly vary under similar conditions (van Oort, 2011). The lack of reliability affects several elements of transit service: the majority of passengers experience long waiting times. At the same time, comfort deteriorates since these passengers experience a full bus that sometimes they cannot board due to bus capacity. From the operator point of view, unreliable services affect the distribution of cycle times. While some buses finish a complete cycle in a short period, others take significantly longer. This factor influences the frequency with which these services can be offered, thus affecting the number of buses and drivers (Delgado et al., 2016; Muñoz et al., 2020).

Improving service reliability requires keeping each vehicle at the desired position in time and space, and in many cases, this depends on the trajectories of the rest of the vehicles in service. Thus, driverless technology is not enough to address this challenge. Improving service reliability requires some sort of connection between vehicles, even if they are AV. Autonomous-and-connected vehicles (V2V) capable of communicating and interacting with each other and with the infrastructure (V2I) are needed. V2I communication allows passengers to receive real-time information of the estimated arrival time of a bus either on their mobile phones or at the stop, reducing passenger uncertainty.

Public transport systems are operated in two ways: according to a predefined schedule, which is typical in services with long headways, or without a schedule, which is common in services with high demand and short headways. Under unscheduled services, public transport system reliability is closely related to providing operation at regular headways between buses. Operating at regular headways is very challenging, mainly because it constitutes an unstable equilibrium where regularity is affected by several factors that add variability into the travel time between consecutive stops across different buses. Some of these factors are associated with the characteristics and personal attitudes of drivers (Ivancevich et al., 2005; Tse et al., 2006; Tao et al., 2017; Martinez-Estupinan et al., 2020), while others are related to external factors: length of the route, presence of traffic lights intersections, congestion (Sterman and Schofer, 1976; Abkowitz and Engelstein, 1983; 1984); travel direction (Strathman et al., 1999; Strathman and Hopper, 1993); time of day (Strathman et al., 1999; Wenquan, 2013); the number of passengers waiting at stops (Hickman, 2001; Bertini and El-Geneidy, 2004; Chen et al., 2009); passenger arrival rates at bus stops, and bus capacity (Delgado et al., 2012); the distance between stops, or the presence of segregated bus lanes (Danés and Muñoz, 2016). AVs should help mitigate the impacts associated with different individual driving skills, by making them more homogeneous across drivers. However, most external factors that cause travel time variability would remain, requiring the use of V2V or V2I associated intelligence to alleviate them.

Regarding V2V communication to improve headway regularity of a bus service, we can think of two schemes: (1) where each vehicle communicates locally with its neighbor vehicles only (predecessor and successor); and (2) all vehicles in the line communicate through a central system. In the first case, the headway control system will operate under a decentralized logic in which each bus takes its best decision knowing only its relative position with the buses immediately behind and ahead (Fu and Yang, 2002; Daganzo, 2009; Daganzo and Pilachowski, 2011; Andres and Nair, 2017). An advantage of this type of control is that it does not require sharing large volumes of information between vehicles or very sophisticated technologies for its implementation. In the second case, centralized and more complex control methods can be implemented. Under this type of control, the decisions to maintain headway regularity of a line are obtained using as input real-time data (depending on the availability) of the position, load and speed of all the buses under operation (Delgado et al., 2012; Sánchez-Martínez et al., 2016). Such a strategy requires a significantly higher volume of data than in the first case, but the decisions obtained should allow a much better performance of the system as a whole. In Delgado et al. (2016) it is shown how implementing a strictly local headway control logic that is not looking ahead in time and is not analyzing the impact in every bus in the line risks overreacting, causing more waiting times in the line. Interestingly, headway control can be implemented in simultaneity with eco-driving, minimizing pollutant emissions and energy consumption (Bueno-Cadena and Munoz, 2017; Xu et al., 2017).

V2V communication opens up possibilities to improve the level of service further. Providing service schedules at every stop becomes more feasible, and their adherence can improve. Also, transfers between vehicles of different routes are easier to program and operate. Providing schedules and coordinated transfers becomes especially important in low-frequency, night-time services (Ibarra-Rojas et al., 2019), in which passengers must transfer at stops that may be perceived as unsafe or under uncomfortable weather conditions.

Headway regularity control would also be favored by communication between vehicles and infrastructure (V2I), primarily through transit signal priority. It has been argued that with AV, traffic lights would be unnecessary at intersections to coordinate the incoming vehicle flows from different directions. However, the car fleet will not just take a long transition until it is fully automated, also traffic lights will still be essential to allow pedestrians to cross streets as well as providing access to public transport stops. Most transit signal priority studies have focused on under which conditions a bus should be given priority by examining the effects at an isolated intersection (Balke et al., 2000; Liao and Davis, 2007; Guo et al., 2019) without considering the impact on subsequent stops. Connecting vehicles to each other and to the infrastructure should allow more sophisticated transit priority systems to be developed. Intervening traffic signals' green and red timing might need to consider the effects on vehicles from different services not only competing in their movements but also in their impact on downstream stops along their services (Skabardonis, 2000; Delgado et al., 2015; Hu et al., 2015). In the case of services sharing the same corridor and serving the same demand, the headway control mechanism might need to consider that some passengers might be indifferent as to which service to take, while others might need just one of these services. In such a case the control tool should keep even headways not only within each service, but also try to keep even headways considering the vehicles of both lines as a single service.

Finally, headway control systems would benefit from real-time information about the number of passengers waiting at each stop or on board each vehicle. This could be achieved through automated passenger counting devices (APC) or the use of video cameras and artificial intelligence algorithms capable of detecting people. Such information would allow the control decisions to be adjusted to minimize the waiting times of the passengers at stops and on the buses. Furthermore, this information might reveal whether any of the passengers waiting require any special attention. For the user, this type of communication will allow them to be informed in real-time and inside the bus on the availability of public bicycles, scooters, and other forms of mobility suitable at the next stop or surrounding area, facilitating and enhancing multimodality.

17.4   ELECTRIC

Using electric vehicles in urban transport systems leads to multiple benefits, mainly from the environmental perspective, due to the zero or reduced emissions for full-electric or hybrid vehicles (see Herrmann and Rothfuss, 2015). Emissions from combustion engine vehicles degrade air quality, causing adverse effects on the health of the nearby population. This is particularly worrying for urban buses, which tend to be used in areas with high concentrations of people. The use of diesel engines can also cause respiratory issues such as asthma. Those who use public transit most often, including children, the elderly, and those without access to a car, are at particular risk. Also, electric public transport systems are more silent and provide a smoother ride than combustion engines, being considered more "neighborhood friendly" and providing a more satisfactory ride for their users. Finally, as long as the energy source is not from fuel fossils, this technology eliminates its carbon emissions at a global scale too.

From the operators' perspective, the maintenance cost of vehicles can be reduced due to the small number of components in electric engines. Besides, electric engines' energy losses are significantly lower than diesel engines' energy losses, so the cost per kilometer of electric bus travel is about a third of the cost of a diesel bus ride (Lajunen, 2014; Ambrose et al., 2017).

Although there are clearly identified benefits of electromobility, implementing an efficient electric bus network is not straightforward. Shen et al. (2019) identified the following challenges when adopting electric fleets: (1) planning charging infrastructure; (2) charging operations; and (3) public policy and business models.

In the case of charging infrastructure, the main problem is the design and operation of the electric grid needed for massive simultaneous vehicle charging. Electricity costs are lower during the night, when most buses would be available for charging. However, most buses would need recharging during the day to serve both morning and afternoon peak periods. Thus, deciding when and where each bus should be recharged must be addressed in coherence with the operational plan for each bus. To prevent causing an electricity demand peak, bus companies should avoid charging their buses simultaneously. Some regulation fostering such coordination that minimizes total electricity costs would be beneficial. Liu and Wang (2017) address this problem through a multi-level location problem for charging stations to minimize a measure of public social costs subject to budget constraints. Another recent study that formulates a location problem for charging infrastructure for electric vehicles in public transport is Gusrialdi et al. (2017). The authors propose a queuing model to minimize waiting time; their numerical results based on a scheduling algorithm show that the proposed solution approach is capable of using charging stations uniformly.

To reduce the complexity of using an electric grid for massive charging, there are alternatives such as battery swapping activities at depots or specific locations in the transit network defined in a planning stage (see for example Chao and Xiaohong, 2013). Indeed, battery swapping can take less than 10 minutes in some cases, which avoids large battery charging times. However, the capacity limits of the swapping stations should be modeled differently, as they are constrained by the number of spare batteries stocked at the stations, and auxiliary equipment requirements for set-up activities, For example, Widrick et al. (2018) propose a Markov decision process that determines the number of batteries to charge/discharge over time at swapping stations (where transport operators could be assisted), the charging capacity, and the inventory of fully charged batteries to maximize the expected total profit over a fixed time horizon (assuming stochastic demands). Numerical results show that the number of fully charged batteries over time and the total number of batteries manipulated in swapping stations are similar across different demand scenarios. Moreover, the cost of swap service at stations must be set appropriately with respect to the seasonal charging costs in order to increase the profit besides the savings due to discharged batteries. Another alternative for planning charging infrastructure is to consider a dynamic scheme in which in some parts of the routes buses receive their energy from batteries, while in the rest they are fed directly from the electric grid. This latter context may happen with trolley buses fed through pantographs in the segments where such an infrastructure is available, or by other technologies such as dynamic wireless charging (DWC), where charging power is directly drawn from the road (see Panchal et al., 2018). Indeed, the use of DWC or "roadway powered" frees electric vehicles from battery shortcomings such as cost, size, weight, and long charging duration (see Buja et al., 2016).

As was mentioned, charging operations must be included in the operational plan for every vehicle. Defining every trip-block for each vehicle in the planning of urban transport networks must consider its autonomy to move without charging. Battery-charging activities can take significantly longer than fuel charging for vehicles with diesel engines. In such scenarios, vehicle scheduling models and algorithms should be fed with data indicating actual energy consumption of each trip type, allowing them to simultaneously determine battery-charging activities between blocks of trips. Few studies address such problems (see, for example, Quttineh et al., 2017 and Liu et al., 2019). One of the main reasons for not tackling vehicle scheduling problems in the context of electric vehicles is that energy consumption is difficult to estimate (see Kavalchuk et al., 2015). The energy consumed by a trip depends on weather conditions (especially if A/C is needed), driver behavior, surface topology, time of day, the weight of the vehicle (which is affected by the batteries inside the vehicle), and sensors requiring high energy consumption rates which may be required to guarantee the vehicle's "connectivity", among others.

Nie and Ghamami (2013) proposed an optimization problem formulated as a nonlinear program to determine which charging mode (slow, medium-speed, fast) should be promoted first by the government in a public transport corridor. The problem minimizes the social cost by determining the ideal battery size and charging capacity, subject to hard constraints for the level of service. The authors show that fast charging (50 percent of full capacity within 10–15 min) could better provide a higher service level and lower social costs than medium-speed charging. Additionally, numerical results show that battery swapping might not be socially optimal due to its huge investment cost in the case study.

In the context of public policies to encourage electromobility, some financial incentives may be needed. In several countries the environmental impact associated with fossil fuels is not captured in its price. Furthermore, in several countries it is subsidized. Thus, a first policy should be to recognize the externalities caused by fossil fuels increasing its cost. Governments should also consider subsidizing the electric charging infrastructure for public transport vehicles. Although the last decade has seen battery costs substantially decreasing every year, electric buses are still significantly more expensive than their diesel equivalent. This is why, outside China, very few cities have an electric bus fleet larger than 100 vehicles. Explaining the slowness of the technology adoption process, Ambrose et al. (2017) claim that, "The big issue is just maintaining two sets of fueling infrastructure." This work addresses a probabilistic approach to studying the tradeoffs between service coverage, frequency, and operating expenses against investments in new technologies. For example, small rural agencies may be forced to increase costs or decrease services to electrify their fleets, and the number of buses that must be purchased by a transit agency will depend on the route structure, the vehicle range per charge, and the charging system.

Despite these challenges, bus operators are starting to perceive electric buses as more cost-effective when their full life is considered, due to the operational and maintenance savings. However, many bus companies lack the financial strength to invest in a more expensive fleet as well as the required accompanying infrastructure, even though it promises to be more convenient in the long run. This can be decisive for small bus operators. Thus, providing some financial credit or facilities for such investments, or reducing the risk associated with an abrupt end of an operational contract for bus operators should be an effective way of encouraging companies to invest in electric buses.

Krawiec et al. (2016) identify the following market-driven scenarios to implement electric vehicles in public transport. First, a passive scenario wherein a public transport company extends the process of fleet exchange, awaiting the expected effect of electric buses' technological maturity. Second, normative scenarios assuming linear or quasi-linear financing and execution of fleet exchange, wherein 50 percent of the conventional fleet is replaced by electric buses in the following decades. Finally, an active scenario wherein the fleet is exchanged, as soon as possible, by getting grants for innovative, environmentally friendly activities. The authors state that due to the multitude of variables affecting the process of fleet exchange, decision support algorithms are expected and needed. For example, game theory has been implemented to define incentive schemes to purchase electric vehicles in competitive supply chains (see Huang et al., 2013 and Nie et al., 2016).

There are strong signs from many countries that after one century of expecting electric vehicles to be a relevant actor in urban mobility, they are becoming a reality. This is great news for cities, public transport users, and the environment.

17.5   SHARED

Most car owners use their vehicle for a very small fraction of the day, so the vehicles spend most of the time parked. In addition, in growing cities space is becoming scarcer and more expensive, which makes parking also costlier for users, particularly close to the most attractive destinations. Therefore, the development of technology to allow users to share their vehicles is a very attractive proposition, so that users will only pay for the amount of time they are using the vehicle. In this context, much of the new technology that has been developed for autonomous vehicles (AV) is predicated on the basis of shared vehicles, also known as shared autonomous vehicles (SAVs). In the meantime, there are some companies providing shared conventional vehicles, such as Car2go, Zipcar, Getaround, Awto, and many others. In this context, an increasing share of users will replace car ownership by using car sharing services, which provide new opportunities for public transport to capture these users as part of their mobility needs. Since for a car owner, the cost of the vehicle and the parking at their home are a sunk cost, the additional cost of using the vehicle for traveling is very small, and is mainly fuel expenses. Thus, unless a car owner is charged according to their use of the roads or for parking at their destination, it is very unlikely that they would prefer to use public transport.

In an urban context, where the land is becoming more expensive, and thus owning a parking space is more difficult, many people are preferring to use shared vehicles. Thus, as with movies or music, most people will prefer not to own a vehicle, but instead to share their use, accessing them only when they need them (Klein and Smart, 2017; Alemi et al., 2018). This should reduce the need for parking space since cars would be sequentially used by different people, liberating space for other urban needs such as bike routes, bus lanes or wider sidewalks. This should also reduce the size of the car fleet in a city since each car could be used by different people even during the peak period. But unless the mode choice for peak-period trips changes, the fleet size will not drop substantially, since most commute trips overlap at some level, leaving little room for a single vehicle to serve two morning commuters. However, if the marginal cost of using the vehicle is higher, one should expect that the mode choice should favor more sustainable transport options, particularly in dense urban areas with good coverage of public transport.

In addition to sharing the vehicle asset, in the last decade we have experienced the impressive entrance and growth of ride-hailing companies, also known as Transportation Network Companies (TNC). TNCs such as Uber, Didi, Lyft, Beat and others provide app-based technology that facilitates requesting a ride from independent drivers who provide a taxi-like service, but increasing the productivity of the driver who is directed to new riders, and improving the experience of the user who can request a ride easily. TNC users can be quoted the price of their trip and upon requesting the service they are given on-line information about waiting time and location of the vehicle for pick-up. This makes the use of TNCs more attractive than traditional taxis. In addition, in many places traditional taxi providers are now also using apps to provide a similar service. These companies have also explored services such as Uber-Pool, Lyft-Line, Didi Express-Pool, etc., in which the vehicle is shared between different riders; thus, if riders accept a small deviation from the shortest path to take other passengers, they can split the cost of their rides. Some companies have taken these shared vehicle services one step further and are operating with bigger vehicles (vans and buses) and the possibility of reserving a seat; some examples of this type of services are UberHOP, Via, and Jetty.mx. These are transit on demand services in which routes are dynamically adjusted and passengers can reserve their seat (Lewis and MacKenzie, 2017; Flores-Dewey, 2019). These services should reduce the number of vehicles operating much more significantly if people opt to share the vehicle with others during their trips. In this case, the resources consumed (fleet size, urban roads, energy) and the externalities created would drop markedly. Unfortunately, if these services reduce the cost of a car trip (as ridesharing companies did with taxis), urban car miles will grow.

In addition to car-sharing systems, there are a growing number of companies providing micro-mobility sharing alternatives, such as bike-sharing and scooter-sharing services in big cities. These public bikes and scooters could play an important role in making public transport more attractive, since they might be used to cover the first and final stage of each trip, which are often highly resisted by potential transit travelers.

These shared services would probably be included in Mobility as a Service (MaaS), in which users would buy weekly or monthly passes, eliminating the out-of-pocket effect. These services should also offer weekly or monthly passes or become integrated with public transport to provide a comprehensive element of urban mobility services (Wong et al., 2019).

The overall impact of TNCs and micro-mobility shared services on public transport is still debatable. This depends largely on whether they influence car ownership, and what types of trips are captured by TNCs. If TNCs can decrease car ownership, they could have a positive impact on public transport, since some users might consider public transport as part of their journey; however, as summarized by Tirachini (2019), the impact of TNCs on car ownership is still not conclusive. In terms of trips captured by TNCs, most studies show that a significant percentage (between 8 percent and 42 percent) are substituting public transport (Tirachini, 2019). This could also happen with micro-mobility modes. Any reduction on public transport ridership has a negative effect on public transport, since either more subsidies are required to maintain the same services, or frequencies (and/or services) need to be reduced to adjust for fewer passengers, thus reducing the level of service and the attractiveness of public transport. Nevertheless, most shared vehicle trips are not regular daily trips. Thus, the net impact of TNCs on public transport will depend on how transit agencies adjust services to this new environment and what type of incentives and disincentives are put in place for the operation of TNCs and shared micro-mobility services.

In this new environment, transit agencies should probably reallocate transit services to high demand corridors and take advantage of new mobility options, which can provide superior service in zones with lower demand. In these areas, demand responsive services and improvements in infrastructure to facilitate active modes should provide efficient mobility, thus solving local trips and giving access to high frequency and reliable transit services for longer trips. In this line, TNCs regulation should internalize the externalities of the use of vehicles in congested areas, thus facilitating their role in local trips, or first or last leg on longer trips in which efficient modes are used in congested areas. For example, local trips on shared bikes could become free given the positive externalities they generate for pollution, accidents, congestion and public health.

17.6   DISCUSSION

Cities worldwide have been declaring that they need to foster the use of public transport but they have faced a century where car use has systematically grown mostly to the detriment of public transport. Cars receive a large share of road space, providing a great ride for its users unless severe congestion has hit. This has made car use an aspiration for most people, which makes authorities' goal of hindering its use difficult.

At the city surface public transport requires the conditions to provide a fast, frequent and reliable service. ACES technologies open the door for the authority to improve it since public transport-only corridors might become more feasible to enforce. Enforcing bus lanes improves speed and headway regularity, which improves level of service and increases transport capacity, which is badly needed in many systems in developing countries. Improving bus lane enforcement might increase the credibility of this solution, creating a virtuous cycle in which badly needed public investment is attracted towards this type of infrastructure in these countries.

The arrival of ACES technologies might also provide an important change in the way we understand transport modes and the level of service they can provide, and the level of public regulation each mode should receive. Indeed, modern Metro lines are not just connected and electric, but are also becoming driverless. Such technologies are used in the Metro to provide a highly reliable service. Collective surface transport would significantly benefit from such technology combination since it would also allow an elusive and key goal to be achieved for user satisfaction: regular headways and timetable schedules. These attributes impact not just user waiting time and reliability, but also comfort, since passengers are better distributed across vehicles. It should avoid having a majority of passengers being extremely dissatisfied with boarding very crowded buses after long waiting times. Notice that user dissatisfaction grows non-linearly with vehicle occupation and wait time experienced, and passengers tend to associate their satisfaction with the worst of their experiences (Munoz et al., 2020). Thus, automated and controlled operations should become decisive for surface collective transport to achieve reliability.

Cities should address this opportunity to encourage the use of massive and non-motorized transport modes. If widely adopted, they will not only provide a more efficient and environmentally friendly transport system. These transport modes also require less road and parking space, which is a major constraint to urban growth and mobility. Note that road space is distributed across different modes and activities according to peak period requirements. And during these periods, when more trips head to similar destinations at the same time, cars are the worst option due to the severe congestion they cause. Thus, during peak periods collective and non-motorized transport should be promoted. Such a move would also leave room for all other activities that give cities their reason to exist. It is in their public space that citizens exploit the opportunities cities provide.

ACES becomes an opportunity for this change. Unfortunately, bus operators worldwide have often been extremely slow at adopting innovative technologies if they do not impact their short-term financial results. This is the case of headway regularity control, which operators rarely consider unless transit authorities associate their revenues with headway regularity performance. This is also the case of electric buses, which demand economic solvency from the operator to adopt them. Thus, if the authorities rely on the operators to implement these technologies, they need either to enforce it through regulation, or to foster it through financial incentives.

Cities must address a key issue: how to provide an economic and infrastructure framework that allows each transport mode to operate efficiently from a social standpoint. In such a challenge, public transport service on the main corridors and in local neighborhoods must become a key element, providing sustainable and convenient service for everyone. ACES technologies might be the last opportunity for city authorities to grasp this vision and make it happen by using their irruption to foster public transport, improve its actual and perceived level of service, and discourage the use of private cars.

NOTE

*   We would like to thank the support by CEDEUS, CONICYT/FONDAP 15110020, and the BRT+ Centre of Excellence funded by VREF. In addition, the second author would like to recognize the support by Fondecyt 1171049.

REFERENCES

Abe, Ryosuke (2019). Introducing autonomous buses and taxis: Quantifying the potential benefits in Japanese transportation systems. *Transportation Research A*, 126: 94–113.

Abkowitz, M. and Engelstein, I. (1983). Factors affecting running time on transit routes. *Transportation Research Part A*, 17A (2), 107–13.

Abkowitz, M. and Engelstein, I. (1984). Methods for maintaining transit service regularity. *Journal of the Transportation Research Board*, 961, 1–8.

Adler, M.W., Peer, S. and Sinozic, T. (2019). Autonomous, connected, electric shared vehicles (ACES) and public finance: An explorative analysis. *Transportation Research Interdisciplinary Perspectives*, 2, 100038.

Alemi, F., Circella, G., Mokhtarian, P. and Handy, S. (2018). Exploring the latent constructs behind the use of ridehailing in California. *Journal of Choice Modelling*, 29, 47–62.

Ambrose, H., Pappas, N. and Kendall, A. (2017). Exploring the costs of electrification for California's transit agencies. Technical report. University of California Institute of Transportation Studies.

Andres, M. and Nair, R. (2017). A predictive-control framework to address bus bunching. *Transportation Research Part B: Methodological*, 104, 123–48.

Balke, K.N., Dudek, C.L. and Urbanik, T. (2000). Development and evaluation of intelligent bus priority concept. *Transportation Research Record*, 1727(1), 12–19.

Becker, F. and Axhausen, K.W. (2017). Literature review on surveys investigating the acceptance of automated vehicles. *Transportation*, 44, 1293–306.

Bertini, R.L. and El-Geneidy, A.M. (2004). Modeling transit trip time using archived bus dispatch system data. *Journal of Transportation Engineering*, 130(1), 56–67.

BRT Centre of Excellence, EMBARQ, IEA and SIBRT (2019). Global BRTData. Version 3.47. Last modified: 22 May 2019. Available at: http://www.brtdata.org.

Bueno-Cadena, C. and Munoz, J.C. (2017). Reducing metro trip times and energy consumption through speed control, holding and boarding limits. *Transportmetrica A: Transport Science*, 13(9), 767–93.

Buja, G., Rim, C. and Mi, C. (2016). Dynamic charging of electric vehicles by wireless power transfer. *IEEE Transactions on Industrial Electronics*, 63(10), 6530–32.

Chao, Z. and Xiaohong, C. (2013). Optimizing battery electric bus transit vehicle scheduling with battery exchanging: Model and case study. *Procedia: Social and Behavioral Sciences*, 96, 2725–36.

Chen, X., Yu, L., Zhang, Y. and Guo, J. (2009). Analyzing urban bus service reliability at the stop, route, and network levels. *Transportation Research Part A: Policy and Practice*, 43(8), 722–34.

Childress, S., Nichols, B., Charlton, B. and Coe, S. (2015). Using an activity-based model to explore the potential impacts of automated vehicles. *Transportation Research Record*, 2493, 99–106.

Correia, G.H.A., Looff, E., van Cranenburgh, S., Snelder, M. and van Arem, B. 2019. On the impact of vehicle automation on the value of travel time while performing work and leisure activities in a car: Theoretical insights and results from a stated preference survey. *Transportation Research Part A: Policy and Practice*, 119, 359–82.

Daganzo, C.F. (2009). A headway-based approach to eliminate bus bunching: Systematic analysis and comparisons. *Transportation Research Part B: Methodological*, 43(10), 913–21.

Daganzo, C.F. and Pilachowski, J. (2011). Reducing bunching with bus-to-bus cooperation. *Transportation Research Part B: Methodological*, 45(1), 267–77.

Danés, C. and Muñoz, J.C. (2016). Public transport's reliability: The case of Santiago, Chile. Paper presented at the 14th International Conference on Competition and Ownership in Land Passenger Transport, Santiago.

Delgado, F., Muñoz, J.C. and Giesen, R. (2012). How much can holding and/or limiting boarding improve transit performance? *Transportation Research Part B*, 46(9), 1202–17.

Delgado, F., Muñoz, J.C. and Giesen, R. (2016). BRRT adding an R for reliability. In J.C. Muñoz and L. Paget-Seekins (eds), *Bus Rapid Transit and the Restructuring of Public Transit*, Bristol: Policy Press, pp. 317–36.

Delgado, F., Muñoz, J.C., Giesen, R. and Wilson, N.H. (2015). Integrated real-time transit signal priority control for high-frequency segregated transit services. *Transportation Research Record*, 2533(1), 28–38.

Duduta, N. and Lindau, L.A. (2015). Road safety impacts of BRT and busway features. In J.C. Munoz and

L. Paget-Seekins (eds), *Bus Rapid Transit and the Restructuring of Public Transit*, Bristol: Policy Press, pp. 355–68.

Flores-Dewey, O. (2019). App-based collective transport service in Mexico City. ITF Discussion Paper.

Fu, L. and Yang, X. (2002). Design and implementation of bus-holding control strategies with real-time information. *Transportation Research Record*, 1791(1), 6–12.

Guo, Y., Ma, J., Xiong, C., Li, X., Zhou, F. and Hao, W. (2019). Joint optimization of vehicle trajectories and intersection controllers with connected automated vehicles: Combined dynamic programming and shooting heuristic approach. *Transportation Research Part C: Emerging Technologies*, 98, 54–72.

Gusrialdi, A., Qu, Z. and Simaan, M.A. (2017). Distributed scheduling and cooperative control for charging of electric vehicles at highway service stations. *IEEE Transactions on Intelligent Transportation Systems*, 8(10), 2713–27.

Herrmann, F. and Rothfuss, F. (2015). Introduction to hybrid electric vehicles, battery electric vehicles, and off-road electric vehicles, in B. Scrosati, J. Garche and W. Tillmetz (eds), *Advances in Battery Technologies for Electric Vehicles*. Cambridge: Woodhead Publishing Series in Energy, pp. 3–16.

Hickman, M.D. (2001). An analytic stochastic model for the transit vehicle holding problem. *Transportation Science*, 35(3), 215–37.

Hu, J., Park, B.B. and Lee, Y.J. (2015). Coordinated transit signal priority supporting transit progression under connected vehicle technology. *Transportation Research Part C: Emerging Technologies*, 55, 393–408.

Huang, J., Leng, J., Liang, L. and Liu, J. (2013). Promoting electric automobiles: Supply chain analysis under a government's subsidy incentive scheme. *IIE Transactions*, 45(8), 826–44.

Ibarra-Rojas, O., Giesen, R., Munoz, J.C. and Knapp, P. (2019), Integrating frequency setting, timetabling, and route assignment to synchronize transit lines. *Journal of Advanced Transportation*. Available at https://doi.org/10.1155/2019/9408595.

Ivancevich, J.M., Konopaske, R. and Matteson, M.T. (2005). *Individual Differences and Work Behaviour*, New York: McGraw Hill.

Kavalchuk, I., Arisoy, H., Stojcevski, A. and Than Oo, A. (2015). Advanced simulation of power consumption of electric vehicles. *International Journal of Computer and Systems Engineering*, 9, 53–9.

Klein, N.J. and Smart, M.J. (2017). Millennials and car ownership: Less money, fewer cars. *Transport Policy*, 53, 20–29.

Krawiec, S., Lazarz, B., Markusik, S., Karón, G., Sierpinski, G., Krawiek, K. and Janecki, R. (2016). Urban public transport with the use of electric buses: Development tendencies. *Transport Problems*, 11(4), 127–37.

Lajunen, A. (2014). Energy consumption and cost-benefit analysis of hybrid and electric city buses. *Transportation Research C*, 38, 1–15.

Lazarus, J., Shaheen, S., Young, S.E., Fagnant, D., Voege, T., Baumgardner, W. and J. Fishelson, J. (2018). Shared automated mobility and public transport. In G. Meyer, and S. Beiker (eds), *Road Vehicle Automation 4: Lecture Notes in Mobility*. Cham: Springer, pp. 141–61.

Lewis, E.O.C. and MacKenzie, D. (2017). UberHOP in Seattle: Who, why, and how? *Transportation Research Record*, 2650(1), 101–111.

Li, T. and Kockelman, K. (2016). Valuing the safety benefits of connected and automated vehicle technologies. Paper presented at the Transportation Research Board 95th Annual Meeting. Washington, DC.

Liao, C.F. and Davis, G.A. (2007). Simulation study of bus signal priority strategy: Taking advantage of global positioning system, automated vehicle location system, and wireless communications. *Transportation Research Record*, 2034(1), 82–91.

Liu, H. and Wang, D. (2017). Locating multiple types of charging facilities for battery electric vehicles. *Transportation Research B*, 103, 30–55.

Liu, Y., Yao, E., Lu, M. and Yuan, L. (2019). Regional electric bus driving plan optimization algorithm considering charging time window. *Mathematical Problems in Engineering*, Article ID 7863290.

Martinez-Estupinan, Y., Delgado, F., Munoz, J.C. and Watkins, K. (2020). Understanding what elements influence a bus driver to use headway regularity tools: Case study of Santiago public transit system. Paper presented at the Transportation Research Board 99th Annual Meeting, Washington, DC.

Metz, D. (2018). Developing policy for urban autonomous vehicles: Impact on congestion. *Urban Science*, 2(2), 33, doi:10.3390/urbansci2020033.

Muñoz, J.C. and Paget-Seekins, L. (2015). *Restructuring Public Transport Through Bus Rapid Transit*. Bristol: Policy Press.

Muñoz, J.C., Soza-Parra, J. and Raveau, S. (2020). A comprehensive perspective of unreliable public transport services' costs. *Transportmetrica A: Transport Science*, 16, pp. 734–48.

NHTSA (2020). National Highway Traffic Safety Administration website. Accessed 12 January 2020 at https://www.nhtsa.gov/technology-innovation/automated-vehicles-safety.

Nie, Y. and Ghamami, M. (2013). A corridor-centric approach to planning electric vehicle charging infrastructure. *Transportation Research Part B*, 57, 172–90.

Nie, Y., Ghamami, M., Zockaie, A. and Xiao, F. (2016). Optimization of incentive policies for plug-in electric vehicles. *Transportation Research Part B*, 84, 103–23.

Panchal, C., Stegen, S. and Lu, J. (2018). Review of static and dynamic wireless electric vehicle charging systems. *Engineering Science and Technology, an International Journal*, 21, 922–37.

Quttineh, N.H., Häll, C.H., Ekström, J. and Ceder, A. (2017). Combined timetabling and vehicle scheduling for electric buses. *Proceedings of the 22nd International Conference of Hong Kong Society for Transportation Studies*.

Sánchez-Martínez, G.E., Koutsopoulos, H.N. and Wilson, N.H. (2016). Real-time holding control for high-frequency transit with dynamics. *Transportation Research Part B: Methodological*, 83, 1–19.

Shen, Z.-J.M., Feng, B., Mao, C. and Ran, L. (2019). Optimization models for electric vehicle service operations: A literature review. *Transportation Research B*, 128, 462–77.

Skabardonis, A. (2000). Control strategies for transit priority. *Transportation Research Record*, 1727(1), 20–26.

Sterman, B. and Schofer, J. (1976). Factors affecting reliability of urban bus services. *Transportation Engineering Journal*, 102, 147–59.

Strathman, J. and Hopper, J. (1993). Empirical analysis of bus transit on-time performance. *Transportation Research Part A*, 27A(2), 93–100.

Strathman, J., Dueker, K.J. and Kimpel, T. (1999). Automated bus dispatching, operations control, and service reliability baseline analysis. *Journal of the Transportation Research Board*, 1666, 28–36.

Sustainable Mobility for All (2017). Global Mobility Report 2017: Tracking sector performance. Washington, DC, License: Creative Commons Attribution CC BY 3.0.

Tao, D., Zhang, R. and Qu, X. (2017). The role of personality traits and driving experience in self-reported risky driving behaviors and accident risk among Chinese drivers. *Accident Analysis and Prevention*, 99, 228–35. Accessed at https://doi.org/10.1016/j.aap.2016.12.009.

Tirachini, A. (2019). Ride-hailing, travel behaviour and sustainable mobility: An international review. *Transportation*, 1–37.

Tse, J.L.M., Flin, R. and Mearns, K. (2006). Bus driver well-being review: 50 years of research. *Transportation Research Part F: Traffic Psychology and Behaviour*, 9(2), 89e114. 89–114.

van Oort, N. (2011). Service reliability and urban public transport design. TRAIL: PhD Thesis Series T2011/2, Delft.

Walker, J. (2011). *Human Transit: How Clearer Thinking about Public Transit Can Enrich Our Communities and Our Lives*. Washington, DC: Island Press.

Wenquan, Z.M.L. (2013). Factors affecting headway regularity on bus routes. *Journal of Southeast University* [English edn], (1), 22.

Widrick, R.S., Nurre, S.G. and Robbins, M.J. (2018). Optimal policies for the management of an electric vehicle battery swap station. *Transportation Science*, 52(1), 59–79.

Wong, Y.Z., Hensher, D.A. and Mulley, C. (2019). Mobility as a service (MaaS): Charting a future context. *Transportation Research Part A: Policy and Practice*.

Xu, Y., Li, H., Liu, H., Rodgers, M.O. and Guensler, R.L. (2017). Eco-driving for transit: An effective strategy to conserve fuel and emissions. *Applied Energy*, 194, 784–97.

18. Research in public transport vehicle scheduling*
Tao Liu and Avishai (Avi) Ceder

18.1 INTRODUCTION

In this chapter we refer to the public transport (PT) operations planning process of a fixed-route system such as bus, rail and passenger ferries. This process commonly includes four basic components, divided into three different levels and usually performed in sequence: (1) network design; (2) timetable development; (3) vehicle scheduling; and (4) crew scheduling and rostering. The framework of this process is shown in Figure 18.1. It is preferable that all four activities be planned simultaneously in order to exploit system capability to the greatest extent and maximize system productivity and efficiency (Ceder 2016). However, since this integrated planning process is extremely cumbersome and complex, especially for medium and large-scale PT agencies, separated treatment is required for each component, with the outcome of one fed as an input into the next component. From the perspective of PT agencies, the highest cost items in the budget are vehicle capital and operating costs, driver wages and fringe benefits. Therefore, it is not surprising to learn that most of the commercially available PT scheduling software packages concentrate primarily on vehicle and crew scheduling activities. In the last fifty years, a considerable amount of effort has been invested in the computerization of the above four components in order to provide more efficient, controllable and responsive PT services.

This chapter focuses on the third PT operations-planning component: vehicle scheduling, which is one of the problems at the operational-planning level. The PT vehicle scheduling problem (VSP) refers to the problem of determining the optimal allocation of vehicles to carry out all the trips of a given timetable. A chain of trips is assigned to each vehicle, although some of them may be deadheading (DH) or empty trips in order to attain optimality. The assignment of vehicle chains to garages should be determined in an efficient manner. The major objective of the PT VSP is to minimize fleet size or, correspondingly, to minimize the total cost comprised of fixed costs (acquisition, salaries, administration, etc.) and variable costs (maintenance, fuels, supplies, etc.). The number of feasible solutions to this problem is extremely high, especially in the case of multiple depots.

Here we are reviewing the latest research works, approaches and computerized software packages to conduct PT vehicle scheduling. The focus is on practical methods and tools for scheduling PT vehicles of transit agencies around the world. We first overview the latest PT vehicle scheduling literature, and secondly describe solution approaches, including exact and heuristic solutions. In doing so several numerical examples are provided to illustrate the solution approaches. In addition, known available PT scheduling software packages, together with their key features and classifications, are reviewed and summarized. Finally, future search directions on VSP are outlined. It is believed that the examination of the PT vehicle scheduling approaches and software packages can benefit PT researchers, schedulers and scheduling software developers.

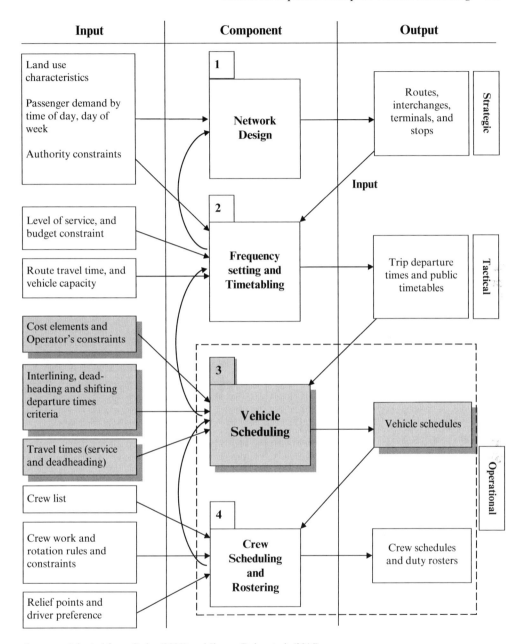

Source: Adapted from Ceder (2001) and Ibarra-Rojas et al. (2015).

Figure 18.1   *Framework of public transport operations-planning process with emphasis on vehicle scheduling*

18.2   LITERATURE REVIEW

Much of the focus in the literature on PT VSPs is on computational issues. During the past few years, a rich body of literature on PT vehicle scheduling has emerged. An early survey by Bodin et al. (1983) provides detailed classifications, mathematical formulations, and solution algorithms of the VSPs. A review of network models and methods for VSPs can be found in Carraresi and Gallo (1984). Daduna and Paixão (1995) reviewed mathematical models for VSPs in PT systems. Recent detailed reviews on model formulations, solution approaches, and algorithm developments for PT VSPs can be found in Desaulniers and Hickman (2007), Bunte and Kliewer (2009), Ibarra-Rojas et al. (2015), Ceder (2016), and Liu and Ceder (2017). The best summary of the software packages, methods developed and knowledge accumulated appeared in a series of books arising from the international Conference on Advanced Systems in Public Transport (CASPT).

Classification of PT Vehicle Scheduling Problems

A good understanding of the characteristics of PT VSPs can help in identifying the appropriate solution approaches. Following a careful examination of the literature, PT VSPs can be generally classified by the following list.

A.   Number of depots
    1.   Single depot
    2.   Multiple depots
B.   Depot capacity constraints
    1.   With depot capacity constraint
    2.   Without depot capacity constraint
C.   Vehicle types
    1.   Single vehicle type (homogeneous fleet)
    2.   Multiple vehicle types (heterogeneous fleet)
D.   Properties of vehicle running times
    1.   Deterministic vehicle running time
    2.   Stochastic vehicle running time
E.   Maximum vehicle running time constraints
    1.   With maximum vehicle running time constraint
    2.   Without maximum vehicle running time constraint
F.   Vehicle departure times
    1.   Fixed departure times
    2.   Variable departure times
G.   Deadheading/interlining operations
    1.   Allowed
    2.   Not allowed
H.   Integrated with other operations planning activities
    1.   Integrated
    2.   Not integrated
I.   Objective function

1. To minimize the number of vehicles, i.e., the fleet size
2. To minimize the total operations cost, including fixed and variable costs

J.   Other problem-dependent characteristics.

The aforementioned characteristics provide a general PT VSPs classification framework. For example, the battery electric PT vehicle scheduling problem belongs to the PT VSP with maximum vehicle running time constraint. This classification framework can also help identify new variants of PT VSPs. Thus, it can help develop new solution approaches.

Solution Approaches

Solution approaches to PT vehicle scheduling world-wide range from primitive decision-making to computerized mathematical-programming techniques. An examination of the existing literature indicates that the PT VSPs solution approaches can be generally classified as follows.

1. *Graphical solution approach.* This approach uses some basic graphical techniques, such as Gantt chart, time–space diagram, and deficit function. The main advantage of the graphical solution approach is its graphical nature and visual simplicity.
2. *Heuristic approach.* This approach uses some practical heuristic methods that provide an opportunity to explore various solution possibilities. Examples of this solution approach include the concurrent scheduler approach, Lagrangian heuristic, improvement/exchange, and interactive optimization.
3. *Meta-heuristic approach.* The meta-heuristic approach extends the heuristic approach by using an efficient computation capacity of computers, allowing a wider exploration of the solution space. Examples are genetic algorithm, ant colony optimization, tabu search, and simulated annealing.
4. *Exact solution approach.* This approach formulates the problem as mathematical programming (MP) models, such as mixed integer programming model, and uses algorithms such as branch-and-bound algorithm, to solve the model and generate exact solutions. Generally speaking, this approach can obtain an optimal solution. However, for large-scale problems, this solution approach may require long computational time, and could even not be feasible to reach the solution in practice. For the latter, heuristic and meta-heuristic solution approaches are employed to attain a near-optimal or an optimal (without a proof) solution.
5. *Simulation-based approach.* This approach generates and evaluates different vehicle schedules by simulating various scenarios with different parameters, such as passenger demand, level of service, and operational cost.
6. *Artificial intelligence (AI)-based solution approach.* This approach uses some AI techniques, such as machine learning, automated reasoning and inference, case-and rule-based reasoning, and expert systems.
7. *Combined solution approach.* The combination of the aforementioned approaches can generate new hybrid solution methods. It can make use of the advantages of different solution approaches. Most PT scheduling computer software packages use this approach.

For small and medium-sized PT VSPs, some existing optimization techniques can provide exact optimal solutions in a reasonable computation time. For large-scale multi-depot PT VSPs, because of the computational complexity, heuristic, meta-heuristic or AI-based solution approaches are usually used to solve the problems with approximated good solutions in an acceptable computation time.

Recent Research Topics

In addition to improving the effectiveness and efficiency of existing solution approaches, recent literature on PT VSPs indicates that there are new emerged research topics. We summarize and review these recent themes in the following sections.

Integrating PT vehicle scheduling with other PT operations-planning activities

Most previous studies on PT vehicle scheduling have treated the problem separately, rather than coupled with other operations planning activities. Recently, there have been a growing number of studies on integrating PT vehicle scheduling with other planning components. Freling et al. (2001) and Huisman et al. (2005) presented an integrated approach for integrating vehicle and crew scheduling for a single bus route. The two problems are first defined separately: the vehicle scheduling problem is formulated as a network-flow problem, in which each path represents a feasible vehicle schedule, and each node a trip. In the combined version, the network problem is incorporated into the same program with a set partitioning formulation of the crew scheduling problem. Haase et al. (2001) formulated another problem that incorporated both crew and vehicle scheduling. For vehicle scheduling, the case of a single depot with a homogeneous fleet is considered. The crew scheduling problem is a set partitioning formulation that includes side constraints for the bus itineraries; these constraints guarantee that an optimal vehicle assignment can be derived afterwards. Steinzen et al. (2010) discussed the integrated vehicle- and crew-scheduling problem in PT with multiple depots. The authors present a new modelling approach that is based on a time–space network representation of the underlying vehicle- and crew-scheduling problem. The suggested methodology is based on a Lagrangian heuristic in conjunction with column generation, where the pricing problem is formulated as a resource-constrained shortest-path problem. It has been illustrated that this proposed network representation for the pricing problem produces favourable results compared with other approaches. The presented method outperforms other methods from the literature in terms of the solution quality and computational time. Ibarra-Rojas et al. (2014) developed a bi-objective optimization model for the complete integration of timetabling and vehicle scheduling problems. Schöbel (2017) proposed a bi-objective model for integrating line planning, timetabling, and vehicle scheduling. Iterative algorithms and an Eigenmodel were developed for the design of re-optimization procedures. Liu et al. (2017) studied the integrated PT vehicle scheduling and timetable synchronization problem. The objectives are to maximize the number of simultaneous vehicle arrivals at the transfer nodes of a PT network, and to minimize the required fleet size. A novel two-stage deficit function (DF)-based method is developed to solve the mathematical model using a human–machine interactive approach. Laporte et al. (2017) integrated users' routings into the integrated timetabling and vehicle scheduling problem within a multi-objective optimization framework. Fonseca et al. (2018) integrated transfer synchronization into the integrated timetabling and vehicle scheduling problem. Carosi et al. (2019) proposed a matheuristic approach to the integrated timetabling and vehicle scheduling problem. The aforementioned studies clearly indicate that integrating PT vehicle scheduling with other operations-planning activities is an emerging and important research problem from the theoretical and practical perspectives.

Electric PT vehicle scheduling
Because of zero emissions and other social and economic benefits, electric vehicles (EVs) are recently being introduced in more and more PT agencies around the world (Häll et al. 2019). The PT electric vehicle scheduling problem (E-VSP) is an extension of the VSP by considering the limited driving range and charging requirement of EVs. The VSP with driving range constraints has been addressed in some previous studies, for example, Freling and Paixão (1995), Haghani and Banihashemi (2002) and Wang and Shen (2007). Desrosiers et al. (1995) provide an earlier overview of optimization methods for the time-constrained vehicle routing and scheduling problem. Recently, Adler and Mirchandani (2016) studied a similar problem by considering the possibility of allowing vehicles to refuel at certain places, which is similar to allowing vehicles to recharge at some charging stations. Zhu and Chen (2013) proposed a non-dominated sorting genetic algorithm (NSGA- II) to optimize battery electric bus transit vehicle scheduling with battery exchanging. Wen et al. (2016) proposed a mixed integer programming (MIP) model for the E-VSP with the aim of minimizing both the total number of vehicles required and the total travel distance. An adaptive large neighbourhood search heuristic algorithm was developed to solve the problem. Wang et al. (2017) developed a mixed integer linear programming model for the electric bus recharging scheduling problem with the objective of minimizing the annual total operating costs of the electric bus recharging system. The math-programming model was solved by using CPLEX. Van Kooten Niekerk et al. (2017) developed two math-programming models for the E-VSP based on different charging processes. For small and medium-sized problems, the two models can be solved using commercial optimization solvers. For large-size problems, two solution methods that are based on column generation and Lagrangian relaxation were developed. Rogge et al. (2018) studied the EV scheduling fleet size and mix problem with optimization of charging infrastructure. A solution framework that is based on a grouping genetic algorithm, coupled with a mixed integer charger optimization, was developed to minimize the total cost of EV fleet ownership. Tang et al. (2019) developed both static and dynamic models within a branch-and-price solution framework for the robust scheduling of electric buses under stochastic road traffic conditions. Li et al. (2019) developed an integer linear programming model using a time–space network concept for the multi-depot and multi-vehicle-type electric bus scheduling problem considering battery range and refuelling constraints. Teng et al. (2020) developed a multi-objective optimization model for the integrated PT timetabling and vehicle scheduling of a single electric bus line, with the objective of smoothing the vehicle departure intervals and minimizing the number of vehicles and total battery-charging costs. A multi-objective particle swarm optimization algorithm was developed to solve the model.

Liu and Ceder (2020) studied the battery-electric transit vehicle scheduling problem with stationary battery chargers installed at transit terminal stations. Yao et al. (2020) developed a genetic algorithm-based heuristic procedure for solving the PT electric vehicle scheduling problem with multiple vehicle types.

Stochastic and dynamic PT vehicle scheduling

Due to traffic disturbances and disruptions, fluctuations in passenger demand, and erroneous behaviour of drivers, PT systems are known to be unstable with stochastic and dynamic characteristics. Some PT vehicle scheduling models and algorithms, considering uncertain input, have been developed over the past years. Huisman et al. (2004) proposed a dynamic formulation of the multi-depot vehicle scheduling problem. The traditional, static vehicle scheduling problem assumes that travel times are a fixed input that enters the solution procedure only once; the dynamic formulation relaxes this assumption by solving a sequence of optimization problems for shorter periods. Naumann et al. (2011) presented a new stochastic programming approach for robust vehicle scheduling in bus transit. The presented approach uses typical disruption scenarios during the optimization to minimize the expected sum of planned costs and costs caused by disruptions. The schedule is represented as a time–space network with all connecting arcs to enable independent penalization of every connection between two consecutive service trips. The results indicate that stochastic programming for the vehicle scheduling problem with disruptions leads to solutions which are of higher quality in terms of total expected costs compared to a simple approach with fixed buffer times. Shen et al. (2016) developed a network flow model for vehicle scheduling considering stochastic trip times. A novel VSP probabilistic model featuring the stochastic trips was proposed with the objectives of minimizing the total cost and maximizing the on-time performance. Shen et al. (2017) further considered adding a new objective of achieving the expected on-time performance in the stochastic PT vehicle scheduling model. He et al. (2018) proposed an approximate dynamic programming approach to formulating the stochastic dynamic vehicle scheduling problem with the objective of tackling the trip time stochasticity, reducing the delay and minimizing the total costs of a PT system. Overall, the stochastic and dynamic PT VSPs will continue to be a hot research theme at the theoretical and practical levels.

On-demand and shared autonomous PT vehicle scheduling

The advent of autonomous vehicles (AVs) and wide use of smartphone apps will have a significant impact on the existing PT systems (Anderson et al. 2014; Rayle et al. 2014; Liu and Ceder 2015; Faisal et al. 2019). The shared use of AVs and smartphone apps will considerably change the current PT systems into far more system-optimal, user-oriented on-demand ones with lower system operation cost and improved level of service. Recently, numerous studies have been appearing in the literature about the scheduling of on-demand and shared autonomous PT vehicles. Tsubouchi et al. (2010) developed cloud computing technology-based vehicle choosing and routing heuristic algorithms for the scheduling of on-demand buses. Lam et al. (2016) formulated the autonomous PT vehicle scheduling problem as a mixed integer linear programming problem, and a genetic algorithm-based method was developed to solve it. Winter et al. (2016) developed a simulation model to determine the optimal and minimum fleet size required for an automated demand-responsive PT system with minimal total operational and travel cost. Pinto et al. (2019) studied the joint transit network redesign and shared-use AV mobility services fleet size determination problem. The problem was formulated as a bi-level mathematical programming model. An iterative agent-based assignment-simulation and heuristic solution procedures are developed to solve the model. Cao and Ceder (2019) developed a binary-variable iteration method-based genetic algorithm for the optimal

scheduling of an autonomous shuttle bus service considering vehicle skip-stop operation. Comprehensively, the on-demand and shared autonomous PT vehicle scheduling
problems will attract more and more research attention.

18.3   THE MINIMUM PT FLEET SIZE PROBLEM

The primal objective of PT vehicle scheduling is to minimize the fleet size, that is, the
number of vehicles required. This is a major concern for PT agencies because it is the most
significant part of their budget. Thus, this is an important task to search for optimization
in finding the minimum fleet size required while complying with all planned trips of the
timetables. Traditionally, equation (18.1) is widely used in the literature to calculate the
minimum fleet size required for a single loop line i:

$$N_i = \left\lceil \frac{T_i}{H_i} \right\rceil \tag{18.1}$$

where N_i is the number of vehicles required for line i; T_i is the cycle time of line i; H_i is the
headway (time elapsed between two consecutive departures) of line i; $\frac{1}{H_i}$ is the frequency
of line i. The bracket is the ceiling function that maps the computed value to the smallest
following integer. For a PT system with 10 lines, the total number of vehicles required, i.e.,
fleet size, is simply calculated by $N = \sum_{i=1}^{10} N_i$.

However, as pointed out by Liu (2020), this fleet size model has some limitations. First,
this model is intended for even-headway PT systems and cannot be used for uneven-
headway PT systems. Second, because of stochastic and uncertain characteristics of PT
systems, the cycle time T_i is not fixed to be a constant for each cycle during the schedule
horizon. Third, this model can only provide approximate, not exact or optimal, solutions
to the minimum fleet size problem. Fourth, it ignores an important fact that the sum of
the fleet size required for each line is not the minimum total fleet size required for the
whole PT network. That is, it does not consider the possibility of allowing interlining
or deadheading operations, which may significantly reduce the network-wide fleet size
required for large-scale PT systems in practice. Because of these limitations, this fleet
size model is not suitable, though used in some studies. One model that can overcome the
limitations of equation (18.1) is the deficit function (DF)-based fleet size model described
as follows.

18.4   DEFICIT FUNCTION APPROACH FOR FLEET SIZING
AND VEHICLE SCHEDULING

Background on the Deficit Function

The concept of the deficit function (DF) was initially proposed in Linis and Maksim (1967),
and used for flight scheduling. The DF concept was formally defined and described in
Gertsbach and Gurevich (1977) and Ceder and Stern (1981). The DF modelling approach
was used to solve the PT minimum fleet size problem by Ceder and Stern (1981) and Ceder

(2002). Ceder (2016) further developed the DF model and applied it to other PT operation planning activities, such as transit network design, crew scheduling, and vehicle parking management. Liu and Ceder (2017) provided a detailed description of the DF model and its major developments of applications over the past 50 years. A DF is defined as a step function that is associated with a transportation terminal. It increases by 1 at the time of each vehicle trip departure and decreases by 1 at the time of each vehicle trip arrival. The main advantage of the DF is its graphical and visual nature. To construct a set of DFs, the only information needed is a timetable of scheduled trips $J = \{j: j = 1, \ldots, n\}$. Let $d(k,t,S)$ denote the DF for terminal k at time t for schedule S. The value of $d(k,t,S)$ represents the total number of departing vehicles minus the total number of arriving vehicles at terminal k, up to and including time t. The maximum value of $d(k,t,S)$ over the schedule horizon $[T_1, T_2]$, designated $D(k,S)$, depicts the deficit number of vehicles required at k. Note that S will be deleted when it is clear which underlying schedule is being considered.

Deficit Function-based Minimum Fleet Size Model

As described in Liu (2020), the minimum fleet size required for a PT system can be calculated according to the following DF-based fleet size theorem:

Theorem 1:   If, for a set of terminals K and a fixed set of required trips J, all vehicle trips start and end within the schedule horizon $[T_1, T_2]$ and no deadheading (DH) insertions are allowed, then the minimum number of vehicles required, i.e., the fleet size, to service all vehicle trips in J is equal to the sum of the deficits across all terminals.

$$Min\, N(S) = \sum_{k \in K} D(k, S) = \sum_{k \in K} \max_{t \in [T_1, T_2]} d(k, t, S) \qquad (18.2)$$

Proof.   A formal proof can be found in Linis and Maksim (1967) and Ceder (2016).

Figure 18.2 illustrates how to use the DF model to determine the minimum fleet size required for a loop-line PT system. The upper part of Figure 18.2 is the schedule with departure/arrival terminals and times; the lower level is the corresponding DF of terminal a. It shows the maximum value of $d(a, t)$ is $D(a)=3$, which indicates the minimum fleet size is three vehicles.

Deficit Function Approach for PT Vehicle Scheduling

The DF model has been developed as a highly graphical human–machine interactive approach for PT vehicle scheduling. It can allow PT schedulers to insert DH vehicle trips and slightly shifting departure times (SDT) of PT vehicle trips to further reduce the minimum fleet size required. In addition, based on the graphical characteristics of DF figures, the vehicle chains can easily be constructed. The SDT is usually bounded by given tolerances. Further explications of the SDT appear in Ceder (2016). Figure 18.3 illustrates how to use the DF model to conduct PT vehicle scheduling. Part (i) of Figure 18.3 shows that the minimum number of vehicles required is five vehicles. Part (ii) shows how to reduce the fleet size by using the SDT procedure with left and right shifting tolerance

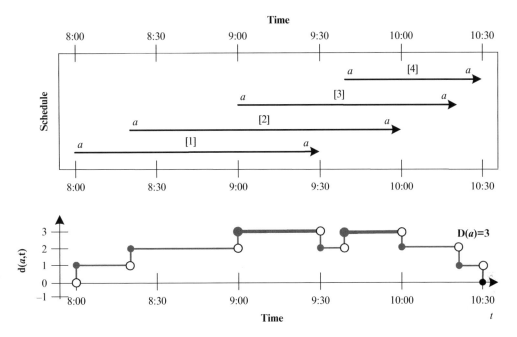

Figure 18.2 *Using DF model to calculate the minimum fleet size*

$\Delta^{i(-)} = \Delta^{i(+)} = \frac{1}{2}$ time unit where the shifts are shown with small arrows and the update DF is marked by a single dash just under the bold line. Part (iii) shows how to apply only the DH procedure with DH times of 2 time units, and part (iv) presents a modified DH (mixed with the SDT) procedure. As can be seen in Figure 18.3 (i), the fixed schedule without DH considerations requires five vehicles. Using SDT allows the fleet size to be reduced to three vehicles. The use of DH allows it to be reduced to four vehicles, and the use of the combined approach requires three vehicles. After determining the minimum fleet size, all of the trips, including the DH trips, are chained together to construct the vehicle blocks.

18.5 NETWORK FLOW APPROACH FOR PT VEHICLE SCHEDULING

In addition to the DF heuristic approach, network flow models can be a useful tool for comprehending the process for finding the minimal number of PT vehicles. In what follows is its description based on the work of Liu and Ceder (2018). A network flow model is employed to estimate the minimum fleet size of a given schedule **s**. A trip joining array for **s** may be constructed by associating the gth row with the arrival event of the gth trip, and the g'th column with the departure event of the g'th trip. Cell (g, g') will be admissible if g and g' can be joined feasibly. Otherwise, (g, g') will be an inadmissible cell. Let $x_{gg'}$ be a

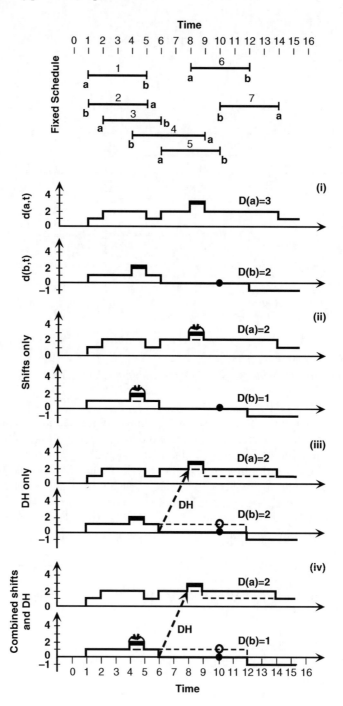

Source: Adapted from Ceder (2002).

Figure 18.3   DF approach for PT vehicle scheduling

0−1 variable associated with cell (g, g') and G be the set of required trips. Then, consider the following problem:

$$Max \ N_1 = \sum_{g \in G} \sum_{g' \in G} x_{gg'} \qquad (18.3)$$

$$\text{s.t.} \sum_{g' \in G} x_{gg'} \leq 1, \ g \in G \qquad (18.4)$$

$$\sum_{g \in G} x_{gg'} \leq 1, \ g' \in G \qquad (18.5)$$

$$\begin{array}{ll} x_{gg'} \in \{0,1\}, \ \text{all} \ (g,g') \ \text{admissible} \\ x_{gg'} = 0, \qquad \text{all} \ (g,g') \ \text{inadmissible} \end{array} \qquad (18.6)$$

A solution with $x_{gg'} = 1$ indicates that trips g and g' are joined. The objective function maximizes the number of such joinings. Constraint (18.4) ensures that each trip may be joined with no more than one successor trip. Similarly, constraint (18.5) indicates that each trip may be joined with no more than one predecessor trip. This problem is equivalent to a special arrangement of the maximum flow (max-flow) problem. The max-flow algorithm that solves the vehicle scheduling problem with DH trips is called an augmenting path algorithm. It is addressed at length in the classic book by Ford and Fulkerson (1962). The vehicle scheduling problem can be transformed to a unit capacity bipartite network in which the solution time has the complexity of $O(n^{1/2} m)$ with n nodes (departure times) and m arcs. The following theorem states that maximizing N_1 is tantamount to minimizing the number of chains for a trip schedule of size n.

Theorem 2 (The max-flow fleet size theorem): Let $N_{MF}(S)$ and n denote the number of chains and trips of schedule s, respectively. Then,

$$Min \ N_{MF}(S) = n - Max \ N_1 \qquad (18.7)$$

Proof: Given a set of $G = \{g: g = 1, ..., n\}$ required trips. Assigning each trip separately to an individual vehicle results in a fleet size of n vehicles. If $x_{gg'} = 1$, then trip g' can be performed after trip g by the same vehicle v_g. Thus, the vehicle $v_{g'}$ assigned to trip g' can be saved. The required fleet size thus can be reduced from n to $n - 1$. Similarly, the value of max-flow $Max \ N_1$ means $Max \ N_1$ vehicles can be saved by linking trips together. Thus, the minimum number of vehicles required to perform all trips in G is $n - Max \ N_1$. This completes the proof.

An Illustrative Example

Consider the three terminal problem defined by the data in Tables 18.1 and 18.2 and Figure 18.4(a). The data in Table 18.1 and Figure 18.4(a) are transformed into the generic diachronic graph in Figure 18.4(c) and network-flow representation in Figure 18.4(d), which has two dummy nodes: a source node s and a sink node t. The nodes, being connected from s, are the arrival times of the example, with an indication, in parentheses, of the arrival terminal. The nodes connected to t are the departure times, with an indication

*Table 18.1 Trip schedule **S** for the example problem*

Trip number g	Departure terminal p^g	Departure time t_s^g	Arrival terminal q^g	Arrival time t_e^g
1	b	6:00	b	6:30
2	a	7:05	c	8:05
3	c	7:10	a	8:00
4	b	8:30	a	9:20
5	a	9:00	b	9:45

Table 18.2 Average DH travel time (minutes) matrix for the example in Table 18.1

		Arrival terminal		
		a	b	c
Departure terminal	a	0	30	50
	b	35	0	45
	c	45	40	0

of the departure terminal. Feasible connections between the arrival and departure times, utilizing the DH data in Table 18.2, establish the arcs between the left and right nodes. Each arc capacity represents the number of connections that can flow through the arc. In our case, there is only a unit capacity assigned to each arc, because only one connection (if any) between a given arrival time and terminal and a given departure time and terminal is possible. The more flow created, the fewer chains will be required, as stated by Theorem 2. The objective function N_1 equals the flow to be created at s and absorbed at t. Since max-flow = minimum s-t cut in the original network flow. This minimum s-t cut is shown in Figure 18.4(d). The result of the example is max-flow = $Max\ N_1$ = 3, and, following Theorem 2, $Min\ N_{MF}(S) = n - MaxN_1 = 5 - 3 = 2$ chains. Restated, the timetable in Table 18.1 can be carried out by a minimum of two vehicles having the connections shown in Figure 18.4(d).

The equivalent DF solution, shown in Figure 18.4(b), also results in two vehicles: $Min\ N_{DF}(S) = D(a) + D(b) + D(c) = 0 + 1 + 1 = 2$. Explicitly the two blocks, by their trip number in 1, are [1-DH$_1$-2-DH$_3$-5] and [3-DH$_2$-4]. These two blocks have three DH trips for connecting arrival and departure terminals: DH$_1(b-a)$ and DH$_3(c-a)$ (in the first block) and DH$_2(a-b)$ (in the second block), with the total of $35 + 45 + 30 = 110$ minutes DH time respectively.

18.6 PT VEHICLE SCHEDULING SOFTWARE

The complexity involved in the PT operations planning process challenged researchers to develop automated computerized procedures, which eventually led to a number of

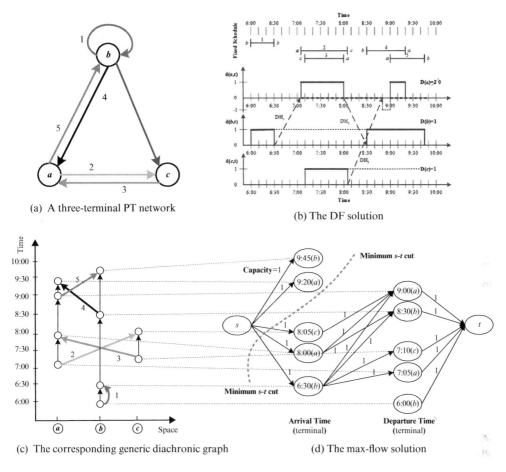

(a) A three-terminal PT network

(b) The DF solution

(c) The corresponding generic diachronic graph

(d) The max-flow solution

Source: Liu and Ceder (2018).

Figure 18.4   *An example vehicle scheduling problem using max-flow technique and its equivalent DF solution*

software packages. An overall view of the architecture of such software is illustrated by Figure 18.5. It is worth mentioning that the evaluation module of such a software package should be based on an external input related to cost coefficients, and performance criteria. The cost coefficients may include: vehicle cost (fixed and variable), driver cost and other costs. The performance criteria may include: level of passenger service, measures for vehicle schedules, and more.

The use of computers in PT scheduling was introduced in the early 1960s (Elias 1964; Wren 1971). Since then, many computer programs have been developed for solving PT scheduling problems. Some of the known software with their internet address and key features are listed in Table 18.3, following Ceder (2016).

In accordance with the approaches used, the computer-aided PT scheduling systems can be classified and grouped into six categories as follows. These categories and the

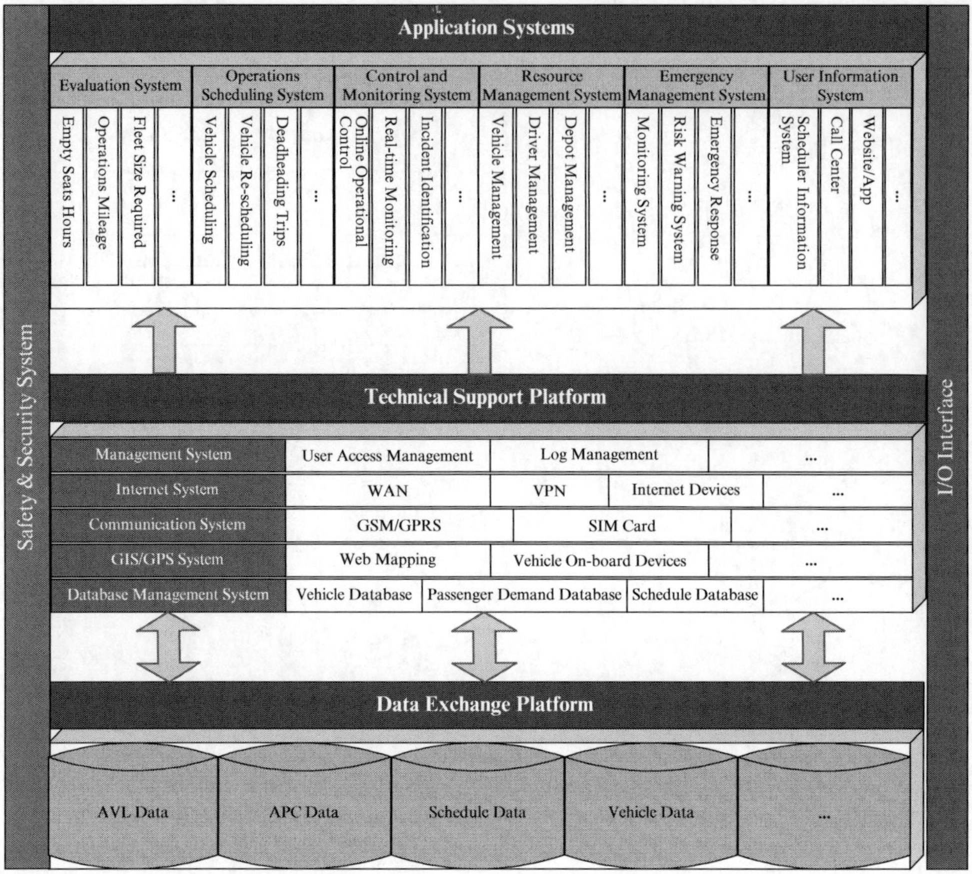

Application Systems

Evaluation System	Operations Scheduling System	Control and Monitoring System	Resource Management System	Emergency Management System	User Information System

Empty Seats Hours · Operations Mileage · Fleet Size Required · …

Vehicle Scheduling · Vehicle Re-scheduling · Deadheading Trips · …

Online Operational Control · Real-time Monitoring · Incident Identification · …

Vehicle Management · Driver Management · Depot Management · …

Monitoring System · Risk Warning System · Emergency Response · …

Scheduler Information System · Call Center · Website/App · …

Technical Support Platform

Management System	User Access Management	Log Management	…
Internet System	WAN	VPN	Internet Devices	…
Communication System	GSM/GPRS	SIM Card	…
GIS/GPS System	Web Mapping	Vehicle On-board Devices	…
Database Management System	Vehicle Database	Passenger Demand Database	Schedule Database	…

Data Exchange Platform

AVL Data · APC Data · Schedule Data · Vehicle Data · …

Safety & Security System

I/O Interface

Source: Adapted from Liu et al. (2017).

Figure 18.5   Architecture of a PT scheduling system

software names mentioned are taken from Wren (1981), Bodin et al. (1983), Wren (1998), Wren (2004) and Liu et al. (2017).

1. *Heuristics-based systems.* These systems were developed early on by using heuristic methods which attempt to simulate the processes adopted by experienced manual schedulers. Examples of such systems include TRACS, VAMPIRES, and TASC.
2. *Mathematical programming-based systems.* By making use of the advances in computer technology, these systems are based on mathematical programming methods, particularly integer linear programming. Examples of such systems include IMPACS and TRACS II.
3. *Graphical human–machine interactive systems.* These systems are based on the deficit function theory developed by using its graphical nature. The scheduling activities are performed in a human–machine interactive mode. Examples of such systems include AUTOBUS and PT-Manager (Liu and Ceder 2017).

Table 18.3   Some known available PT scheduling software

Software	Internet Address	Features
GIRO "HASTUS"	http://www.giro.ca/en	Vehicle Assignment Crew Assignment
Merakas "PIKAS"	http://www.merakas.lt/26en/	Timetable Calculation Trips Assignment Shifts cutting
PTV	http://www.ptv.de	Network Planning Simulation of Vehicle Running
ROUTELOGIC	http://www.routelogic.com/ FeaturesScheduling.html	Vehicle Assignment Planning and Analysis Operations Management Crew Assignment
Routematch	http://www.routematch.com/	Vehicle Assignment Planning and Analysis Operations Management Crew Assignment Service Management
NEMSYS "Routemate"	http://www.nemsys.it/	Transportation Planning Vehicle Scheduling
Optibus	www.optibus.co	Real-time Rescheduling, Vehicle Assignment, Crew Assignment, Interactive Scheduling, Planning and Analysis
SYSTRA	http://www.systra.com	Transportation Planning Simulation
Tracsis	http://www.tracsis.com/	Demand Forecasting Capacity Planning Timetable Development Rolling Stock Planning Crew Scheduling
Enghouse Transportation "TranSched"	http://www.enghousetransportation.com/	Scheduling Vehicle Blocking Optimized Run-cutting and Rostering Workforce Management
Trapeze	http://www.trapezegroup.com	Vehicle Assignment Planning and Analysis Operations Crew Assignment
init	https://www.initse.com/ende/home.html	Integrated Planning, Dispatching, Telematics and Ticketing Systems for Buses and Rail
MENTZ	https://www.mentz.net/en/	Vehicle- and Duty Scheduling, Vehicle Monitoring – AVM Light, Data Management, Electronic Journey Planner
IVU	https://www.ivu.com/	Service Management, Fleet Management, Ticketing, Personnel/Vehicle Deployment, Passenger Information
LinTim	https://lintim.math.uni-goettingen.de/ index.php?go=main.php&lang=en	Line Planning, Timetabling, Delay Management, and Rolling Stock Circulation

4. *Metaheuristics-based systems.* Driven by the need to obtain acceptable results quickly for large-scale scheduling problems, a number of metaheuristics, such as genetic algorithm (Wren and Wren 1995), tabu search (Shen 2001), and variable neighbourhood search, have been proposed for resolving PT vehicle scheduling problems.
5. *Artificial intelligence-based systems.* With the rapid development of information and computation technologies, recently some researchers have been attempting to develop bus transit scheduling systems using AI techniques, such as machine learning, expert system, case-based and rule-based reasoning.
6. *Combinatorial methods-based systems.* These systems are developed by using a mixture of the aforementioned methods. For example, HASTUS and HOT are based on a mixture of heuristics and mathematical programming. These combinatorial methods-based systems are believed to generate better performances (Wren 1998).

18.7   FUTURE RESEARCH DIRECTIONS

Recently we have been observing considerable changes in our PT systems. Emerging technologies such as autonomous vehicles, electric vehicles, and information and communication technologies, together with new business models, have great potential of transforming our existing PT systems to considerably more efficient and effective systems. That is, making the systems far more user-oriented, system-optimal, smart and sustainable with increased service connectivity, synchronization and coordination and with improved user satisfaction. There is no doubt that PT agencies need to adjust the PT scheduling process to harness the innovative emerging technologies. New methods and tools should be developed to meet the challenges of future PT vehicle scheduling problems. Future research on PT vehicle scheduling may focus on the following new research directions.

- Scheduling of autonomous and connected PT vehicles;
- Scheduling of electric and alternative-fuel PT vehicles;
- Scheduling of modular PT vehicles;
- PT vehicle scheduling in a connected vehicle environment;
- Demand-responsive/on-demand PT vehicle scheduling;
- PT vehicle scheduling in the era of mobility as a service;
- Integrated PT vehicle scheduling with timetabling, crew scheduling, network design and passenger demand assignment;
- Dynamic and real-time rescheduling of PT vehicles;
- Emergency PT vehicle scheduling;
- Coordinated scheduling of multi-modal PT vehicles.

These directions strive for the development of constructive and efficient new models and solution algorithms.

18.8   CONCLUSIONS

Public transport (PT) vehicle scheduling is one of the most time-consuming and cumbersome tasks in PT operations planning. In practical PT vehicle scheduling, schedulers attempt to allocate vehicles in the most efficient manner possible. However, these scheduling tasks are complex and time-consuming, thus requiring the services of imaginative and experienced schedulers. The application of advanced computer-aided scheduling software packages in PT vehicle scheduling can produce more efficient timetables and vehicle schedules to ultimately result in savings of the total operations costs and improving users' level of service.

This chapter reviews the latest research on PT vehicle scheduling, including several new research topics, such as integrated PT vehicle scheduling, electric PT vehicle scheduling, stochastic and dynamic PT vehicle scheduling, and on-demand and shared autonomous PT vehicle scheduling. One of its most important tasks is to determine the minimum fleet size required. A deficit function-based fleet size model is introduced to overcome the limitations of a traditional fleet size model. A network-flow model for PT vehicle scheduling is described, together with illustrative examples. A systematic review and classification of the PT vehicle scheduling software packages are also provided.

George Bernard Shaw once said: "We are made wise not by the recollection of our past, but by the responsibility for our future." Recently, new technologies have been emerging and becoming part of our lives at an increased pace, which will affect all aspects of daily life, including PT service planning and operations. This chapter further points out a set of new and challenging PT vehicle scheduling problems for possible future research. We cannot change the direction of the wind, with respect to the evolution of new technologies and future urban mobility patterns. We can, however, adjust the sails and create efficient and successful PT vehicle scheduling systems that will naturally improve PT operations and users' level of service.

NOTE

* The first author is supported by the National Natural Science Foundation of China (Grant No. 61903311, No. 62011530435), and the Chunhui Cooperative Research Project of the Ministry of Education of P.R. China (No. CH2019lt).

REFERENCES

Adler, J.D. and P.B. Mirchandani (2016), 'The vehicle scheduling problem for fleets with alternative-fuel vehicles', *Transportation Science*, **51**(2), 441–56.
Anderson, J.M., K. Nidhi, K.D. Stanley, P. Sorensen, C. Samaras and O.A. Oluwatola (2014), *Autonomous Vehicle Technology: A Guide for Policymakers*. Rand Corporation, Document Number: RR-443-2-RC.
Bodin, L.D., B.L. Golden, A. Assad and M. Ball (1983), 'Routing and scheduling of vehicles and crews: The state of the art', *Computers and Operations Research*, **10**, 69–211.
Bunte, S. and N. Kliewer (2009), 'An overview on vehicle scheduling models', *Public Transport*, **1**(4), 299–317.
Cao, Z. and A. Ceder (2019), 'Autonomous shuttle bus service timetabling and vehicle scheduling using skip-stop tactic', *Transportation Research Part C: Emerging Technologies*, **102**, 370–95.
Carosi, S., A. Frangioni, L. Galli, L. Girardi and G. Vallese (2019), 'A matheuristic for integrated timetabling and vehicle scheduling', *Transportation Research Part B: Methodological*, **127**, 99–124.

Carraresi, P. and G. Gallo (1984), 'Network models for vehicle and crew scheduling', *European Journal of Operational Research*, **16**(2), 139–51.

Ceder, A. (2001), 'Public transport scheduling', in D. Hensher and K. Button (eds), *Handbook of Transport Systems and Traffic Control*, New York: Pergamon Imprint, Elsevier Science, pp. 539–58.

Ceder, A. (2002), 'A step function for improving transit operations planning using fixed and variable scheduling', in M.A.P. Taylor (ed.), *Transportation and Traffic Theory in the 21st Century: Proceedings of the 15th International Symposium on Transportation and Traffic Theory*, Bingley: Emerald Group, pp. 1–21.

Ceder, A. (2016), *Public Transit Planning and Operation: Modeling, Practice and Behavior*, 2nd edn. Boca Raton, FL: CRC Press.

Ceder, A. and H.I. Stern (1981), 'Deficit function bus scheduling with deadheading trip insertion for fleet size reduction', *Transportation Science*, **15**(4), 338–63.

Daduna, J.R. and J.M.P. Paixão (1995), 'Vehicle scheduling for public mass transit: An overview', in J.R. Daduna and A. Wren (eds), *Computer-aided Transit Scheduling*, Berlin and Heidelberg: Springer, pp. 76–90.

Desaulniers, G. and M. Hickman (2007), 'Public transit', in C. Barnhart and G. Laporte (eds), *Transportation: Handbooks in Operations Research and Management Science*, vol. **14**, Amsterdam: North-Holland, pp. 69–128.

Desrosiers, J., Y. Dumas, M.M. Solomon and F. Soumis (1995), 'Time constrained routing and scheduling', in M.O. Ball, T.L. Magnanti, C.L. Monma and G.L. Nemhauser (eds), *Network Routing: Handbooks in Operations Research and Management Science*, vol. **8**, Amsterdam: Elsevier, pp. 35–139.

Elias, S.E.G. (1964), 'The use of digital computers in the economic scheduling for both man and machine in public transportation', *Kansas State University Bulletin, Special Report No. 49*, Manhattan, KS.

Faisal, A., T. Yigitcanlar, M. Kamruzzaman and G. Currie (2019), 'Understanding autonomous vehicles: A systematic literature review on capability, impact, planning and policy', *Journal of Transport and Land Use*, **12**(1), 45–72.

Fonseca, J.P., E. van der Hurk, R. Roberti and A. Larsen (2018), 'A matheuristic for transfer synchronization through integrated timetabling and vehicle scheduling', *Transportation Research Part B: Methodological*, **109**, 128–49.

Ford Jr, L.R. and D.R. Fulkerson (1962), *Flows in Networks*, Princeton, NJ: Princeton University Press.

Freling, R. and J.M.P. Paixão (1995), 'Vehicle scheduling with time constraint', in J.R. Daduna, I. Branco and J.M.P. Paixão (eds), *Computer-Aided Transit Scheduling*, Berlin and Heidelberg: Springer, pp. 130–44.

Freling, R., D. Huisman and A.P.M. Wagelmans (2001), 'Applying an integrated approach to vehicle and crew scheduling in practice', in S. Voss and J.R. Daduna (eds), *Computer-Aided Scheduling of Public Transport: Lecture Notes in Economics and Mathematical Systems*, **505**, Heidelberg: Springer-Verlag, pp. 73–90.

Gertsbach, I. and Y. Gurevich (1977), 'Constructing an optimal fleet for a transportation schedule', *Transportation Science*, **11**(1), 20–36.

Haase, K., G. Desaulniers and J. Desrosiers (2001), 'Simultaneous vehicle and crew scheduling in an urban mass transit system', *Transportation Science*, **35**(3), 286–303.

Haghani, A. and M. Banihashemi (2002), 'Heuristic approaches for solving large-scale bus transit vehicle scheduling problem with route time constraints', *Transportation Research*, **36A**, 309–33.

Häll, C.H., A. Ceder, J. Ekström and N.H. Quttineh (2019), 'Adjustments of public transit operations planning process for the use of electric buses', *Journal of Intelligent Transportation Systems*, **23**(3), 216–30.

He, F., J. Yang and M. Li (2018), 'Vehicle scheduling under stochastic trip times: An approximate dynamic programming approach', *Transportation Research Part C: Emerging Technologies*, **96**, 144–59.

Huisman, D., R. Freling and A.P.M. Wagelmans (2004), 'A robust solution approach to the dynamic vehicle scheduling problem', *Transportation Science*, **38**(4), 447–58.

Huisman, D., R. Freling and A.P.M. Wagelmans (2005), 'Models and algorithms for integration of vehicle and crew scheduling', *Transportation Science*, **39**, 491–502.

Ibarra-Rojas, O.J., R. Giesen and Y.A. Rios-Solis (2014), 'An integrated approach for timetabling and vehicle scheduling problems to analyze the trade-off between level of service and operating costs of transit networks', *Transportation Research Part B: Methodological*, **70**, 35–46.

Ibarra-Rojas, O.J., F. Delgado, R. Giesen and J.C. Muñoz (2015), 'Planning, operation, and control of bus transport systems: A literature review', *Transportation Research Part B: Methodological*, **77**, 38–75.

Lam, A.Y., Y.W. Leung and X. Chu (2016), 'Autonomous-vehicle public transportation system: Scheduling and admission control', *IEEE Transactions on Intelligent Transportation Systems*, **17**(5), 1210–26.

Laporte, G., F.A. Ortega, M.A. Pozo and J. Puerto (2017), 'Multi-objective integration of timetables, vehicle schedules and user routings in a transit network', *Transportation Research Part B: Methodological*, **98**, 94–112.

Li, L., H.K. Lo and F. Xiao (2019), 'Mixed bus fleet scheduling under range and refueling constraints', *Transportation Research Part C: Emerging Technologies*, **104**, 443–62.

Linis, V.K. and M.S. Maksim (1967), 'On the problem of constructing routes', *Proceedings of the Institute of Civil Aviation Engineering*, **102**, 36–45 [in Russian].

Liu, T. (2020), 'Continuous approximation of deficit functions for fleet size calculation', *Journal of Transportation Engineering, Part A: Systems*, **146**(2), 04019064, DOI: 10.1061/JTEPBS.0000302.

Liu, T. and A. Ceder (2015), 'Analysis of a new public-transport-service concept: Customized bus in China', *Transport Policy*, **39**, 63–76.

Liu, T. and A. Ceder (2017), 'Deficit function related to public transport: 50-year retrospective, new developments, and prospects', *Transportation Research Part B: Methodological*, **100**, 1–19.

Liu, T. and A. Ceder (2018), 'Integrated public transport timetable synchronization and vehicle scheduling with demand assignment: A bi-objective bi-level model using deficit function approach', *Transportation Research Part B: Methodological*, **117**, 935–55.

Liu, T. and A. Ceder (2020), 'Battery-electric transit vehicle scheduling with optimal number of stationary chargers', *Transportation Research Part C: Emerging Technologies*, **114**, 118–39.

Liu, T., A. Ceder and S. Chowdhury (2017), 'Integrated public transport timetable synchronization with vehicle scheduling', *Transportmetrica A: Transport Science*, **13**(10), 932–54.

Liu, T., A. Ceder, J.H. Ma, W. Guan and L.J. Zhou (2017), 'Graphical human–machine interactive approach for integrated bus transit scheduling: Lessons gained from a large bus company', *IEEE Transactions on Intelligent Transportation Systems*, **18**(4), 1023–8.

Naumann, M., L. Suhl and S. Kramkowski (2011), 'A stochastic programming approach for robust vehicle scheduling in public bus transport', *Procedia – Social and Behavioral Sciences*, **20**, 826–35.

Pinto, H.K., M. F. Hyland, H.S. Mahmassani and I.Ö. Verbas (2019), 'Joint design of multimodal transit networks and shared autonomous mobility fleets', *Transportation Research Part C: Emerging Technologies*, forthcoming.

Rayle, L., S.A. Shaheen, N. Chan, D. Dai and R. Cervero (2014), 'App-based, on-demand ride services: Comparing taxi and ridesourcing trips and user characteristics in San Francisco' (No. UCTC-FR-2014-08), Berkeley, CA: University of California Transportation Center.

Rogge, M., E. van der Hurk, A. Larsen and D.U. Sauer (2018), 'Electric bus fleet size and mix problem with optimization of charging infrastructure', *Applied Energy*, **211**, 282–95.

Schöbel, A. (2017), 'An eigenmodel for iterative line planning, timetabling and vehicle scheduling in public transportation', *Transportation Research Part C*, **74**, 348–65.

Shen, Y.D. (2001), *Tabu Search for Bus and Train Driver Scheduling with Time Windows*. Doctoral dissertation, University of Leeds, Leeds.

Shen, Y., J. Xu and J.P. Li (2016), 'A probabilistic model for vehicle scheduling based on stochastic trip times', *Transportation Research Part B*, **85**, 19–31.

Shen, Y., J. Xu and X. Wu (2017), 'Vehicle scheduling based on variable trip times with expected on-time performance', *International Transactions in Operational Research*, **24**(1–2), 99–113.

Steinzen, I., V. Gintner, L. Suhl and N. Kliewer (2010), 'A time–space network approach for the integrated vehicle-and crew-scheduling problem with multiple depots', *Transportation Science*, **44**(3), 367–82.

Tang, X., X. Lin and F. He (2019), 'Robust scheduling strategies of electric buses under stochastic traffic conditions', *Transportation Research Part C: Emerging Technologies*, **105**, 163–82.

Teng, J., T. Chen and W.D. Fan (2020), 'Integrated approach to vehicle scheduling and bus timetabling for an electric bus line', *Journal of Transportation Engineering, Part A: Systems*, **146**(2), 04019073.

Tsubouchi, K., H. Yamato and K. Hiekata (2010), 'Innovative on-demand bus system in Japan', *IET Intelligent Transport Systems*, **4**(4), 270–79.

van Kooten Niekerk, M.E., J.M. van den Akker and J.A. Hoogeveen (2017), 'Scheduling electric vehicles', *Public Transport*, **9**(1–2), 155–76.

Wang, H. and J. Shen (2007), 'Heuristic approaches for solving transit vehicle scheduling problem with route and fueling time constraints', *Applied Mathematics and Computation*, **190**(2), 1237–49.

Wang, Y., Y. Huang, J. Xu and N. Barclay (2017), 'Optimal recharging scheduling for urban electric buses: A case study in Davis', *Transportation Research Part E: Logistics and Transportation Review*, **100**, 115–32.

Wen, M., E. Linde, S. Ropke, P. Mirchandani and A. Larsen (2016), 'An adaptive large neighborhood search heuristic for the electric vehicle scheduling problem', *Computers & Operations Research*, **76**, 73–83.

Winter, K., O. Cats, G.H.D.A. Correia and B. van Arem (2016), 'Designing an automated demand-responsive transport system: Fleet size and performance analysis for a campus–train station service', *Transportation Research Record*, **2542**, 75–83.

Wren, A. (1971), *Computers in Transport Planning and Operation*, London: Ian Allan.

Wren, A. (1981), 'General review of the use of computers in scheduling buses and their crews', in A. Wren (ed.), *Computer Scheduling of Public Transport*, Amsterdam: North-Holland, pp. 3–17.

Wren, A. (1998), 'Heuristics ancient and modern: Transport scheduling through the ages', *Journal of Heuristics*, **4**(1), 87–100.

Wren, A. (2004), 'Scheduling vehicles and their drivers: Forty years' experience', Technical Report, School of Computing Research Report Series, Report 2004.03, University of Leeds, Leeds.

Wren, A. and D.O. Wren (1995), 'A genetic algorithm for public transport driver scheduling', *Computers & Operations Research*, **22**(1), 101–110.

Yao, E., T. Liu, T. Lu and Y. Yang (2020), 'Optimization of electric vehicle scheduling with multiple vehicle types in public transport', *Sustainable Cities and Society*, **52**, 101862, 1–10.

Zhu, C. and X. Chen (2013), 'Optimizing battery electric bus transit vehicle scheduling with battery exchanging: Model and case study', *Procedia – Social and Behavioral Sciences*, **96**, 2725–36.

PART V

SERVICE DEVELOPMENT AND FUTURE PERSPECTIVES

19. Incorporating Mobility-on-Demand (MOD) and Mobility-as-a-Service (MaaS) automotive services into public transportation
Emma Lucken and Susan Shaheen

19.1 INTRODUCTION

As smartphone-enabled mobility services have gained prominence around the world, public transportation agencies have started experimenting with strategies to incorporate elements of these innovative mobility options to make public transit services more attractive and efficient. In the United States (US), the emerging transportation services have been conceptualized as Mobility on Demand (MOD), in which consumers have on-demand access to both passenger and goods movement through an integrated multimodal network (Shaheen et al., 2017a). In Europe, the prevalent terminology is Mobility as a Service (MaaS), which involves the provision of an array of aggregated passenger mobility services as bundled subscription options (Shaheen and Cohen, 2019). Both MOD and MaaS involve the concept of providing a single user interface for trip planning and booking, real-time information, and fare payment.

While MOD and MaaS services offer the possibility of more convenient travel and a reduction in private-vehicle ownership, they also raise several concerns about their potential societal impacts. These include drawing riders away from public transportation, thereby increasing congestion and vehicle miles/kilometres travelled (VMT/VKT), and creating barriers to equitable service for transit-dependent disabled, older adult, and low-income populations. Implementing MOD and MaaS services in ways that promote the public good will require public transportation agencies to address these environmental and equity challenges.

This chapter focuses primarily on MOD services, particularly microtransit and transportation network companies (TNCs, also known as ridesourcing and ridesharing), and their integration with public transportation service in the US. For an overview on MaaS services and research, Kamargianni et al. (2016), Jittrapirom et al. (2017), Durand et al. (2018), and Wong et al. (2018) are valuable resources. In the next section, we discuss existing research on the impacts from MOD companies on public transit ridership. Section 19.3 provides a detailed analysis of partnerships between MOD companies and public transportation agencies (MOD PPPs) in the US, including proposed typologies for such partnerships and research on associated benefits, challenges and recommendations. Section 19.4 presents the state of the research on modelling the impacts on the transportation system from integrating MOD services with public transportation. We conclude with a section on new research frontiers. The following definitions for terms used throughout the chapter are from the US Federal Highway Administration (FHWA) 2017 report, "Mobility on Demand: Operational Concept Report":

- *Mobility on Demand (MOD):* Transportation concept where consumers can access mobility, goods, and services on demand by dispatching or using shared mobility, courier services, unmanned aerial vehicles, and public transportation solutions. Passenger modes facilitated through MOD providers can include: shared modes, public transportation, and other emerging transportation solutions (e.g., aerial taxis). Goods delivery through MOD can include app-based and aerial delivery services (e.g., drones).
- *Mobility as a Service (MaaS):* MaaS emphasizes mobility aggregation, smartphone and app-based subscription access, and multimodal integration (infrastructure, information, and fare integration). MaaS tends to emphasize the integration and convergence of passenger mobility services, mobile devices, real-time information, and payment mechanisms.
- *Public Transportation:* Any transport system available to the public with set fares.
- *Shared Mobility:* Transportation strategy that enables users to have short-term access to a transportation mode (e.g., vehicle, bicycle, or other low-speed travel mode) on an as-needed basis. Shared mobility can include: roundtrip services (vehicle, bicycle, or other low-speed mode is returned to its origin); one-way station-based services (vehicle, bicycle, or low-speed mode is returned to a different designated station location); and one-way free-floating services (vehicle, bicycle, or low-speed mode can be returned anywhere within a geographic area).
- *Microtransit:* A privately owned and operated shared transportation system that can have fixed routes and schedules, as well as flexible routes and on-demand scheduling. The vehicles generally include vans and mini-buses.
- *TNCs:* TNCs (also known as ridehailing and ridesourcing, e.g. Lyft, Uber) provide prearranged and on-demand transportation services for compensation, which connect drivers of personal vehicles with passengers. Smartphone mobile applications are used for booking, ratings (for both drivers and passengers), and electronic payment. TNCs also include "ridesplitting" (or pooling), in which customers can choose to split a ride and fare in a TNC vehicle (where available).

19.2   MOD COMPANY IMPACTS ON PUBLIC TRANSPORTATION RIDERSHIP

An examination of the integration of MOD services with public transportation prompts the question of MOD companies' current impacts on public transit ridership. After reaching a peak in 2014, total public transit ridership in the US declined 7.2 per cent by 2019 (American Public Transportation Association, 2014; 2019). The literature is mixed as to whether MOD companies have contributed to this decline. Empirical studies in this area focus on ride-alone TNCs, with no conclusive studies on the impacts on public transit ridership from TNC pooled services (e.g., Lyft Shared rides or UberPool) or microtransit vans.

Some studies found a relatively modest effect from TNCs on public transportation ridership. An American Public Transportation Association (APTA) survey of 4500 people who used shared modes (including public transit, bikesharing, carsharing, and TNCs) in Austin, Boston, Chicago, Los Angeles, San Francisco, Seattle and Washington, DC found that TNC use is higher at weekends than on weekdays and peaks between 8 pm and 4 am, when public transit is less available, indicating TNCs may complement public transit by providing service during off-peak times (Murphy and Feigon, 2016). Among respondents who listed TNCs as their preferred mode: 34 per cent would drive alone or with a friend if TNCs were not an option, 24 per cent would choose carsharing, 8 per cent would take a taxi, and 14 per cent would take a public bus or train. Fewer than 1 per cent said they would not have made the trip. While these numbers suggest that very frequent TNC users primarily transfer away from car-based modes rather than from public transit, the results are not representative of less frequent TNC users. These results do indicate a disproportional shift away from public transit; in most US cities, public transit has a less than 14 per cent mode share, while the combination of drive alone, carpool, and carshare has a greater than 58 per cent mode share. Moreover, the authors ask what mode respondents most often use TNCs to replace, rather than asking the mode they replaced with their most recent trip. This could result in lower replacement rates for less commonly replaced modes. Finally, aggregating across cities hides land-use and built environment effects that differ by city. Hampshire et al. (2017) surveyed 1840 former Lyft and/or Uber users in Austin, TX to learn what modes they chose after the two companies suspended service in the city in May 2016. They found that 42 per cent of respondents switched to another TNC, 41 per cent to a personal vehicle, and 3 per cent to public transit. Leaving out the switch to other TNCs, which does not convey additional information about TNC impacts on public transit ridership, the switch away from public transit is disproportionately high: 3.6 per cent of Austin residents commuted to work by public transit in 2016 (about the same percentage as those that switched to public transit from Uber and Lyft), but 73.5 per cent commuted by driving alone (almost twice as many as switched to personal vehicles) (American Community Survey, 2016).

Other research has found a stronger negative impact on public transit ridership. Rayle et al. (2016) surveyed 380 TNC users in San Francisco in 2014 and found that, if TNCs were not available, 39 per cent would have taken a taxi, 7 per cent would have driven alone or with a friend, 24 per cent would have taken a public bus, and 9 per cent would have taken public rail. They also found that 8 per cent would not have taken the trip at all, reflecting a greater induced travel effect than the APTA study described above. Five per cent used their TNC trip as a first-mile/last-mile strategy to get to or from public transit, while 40 per cent of respondents who owned a car reported driving less as a result of TNCs. Study limitations include surveying respondents at three heavily used TNC locations during the evening, thus capturing mainly social trips but not commute, school, errand or airport trips. Another survey of 311 Lyft and Uber riders in the Denver area found that 40 per cent used public transit less as a result of TNCs, 5 per cent used public transit more, 32 per cent drove less, and 2 per cent drove more (Henao, 2017). A survey of 4094 urban and suburban residents of Boston, Chicago, Los Angeles, New York, the San Francisco Bay Area, Seattle, and Washington, DC, 21 per cent of whom use TNCs, found that TNC users decrease their bus use by 6 per cent and light rail use by 3 per cent, while increasing heavy rail use by 3 per cent (Clewlow and Mishra, 2017). This suggests that, on average, TNCs compete with bus and light rail but complement heavy rail, perhaps by offering more convenient first-mile/last-mile service to heavy rail stations. Nine per cent of TNC users reported getting rid of a vehicle due to TNCs. Results also showed that 22 per cent of TNC trips were induced trips, 21 per cent would have been made by private vehicle, 18 per cent would have been by carpool, 1 per cent by taxi, and 15 per cent by public transit. Limitations of this study include aggregating across cities, which could obscure city-specific trends, as well as asking respondents what mode they generally use TNCs to replace, rather than the mode they replaced with their most recent TNC trip. This approach may yield artificially low replacement rates for less commonly replaced modes, including public transit and taxis.

Outside of survey-based research, several studies have examined how public transit ridership changes in relation to various measures that approximate TNC use. Results from the strongest of these analyses suggest that TNCs negatively impact public transit ridership. One study used a difference-in-differences analysis of all 196 US Metropolitan Statistical Areas (MSAs) that have both Uber and public transit to examine the impact of Uber entry in the MSA on public transit ridership (Hall et al., 2018). This study also analysed the impact of Uber penetration, as measured by the number of Google searches for "Uber", which correlates with the number of Uber drivers per capita. The authors found that, after the arrival of Uber, public transit ridership in MSAs of below median population (280000 people) decreased by 5.9 per cent, while ridership in MSAs of above median population increased by 0.8 per cent. A standard deviation increase in Uber penetration, meanwhile, correlated with a 0.5 per cent decrease in public transit ridership among agencies in smaller MSAs and a 1.8 per cent increase in ridership among agencies in larger MSAs. A drawback of this work is the use of two imperfect measures of Uber use: Uber entry does not account for changing impact over time, while Google searches are an inexact approximation of ridership. A more recent publication improves on these measures by using year since TNC entry as its independent variable, thereby combining an exact measure (date of entry) with a ridership approximation that accounts for changes over time (this measure assumes ridership increases linearly by year). In this study, a longitudinal analysis of the determinants of public transit ridership in 22 large US cities from 2002 to 2018 found that heavy rail ridership decreased by 1.29 per cent for each year after TNCs began operating in the service area, while bus ridership decreased by 1.70 per cent per year (Graehler Jr et al., 2019). The authors note that impacts may differ in smaller and medium cities. Results from both studies would benefit greatly from data on TNC ridership by city. In NYC, where TNC ridership data are available, a separate analysis indicated that as TNC ridership increased by 7 million, 17 million and 29 million in 2014, 2015 and 2016, respectively, bus ridership decreased by 10, 17, and 12 million, and subway ridership increased by 43 million and 11 million before decreasing by 7 million in 2016 (Schaller, 2017). This represents a reversal of over a decade of transit-led growth in the city. The author attributes the change to TNCs but did not provide causal evidence to support this conclusion.

19.3 PUBLIC TRANSPORTATION AGENCY PARTNERSHIPS WITH MOD COMPANIES

As of April 2019, 47 public agencies in the US, including public transportation agencies, public transportation authorities, and cities, have partnered with private companies to provide 62 MOD services that meet the US Federal Transit Administration (FTA) definition of public transportation: "regular, continuing shared-ride surface transportation services that are open to the general public or open to a segment of the general public defined by age, disability, or low income" (FTA, 2016a). Some of these MOD public–private partnerships (MOD PPPs) have received support from the MOD Sandbox Program, which the FTA started in 2016 to provide $8 million in funding to public transportation agencies that integrate MOD services, including partnerships with TNCs and microtransit (FTA, 2016b; Lucken et al., 2019). The federal programme aims to generate best practices for how to develop such partnerships; measure MOD impacts on the transportation system; and determine government requirements, regulations and policies that help or hinder the integration of MOD services with public transit.

Outside the US, the European Union (EU) MaaS4EU, EU MaaS Alliance, and Australia Future Transport Digital Accelerator are all government-supported initiatives that promote research into implementing MaaS in ways that meet societal goals. Among other locations, MaaS services that incorporate public and private modes have been piloted in Gothenburg, Sweden (2013 to 2014); Hannover, Germany (2014); Turku, Finland (2015); Italy (2015); Germany (2016); Helsinki, Finland (2016); Birmingham, UK (2017); Amsterdam/Nijmegen, the Netherlands (2017); Singapore (2017 to 2018); and Antwerp, Belgium (2018) (Jittrapirom et al., 2017; Wong et al., 2018).

In the following subsections, we present typologies for the 62 US MOD PPPs as well as qualitative benefits, challenges and recommendations for these partnerships as identified in the literature. Sections 19.4 and 19.5 discuss quantitative research into the impacts of incorporating MOD services with public transportation.

19.3.1 Overview of MOD PPPs in the US

Several reports have proposed typologies for US partnerships between public agencies and MOD companies, including Lucken et al. (2019), Curtis et al. (2019), the US Government Accountability Office (GAO) (2018), Schwieterman et al. (2018), and Blodgett et al. (2017). Table 19.1 indicates the differences among the proposed typologies. The three potential types of MOD companies considered in the publications as MOD PPP participants include TNCs, van-based microtransit services, and companies that provide ride-matching and routing software for public agencies to operate their own MOD services. The four main categories of service provided by MOD PPPs include first-mile/last-mile (FMLM) connections to fixed-route public transit, gap-filling services in low-density areas, off-peak services during times when fixed-route service is not available, and paratransit for disabled and older adult populations.

In addition to categorizing MOD PPPs by the service provided, Blodgett et al. (2017) include payment structure as a dimension in their typology, with four categories: (1) city pays all; (2) city pays a fixed fraction; (3) customer pays a fixed amount; and (4) tailored to customer. In Lucken et al. (2019), the authors introduced two additional analysis dimensions: (1) the assets each partner contributes to enable service; and (2) the vehicle type used to provide the service. The two asset contribution models include: (1) Agency-Operated MOD, in which the public partner uses its own vehicles and drivers and the private partner provides the ride-matching and routing algorithm; and (2) Agency-Subsidized Private MOD, in which the private partner provides the vehicles and drivers as well as the MOD algorithm. The three vehicle types include: vans, taxis, and TNC drivers' personal vehicles. While the type of service provided impacts the risk that a MOD PPP

Table 19.1 Publications proposing typologies of MOD PPPs

| Publication | MOD Companies Considered | | | | Service Models Considered | | | | |
	TNCs	Van-Based	Software	First-Mile/ Last-Mile	Low- Density	Off- Peak	Paratransit	Other(s)
Lucken et al. (2019)	X	X	X	X	X	X	X	None. Considers alleviation of parking demand as a possible impact of MOD PPPs. Considers the other categories below as strategies to support the four core service models to the right
Curtis et al. (2019)	X			X	X	X	X	Guaranteed Rides Home
US GAO (2018)	X	X	X	X	X	X	X	Trip Planning & Fare Integration, Marketing
Schwieterman et al. (2018)	X			X		X	X	Trip Planning & Fare Integration, Data Sharing, Alleviation of Parking Demand
Blodgett et al. (2017)	X			X	X	X	X	None

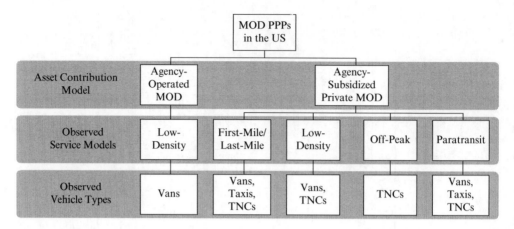

Source: Lucken et al. (2019).

Figure 19.1   MOD PPP typology

will compete with fixed-route transit, the asset contribution model impacts each partner's control over service operations and data, and the vehicle type affects operational costs and potential impacts on congestion, VMT and emissions. Figure 19.1 illustrates the existing combinations of asset contribution models, service models and vehicle types among MOD PPPs in the US.

Figure 19.2 shows the locations of 62 MOD PPPs by US public transit agencies, transportation authorities and cities, as well as each partnership's asset contribution model and service model. Table 19.2 provides additional information on public transit agency MOD PPPs.

19.3.2   Benefits

A growing number of qualitative analyses suggest that incorporating MOD services offers a range of potential benefits to public transit agencies. The primary benefit to public transportation agencies is the ability to offer on-demand versions of the services identified in the previous section, sometimes at a lower cost than fixed-route or traditional paratransit service. For instance, Shaheen and Chan (2016) assert that TNCs can complement public transit by providing a FMLM strategy during off-peak times or in less-served areas, while microtransit could also provide FMLM service and reduce overcrowding on high-ridership bus routes. Lazarus et al. (2018) recommend that public transportation agencies could reduce costs and improve transit access by replacing low-ridership bus routes and offering FMLM strategies with subsidized TNC trips. The authors identify partnership opportunities as those times when and areas where public transit service is inefficient and TNC driver pools are available. They also advise public transportation agencies to take advantage of such partnerships to concentrate fixed-route service along high-volume corridors. Shaheen and Cohen (2018a) recommend the use of MOD PPPs to right-size transit vehicles, reduce operating costs, and optimize passenger experience to compete with private-vehicle ownership, particularly with the onset of vehicle automation. Schaller

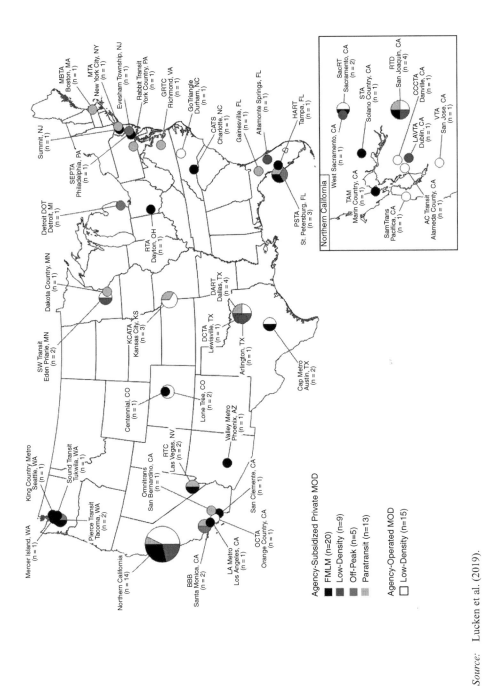

Source: Lucken et al. (2019).

Figure 19.2   Map of MOD PPPs in the US through to April 2019

417

Table 19.2   *Number of public transit agency MOD PPPs in the US through to April 2019*

Service Model & Start Date	Agency-Operated MOD	Agency-Subsidized Private MOD			
	Microtransit Vans	Microtransit Vans	Taxi	TNC (Personal Vehicles)	Total:
FMLM		2	1	11[a]	14
2016			Tampa*	St Petersburg (FL), Philadelphia*, Sacramento*	
2017				Dayton, San Joaquin (CA), Phoenix*	
2018		Seattle		Charlotte, Tacoma, Austin, Las Vegas	
2019[†]		Seattle		Los Angeles	
Low-Density	13[b]	0[c]		6[d]	19
2015	Eden Prairie (MN)				
2016	San Jose*, Kansas City*, Alameda County (CA)			Dallas*, Lewisville (TX)	
2017	Austin*, Dallas			Dublin (CA), San Joaquin (CA)	
2018	Sacramento, Durham, Contra Costa (CA)*, San Joaquin (CA), Orange County			Eden Prairie (MN)*	
2019[†]	Kansas City, Pacifica (CA)			Dallas	
Off-Peak				4[e]	4
2016				St Petersburg (FL)	
2017				*Santa Monica*	
2018				Tacoma, *Detroit*	
Paratransit		1	2	8[f]	11
2016				Boston	
2017		San Joaquin (CA)	NYC, Kansas City	York County (PA), Richmond (VA), Dallas	
2018				Las Vegas, San Bernardino (CA), Santa Monica, St Petersburg (FL)	
Total:	13	3	3	29	48

Table 19.2   (continued)

Notes:
*   MOD PPP has ended.
†   Through to April 2019.
This table excludes PPPs with transportation authorities and cities, focusing on public transportation agencies only. PPPs with transportation authorities and cities are listed in the footnotes below. In the table, the italicized Off-Peak partnerships employ FMLM restrictions, as opposed to point-to-point service.
a   Also includes four MOD partnerships with cities and two with transportation authorities: (1) Centennial, CO (2016*); (2) Summit, NJ (2016); (3) San Clemente, CA (2016); (4) Mercer Island, WA (2018*); (5) Solano Transportation Authority, CA (2017); and (6) Transportation Authority of Marin, CA (2017).
b   Includes Lone Tree, CO (2017* and 2019).
c   Includes: (1) Arlington, TX (2017) and (2) West Sacramento, CA (2018).
d   Also includes: (1) Altamonte Springs, Lake Mary, Longwood, Maitland, and Sanford in Florida (2016*) and (2) Monrovia, CA (2018).
e   Also includes Evesham Township, NJ (2015).
f   Also includes: (1) Gainesville, FL (2015) and (2) Dakota County, MN (2019).

Source: Lucken et al. (2019).

(2018) identifies paratransit service, FMLM connections and dispersed travel markets as the main opportunities for public benefit from MOD services. Kuhr et al. (2017) state that partnerships between public transportation agencies and TNCs allow the public sector to innovate while sharing risk.

19.3.3   Challenges and Recommendations

Our literature analysis yielded four main categories of challenges and recommendations for MOD PPPs: (1) equity; (2) data sharing; (3) regulations and liability; and (4) labour-management relationships. We discuss recommendations from the literature in the context of these categories. Figure 19.3 provides an overview of the recommendations within each category.

Several reports offer high-level analysis of challenges and recommendations for partnerships between public transit agencies and MOD companies. These include the TransitCenter's September 2016 report, *Private Mobility, Public Interest: How public agencies can work with emerging mobility providers* (Tsay et al., 2016). The authors conducted over 100 interviews with public- and private-sector representatives, including those involved in early partnerships between public transit agencies and MOD companies, over the course of 2015 and 2016. They provide extensive analysis of these early partnerships and offer many detailed recommendations under four overarching guidelines: (1) partner to reinforce public transit's strengths; (2) leverage agency-controlled assets; (3) plan for a streamlined user experience; and (4) be open to new ways of providing useful transit. Another resource is the Federal Highway Administration (FHWA) April, 2016 report, *Shared Mobility: Current Practices and Guiding Principles*, which examines many shared modes but includes recommendations specific to TNCs as they relate to equity, data sharing, multimodal integration, insurance requirements, and leveraging public agency resources (Shaheen et al., 2016). The American Planning Association (APA) July 2016 report, *Planning for Shared Mobility*, offers further analysis of the way public agencies can use public rights-of-way, incentive zoning, and transportation demand management to

Figure 19.3   Challenges and strategies for MOD PPPs

influence MOD companies for the public good, with case studies from eight cities (Cohen and Shaheen, 2016). Finally, the National Research Council (NRC) and Transportation Research Board (TRB) 2015 report, *Between Public and Private Mobility: Examining the Rise of Technology-Enabled Transportation Services*, provides an in-depth look at the equity, insurance and labour issues surrounding TNCs and microtransit, as well as recommendations for public agencies on how to address them (Taylor et al., 2015).

Overarching requirements and recommendations
To use federal funds for Agency-Subsidized Private MOD, public transportation agencies in the US must ensure the service meets the definition of public transportation – "regular, continuing shared-ride surface transportation services that are open to the general public" – or is an alternative to public transportation, as in job access and reverse commute programmes (FTA, 2016c).

Two overarching strategies often recommended include: (1) leveraging agency-controlled assets in negotiations with MOD companies; and (2) sharing lessons learned with other agencies. Leveraging financial resources, kerb access for passenger loading zones, and off-street parking for waiting zones could help public transit agencies secure desired data or other requests, such as the procurement of wheelchair-accessible vehicles (WAVs), in their partnerships with MOD companies (Shaheen et al., 2016; Tsay et al., 2016). Exchanging lessons learned with other public transit agencies involved in similar partnerships can suggest additional best practices and facilitate the learning process in preparing, implementing and adjusting or expanding pilot projects.

Equity in MOD PPPs

Equity is a primary area of study and concern relating to MOD companies in general and also to MOD PPPs. Partnering with MOD companies presents many equity-related challenges, including limited WAV availability, lack of driver training to assist disabled passengers to the vehicle, the potential for race-based discrimination by MOD company drivers, barriers for people without bank accounts or smartphones, and lack of driver availability in rural areas.

However, such partnerships also offer significant opportunities to improve service for low-income, disabled, older adult, and rural populations. Indeed, these opportunities are one of the main motivations for public transportation agencies to partner with MOD companies. By partnering with MOD companies to replace or supplement service that the public agency struggles to provide efficiently, such as paratransit or low-ridership bus routes in less dense areas, agencies can save money while simultaneously improving transportation quality for the populations that previously relied on the inefficient service.

Public agencies in the US that receive federal funding must ensure their services do not discriminate by race, colour, or national origin, as dictated by Title VI Statute of the Civil Rights Act of 1964. All transportation services must also abide by the Americans with Disabilities Act (ADA) of 1990, which requires equitable service for those with physical or mental disabilities. Public transportation agencies need any service they provide through MOD company partnerships to abide by Title VI and ADA regulations as well (FTA, 2016d). The USDOT has specifically required that public transportation agencies in MOD PPPs provide alternative methods of payment and reservations for individuals without bank accounts or smartphones; offer WAV access; and ensure the same level of service for all users with regard to fares, response times, and areas and times of service (Foxx, 2016; FTA, 2016d; Shaheen and Cohen, 2018b). To evaluate the equity of potential or existing MOD PPPs, public transportation agencies can use the FHWA STEPS (Spatial – Temporal – Economic – Physiological – Social) framework to analyse the service along spatial, temporal, economic, physiological and social dimensions (Shaheen et al., 2017b).

A few notable resources offer substantial analysis of the barriers and opportunities MOD service poses for equitable transportation quality and access. The New York University Ruden Center for Transportation Policy and Management's 2016 report (Kaufman et al., 2016), analyses the potential for MOD technology to enhance paratransit, identifying the need for collaboration between MOD companies and paratransit agencies. The Citizens Budget Commission of New York published a report analysing the obstacles to and potential benefits from public transit agencies partnering with MOD companies to provide paratransit service (*Access-A-Ride*, 2016). An APTA report, *Shared Mobility and the Transformation of Public Transit*, includes a chapter on the same topic. The Brookings Institution also performed an economic analysis suggesting substantial cost savings to public transit agencies from offering paratransit service through partnerships with MOD companies (Kane et al., 2016). Finally, the Institute for Transportation and Development Policy (ITDP) report, *Connecting Low-Income People to Opportunity with Shared Mobility*, provides a comprehensive review of the challenges low-income communities face in accessing shared mobility, including MOD services, as well as the challenges shared mobility providers face in serving such communities (Kodransky and Lewenstein, 2014). The report offers recommendations for addressing these challenges, including launching pilot projects based on research on low-income community transportation needs, and concludes that programmes to help low-income individuals benefit from shared mobility should address at least three barriers to be successful.

Table 19.3 offers an in-depth examination of equity-related challenges and recommendations, while Table 19.4 presents existing literature on operational challenges and recommendations.

19.4   EXISTING METHODS FOR ESTIMATING DEMAND FOR VEHICULAR MOD SERVICES

To quantify the impacts of MOD PPPs on a variety of public goals, including VMT reduction, an increase in accessibility, and improved equity, a method is required for measuring the replaced modes and induced demand from existing MOD PPP services. Beyond measuring existing impacts, estimating the demand for new MOD services is a necessary step for: (1) identifying the potential impacts on VMT, accessibility and equity from MOD PPP implementation on a broader scale; and (2) identifying the best locations, densities, and land-use mixes in which to implement MOD PPPs to most advance these societal goals. Regarding the second objective, estimating how demand for MOD services varies throughout a public transportation agency's service area is also essential for selecting MOD PPP locations that entail a manageable level of public subsidy, thereby improving the chances the service will remain financially sustainable in the long term.

Thus far, the two main approaches to achieving the objectives described above have been agent-based simulation and stated preference surveys. Agent-based simulation has been a popular approach to exploring the impacts of MOD services on travel times and VMT. These studies vary in their focus on MOD or automated MOD (AMOD) services, including shared automated vehicles (SAVs), and on single-passenger or shared MOD services. Table 19.5 presents a synopsis of this research, which has focused on optimizing the design of MOD and AMOD services, simulating the integration of MOD and AMOD services with fixed-route transit, and incorporating synthetic mode choice models into MOD and AMOD simulation. Drakoulis et al. (2018) and Inturri et al. (2018) also simulated shared-ride MOD services, while Tsao et al. (2019), Winter et al. (2018), and Archetti et al. (2018) simulated shared-ride AMOD services. Other simulation-based research on shared-ride, intermodal MOD includes Stiglic et al. (2018). Single-passenger, intermodal AMOD simulations include Salazar et al. (2018) and Bischoff et al. (2017), while Martinez and Viegas (2017) simulated a shared-ride, intermodal AMOD system in Lisbon, Portugal. The Intermodal Transport Forum's 2015 report, *Urban Mobility System Upgrade*, provides an overview of early SAV simulations and includes an additional simulation comparing VMT impact in scenarios with shared-ride or single-passenger SAV fleets and with or without high-capacity public transportation (Martínez, 2015). The research described in this paragraph has all assumed exogenous demand or used synthetic mode choice models rather than estimating a mode choice model from real-world data. The results thus lack support from observed mode choice behaviour and also cannot provide estimates for induced demand, a crucial element in predicting the use of MOD services.

A few studies have begun estimating models for MOD demand based on stated

Table 19.3   Equity-related challenges and recommendations for MOD PPPs

Vulnerable Population	Challenges	Recommendations
Individuals with Disabilities (NCMM, 2018; Foxx, 2016; Blake et al., 2016; Danielsen, 2016; Taylor et al., 2015)	• *Low WAV availability* in MOD company fleets • Higher fares and wait times • MOD companies may decrease the number of WAVs in a city, if they drive taxi companies out of business • MOD company *drivers often lack training* in assisting disabled passengers	• In-app options to request WAVs (e.g., uberWAV, Lyft Access Mode) or request drivers with specialized training (e.g., uberASSIST) • Contract with third-party WAV providers like taxi companies • Use an agency's existing WAVs • Require MOD company to meet a specified number of WAVs before entering into MOD PPP
Minorities (Ge et al., 2016)	• MOD company drivers may cancel trips more often for passengers with pictures and/or names associated with racial minorities	• Remove the rider's picture and/or name from MOD apps • Drivers could still cancel after seeing the passenger in person, leading to even longer wait times for these passengers
Seniors (NCMM, 2018; Shirgaokar, 2018; SUMC, 2016)	• Barriers by age may include *need for assistance to the vehicle* or *lack of access to/ comfort with smartphones*	• Train drivers to assist passengers to board vehicles, offer training on how to use the app, and/or provide alternatives to smartphones
Low-Income Individuals (Smith, 2016)	• MOD services often have high fares	• Offer subsidized rides to low-income individuals
Unbanked/ Underbanked Individuals (Kodransky and Lewenstein, 2014)	• MOD services often *require payment by credit card* • 20% of US households do not have access to a credit card (FDIC, 2016)	• Purchase Uber and Lyft *gift cards* with cash • *Partner with a local credit union or bank* that can provide accounts and debit or credit cards for unbanked individuals
Individuals without Smartphones	• MOD services often *require smartphones to request rides* • Less than half of low-income Californians own smartphones (Chang, 2015)	• Through centralized call centres (e.g., Uber Central, Lyft Concierge), organizations can order rides for their constituents
Rural Populations (Rodier and Podolsky, 2017; Shaheen et al., 2017b; Shaheen et al., 2016)	• Lower driver availability • Unreliable mobile phone service	• Subsidize service in rural areas • Use community gathering places, such as faith-based buildings, as MOD hubs

preference choice experiments. Frei et al. (2016) conducted a stated preference survey with 183 respondents who completed 1997 choice experiments comparing drive alone, indirect shared MOD service, and fixed-route transit, although the sample is biased toward current public transit riders due to survey collection within a university

Table 19.4   Operational challenges and recommendations for MOD PPPs

Challenge	Description	Recommendations
Data Sharing (GAO, 2018; Tsay et al., 2016; Corey et al., 2017; Uber, 2016; Shaheen et al., 2016)	• MOD companies avoid sharing data due to *proprietary concerns* and the need to *protect customer information*. • Public transportation agencies entering into MOD PPPs need access to data on the rides they are subsidizing to *analyse the partnership's success* and further improve service.	• *Clearly define the desired data*, how to use the data to answer specific questions, and how to ensure data security and privacy. • *Obtain data through regulation* rather than voluntary agreements. • *Leverage agency-controlled assets* in negotiations for data access. • Seek *data analysis through a third party*, such as an academic institution. • *Set industry-wide standards* for "data formats, data sharing protocols, and privacy protections". • Develop a *nationwide, neutral MOD company data platform*.
Regulations and Liability: Drug and Alcohol Testing (FTA, 2016e)	• Public agencies that receive funds under the FTA's Urbanized Area, Capital Investment Grant, and Rural Area programmes must ensure *drug and alcohol testing* of the partner company's drivers.	• Consider partnering with *more than one MOD company* and/or taxi company and allow the *passenger to choose which service to use*, as this exempts the partnership from FTA drug and alcohol testing requirements.
Insurance Coverage and Background Checks	• Public agencies may have *concerns around liability* with regard to insurance coverage or driver background checks by their MOD company partner.	• Work with state and local governments to set *regulations and requirements regarding insurance and background checks* by MOD companies (Shaheen et al., 2016; Schaller, 2016).
Procurement Requirements (Tsay et al., 2016)	• Public agencies may need to *modify or waive their existing procurement requirements* to enable MOD PPPs.	• Negotiate the partnership through a company with which the public agency already has a contract, such as *trip-planning providers* like TransLoc (recently acquired by Ford).
Instability of MOD companies and prices	• Public agencies assume risk by subsidizing trips in the volatile MOD market (Tsay et al., 2016).	• Minimize risk by conducting short pilotsProtect against surge pricing by capping trip subsidies.
Labour–Management Relationships	• Existing contracts and relationships with unionized labour can financially, legally and politically restrict agencies from entering into MOD PPPs (Tsay et al., 2016).	• Procure software to provide Agency-Operated MOD service. • Partner with a local transportation provider alongside a MOD company. • Ensure the new service will complement, not replace, existing services.

Table 19.5   Literature on agent-based simulation of MOD and AMOD services

Subject	Journal Article(s)	Main Empirical or Methodological Contribution
Optimizing MOD service design	Alonso-Mora et al., 2017	Showed efficiency gains from 4-passenger and 10-passenger MOD services compared to existing taxi demand in Manhattan, New York
	Fiedler et al., 2017	Found increased congestion and VMT from single-passenger MOD service
	Djavadian and Chow, 2017a, 2017b	Simulated two-sided market equilibrium from dynamic adjustment by MOD operator in Oakville, Ontario
	Martinez et al., 2015	Tested passenger-vehicle matching scheme for a shared-taxi system in Lisbon, Portugal
	Santi et al., 2014	Showed efficiency gains from a two-passenger shared MOD service
	Ma et al., 2013	Proposed dispatching strategy for a MOD fleet
Optimizing AMOD service design	Fagnant and Kockelman, 2018, 2014	Simulated SAV fleet size and VMT impacts for single-passenger (2014) and shared (2018)
	Leich and Bischoff, 2018	Found higher operating costs and slight travel time savings from replacing buses with SAVs
	Dia and Javanshour, 2017	Optimized SAV fleet size in Melbourne, Australia
	Zhang and Guhathakurta, 2017, 2015	Calculated SAV impact on parking needs
	Fagnant et al., 2016	Found SAVs can meet current demand in Austin, Texas with one-tenth the current number of privately owned vehicles
Integrating MOD and AMOD services with fixed-route transit	Ma, 2017	Proposed dispatching system for efficient MOD service integration with fixed-route transit in and around Luxembourg City
	Vakayil et al., 2017	Simulated AMOD service with fixed-route transit in Washington, DC
	Shen et al., 2017	Simulated SAVs as a FMLM service in Singapore, identified bus routes to keep
	Moorthy et al., 2017	Simulated SAV fleet as FMLM service in Ann Arbor, Michigan
Integrating synthetic endogenous demand models in MOD and AMOD simulation	Basu et al., 2018	– Added AMOD to mode choice model with nests of private modes (drive alone, carpool, motorcycle), fixed-route transit (bus, rail), and on-demand (taxi) – Set the AMOD utility equation and parameters equal to those of taxi, with adjusted fares and travel times
	Hao and Yamamoto, 2017	Estimated model for SAV use and the sharing of privately owned vehicles in Meito Ward, Nagoya, Japan
	Hörl et al., 2016	Simulated single-passenger SAV system in which demand varies based on traffic
	Atasoy et al., 2015	Included mode choice model with options of taxi, shared taxi, and minibus

Source: Adapted and expanded from Liu et al. (2019).

community and through a public transportation agency website. They estimated a mode choice model that included: income, age, gender, trip and parking costs, in-vehicle time as well as walk and wait time, number of transfers, trip distance, distance to the nearest public transit stop, the weather and season, and a variety of opinions and preferences. Lazarus et al. (forthcoming) drew on a stated preference survey with 2398 respondents from Sacramento, San Francisco, Los Angeles and San Diego, California. The survey resulted in 10 912 choice experiments comparing single-passenger, shared door-to-door, and shared indirect TNC services, thereby estimating travellers' choice between TNC modes but not the choice of TNCs over other modes. The mode choice model they estimated included explanatory variables similar to those in Frei et al. (2016) as well as frequency of TNC use, trip purpose, and three categories of promotional offers. Aside from mode choice models, a few studies have used stated preference choice experiments to estimate models for related aspects of MOD service. Alemi et al. (2019) used a survey of 1975 California millennials and members of Generation X to estimate a model for the use frequency of Uber and Lyft, although the use of coarse frequency categories may have masked the impacts of geographic region and sociodemographic character-istics on frequency of use. Bansal et al. (2016) and Krueger et al. (2016) estimated how demographic, social, and service characteristics impact willingness to pay for shared and single-passenger SAV services. Matyas and Kamargianni (2019a; 2019b) estimated models for the choice of MaaS subscription bundles and find that respondents do not prefer bundles with shared modes but would be more willing to try shared modes after subscribing to bundles that include these services.

One study has combined stated preference choice experiments and agent-based simula-tion, enabling realistic demand estimates, supply-side optimization, and the identification of a supply–demand equilibrium. Liu et al. (2019) conducted a stated-preference survey of 1507 New York City residents, who each answered one choice experiment compar-ing single-passenger Uber, UberPool, and the respondents' current mode: drive-alone car, carpool, or fixed-route transit. Explanatory variables included walk and wait time, in-vehicle travel time, trip cost, parking cost, and whether the vehicle was electric and/or automated. With NYC taxi trip data providing a set level of demand, the authors estimated mode share between fixed-route transit and three MOD modes, using the utility equation for single-passenger Uber to estimate demand for a single-passenger MOD mode and the utility equation for UberPool to estimate demand for 4-passenger and 10-passenger MOD modes. Agent-based simulation provided travel and wait times based on the fleet sizes and demand for each MOD mode. They assumed all three MOD modes are operated by a profit-maximizing service provider, and used Bayesian optimization to determine this pro-vider's five decision variables: the fleet size for each MOD mode and the discount factors for the two shared-ride MOD modes. Through an iterative process, the authors identify a supply–demand equilibrium with mode share, fleet sizes and fares for each mode. This research does not consider induced demand or competition with traditional drive modes.

19.5   NEW RESEARCH FRONTIERS

Understanding of MOD PPPs could benefit from further research in several areas, including: (1) quantitative analysis of existing partnerships on how agency cost, VMT, accessibility, and equity impacts vary by service design; (2) estimation of induced demand from MOD PPP services; (3) the appropriate service environment (e.g., density, land use) for each MOD PPP service model and vehicle size, as well as the policy levers that encourage the best match of service environment and MOD PPP design; and (4) evaluation of how MOD PPP impacts may change with the transition to automated vehicles.

Section 19.3 and section 19.4 highlight a clear research gap: the use of data from existing MOD PPPs to provide guidance for public transportation agencies on how best to integrate MOD services with fixed-route transit to meet societal goals at a sustainable level of public subsidy. As described at the start of section 19.4, determining replaced modes and induced demand from existing partnerships is a crucial step to enable accurate estimates of ridership and thus VMT impacts and required subsidies. None of the research reviewed in section 19.4 includes a method to estimate induced demand. As indicated by the research on general TNC impacts in section 19.2, one way to estimate replaced modes and induced demand is to ask passengers of MOD PPP services what mode they would have used for their last trip on the service or if they would not have made the trip if the service were not available. More work like Liu et al. (2019) and Lazarus et al. (forthcoming) is needed to estimate mode choice models that include single-passenger and shared MOD modes, fixed-route transit, traditional drive modes, and non-motorized modes and draw on revealed or stated preference data from people familiar with MOD modes, such as residents in MOD PPP service areas. The surveys to estimate induced demand and mode choice must include demographic data to enable analysis of equity impacts, including relative travel time and wait time changes by income, race, age, ability and geographic location.

Another area of needed research involves determining the most appropriate service environment for each type of partnership between public transportation agencies and MOD companies: FMLM, Low-Density, Off-Peak, and Paratransit services, with vehicle sizes of 4-passenger, 10-passenger, or larger. After drawing on data from existing MOD PPPs to estimate induced demand and mode choice models that include demographic variables, researchers can expand on the work by Liu et al. (2019) and use agent-based simulation and supply-side optimization to determine the optimal service type and vehicle size by density and land use. In this context, the supply-side optimization would focus not on maximizing profit but rather on maximizing societal goals, including VMT reduction, equity and accessibility, subject to a maximum acceptable public subsidy.

Future research is also needed to identify policy levers that encourage the ideal distributions of MOD PPP services and vehicle sizes. This could involve testing outcomes under status-quo policies as well as combinations of: (1) subsidies to support socially desirable MOD uses like service in unprofitable low-income and rural areas; (2) fees to penalize undesirable uses like single-occupancy trips in high-traffic areas and times; and (3) dedicated infrastructure policies like assigning curb and road space to favour desirable modes and restrict MOD modes from competing with public transit along high-volume corridors.

Finally, the research outlined in this section can inform work on estimating social equity, accessibility, VMT, and cost impacts as MOD modes transition to automated services.

19.6   CONCLUSION

Survey-based and econometric analysis suggests negative impacts from TNCs on public transit ridership. In light of this competition, public transportation agencies are experimenting with the provision of smartphone-enabled, on-demand service by partnering with MOD companies, including TNCs, van-based microtransit, and ride-matching and routing software companies. The four main service models provided include FMLM, low-density, off-peak, and paratransit service. These partnerships aim to fill gaps or replace existing service in scenarios in which demand is too low or dispersed to support fixed-route service. Agencies implementing MOD PPPs face challenges such as ensuring equitable access, reaching data-sharing agreements with the private partner to enable in-house evaluation of the service, navigating regulations like driver background checks and drug tests, and addressing concerns from public transit labour unions about contracting with outside providers.

Most quantitative analyses on the impacts of shared-ride MOD services have involved agent-based simulation. These studies have primarily optimized MOD service design to minimize costs, evaluated travel time and VMT impacts, and assumed exogenous demand or synthetic mode choice models. A few research groups have used stated preference surveys to estimate mode choice models that include drive alone, ride-alone MOD, shared-ride MOD, and fixed-route public transit. A single study has used such a model in combination with agent-based simulation to identify a supply–demand equilibrium with mode share, fleet sizes, and fares for each mode. While this work has begun to address methods for designing intermodal MOD and fixed-route services, further research is needed on the impacts of existing and planned MOD PPPs.

In particular, none of the research described in this chapter has used trip data or surveys from existing MOD PPPs to evaluate how travel time and cost impacts vary by demographic group – a crucial step to ensuring benefits of the new service model are distributed equitably and meet the needs of transit-dependent populations. Moreover, none of the research includes a method to estimate induced demand, which is necessary to accurately analyse VMT impacts from existing MOD PPPs and to project ridership and agency costs for new partnerships. Additional research is also needed to identify the appropriate service environment for each type of MOD PPP, policy levers to encourage the socially optimal design of intermodal MOD services, and guidance for managing the transition to automated vehicles. While MOD PPPs offer the potential to improve travel times and reduce operational costs, public transit agencies and researchers must carefully monitor impacts to ensure these partnerships not only attract new ridership but also support fixed-route public transit service, lower overall VMT, and meet the needs of vulnerable populations.

REFERENCES

Access-A-Ride 2016. Citizens Budget Commission of New York [online]. Accessed at https://cbcny.org/research/access-ride.

Alemi, F., Circella, G., Mokhtarian, P. and Handy, S. 2019. What drives the use of ridehailing in California? Ordered probit models of the usage frequency of Uber and Lyft. *Transportation Research Part C: Emerging Technologies* 102, 233–48. Accessed at https://doi.org/10.1016/j.trc.2018.12.016.

Alonso-Mora, J., Samaranayake, S., Wallar, A., Frazzoli, E. and Rus, D. 2017. On-demand high-capacity ride-sharing via dynamic trip-vehicle assignment. *Proceedings of the National Academy of Sciences* 114, 462–7. Accessed at https://doi.org/10.1073/pnas.1611675114.

American Community Survey 2016 [online]. Means of transportation to work in Austin City, TX in 2016. Accessed at https://factfinder.census.gov/faces/tableservices/jsf/pages/productview.xhtml?pid=ACS_16_1YR_B08301 &prodType=table.

American Public Transportation Association 2014. Transit Ridership Report: Second Quarter 2014 [online]. Accessed at https://www.apta.com/wp-content/uploads/Resources/resources/statistics/Documents/Ridership/2014-q2-ridership-APTA.pdf.

American Public Transportation Association 2019 [online]. Transit Ridership Report: Second Quarter 2019. Accessed at https://www.apta.com/wp-content/uploads/2019-Q2-Ridership-APTA.pdf.

Archetti, C., Speranza, M.G. and Weyland, D. 2018. A simulation study of an on-demand transportation system. *International Transactions in Operational Research* 25, 1137–61. Accessed at https://doi.org/10.1111/itor.12476.

Atasoy, B., Ikeda, T. and Ben-Akiva, M. 2015. Optimizing a flexible mobility on demand system. *Transportation Research Record* 2536, 76–85. Accessed at https://doi.org/10.3141/2536-10.

Bansal, P., Kockelman, K.M. and Singh, A. 2016. Assessing public opinions of and interest in new vehicle technologies: An Austin perspective. *Transportation Research Part C: Emerging Technologies* 67, 1–14. Accessed at https://doi.org/10.1016/j.trc.2016.01.019.

Basu, R., Araldo, A., Akkinepally, A.P., Nahmias Biran, B.H., Basak, K., Seshadri, R., Deshmukh, N. et al. 2018. Automated mobility-on-demand vs. mass transit: A multi-modal activity-driven agent-based simulation approach. *Transportation Research Record* 2672, 608–18. Accessed at https://doi.org/10.1177/0361198118758630.

Bischoff, J., Kaddoura, I., Maciejewski, M. and Nagel, K., 2017. Re-defining the role of public transport in a world of Shared Autonomous Vehicles. Paper presented at the Symposium of the European Association for Research in Transportation (hEART), Israel Institute of Technology.

Blake, C., Franklin, S., McFadden-Resper, S., Muhammad, K., Abdul-Mateen, S. and Dash, A. 2016. Annual Report on Accessible Vehicle for Hire Service [online]. Accessed 1 December 2017 at https://dfhv.dc.gov/sites/default/files/dc/sites/dc%20taxi/page_content/attachments/DFHV%20Accessibility%20Advisory%20Committee%202016%20Annual%20Report%20120216%20FINAL%20Update.pdf.

Blodgett, M., Khani, A., Negoescu, D. and Benjaafar, S. 2017 [online]. Public/Private Partnerships in transit: Case studies and analysis (Report). Minnesota Council on Transportation Access. Accessed at http://conservancy.umn.edu/handle/11299/192846.

Chang, T. 2015. Crossing the digital and income divide [online]. Paper presented at the *Crossing the Digital and Income Divide: Making Mobility Innovations Accessible to All* meeting, San Francisco, CA, 18 February. Accessed at http://innovativemobility.org/?project=crossing-the-digital-and-income-divide-making-mobility-innovations-accessible-to-all-workshop-summary.

Clewlow, R.R. and Mishra, G.S. 2017. Disruptive transportation: The adoption, utilization, and impacts of ride-hailing in the United States [online]. Accessed at https://trid.trb.org/view.aspx?id=1485471.

Cohen, A. and Shaheen, S. 2016. Planning for shared mobility (PAS 583) [online]. American Planning Association. Accessed at https://www.planning.org/publications/report/9107556/.

Corey, E., Hastings, A., Krawczyk, T., de la Pena, B., Thompson, M., Hobson, M. and Kubly, S. 2017. New mobility playbook. Seattle Department of Transportation.

Curtis, T., Merritt, M., Chen, C., Perlmutter, D., Berez, D. and Ellis, B. 2019. Partnerships between transit agencies and transportation network companies. The National Academies of Sciences.

Danielsen, C. 2016. Groundbreaking settlement to end discrimination against blind Uber riders who use guide dogs [online]. National Federation of the Blind. Accessed 1 December 2017 at https://nfb.org/groundbreaking-settlement-end-discrimination-against-blind-uber-riders-who-use-guide-dogs.

Dia, H. and Javanshour, F. 2017. Autonomous shared Mobility-On-Demand: Melbourne pilot simulation study. 19th EURO Working Group on Transportation Meeting, EWGT2016, 5–7 September 2016, Istanbul, Turkey, *Transportation Research Procedia*, 22, 285–96. Accessed at https://doi.org/10.1016/j.trpro.2017.03.035.

Djavadian, S. and Chow, J.Y.J. 2017a. Agent-based day-to-day adjustment process to evaluate dynamic flexible transport service policies. *Transportmetrica B: Transport Dynamics* 5, 281–306. Accessed at https://doi.org/10.1080/21680566.2016.1190674.

Djavadian, S. and Chow, J.Y.J. 2017b. An agent-based day-to-day adjustment process for modeling "Mobility as a Service" with a two-sided flexible transport market. *Transportation Research Part B: Methodological* 104, 36–57. Accessed at https://doi.org/10.1016/j.trb.2017.06.015.

Drakoulis, R., Bellotti, F., Bakas, I., Berta, R., Paranthaman, P.K., Dange, G.R., Lytrivis, P. et al. 2018. A gamified flexible transportation service for on-demand public transport. *IEEE Transactions on Intelligent Transportation Systems* 19, 921–33. Accessed at https://doi.org/10.1109/TITS.2018.2791643.

Durand, A., Harms, L., Hoogendoorn-Lanser, S. and Zijlstra, T. 2018. Mobility-as-a-Service and changes in travel preferences and travel behaviour: A literature review. Accessed at https://doi.org/10.13140/RG.2.2.328 13.33760.

Fagnant, D.J. and Kockelman, K.M. 2014. The travel and environmental implications of shared autonomous vehicles, using agent-based model scenarios. *Transportation Research Part C: Emerging Technologies* 40, 1–13. Accessed at https://doi.org/10.1016/j.trc.2013.12.001.

Fagnant, D.J. and Kockelman, K.M. 2018. Dynamic ride-sharing and fleet sizing for a system of shared autonomous vehicles in Austin, Texas. *Transportation* 45, 143–58. Accessed at https://doi.org/10.1007/s1111 6-016-9729-z.

Fagnant, D.J., Kockelman, K.M. and Bansal, P. 2016. Operations of shared autonomous vehicle fleet for Austin, Texas market. *Transportation Research Record* 2563, 98–106. Accessed at https://doi.org/10.3141/2536-12.

FDIC 2016. FDIC National survey of unbanked and underbanked households. Federal Deposit Insurance Corporation.

Fiedler, D., Cáp, M. and Certický, M. 2017. Impact of mobility-on-demand on traffic congestion: Simulation-based study. Paper presented at the *2017 IEEE 20th International Conference on Intelligent Transportation Systems ITSC* 1–6. Accessed at https://doi.org/10.1109/ITSC.2017.8317830.

Foxx, A. 2016. DOT Dear Colleague Letter (Equity, Access for Shared Mobility Initiatives) [online]. FTA. Accessed 1 December 2017 at https://www.transit.dot.gov/regulations-and-guidance/policy-letters/ dot-dear-colleague-letter-equity-access-shared-mobility.

Frei, C., Hyland, M. and Mahmassani, H.S. 2016. Assessing the potential for demand adaptive transit via a stated preference choice survey. Paper presented at the Transportation Research Board 95th Annual Meeting.

FTA 2016a. Shared mobility definitions [online]. Federal Transit Administration. Accessed 7 May 2019 at https://www.transit.dot.gov/regulations-and-guidance/shared-mobility-definitions.

FTA 2016b. Mobility on Demand (MOD) Sandbox Program [online]. Federal Transit Administration. Accessed 25 November 2017 at https://www.transit.dot.gov/research-innovation/mobility-demand-mod-sand box-program.html.

FTA 2016c. Shared mobility Frequently Asked Questions [online]. Federal Transit Administration. Accessed 2 December 2017 at https://www.transit.dot.gov/regulations-and-guidance/shared-mobility-frequently-asked-questions.

FTA 2016d. Shared Mobility FAQs: Americans with Disabilities Act (ADA) [WWW Document]. Federal Transit Administration. Accessed 2 December 2017 at https://www.transit.dot.gov/regulations-and-guidance/ shared-mobility-faqs-americans-disabilities-act-ada.

FTA 2016e. Shared mobility FAQs: Controlled substance and alcohol testing requirements [online]. Federal Transit Administration. Accessed 2 December 2017 at https://www.transit.dot.gov/regulations-and-guidance/ shared-mobility-faqs-controlled-substance-and-alcohol-testing-requirements.

GAO 2018. Public transit partnerships: Additional information needed to clarify data reporting and share best practices. GAO-18-539. US Government Accountability Office.

Ge, Y., Knittel, C.R., MacKenzie, D. and Zoepf, S., 2016. Racial and gender discrimination in transportation network companies (Working Paper No. 22776). National Bureau of Economic Research. Accessed at https:// doi.org/10.3386/w22776.

Graehler Jr, M., Mucci, R.A. and Erhardt, G.D. 2019. Understanding the recent transit ridership decline in major US cities: Service cuts or emerging modes? Paper presented at the *Transportation Research Board 98th Annual Meeting*.

Hall, J.D., Palsson, C. and Price, J. 2018. Is Uber a substitute or complement for public transit? *Journal of Urban Economics* 108, 36–50. Accessed at https://doi.org/10.1016/j.jue.2018.09.003.

Hampshire, R., Simek, C., Fabusuyi, T., Di, X. and Chen, X. 2017. Measuring the impact of an unanticipated suspension of ride-sourcing in Austin, Texas (SSRN Scholarly Paper No. ID 2977969). Social Science Research Network, Rochester, NY.

Hao, M. and Yamamoto, T., 2017. Analysis on supply and demand of shared autonomous vehicles consider-ing household vehicle ownership and shared use. Paper presented at the *2017 IEEE 20th International Conference on Intelligent Transportation Systems (ITSC)*, pp.185–190. Accessed at https://doi.org/10.1109/ ITSC.2017.8317920.

Henao, A. 2017. Impacts of ridesourcing – Lyft and Uber – on transportation including VMT, mode replace-ment, parking, and travel behavior (PhD). University of Colorado at Denver, CO.

Hörl, S., Erath, A. and Axhausen, K.W. 2016. Simulation of autonomous taxis in a multi-modal traffic scenario with dynamic demand (Working Paper). IVT, ETH Zurich. Accessed at https://doi.org/10.3929/ ethz-b-000118794.

Inturri, G., Giuffrida, N., Ignaccolo, M., Le Pira, M., Pluchino, A. and Rapisarda, A. 2018. Testing demand responsive shared transport services via agent-based simulations. In P. Daniele and L. Scrimali (eds), *New Trends in Emerging Complex Real Life Problems*. Cham: Springer International Publishing, pp.313–20. Accessed at https://doi.org/10.1007/978-3-030-00473-6_34.

Jittrapirom, P., Caiati, V., Feneri, A.-M., Ebrahimigharehbaghi, S., González, M.J.A. and Narayan, J. 2017.

Mobility as a Service: A critical review of definitions, assessments of schemes, and key challenges. *Urban Planning* 2, 13–25. Accessed at https://doi.org/10.17645/up.v2i2.931.

Kamargianni, M., Li, W., Matyas, M., Schäfer, A. 2016. A critical review of new mobility services for urban transport. *Transportation Research Procedia* 14, 3294–303. Accessed at https://doi.org/10.1016/j.trpro.2016.05.277.

Kane, J., Tomer, A. and Puentes, R. 2016. How Lyft and Uber can improve transit agency budgets. The Brookings Institution.

Kaufman, S., Smith, A., O'Connell, J. and Marulli, D. 2016. Intelligent paratransit. New York University Rudin Center for Transportation Policy and Management.

Kodransky, M. and Lewenstein, G. 2014. Connecting low-income people to opportunity with shared mobility. Institute for Transportation and Development Policy.

Krueger, R., Rashidi, T.H. and Rose, J.M. 2016. Preferences for shared autonomous vehicles. *Transportation Research Part C: Emerging Technologies* 69, 343–55. Accessed at https://doi.org/10.1016/j.trc.2016.06.015.

Kuhr, J., Bhat, C.R., Duthie, J. and Ruiz, N. 2017. Ridesharing & public–private partnerships: Current issues, a proposed framework and benefits. Paper presented at the *Transportation Research Board 96th Annual Meeting*.

Lazarus, J., Caicedo, J., Bayen, A., Shaheen, S. forthcoming. To pool or not to pool? Understanding opportunities and challenges to expand the market for pooling (under review).

Lazarus, J., Shaheen, S., Young, S.E., Fagnant, D., Voege, T., Baumgardner, W., Fishelson, J. et al. 2018. Shared automated mobility and public transport. In *Road Vehicle Automation 4, Lecture Notes in Mobility*. Cham: Springer, pp. 141–61. Accessed at https://doi.org/10.1007/978-3-319-60934-8_13.

Leich, G. and Bischoff, J. 2018. Should autonomous shared taxis replace buses? A simulation study. Accessed at https://doi.org/http://dx.doi.org/10.14279/depositonce-8478.

Liu, Y., Bansal, P., Daziano, R. and Samaranayake, S. 2019. A framework to integrate mode choice in the design of mobility-on-demand systems. *Transportation Research Part C: Emerging Technologies* 105, 648–65. Accessed at https://doi.org/10.1016/j.trc.2018.09.022.

Lucken, E., Trapenberg Frick, K. and Shaheen, S.A. 2019. "Three Ps in a MOD": Role for mobility on demand (MOD) public–private partnerships in public transit provision. *Research in Transportation Business & Management* 32, 100433.

Ma, S., Zheng, Y. and Wolfson, O. 2013. T-share: A large-scale dynamic taxi ridesharing service. Paper presented at the *International Conference on Data Engineering*, pp. 410–21. Accessed at https://doi.org/10.1109/ICDE.2013.6544843.

Ma, T.-Y. 2017. On-demand dynamic Bi-/multi-modal ride-sharing using optimal passenger-vehicle assignments. *2017 IEEE International Conference on Environment and Electrical Engineering and 2017 IEEE Industrial and Commercial Power Systems Europe EEEIC/ICPS Europe*, pp. 1–5. Accessed at https://doi.org/10.1109/eeeic.2017.7977646.

Martínez, L. 2015. Urban mobility system upgrade (Text). *International Transport Forum*.

Martinez, L.M. and Viegas, J.M. 2017. Assessing the impacts of deploying a shared self-driving urban mobility system: An agent-based model applied to the city of Lisbon, Portugal. *International Journal of Transportation Science and Technology, Connected and Automated Vehicles: Effects on Traffic, Mobility and Urban Design* special issue 6, 13–27. Accessed at https://doi.org/10.1016/j.ijtst.2017.05.005.

Martinez, L.M., Correia, G.H.A. and Viegas, J.M. 2015. An agent-based simulation model to assess the impacts of introducing a shared-taxi system: An application to Lisbon (Portugal). *Journal of Advanced Transportation* 49, 475–95. Accessed at https://doi.org/10.1002/atr.1283.

Matyas, M. and Kamargianni, M. 2019a. Survey design for exploring demand for Mobility as a Service plans. *Transportation* 46, 1525–58. Accessed at https://doi.org/10.1007/s11116-018-9938-8.

Matyas, M. and Kamargianni, M. 2019b. The potential of mobility as a service bundles as a mobility management tool. *Transportation* 46, 1951–68. Accessed at https://doi.org/10.1007/s11116-018-9913-4.

Moorthy, A., Kleine, R.D.D., Keoleian, G.A., Good, J. and Lewis, G. 2017. Shared autonomous vehicles as a sustainable solution to the last mile problem: A case study of Ann Arbor-Detroit area. University of Michigan, CSS publication. Accessed at https://doi.org/10.4271/2017-01-1276.

Murphy, C. and Feigon, S. 2016. Shared mobility and the transformation of public transit. American Public Transportation Association.

NCMM 2018. Considerations for TNC partnerships: Seniors and individuals with disabilities. National Center for Mobility Management.

Rayle, L., Dai, D., Chan, N., Cervero, R. and Shaheen, S. 2016. Just a better taxi? A survey-based comparison of taxis, transit, and ridesourcing services in San Francisco. *Transport Policy* 45, 168–78. Accessed at https://doi.org/10.1016/j.tranpol.2015.10.004.

Rodier, C. and Podolsky, L. 2017. Opportunities for shared-use mobility services in rural disadvantaged communities in California's San Joaquin valley: Existing conditions and conceptual program development. National Center for Sustainable Transportation.

Salazar, M., Rossi, F., Schiffer, M., Onder, C.H. and Pavone, M. 2018. On the interaction between autonomous mobility-on-demand and public transportation systems. Paper presented at the *2018 21st International Conference on Intelligent Transportation Systems (ITSC)*, pp. 2262–9. Accessed at https://doi.org/10.1109/ITSC.2018.8569381.

Santi, P., Resta, G., Szell, M., Sobolevsky, S., Strogatz, S. and Ratti, C. 2014. Quantifying the benefits of vehicle pooling with shareability networks. *Proceedings of the National Academy of Sciences of the United States of America* 111(37). Accessed at https://doi.org/10.1073/pnas.1403657111.

Schaller, B. 2016. Unfinished business: A blueprint for Uber, Lyft and taxi regulation. Schaller Consulting.

Schaller, B. 2017. Unsustainable? The growth of app-based ride services and traffic, travel and the future of New York City. Schaller Consulting.

Schaller, B. 2018. The new automobility: Lyft, Uber and the future of American cities. Schaller Consulting.

Schwieterman, J.P., Livingston, M. and Van der Slot, S. 2018. Partners in transit: A review of partnerships between transportation network companies and public agencies in the United States. DePaul University.

Shaheen, S. and Chan, N. 2016. Mobility and the sharing economy: Potential to facilitate the first- and last-mile public transit connections. *Built Environment* 42, 573–88. Accessed at https://doi.org/10.2148/benv.42.4.573.

Shaheen, S. and Cohen, A. 2018a. Is it time for a public transit renaissance?: Navigating travel behavior, technology, and business model shifts in a brave new world. *Journal of Public Transportation* 21. https://doi.org/https://doi.org/10.5038/2375-0901.21.1.8.

Shaheen, S. and Cohen, A. 2018b. Equity and shared mobility. ITS Berkeley Policy Briefs 2018. Accessed at https://doi.org/10.7922/G2MC8X6K.

Shaheen, S. and Cohen, A. 2019. Mobility on Demand (MOD) and Mobility as a Service (MaaS): How are they similar and different? [online]. Medium. Accessed 26 October 2019 at https://medium.com/move-forward-blog/mobility-on-demand-mod-and-mobility-as-a-service-maas-how-are-they-similar-and-different-a853c853b0b8.

Shaheen, S., Cohen, A. and Zohdy, I. 2016. Shared mobility: Current practices and guiding principles. Federal Highway Administration.

Shaheen, S., Bell, C., Cohen, A. and Yelchuru, B. 2017b. Travel behavior: Shared mobility and transportation equity. Federal Highway Administration.

Shaheen, S., Cohen, A., Yelchuru, B. and Sarkhili, S. 2017a. Mobility on demand operational concept Report (No. FHWA-JPO-18-611). Federal Highway Administration.

Shen, Y., Zhang, H. and Zhao, J. 2017. Embedding autonomous vehicle sharing in public transit system: An example of last-mile problem. Paper presented at the *Transportation Research Board 96th Annual Meeting*.

Shirgaokar, M. 2018. Expanding seniors' mobility through phone apps: Potential responses from the private and public sectors. *Journal of Planning Education and Research* 36(2), 210–24. Accessed at 0739456X18769133. https://doi.org/10.1177/0739456X18769133.

Smith, A. 2016. Shared, collaborative and on demand: The new digital economy. Pew Research Center. Accessed 25 November 2017 at http://www.pewinternet.org/2016/05/19/the-new-digital-economy/.

Stiglic, M., Agatz, N., Savelsbergh, M. and Gradisar, M. 2018. Enhancing urban mobility: Integrating ride-sharing and public transit. *Computers & Operations Research* 90, 12–21. Accessed at https://doi.org/10.1016/j.cor.2017.08.016.

SUMC 2016. 7 services expanding mobility for aging Americans. *Shared-Use Mobility Center*. Accessed 1 December 2017 at http://sharedusemobilitycenter.org/news/7-new-services-expanding-mobility-for-aging-americans/.

Taylor, B., Chin, R., Crotty, M., Dill, J., Hoel, L. and Manville, M. 2015. Between public and private mobility: Examining the rise of technology-enabled transportation services. National Resource Council, *Transportation Research Board*. Accessed at https://doi.org/10.17226/21875.

Tsao, M., Milojević, D., Ruch, C., Salazar, M., Frazzoli, E. and Pavone, M. 2019. Model predictive control of ride-sharing autonomous mobility-on-demand systems. Paper presented at the *2019 International Conference on Robotics and Automation (ICRA)*, pp. 6665–71. Accessed at https://doi.org/10.1109/ICRA.2019.8794194.

Tsay, S., Accuardi, Z., Schaller, B. and Hovenkotter, K. 2016. Private mobility, public interest. TransitCenter.

Uber, 2016. Transparency report. Uber.

Vakayil, A., Gruel, W. and Samaranayake, S. 2017. Integrating shared-vehicle mobility-on-demand systems with public transit. Paper presented at the *Transportation Research Board 96th Annual Meeting*.

Winter, K., Cats, O., Correia, G. and van Arem, B. 2018. Performance analysis and fleet requirements of automated demand-responsive transport systems as an urban public transport service. *International Journal of Transportation Science and Technology* 7, 151–67. Accessed at https://doi.org/10.1016/j.ijtst.2018.04.004.

Wong, Y.Z., Hensher, D.A. and Mulley, C. 2018. Emerging transport technologies and the modal efficiency framework: A case for mobility as a service (MaaS). Working Paper.

Zhang, W. and Guhathakurta, S. 2017. Parking spaces in the age of shared autonomous vehicles: How much parking will we need and where? *Transportation Research Record* 2651, 80–91. Accessed at https://doi.org/10.3141/2651-09.

Zhang, W., Guhathakurta, S., Fang, J. and Zhang, G. 2015. Exploring the impact of shared autonomous vehicles on urban parking demand: An agent-based simulation approach. *Sustainable Cities and Society* 19, 34–45. Accessed at https://doi.org/10.1016/j.scs.2015.07.006.

20. Large increases in bus use in Sweden: lessons learned

Maria Börjesson, Margareta Friman and Masoud Fadaei

1. INTRODUCTION

For decades, improved public transport has been seen as an important measure to increase accessibility and combat negative effects of car use (see for instance the European Commission's White Paper on transport, 2011). In 2007, the Swedish public transport sector adopted the objective of doubling public transport use between 2008 and 2020, and this target was also adopted by the Swedish Government (Government Bill 2015/16:100). Public transport demand also increased by 30 per cent over the first decade after 2008. In the period 2002–17 public transport use increased by nearly 50 per cent while the increase in the European Union was only 8 per cent (UITP, 2016). In this chapter we show and analyse the aggregated trends in the Swedish public transport sector regarding demand, supply, costs, fares and car use. As a complement, we analyse public transport use and satisfaction from two cities that have adopted different strategies and measures to increase public transit use. The chapter aims at summarizing lessons learned from development of the Swedish public transport sector.

While there is ample evidence that increased public transport supply increases accessibility and use, there is still little conclusive evidence on what type of softer improvements are most effective in increasing use and satisfaction of public transport (e.g., Balcombe et al., 2004; Richter et al., 2010; Bamberg et al., 2011). The extent to which increased public transport use has a long-term impact on car use, energy use and emissions is even more uncertain. In section 2 of this chapter, we describe the aggregate trends in public transport from Sweden as a whole, Stockholm and the smaller city of Karlstad. We show trends regarding the number of trips, public transport supply (seat kilometres), production costs and monthly ticket fares. A key driver of the rapid increase in public transport in Sweden is a large expansion in public transport supply, but also softer measures such as customer-oriented design and marketing have been applied to increase the attractiveness of public transport.

In addition, we show trends in car use. Although aggregate descriptive statistics cannot reveal causality, we conclude that car use per capita has not declined as public transport has increased. Although public transport may be very important for increasing equality and accessibility, measures directly targeting car use itself are more efficient in reducing car use. Moreover, in line with several other studies, we find that the cost efficiency of public transport is reduced over time (Holmgren, 2013; Li et al., 2015). In other words, production cost has increased faster than both demand and supply, implying increased fares and a greater burden on taxpayers.

To increase the understanding of what measures are most effective for increasing public transport satisfaction and use, section 3 analyses data on public transport use and satisfaction from two cities that have adopted different strategies and measures to increase public transport use and satisfaction. It shows how travel satisfaction and travel behaviour changed over time in the two cities. Section 4 concludes.

2.   AGGREGATE TRENDS

In Sweden, local and regional public transport is subsidized and provided by the 21 regions' Public Transport Authorities (PTA). On average, the subsidy rate (and cost recovery) is 50 per cent. The PTAs can operate the traffic themselves (approximately 5 per cent of the traffic) or provide the traffic by competitive tendering (approx. 90 per cent). Fully commercial public transport services are also allowed, but in practice rare (5 per cent). Three contract types are applied in Sweden: gross-cost without incentives, with incentives, and net-cost contracts.

Figures 20.1 to 20.3 show how the demand, supply, cost, price of the monthly ticket and population have developed in Sweden, in the capital Stockholm and in Karlstad (a

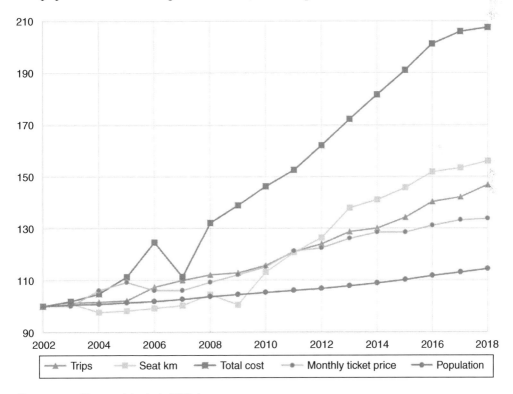

Data source: Transport Analysis (2020a).

Figure 20.1   *The development (percentage changes) of demand for bus trips (on-board counts), supply (seat kilometres), total production cost, price of a monthly ticket, and total population in Sweden: prices and costs changes are in real terms (same price level)*

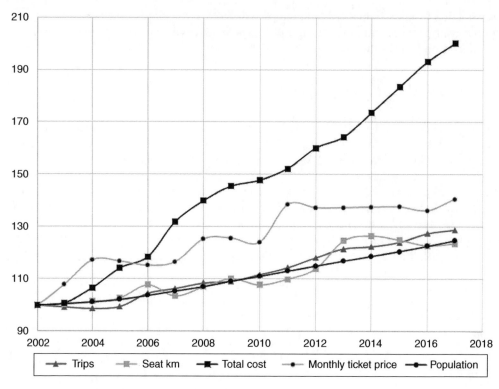

Note: Prices and costs changes are in real terms.

Source: Own processing of data from Eliasson (2019).

Figure 20.2   *The development (percentage changes) of demand for bus trips (on-board
counts), supply (seat kilometres), total production cost, price of the
monthly ticket, and total population in Stockholm*

medium-sized city with approximately 90 000 inhabitants) from 2002 to 2018 or 2014
(depending on data availability). As much as 53 per cent of the total public transport
travel in Sweden takes place in the Stockholm region, and together 83 per cent of all public
transport journeys are made in the three metropolitan regions (Stockholm, Gothenburg
and Malmö regions, making up approximately 50 per cent of the Swedish population).
Hence, the trend for Sweden (Figure 20.1) is heavily influenced by the trends in the three
metropolitan regions.

   The most conspicuous trend in all figures is the rapid increase in total production
cost (in real terms[1]). As shown, the cost increased faster than both supply and demand
in Sweden (Figure 20.1) and in Stockholm (Figure 20.2). The cost of public transport
doubled in 15 years, whereas the supply increased by 30 per cent in Stockholm and 50
per cent in Sweden. Hence, the cost efficiency decreased over time. In Karlstad, the cost
increased faster and had already doubled in 2013, but the supply had also increased even
faster (67 per cent in 2013; see Figure 20.3). The rate of the cost increase in Karlstad is
roughly equal to the rate of the supply increase until 2013, when new buses were acquired.

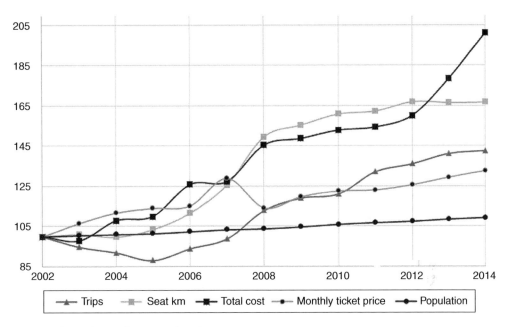

Note: Prices and costs changes are in real terms.

Data source: Pyddoke and Swärdh (2017) and Statistics Sweden.

Figure 20.3 *The development (percentage changes) of demand for bus trips (on-board counts), supply (seat kilometre), total production cost, price of the monthly ticket, and population in Karlstad*

After this, the increase in the number of travellers and the supply levelled out, whereas the costs continued to increase. Hence, after 2013 the cost of the bus system increased faster than the supply and demand, as in the rest of Sweden.

In Stockholm, the number of travellers increased at the same rate as the supply between 2002 and 2018, maintaining the average occupancy rate. In Karlstad, supply increased faster than demand, implying that the average occupancy rate declined over time. In Sweden as a whole, the occupancy rate increased until 2009, but has declined since. The cost increased faster than the number of travellers, and since a cost subsidy rate of 50 per cent was maintained, the fares also increased. In Karlstad, Stockholm and in the rest of Sweden, the price of the monthly ticket increased by just above 40 per cent (in real terms). Fares have increased further since 2017; in the period 2002–20, the price of a monthly ticked has increased by 52 per cent in Stockholm and by 57 per cent in Karlstad. The increase in fares and the increased burden for the taxpayers imply that the equity of public transport may have been reduced. Hence, a negative consequence of increased supply and production costs may be a weakened equity of public transport. Moreover, the price of single tickets has increased even faster than the monthly tickets. In passing, we note that expensive single tickets might reduce equity even more, since low-income people benefit less from the higher subsidy rate for monthly tickets than for single tickets (Bondemark et al., 2020).

Why Does the Cost Increase?

A key question is why the costs have been increasing so much faster than supply in Swedish public transport. Holmgren (2013) showed that the cost efficiency decreased substantially in Sweden between 1986 and 2009, but due to lack of data the cost drivers could not be identified. Moreover, Li et al. (2015) found that the operational cost of buses has not declined over time to the same extent as cars. According to the empirical analysis of the US bus fleet, environmental and employment regulations and capital costs of the buses are the main reasons for the slow decline in operational and capital costs for buses.

Several authors have found higher cost efficiency for privately owned operators and a higher degree of outsourcing (Ottoz et al., 2009; Walter, 2011). In line with these studies, cost efficiency also increased when competitive tendering was introduced in Sweden in the late 1980s (Alexandersson and Pyddoke, 2010) (but has since then decreased over time). Dalen and Gómez-Lobo (2003) and Piacenza (2006) found that using contracts with strong incentives increased cost-efficiency. However, Vigren (2016) found no effect on cost efficiency of incentives in public transport contracts in Sweden. Moreover, Vigren found lower cost efficiency in regions with higher population density.

There are a limited number of studies investigating how contract design factors impact cost efficiency in Sweden. The key reason for this seems to be lack of data. For instance, Nilsson (2011) observed how the public transport providers omitted to demand monitoring of traffic outcomes in the contract. For this reason, new types and designs of contracts are often introduced without any evidence of what effects they might have on costs or services, and without an evaluation plan. Camén and Lidestam (2016) conclude, based on interviews with operators as well as the PTAs, that many cost drivers are related to the procurement and specifically a wider range of specific requirements from the public transport authority in the public procurement process. The wide range of specific requirements may include a certain colour for the seats or curtains, the colour of the bus, or spacing of the chairs. If the bus operator loses the subsequent tender, the value of the buses will drop substantially, and they will need to be redesigned at high cost. Age and fuel requirements are other factors that can cause well-functioning buses to be scrapped prematurely.

A telling example of this is in Karlstad, where the trips increased at the same rate even before new vehicles were bought and brought into service in 2013. Hence, there is no strong evidence showing that new "green/sustainable" buses are important for an increase in trip demand. The story of the super bus project in Malmö (see the following section) is another telling example. A main cost driver of the new "super buses" was the specification requirements, implying that there was only one manufacturer able to deliver the bus (Van Hool).[2] The purchase price was 8 million SEK, compared to the price for a standard 18-metre-long city bus, which was 3–4 million SEK. This demonstrates how procurement and political specifications drive certain costs with limited effects on both passenger volumes and operation costs. Inevitably, this would hurt low-income groups more, since fares and the burden on taxpayers increase.

An interesting question is whether the unilateral objective of doubling public transport, which was a goal launched in 2008, has contributed to the cost increase and reduced occupancy rate. This cannot be proven, but it is possible that the cost control become less of an issue with such a strong objective. In any case, the occupancy rates started to fall after 2009 in Sweden.

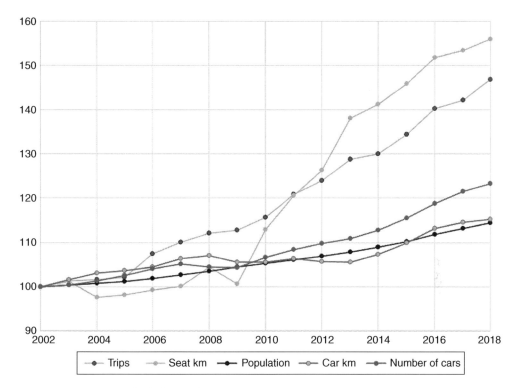

Data source: Transport Analysis (2020a).

Figure 20.4   *The development of demand for public transport trips, public transport supply and car use in Sweden*

Effects on Car Use . . .

Measures to increase public transport use are often motivated by the aim of reducing car and energy use. Figure 20.4 shows the trend in car use and car ownership, together with the public transport demand and supply and population growth in 2002–18. On average, car use increased slightly faster than the population in 2002–17. The car use increased fastest in 2002–08. During the subsequent period of the economic crisis 2008–12 car use declined, while population continued to increase. This seems to have been caused by falling GDP and increased fuel prices in Sweden and in many other countries (Bastian et al., 2016), rather than increased public transport use. Since 2013, car use has increased slightly faster than the population.

So, whereas public transport use has increased substantially faster than car use since 2002, the trend in car use seems to follow the economic development rather than the trends in public transport use, so the causality cannot be proven. Although public transport increased by nearly 50 per cent in 2002–17, as compared to the increase in the EU of 8 per cent in 2000–14, car use development in Sweden does not stand out compared to other comparable countries (OECD/ITF, 2020). Moreover, car use per capita has *not declined* as public transport use has increased. Hence, as a means to reduce car use, public transport extensions can be questioned. However, a worrying trend is that cycling distance per capita has fallen by 10 per cent in Sweden in 2000–17 (Transport Analysis, 2020b). Now, the decline in cycling might clearly not be caused by a direct diversion of trips from cycling to public transport. But the fact remains that as public transport trips have increased rapidly, car use per capita has remained constant or increased slightly, whereas cycling per capita has decreased.

Even if some car trips were replaced by public transport trips, this would still have a small effect on car use – simply because car use is so much greater, as shown in Figure 20.7. For instance, the bus person kilometres were only 5 per cent of the car person kilometres in 2017. For this reason, if bus use were to increase by 10 per cent and if all of these were directly diverted from the car, the car kilometres would only decrease by 0.5 percent.

A contributing factor to the faster increase in public transport trips than in car use (and cycling) could be the large migration to Sweden. Population growth since the turn of the century has been 16 per cent, and migration has constituted the biggest contribution to the population growth during this period (Statistics Sweden, 2020). Moreover, car use and car ownership are probably much lower among migrants (there are no data on car use among migrants; but migrants have on average lower incomes, lower driving licence holdings and tend to live in urban areas, which are all correlated with lower car use and ownership).

Turning to Stockholm, Figure 20.5 shows that car use developed faster than the number of public transport trips and population 2002–08. During the period of the economic crisis 2008–12 car use declined, whereas public transport and population continued to

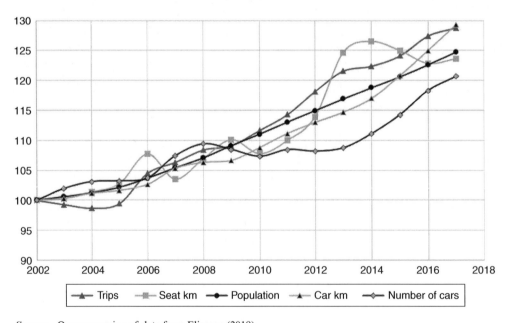

Source: Own processing of data from Eliasson (2019).

Figure 20.5   The development of demand for public transport trips, public transport supply and car use in Stockholm

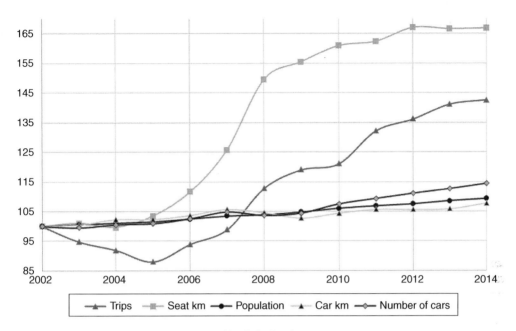

Data source: Pyddoke and Swärdh (2017) and Statistics Sweden.

Figure 20.6 *The development of demand for public transport trips, public transport*
supply and car use in Karlstad

increase. Since 2012, car use has increased more rapidly than public transport and population. Hence, again we find that whereas public transport increases in line with supply, car
use is much more dependent on the economy, employment and fuel prices. But again, it is
hard to detect a transfer from the car to public transport, even if it cannot be ruled out.

Figure 20.6 shows that in Karlstad car use increased slightly faster than the population
before 2007 and after 2009, and decreased in the period in between. The change in car use
is dwarfed by the large increase in public transport since 2005. Again, public transport
supply has increased even more rapidly, which indicates that this is the main cause.

Turning to the research literature on how public transport improvements reduce car
use, Wardman et al. (2018) conducted a meta-study to deduce cross-elasticities from a
large number of empirical studies. Cross-elasticities convey how car use declines as public
transport supply or fares increase. Wardman et al. based the study on 1096 estimates of
cross-elasticity from 93 studies and 20 countries (almost all in Europe and with a focus on
northern Europe), and found cross-elasticities of 6 per cent for trip headway, fare and travel
time in the vehicle. Hence, if the headway, ticket price or travel time in the vehicle decreases
by 1 per cent, the car trips will decrease by 0.06 per cent. The Swedish and Danish national
transport models produce similar cross-elasticities. Note, however, that cross-elasticities
are not one number but are context-dependent. The effect on car use of a public transport
improvement is in general lower if the initial market share for public transport is low.

The key problem with most studies on cross-elasticities, however, is that they disregard
self-selection (spatial sorting), which will tend to overestimate the effect on car use of

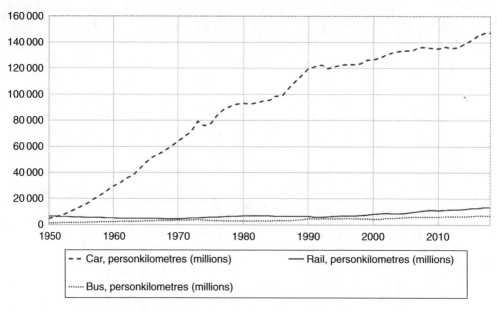

Data source: Transport Analysis (2020a).

Figure 20.7   Trends in person km for bus, rail and car in Sweden

improvement in public transport. Spatial sorting means that individuals with a relatively higher preference for public transport use will tend to self-select into places with improved public transport. Moreover, second-order effects from reduced car use can generate new car demand. That is, if travel time is reduced when car users divert to public transport, the reduced car travel time is likely to generate new car use. Such second-order effects are also often neglected in empirical studies, which again will tend to overestimate elasticities. The weakness of the aggregate trends shown in the present chapter is that they cannot be used to infer causality. However, one strength is that the aggregate trends take into account self-selection and second-order effects on car use.

Furthermore, the own elasticity of public transport is significantly greater than the cross-elasticity between car and public transport, often around 40 per cent for fares and just over 100 per cent for travel time in vehicles (Dunkerley et al., 2018). This may explain the trends we see in the figures above: most of the new public transport journeys that arise after an improvement will be generated travel rather than replaced car journeys. Own elasticities for car use regarding fuel price (Graham and Glaister, 2004) and congestion charges (Börjesson and Kristoffersson, 2018) are also substantially higher than the cross-elasticities. Hence, to reduce carbon emissions from car use, fuel tax, registration tax and congestion charges are more efficient.

. . . and Carbon Emissions

It is not only car use that consumes energy, so do buses. The figures show that the public transit supply has increased faster than demand in Karlstad and Sweden, which means

Table 20.1   Energy consumption per person kilometre for bus and car

	Bus	Car
Litre per 100 km	44 Basic requirements for standard buses up to 13.5 metres (The Swedish Public Transport Association, 2018)	3.9 Average per diesel car from 2016[a] (The Swedish Transport Agency, 2019)
Seating per vehicle	44 on average (The Swedish Confederation of Transport Enterprises, 2015)	5
Number of persons in each bus	11.4 (SKL, 2018)	2.1 Analysis of the national travel customs survey RES 2005–2006 (Transport Analysis, 2020b)
Average fuel per person kilometre	3.9 (44/11.4)	1.8 (3.9/2.1)

Note: a.   The Swedish Transport Agency specifies average emissions from diesel cars sold in 2016 as 129.54 g/km. Conversion to the consumption of diesel per kilometre has been done on the basis of 95.1 g of carbon dioxide equivalents per megajoule and 35.3 megajoules per litre of diesel. These figures originate from the Swedish Energy Agency.

that the occupancy rates decrease over time. This is worrying not only from an economic perspective but also from the perspective of energy use. Now, the average occupancy rate is already low (on average it is roughly 25 per cent for Swedish buses, if not counting the kilometres driven when the buses are not in revenue service which would reduce occupancy further). For this reason, energy consumption per kilometre is *on average* higher for buses than for cars in Sweden. To show this, Table 20.1 calculates energy consumption per passenger kilometre for bus and car use in Sweden.

A standard bus uses an average of 44 litres of diesel per 100 km. The average number of passengers in the buses per supply kilometre is 11.4. The fuel consumption is thus 3.9 litres of diesel per 100 km per person. But since the distance covered when the bus is not in revenue service is not considered when calculating occupancy, the fuel consumption per passenger kilometre is higher. A diesel car purchased in 2016 consumes an average of 3.9 litres of fuel per 100 km. Moreover, considering that there are on average 2.1 individuals in each passenger car, there will be significantly lower fuel consumption per person and kilometre in the car.

Of course, this does not mean that public transport does not reduce carbon emissions anywhere. In places where the occupancy rate is high, emissions are significantly lower per bus passenger kilometre than for a car passenger kilometre. And where there is congestion, buses are far more space-efficient than cars. In addition, they offer travel opportunities to people who do not have access to a car. There are thus many arguments in favour of buses at the right time and place. But as a means to reduce carbon dioxide emissions in all parts of the country, it does not seem to work.

3.   MEASURES AND STRATEGIES FOR INCREASING SATISFACTION AND USE

Essentially, there are two main strategies to reduce car use. One strategy is to use direct measures to reduce car use by implementing measures that increase the cost of, or accessibility to, driving (Richter et al., 2010). A common measure is to implement different pricing mechanisms, making it difficult to own and drive a car. Taxing car use further, however, is often not politically feasible or considered to be enough;[3] thus an alternative strategy to reduce car use is to focus on indirect measures, for instance, improved attractiveness and service level and use of public transport. By increasing the attractiveness of the service, people's attitudes towards public transport are becoming more positive and accessibility increases. A positive attitude and increased public transport accessibility increase the likelihood for switching behaviour, frequency of use, loyalty and positive word-of-mouth (Gärling et al., 2018).

From the quantitative transport literature, it is also fairly well-known how measures impacting travel cost or different travel time components (in-vehicle time, waiting and access time, travel time reliability) impact mode choice. It is also evident from the increase in Swedish use of public transport, that the increased supply (impacting different travel time components) has been a major driving factor. The impact of softer measures, such as travel information, contact with drivers and cleanliness, on the use of public transport seems to be more uncertain and context-specific.

Also, a review of psychological public transport research shows that measures increasing accessibility, reliability and availability of services are important for attractiveness (Redman et al., 2013). The same review also shows that context as well as user segments and type of public transport mode determine which factors are most important. Eriksson et al. (2010) also showed that good access to bus stops increases bus use and reduces car use among car users. Börjesson and Rubensson (2019) show that the hard attributes of reliability and frequency are the most important attributes for total satisfaction with public transport. It has been shown that users value access to bus stops, wait time, trip length (but also vehicle design, driver skill, and correct and timely information) (Prioni and Hensher, 2000).

Friman et al. (2001) as well as Friman and Gärling (2001) identified treatment by employees (i.e., willingness to serve, knowledge and competence), simplicity of information (e.g., accessibility of departure and destination information), reliability of service, and design of vehicles and space (relating to comfort, security and cleanliness) as important for satisfaction with public transport. A European study (Friman and Fellesson, 2009) confirmed earlier results by demonstrating the impact on satisfaction with public transport of safety, security, frequency and reliability of service, comfort, and quality of staff behaviour. A research synthesis by Currie and Rose (2008) suggests that reliability, service levels and fares are the principal tools to increase use of public transport. Also, Currie and Wallis (2008) conclude that fares are related to use of service, particularly in certain groups and in relation to service received.

Mouwen (2015) showed that travellers with access to a car are more sensitive to security issues, cleanliness of stations, and user information than those with no such access. Furthermore, young, female, and low-income or unemployed travellers differ in which features of satisfaction they value for various public transport modes (Susilo and Cats,

2014). Different mode users (rail, metro, bus) value different aspects; for instance, on-board information and fare prices are more important for metro users, whereas regional train users emphasize reliability and speed (Mouwen, 2015).

Lessons Learned from Malmö and Karlstad

Two cities in Sweden implemented different strategies to increase public transport use. In Karlstad (a medium-sized city), the route network was redesigned, and transfers between different routes were improved. A new system map was launched with a simple and clear layout. The physical design of bus stops was redesigned, and a real-time information system was introduced. The bus fleet was replaced by new biogas buses, with improved air conditioning, low floors, free Wi-Fi and Bus TV. The buses were equipped with surveillance cameras. Also, incentives in tendered contracts were set up with bonuses and penalties linked to service quality as well as to the number of travellers.

In Malmö (the third largest city in Sweden, with approximately 330000 inhabitants), a super bus line with an exclusive tram-like design was implemented, requiring large infrastructure investments. To reduce travel time, the passengers could enter and exit at all doors. A new traffic signal system also gave priority to the new bus line. There was also some indication that the travel time reliability increased, but the average bus speed remained unchanged. The capacity of the super bus is larger than that of a standard bus, and the headway was therefore slightly increased (to 5 minutes), such that total capacity remained. There was some indication that the travel time reliability increased, but the average travel time remained unchanged.

The strategy in Karlstad was to take small steps with minor improvements over many (10) years, while the strategy in Malmö included a major infrastructural change during a much shorter time frame, focusing on the new super bus concept and vehicles. By analysing available data from the two cities regarding travel satisfaction and travel behaviour, we discuss what lessons can be learnt.

Since Karlstad participates in an annual national survey it is possible to compare the development in travel satisfaction during the 10-year period with six other comparable Swedish cities (similar in size, socio-economic status and car ownership). The result showed an increase in overall satisfaction in Karlstad and a decrease in the reference cities (Figure 20.8) that did not implement a similar programme. The positive development in Karlstad could be explained by the substantial increase in supply (see Figure 20.6). Moreover, in Malmö the overall travel satisfaction was higher after the implementation of the super bus than before (see Table 20.3).

The satisfaction with a number of different service quality attributes showed a positive development in Karlstad and Malmö. The satisfaction with different service attributes increased significantly in Karlstad (reported in Table 20.2, with a comparison between the start (2004) and end (2014) of the programme) as well as in Malmö (reported in Table 20.3, with a comparison between before and after the implementation of the new super bus). Still, Karlstad has (for many attributes) larger increases in satisfaction levels than Malmö (t-statistics in Table 20.2 and Table 20.3). A possible explanation is the focus on many different measures during an extended time frame, while Malmö concentrated on the super bus. Another explanation is that the traffic supply extended substantially in Karlstad, but not in Malmö. The investment in supply resulted in reduced waiting

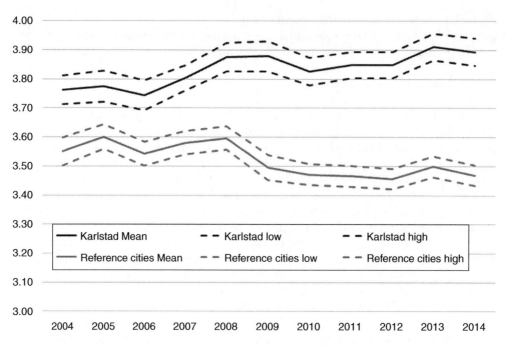

Figure 20.8   Bus users' overall satisfaction trend over time, mean and 95% confidence intervals

times, reduced travel time and shorter distances to bus stops, factors that will increase satisfaction according to research. A third explanation is that, for example, the driver's behaviour as a service function changes in longer super buses, where people can board both at the front and at the middle of the bus, compared to the role in traditional buses, as in Karlstad. The conclusion is that both a long-term programme including several types of measures implemented over several years and a super bus project including major infrastructure changes implemented during a much shorter time frame are related to increased travel satisfaction with public transport. However, we cannot conclude that the positive trend in travel satisfaction relating to the super bus project in Malmö has a long-term effect since we only have two years' worth of data. The long-term effect is, however, significant in Karlstad.

In Malmö, a stated preference survey was distributed on board the super bus with the aim of investigating preferences for different travel modes (super bus, tram, standard bus). The stated preference survey included eight choices differing in in-vehicle travel time, frequency/waiting time and fare. The respondent could choose one of the two options or rate them as equivalents. The value of in-vehicle travel time and waiting time did not differ significantly between the two buses or the tram (Table 20.4). A mode constant for the standard bus and the super bus were included in the analysis so that the tram acted as a reference alternative. The constants showed that there is no significant difference in the preferences for the standard bus compared to the super bus. However, the preference for both buses surpasses the preference for the tram. The analyses of satisfaction with service quality attributes in Malmö showed a positive development; however, the preference does

Table 20.2   The average satisfaction score of service quality attributes and the contribution of each attribute (parameter estimate in brackets) to overall satisfaction (T-statistics before (2004) and after (2014) the bus system changes in Karlstad)

Service quality attribute	2004, Md	2014, Md	t-statistics
It is easy to find information about departure times[a]	4.27 (0.42)*	4.38 (0.18)*	2.6*
It is easy to buy tickets	4.10 (0.33)*	3.45 (0.21)*	−12.6*
The scheduled departure times match my needs	3.47 (0.47)*	3.64 (0.34)*	3.1*
The bus routes provide the closest paths to my destination	3.40 (0.20)*	3.58 (0.34)*	3.0*
The buses are clean and tidy	3.72 (0.32)*	4.31(ns)	14.7*
The drivers and staff behave well	3.78 (0.64)*	4.05 (0.58)*	6.6*
I feel comfortable on the trip	3.61 (0.22)*	4.18 (0.27)*	13.6*
It is fast to travel by bus	3.47 (0.57)*	3.79 (0.60)*	6.8*
Departure times are reliable	3.97 (0.57)*	3.98 (0.53)*	− (ns)
The information about changes to schedules and lines is good	3.83 (0.20)*	3.56 (ns)	−5.1*
The information about delays works well	2.81 (ns)	3.05 (0.19)*	3.9*
The service provider listens to my feedback	3.15 (0.56)*	3.27 (0.38)*	2.0*
Overall satisfaction	3.76	3.89	3.8*
Number of estimated parameters:	15	14	
Number of observations:	998	1199	
Null log-likelihood:	−1606.22	−1929.716	
Final log-likelihood:	−664.21	−936.576	
Rho-square:	0.586	0.515	

Notes:
a.   Responses were made on a seven-point Likert scale (ranging from 1 = strongly disagree to 7 = strongly agree).
*p < .05.

not differ for any type of bus. Thus, it cannot be concluded that a super bus reduces generalized cost of travelling.

An important question is whether the investments in service quality have generated an increase in bus travel in Karlstad and Malmö. To answer this question, we analysed travel data collected in each city. In Karlstad, there was a significant increase in the number of bus trips between 2004 and 2014. This increase, however, cannot be explained by a transfer of car drivers to public transport. As shown in Table 20.5, travel as a "car driver" or "car passenger" remained unchanged between 2004 and 2014. The average number of journeys by bus increased from 0.1 to 0.21 per person per day. These numbers are fairly consistent with Figure 20.6 based on aggregate data. Women increased their number of bus trips; they also increased their total number of trips. Men did not increase their number of bus trips. However, they reduced their number of car trips as driver, and their total number of trips.

In Malmö, the total number of travellers on the super bus line increased (10 per cent) in the peak (7:00–8:30 am) compared to the replaced standard bus line (in a travel count).

Table 20.3   The average satisfaction score of service quality attributes and the contribution of each attribute (parameter estimate in brackets) to overall satisfaction (T-statistics before (spring 2014) and after (spring 2015) the introduction of the super bus in Malmö: ordinal logit model including all satisfaction data (2014 and 2015))

Service quality attribute	Spring 2014 (n = 309) M	Autumn 2014 (n = 288) M	Spring 2015 (n = 250) M	Autumn 2015 (n = 230) M	t-statistics difference in mean value spring 2014 and spring 2015	Ordinal logit parameter. All data (n = 1077)
My impression of the vehicle exterior[a]	7.19 (ns)	9.29 (ns)	9.03 (0.40)*	9.20 (ns)	8.48*	0.12*
Information of destination and route number	8.48 (0.12)*	9.65 (ns)	9.11 (ns)	9.47 (ns)	2.84*	0.08*
Driving behaviour	8.32 (ns)	8.24 (0.21)*	7.96 (ns)	8.45 (0.39)*	−1.63 (ns)	0.14*
Traffic safety	8.11 (ns)	8.03 (ns)	8.23 (0.29)*	8.83 (ns)	0.51 (ns)	0.11*
Punctuality	7.73 (ns)	7.20 (0.10)*	8.60 (ns)	8.87 (ns)	3.27*	0.04*
Announcements on-board	8.31 (ns)	9.69 (0.15)*	9.04 (ns)	9.53 (0.34)*	3.15*	0.09*
My impression of the vehicle interior	7.54 (0.25)*	9.01 (ns)	8.97 (ns)	9.17 (0.24)*	7.03*	0.12*
Safety on-board	8.36 (0.19)*	8.76 (0.12)*	8.69 (0.30)*	9.22 (0.34)*	1.55 (ns)	0.20*
Space on-board	8.41 (0.14)*	8.84 (0.23)*	8.75 (0.18)*	8.86 (0.19)*	1.54 (ns)	0.18*
Overall satisfaction	8.48 (ns)	9.04 (ns)	8.87 (ns)	9.34 (ns)	1.99*	

Notes:
a.   Responses were made on an eleven-point Likert scale (ranging from 0 = strongly disagree to 10 = strongly agree).
* p < .01.

However, the number of users declined on other buses in the Malmö public transport system. A likely explanation is that the super bus induced a route choice change within the bus system. This conclusion is supported by counts of the total number of bus trips in Malmö, showing no increase in bus trips between 2013 and 2014. In fact, the total number of bus trips declined by 0.3 per cent in 2014 (City of Malmö, 2016). This was unexpected, since in the years before and after 2014, the number of bus trips increased by 4 to 10 per cent per year. To conclude, the new super bus seems to have induced a route choice but no increase in the use of public transport in Malmö.

Analyses of travel behaviour before and after the changes in Karlstad and Malmö showed a positive development in Karlstad concerning bus travel and a neutral to slightly negative development in Malmö. At the same time, there were no changes in car travel during the same period in Karlstad.

Table 20.4 Test of stated preference choices with the tram as the reference alternative

Variable Name	Value	Robust t-test
Constant super bus	0.5830	3.56, p < .005
Constant standard bus	0.3890	2.06, p < .005
α Travel time [min]	−0.0715	−5.37, p < .005
β Fare [€]	−0.942	−8.62, p < .005
γ In-vehicle travel time [min]	−0.1040	−7.94, p < .005
Value of in-vehicle time [€/h]:	6.6	$60 \cdot \alpha / \beta$
Value of waiting time [€/h]:	9.1	$2.60 \cdot \gamma / \beta$
Number of estimated parameters:	5	
Number of observations:	526	
Null log-likelihood:	74	
Final log-likelihood:	−364.595	
Rho-square:	0.185	

Note: The value of waiting time is twice the value of travel time since travellers are assumed to arrive randomly at the bus stop.

Table 20.5 Number of trips by mode, gender and total in the 2004 and 2014 Karlstad survey

Gender	Travel mode	2004	2014	Mean difference 2004–14	t-statistics
Women	Bus	0.14	0.30	0.16	2.1*
	Car Driver	0.71	0.81	0.10	1.2
	Car Passenger	0.16	0.26	0.10	1.2
	Other[a]	0.01	0.01	0.00	0.1
	Total	1.79	2.14	0.35	4.5**
Men	Bus	0.07	0.12	0.05	0.7
	Car Driver	0.92	0.75	−0.17	−2.1*
	Car Passenger	0.08	0.04	−0.04	−0.5
	Other	0.01	0.00	−0.01	−0.1
	Total	1.63	1.47	−0.16	−2.0*
Total	Bus	0.11	0.22	0.11	2.0*
	Car Driver	0.81	0.78	−0.03	−0.6
	Car Passenger	0.12	0.15	0.03	0.6
	Other	0.01	0.00	−0.01	−0.1
	Total	1.71	1.82	0.11	1.9

Notes:
a. Taxi, motorcycle and special transport services for elderly and disabled travellers.
*p < .05; **p <. 001.

4.   CONCLUSIONS

The public transport supply and the number of trips have increased by nearly 50 per cent in Sweden in the period 2002–17, as compared to an 8 per cent increase for the EU (2020–14). However, the supply has increased more rapidly than demand, so that the average occupancy rate has fallen. The production costs have increased more quickly than both supply and demand, increasing subsidies from taxpayers and fares. This chapter has aimed at summarizing the lessons learned from the aggregate trends in the Swedish public transport sector.

One key lesson is that it is difficult to expand public transport outside the big cities while maintaining a high occupancy rate. Large buses simply cannot be filled in less densely populated areas, particularly not in the off-peak hours. It might be possible to use smaller and more flexible vehicles in some places, but then energy gain compared to private car use or carpooling would diminish. Moreover, the UK Commission for Integrated Transport, reviewing on-demand public transport, found that large subsidies are still needed in the UK and mainland Europe (Commission for Integrated Transport, 2008). One of the earliest on-demand public transport services in rural Scotland reverted to a standard bus route because of high cost (Derek Halden Consultancy et al., 2006).

Like many other countries, Sweden has experienced declining cost efficiency in the public transport sector. One contributing factor is probably the political pressure to expand supply in less dense areas and to adopt vehicles with a particular design and fuel type to reduce carbon emissions. However, a second lesson is that the consequences of such requirements need to be explored further in several dimensions. One important dimension is equality. Increased costs due to reduced occupancy rate and new procurement requirements generate increased production cost per passenger. Increased production costs per passenger will eventually hurt low-income people the most through increased fares and possibly through the transfer of public money to public transport from other public sectors such as health and education. We believe that this is an aspect that has not received enough attention.

An expanded public transport system is often motivated by environmental concerns. Indeed, it is often taken for granted that public transport contributes to reduced carbon emissions and energy use. However, this implicitly assumes that generated public transport trips are diverted car trips, and not new trips or trips diverted from slow modes. The aggregate Swedish trends show that although public transport supply has increased, car use per capita has not declined. At the same time, cycling per capita has declined. This is consistent with the finding that it has proven to be difficult to reduce car use by only increasing public transport supply in most cities in the Western world (Gendron-Carrier et al., 2018).

The transition to sustainable systems will entail a customer-oriented approach. What measures are then needed to attract car users to public transport? The development in Karlstad provides some guidance. First is the importance of a long-term perspective and endurance that includes continuous quality improvements. Investments in supply will reduce waiting times and travel times as well as distances to the nearest bus stop. An increase in supply will eventually have a positive effect on customer satisfaction since it aims at improving those attributes that travellers value most. Thus, our analysis confirms what has been observed in previous research. Furthermore, small changes in service (e.g., offering free Wi-Fi or bus TV) seem to have a long-term effect when it comes to attracting new users. The importance of providing information is already known, especially if it is adapted to people who are somewhat motivated and prepared to change their travel behaviour (see Friman et al., 2017).

Swedish policy makers have focused on the short term: impressive public transport initiatives, prestige purchases of new vehicles and the signal value of sustainability initiatives. Whilst that has a value, we also need to keep an eye on various long-term effects. One problem is that investments in public transport are rarely monitored and analysed. Monitoring and evaluations require systematic data collection of good quality. In our in-depth analyses of the developments in two different cities, we were surprised by the lack of data and its quality. We therefore underscore the lesson that when implementing costly public transport improvements, the authorities have much to gain from making more of an effort to evaluate the effects against the intended objectives and targets. Systematic evaluations provide the opportunity to learn from mistakes and success stories, which in the long run can improve both accessibility and environmental, social and economic sustainability.

NOTES

1. In this chapter, all prices and costs have been adjusted for inflation. The real prices and costs are calculated by dividing the nominal (observed) price or costs by the consumer price index (CPI) for Sweden. Since CPI has increased over time, the nominal prices and cost have increased faster than the real prices and costs that we present.
2. The requirements included a large size (24 m) and compressed Natural Gas (CNG)–electric hybrid.
3. Virtually all the 43 OECD and G20 countries apply fuel taxes, and many countries have also increased them over time (OECD, 2019).

REFERENCES

Alexandersson, G. and Pyddoke, R. (2010). Bus deregulation in Sweden revisited: Experiences from 15 years of competitive tendering. In "The Accidental Deregulation" (PhD thesis). Doctoral dissertation by G. Alexandersson, Stockholm School of Economics.

Balcombe, R., Mackett, R., Paulley, N., Preston, J., Shires, J., Titheridge, H., Wardman, M. et al. (2004). *The Demand for Public Transport: A Practical Guide*. Wokingham: TRL.

Bamberg, S., Fujii, S., Friman, M. and Gärling, T. (2011). Behaviour theory and soft transport policy measures. *Transport Policy*, 18, 228–35.

Bastian, A., Börjesson, M. and Eliasson, J. (2016). Explaining "peak car" with economic variables. *Transportation Research Part A: Policy and Practice*, 88, 236–50. Accessed at https://doi.org/10.1016/j.tra.2016.04.005.

Bondemark, A., Andersson, H., Wretstrand, A. and Brundell-Freij, K. (2020). Is it expensive to be poor? Public transport in Sweden. *Transportation*, 1–26.

Börjesson, M. and Kristoffersson, I. (2018). The Swedish congestion charges: Ten years on. *Transportation Research Part A: Policy and Practice*, 107, 35–51. Accessed at https://doi.org/10.1016/j.tra.2017.11.001.

Börjesson, M. and Rubensson, I. (2019). Satisfaction with crowding and other attributes in public transport. *Transport Policy*, 79, 213–22. Accessed at https://doi.org/10.1016/j.tranpol.2019.05.010.

Camén, C. and Lidestam, H. (2016). Dominating factors contributing to the high(er) costs for public bus transports in Sweden. *Research in Transportation Economics, Competition and Ownership in Land Passenger Transport* (selected papers from the Thredbo 14 conference) 59, 292–6. Accessed at https://doi.org/10.1016/j.retrec.2016.07.021.

City of Malmö (2016). Systemanalys för lokal kollektivtrafik i Malmö: För buss, dubbelledbuss och spårvagn. [System analysis for local public transport in Malmö: For bus, double articulated bus and tram]. PM update for 2015, Malmö.

Commission for Integrated Transport (2008). A new approach to rural public transport – Report.

Currie, G. and Rose. J. (2008). Growing patronage: Challenges and what has been found to work. *Research in Transportation Economics*, 22(1), 5–11.

Currie, G. and Wallis, I. (2008). Effective ways to grow urban bus markets: A synthesis of evidence. *Journal of Transport Geography, Growing Public Transport Patronage*, 16, 419–29. Accessed at https://doi.org/10.1016/j.jtrangeo.2008.04.007.

Dalen, D.M. and Gómez-Lobo, A. (2003). Yardsticks on the road: Regulatory contracts and cost efficiency in the Norwegian bus industry. *Transportation*, 30, 371–86. Accessed at https://doi.org/10.1023/A:102478451 7628.

Derek Halden Consultancy, The TAS Partnership and The University of Aberdeen (2006). Review of Demand Responsive Transport in Scotland, Technical report, Scottish Government.

Dunkerley, F., Wardman, M., Rohr, C. and Fearnley, N. (2018). Bus fare and journey time elasticities and diversion factors for all modes. RAND Corporation.

Eliasson, J. (2019). Stockholms transportsystem: 45 punkter för bättre Stockholmstrafik [Stockholm transport system: 45 bullets for better traffic]. Stockholm Chambers of Commerce, Stockholm.

Eriksson, L., Ettema, D., Friman, M., Gärling, T. and Fujii, S. (2010). Experimental simulation of car users' switching to public transport. *Transportation Letters*, 2, 145–55.

European Commission, Directorate-General for Mobility and Transport (2011). White Paper on Transport: Roadmap to a Single European Transport Area: Towards a Competitive and Resource-efficient Transport System. Publications Office of the European Union.

Friman, M. and Fellesson, M. (2009). Service supply and customer satisfaction in public transportation: The quality paradox. *Journal of Public Transportation*, 12(4), 4.

Friman, M. and Gärling, T. (2001). Frequency of negative critical incidents and satisfaction with public transport services. II. *Journal of Retailing and Consumer Services*, 8, 105–14.

Friman, M., Edvardsson, B. and Gärling, T. (2001). Frequency of negative critical incidents and satisfaction with public transport services. I. *Journal of Retailing and Consumer Services*, 8, 95–104.

Friman, M., Huck, J. and Olsson, L.E. (2017). Transtheoretical model of change in travel behavior interventions: An integrative review. *International Journal of Environmental Research and Public Health*, 14(6), 581.

Gärling, T., Bamberg, S. and Friman, M. (2018). The role of attitude in choice of travel, satisfaction with travel, and change to sustainable travel. In D. Albarracin and B.T. Johnson (eds), *Handbook of Attitudes, Volume 2: Applications* (pp. 562–86). London: Routledge.

Gendron-Carrier, N., Gonzalez-Navarro, M., Polloni, S. and Turner, M.A. (2018). Subways and urban air pollution (Working Paper No. 24183), Working Paper Series. National Bureau of Economic Research. Accessed at https://doi.org/10.3386/w24183.

Government Bill (2015/16:100) Ministry of Finance, Stockholm, Sweden.

Graham, D.J. and Glaister, S. (2004). Road traffic demand elasticity estimates: A review. *Transport Reviews*, 24, 261–74.

Holmgren, J. (2013). The efficiency of public transport operations: An evaluation using stochastic frontier analysis. *Research in Transportation Economics, THREDBO 12: Recent Developments in the Reform of Land Passenger Transport*, 39, 50–57. Accessed at https://doi.org/10.1016/j.retrec.2012.05.023.

Li, S., Kahn, M.E. and Nickelsburg, J. (2015). Public transit bus procurement: The role of energy prices, regulation and federal subsidies. *Journal of Urban Economics*, 87, 57–71. Accessed at https://doi.org/10.1016/j.jue.2015.01.004.

Mouwen, A. (2015). Drivers of customer satisfaction with public transport services. *Transportation Research Part A: Policy and Practice*, 78, 1–20. Accessed at https://doi.org/10.1016/j.tra.2015.05.005.

Nilsson, J.-E. (2011). Kollektivtrafik utan styrning, ESO. Finansdepartementet, Regeringskansliet.

OECD (2019). *Taxing Energy Use 2019: Using Taxes for Climate Action*. OECD iLibrary.

OECD/ITF (2020). Transport – Passenger transport – OECD Data [online]. Accessed 27 March 2010 at http://data.oecd.org/transport/passenger-transport.htm.

Ottoz, E., Fornengo, G. and Giacomo, M.D. (2009). The impact of ownership on the cost of bus service provision: An example from Italy. *Applied Economics*, 41, 337–49. Accessed at https://doi.org/10.1080/00036840601007260.

Piacenza, M. (2006). Regulatory contracts and cost efficiency: Stochastic frontier evidence from the Italian local public transport. *Journal of Productivity Analysis*, 25, 257–77. Accessed at https://doi.org/10.1007/s11 123-006-7643-7.

Prioni, P. and Hensher, D.A. (2000). Measuring service quality in scheduled bus services. *Journal of Public Transportation*, 3(2), 4.

Pyddoke, R. and Swärdh, J.-E. (2017). The influence of demand incentives in public transport contracts on patronage and costs in medium sized Swedish cities, K2 Working Paper 2017:10.

Redman, L., Friman, M., Gärling, T. and Hartig, T. (2013). Quality attributes of public transport that attract car users: A research review. *Transport Policy*, 25, 119–27.

Richter, J., Friman, M. and Gärling, T. (2010). Review of evaluations of soft transport policy measures. *Transportation: Theory & Application*, 2, 5–18.

Statistics Sweden (2020). Sveriges befolkning [online]. Statistics Sweden. Accessed 14 March 2020 at http://www.scb.se/hitta-statistik/sverige-i-siffror/manniskorna-i-sverige/sveriges-befolkning/.

Susilo, Y.O. and Cats, O. (2014). Exploring key determinants of travel satisfaction for multi-modal trips by different traveler groups. *Transportation Research Part A: Policy and Practice*, 67, 366–80.

The Swedish Association of Local Authorities and Regions (2018). Öppna jämförelser: Kollektivtrafik [Open comparisons: Public transport]. The Swedish Association of Local Authorities and Regions, SKL.

The Swedish Confederation of Transport Enterprises (2015). Fakta och statistik om bussbranschen [Facts and statistics about the bus industry]. Accessed at https://www.yumpu.com/sv/document/view/44983899/statistik-om-bussbranschen-2015-05-final.

The Swedish Public Transport Association (2018). Miljökrav vid trafikupphandling: En bilaga till Avtalsprocessen inom Partnersamverkan för en förbättrad kollektivtrafik [Environmental requirements for traffic procurement: An appendix to the Partnership for improved public transport], Stockholm.

The Swedish Transport Agency (2019). Statistik över koldioxidutsläpp [online]. Accessed 7 August 2019 at https://www.transportstyrelsen.se/sv/vagtrafik/statistik/Statistik-over-koldioxidutslapp/.

Transport Analysis (2020a). Regional scheduled public transport. Data tables [online]. Accessed 25 March at https://www.trafa.se/en/public-transport-and-publicly-financed-travel/regional_scheduled_public_transport/.

Transport Analysis (2020b). Travel survey statistics [online]. Accessed 28 March 2020 at https://www.trafa.se/en/travel-survey/travel-survey/.

UITP (2016). Local public transport in the European Union Statistics Brief. Accessed at https://www.uitp.org/sites/default/files/cck-focus-papers-files/UITP_Statistics_PT_in_EU_DEF_0.pdf.

Vigren, A. (2016). Cost efficiency in Swedish public transport. *Research in Transportation Economics, Competition and Ownership in Land Passenger Transport (selected papers from the Thredbo 14 conference)*, 59, 123–32. Accessed at https://doi.org/10.1016/j.retrec.2016.05.009.

Walter, M. (2011). Some determinants of cost efficiency in German public transport [online]. Accessed 13 March 2020 at https://www.ingentaconnect.com/content/lse/jtep/2011/00000045/00000001/art00001.

Wardman, M., Toner, J., Fearnley, N., Flügel, S. and Killi, M. (2018). Review and meta-analysis of inter-modal cross-elasticity evidence. *Transportation Research Part A: Policy and Practice*, 118. Accessed at https://doi.org/10.1016/j.tra.2018.10.002.

21. Advances in transit customer information
Kari Watkins, Candace Brakewood, Sean Barbeau and Aaron Antrim

21.1 INTRODUCTION

"*Scientia potentia est*": knowledge is power. Knowledge can enable you to succeed in your endeavors, such as the value of education to your career. But the power of knowledge can help in even the smallest of endeavors, such as a simple trip from Point A to Point B. Although increased transit use could have substantial positive impacts for society, users face many barriers when making the transit choice. Relying on someone else for transportation has inherent risks. Will the bus come? Will it come in time to make my appointment? Where does the bus run? Where do I catch it? How do I board and pay and tell the driver I need to get off? Where should I get off? These simple issues can be overwhelming when deciding to try a new mode. However, many of the inherent difficulties in transit use can be overcome through better information. If high ridership transit service is a more sustainable means for transportation, then through better information, we can better serve individual needs and deliver better outcomes for our society.

From a customer perspective, a mobility choice is only a choice if it is fast, comfortable, affordable and reliable. However, there is inherent travel time unreliability in public transportation (e.g., impacts on bus headways due to traffic), and indeed all transportation modes, that would require substantial investments in infrastructure to overcome. Minor infrastructure and service improvements will only go so far in improving speed and reliability. Without substantial buffer time, a schedule cannot be met, but substantial buffer time creates long inefficient travel times. How then can this inherent unreliability be overcome? The answer is through the power of information.

This chapter first addresses the history and benefits of transit information as we have evolved from printed schedule materials to ubiquitous real-time information. It then dives deeper into the standardized data formats that have enabled the transit data revolution as well as applications that have resulted. Finally, the future of transit information is addressed as we move into Mobility-as-a-Service (MaaS) applications that combine real-time information with fare payments and subscription plans that place transit as the backbone of a seamless, multimodal transportation system.

21.2 HISTORY OF TRANSIT INFORMATION

The past two decades have brought about multiple technology enhancements that have made the provision of transit information easier, less costly and more impactful for transit agencies. Three major advancements have revolutionized transit information. The first transit information gain came in the year 2000 with the worldwide deactivation of selective availability for GPS (US National Coordination Office for Space-Based Positioning, Navigation, and Timing, 2018), which increased the accuracy of GPS devices for civilian purposes and soon thereafter decreased the cost and availability of GPS devices. By making GPS more readily available, the number of transit agencies able to equip their vehicles with automatic vehicle location systems increased and agencies switched from using expensive signpost and beacon-based systems. By 2011, in a survey of 28 North American transit agencies representing a cross-section of the industry, 82 percent had some type of automatic vehicle location system (Schweiger, 2011). Usage of vehicle location data has only grown since that time.

The second advancement in transit information began in 2005, when Google and TriMet, the transit agency in Portland, Oregon, began an effort to standardize transit schedule data in the form of the General Transit Feed Specification (GTFS) (Roth, 2010). The goal of the project was to make it easier for transit agencies to share their data to populate Google's transit trip planner, but this effort to standardize transit schedule data kicked off a revolution in transit information. The specification was designed to be simple for agencies to create data, easy for programmers to access, and comprehensive enough to describe essential information for journey planning. GTFS identifies a series of comma-separated files which together describe the stops, trips, routes and fare information about an agency's service, described in greater detail in the following section. Google opened the specification for general use in mid-2007 and it propagated widely as agencies translated their transit schedules into the format. Today, GTFS is the most widely used format for static transit data exchange in the world (Barbeau, 2013; McHugh, 2016). In addition, the move to standardize transit schedule data eventually led to greater awareness and adoption of transit data standards in general, including GTFS-realtime and the Standard Interface for Real-time Information (SIRI), that allow agencies to share their real-time data feeds with developers (Reed, 2013).

In a similar timeframe, smartphones such as the BlackBerry and Nokia models began to create a market for mobile devices. The introduction of the iPhone revolutionized the market, leading to the eventual ubiquity of smartphones with mobile applications (or "apps") across the world. As shown in Figure 21.1, according to Pew Internet Research data, smartphone usage is now above 80 percent in the United States (Pew Research, 2019). Deloitte reports similar usage rates near 80 percent for smartphones across Europe, Australia, China, India and much of South America (Deloitte, 2017). Such devices have made mobile access to data easy for most transit riders (Windmiller et al., 2014). This has resulted in wide interest on the part of transit agencies to provide their customers with access to information about transit services in the palm of the rider's hand and in turn has increased the interest on the part of third-party developers to create applications for transit riders based on this information. With more and more transit agencies releasing their data feeds as part of the push for open data, developers have easy access to a multitude of transit data feeds from across the world, allowing their applications to reach more potential riders (Wong et al., 2013).

21.3   BENEFITS OF TRANSIT INFORMATION

The increased provision of transit information that is real-time, standardized and ubiquitous has brought about several benefits to both the agencies providing the data

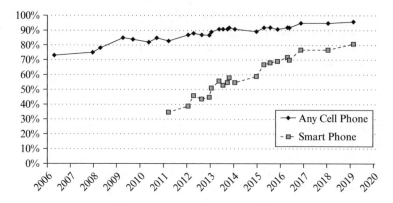

Source: Based on Pew Internet data.

Figure 21.1   US mobile phone ownership over time

and to riders using it. The benefits of real-time information to passengers specifically are summarized in Brakewood and Watkins (2019). The provision of real-time information decreases both actual and perceived wait times, resulting in increased transit ridership in some situations and improved satisfaction in most cases.

The authors' own research found multiple positive outcomes: 92 percent of riders reporting increased or greatly increased satisfaction with public transportation, along with an increased number of transit trips per week, increased feelings of safety (for example while waiting at night), and even additional walking, which has a public health benefit (Ferris et al., 2010). An additional study of perceived and actual wait times (Watkins et al., 2011) found that for riders without real-time information, perceived wait time is greater than measured wait time, but having real-time information brings perceived wait time in line with actual wait time. In addition, mobile real-time information users in the study were observed to wait almost two minutes less than those arriving using traditional schedule information. Using web-based surveys before and after the introduction of real-time information, Brakewood et al. (2014) found "usual" wait times decreased nearly two minutes and levels of anxiety and frustration decreased for real-time information users compared to a control group.

Perhaps most critically, in some cases, real-time information has been shown to contribute to an increase in ridership (Tang and Thakuriah, 2012). In New York City, the gradual rollout of real-time information allowed for a natural experiment in which routes with real-time information could be compared to those without it to model bus ridership at an aggregate level over time (Brakewood et al., 2015). Real-time information showed a median increase of 1.7 percent of weekday route-level ridership, which could equate to almost 100 000 new weekday trips systemwide. Additional results suggest that real-time information may have the greatest impact in areas with higher levels of service, such as frequent routes in larger transit-oriented cities. Self-report studies in Seattle have verified these increases in ridership (Ferris et al., 2010; Gooze et al., 2013). However, studies in Tampa and Atlanta did not find a substantial change in transit travel associated with use of real-time information, although the methodologies used did not consider completely new transit riders (Brakewood et al., 2014).

Of equal importance to real-time data availability to riders is data quality. In fact, accuracy of real-time information is a key concern of transit riders. A survey of riders of a mobile transit app showed that 84 percent rely solely on real-time information instead of using the schedule (Gooze et al., 2013). Errors in predictions create a negative perception of the mobile app providing the information as well as the transit agency. For example, 74 percent of surveyed Puget Sound transit riders considered a difference between actual and estimated arrival times greater than four minutes as an "error". In addition, 9 percent of surveyed riders said that they took the bus less often due to errors they experienced (Gooze et al., 2013). Prediction errors can also lead to reduced system performance if operators are making decisions based on this data.

21.4   DATA STANDARDS AND FORMATS

For mobile applications to scale easily across multiple geographic areas to serve more transit riders, a standardized format for public transportation stops, routes, timetables, and more must exist. GTFS and its real-time counterpart, GTFS-realtime, have become de facto standards for transit data. The following sections discuss GTFS and GTFS-realtime in detail. Efforts to expand the current features of GTFS and GTFS-realtime are also discussed, as well as other multimodal data formats inspired by GTFS and its governance process.

General Transit Feed Specification (GTFS)

Since its creation in 2005, GTFS has become the most widely used data format to describe fixed-route transit services in the world (Barbeau, 2013; McHugh, 2016). Most agencies have decided to share their GTFS data openly with the public, while some choose to restrict access only to select partners (e.g., Google Maps). There are over 2500 transit operators worldwide that share their GTFS data openly with the general public (Transitland, 2019). As a result of third-party developer innovation, GTFS data is now being used by a variety of third-party software applications for many different purposes, including trip planning, timetable creation, mobile data, data visualization, accessibility, analysis tools for planning, and real-time information systems. In 2010, the GTFS format name was changed to the General (instead of "Google") Transit Feed Specification to accurately represent its use in many different applications outside of Google products. Transit agencies can publicly share transit data in GTFS format and leverage a wealth of new services based on this information, typically at little to no cost to the agency.

GTFS gained popularity to become a de facto standard due to several factors. Early support from Google created an impetus for transit providers to develop GTFS datasets in order to be included in Google Maps. Because transit agencies, who produce GTFS data, and application developers, who use the data, worked together to create and maintain the GTFS format, GTFS was designed to be very practical – all elements of the format were tested in real-world systems before being adopted in the specification. The resulting simplicity of GTFS has reduced barriers to producing and maintaining data. Finally, because Google released GTFS under an open license and embraced an open online community to continue to improve the format, other companies and organizations have been able to utilize the data specification in their products and contribute to its further development (Antrim, 2017).

Dataset description
GTFS data is implemented as a set of comma-delimited text files added to a single zip file. A subset of the full GTFS specification is required for a GTFS-realtime feed – the following are key for understanding real-time information:

- *stops.txt* – All bus stops included in a feed, with each record including a stop_id (identifier internal to agency), stop_code (rider-facing stop identifier), stop location, location_type (a single stop or station with multiple stops), etc. For some agencies, stop_id and stop_code may be the same.
- *routes.txt* – All routes defined for an agency, including a route_id and short and long name.
- *calendar.txt and calendar_dates.txt* – Includes service days and times, each identified via a service_id, that the agency provides service.
- *trip.txt* – All trips defined for an agency, including to which route_id each trip belongs. A route may have multiple trip patterns, depending on the day and/or time. The day/time that each trip is operational is defined by a service_id that relates to calendar.txt and/or calendar_dates.txt.
- *stop_times.txt* – The core schedule file that defines, for each trip_id, the ordered list of bus stops that will be visited, along with a scheduled arrival and departure time, and whether each stop is a timepoint (optional).

A full explanation of all GTFS files and data fields is available on the GTFS reference website at https://github.com/google/transit and the TransitWiki GTFS page at https://www.transitwiki.org/TransitWiki/index.php/General_Transit_Feed_Specification.

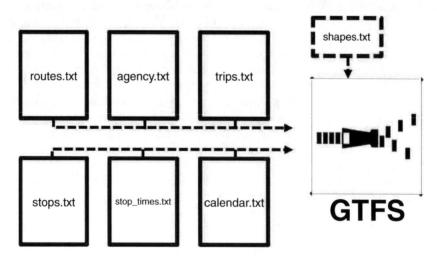

Source: Landon Reed.

Figure 21.2   File components of General Transit Feed Specification (GTFS)

Creation and maintenance
Transit agencies must make the decision whether to create and maintain a GTFS dataset using their own personnel, or if they are going to outsource this task. It is important to consider that a new GTFS dataset will need to be produced every time there is a change to the schedule to keep the applications based on GTFS data up to date. If the agency has enough in-house technical expertise, they may wish to produce and maintain the GTFS feed themselves. Industry-standard scheduling software packages from vendors such as Trapeze, HASTUS, Connexionz, Optibus and TripSpark (formerly Mentor Engineering) can often export agency data into the GTFS format, facilitating the GTFS creation and maintenance process. However, agencies should not necessarily assume that the output of these tools produces perfect GTFS data, as agencies have indicated that they often still need to perform manual data processing on the GTFS data exported from these tools before it will be acceptable for application use (Barbeau et al., 2010).

For agencies that do not have access to scheduling software, there are a variety of open source and vendor-based tools that can be used for creating and maintaining GTFS data. Some simple tools have been spreadsheet-based (Heitzman, 2012; National Rural Transit Assistance Program, 2020), while others are full-blown websites and databases (Center for Urban Transportation Research, 2019a; Trillium, 2020; Conveyal, 2019a; IBI Group, 2019). For agencies without high-quality bus stop inventories, there are tools that can help crowd-source bus stop and route locations (Tran et al., 2011; Conveyal, 2019b). There are also many educational and open source resources available online from the transit developer community for agencies interested in creating a GTFS feed (GoogleTransitFeed, 2020; Google Inc., 2020; Center for Urban Transportation Research, 2019b). An open list of vendors, populated by the open data community that provide both self-service and full-service products and services for GTFS creation and maintenance can be found online in the "Vendors Providing GTFS Creation/Maintenance Services" document (Barbeau, 2016). The awesome-transit list is an open directory of tools to create and maintain GTFS datasets (Center for Urban Transportation Research, 2019a).

In order to create and maintain GTFS, it is necessary to develop an understanding of the specification. Several GTFS training materials are available on TransitWiki.org, including a collection of simplified example GTFS datasets that represent various transit scenarios.

GTFS leaves many options available for describing transit services. See the GTFS Best Practices (https://gtfs.org/best-practices/) for recommendations that will provide the best results in applications. After GTFS data is created, it should be validated using one of the several GTFS validator tools available (Center for Urban Transportation Research, 2019c), both by the vendor and agency.

Once an agency has determined a method for producing and maintaining GTFS datasets, they must consider who they will share the data with. In the United States, the Federal Transit Administration released open data guidance encouraging the use of the GTFS format in 2016 (Catalá, 2016). Schweiger (2015) and Wong et al. (2013) provide an extensive discussion of the industry status and benefits of open data, including significant cost savings to the agencies.

GTFS-realtime

The basic GTFS format contains only static (i.e., infrequently changing) transit information such as schedules, routes and bus stops. Therefore, a GTFS dataset alone will not enable real-time transit information services for a transit agency. A real-time counterpart to GTFS, GTFS-realtime, was released in 2015 and has emerged as a de facto worldwide standard for real-time transit information. Previously, real-time transit information had only been shared in proprietary formats specific to each vendor or agency. GTFS-realtime offers the opportunity for developers to create mobile apps that can function across a large number of cities and agencies, and for practitioners and researchers to be able to easily study and compare actual system performance across different transit systems using the same tools, without the overhead of manually transforming data into a consistent format. Having real-time transit data available in a common format is a key pillar for real-time multimodal information systems.

The GTFS-realtime specification can be broken down into three types of elements:

- *Trip Updates* – Real-time predictions for when vehicles arrive and depart. Predictions (stop_time_updates) are represented as an update to the time that the vehicle was scheduled to arrive or depart (defined in GTFS stop_times.txt), either as a relative "delay" or "time". stop_time_updates are identified using a trip ID from GTFS trips.txt.
- *Vehicle Positions* – Real-time vehicle location, trip assignment (defined using the trip ID from GTFS trips.txt), and occupancy information.
- *Service Alerts* – A human-readable description of events that affect transit service, along with the transit stops/routes that the event impacts. For example, "Route 5 is on detour due to flooding".

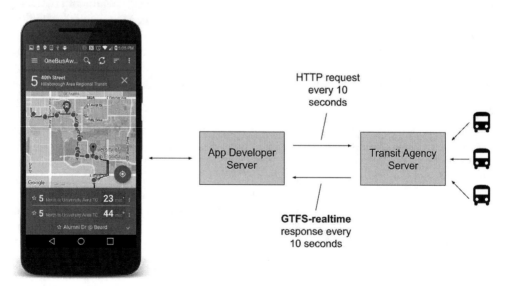

Figure 21.3   Typical real-time information flow from a transit agency to a mobile app

While GTFS datasets are typically updated 3–4 times per year (e.g., when new schedules are published), a GTFS-realtime Trip Updates and Vehicle Positions feed can be updated as often as every few seconds and are typically driven by an automatic vehicle location (AVL) system. For example, from a sample taken in March 2020, the Massachusetts Bay Transportation Authority's GTFS-realtime feed contained data for 406 vehicles with independent arrival or departure predictions for most stops on active trips refreshed around every five seconds.

GTFS-realtime datasets are formatted in the Protocol Buffer format, which is a very efficient binary representation of the information in the feed. As a result, the actual GTFS-realtime messages produced and consumed by applications require special software to convert them to human-readable plain text.

Both the frequency of real-time updates as well as the required conversion from binary to a plain text make it very challenging to manually identify and troubleshoot problems in the feed. Vendors and transit agencies are strongly encouraged to use validation tools to test and troubleshoot GTFS-realtime feeds (Center for Urban Transportation Research, 2019c).

Expanding GTFS Functionality

In 2017, the Rocky Mountain Institute convened and facilitated a working group of GTFS stakeholders to establish a set of GTFS Best Practices (https://gtfs.org/best-practices). This coordination led to the formation of MobilityData (MobilityData IO, 2020a), a non-profit supported by various private and public sector stakeholders in the GTFS community that helps advance new features within the GTFS governance process. In 2019, MobilityData, with the help of the GTFS community, has developed draft extensions to GTFS in several areas (MobilityData IO, 2020b), including:

- *Pathways* – Describes step-free accessibility and walkable paths within transit stations, including dynamic changes such as elevators being out of service;
- *Fares* – Support for more complex fare structures, including differences based on transit mode, time of day, origin-destination pair, transfers, etc.;
- *Demand responsive transit* – Describes transit service that is "flexible" in time or geography (i.e., do not operate on fixed routes, schedules, or stops);
- *Service changes* – Describes detours and other real-time changes to trip attributes or structure within GTFS-realtime;
- *Branding* – Support for more complex branding attributes to more clearly differentiate components of the transit system for riders;
- *Vehicles* – Describes occupancy status, bike capacity, boarding restrictions, accessibility and more features of transit vehicles;
- *Disallowed travel* – Support for better describing services with certain travel restrictions (e.g., intercity buses that do not allow travel within a city);
- *Translations* – Expanded support for multiple languages and translations within GTFS feeds.

Each of these extensions is being evaluated by several different producers and consumers of GTFS and GTFS-realtime data, and will be officially adopted following implementation and a final GTFS community vote.

GTFS-inspired Formats

GTFS has demonstrated far-reaching benefits of a broadly adopted data specification: lower barriers to entry in the development of software in many categories has facilitated innovation, reduced costs for some applications, and supported the development of multimodal applications. More importantly, the GTFS community has produced a light-weight governance process (Google, 2019) that has resulted in a streamlined, pragmatic and laser-focused data specification. As a result, other data standardization efforts are now looking to replicate GTFS's success. For example, TCRP Web-Only Document G-62 cites GTFS as "an example of a mature process of developing standards" (O'Neill and Teal, 2013) and a specification on which to model creating data standards for demand-responsive transportation (Teal et al., 2019). Rocky Mountain Institute's report on Interoperable Transit Data (Carlin et al., 2015) described further roles for GTFS and the GTFS governance process in the future paradigm of mobility-as-a-service, which will be realized by integrating:

- transportation modes (transit, bikeshare, taxis and ridesourcing, etc.);
- traveler functions (trip planning, real-time, payment);
- planning functions (operations performance, ridership reporting, and demand analysis).

The following sections discuss other data formats that are inspired by GTFS.

General Bikeshare Feed Specification
In 2015, the North American Bikeshare Association (NABSA) released the General Bikeshare Feed Specification (GBFS) (North American Bike Share Association, 2019a). GBFS allows micromobility providers to share the real-time availability and position of lightweight personal vehicles (e.g., bikes, scooters) that customers can rent. These vehicles can then be shown in third party applications in combination with other modes such as transit. While the lightweight design of GBFS was inspired by GTFS, no governance process was initially defined for improvements to GBFS. In 2019, NABSA selected MobilityData to lead an effort to update and enhance GBFS (North American Bike Share Association, 2019b), which included applying a GTFS-inspired governance process to GBFS.

Mobility Data Specification
Originally created by the Los Angeles Department of Transportation (LADOT) in 2018, the Mobility Data Specification is a data format designed to help municipalities oversee and control mobility within their jurisdiction. MDS allows the exchange of information and instructions between micromobility providers and regulators, including:

- Historical usage data of vehicles from the provider to the regulator;
- Events such as a trip start or vehicle status change from the provider to the regulator;
- Policies that may affect the operation of vehicles from the regulator to the provider.

In 2019 the stewardship of MDS was transferred to the Open Mobility Foundation (Open Mobility Foundation, 2019).

Other *Transit* Data Formats

The European Committee for Standardization (CEN) has produced several standards related to public transportation to standardize transit data in the European Union. These include NeTEx (NeTEx, 2019) for transit schedule data as well as SIRI (Transmodel, 2019a) for real-time data. NeTEx and SIRI both use the CEN Transmodel (Transmodel, 2019b) terminology for describing various features of public transportation and attempt to provide a unified EU framework that could replace national standards such as German Transport Companies (VDV) VDV 452 (VDV, 2019) and United Kingdom Department of Transport's TransXChange (Department for Transport, 2019). The American Public Transportation Association (APTA) similarly created the Transit Communication Interface Profile (TCIP) to standardize transit agency internal communications in the United States (US Department of Transportation, 2019). NeTEx, SIRI, TCIP, TransXChange and VDV differ from GTFS in that these are *de jure* standards voted on and endorsed by a standards body, while GTFS has emerged as a de facto standard based on its worldwide use. GTFS is also focused on data exchange between a transit agency and external applications, while many of the above formats focus on standardization within a transit agency's internal information system.

The Japanese government endorsed GTFS-JP (https://www.gtfs.jp/) as its official public transportation data format in 2017. GTFS-JP is an expansion of GTFS to meet some specific Japanese transit administrative and operational use cases. In March 2019, the Japanese government officially endorsed the GTFS-realtime format (without any changes specific to Japan).

Beyond Rider Information

In addition to the multitude of rider applications developed that rely on GTFS data, some public entities are using the data for internal analysis. The Delaware Valley Regional Planning Commission (DVRPC) modeling group uses GTFS data in its regional forecasting model, citing the advantages of GTFS feeds to avoid manual coding errors, ease data integration among multiple providers, and improve general data quality (Puchalsky et al., 2011). Researchers in San Francisco are likewise using GTFS data as part of their transit assignment model for use as a component in other planning models (Khani et al., 2013). A study from École Polytechnique de Montréal used GTFS to build public transit trip-generation models (Nazem et al., 2013). A study from the University of Arizona used GTFS data to explore transit route restructuring plans (Lee et al., 2013). In all instances, research focused on the use of a GTFS feed as a data set for one region, rather than the use of multiple feeds to represent multiple agencies whose metrics could be compared.

Transit planning studies often require a variety of quantitative analyses and metrics to support local decision making and to evaluate a transit system among its peers (Ryus et al., 2003). The Brookings Study of Transit and Jobs in America (Tomer et al., 2011) and the University of Minnesota's Accessibility Observatory (Owen and Murphy, 2020) have both used GTFS data to determine how well transit connects people with their jobs. Catalá, Downing and Hayward (2011) explain the potential for GTFS to be used as a data source in various business activities including, most significantly, service evaluations and planning. GTFS is a standard that is shared by hundreds of transit service providers around the world; therefore any methodology that effectively utilizes data in that format can be applied to a vast number of agencies and services. This provides new opportunities for performance measurement, benchmarking and research. For example, modes can be characterized based on their service frequencies, route lengths and stop densities in a way that was previously impractical due to the non-digitized and un-standardized format of transit information.

The Oregon Department of Transportation (ODOT) and Oregon State University (OSU) have undertaken a research project to define a format called GTFS-ride to attach ridership data to GTFS (https://www.gtfs-ride.org/). This could further enhance the use of the standard in analysis, but also possibly in rider information about fullness on transit vehicles.

21.5   TRANSIT INFORMATION APPLICATIONS

Using these data standards, transit agencies and developers have created many different types of applications to provide information to customers and allow agencies to manage their resources. An overview of these different types of applications is provided in this section:

- *Trip planning and maps* – applications that assist a transit customer in planning a trip from one location to another using public transportation;
- *Timetable creation* – applications that create a printed list of the agency's schedule in a timetable format;
- *Data visualization* – applications that provide graphic visualizations of transit routes, stops and schedule data;
- *Accessibility* – applications that assist transit riders with disabilities in using public transportation;
- *Planning analysis* – applications that assist transit professionals in assessing the current or planned transit network, including ridership forecasting;
- *Real-time transit information* – applications that use GTFS data along with a real-time information source to provide estimated arrival information to transit riders.

It should be noted that only a subset of all applications are presented Table 21.1, shown below, and new applications are constantly emerging. This discussion focuses on examples of applications that provide services based on many transit agencies' GTFS data, and therefore are relevant on a larger scale beyond a specific city-sized geographic area. Presented applications were selected to demonstrate and map the range of application functions and approaches. It is estimated that hundreds of GTFS-based applications exist around the world and provide information for only one or a handful of local agencies within a metro area. Other GTFS-consuming applications can be found at TransitWiki.

Open Source Software

The software industry increasingly relies on open-source software as a critical part of systems and tools. Open-source software (OSS) is a software application whose source code

Table 21.1   Examples of transit information-related web and mobile applications

Application name	Link	License/service type	Notes
Examples of Trip Planning and Maps (some with Real-time Information)			
Google Maps	http://maps.google.com	Free commercial	Available worldwide (https://maps.google.com/landing/transit/cities/index.html)
OpenTripPlanner	http://www.opentripplanner.org	Open source	Deployed for multi-modal trip planning by many transit agencies around the world (http://docs.opentripplanner.org/en/latest/Deployments/)
Bing Maps	http://www.bing.com/maps/	Free commercial	Available worldwide (https://docs.microsoft.com/en-us/bingmaps/coverage/transit-coverage)
Apple Maps	http://www.apple.com/ios/maps/	Free commercial	Available worldwide (https://www.apple.com/ios/feature-availability/#maps-transit)
Transit	http://transitapp.com/	Free commercial	Available worldwide (https://transitapp.com/region/#all-regions)
Citymapper	https://citymapper.com/	Free commercial	Available worldwide (https://citymapper.com/cities)
rome2rio	http://www.rome2rio.com/	Free commercial	An international travel search site. Shows options between two given locations in the world by commercial air flights, rail, bus, driving, or a combination of modes
Examples of Timetable Creation			
TimeTable Publisher	https://github.com/OpenTransitTools/ttpub	Open source	Used by TriMet and Hampton Roads Transit to produce their own PDF and HTML timetables
GTFS-to-HTML	https://github.com/BlinkTagInc/gtfs-to-html	Open source	Used by several transit agencies to generate schedule pages for websites (https://github.com/BlinkTagInc/gtfs-to-html#current-usage)
Examples of Data Visualization			
Walk/Bike/Transit Score	https://www.walkscore.com/	Free commercial	Indicates the number of nearby amenities that are within walking/biking/transit distance
Mapnificent	http://www.mapnificent.net/	Hosted/open source	Shows how far it is possible to travel on public transportation from a given location
Examples of Accessibility			
Sendero Group BrailleNote GPS	http://www.senderogroup.com/	Commercial	Braille devices and apps for visually-impaired (include bus stop locations)
1-Click	http://1-click.camsys-apps.com/	Open source	Provides trip planning options for fixed-route and demand-response transit system
Examples of Planning and Analysis Tools			
Remix	https://www.remix.com/	Purchased commercial – hosted service	Planning software for route-level analysis

Table 21.1   (continued)

Application name	Link	License/service type	Notes
Conveyal Analysis	https://www.conveyal.com/analysis	Open source/ purchased commercial hosting	Evaluates changes to public transport systems using accessibility indicators
R5	https://github.com/conveyal/r5	Open source	Routing engine for multimodal (transit/ bike/walk/car) networks that emerged from work on the OpenTripPlanner and RRRR project
ODOT Transit Network Explorer Tool	https://github.com/ODOT-PTS/TNExT	Open source	Web-based software tool developed for the visualization, analysis, and reporting of regional and statewide transit networks in the state of Oregon
Transit Boardings Estimation and Simulation Tool (TBEST)	http://tbest.org/	Free to download	Supported by the Florida Department of Transportation
TransCAD 6.0	http://www.caliper.com/Press/pr20120814.htm	Commercial – packaged software	Travel demand forecasting software product
FTA STOPS	https://www.transit.dot.gov/funding/grant-programs/capital-investments/stops	Free for sponsors of New Starts and Small Starts projects	A limited implementation of the conventional "4-step" travel model
Citilabs	https://www.citilabs.com/	Purchased commercial	Tool to score multimodal accessibility
Transport Foundry Citycast	https://citycast.io/	Purchased commercial	Travel demand modeling using data from consumer sources
Examples of Real-time Transit Information			
OneBusAway	http://onebusaway.org/	Open source	Deployed by several transit agencies around the world (https://onebusaway.org/onebusaway-deployments/). Supported by the non-profit Open Transit Software Foundation (http://opentsf.org/)
TheTransitClock	https://thetransitclock.github.io/	Open source	Generates arrival predictions from vehicle location information
Tiramisu	http://www.tiramisutransit.com/	Free, limited deployment (Pittsburgh, New York City)	Research project by Carnegie Mellon University targeted at transit accessibility
Moovit	http://moovit.com/	Free commercial	Available worldwide (https://company.moovit.com/moovit-cities/)

has been openly shared so that others can modify the functionality and appearance of the software, and then run it themselves. The goal of OSS is to increase collaboration among stakeholders with common goals to avoid duplication of efforts and therefore reduce the overall cost of creating and maintaining a project. OSS projects in the general software industry include Linux (Finley, 2016), used as the operating system for two-thirds of the world's web servers, Android (Popper, 2017), a smartphone operating system with over 2 billion monthly active devices, and the web browsers FireFox and Chrome (based on the Chromium open source project). Foundations such as the Apache Software Foundation and the Linux Foundation support a variety of open-source projects by providing a legal and governance structure. Code for America is an organization that assists the government with OSS.

The transit industry has also followed the OSS trend, with many different OSS projects, both large and small, emerging on popular code hosting sites like GitHub (Center for Urban Transportation Research, 2019b). OpenTripPlanner (http://opentripplanner.org) and OneBusAway (http://onebusaway.org), both included in Table 21.1 above, are two examples of OSS projects that started in the mid-2000s with a small set of key stakeholders but quickly grew to be deployed by a large number of users around the world.

OpenTripPlanner started as a project of TriMet, the transit agency in Portland, Oregon, based on a Regional Travel Options grant in 2009 with a goal to help riders find a transit trip from one location to another. As of 2020, over ten countries have OpenTripPlanner-based deployments, some of them country-wide. OpenTripPlanner is governed through the Software Freedom Conservancy (https://sfconservancy.org/). In October 2016, two of the projects funded by the Federal Transit Administration (FTA) under the Mobility on Demand (MOD) Sandbox project focused on adding new capabilities to OTP. TriMet's project focused on adding real-time shared use mobility (e.g., bikeshare, ridesourcing providers) to trip plans as well as improved transit point-of-interest search. The Vermont Agency of Transportation (VTrans) project focused on adding support for certain demand-responsive services.

OneBusAway started as a graduate student project at the University of Washington in 2008 with a goal of providing transit riders easy access to real-time arrival information and became the focus of two PhD dissertations. Since then it has grown into a project deployed by multiple transit agencies, including MTA in New York City, San Diego Metropolitan Transit System in California, and Washington Metropolitan Area Transit Authority. Countries deploying OneBusAway outside of the United States include Poland and Argentina. In mid-2019, the Open Transit Software Foundation, a 501(c)3 nonprofit, was created by OneBusAway project members to serve as a long-term home for the above project assets and licenses. Transit agencies benefiting from the OneBusAway project are voluntarily contributing funds to the project, which will help with overheads in managing the project as a whole, including the maintenance of the native OneBusAway iOS and Android apps that are deployed across the multiple OneBusAway regions and available to download from Google Play and the Apple App Store. The Open Transit Software Foundation hopes to include other similar rider-oriented information applications over time.

Transit agencies who have used the above open-source project have reported positive experiences (Barbeau and Polzin, 2020). They also stated a strong preference for coordinating with other public and private sector organizations with OSS to avoid duplicating efforts and getting the best return on the investment of taxpayer dollars. Open-source projects can be deployed directly by a transit agency if they have the technical resources, or transit agencies may coordinate with vendors, consultants or universities (or other public sector partners). If an agency would like assistance deploying or modifying an open-source project, there is an open list of vendors maintained by the GTFS community online (Barbeau, 2016).

21.6   MOVING INTO MAAS: FARE PAYMENT AND MORE

Imagine a day when you could wake up and simply type into your phone your first destination for the day and your required arrival time. Based on your location and the current conditions of the transportation system, the phone would tell you where you should go to catch the bus and at what time. If conditions change en route, the phone would warn you to change your path or your mode of transportation. Once work or school was done for the day, you could type in "Thai for dinner" and the phone would give a suggested list of places that were easy to access from your location, based again on the current conditions. After dinner, it would automatically direct you how to get home, and it would enable payment for the entire day (or month) of travel across multiple modes of transportation. With some additional enhancements to existing tools and integration of components already introduced, we are not far from this situation.

The concept of Mobility as a Service (MaaS) combines private and public transportation services seamlessly to enable travel without personal vehicle ownership. MaaS uses public transportation as the backbone of the service. When the local transit agency cannot serve a trip, the user can access any number of alternative shared mobility providers such as ridesourcing (e.g., Lyft/Uber) or taxis, bikeshare, carshare, and more recently, scooter sharing. MaaS is similar to ridesourcing in that it uses apps to plan a trip, locate or hail a vehicle, and pay for the trip, all in one place. To date, both Sweden and Finland have implemented MaaS successfully (UbiGo, 2017). This kind of seamless travel with collective transportation as the backbone must be the basis for transportation into the future. Such services use the best of high-capacity public transportation for the bulk of travel distances, with localized services for short trips and first mile/last mile connectivity. The name behind MaaS is perhaps the biggest key. Mobility must be transformed to be perceived as a high-quality utility. The connection from one service to another must be efficient and pleasant, with good information and minimal delay. In addition to good information, the ability to pay for the service in the same application is critical to facilitating a seamless user experience.

In North America, there are currently numerous applications that provide real-time information about multimodal, shared transportation services (public transportation, ridesourcing, bikeshare, scooter sharing, etc.) across multiple cities and regions. However, a critical missing link is the ability to pay for all of these services in a single place. If public transportation is the backbone of this MaaS transportation system, then transit fare payments – and the technologies and standards that enable them – are a critical next step in moving toward MaaS. Efforts are currently underway in numerous locations (e.g., California) to move to increased standardization and integration of fare payments (Cal-ITP, 2020).

One emerging technology in the transit industry is the use of Software Development Kits (SDKs) for mobile fare payments. SDKs include application programming interfaces (APIs), additional tools, libraries, and/or documentation, and vendors are beginning to make them available to transit agencies to integrate fare payments into various apps. For example, a vendor (Masabi) provides a fare payment SDK that is used by the transit agency in Denver (known as the Regional Transportation District) and has been integrated into the multimodal smartphone app known as Transit and into the Uber app (Brakewood, 2020). While this type of mobile fare payment integration is still relatively new in the transit industry, it is likely to be an area with significant innovation and adoption in the near future.

In addition to changing technologies, it is likely that we will see a shift in the pricing structure for transit as part of MaaS. It is likely that subscription plans – e.g., a monthly fee – will include not only public transit but other supporting shared transportation services, such as ridesourcing, carsharing, bikesharing and/or scooter sharing, that can be tailored to the individual traveler's preferences. These multimodal subscription MaaS plans will – hopefully – lead to reductions in individual vehicle ownership and move toward a more sustainable transportation system.

Finally, it should be noted that the term MaaS is closely related to the concept of Mobility on Demand (MOD), which focuses on the "commodification of passenger mobility and goods delivery and transportation systems management, whereas MaaS primarily focuses on passenger mobility aggregation and subscription services" (Shaheen and Cohen, 2019).

21.7   CONCLUSIONS

This chapter first addressed the history and benefits of transit information as we have evolved from printed schedule materials to ubiquitous real-time transit information. Three key technology advances occurred during the last few decades that have led to significant advances in transit information provision, including the widespread availability of GPS devices used by transit agencies to track vehicles, the rapid adoption of smartphones by transit riders, and the standardization of transit schedule data in the form of the General Transit Feed Specification (GTFS).

Because of its widespread use and numerous applications, GTFS was discussed in substantial detail in this chapter. GTFS identifies a series of comma-separated files that together describe the stops, trips, routes and fare information about a transit agency's service. The basic GTFS format contains only static (i.e., infrequently changing) transit information such as schedules, routes and bus stops. A real-time counterpart to GTFS, GTFS-realtime, has more recently emerged as a de facto worldwide standard for real-time transit information.

Using these data standards, transit agencies and software developers have created many different types of web and mobile applications to provide information to transit customers and allow agencies to manage their resources. Different types of applications discussed in this chapter include those for trip planning and maps, real-time transit information provision, timetable creation, data visualization, and planning analysis.

Finally, the future of transit information was addressed as we move into Mobility as a Service (MaaS) applications that combine private and public transportation services seamlessly to enable travel without personal vehicle ownership. This type of application currently provides real-time information on a variety of shared transportation modes, such as ridesourcing, bikeshare, carshare, and scooter sharing, with transit as the backbone of the service. However, a critical missing link is the ability to pay for all of these services in a single place. If public transportation is the backbone of this MaaS transportation system, then transit fare payments – and the technologies and standards that enable them – are a critical next step in moving toward MaaS.

REFERENCES

Antrim, A. (2017). Life and growth of transport data standards: Lessons from 12 years of GTFS. Accessed 20 March 2020 at https://trilliumtransit.com/2017/12/31/life-of-data-standards/.

Barbeau, S. (2013). Open transit data – A developer's perspective. *APTA TransITech 2013*, Phoenix, AZ.

Barbeau, S. (2016). Entities providing transportation software development consulting services?, Transit Developers Google Group. Accessed 30 December 2019 at https://groups.google.com/d/msg/transit-develo pers/0yIkh37l3MU/R_SQs7MpCwAJ.

Barbeau, S. and S. Polzin (2020). *Open Source Software in Public Transportation: A Case Study*. Paper presented at the *Transportation Research Board (TRB) 99th Annual Meeting*, Washington, DC.

Barbeau, S., N.L. Georggi and P. Winters (2010). Travel Assistance Device (TAD) deployment to transit agencies. National Center for Transit Research.

Brakewood, C. (2020). TCRP synthesis: Mobile fare apps business models. Transit Cooperative Research Program, Transportation Research Board of the National Academies, Washington, DC.

Brakewood, C. and K. Watkins (2019). A literature review of the passenger benefits of real-time transit information, *Transport Reviews*, 39(3).

Brakewood, C., S. Barbeau and K. Watkins (2014). An experiment validating the impacts of transit information on bus riders in Tampa, Florida. *Transportation Research Part A*, 69, 409–22.

Brakewood, C., G. Macfarlane and K. Watkins (2015). The impact of real-time information on bus ridership in New York City, *Transportation Research Part C*, 53, 59–75.

Cal-ITP (2020). California integrated travel project. Accessed 2 March 2020 at https://www.californiaintegrat edtravel.org/.

Carlin, K., B. Rader and G. Rucks (2015). Interoperable transit data: Enabling a shift to mobility as a service. Rocky Mountain Institute. Accessed 30 December 2019 at https://rmi.org/wp-content/uploads/2017/04/ RMI-Mobility-InteroperableTransitData-FullReport-2.pdf.

Catalá, M. (2016). FTA Open Data Policy Guidelines, FTA Research, Federal Transit Administration. Accessed 30 December 2019 at https://www.transit.dot.gov/sites/fta.dot.gov/files/FTA_Report_No._0095.pdf.

Catalá, M., S. Downing and D. Hayward (2011). *Expanding the Google Transit Feed Specification to Support Operations and Planning*. National Center for Transit Research, Tampa, FL. Accessed 30 December 2019 at https://www.nctr.usf.edu/wp-content/uploads/2012/02/77902.pdf.

Center for Urban Transportation Research (2019a). *GTFS Data Collection and Maintenance Tools*, awesome-transit, GitHub Repository. Accessed 30 December 2019 at https://github.com/CUTR-at-USF/awesome-transit#gtfs-data-collection-and-maintenance-tools.

Center for Urban Transportation Research (2019b). GTFS, awesome-transit, GitHub Repository. Accessed 30 December 2019 at https://github.com/CUTR-at-USF/awesome-transit#gtfs.

Center for Urban Transportation Research (2019c). GTFS Validators, awesome-transit, GitHub Repository. Accessed 30 December 2019 at https://github.com/CUTR-at-USF/awesome-transit#gtfs-validators.

Conveyal (2019a). *GTFS Editor*, GitHub Repository. Accessed 30 December 2019 at https://github.com/convey al/gtfs-editor.

Conveyal (2019b). *transit-wand*, GitHub Repository. Accessed 30 December 2019 at https://github.com/convey al/transit-wand.

Deloitte (2017). *Global Mobile Customer Trends*, 2nd edn. Accessed 30 December 2019 at https://www2.deloitte. com/content/dam/Deloitte/us/Documents/technology-media-telecommunications/us-global-mobile-consum er-survey-second-edition.pdf.

Department for Transport (2019). TransXChange. Accessed 30 December 2019 at http://naptan.dft.gov.uk/tra nsxchange/.

Ferris, B., K. Watkins and A. Borning (2010). OneBusAway: Results from providing real-time arrival information for public transit. In *Proceedings of the Association for Computing Machinery Conference on Human Factors in Computing Systems (CHI)*, April.

Finley, K. (2016). Linux took over the web. Now, it's taking over the world. *Wired*, 25 August. Accessed 25 June 2019 at https://www.wired.com/2016/08/linux-took-web-now-taking-world/.

GoogleTransitFeed (2020). Library for reading, validating, and writing GTFS data. Accessed at https://github.com/google/transitfeed.

Google, Inc. (2020). Google Transit Partners Help. Accessed at https://support.google.com/transitpartners#topic=3521043.

Google (2019). Specification Amendment Process, transit, GitHub Repository. Accessed 30 December 2019 at https://github.com/google/transit/blob/master/gtfs/CHANGES.md.

Gooze, A., K. Watkins and A. Borning (2013). Benefits of real-time transit information and impacts of data accuracy on rider experience. *Transportation Research Record*, 2351, 95–103.

Heitzman, B. (2012). XLS Tools for Google Transit. Accessed 30 December 2019 at https://sites.google.com/site/rheitzman/.

IBI Group (2019). Datatools-iu, GitHub repository. Accessed 30 December 2019 at https://github.com/ibi-group/datatools-ui.

Khani, A., E. Sall, L. Zorn and M. Hickman (2013). Integration of the FAST-TrIPs person-based dynamic transit assignment model, the SF-CHAMP regional, activity-based travel demand model, and San Francisco's citywide dynamic traffic assignment model. Paper presented at the *92nd Annual Meeting of the Transportation Research Board*. Washington, DC: Transportation Research Board.

Lee, S., D. Tong and M. Hickman (2013). A comparative study of alternative methods for generating route-level mutually exclusive service areas. Paper presented at the *92nd Annual Meeting of the Transportation Research Board*. Washington, DC: Transportation Research Board.

McHugh, B. (2016). Pioneering open data standards: The GTFS story. Accessed 30 December 2019 at http://beyondtransparency.org/chapters/part-2/pioneering-open-data-standards-the-gtfs-story/.

MobilityData IO (2020a). MobilityData. Accessed 18 March 2020 at https://mobilitydata.org/.

MobilityData IO (2020b). What we do. Accessed 18 March 2020 at https://mobilitydata.org/what-we-do/.

National Rural Transit Assistance Program (2020). GTFS Builder. Accessed at https://nationalrtap.org/Web-Apps/GTFS-Builder.

Nazem, M., M. Trepanier and C. Morency (2013). Integrated intervening opportunities model for public transit trip generation-distribution: A supply-dependent approach. Paper presented at the *92nd Annual Meeting of the Transportation Research Board*. Washington, DC: Transportation Research Board.

NeTEx (2019). Welcome. Accessed 30 December 2019 at http://netex-cen.eu/.

North American Bike Share Association (2019a). GBFS, GitHub Repository. Accessed 30 December 2019 at https://github.com/NABSA/gbfs.

North American Bike Share Association (2019b). Help shape the future of GBFS & open data for bikeshare. Accessed 30 December 2019 at https://nabsa.net/2019/07/17/gbfsprojectannouncement/.

O'Neill, S. and R. Teal (2013). TCRP web-only document 62: Standardizing data for mobility management. Transit Cooperative Research Program, Transportation Research Board of the National Academies, Washington, DC.

Open Mobility Foundation (2019). The future of mobility. Accessed 30 December 2019 at https://www.openmobilityfoundation.org/.

Owen, A. and Murphy, B. (2020). Access across America: Transit 2018. Data Repository for the University of Minnesota. Accessed 17 March 2020 at http://www.cts.umn.edu/Publications/ResearchReports/reportdetail.html?id=2894.

Pew Research (2019). Mobile fact sheet. Pew Internet and Technology. Accessed 30 December 2019 at https://www.pewresearch.org/internet/fact-sheet/mobile/.

Popper, B. (2017). Google announces over 2 billion monthly active devices on Android. *The Verge*, 17 May. Accessed 25 June 2019 at https://www.theverge.com/2017/5/17/15654454/android-reaches-2-billion-monthly-active-users.

Puchalsky, C., D. Joshi and W. Scherr (2011). Development of a regional forecasting model based on Google Transit Feed. Paper presented at the *13th TRB Planning Application Conference*, May. Reno, NV: Transportation Research Board.

Reed, L. (2013). Real-time transit passenger information: A case study in standards development. Thesis, Georgia Institute of Technology.

Roth, M. (2010). How Google and Portland's TriMet set the standard for open transit data. *Streetsblog San Francisco*, 5 January. Accessed 30 December 2019 at https://sf.streetsblog.org/2010/01/05/how-google-and-portlands-trimet-set-the-standard-for-open-transit-data/.

Ryus, P., M. Connor, S. Corbett, A. Rodenstein, L. Wargelin, L. Ferreira, Y. Nakanishi et al. (2003). *TCRP Report 88: A Guidebook for Developing a Transit Performance-Measurement System*. Transit Cooperative Research Program, Transportation Research Board of the National Academies, Washington, DC.

Schweiger, C. (2011). *TCRP Synthesis 91: Use and Deployment of Mobile Device Technology for Real-Time*

Transit Information. Transit Cooperative Research Program, Transportation Research Board of the National Academies, Washington, DC.

Schweiger, C. (2015). Open data: Challenges and opportunities for transit agencies. TCRP Synthesis 115. Accessed at https://trid.trb.org/view/1347041.

Shaheen, S. and Cohen, A. (2019). Mobility on Demand (MOD) and Mobility as a Service (MaaS): How are they similar and different? *Medium*, 7 March. Accessed 2 March 2020 at https://medium.com/move-forward-blog/mobility-on-demand-mod-and-mobility-as-a-service-maas-how-are-they-similar-and-different-a853c853b0b8.

Tang, L. and P. Thakuriah (2012). Ridership effects of real-time bus information system: A case study in the city of Chicago. *Transportation Research Part C*, 22, 146–61.

Teal, R., N. Larsen, D. King, C. Brakewood, C. Frei and D. Chia (2019). *TCRP Report 210: Development of Transactional Data Specification for Demand-Responsive Transportation*. Transit Cooperative Research Program, Transportation Research Board of the National Academies, Washington, DC: National Academies Press.

Tomer, A., E. Kneebone, R. Puentes and A. Berube (2011). Missed opportunity: Transit and jobs in metropolitan America. Metropolitan Policy Program at Brookings. Accessed 30 December 2019 at https://www.brookings.edu/wp-content/uploads/2016/06/0512_jobs_transit.pdf.

Tran, K., E.L. Hillsman, S. Barbeau and M.A. Labrador (2011). GO-Sync: A framework to synchronize crowd-sourced mapping contributions from online communities and transit agency bus stop inventories. *Proceedings of the ITS World Congress*, Orlando, FL.

Transitland (2019). Feed registry. Accessed 30 December 2019 at https://transit.land/feed-registry/.

TransitWiki (2016). Category:GTFS-consuming applications. Accessed 30 December 2019 at http://www.transitwiki.org/TransitWiki/index.php?title=Category:GTFS-consuming_applications.

Transmodel (2019a). SIRI Standard. Accessed 30 December 2019 at http://www.transmodel-cen.eu/standards/siri/.

Transmodel (2019b). CEN European reference data model for public transport information. Accessed 30 December 2019 at http://www.transmodel-cen.eu/.

Trillium (2020). GTFS Manager. Accessed 20 March 2020 at https://trilliumtransit.com/gtfs/gtfs-manager/.

UbiGo (2017). Gothenburg, Sweden. Accessed 30 December 2019 at http://ubigo.se/.

US Department of Transportation (2019). APTA TCIP-S-001: Standard for Transit Communications Interface Profiles (TCIP), ITS Standards Fact Sheets. Accessed 30 December 2019 at https://www.standards.its.dot.gov/Factsheets/Factsheet/37.

US National Coordination Office for Space-Based Positioning, Navigation, and Timing (2018). Selective availability. Accessed 30 December 2019 at http://www.gps.gov/systems/gps/modernization/sa/.

VDV (2019). Die Verkehrsunternehmen. Accessed 30 December 2019 at https://www.vdv.de/oepnv-datenmodell.aspx.

Watkins, K., B. Ferris, A. Borning, G. Rutherford and D. Layton (2011). Where is my bus? Impact of mobile real-time information on the perceived and actual wait time of transit riders. *Transportation Research Part A*, 45(8), 839–48.

Windmiller, S., T. Hennessy and K. Watkins (2014). Accessibility of communication technology and the rider experience: Case study of St. Louis Metro. *Transportation Research Record*, 2415, 118–26.

Wong, J., L. Reed, K. Watkins and R. Hammond (2013). Open Transit Data: State of the practice and experiences from participating agencies in the United States. Paper presented at the *92nd Annual Meeting of the Transportation Research Board*. Washington, DC: Transportation Research Board.

Index

Printed and bound by CPI Group (UK) Ltd, Croydon, CR0 4YY

17/04/2025

14658905-0001